Pro Exchange Administration

Understanding On-premises and Hybrid Exchange Deployments

Third Edition

Jaap Wesselius
Michel de Rooij

Apress®

Pro Exchange Administration: Understanding On-premises and Hybrid Exchange Deployments, Third Edition

Jaap Wesselius
MARKNESSE, Flevoland, The Netherlands

Michel de Rooij
VLEUTEN, Utrecht, The Netherlands

ISBN-13 (pbk): 978-1-4842-9590-8
https://doi.org/10.1007/978-1-4842-9591-5

ISBN-13 (electronic): 978-1-4842-9591-5

Managing Director, Apress Media LLC: Welmoed Spahr
Acquisitions Editor: Smriti Srivastava
Development Editor: Laura Berendson
Editorial Project Manager: Mark Powers

Cover designed by eStudioCalamar

Cover image by Jon Wicks on Pixabay (www.pixabay.com)

Distributed to the book trade worldwide by Springer Science+Business Media New York, 1 New York Plaza, Suite 4600, New York, NY 10004-1562, USA. Phone 1-800-SPRINGER, fax (201) 348-4505, e-mail orders-ny@springer-sbm.com, or visit www.springeronline.com. Apress Media, LLC is a California LLC and the sole member (owner) is Springer Science + Business Media Finance Inc (SSBM Finance Inc). SSBM Finance Inc is a **Delaware** corporation.

For information on translations, please e-mail booktranslations@springernature.com; for reprint, paperback, or audio rights, please e-mail bookpermissions@springernature.com.

Apress titles may be purchased in bulk for academic, corporate, or promotional use. eBook versions and licenses are also available for most titles. For more information, reference our Print and eBook Bulk Sales web page at http://www.apress.com/bulk-sales.

Any source code or other supplementary material referenced by the author in this book is available to readers on GitHub (github.com/apress). For more detailed information, please visit https://www.apress.com/gp/services/source-code.

Paper in this product is recyclable

Table of Contents

About the Authors

Jaap Wesselius is an independent consultant based in the Netherlands. As a consultant, Jaap has been working with Exchange Server since Exchange 5.0 in 1997. After working for Microsoft, he became an independent consultant in 2006. For his work in the (Exchange) community, primarily his blog on jaapwesselius.com and presentations on Microsoft events like TechEd and MEC, Jaap has received a Microsoft MVP award in 2007, an award he still holds in 2023. The first MVP category was Exchange Server, but over the years that has changed to Office Apps and Services. Besides working with Exchange, Jaap also works with Office 365, identity management, privacy, and security. Jaap is 56 years old and married, has three grown sons, and likes to ride his motorcycle, when possible.

Michel de Rooij is a consultant and Microsoft MVP since 2013. He lives in the Netherlands and has been working in the IT industry for over 20 years. Michel helps customers with their journeys related to Microsoft 365, with a focus on Exchange and Identity, but also related technologies such as Microsoft Teams or email in general. Michel has a developer background, but after a long-term Exchange-related project for a large multinational switched to Exchange and never looked back. Michel is also an enthusiastic fan of automating processes and procedures related to infrastructure, whether supporting projects or automating administrator tasks. Michel is active in online communities, such as the Microsoft Tech Community, or on social media such as Twitter (@mderooij). He runs a blog at eightwone.com, guest authors for several other sites, and speaks at international events.

About the Technical Reviewer

 **Vikas Sukhija** has nearly two decades of IT infrastructure experience. He is Microsoft certified and has worked on various Microsoft and related technologies.

He has been awarded seven times with the Microsoft Most Valuable Professional title.

Vikas is a lifelong learner, always eager to explore new technologies and expand his knowledge. He keeps himself up to date with the latest trends and developments in the field, ensuring that his reviews reflect the current best practices and industry standards. His commitment to continuous improvement and his passion for sharing knowledge make him an invaluable resource for technical content creators and readers alike.

With a strong foundation in Microsoft technologies, Vikas has continuously expanded his knowledge and skills throughout his career, adapting to the ever-evolving landscape of cloud. His deep understanding of the Microsoft ecosystem, including Windows Server, SQL Server, Exchange Server, Active Directory, and other technologies, allows him to provide comprehensive and insightful reviews of technical materials.

Vikas's passion for automation and scripting led him to specialize in PowerShell and Python, where he has honed his skills in developing efficient and robust scripts for various administrative tasks. His expertise in PowerShell/Python ranges from simple automation scripts to complex solutions, empowering organizations to streamline their processes and enhance productivity.

His contributions can be browsed at the following sites and pages, of which he is the owner and author:

http://TechWizard.cloud
http://SysCloudPro.com
www.facebook.com/TechWizard.cloud

Introduction

A book about Exchange 2019—that is not something one would expect to be released, but after all these years, we are still amazed by the amount of Exchange deployments on-premises. We must admit though that most deployments are in a hybrid configuration, where mailboxes reside in Exchange on-premises or in Exchange Online (EXO) or both.

At the same time, we see a lot of old versions of Exchange Server on-premises, and these are all subject to upgrade anytime soon. Since Exchange 2019 is the only version that is currently in Microsoft mainstream support, this is also the version most customers migrate to.

This book is the third version of our Exchange on-premises book, but we have removed most of the Exchange 2016 content since Exchange 2016 is no longer in mainstream support, so the book only focuses on Exchange 2019. There is also a strong focus on hybrid scenarios, identity management, and security. It has the following chapters:

1. "Exchange 2019 Introduction": This chapter covers the Exchange Server versions, licenses, and features that come and go in the product. Since an update of Exchange 2019 is released two times per year, new features are introduced in the same cadence. At the same time, features are deprecated as well, especially when it is about security. Part of the introduction is networking where Active Directory sites and services are discussed, with a focus on virtual networking in Microsoft Azure to host your on-premises Exchange servers in the Azure cloud.

2. "Exchange Infrastructure": Chapter 2 is about installing and designing and building a solid Exchange 2019 infrastructure, including high availability.

3. "Managing Exchange": An important chapter where not only the management of Exchange Server is discussed but also the management of all recipients in Exchange 2019.

4. "Azure AD Identities" covers the identity models supported when deploying hybrid identities.

5. "Exchange Online" talks about Exchange hybrid topologies, deploying Exchange hybrid, and some of the key topics in those scenarios.

6. "Publishing Exchange Server" talks about publishing Exchange, namespaces, availability, and how features such as Autodiscover need to be configured properly for the smoothest client connectivity experience. We also talk about using Azure Application Proxy to securely publish internal web applications such as Outlook on the Web.

7. "Email Authentication": This chapter discusses Sender Policy Framework (SPF), DomainKeys Identified Mail (DKIM), and Domain-based Message Authentication, Reporting & Conformance (DMARC). These are the most basic email authentication mechanisms that are more and more in use. Although these can hardly be used in Exchange 2019, they are used in Exchange Online. After discussing these topics, Domain Name System Security Extensions (DNSSEC), DNS-based

Authentication of Named Entities (DANE), and Mail Transfer Agent Strict Transport Security (MTA-STS) are discussed briefly—briefly, because these are mechanisms that are still in development, even in Exchange Online.

8. "Message Hygiene and Security": Chapter 8 discusses anti-spam and anti-phishing measures in Exchange Online Protection. This is by default available for mailboxes in Exchange Online, but Exchange Online Protection can also be purchased to be used in front of Exchange 2019.

9. "Authentication" talks about Hybrid Modern Authentication (HMA) to handing off authentication for your Exchange on-premises to Azure Active Directory with all additional benefits such as multifactor authentication (MFA) and Conditional Access. We also discuss Client Access Rules, SMTP AUTH, and certificate-based authentication and end with Windows Extended Protection to counter man-in-the-middle attacks.

10. "Permissions and Access Control" talks about Role-Based Access Control (RBAC) and when you might want to consider the split permissions model.

11. "Backup and Restore": This is a traditional and Exchange 2019 on-premises chapter where the technologies and procedures around backup and restore in Exchange 2019 are discussed, not only backing up mail data but also restoring entire Exchange servers.

12. "Policy and Compliance": This is a topic that is gaining more and more importance. The chapter discusses the options available in Exchange 2019 to safeguard your email data and make sure it is kept the right way and no data leakage can take place. Although these technologies are also available in Exchange Online, we only discuss them for Exchange 2019 since the approach in Exchange Online is so much different.

If you are in an Exchange hybrid scenario and want to manage your Exchange 2019 environment, this book can be very useful since it covers the most important topics in any Exchange deployment.

PART I

Infrastructure and Exchange Server

CHAPTER 1

Exchange 2019 Introduction

Exchange Server 4.0 was introduced in 1996, more than 25 years ago! Now, in 2023, Exchange Server is still around and still alive, despite the massive migrations to Exchange Online.

I must admit though that for a hybrid configuration, you need at least one Exchange server on-premises, but lots of customers still have mailboxes in Exchange Server on-premises. There are also customers that are legally not allowed to move their data to the cloud, and they must keep Exchange servers on-premises.

For these customers Microsoft has released its Exchange Server Roadmap, which you can find on `https://bit.ly/ExchRoadmap`. This roadmap outlines that Exchange Server is still alive and that Microsoft is still investing in Exchange Server.

At the time of writing, mid-2023, the only version of Exchange Server in mainstream support is Exchange 2019. This means that Microsoft is only developing new features and bug fixes for Exchange 2019. For Exchange 2016 there are no more developments going on, but Security Updates are still released for Exchange 2016.

© Jaap Wesselius and Michel de Rooij 2023
J. Wesselius and M. de Rooij, *Pro Exchange Administration*,
https://doi.org/10.1007/978-1-4842-9591-5_1

In October 2025, support for both Exchange 2016 and Exchange 2019 will end, and a new version of Exchange Server will be released, at this moment with codename "Exchange vNext." If you check the Exchange Server roadmap on a regular basis, you'll see upcoming changes for the product, both Exchange 2019 and Exchange vNext.

Looking back over the years, three real major infrastructural changes can be identified in Exchange Server:

- *Use of Active Directory*: The first versions of Exchange Server had their own X.500 directory, which was used in combination with the NT4 directory. User accounts were created in the NT4 domain, and mailboxes were created in the Exchange directory. Exchange 2000 was the first version of Exchange that used Active Directory, and it still is up to today.

- *64-bit architecture*: Exchange Server 2007 was the first version that was built on the x64 platform, although a 32-bit version for testing purposes was still available. Exchange Server was growing tremendously, and it hit the boundaries of the 32-bit architecture of Exchange Server 2003, which resulted in major performance issues. By moving to a 64-bit architecture, Microsoft was able to work on the performance issues, and performance has been improved with each new version.

- *Managed code*: Exchange Server 2013 was the first version that was 100% built on top of the .NET Framework, and as such it was really built from the ground up. I do not want to sound like a marketing guy, but this really was a big change. Another big change with the introduction of Exchange Server 2013 was that Exchange Server 2013 and Exchange Online shared

4

the same codebase, which means that all releases and Cumulative Updates (CUs) of Exchange Server 2013 are a spin-off of Exchange Online. This was continued with Exchange Server 2016 but stopped with Exchange 2019, which now is a separate product compared with Exchange Online. This was clearly visible when the HAFNIUM vulnerability hit. Exchange servers on-premises were vulnerable, but Exchange Online was not.

Starting with Exchange Server 2013, Microsoft introduced a new servicing model based on Cumulative Updates or CUs. Microsoft releases a CU two times a year, and a CU contains fixes and new features when available. Microsoft stepped away from the concept of service packs; all features are now included in CUs. Because of the cumulative nature of the CUs, a CU contains all features and fixes of earlier CUs. Therefore, you can "jump" over several CUs, for example, from Exchange Server 2019 CU10 to Exchange Server 2019 CU13. There is no need to install CUs that are between those versions.

CUs are only released when the product is in mainstream support. When critical security issues are found and a product is in extended support, a Security Update (SU) is released. This happened in March 2021, when Microsoft released Security Updates for all Exchange servers in mainstream and in extended support for the HAFNIUM vulnerability. SUs are also cumulative, so the August 2023 Security Updates contain all previous Security Updates for the same CU. SUs are also CU specific, so a SU for Exchange Server 2019 CU13 is different from a SU for Exchange Server 2019 CU12. Microsoft typically releases SUs only for the current CU and the previous CU. For the HAFNIUM vulnerability, an exception was made. Because of the critical and dangerous nature of the HAFNIUM vulnerability, SUs were released for older CUs and even out-of-support Exchange builds as well, but this should really be considered an exception.

Exchange Server 2013, 2016, and 2019 are very similar and to some extent compatible. Over the years, there have not been major infrastructural changes to the product, but more lots of improvements.

The first area of improvement is security with support for Windows Server Core, TLS 1.2, and blockage of the Exchange Control Panel (ECP) and Exchange Management Shell (EMS) externally.

Another area of improvement is performance and reliability. Performance improvement in Exchange Server 2019 is achieved by modern hardware support (Exchange Server 2019 now supports up to 256 GB memory!), a new search engine (which also improves failover times), and the MetaCache database (MCDB), a combination of large JBODs and SSDs.

There are also several client improvements, such as the "Do not forward" option in meeting invites, improved out-of-office support, and the option to remove calendar events (using PowerShell), possibly the most requested feature.

From a security perspective, Microsoft introduced new features, like Modern Authentication (CU13), the Exchange Emergency Mitigation Service (EEMS, CU11), or the Windows Antimalware Scan Interface (AMSI, CU10).

Of course, there are differences between Exchange Server 2013, 2016, and 2019, especially when it comes to features. But these versions also work together quite well. For example, it is possible to create a load-balanced array for Exchange servers with all three versions in this array. It does not matter on which Exchange server a client connection is terminated; the request is automatically proxied to the correct Mailbox server. This is extremely useful when upgrading your Exchange environment from Exchange 2013 or Exchange 2016 to Exchange Server 2019.

There is one major difference between Exchange Server 2013 on one hand and Exchange Server 2016 and 2019 on the other hand. Exchange Server 2013 does have two server roles, the Client Access server role and the Mailbox server role. In Exchange Server 2016 and up, these two roles are combined, and only the Mailbox server role is available. The different components are still there, but only available in one server role. The Edge Transport server role is still available in Exchange 2019.

Exchange Server 2019 is targeted toward large enterprise customers. Smaller customers can still use Exchange Server 2019 or move to Exchange Online, not surprisingly the Microsoft recommended approach. Exchange Online contains the latest and greatest features, Exchange Server 2019 is the rock-solid solution for enterprise customers that need a solid on-premises mail environment.

Exchange Server 2019 Editions

Exchange 2019 is available in two editions:

- *Exchange 2019, Standard Edition*: This is a "normal" Exchange 2019 but limited to five (5) mailbox databases per Mailbox server.

- *Exchange 2019, Enterprise Edition*: This version can host up to 100 mailbox databases per Mailbox server.

Except for the number of mailbox databases per Exchange server, there are no differences between the two versions; the binaries are the same.

Entering the Exchange 2019 license key changes the limit of maximum mailbox databases for that server. Besides the Exchange 2019 server license, there is also a Client Access license (CAL), which is required for each user or device accessing the server software.

There are two types of CALs available:

- *Standard CAL*: This CAL offers standard email functionality from any platform. The license is for typical Exchange and Outlook usage.

- *Enterprise CAL*: This more advanced CAL offers functionality such as integrated archiving, compliance features, and information protection capabilities. The CAL is an add-on to the Standard CAL, so both licenses need to be purchased!

This is not a complete list of all available features for the different CALs. For a complete overview, visit the Microsoft licensing page at https://bit.ly/X2019Licensing.

Note   An Exchange Server 2019 server license is always needed. But an Exchange Online P1 or P2 of Office 365 E1 or E3 license can also be used for a CAL. When an Exchange 2019 server is used in a hybrid environment, and all mailboxes are in Exchange Online, customers might be eligible for a free "hybrid server license" from Microsoft.

What's New in Exchange Server 2019

So what are the new features and improvements in Exchange Server 2019? Twice a year Microsoft releases a Cumulative Update for Exchange 2019, so new features are added twice a year as well. This book is written based on Exchange 2019 Cumulative Update 13, which has a lot of new features compared with the initial release of Exchange 2019 by the end of 2018. Let's discuss the most interesting features, listed from new to older:

- *Modern Authentication* (CU13): Modern Authentication is introduced in Exchange 2019 CU13 and is targeted toward customers that do not have any cloud integration and as such cannot use Hybrid Modern Authentication. Traditionally Exchange Server

8

used basic authentication, NTLM, or Kerberos for authentication, but Modern Authentication is claims-based authentication. Modern Authentication replaces basic authentication and is much more secure than older, legacy authentication methods.

- *Configuration Preservation* (CU13): Configuration Preservation is introduced in Exchange 2019 CU13 and is a long-requested feature in Exchange. When you have made manual changes to configuration files in Exchange, they are no longer overwritten when installing a new CU, but they are kept.

- *Removal of UNC paths in PowerShell commands* (CU12): For security reasons, the use of UNC paths in PowerShell commands has been decommissioned, starting in Exchange 2019 CU12. Using a UNC path in a PowerShell command to read contents of a file no longer works directly. Instead, you need to read the contents of a file into a variable and use that variable in the PowerShell command. This makes it much more difficult for a malicious user to read the contents of a (deliberately placed) file and manipulate the Exchange server.

- *Exchange Emergency Mitigation Service* (EEMS, CU11): The Exchange Emergency Mitigation Service or EEMS is introduced in Exchange 2019 CU11, shortly after the ongoing security issues that were found in Exchange. It's a service that runs on an Exchange server and that stays online with Microsoft. When a security issue is found, Microsoft can push a rewrite rule to the Exchange server, mitigating the vulnerability.

9

EEMS is using the IISRewrite module, hence the additional prerequisite software in Exchange 2019 CU11 and later. Please note that EEMS is also available for Exchange 2016.

- *Windows Antimalware Scan Interface (AMSI)* (CU10): Support for AMSI, or the Windows Antimalware Scan Interface, is introduced in Exchange 2019 CU10. AMSI is an interface that allows applications and services to interact with any antimalware vendor. For Exchange, it means that an antimalware application can scan the content of any HTTP request performed against the Exchange server and act appropriately. This happens in real time, so it's an extra layer of security against malicious attacks on the Exchange web services.

- *Support for Windows Server Core*: Exchange Server 2019 is supported on Windows 2022 and Windows 2019, both Desktop Experience and Server Core. Windows 2022 Server Core is the recommended operating system for Exchange Server 2019 because of the lower footprint and improved security. Exchange 2019 is only supported on Windows 2022 and Windows 2019; Windows 2016 is **NOT** supported for Exchange 2019.

- *TLS 1.2*: To improve the client-to-server connections, the default protocol for encrypting traffic between clients and the Exchange Server 2019 server. Older versions are still available but are disabled by default. Please note that a client in this respect can also be another (Exchange) server that is communicating with the Exchange Server 2019 server. Unfortunately, TLS 1.3 is supported on Windows 2022, but still not supported

in Exchange 2019 CU13. Support for TLS 1.3 is expected
in a future Exchange 2019 CU.

- *Blocking external access to ECP and EMS*: In Exchange
  Server 2019, it is possible to block external access
  to the Exchange Control Panel (ECP) and Exchange
  Management Shell (EMS) using Client Access Rules.
  Based on conditions, exceptions, and actions, Client
  Access Rules help you control access to ECP and EMS
  in a very granular manner.

- *Improved search infrastructure*: The search
  infrastructure in Exchange Server 2019 is improved
  and is now based on the Bing search technology. Its
  codename is "Big Funnel," something you can still
  see in Exchange Server 2019 under the hood. Search
  indexes are no longer stored in a separate directory on
  the disk containing the mailbox database, but they are
  stored in the user's mailbox. Because of this, search
  data replication is always up to date, and mailbox
  database failover is much faster, therefore improving
  the performance of the Exchange Server 2019 server.

- *Modern hardware support*: Exchange Server 2019
  supports more modern hardware, up to 256 GB
  memory, and up to 48 CPU cores. The minimum
  recommended amount of memory for Exchange
  Server 2019 is also 128 GB (it can run with less memory
  though), and performance greatly benefits from this
  large amount of memory. Large memory and multiple
  processor cores also enable switching from Workstation
  Garbage Collection (GC) to Server GC. This setting in
  the .NET Framework can handle more requests per
  second, thus improving performance.

- *MetaCache database*: Exchange Server 2019 has a new feature called MetaCache database (MCDB). This feature uses SSDs to cache frequently accessed data from mailbox databases. Mailbox databases are still stored on slow JBODs, but frequently accessed data can now be cached on SSDs. For every four (slow) JBODs, one SSD is used to cache information. This greatly improves performance and latencies, which is very beneficial for remote desktop or Citrix environments where Outlook clients are running in online mode. The downside is that MCDB only works in bare-metal deployments of Exchange 2019.

- *Dynamic database cache*: Mailbox database information is kept in memory. While this is useful for active mailbox databases, it does not make much sense for passive mailbox databases in a Database Availability Group (DAG). Previous versions of Exchange did not differentiate between these two, therefore "wasting" valuable memory on passive mailbox databases. Exchange Server 2019 has a dynamic database cache, which means that passive mailbox database use less memory than active mailbox databases. In other words, active mailbox databases in Exchange Server 2019 can use more memory than they could in Exchange Server 2016. This also improves overall Exchange Server 2019 performance.

Of course, there are more new features in Exchange 2019, but these are the most important and interesting ones.

What Has Been Discontinued or Deprecated in Exchange Server 2019

Every new version of Exchange Server introduces new features, but at the same time, other features are discontinued, deprecated, or available only in some other form or scenario. When you are upgrading from Exchange 2013 or Exchange 2016, here's a list of most important changes or discontinued features in Exchange 2019:

- *Unified Messaging (UM) server role*: The Unified Messaging (UM) server role has been removed from Exchange Server 2019 but is still available in Exchange Server 2016. Since the UM role is no longer available in Exchange Server 2019, it is out of scope for this book. The UM role in Exchange Server 2016 has not changed since Exchange Sever 2013, so when information is needed about the UM role, you are kindly referred to our *Pro Exchange Server 2013 SP1 PowerShell Administration* book.

- *Separate server roles*: Exchange 2013 had a separate Client Access server role and a Mailbox server role. In these days it is a best practice to combine these roles into a multi-server role. In Exchange 2016 and Exchange 2019, the separate server roles are no longer available; only the Exchange 2019 Mailbox server role is available. Under the hood you can still see the two different server roles if you look closely.

- *MAPI/CDO library*: When moving from Exchange Server 2013 to Exchange Server 2019, you will see that the MAPI/CDO library is no longer available. The functionality of the MAPI/CDO library has been replaced by Exchange Web Services (EWS), Exchange ActiveSync (EAS), or REST APIs.

13

- *RPC/HTTP*: RPC/HTTP (also known as **Outlook Anywhere**) is deprecated in Exchange Server 2019 and is replaced by Mapi/Http for Outlook client communications. Although being deprecated, this is still a requirement for installing Exchange 2019 for compatibility purposes.

- *Cluster administrative access points for DAGs*: Database Availability Groups in Exchange 2019 no longer use a cluster administrative access point, so when creating a DAG, there's no need any more to pre-create the cluster object before creating the DAG. As a result, the DAG must be managed using the Exchange Admin Center or Exchange PowerShell. Please note that this is already the recommended approach to managing a DAG.

Exchange 2019 and Active Directory

Active Directory is the foundation for Exchange Server 2019, as it has been for Exchange Server since Exchange 2000 was released 24 years ago. Earlier versions of Exchange Server—that is, Exchange 5.5 and earlier—relied on their own directory, which was separate from the (NT4) user directory. Active Directory stores most of Exchange's configuration information, both for server/organization configuration and for mail-enabled objects.

A Microsoft Windows ADDS, or Active Directory Domain Services, is best described as a forest; this is the highest level in the directory service and is the actual security boundary. The forest contains one or more Active Directory domains; a domain is a logical grouping of resources, such as users, groups, and computers. An Exchange 2019 organization is bound to one forest, so even if you have an environment with one Active Directory forest and over 100 Active Directory domains, there is only one Exchange organization.

Active Directory sites also play an important role in Exchange deployment. An Active Directory site can be seen as a location, well connected with high bandwidth and low latency—for example, a data center or an office. Active Directory sites can contain multiple Active Directory domains, but an Active Directory domain can also span multiple Active Directory sites.

Exchange 2019 depends heavily on ADDS, and ADDS depends heavily on DNS (Domain Name Service). Obviously, both need to be healthy. For Exchange 2019, the minimum levels in ADDS need to be Windows 2012 R2 Forest Functional Level (FFL) and Windows 2012 R2 Domain Functional Level (DFL). The Domain Controllers need to be at a minimum level of Windows Server 2012 R2.

Integration with Active Directory

As mentioned in the previous section, Exchange 2019 relies heavily on Active Directory, and the following topics can be identified:

- Active Directory partitions
- Active Directory permissions
- Active Directory sites

These are discussed in the next sections.

Active Directory Partitions

A Microsoft Windows ADDS consists of three system-provided partitions:

- *Schema partition*: The schema partition is the blueprint for all objects and properties that are available in Active Directory. For example, if a new user is created, a user object is instantiated from the schema, the required properties are populated, and the user

15

account is stored in the Active Directory database. All objects and properties are in the schema partition, and therefore, it depends on which version is used. Windows 2019 Active Directory has much newer objects and newer (and more) properties than, for example, Windows 2012 R2 Active Directory. The same is true, of course, for applications like Exchange Server. Exchange 2019 adds a lot of new objects and attributes to Active Directory that make it possible to increase functionality. Therefore, every new version of Exchange Server, or even the Cumulative Updates or service packs, needs to make schema changes. There is only one schema partition in the entire Active Directory forest. Even if you have an Active Directory forest with 100 domains and 250 sites worldwide, there is only one schema partition. This partition is replicated among all Domain Controllers in the entire Active Directory forest. The most important copy of the schema partition is running on the schema master, which is typically the first Domain Controller installed in the forest. This copy is the only read-write copy in the entire Active Directory forest.

- *Configuration partition*: The configuration partition is where all non-schema information is stored that needs to be available throughout the Active Directory forest. Information that can be found in the configuration partition is, for example, about Active Directory sites, about public key infrastructure, about the various partitions that are available in Active Directory, and of course about Exchange Server. Just like the schema partition, there is only one configuration partition. It replicates among all Domain Controllers in the entire Active Directory environment so that all the Exchange servers have access to the same, consistent set of information. All information regarding the Exchange server configuration, like the Exchange servers themselves, the routing infrastructure, or the number of domains that Exchange Server is responsible for, is stored in the configuration partition.

- *Domain partition*: The domain partition is where all domain-specific information is stored. There is one partition per domain, so if you have 100 domains in your Active Directory forest, you have 100 separate domain partitions. User objects, contacts, and security groups and Distribution Groups are stored in the domain partition.

The best tool for viewing the three Active Directory partitions is the ADSI Edit MMC (Microsoft Management Console) snap-in, which is shown in Figure 1-1.

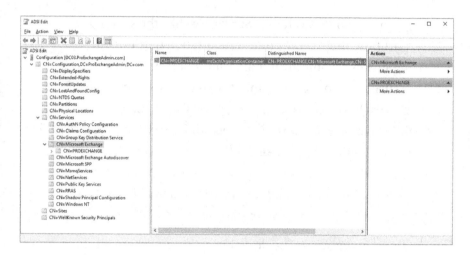

Figure 1-1. *The Exchange information is stored in the configuration partition*

Warning   There is very little safeguarding in this tool, so it is easy to destroy critical parts in Active Directory when you are just clicking around!

In Windows Server 2019, the Active Directory Administrative Center (ADAC) is the preferred tool to manage the Active Directory environment, but Active Directory Users and Computers (ADUC) can also be used. Using either tool is relatively safe since the tool prevents messing around with objects in a way that Active Directory does not like.

Tip   Enable the Active Directory recycle bin. Using the Active Directory Administrative Center, it is possible to restore (accidentally) deleted objects.

The Active Directory Sites and Services (ADSS) MMC snap-in reads and writes information from the configuration partition. All changes made here are visible to all domains in the forest; the same is true for the Active Directory Domains and Trusts MMC snap-in.

A very powerful tool regarding Active Directory is the Schema MMC snap-in, which is usually run on the Domain Controller that holds the schema master role. Using the Schema MMC snap-in, it is possible to make changes to the Active Directory schema partition.

Warning   Only do this when you are absolutely sure of what you are doing and when you have proper guidance—for example, from Microsoft support. Changes made to the Active Directory schema are irreversible!

Domain Controllers also have tools like LDIFDE and CSVDE installed as part of the AD management tools. These are command-line tools that can be used to import and export objects into or out of Active Directory. LDIFDE can also be used to make changes to the Active Directory schema, and the Exchange 2019 setup application uses the LDIFDE tool to configure Active Directory for use with Exchange 2019. These tools are beyond the scope of this book.

When promoting a server to a Domain Controller or when installing the Remote Server Administration Tools (RSAT) for Active Directory Directory Services (ADDS), the PowerShell Active Directory module is installed as well. This module enables Active Directory functionality in PowerShell, making it possible to manage Active Directory using PowerShell cmdlets.

Active Directory Permissions

There are three partitions in Active Directory. Each of these partitions has separate permission requirements, and not everybody has (full) access to these partitions. The following are the default administrator accounts or security groups that have access to each partition:

- *Schema Admins security group*: The Schema Admins have full access to the schema partition. The first administrator account is the top-level domain, which is the first domain created. To make the necessary changes to the schema partition for installing Exchange Server, the account that is used needs to be a member of this security group. Any other domain administrator in the forest is, by default, not a member of this group.

- *Enterprise Admins security group*: The Enterprise Admins have full access to the configuration partition. Again, the first administrator account in the top-level domain is a member of this group and as such can make changes to the configuration partition. Since all Exchange Server configuration information is stored in the configuration partition, the account used for installing Exchange Server needs to be a member of this group. Please note that the Enterprise Admins security group does not have permission to make changes to the schema partition.

- *Domain Admins security group*: The Domain Admins have full access to the domain partition of the corresponding domain. If there are 60 domains in an Active Directory environment, there are 60 domain partitions and thus 60 different Domain Admins security groups. The first administrator account in the top-level domain is a member of the Domain Admins security group in this top-level domain.

Why is this important to know? In the early days of Active Directory, Microsoft recommended using multiple domains in an Active Directory forest, preferably with an empty root domain. This empty root domain was a domain without any resources, and its primary purpose was for Active Directory management. All resources like servers, computers, users, and groups were in child domains. This has some implications for the use of various administrator accounts. It is a delegated model, where the administrator accounts in the top-level domain have control over all Active Directory domains, whereas the administrators in the other domains have administrative rights only in their respective Active Directory domains. These other administrators do not have administrative privileges in other domains, let alone permission to modify the configuration partition or the schema partition.

But things have changed, and although an empty root Active Directory domain environment can still be used, it is no longer actively recommended. Mostly recommended these days is a "single-forest, single-domain" environment unless there are strict legal requirements that dictate using another Active Directory model.

Active Directory Sites

Active Directory sites play an important role in any Exchange Server deployments. As stated earlier, an Active Directory site can be seen as a (physical) location with good internal network connectivity, high bandwidth, and low latency—that is, a local LAN. An office or data center is typically a good candidate for an Active Directory site.

An organization can have multiple locations, multiple data centers, or a virtual data center in Microsoft Azure, resulting in multiple Active Directory sites. Sites are typically interconnected, with lower bandwidth and higher latency connections. An Active Directory site can also have multiple domains, but at the same time, an Active Directory domain can span multiple sites.

An Active Directory site also is a replication boundary. Domain Controllers in an Active Directory site replicate their information almost immediately among Domain Controllers in the same site. If a new object is created or if an object is changed, the other Domain Controllers in that same site are notified immediately, and the information is replicated within seconds. All Domain Controllers in an Active Directory site must contain the same information.

Information exchanged between Domain Controllers in different Active Directory sites is replicated on a timed schedule, defined by the administrator. A typical timeframe can be 15 minutes, but depending on the type of connection or the bandwidth used to a particular location (you do not want your replication traffic to interfere with normal production bandwidth), it can take up to several hours. This means that when changes are made to Active Directory—for example, when installing Exchange 2019—it can take a serious amount of time before all the information is replicated across all the Domain Controllers and the new changes are visible to the entire organization.

Active Directory sites are created using the Active Directory Sites and Services MMC snap-in. The first step is to define the network subnets in the various locations in the snap-in and then tie the actual Active Directory site to the network subnet. For example, a data center in the Amsterdam site has IP subnet 10.83.4.0/24, while the network in Microsoft Azure has IP subnet 172.16.0.1/24. This is shown in Figure 1-2.

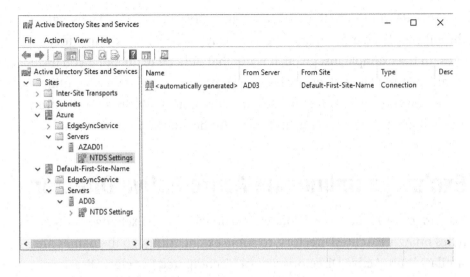

Figure 1-2. *Two different subnets and sites, as shown in Active Directory Sites and Services*

A location like a data center in Amsterdam or Microsoft Azure (which corresponds with the Active Directory site) can be "Internet facing" or "non-Internet facing," a descriptor that indicates whether the location has Internet connectivity or not. This is important for Exchange 2019, since it determines how namespaces are configured and thus how external clients are connected to their mailboxes in the different locations.

For example, the environment in Figure 1-2 has two Active Directory sites. If the data center in Microsoft Azure has an Internet connection and the data center in Amsterdam does not, all clients from the Internet are connected initially to the Exchange 2019 servers in Microsoft Azure. If a user's mailbox is in Amsterdam, the client request is proxied to the Exchange 2019 servers in Amsterdam.

But, if the data center in Amsterdam also has an Internet connection and the Exchange servers are configured accordingly, the Amsterdam-based clients can access the Exchange 2019 servers from the Internet in Amsterdam, though the request will be redirected from the Exchange 2019 servers in Azure and thus connect directly to the servers in Amsterdam.

23

Also, the routing of Simple Mail Transfer Protocol (SMTP) messages through the Exchange organization is partly based on Active Directory sites. In the example just given, it is not that difficult to do, but if you have an environment with dozens of Active Directory sites, the SMTP routing will follow the Active Directory site structure unless otherwise configured. This will be the case in a hub and spoke model for routing, for example.

Exchange Online and Azure Active Directory

Exchange 2019 relies heavily on Active Directory, and Exchange Online relies on Azure Active Directory, to some extent. Although the names are similar, Azure Active Directory cannot be compared to Active Directory, but it can better be compared to Active Directory Lightweight Directory Services (AD LDS) as used in an Edge Transport server. AD LDS is pretty much an LDAP directory.

Accounts in Azure Active Directory can be

- *Cloud identities*: These are accounts that are created directly in Azure Active Directory and do not have any correlation with an on-premises Active Directory. They are entirely managed in the cloud, using tools like the Azure Active Directory portal, the Microsoft Online Portal, or the Azure Active Directory PowerShell module.

- *Synced identities*: These are accounts that are created and managed in the on-premises Active Directory. Using an Azure AD Connect server, the identities are synchronized with Azure Active Directory. Important to keep in mind is that they are managed on-premises and NOT in the cloud. This implies that mailboxes in Exchange Online in this situation are also managed on-premises, hence the reason you need an Exchange server on-premises when using synced identities and Azure AD Connect.

Applications like Exchange Online have their own (hidden) Active Directory, the Exchange Online Directory Services (EXODS). There is a forward sync from Azure AD to this EXODS, and there's a slight delay between the two. You can see this when managing accounts in Azure AD directly. When making changes in Azure AD, it can take some time before these changes are visible in Exchange Online.

Chapter 4 goes more into detail about Azure AD and Exchange Online.

Exchange Server 2019 Architecture

Exchange 2019 Services

In Exchange 2013 there were three so-called building blocks available:

- Client Access server

- Mailbox server

- Edge Transport server

In Exchange 2013 it was already recommended to combine the Client Access and Mailbox servers into a multi-role server. In Exchange 2016 a multi-role server is enforced, and this is continued in Exchange Server 2019. In Exchange 2019 two building blocks are available:

- *Mailbox server*: As just explained, the Exchange 2019 Mailbox server contains previous Client Access and Mailbox server roles, but now there are more services:

    - *Client Access service*: The Client Access service (CAS) is the server where all clients connect. The CAS consists of two parts: Client Access Front

25

End (CAFE) and the Front-End Transport service
(FETS). The CAS performs authentication of a
client request, it locates the location of the client's
mailbox, and it proxies or redirects the client
request to the appropriate Mailbox server, where
the actual client mailbox is located. The CAS in
Exchange 2019 is sometimes also referred to as the
"front end."

- *Mailbox service*: The Mailbox service is the
  component where the actual mailbox data is stored.
  Clients do not access the Mailbox service directly;
  all requests are routed through the CAS. The
  Mailbox service in Exchange 2019 is sometimes
  also referred to as the "back end." Rendering for
  clients like Outlook Web App (OWA), transport
  transcoding for SMTP always takes place on the
  back end.

- *Edge Transport server*: The Edge Transport server acts
  as an SMTP gateway between your internal Exchange
  environment and the Internet, typically situated in the
  perimeter network. When an Edge Transport server is
  used, all messages are routed through this server. Using
  an Edge Transport server is not mandatory; there are
  lots of customers who have decided not to use an Edge
  Transport server and use a third-party solution instead
  or route SMTP messages directly from a cloud message
  hygiene solution into the Mailbox servers.

Exchange 2019 Client Access Services

The Client Access service (CAS) performs only authentication of a client request; after authentication, the client request is proxied to the Mailbox server where the destination mailbox is located. The CAS does not perform any processing with respect to mail data. According to Microsoft, its connections are stateless, but the connections are not really stateless because the SSL connection is terminated at the CAS and then processed. If a CAS goes offline, all connections are terminated and must be set up again on another CAS (which would not be the case in a true stateless setup). The reason that Microsoft calls it "stateless" is that there is no persistent storage on Exchange 2019 CAS.

Client connections are proxied from the CAS to the Mailbox server hosting the user's mailbox. This can be the same server, but it can also be another Exchange Server 2019 server in the same organization. The protocol used to communicate with the Mailbox server is the same as the client connection, so when a client uses HTTP to connect to the CAS, the HTTP request is proxied to the correct Mailbox server. The only difference is the port that is used. The client uses port 443 to connect to the CAS; the CAS uses port 444 to connect to the Mailbox server. This is also true for other protocols like POP3, IMAP4, and SMTP. Figure 1-3 shows two Exchange 2019 servers (EXCH01 and EXCH02) with the Exchange services.

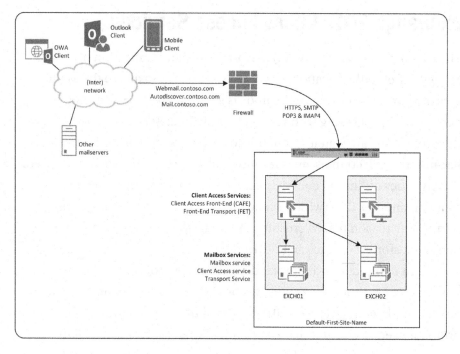

Figure 1-3. *CAS and Mailbox service in an Exchange 2019 Mailbox server*

As stated before, the CAS is a "thin" service and does not store any information from the sessions, except for the various protocol logs like Autodiscover, Outlook Anywhere, or IIS logging. This is true for both regular client requests and SMTP requests.

The Front-End Transport service is responsible for handling SMTP messages and does not store messages on the server itself but passes the SMTP messages directly to the appropriate Mailbox server where the intended recipient's mailbox is located. The Front-End Transport service does not inspect message content, but it does perform protocol logging for troubleshooting purposes.

Exchange 2019 Mailbox Services

The Mailbox service is where all the processing regarding messages takes place. Clients connect to the CAS, but the requests are proxied or redirected to the appropriate Mailbox service. All message rendering takes place on the Mailbox server.

SMTP Transport is also located on the Mailbox server and consists of three separate services:

- The Transport service

- The Mailbox Transport Delivery service

- The Mailbox Transport Submission service

The Transport service handles all SMTP message flow within the organization, such as routing, queuing, bifurcation, message categorization, and content inspection. Important to note is that the Transport service never communicates directly with the mailbox databases.

Communication between the Transport service and the mailbox database is performed by the Mailbox Transport Delivery service and the Mailbox Transport Submission service. These services connect directly to the mailbox database to deliver or retrieve messages to or from the mailbox database. As with the Front-End Transport service, the Mailbox Transport Delivery and Mailbox Transport Submission services do not queue any messages on the Mailbox server; the Transport service does queue information on the Mailbox server.

The most important part of this, of course, is the mailbox components that run on the Mailbox server. The Information Store, or store process, is responsible for handling all mailbox transactions and for storing these transactions in a mailbox database. The database is not a relational database like SQL Server; it is running on its own engine, the extensible storage engine or ESE. The ESE database engine has been fully optimized for the past 25 years for use with Exchange Server, so it performs very well and is very reliable. The ESE database is a transactional database using a database, log files, and a checkpoint file.

The Exchange Replication service is another important service running on the Mailbox server. This service is responsible for replicating mailbox data from one mailbox database on one Mailbox server to a mailbox database running on another Mailbox server. The collection of Mailbox servers replicating data between each other is called the Database Availability Group, or DAG. A DAG can take up to 16 Exchange 2019 Mailbox servers. Each mailbox database has one active mailbox database copy and may have up to 16 mailbox database copies. There is always one active mailbox database copy, with up to 15 passive mailbox database copies.

Note   An Exchange Server 2019 DAG can only contain Exchange Server 2019 Mailbox servers. Adding a previous version of Exchange is not supported and will not work. As mentioned earlier, Exchange 2019 will only support Exchange Server vNext in hosting copies of the same database on different product versions.

Exchange Server 2019 Management

There are two options for managing your Exchange 2019 environment:

- *Exchange Admin Center*: The HTML-based GUI that offers the most basic options for managing your Exchange 2019 environment

- *Exchange Management Shell*: The command-line interface running on top of Windows PowerShell and offering all nitty-gritty options when managing your Exchange 2019 environment

I will discuss these in more detail in the following sections.

Exchange Admin Center

The Exchange Admin Center (EAC) is the web-based administration portal for managing your Exchange 2019 environment. The EAC can be managed from the internal network as well as from the external network. From a safety perspective, it is recommended to disable external access to the EAC. The EAC is accessible via a URL like https://exch01/ecp internally or `https://webmail.contoso.com` externally.

When the EAC is opened, a window like the one shown in Figure 1-4 appears.

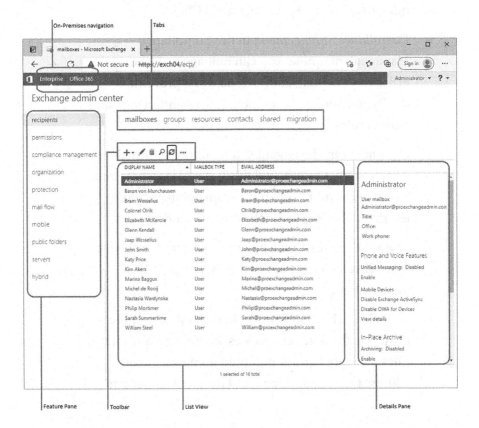

Figure 1-4. *The Exchange Admin Center in Exchange Server 2019*

In the left-hand menu, there are various components of Exchange Server 2019 that can be managed in the EAC. The left-hand menu is also called the "Feature pane" and consists of the following features:

- *Recipients*: All recipients, like mailboxes, groups, contacts, shared mailboxes, and resource mailboxes, are managed from the Recipients option.

- *Permissions*: In the Permissions option, you can manage administrator roles, user roles, and Outlook Web App policies. The first two roles are explained in more detail in the RBAC section in Chapter 10.

- *Compliance Management*: In the Compliance Management option, you can manage In-Place eDiscovery & Hold, auditing, data loss prevention (DLP), retention policies including retention tags, and journal rules.

- *Organization*: The Organization option is the highest level of configuration, and this is the place where you will manage your Exchange organization, including federated sharing, Outlook apps, and address lists.

- *Protection*: In the Protection option, you can manage antimalware protection for the Exchange 2019 organization.

- *Mail Flow*: The Mail Flow option contains all choices regarding the flow of messages, including transport rules, delivery reports, accepted domains, email address policies, and send and Receive Connectors.

- *Mobile*: All settings regarding mobile devices are managed from the Mobile option. You can manage mobile device access and mobile device mailbox policies.

- *Public Folders*: From the Public Folders option, you can manage Exchange 2019 public folders.

- *Servers*: The Exchange 2019 servers can be managed from the Servers option. This also includes databases, Database Availability Groups (DAGs), virtual directories, and certificates.

- *Hybrid*: In this section you can connect to Office 365, download the Hybrid Configuration Wizard (HCW), and create a hybrid environment.

Note   Functions available in the EAC are limited by the permissions enforced by Role-Based Access Control.

When working with the EAC, all actions are translated to PowerShell commands and then executed. The EAC has a command logging option so you can see what commands are executed. This is great for learning PowerShell and understanding what is happening under the hood.

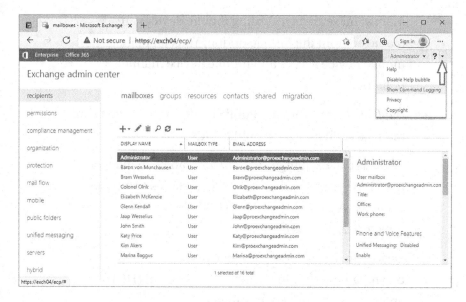

Figure 1-5. *The command log is available in the upper-right menu in the EAC*

The tabs in the top-level menu are context sensitive. In other words, they change when a different feature in the Feature pane is selected.

All actions are associated with an icon. Table 1-1 describes each of the icons.

Table 1-1. *Available Options (Icons) in the EAC Toolbar*

Icon	Name	Description
✚ ▾	Add, New	Use this for adding a new object. Sometimes a down arrow is shown like here; this means multiple options are available for creating a new object.
✏	Edit	Use this for editing a selected object.

(continued)

Table 1-1. (*continued*)

Icon	Name	Description
🗑	Delete	Use this for deleting a selected object.
🔍	Search	Use this for searching for a particular object.
↻	Refresh	Use this for refreshing the objects listed in the list view.
•••	More options	This is shown when more action options are available. For example, in **Recipients ➤ Mailboxes**, the following additional options are available: Add/Remove columns, Export data to a CSV file, Connect a mailbox, and Advanced search.
↑↓	Up/Down	Use this option when changing the priority of an object in the list view. You will find this, for example, in **Mail Flow ➤ Email Address Policies**.
📑	Copy	Use this to copy an object to a new object and start editing this new object. The original object will be kept and not changed.
╋ ━	Add/Remove	Use to add or remove an item to or from a list. For example, the Remove option is available in the Public Folders Permissions dialog box to remove users from the allowed users list.

The EAC can list up to 500 objects in one page at the same time, and if you want to view objects that aren't listed in the Details pane, you need to use Search and Filter options to find those specific objects. In Exchange 2019, the viewable limit from within the EAC list view is approximately 20,000 objects. In addition, paging is included so you can page to the results. In the Recipients list view, you can also configure page size and export the data to a CSV file.

When you select an object from the list view, information about that object is displayed in the Details pane. In some cases (e.g., with mailboxes), the Details pane includes quick management tasks. For example, if you navigate to Recipients and then Mailboxes and select a mailbox from the list view, the Details pane displays an option to enable or disable the archive for that mailbox. The Details pane can also be used to bulk-edit several objects.

Simply press the Ctrl key, select the objects you want to bulk-edit, and use the options in the Details pane. For example, selecting multiple mailboxes allows you to bulk-update users' contact and organization information, custom attributes, mailbox quotas, Outlook Web App settings, and more.

Exchange Admin Center in Exchange Online

For years, the Exchange Admin Center in Exchange Online has been used for managing Exchange Online; the look and feel was almost identical to the Exchange Admin Center in Exchange Server.

But in 2022 the new Exchange Admin Center was introduced, and the new Exchange Admin Center is more in line with the other Microsoft Online portals. The Exchange Online Admin Center can be found on `https://admin.exchange.microsoft.com` and is shown in Figure 1-6.

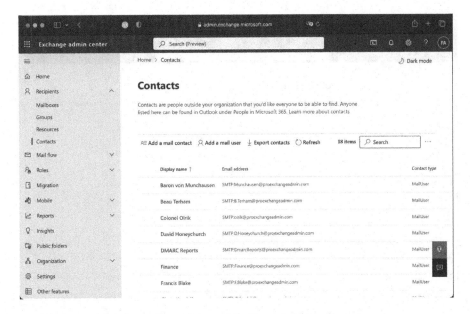

Figure 1-6. The *"new" Exchange Online Admin Center*

Please note that when you are in a hybrid configuration, recipients are managed in the on-premises Exchange Admin Center and that all changes to recipients are synchronized with Exchange Online using Azure AD Connect.

All Exchange Online–related configuration can be done in the Exchange Admin Center, but the security configuration has been removed from the Exchange Admin Center. Security settings can now be found in the Microsoft Defender Portal, which you can find on https://security. microsoft.com. This is shown in Figure 1-7.

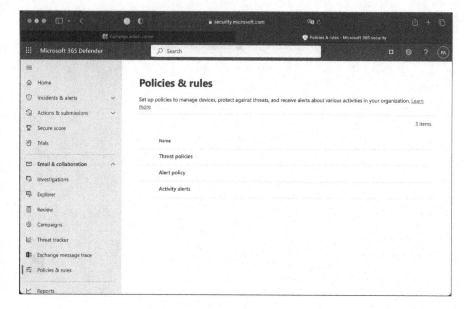

Figure 1-7. *Exchange security settings in the Microsoft Defender Portal*

Security configuration settings are discussed in detail in Chapter 7.

Exchange Management Shell

The Exchange Management Shell (EMS) is the core of Exchange Server management. This is the place where you can configure everything—every little, tiny tidbit of Exchange Server. EMS is not new; its first version appeared with Exchange Server 2007, and EMS has become more and more important over the years. There remain features that are only manageable from using EMS, and not from the EAC, such as the Client Access Rules.

EMS runs on top of Windows PowerShell, and as such it can use all functionality that is available in PowerShell, like pipelining, formatting output, saving to local disk, ordering the output, or using filtering techniques.

We will discuss the most important basics here but also at various points throughout this book.

PowerShell

Lots of Microsoft server applications have their own management shell, and all are running on top of Windows PowerShell; and whether you like it or not, PowerShell is an industry standard for Windows management and for applications that run on top of Windows. And it is not only Microsoft that is using PowerShell for managing their applications; third-party vendors are also writing PowerShell add-ons for their products. Examples of these are HP, for their EVA storage management solutions; VMware, for their virtualization platform; and KEMP, for their load-balancing solutions.

PowerShell is a command-line shell and scripting environment, and it uses the power of the .NET Framework. But PowerShell is not text based; it is object based, and as such it supports nice features such as pipelining, formatting, or redirecting the output. All objects have properties or methods that can be accessed and used in PowerShell.

Additional Modules

PowerShell is interesting to use, but it gets more interesting when you are using additional modules. The Server Manager module is used, for example, to use Server Manager features using PowerShell. When installing Exchange 2019, you need to install the prerequisite Server Roles and Features. You can do this using the Server Manager, but you can also load the Server Manager module in PowerShell, followed by the server role or server feature you want to install. For example, if you want to install the Remote Server Administration Tools, you can use the following commands:

```
[PS] C:\> Import-Module ServerManager
[PS] C:\> Install-WindowsFeature RSAT-ADDS
```

To install the IIS web server, you can use commands similar to the following:

```
[PS] C:\> Import-Module ServerManager
[PS] C:\> Install-WindowsFeature Web-Server
```

Note   In Windows Server 2019 and 2022, the Server Manager module is automatically loaded. It is referenced here for clarity.

Another interesting module when administering your Exchange 2019 environment is the Active Directory module, which can be loaded using the following command:

```
[PS] C:\> Import-Module ActiveDirectory
```

When the Active Directory module is loaded, the following options will be available in PowerShell:

- Account management

- Group management

- Organizational Unit management

- Searching and modifying objects in Active Directory

- Forest and domain management

- Domain Controller management

- Operations Master management

To create a new user in Active Directory called "Sarah Summertime" in the OU=Users in the Accounts Organizational Unit, a command similar to the following can be used:

```
[PS] C:\> Import-Module ActiveDirectory
[PS] C:\> New-ADUser -SamAccountName Sarah -Name "Sarah
Summertime" -GivenName Sarah -SurName Summertime -
AccountPassword (ConvertTo-SecureString -AsPlainText
"Pass1word" -Force) -Enabled $TRUE -Path "OU=Users,OU=Account,
DC=Proexchangeadmin,DC=COM"
```

Note   The ConvertTo-SecureString is used because the AccountPassword parameter does not accept any clear text as input for a password. In addition, AsPlainText and Force are required to convert plain text to a secure string.

Another module that is often used in Exchange management using PowerShell is the Web Administration module. Using this module, you can manage websites and their properties on your Exchange 2019 server. For example, to load the Web Administration module and clear the SSL offloading flag on the OWA Virtual Directory, you can use the following commands:

```
[PS] C:\> Import-Module WebAdministration
[PS] C:\> Set-WebConfigurationProperty -Filter //security/
access -name sslflags -Value "None" -PSPath IIS:\ -Location
"Default Web Site/OWA"
```

The last module I want to discuss is the Exchange module. The Exchange System Manager (ESM) is best started using the EMS icon on the Start menu. This will make sure the binaries are loaded correctly. What basically happens is that PowerShell is started, a special Exchange management script is loaded, and the session is connected to an Exchange 2019 server. This can be the local Exchange server you are logged onto, but it can also be another server, as long as it is in the same Active Directory site. This is called remote PowerShell, even when it is connected locally.

Remote PowerShell

When you open the EMS on the Exchange server, it is running on the local server, and you need access to the console of the server. But it is possible to use a remote PowerShell as well, thereby making connection a local Windows PowerShell instance to an Exchange server at a remote location. The workstation does not have to be in the same domain; if the proper credentials and authentication method are used, it will work. With this kind of function, it is now as easy to manage your Exchange 2019 servers in other parts of the building as those servers in data centers in other parts of the country. Needless to say, if you are using a non-domain-joined client for remote PowerShell, you cannot use Kerberos. You must change authentication on the PowerShell Virtual Directory to basic authentication for this to happen.

When the Exchange Management Shell is opened, it will automatically try to connect to the PowerShell Virtual Directory on the Exchange 2019 server you are logged onto. However, this is only true if you are logged onto an Exchange server (Console or RDP) at the time. If you are on a management workstation with the Exchange management tools installed, it will choose any Exchange server within your Active Directory site. Alternatively, by using the remote option, it is possible to connect to a remote Exchange server at this stage.

To use the remote PowerShell with Exchange 2019, make sure that the workstation (or server) supports remote signed scripts. Owing to security constraints, this is disabled by default. You can enable the support for remote signed scripts by opening a PowerShell command prompt with elevated privileges and entering the following command:

```
[PS] C:\> Set-ExecutionPolicy RemoteSigned
```

The next step is to create a session that will connect to the remote Exchange server. When the session is created, it can be imported into PowerShell:

```
[PS] C:\> $Session = New-PSSession -ConfigurationName
Microsoft.Exchange
-ConnectionUri "https://exch01.proexchangeadmin.com/powershell"
-Authentication Kerberos
[PS] C:\> Import-PSSession $Session
```

Note   When using Kerberos authentication, it is only possible to use the FQDN to connect to a specific Exchange server. Also, when using HTTPS to connect to a specific Exchange server requires a valid SSL certificate. Using a more general FQDN like webmail. proexchangeadmin.com is not possible with Kerberos authentication, unless the Service Principle Name (SPN) is registered to that system. If not, basic authentication must be used.

The PowerShell on the workstation will now connect to the remote Exchange server using a default SSL connection and, RBAC permitting, all Exchange cmdlets will be available. It is incredibly easy, as can be seen in Figure 1-8.

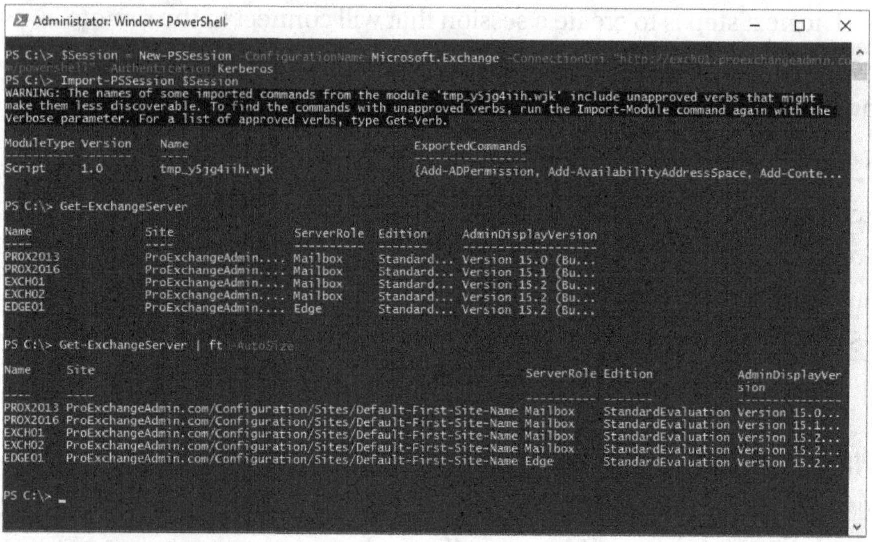

Figure 1-8. *Using remote PowerShell on a local workstation to manage Exchange 2019*

To end the remote PowerShell session, just enter the command

```
[PS] C:\> Remove-PSSession $session
```

Note   It is also possible to set up an Exchange session using the Add-PSSnapin Microsoft.Exchange.Management.PowerShell.E2010 command. While the result looks similar, it is not. This does connect, but it bypasses the RBAC configuration and it is not supported.

The example in Figure 1-8 is from a Windows 11 workstation that is also a member of the same Active Directory domain. To connect to a remote Exchange 2019 from a non-domain-joined workstation, Kerberos authentication cannot be used. Instead, basic authentication must be used.

The first step is to create a variable $Credential in the PowerShell session that contains the username and password for the remote session. When using the Get-Credential command, a pop-up box will appear, requesting a username and password for the remote Exchange environment. Once you have filled in the credentials, the following command will create a new session that will set up a connection to the Exchange environment. The $Credential variable is used to pass the credentials to the Exchange environment, and then the session is imported into PowerShell:

```
[PS] C:\> $Credential = Get-Credential
[PS] C:\> $Session = New-PSSession -ConfigurationName
Microsoft.Exchange
-ConnectionUri "https://webmail.proexchangeadmin.com"
-Authentication Basic
-Credential $Credential
[PS] C:\> Import-PSSession $Session
```

Note   If you want to use basic authentication with remote PowerShell, do not forget to enable basic authentication on the PowerShell Virtual Directory. Using remote PowerShell via the Internet is possible, but not recommended from a security perspective.

These examples were for the Active Directory domain administrator, who automatically has the Remote Management option enabled. To enable another account for remote management, you can use the following command:

```
[PS] C:\> Set-User <username> -RemotePowerShellEnabled $True
```

Tip   You can use the Prefix parameter with Import-PSSession to prefix imported cmdlets. This may come in handy when working against multiple Exchange environments or Exchange on-premises and Exchange Online. For example, when using -Prefix Contoso, all imported Exchange cmdlets for that session are prefixed with ProExchange, e.g., Get-ProExchangeMailbox. Do note that while convenient, it also means things like scripts need to be adjusted accordingly.

PowerShell ISE

When you want to create PowerShell scripts, you can use a basic tool like Notepad or Notepad++, but you can also use the PowerShell Integrated Scripting Environment, or ISE. Using ISE, you can run single commands, but you can also write, test, and debug PowerShell scripts. ISE supports multiline editing, tab completion, syntax coloring, and context-sensitive help. When debugging, you can set a breakpoint in a script to stop execution at that point. Windows PowerShell ISE can be found at the Administrative Tools menu, but when selecting a PowerShell script in Windows Explorer, you can also edit the script using ISE.

It is fully supported to use the remote PowerShell functionality and import Exchange sessions as explained in the previous section in ISE, making it possible to use all Exchange 2019–related cmdlets in ISE and to create your own Exchange 2019 scripts. This is shown in Figure 1-9.

```
Administrator: Windows PowerShell                                              —    □    ×
PS C:\> $Credential = Get-Credential ProExchange\Administrator
PS C:\> $Session = New-PSSession -ConfigurationName Microsoft.Exchange -ConnectionUri https://webmail.proexchangeadmin.c
om/PowerShell -Authentication Basic -Credential $Credential
PS C:\> Import-PSSession $Session
WARNING: The names of some imported commands from the module 'tmp_m4ifjig0.m3b' include unapproved verbs that might
make them less discoverable. To find the commands with unapproved verbs, run the Import-Module command again with the
Verbose parameter. For a list of approved verbs, type Get-Verb.

ModuleType Version     Name                              ExportedCommands
---------- -------     ----                              ----------------
Script     1.0         tmp_m4ifjig0.m3b                  {Add-ADPermission, Add-AvailabilityAddressSpace, Add-Conte...


PS C:\> Get-ExchangeServer

Name              Site                  ServerRole  Edition    AdminDisplayVersion
----              ----                  ----------  -------    -------------------
EXCH03            ProExchangeAdmin....  Mailbox,... Standard... Version 15.0 (Bu...
EXCH04            ProExchangeAdmin....  Mailbox,... Standard... Version 15.1 (Bu...
edge01            ProExchangeAdmin....  Edge        Standard... Version 15.2 (Bu...


PS C:\> _
```

Figure 1-9. *Using remote PowerShell in ISE to get access to the Exchange 2019 modules*

While ISE is convenient as it is available out of the box on Windows servers, other tools for writing and maintaining PowerShell code are available as well. Another popular one is Visual Studio Code or VSCode, which is freely available from Microsoft at code.visualstudio.com. This environment is extensible and also has add-in support for things such as GitHub or PSScriptAnalyzer for quickly analyzing your scripts and supports other languages and file types as well (e.g., C, XML, JSON).

Exchange Online PowerShell

Exchange Online can also be managed using PowerShell. Microsoft has an Exchange Online PowerShell module available.

To check if there are any PowerShell modules installed on the (management) server, you can use the Get-InstalledModule PowerShell cmdlet. If no Exchange Online module is installed, you can use the Install-Module command:

```
PS C:\> Install-Module -Name ExchangeOnlineManagement
-RequiredVersion 3.0.0
```

Sometimes, if you want to install this on an older Windows 2016 server, the installation fails with warning messages similar to

```
WARNING: MSG:UnableToDownload «https://go.microsoft.com/
fwlink/?LinkID=627338&clcid=0x409» «»
WARNING: Unable to download the list of available providers.
Check your internet connection.
WARNING: Unable to download from URI 'https://go.microsoft.com/
fwlink/?LinkID=627338&clcid=0x409' to ''.
```

These are usually caused by TLS 1.2 issues on your management server. To have PowerShell use a TLS 1.2 session, execute the following command before running the Install-Module cmdlet:

```
PS C:\> [Net.ServicePointManager]::SecurityProtocol =
[Net.SecurityProtocolType]::Tls12
```

Of course, a better solution is to use Windows 2019, Windows 2022, or Windows 11 for remote management purposes.

To set up a PowerShell connection to Exchange Online, execute the Connect-ExchangeOnline cmdlet after you have installed the Exchange Online PowerShell module. Starting in January 2023, Microsoft only supports Modern Authentication, so an additional authentication window is shown. After entering your administrator credentials and using MFA, you have set up a connection:

```
PS C:\> Connect-ExchangeOnline
```

This V3 EXO PowerShell module contains new REST API backed
Exchange Online cmdlets which doesn't require WinRM for Client-
Server communication. You can now run these cmdlets after
turning off WinRM Basic Auth in your client machine thus making
it more secure.

Unlike the EXO* prefixed cmdlets, the cmdlets in this module
support full functional parity with the RPS (V1) cmdlets.

V3 cmdlets in the downloaded module are resilient to transient
failures, handling retries and throttling errors inherently.

However, REST backed EOP and SCC cmdlets are not available yet.
To use those, you will need to enable WinRM Basic Auth.

For more information check https://aka.ms/exov3-module

PS C:\>

And you can start using Exchange Online PowerShell cmdlets. For
example, to retrieve a list of mail-enabled users (MEUs; which correspond
to mailboxes in Exchange 2019 because of Azure AD Connect), you can use
the Get-MailUser cmdlet:

PS C:\> Get-MailUser | Select DisplayName,Alias,UserPri
ncipalName

DisplayName	Alias	UserPrincipalName
Baron von Munchausen	Munchausen	Munchausen@ ProExchangeAdmin.com
Beau Terham	B.Terham	B.Terham@ ProExchangeAdmin.com

Colonel Olrik	olrik	olrik@ProExchangeAdmin.com
David Honeychurch	D.Honeychurch	D.Honeychurch@ ProExchangeAdmin.com
DMARC Reports	DmarcReports	DmarcReports@ ProExchangeAdmin.com
Finance	Finance	Finance@ProExchangeAdmin.com
Francis Blake	F.Blake	F.Blake@ProExchangeAdmin.com
Glenn Kendall	G.Kendall	G.Kendall@ ProExchangeAdmin.com
Jaap Wesselius	j.wesselius	j.wesselius@ ProExchangeAdmin.com
Jimmy Tcheng	J.Tcheng	J.Tcheng@ ProExchangeAdmin.com
John Smith	J.Smith	J.Smith@ProExchangeAdmin.com
Karen Young	K.Young	K.Young@ProExchangeAdmin.com
Michel De Rooij	M.deRooij	M.deRooij@ ProExchangeAdmin.com
Philip Mortimer	P.Mortimer	P.Mortimer@ ProExchangeAdmin.com
Professor Labrousse	P.Labrousse	P.Labrousse@ ProExchangeAdmin.com
Sarah Summertown	S.Summertown	S.Summertown@ ProExchangeAdmin.com
TLS Reports	TLSReports	TLSReports@ ProExchangeAdmin.com

```
PS C:\>
```

When you are finished using Exchange Online PowerShell, it is a good practice to disconnect from Exchange Online using the Disconnect-ExchangeOnline cmdlet.

Note   In older blogposts available on the Internet, you can find information on how to connect to Exchange Online PowerShell by setting up a $Session connection to Exchange Online and importing this into PowerShell. This is using basic authentication and no longer works. Only Modern Authentication is supported for Exchange Online PowerShell.

Virtualization

When looking at the minimum recommended hardware, you might think that virtualizing Exchange 2019 is no longer supported. But that is not the case. A virtualized Exchange Server 2019 server is fully supported as long as your virtualization platform is supported via the SVVP.

Running your Exchange 2019 servers in Microsoft Azure is also fully supported. The only additional requirement for Exchange 2019 servers in Microsoft Azure is that all data is stored on premium SSD storage.

Summary

At the time of writing, Exchange has been around for almost 25 years. The current version is Exchange Server 2019, but a successor with codename Exchange vNext is already announced. If you want the latest and greatest of Exchange features, you should move to Exchange Online. If you want a rock-solid messaging platform without too many bells and whistles, you can implement Exchange Server 2019.

Exchange Server 2019 has been a continuous development and improvement from Exchange Server 2013. Differences with Exchange Server 2016 are minor when it comes to user features, but there are improvements when it comes to security and performance. Examples of this are default support for TLS 1.2, support for Windows 2022 Server Core, modern hardware support, and the MetaCache database and Modern Authentication.

The next chapter is about designing your Exchange 2019 infrastructure and installing Exchange 2019.

CHAPTER 2

Exchange Infrastructure

In the previous chapter, we have discussed some of the basics of Exchange 2019. This chapter will cover the infrastructure of Exchange 2019, which consists of the following sections:

- "Designing Your Exchange 2019 Environment": In this section we will discuss designing a 2,000-mailbox fictitious company called ProExchangeAdmin.com.

- "Installation of Exchange 2019": In this section we will discuss installing Exchange 2019 on Windows Server 2022. As per Microsoft recommendation, we will use the Server Core edition and use an unattended setup of Exchange 2019.

- "Configuring Exchange 2019": In this section we will discuss the post-installation configuration, so everything you must do after the initial installation. This includes setting virtual directories, installing certificates, relocation files etc.

- "High Availability": In this section we will discuss the high availability features in Exchange 2019. This covers the Database Availability Group (DAG), including the AutoReseed and MetaCache database (MCDB) features. Furthermore, we will discuss protocol load balancing as part of the high availability solutions.

© Jaap Wesselius and Michel de Rooij 2023
J. Wesselius and M. de Rooij, *Pro Exchange Administration*,
https://doi.org/10.1007/978-1-4842-9591-5_2

- "Exchange Transport": In this section we will discuss SMTP Transport in Exchange 2019, including Send Connectors and Receive Connectors, which covers SMTP relay as well. The Exchange 2019 Edge Transport server is discussed as well as it is installed in the perimeter network. As such, it acts as a gateway between the Exchange 2019 Mailbox servers and Exchange Online Protection for message hygiene or cross-premises communications in case of a hybrid deployment.

- "Upgrading from Exchange 2013 or Exchange 16": If you are running a previous version of Exchange Server, you can use this section for upgrading to Exchange 2019.

Designing Your Exchange 2019 Environment

When you want to deploy Exchange 2019 for any number of users, you must make a proper design of your Exchange Server environment. You must do an inventory of all business and legal requirements and write these down in a design document. Together with the user requirements, such as the number of users (i.e., mailboxes), the mailbox sizing, and so on, you create a design of your Exchange 2019 environment based on the proper design decisions. If you fail to do so, most likely you will run into capacity issues when you run your Exchange 2019 environment.

Business, legal, and user requirements include answers to the following questions:

- What is the average mailbox size?

- What is your backup strategy?

- If you have backups, how long do you need to keep these backups, and do you need to store the backups at an off-site location?

- What is the average message size used by your users, and how many messages are sent and received on average?

- What are the normal business hours?

- What does your service-level agreement (SLA) look like? In your SLA you will define your answers to such questions as the following:

  - Is there a need for 24 × 7, or will 5 × 12 do as well?

  - How long does it take to create a backup and, more important, how long does it take to restore data, and what type of data can be restored (e.g., mailbox or item level)?

  - In case of an emergency, what amount of data are you allowed to lose, or is it allowed to resume with initial empty mailboxes where data will be restored to over time (dial-tone recovery)?

  - How long does it take to restore a mailbox, a mailbox database, or an entire Exchange 2019 server?

  - Are there guaranteed delivery times for messages?

- What is the user concurrency? That is, how many users are online at the same time?

These are some of the questions you need to answer when designing a proper Exchange 2019 environment. They are a different kind of question from the ones you, as an Exchange administrator, are accustomed to answering, such as "Can I virtualize my Exchange server?", "How much memory do I need in my server?", or "How about the disk configuration of my Exchange 2019 server?"

In our fictitious ProExchangeAdmin.com company, we have 2,000 users, we anticipate a 5 GB mailbox for each user, and, for high availability purposes, we will use two Exchange 2019 servers in a Database Availability Group.

Exchange 2019 Server Role Requirements Calculator

One of the best tools to determine the sizing of your Exchange 2019 server is the Exchange 2019 Server Role Requirements Calculator. This is basically a spreadsheet created by the Microsoft Exchange product group that will perform the sizing calculations for an Exchange 2019 deployment based on the requirements, which you must provide as input. Initially, the Exchange 2019 requirements calculator was only made available via the Exchange 2019 ISO image. However, after customer complaints the calculator for Exchange 2019 is also available as a separate download via `https://aka.ms/excalc`.

When you open the calculator, you will see an Excel spreadsheet with nine tabs. The first tab is where you enter the requirements that will be used as input for the actual design.

Important requirements you must enter here are, for example

- *If you are virtualizing your Exchange servers*:
  Virtualizing your Exchange 2019 servers is not a problem if the virtualization solution is validated in the SVVP and the virtualization vendor supports running Exchange 2019 in its solution.

- *How many Mailbox servers you will use*: This is a tricky matter; the number you choose depends on the number of mailboxes you will be hosting on your Mailbox server. You must start somewhere, and as a rule of thumb, I always start with approximately 2,500 mailboxes on one Mailbox server, so for 10,000 mailboxes, I start with four Mailbox servers. Depending on the sizing that comes out of the requirements calculator, you can always adjust the number of Mailbox servers.

- *How many mailboxes in your environment*: This is a hard number to ascertain for setting your requirements. When you are designing your Exchange 2019 environment, keep future growth in mind. You can define a percentage growth in the calculator for this.

- *How many messages sent and received per mailbox each day*: This number is also known as the usage profile, and it might be quite difficult to ascertain. One way to find good numbers for this is to analyze message tracking in your existing environment and calculate average values for this.

- *The mailbox size*: In our ProExchangeAdmin.com environment, we set this to 5 GB. Quite a lot of people still have doubts about large mailboxes, but Exchange 2019 does not have trouble with 50 GB mailboxes, especially not if the MetaCache database is used (more about this later in this chapter).

- *The backup architecture*: A traditional backup is VSS based, whether it is a hardware VSS solution or a software VSS one. There is a backup server running in your network and backup clients on your Exchange servers. Microsoft System Center DPM is an example of this, but there are a lot more from Symantec, IBM, HP, and others. Exchange Native Data Protection is another way of safeguarding your information, sometimes also referred to as a "backup-less" environment.

In our ProExchangeAdmin environment, the requirements are based on an HP DL380 Gen11 server with a dual Intel Xeon Gold 6418H processor with 48 cores, running at 2.1 GHz. The SPECint2017 value for this server is 569. This data is fed into the requirements calculator as listed in Table 2-1. For the Exchange server, we are not using any virtualization solution.

Table 2-1. *Requirements Used as Input for the ProExchangeAdmin Exchange Server Configuration*

Requirement	Value
Server Role Virtualization	No
High Availability Deployment	Yes
Site Resilient Deployment	No
Use MetaCache Database	Yes
Number of Non-lagged Copies	2
Number of Lagged Copies	0

(continued)

Table 2-1. (*continued*)

Requirement	Value
Number of Mailboxes	2,000
Number of Days per Workweek	5
Total Send/Receive Messages per Mailbox per Day	50
Average Message Size	75 KB
Initial Mailbox Size	2.5 GB
Mailbox Size Limit	5 GB
Deleted Items Retention Window (days)	30
Single Item Recovery Enabled	Yes
Maximum Database Size	1 TB
Backup Methodology	Software VSS backup/restore
System and Boot Disk	600 GB, 15 krpm SAS
Database Disk	4 TB, 7200 RPM, 3½-inch SAS disk
Log Disk	4 TB, 7200 RPM, 3½-inch SAS disk
Restore Volume	4 TB, 7200 RPM, 3½-inch SAS disk
Server SPECint2017 Rate Value[1]	569
Process Cores/Server	48
Number of Mailbox Servers Hosting Mailboxes	2

---

[1] You can find the SPECint2017 value for your own hardware on the www.spec.org/cpu2017/results/ website.

These are the most important settings for the first page of the requirements calculator; all other requirements can be left at their default settings at this point.

When you have entered all data into the requirements calculator, you can navigate to the second tab for viewing the role requirements. On this sheet, you will find the sizing of the Exchange 2019 servers, based on the input you have just entered.

You will find the number of mailboxes, the number of mailbox databases, the IOPS generated, and the amount of memory needed in the Exchange server, just to name a few. In our example, the most important results are listed in Table 2-2.

Table 2-2. *Calculated Requirements of Our ProExchangeAdmin Exchange 2019 Environment*

Requirement	Value
Number of Mailboxes	2,000
Number of Mailboxes per Database	164
Transaction Logs Generated per Mailbox per Day	10
IOPS Profile per Mailbox	0,03
Number of Mailbox Databases	14
Available Database Cache per Mailbox	10.7
Recommended RAM Configuration	96 GB
Server CPU Megacycles Requirement	9424
Number of Processor Cores Utilized	3
Primary Data Center Server CPU Utilization	5%
Database Space Required (per Database)	1023 GB
Log Space Required (per Database)	10 GB

(continued)

Table 2-2. (*continued*)

Requirement	Value
Database Space Required (per Server)	14,324 GB
Log Space Required (per Server)	137 GB
Total Database Required IOPS (per Server)	79
Total Log Required IOPS (per Server)	45

As you can see, Exchange 2019 needs quite some resources according to the requirements calculator; on the other hand, it could be said that this calculation is a worst-case scenario in which all resources are stressed to the max. But compared with previous versions of Exchange, or when not including the MetaCache database, the numbers are a lot lower. In real life, the resources used by Exchange 2019 are probably much less, but when your design is according to the requirements calculator, you know it is fully supported. When you assign fewer resources to your Exchange 2019 server, especially memory, there is a serious risk of experiencing performance issues.

So 14 mailbox databases are used by these Exchange 2019 servers. The "Volume Requirements" tab in the requirements calculator shows the number of mailbox databases and the volumes used where the mailbox databases are stored. Since Exchange 2019 supports multiple mailbox databases on one volume, only seven volumes are used, and the mailbox databases are spread across these seven volumes.

The "Storage Design" tab in the requirements calculator tells you how many disks are used for each volume. For the mailbox databases, six disks are used, in a RAID-1/0 configuration. The transaction log files of all mailbox databases are stored on a separate volume, consisting of two disks in a RAID-1/0 configuration.

A special volume is used for restoring purposes. If you want to restore one or more mailbox databases from backup, a special volume is used for this. In our example, three disks in a RAID-5 configuration are used to create this restore volume.

So, in total, this Exchange 2019 server is using 11 physical disks of 6 TB each for storing 2,000 mailboxes of max 5 GB in size each. The server itself is using two disks in a RAID-1 configuration for the operating system and the Exchange 2019 server software and the transport queue database. A graphic representation of this distribution is shown in Figure 2-1.

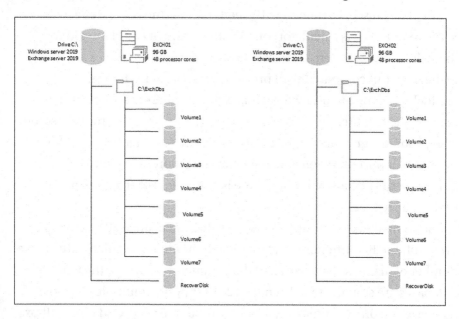

Figure 2-1. *The Exchange 2019 server design for a 2,000-mailbox ProExchangeAdmin environment*

For smaller Exchange servers, drive letters can be used for the disks holding the mailbox databases. For larger environments, it is recommended to use mount points. When using mount points, a structure like this is used:

- C:\ExchDbs\Volume1

- C:\ExchDbs\Volume2

- C:\ExchDbs\Volume3

- C:\ExchDbs\Volume4

- Etc.

When using mount points, it is also possible to use features like AutoReseed and the MetaCache database. AutoReseed and MetaCache database are discussed later in this chapter as part of the high availability section.

Microsoft has published articles and whitepapers on sizing Exchange 2013 and Exchange 2016 that can be found at `https://bit.ly/X2016Sizing`. These are old whitepapers, but the overall technology has not changed over the years.

Installation of Exchange 2019

When you are installing Exchange 2019, you must meet several requirements regarding hardware, the operating system where Exchange Server will be installed, and the version of Active Directory Directory Services (ADDS) that will be used. There is also some prerequisite software that needs to be installed in advance, including Windows Server Roles and Features.

Hardware Requirements

Exchange 2019 has the following hardware requirements, based on Microsoft's experience from Exchange Online. One could think that these requirements seem to have been established by a marketing department. As we have seen in the previous section, the normal hardware requirements are a bit different, depending on the expected usage. The following are the Microsoft recommended bare-minimum requirements for a supported Exchange 2019 deployment:

- x64 architecture from Intel or AMD.

- 128 GB of RAM for the Mailbox server. Exchange has large memory support up to 256 GB.

- 64 GB of RAM for the Edge Transport server.

- At least 30 GB of free space where Exchange 2019 will be installed. (Add 500 MB for every UM language pack. All disks must be formatted with the NTFS or ReFS.)

- An additional hard disk of 500 MB where the transport queue database is stored.

For a full and up-to-date overview of all Exchange 2019 requirements, visit the Exchange Server system requirements on Microsoft docs at https://bit.ly/Ex2019Requirements.

Note   The requirements look substantial at first sight, especially when comparing with previous versions of Exchange. Please bear in mind that these numbers are based on Exchange Online experiences, where the previous numbers were dictated by the marketing department. These numbers are a recommendation. Your mileage may vary though, depending on the storage calculator as discussed in the previous section. Also keep in mind Exchange is now designed with the end user experience in mind, which translates to low latencies made possible by plenty of resources and substantial caching of data.

Software Requirements

Exchange 2019 can be installed on the following Windows operating systems:

- Windows Server 2022, Datacenter or Standard. Server Core is recommended. Desktop Experience is no longer required, but fully supported.

- Windows Server 2019, Datacenter or Standard, with both Server Core and Desktop Experience. Nano Server is not supported.

Note   Exchange 2019 is only supported on Windows Server 2022 and Windows Server 2019. It will not work on Windows Server 2016.

The Exchange 2019 management tools can be installed on the following Windows operating systems:

- Windows Server 2022, Datacenter or Standard
- Windows Server 2019, Datacenter or Standard
- Windows 10 or Windows 11, 64-bit edition

When it comes to Active Directory, the following requirements can be identified:

- Domain Controllers must be Windows 2012 R2 or higher.

- Active Directory functional level must be Windows 2012 R2 or higher.

- The Active Directory site where Exchange 2019 is installed should have at least one writeable Domain Controller that also holds the Global Catalog server.

Several DNS namespace scenarios are supported in Exchange 2019, although these requirements have not changed in years. The following namespaces can be used with Exchange 2019:

- *Contiguous namespace*: This is a normal namespace where all domain names in the environment are contiguous. For example, a root domain would be proexchangeadmin.com, and the child domains would be emea.proexchangeadmin. com, na.proexchangeadmin.com, or asia. proexchangeadmin.com. Go one level deeper, and it would be prod.emea.proexchangeadmin.com and rnd. na.proexchangeadmin.com.

- *Non-contiguous namespace*: This is a namespace where the different trees in an Active Directory forest do not have similar names. For example, one tree in the Active Directory forest can be proexchangeadmin.com, while another tree in the same Active Directory forest can be Exchange2019.nl, and a third tree can be Exchangelabs. nl. They form separate domain trees in one forest.

  A special example of a non-contiguous namespace is where one tree would be proexchangeadmin. com and another tree would be proexchangeadmin. net. In this scenario, you would run into problems with the NetBIOS name of these domains. By default, the NetBIOS name of the domains would be proexchangeadmin, but since you cannot have two identical NetBIOS names in one network, you have to have another NetBIOS name for the second proexchangeadmin domain.

- *Single-label domain*: A single-label domain is a domain name that does not contain a DNS suffix—for example, no .com, .net, .org, or .corp. A normal domain name would be proexchangeadmin.com, but a single-label domain would be proexchangeadmin. A single-label domain is supported by Exchange 2019, but the use of single-label domains is not recommended by Microsoft.

- *Disjoint namespace*: A disjoint namespace is a namespace where the primary DNS suffix of a server does not match the DNS name of the Active Directory domain. For example, you can have an Exchange server called AMS-EXCH01 with a primary DNS suffix research.proexchangeadmin.com in the Active Directory domain emea.proexchangeadmin.com.

For a complete overview of supported DNS namespaces and additional resources, you can check the support for DNS namespace planning in the Microsoft server products article at `https://bit.ly/ExNamespace`.

Note   Installation of Exchange 2019 on Domain Controllers is supported but not recommended. The recommended way of installing Exchange 2019 is on a member server in an Active Directory domain.

Installing Exchange 2019

One of the requirements of Exchange 2019 is that it can only be installed on Windows Server 2022 or Windows Server 2019. Windows Server Core is recommended, but not required. The Desktop Experience feature can be used as well. Although more difficult to manage for the more traditional

Windows GUI administrator, I always recommend using Server Core because of the lower footprint and attack surfaces. The prerequisites for Windows 2019 Server Core and Desktop Experience are similar, but where needed information for Desktop Experience is added.

Note   Take special care when deciding whether to use Server Core or Desktop Experience; it is not possible to change between the two after installation.

Exchange uses multiple disks for its operation. Of course, there is the system and boot disk (drive C:\), but there are also disks for storing the SMTP queue database and the mailbox databases.

For small deployments you can use regular drive letters for the mailbox database disks, but for larger deployments, mount points are recommended to avoid running out of drive letters. Also, when using mount points, you can take advantage of interesting features like AutoReseed and MetaCache database. Throughout this book we will be using drive D:\ as the disk holding the SMTP Transport database and SMTP log files, and drive Z:\ will be assigned to the DVD drive. Mailbox databases will be stored on disks configured as mount points, located in C:\ExchDbs\Volume1, C:\ExchDbs\Volume2, C:\ExchDbs\Volume3, etc. The commands in the following sections are PowerShell commands for Windows Server 2022 Core but can be used on Windows 2022 Desktop Experience and both versions of Windows 2019.

Note   For the following sections, I assume you already have installed Windows Server 2022 Server Core, joined it to a domain, and configured network settings, remote desktop, and date and time settings and that the server is fully patched.

Disk Configuration

To assign drive letter Z: to the DVD drive, use the following PowerShell command:

```
PS C:\> Get-WmiObject -Class Win32_volume -Filter "DriveType=5" |
Select -First 1 | Set-WmiInstance -Arguments @{DriveLetter="Z:"}
```

To get an overview of the disks that are available on Windows Server 2022, you can use the Get-Disk command in PowerShell as shown in the following output:

```
PS C:\> Get-Disk | ft -a

Number Friendly Name       Serial Number    HealthStatus   OperationalStatus
Total Size    Partition Style
------ ------------------  -------------    ------------   -----------------
---------     ---------------
0      HP LOGICAL VOLUME   PDNLHOBRH47487   Healthy        Online
186.28 GB    MBR
1      HP LOGICAL VOLUME   PDNLHOBRH47487   Healthy        Online
279.37 GB    RAW
2      HP LOGICAL VOLUME   PDNLHOBRH47487   Healthy        Online
279.37 GB    RAW
3      HP LOGICAL VOLUME   PDNLHOBRH47487   Healthy        Online
279.37 GB    RAW
4      HP LOGICAL VOLUME   PDNLHOBRH47487   Healthy        Online
279.37 GB    RAW
5      HP LOGICAL VOLUME   PDNLHOBRH47487   Healthy        Online
279.37 GB    RAW
6      HP LOGICAL VOLUME   PDNLHOBRH47487   Healthy        Online
447.1 GB     RAW
```

Disk number 0 is the boot and system disk. Disk number 1 will be used for storing the SMTP queue database, which will be drive D:\. Disks 2, 3, 4, and 5 are also database disks. Disk 6 is a SSD disk that will be used for the MetaCache database. This disk must not be initialized and formatted. The MetaCache database needs a raw SSD disk.

To configure the SMTP queue disk, bring it online, initialize, and format it using the following PowerShell commands:

```
PS C:\> Get-Disk -Number 1 | Initialize-Disk
-PartitionStyle GPT
PS C:\> New-Partition -DiskNumber 1 -UseMaximumSize

    DiskPath: \\?\scsi#disk&ven_hp&prod_logical_volume#5&22eb63&
0&000500#{53f56307-b6bf-11d0-94f2-00a0c91efb8b}
```

PartitionNumber	DriveLetter	Offset	Size	Type
2		16777216	279.35 GB	Basic

```
PS C:\> Add-PartitionAccessPath -DiskNumber 1 -PartitionNumber
2 -AccessPath D:
PS C:\> Get-Partition -DiskNumber 1 -PartitionNumber 2 |
Format-Volume -FileSystem NTFS -NewFileSystemLabel "Queue
Database" -AllocationUnitSize 65536 -Confirm:$false
```

DriveLetter	FriendlyName	FileSystemType	DriveType	HealthStatus
OperationalStatus	SizeRemaining	Size		
D	Queue Database	NTFS	Fixed	Healthy
OK	279.26 GB	279.35 GB		

For formatting the disks that will hold the mailbox databases in mount points, the process is similar. When using the Add-PartitionAccessPath command in PowerShell, the -AccessPath option will have the value "C:\ExchDbs\Vol1" instead of a drive letter. This will result in the following:

```
PS C:\> New-Item C:\ExchDbs\Vol1 -ItemType Directory

    Directory: C:\ExchDbs
```

```
Mode                LastWriteTime          Length Name
----                -------------          ------ ----
d-----      2/6/2023    4:30 PM                   Volume1
```

```
PS C:\> Get-Disk -Number 2 | Initialize-Disk -PartitionStyle GPT
PS C:\> New-Partition -DiskNumber 2 -UseMaximumSize
```

```
    DiskPath: \\?\scsi#disk&ven_hp&prod_logical_volume#5&22eb63&
0&000600#{53f56307-b6bf-11d0-94f2-00a0c91efb8b}
```

```
PartitionNumber DriveLetter Offset     Size      Type
--------------- ----------- ------     ----      ----
2                           16777216   279.35 GB Basic
```

```
PS C:\> Add-PartitionAccessPath -DiskNumber 2 -PartitionNumber
2 -AccessPath "C:\ExchDbs\Vol1"
PS C:\> Get-Partition -Disknumber 2 -PartitionNumber 2 |
Format-Volume -FileSystem NTFS -NewFileSystemLabel "Vol1"
-AllocationUnitSize 65536 -Confirm:$false
```

```
DriveLetter FriendlyName FileSystemType DriveType HealthStatus
OperationalStatus SizeRemaining      Size
----------- ------------ -------------- --------- ------------
----------------- -------------      ----
            Vol1         NTFS           Fixed     Healthy
OK                279.26 GB          279.35 GB
```

Repeat this for the other disks that will contain databases.

Note   If you made an error and need to clean up a disk configuration, you can use the Remove-Partition and Clear-Disk commands in PowerShell.

Installing Prerequisite Software

When installing the Exchange 2019 Mailbox server on Windows 2022, the following prerequisite Windows features as well as additional runtimes are required:

- Windows Server Roles and Features and the Active Directory Remote Server Administration Tools (RSAT-ADDS)

- Visual C++ Redistributable package for Visual Studio 2012

- Visual C++ Redistributable package for Visual Studio 2013

- Microsoft Unified Communications Managed API 4.0 Core Runtime

---

Note   When installing Exchange 2019 on Windows Sever 2019, the .NET Framework 4.8 must be installed as well. The .NET Framework 4.8 is installed by default on Windows Server 2022.

To install Windows Server Roles and Features on Windows 2022 Server Core, use the following command:

```
PS C:\> Install-WindowsFeature Server-Media-Foundation, NET-
Framework-45-Features, RPC-over-HTTP-proxy, RSAT-Clustering,
RSAT-Clustering-CmdInterface, RSAT-Clustering-PowerShell,
WAS-Process-Model, Web-Asp-Net45, Web-Basic-Auth, Web-Client-
Auth, Web-Digest-Auth, Web-Dir-Browsing, Web-Dyn-Compression,
```

Web-Http-Errors, Web-Http-Logging, Web-Http-Redirect, Web-Http-Tracing, Web-ISAPI-Ext, Web-ISAPI-Filter, Web-Metabase, Web-Mgmt-Service, Web-Net-Ext45, Web-Request-Monitor, Web-Server, Web-Stat-Compression, Web-Static-Content, Web-Windows-Auth, Web-WMI, RSAT-ADDS, Telnet-Client

To install Windows Server Roles and Features on Windows 2022 Desktop Experience, use the following command:

PS C:\> Install-WindowsFeature Server-Media-Foundation, NET-Framework-45-Features, RPC-over-HTTP-proxy, RSAT-Clustering, RSAT-Clustering-CmdInterface, RSAT-Clustering-Mgmt, RSAT-Clustering-PowerShell, WAS-Process-Model, Web-Asp-Net45, Web-Basic-Auth, Web-Client-Auth, Web-Digest-Auth, Web-Dir-Browsing, Web-Dyn-Compression, Web-Http-Errors, Web-Http-Logging, Web-Http-Redirect, Web-Http-Tracing, Web-ISAPI-Ext, Web-ISAPI-Filter, Web-Lgcy-Mgmt-Console, Web-Metabase, Web-Mgmt-Console, Web-Mgmt-Service, Web-Net-Ext45, Web-Request-Monitor, Web-Server, Web-Stat-Compression, Web-Static-Content, Web-Windows-Auth, Web-WMI, Windows-Identity-Foundation, RSAT-ADDS, Telnet-Client

---

Note   The Telnet-Client is not a prerequisite for any version of Exchange, but it is a very useful tool for basic troubleshooting of Exchange, so I install it on any Exchange server.When the Exchange server is configured to be a member of a Database Availability Group, the Failover-Clustering features must be included in both commands as well.

The easiest way to download and install any prerequisite software is using PowerShell. Log onto the Windows 2022 server with an administrative account and execute the following commands in a PowerShell command window with elevated privileges.

To download the Visual C++ Redistributable package for Visual Studio 2012

```
PS C:\> New-Item C:\Install\VS2012 -ItemType Directory
PS C:\> Start-BitsTransfer -Source "https://download.microsoft.
com/download/1/6/B/16B06F60-3B20-4FF2-B699-5E9B7962F9AE/VSU_4/
vcredist_x64.exe" -Destination C:\Install\VS2012
```

To download the Visual C++ Redistributable package for Visual Studio 2013

```
PS C:\> New-Item C:\Install\VS2013 -ItemType Directory
PS C:\> Start-BitsTransfer -Source "https://download.
visualstudio.microsoft.com/download/pr/10912041/
cee5d6bca2ddbcd039da727bf4acb48a/vcredist_x64.exe" -Destination
C:\Install\VS2013
```

Finally, to download the Microsoft Unified Communications Managed API 4.0 Core Runtime, 64-bit (Desktop Experience Only)

```
PS C:\> Start-BitsTransfer -Source "http://download.microsoft.
com/download/2/C/4/2C47A5C1-A1F3-4843-B9FE-84C0032C61EC/
UcmaRuntimeSetup.exe" -Destination C:\Install
```

For Windows Server 2019, download the .NET Framework 4.8:

```
PS C:\> New-Item C:\Install -ItemType Directory
PS C:\> Start-BitsTransfer -Source "https://download.
visualstudio.microsoft.com/download/pr/7afca223-55d2-470a-
8edc-6a1739ae3252/abd170b4b0ec15ad0222a809b761a036/ndp48-
x86-x64-allos-enu.exe" -Destination C:\Install
```

Note   All PowerShell commands in this book are available via the
Apress GitHub.

The Microsoft Unified Communications Managed API 4.0 Core
Runtime, 64-bit, needs to be downloaded for the Desktop Experience
version of Windows 2022 only. For Windows 2022 Server Core, there is
a special Server Core version of the Microsoft Unified Communications
Managed API 4.0 available on the Exchange 2019 installation media in the
\UCMARedist folder.

Make sure that the directories where the installation files are
downloaded exist. Both Visual C++ Redistributable packages have
identical names, so they need to be stored in separate directories or
renamed after downloading.

To install the .NET Framework 4.8 on Windows Server 2019, use the
following PowerShell command:

```
PS C:\> Start-Process -FilePath "C:\Install\ndp48-x86-x64-
allos-enu.exe"
-ArgumentList "/q" -Wait
```

To install the other prerequisite software, use the following PowerShell
commands:

```
PS C:\> Start-Process -FilePath "C:\Install\VS2012\vcredist_
x64.exe" -ArgumentList "/q" -Wait
PS C:\> Start-Process -FilePath "C:\Install\VS2013\vcredist_
x64.exe" -ArgumentList "/q" -Wait
PS C:\> Start-Process -FilePath "C:\Install\rewrite_amd64_en-
US.msi" -ArgumentList "/q" -Wait
```

For Windows Server 2019 Server Core

```
# When needed, mount an ISO image
Mount-DiskImage -ImagePath "C:\Install\ExchangeServer2019-x64-
cu13.iso"
PS C:\> Start-Process -FilePath "Z:\UcmaRedist\setup.exe"
-ArgumentList "/q" -Wait
```

For Windows Server 2019 Desktop Experience

```
PS C:\> Start-Process -FilePath "C:\Install\UcmaRuntimeSetup.
exe" -ArgumentList "/q" -Wait
```

When the prerequisite software is installed, you can continue with preparing Active Directory and installing the Exchange 2019 server.

Exchange 2019 Unattended Setup

When the prerequisite software and Server Roles and Features are installed and the Windows server is fully patched, the Exchange 2019 Mailbox server can be installed.

As discussed in Chapter 1, Exchange Server depends heavily on Active Directory, and before Exchange can be installed, Active Directory needs to be prepared. This consists of three different consecutive steps:

- Prepare the schema partition.

- Prepare the configuration partition.

- Prepare the domain partition.

This will be discussed in the following sections.

Note The Exchange GUI setup as well as unattended setup can also take care of this, but for clarity in the process and since many organizations have different teams and thus change processes for Active Directory and Exchange, we will describe the manual process here.

Prepare the Schema Partition

To prepare the schema for Exchange 2019, log in using an account that is part of the Schema Admins security group. Then, open a command prompt with elevated privileges and enter the following command:

```
PS Z:\> .\Setup.EXE /PrepareSchema /
IAcceptExchangeServerLicenseTerms_DiagnosticDataOn

Microsoft Exchange Server 2019 Cumulative Update 13
Unattended Setup

Copying Files...
File copy complete. Setup will now collect additional
information needed for installation.

Performing Microsoft Exchange Server Prerequisite Check

    Prerequisite Analysis                        COMPLETED

Configuring Microsoft Exchange Server

    Extending Active Directory schema            COMPLETED

The Exchange Server setup operation completed successfully.
```

The read-write copy of the Active Directory schema partition is hosted on the Domain Controller that hosts the schema master FSMO role. Therefore, this command must be run on the Domain Controller holding the schema master FSMO role, not on any other Domain Controller in the same Active Directory site as where the schema master is installed. Of course you can also run it on the new Windows 2022 server that will hold the Exchange server, as long as it is in the same Active Directory site as where the schema master is hosted. In a multi-domain environment, this must be run in the root domain.

If you try to prepare the schema partition from a server in a different Active Directory site, the error message is returned on the console:

```
Setup encountered a problem while validating the state of
Active Directory: Exchange organization-level objects have not
been created, and setup cannot create them because the local
computer is not in the same domain and site as the schema
master. Run setup with the /PrepareAD parameter on a computer
in the domain <contoso> and site Default-First-Site-Name, and
wait for replication to complete. See the Exchange setup log
for more information on this error.
```

How do you know this worked? First, if you do not see any error messages on the console, you can be sure that it worked correctly.

You can also use PowerShell to check the version of the Active Directory schema. Every Exchange version makes changes to Active Directory, and each version has its own consecutive version. To check the current version, run the following PowerShell commands:

```
PS C:\> $Root = [ADSI]"LDAP://RootDSE"
PS C:\> ([ADSI]("LDAP://CN=ms-Exch-Schema-Version-Pt," + $Root.
schemaNamingContext)).rangeUpper
```

This will return the value of the rangeUpper property.

For your reference, Table 2-3 lists the Active Directory versions of the most recent Exchange versions.

Table 2-3. *Overview of Active Directory Versions*

Exchange Version	rangeUpper (Schema)	objectVersion (Configuration)	objectVersion (Domain)
Exchange 2019 CU13	17003		
Exchange 2019 CU12	17003	16760	13243
Exchange 2019 CU11	17003	16759	13242
Exchange 2016 CU23	15334	16223	13243
Exchange 2016 CU22	15334	16222	13242
Exchange 2016 CU21	15334	16221	13241
Exchange 2013 CU23	15312	16133	13237
Exchange 2013 CU22	15312	16131	13236
Exchange 2013 CU21	15312	16130	13236

You can also check the Active Directory schema version using ADSI Edit. To do this, open ADSI Edit and navigate to the ms-Exch-Schema-Version-Pt attribute. Open its properties and check the rangeUpper property as shown in Figure 2-2.

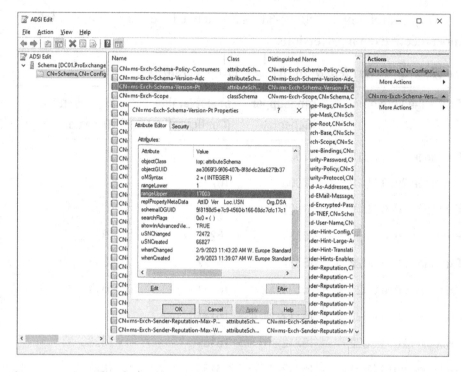

Figure 2-2. *Checking the schema version using ADSI Edit*

For an up-to-date list of all Active Directory schema, configuration, and domain versions, you can check the Active Directory version information on Microsoft docs at `https://bit.ly/ExADVersions`.

Prepare the Configuration Partition

When the Active Directory schema partition is prepared for Exchange and all changes have been replicated throughout the forest, you can continue with preparing the Active Directory configuration partition. This partition holds information about the entire Exchange configuration.

The configuration partition can be prepared using the following command, started in an elevated command prompt and using an account that is a member of the Enterprise Admins security group:

```
PS Z:\> Setup.exe /PrepareAD /
IAcceptExchangeServerLicenseTerms_DiagnosticDataOn
```

Microsoft Exchange Server 2019 Cumulative Update 13
Unattended Setup

Copying Files...
File copy complete. Setup will now collect additional
information needed for installation.

Performing Microsoft Exchange Server Prerequisite Check

    Prerequisite Analysis   COMPLETED

Setup will prepare the organization for Exchange Server 2019 by
using 'Setup /PrepareAD'. No Exchange Server 2016 roles
have been detected in this topology. After this operation, you
will not be able to install any Exchange Server 2016
roles.
For more information, visit: https://learn.microsoft.com/
Exchange/plan-and-deploy/deployment-ref/ms-exch-setupreadiness-
NoE16ServerWarning?view=exchserver-2019

Setup will prepare the organization for Exchange Server 2019 by
using 'Setup /PrepareAD'. No Exchange Server 2013 roles
have been detected in this topology. After this operation, you
will not be able to install any Exchange Server 2013
roles.
For more information, visit: https://learn.microsoft.com/
Exchange/plan-and-deploy/deployment-ref/ms-exch-setupreadiness-
NoE15ServerWarning?view=exchserver-2019

Configuring Microsoft Exchange Server

    Organization Preparation   COMPLETED

The Exchange Server setup operation completed successfully.

If this is a greenfield scenario where you did not install any Exchange server previously, the Exchange organization must be created in Active Directory. This is achieved by adding the /OrganizationName:<OrgName> in the preceding command. This will make sure the organization is created. You can use any name for the organization that you want; it is completely transparent for users. The only time you see it is when using ADSI Edit or when creating (complex) PowerShell scripts that access Exchange.

When running this command when there are no (previous) Exchange servers in the organization, a warning message is displayed on the console that no servers were found. This is an example of the warning message:

```
Setup will prepare the organization for Exchange Server 2019 by
using 'Setup /PrepareAD'. No Exchange Server 2016 roles have
been detected in this topology. After this operation, you will
not be able to install any Exchange Server 2016 roles.
For more information, visit: https://learn.microsoft.com/
Exchange/plan-and-deploy/deployment-ref/ms-exch-setupreadiness-
NoE16ServerWarning?view=exchserver-2019

Setup will prepare the organization for Exchange Server 2019 by
using 'Setup /PrepareAD'. No Exchange Server 2013 roles have
been detected in this topology. After this operation, you will
not be able to install any Exchange Server 2013 roles.
For more information, visit: https://learn.microsoft.com/
Exchange/plan-and-deploy/deployment-ref/ms-exch-setupreadiness-
NoE15ServerWarning?view=exchserver-2019
```

This warning makes sense since care must be taken. If there are any applications or services that require Exchange 2013 or Exchange 2016 in your organization, then you must install these servers first before continuing. If you do not, the setup application will not allow you to install any previous version of Exchange in your environment.

Again, when no error message is returned on the console, you can be sure that no errors occurred while preparing the Active Directory configuration partition.

You can check the version of the configuration partition using the following commands in PowerShell:

```
PS C:\> $Root = [ADSI]"LDAP://RootDSE"
PS C:\> ([ADSI]("LDAP://CN=<OrganizationName>,CN=Microsoft
Exchange,CN=Services," + $Root.configurationNamingContext)).
objectVersion
```

You can also check this version in ADSI Edit. Open the configuration partition and navigate to the CN=Microsoft Exchange object through CN=Configuration,DC=Domain,DC=Com ➤ CN=Services and check the value of the objectVersion property. This is shown in Figure 2-3.

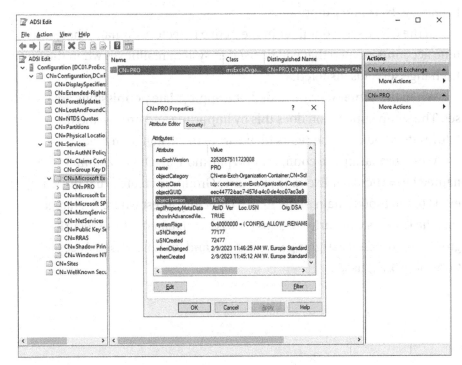

Figure 2-3. *Checking the version of the Active Directory configuration partition*

Possible values for the objectVersion property are listed in Table 2-3 earlier in this chapter.

When the configuration partition is prepared for Exchange, a container named CN=Microsoft Exchange is created under CN=Services, CN=Configuration, DC=, DC=com. This container is created in a greenfield scenario where no Exchange information is available in Active Directory. When it is already available from a previous version of Exchange, it is updated with the latest information.

The /PrepareAD step also creates a hidden container called CN=Microsoft Exchange System Objects in the Active Directory root domain when not available from a previous setup. At this stage it only contains a security group called Exchange Install Domain Servers and another container called Monitoring Mailboxes, which is still empty. This container is only visible when View Advanced Features is selected in Active Directory Users and Computers.

In the CN=Users container in the Active Directory domain, there are nine accounts created that will be used as system mailboxes when the first Exchange server is installed.

When the containers are added, the appropriate permissions are set. The setup application does this by importing and processing the information found in the rights.ldf file from the installation media.

When preparing the configuration partition, an Organizational Unit named OU=Microsoft Exchange Security Groups is created (if it does not exist) in the root domain of the Active Directory forest where Exchange-specific Universal Security Groups (USGs) are created. These security groups are used for assigning permissions and for Role-Based Access Control (RBAC) usage.

Prepare the Domain Partition

The last step in preparation before installing Exchange 2019 is preparing the Active Directory domain partition, or partitions if you have multiple domain partitions that contain mail-enabled objects.

To prepare the Active Directory domain partition, execute the following command in an elevated command prompt:

```
PS Z:\> .\Setup.EXE /PrepareDomain /
IAcceptExchangeServerLicenseTerms_DiagnosticDataOn

Microsoft Exchange Server 2019 Cumulative Update 13
Unattended Setup

Copying Files...
File copy complete. Setup will now collect additional
information needed for installation.

Performing Microsoft Exchange Server Prerequisite Check

    Prerequisite Analysis                          COMPLETED

Configuring Microsoft Exchange Server

    Prepare Domain Progress                        COMPLETED

The Exchange Server setup operation completed successfully
```

This command should be run in every domain in Active Directory that contains mail-enabled recipients. The setup application has an option to prepare all domains in just one command by using the / PrepareAllDomains switch.

You can check the version of the Active Directory domain partition with the following PowerShell commands:

```
PS C:\> $RootDSE= ([ADSI]"").distinguishedName
PS C:\> ([ADSI]("LDAP://CN=Microsoft Exchange System
Objects,$RootDSE")).objectVersion
```

85

This will show the value of the objectVersion property.

To check this version in ADSI Edit, navigate to the CN=Microsoft Exchange System Objects container in Active Directory and retrieve its properties. The objectVersion property should have a value listed in Table 2-3. Checking the objectVersion property is shown in Figure 2-4.

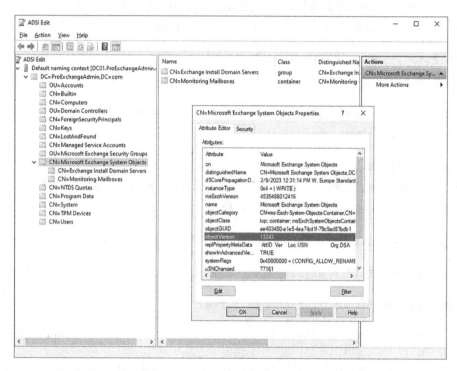

Figure 2-4. *Checking the domain version after preparing for Exchange 2019 CU8*

When Active Directory is fully prepared, the Exchange servers themselves can be installed. This can be done using the setup application in graphical mode (GUI setup) or from the command line (unattended setup). This will be discussed in the following sections.

Exchange 2019 Unattended Setup

Exchange 2019 can be installed using the GUI when Windows 2019 Desktop Experience is used. When using Windows 2019 Server Core, this is not possible of course, and an unattended setup is always used.

The setup application accepts several parameters:

- /Mode: Defines the action that setup uses. Options are install, remove, or upgrade.

- /Roles: Defines the Exchange server that will be installed. Options are Mailbox or EdgeTransport. Unlike Exchange 2013, Exchange 2016 and Exchange 2019 are multi-role only and no longer accept the ClientAccess option.

- /MdbName: The name of the first mailbox database that will be created on this server.

- /DbFilePath: The path and name of the mailbox database file.

- /LogFolderPath: The location of the transaction log files of the mailbox database.

- /InstallWindowsComponents: Installs Windows components that the Exchange server needs. These components can also be installed as part of the prerequisite software installation.

- /IAcceptExchangeServerLicenseTerms: Indicates you agree to the Microsoft license terms.

To install an Exchange 2019 Mailbox server unattended, run the following command from the command line:

```
Z:\> Z:\>Setup.exe /Mode:Install /Roles:Mailbox /
MdbName:"MDB01" /DbFilePath:"C:\ExchDbs\MDB01\MDB01.
edb" /LogFolderPath:"C:\ExchDbs\MDB01\LogFiles" /
InstallWindowsComponents /IAcceptExchangeServerLicenseTerms_
DiagnosticDataOn

Microsoft Exchange Server 2019 Cumulative Update 13
Unattended Setup

Copying Files...
File copy complete. Setup will now collect additional
information needed for installation.

Languages
Management tools
Mailbox role: Transport service
Mailbox role: Client Access service
Mailbox role: Mailbox service
Mailbox role: Front End Transport service
Mailbox role: Client Access Front End service

Performing Microsoft Exchange Server Prerequisite Check

    Configuring Prerequisites                    COMPLETED
    Prerequisite Analysis                        COMPLETED

Configuring Microsoft Exchange Server

    Preparing Setup                              COMPLETED
    Stopping Services                            COMPLETED
    Copying Exchange Files                       COMPLETED
    Language Files                               COMPLETED
```

```
Restoring Services                          COMPLETED
Language Configuration                      COMPLETED
Exchange Management Tools                   COMPLETED
Mailbox role: Transport service             COMPLETED
Mailbox role: Client Access service         COMPLETED
Mailbox role: Mailbox service               COMPLETED
Mailbox role: Front End Transport service   COMPLETED
Mailbox role: Client Access Front End service  COMPLETED
Finalizing Setup                            COMPLETED
```

The Exchange Server setup operation completed successfully. Setup has made changes to operating system settings that require a reboot to take effect. Please reboot this server prior to placing it into production.

When the server is rebooted, the Exchange 2019 server can be configured.

Exchange 2019 Graphical Setup

Instead of using the command line for an unattended setup, it is also possible to use the GUI version of Exchange setup. The GUI setup is a very basic wizard that asks some questions regarding the installation and installs Exchange on your server. It is straightforward, not much room for error, and requires additional configuration after the initial install. The additional configuration is a bit more than when using the unattended setup.

In the previous sections, preparation of Active Directory for Exchange was explained. Preparing Active Directory in advance is recommended for large deployments of Active Directory and Exchange or for organizations that have different departments for managing Active Directory and for Exchange Server.

The GUI setup will automatically prepare Active Directory as part of the setup application and is perfectly suited for smaller organizations that do not have the need for separate management of Active Directory and Exchange or organizations that do not have large and complex Active Directory deployments.

You can start the GUI setup by double-clicking setup.exe on the installation media or by launching setup.exe from the command line without any parameters. The first window that is shown is the Check for Updates window, which will check for newer Cumulative Updates than the one you are currently installing.

Follow the wizard, and in the "Accept the License Agreement" window, you can choose between the following options:

- I accept the license agreement and will share diagnostic data with Microsoft (recommended).

- I accept the license agreement, but I'm not ready to share diagnostic data with Microsoft.

- I do not accept the license agreement.

The first and recommended option is sharing diagnostic data with Microsoft. In this case, information regarding the setup is sent to Microsoft. Be aware that this is only diagnostic data regarding the setup application and NOT any personal or organizational information.

The next window is the "Server Role Selection" as shown in Figure 2-5.

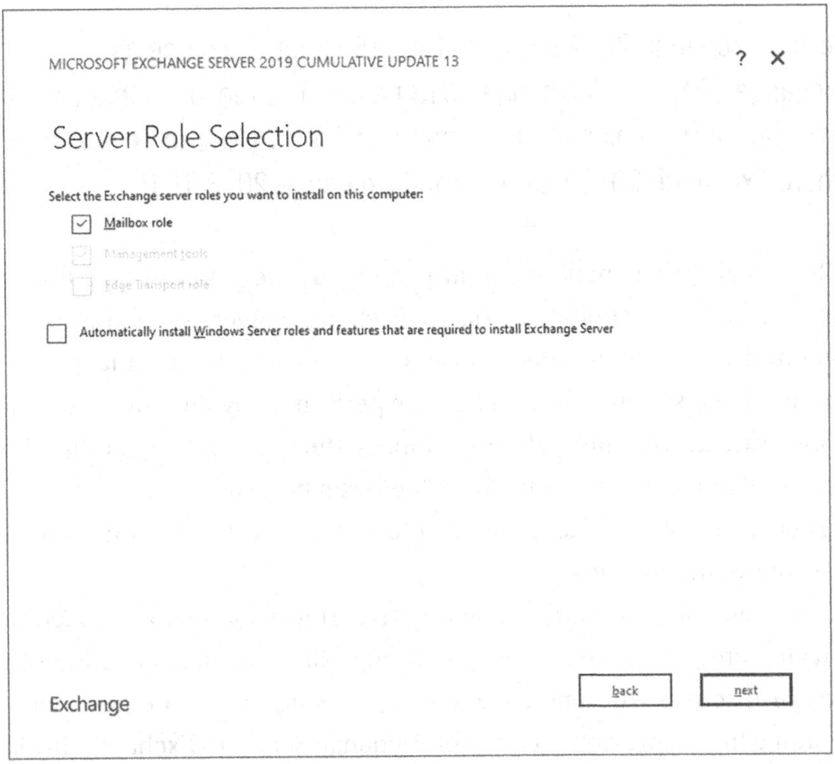

MICROSOFT EXCHANGE SERVER 2019 CUMULATIVE UPDATE 13   ?   ✕

Server Role Selection

Select the Exchange server roles you want to install on this computer:

- [✓] Mailbox role
- [ ] Management tools
- [ ] Edge Transport role

- [ ] Automatically install Windows Server roles and features that are required to install Exchange Server

Exchange

[back]   [next]

Figure 2-5. *Server role selection*

Server roles are mutually exclusive. When the Mailbox role is selected, the Edge Transport role is automatically grayed out. Also, when the Mailbox role is selected, the management tools are automatically included. Check the Automatically install Windows Server Roles and Features checkbox when prerequisite Server Roles and Features are not installed in advance. I always check this box, even when Server Roles and Features are installed, just in case a server role or feature is accidentally not installed.

The default location for installing Exchange is C:\Program Files\ Microsoft\Exchange Server\V15, but any other location can be used. The advantage of using another disk for installing Exchange is that the system disk is not filled up with Exchange information, causing the server to stop unexpectedly.

Note   Exchange 2019 still uses the V15 folder, the same as Exchange 2016 and Exchange 2013 before. The reason is that the Exchange 2019 major version number still is 15 (15.2 to be exact), where Exchange 2016 was 15.1 and Exchange 2013 15.0.

Exchange 2019 comes with built-in antimalware scanning, and this is provided by a transport agent on the Exchange server. Antimalware is scanning messages in transit and as such does not scan any mailbox database or file system. The latter can be performed by Windows Defender.

Be aware that for antimalware scanning, the Exchange server must be able to download the signature files. These can be downloaded from the Internet or from a local file share. Needless to say, enabling antimalware is the recommended option.

At the end of the wizard, the setup will perform a prerequisite check to see if all prerequisites for installing Exchange 2019 are met. Sometimes the prerequisite check will generate a warning message. For example, when upgrading from a previous version of Exchange Server to Exchange 2019, a warning message will be shown that the Exchange organization does not have MAPI over HTTP enabled.

Warning messages can be ignored, but error messages must be fixed before installation can continue. If no errors are generated, click Install to start the installation of Exchange. The installation of Exchange consists of 14 different steps, and these can take a considerable amount of time.

When installation is complete, you can check the Launch Exchange Administration Center after finishing Exchange setup checkbox to launch the Exchange Admin Center (EAC). I always recommend rebooting the server first and then continuing with the configuration.

When the server is rebooted, the Exchange 2019 server can be configured.

Configuring the Exchange 2019 Server

After installing the Exchange server and the reboot, how do you know
the installation completed successfully? First, if you did not get any error
messages on the console, the installation itself went well.

Next, check if all Exchange services are started successfully. To do this,
start PowerShell and execute the Get-Service command as shown in the
following output:

```
PS C:\> Get-Service MSExchange* | ft -a

Status  Name                          DisplayName
------  ----                          -----------
Running MSExchangeADTopology          Microsoft Exchange Active
                                      Directory Topology
Running MSExchangeAntispamUpdate      Microsoft Exchange Anti-
                                      spam Update
Running MSExchangeCompliance          Microsoft Exchange
                                      Compliance Service
Running MSExchangeDagMgmt             Microsoft Exchange DAG
                                      Management
Running MSExchangeDelivery            Microsoft Exchange Mailbox
                                      Transport Delivery
Running MSExchangeDiagnostics         Microsoft Exchange
                                      Diagnostics
Running MSExchangeEdgeSync            Microsoft Exchange
                                      EdgeSync
Running MSExchangeFastSearch          Microsoft Exchange Search
Running MSExchangeFrontEndTransport   Microsoft Exchange
                                      Frontend Transport
Running MSExchangeHM                  Microsoft Exchange
                                      Health Manager
```

```
Running MSExchangeHMRecovery           Microsoft Exchange Health
                                       Manager Recovery
Stopped MSExchangeImap4                Microsoft Exchange IMAP4
Stopped MSExchangeIMAP4BE              Microsoft Exchange
                                       IMAP4 Backend
Running MSExchangeIS                   Microsoft Exchange
                                       Information Store
Running MSExchangeMailboxAssistants    Microsoft Exchange Mailbox
                                       Assistants
Running MSExchangeMailboxReplication   Microsoft Exchange Mailbox
                                       Replication
Running MSExchangeMitigation           Microsoft Exchange
                                       Emergency
                                       Mitigation Service
Stopped MSExchangePop3                 Microsoft Exchange POP3
Stopped MSExchangePOP3BE              Microsoft Exchange
                                       POP3 Backend
Running MSExchangeRepl                 Microsoft Exchange
                                       Replication
Running MSExchangeRPC                  Microsoft Exchange RPC
                                       Client Access
Running MSExchangeServiceHost          Microsoft Exchange
                                       Service Host
Running MSExchangeSubmission           Microsoft Exchange Mailbox
                                       Transport Submission
Running MSExchangeThrottling           Microsoft Exchange
                                       Throttling
Running MSExchangeTransport            Microsoft Exchange
                                       Transport
Running MSExchangeTransportLogSearch   Microsoft Exchange
                                       Transport Log Search
```

Tip On Windows 2019 Server Core, you can start PowerShell by executing the command "PowerShell" on the command prompt. On Windows 2022 Server Core, when you exit the SCONFIG utility, it will automatically launch a PowerShell window. To launch the Exchange Management Shell (EMS), execute the command "LaunchEMS".

All services should be running and have set the Startup Type to Automatic, except

- Microsoft Exchange IMAP4

- Microsoft Exchange IMAP4 Backend

- Microsoft Exchange POP3

- Microsoft Exchange POP3 Backend

- Microsoft Exchange Server Extension for Windows Server Backup

These services have set their Startup Type to Manual right after installation and thus should not be running.

Another server-side test is to use the EMS command Get-ServerComponentState, which is a part of Microsoft Managed Availability and checks the state of all Exchange components. To check this, execute the Get-ServerComponentState command as shown in the following output:

```
[PS] C:\>Get-ServerComponentState -Identity EXCH01

Server                         Component          State
------                         ---------          -----
EXCH01.ProExchangeAdmin.com ServerWideOffline     Active
EXCH01.ProExchangeAdmin.com HubTransport          Active
EXCH01.ProExchangeAdmin.com FrontendTransport     Active
```

EXCH01.ProExchangeAdmin.com	Monitoring	Active
EXCH01.ProExchangeAdmin.com	RecoveryActionsEnabled	Active
EXCH01.ProExchangeAdmin.com	AutoDiscoverProxy	Active
EXCH01.ProExchangeAdmin.com	ActiveSyncProxy	Active
EXCH01.ProExchangeAdmin.com	EcpProxy	Active
EXCH01.ProExchangeAdmin.com	EwsProxy	Active
EXCH01.ProExchangeAdmin.com	ImapProxy	Active
EXCH01.ProExchangeAdmin.com	OabProxy	Active
EXCH01.ProExchangeAdmin.com	OwaProxy	Active
EXCH01.ProExchangeAdmin.com	PopProxy	Active
EXCH01.ProExchangeAdmin.com	PushNotificationsProxy	Active
EXCH01.ProExchangeAdmin.com	RpsProxy	Active
EXCH01.ProExchangeAdmin.com	RwsProxy	Active
EXCH01.ProExchangeAdmin.com	RpcProxy	Active
EXCH01.ProExchangeAdmin.com	XropProxy	Active
EXCH01.ProExchangeAdmin.com	HttpProxyAvailabilityGroup	Active
EXCH01.ProExchangeAdmin.com	ForwardSyncDaemon	Inactive
EXCH01.ProExchangeAdmin.com	ProvisioningRps	Inactive
EXCH01.ProExchangeAdmin.com	MapiProxy	Active
EXCH01.ProExchangeAdmin.com	EdgeTransport	Active
EXCH01.ProExchangeAdmin.com	HighAvailability	Active
EXCH01.ProExchangeAdmin.com	SharedCache	Active
EXCH01.ProExchangeAdmin.com	MailboxDeliveryProxy	Active
EXCH01.ProExchangeAdmin.com	RoutingUpdates	Active
EXCH01.ProExchangeAdmin.com	RestProxy	Active
EXCH01.ProExchangeAdmin.com	DefaultProxy	Active
EXCH01.ProExchangeAdmin.com	Lsass	Active
EXCH01.ProExchangeAdmin.com	RoutingService	Active
EXCH01.ProExchangeAdmin.com	E4EProxy	Active
EXCH01.ProExchangeAdmin.com	CafeLAMv2	Active
EXCH01.ProExchangeAdmin.com	LogExportProvider	Active

Note   All components should return Active for their state, except the ForwardSyncDeamon and ProvisioningRps components. These are not actively used in Exchange 2019.

Another check is to see if you can open OWA in the browser using https://exch01/owa and log on as the account you used to install the Exchange server. You can ignore the SSL certificate warning; this is caused by using a self-signed SSL certificate on the Exchange server. After logging on and selecting the region and language, you should see OWA as shown in Figure 2-6.

Figure 2-6. *Outlook for the Web directly after installation*

When the URL is changed to https://exch01/ecp as shown in Figure 2-7, the Exchange Admin Center is shown. This is used for configuration of the Exchange server.

Figure 2-7. *Exchange Admin Center right after installation*

At this point we can conclude that the installation of the Exchange server finished successfully and configuration of the Exchange server can be started.

Configuring Exchange 2019

The following items must be configured to get to a fully operational Exchange server:

- Virtual directories

- SSL certificate

- Send Connector

- Accepted domains

- Email address policies

- Mailbox database location (optional)

- SMTP queue database location (optional)

- IIS log file location (optional)

- Exchange 2019 product key

Configuring these items will be discussed in the following sections.

Virtual Directories

When you are deploying Exchange 2019, all internal virtual directories on the server are configured with their local FQDN, for example, `https://exch01.proexchangeadmin.com`. The external virtual directories on the server are always empty right after installation of the Exchange 2019 server.

If you have only one Exchange server, you can configure the external virtual directory with the same FQDN. If you have multiple Exchange servers, using an individual FQDN on each server becomes challenging, and a more general FQDN like webmail.proexchangeadmin.com can be used. In the example of OWA, this can be `https://webmail.proexchangeadmin.com`.

Microsoft recommends that you use one namespace for both external URLs and internal URLs for all virtual directories. This means that webmail.proexchangeadmin.com on the Internet points to your public IP address on the Internet. At the same time, webmail.proexchangeadmin.com points to the private IP address on the internal network. This is called a "split DNS" configuration.

In Exchange 2019, the following directories need to be configured:

- OWA Virtual Directory

- ECP Virtual Directory

- EWS (Web Services) Virtual Directory

- ActiveSync Virtual Directory

- OAB (Offline Address Book) Virtual Directory

- PowerShell Virtual Directory

- Mapi/Http Virtual Directory

Note   In previous versions of Exchange, Outlook Anywhere was configured as well, but as discussed in Chapter 1, Outlook Anywhere is deprecated and replaced by Mapi/Http.

Table 2-4 lists the values for the InternalURL and ExternalURL properties for all virtual directories in Exchange 2019. For our proexchangeadmin installation, the same URL is used for the InternalURL and ExternalURL properties.

Table 2-4. *Virtual Directory Settings*

Virtual Directory	InternalURL and ExternalURL Settings
OWA	https://webmail.proexchangeadmin.com/owa
ECP	https://webmail.proexchangeadmin.com/ecp
ActiveSync	https://webmail.proexchangeadmin.com/Microsoft-Server-ActiveSync
EWS	https://webmail.proexchangeadmin.com/ews/exchange.asmx
OAB	https://webmail.proexchangeadmin.com/oab
PowerShell	https://webmail.proexchangeadmin.com/PowerShell
Mapi	https://webmail.proexchangeadmin.com/mapi

When you look closely at Table 2-4, you will notice that the Autodiscover Virtual Directory is not mentioned. This is correct because there is no need to set the internal URL and external URL properties of this virtual directory.

You can change these virtual directory settings using PowerShell commands like Set-OWAVirtualDirectory, Set-ECPVirtualDirectory, or Set-MAPIVirtualDirectory. Personally, I find it easier to combine the Set-command with the corresponding Get- command.

To configure all virtual directories on an Exchange 2019 server, you can use the following commands:

```
[PS] C:\> Set-OWAVirtualDirectory -Identity "EXCH01\
OWA (Default Web Site) " -InternalURL https:// webmail.
proexchangeadmin.com/owa -ExternalURL https:// webmail.
proexchangeadmin.com/owa
[PS] C:\> Set-ECPVirtualDirectory -Identity "EXCH01\
Ecp (Default Web Site)" -InternalURL https://webmail.
proexchangeadmin.com/ecp -ExternalURL https://webmail.
proexchangeadmin.com/ecp
[PS] C:\> Set-WebServicesVirtualDirectory -Identity "EXCH01\
EWS (Default Web Site)" -InternalURL https://webmail.
proexchangeadmin.com/ews/exchange.asmx -ExternalURL https://
webmail.proexchangeadmin.com /ews/exchange.asmx
[PS] C:\> Set-ActiveSyncVirtualDirectory -Identity "EXCH01\
Microsoft-Server-ActiveSync (Default Web Site)" -InternalURL
https://webmail.proexchangeadmin.com/Microsoft-Server-
ActiveSync -ExternalURL https://webmail.proexchangeadmin.com/
Microsoft-Server-ActiveSync
[PS] C:\> Set-OABVirtualDirectory -Identity "EXCH01\
OAB (Default Web Site)" -InternalURL https://webmail.
proexchangeadmin.com/oab -ExternalURL https://webmail.
proexchangeadmin.com/oab
[PS] C:\> Set-MapiVirtualDirectory -Identity "EXCH01\
Mapi (Default Web Site)" -InternalURL https://webmail.
proexchangeadmin.com/mapi -ExternalURL https://webmail.
proexchangeadmin.com/mapi
```

```
[PS] C:\> Set-PowerShellVirtualDirectory -Identity "EXCH01\
PowerShell (Default Web Site)" -InternalURL https://webmail.
proexchangeadmin.com/PowerShell -ExternalURL https://webmail.
proexchangeadmin.com/PowerShell
```

You can play around a bit with variables in the commands mentioned previously. For example, the FQDN of the server is always identical in this example, so it makes sense to use a variable called $FQDN. The server name in this example is also always EXCH01, so you can use a variable called $Server for this as well.

Combined with the other commands, we will get something like

```
[PS] C:\> $FQDN = "webmail.proexchangeadmin.com"
[PS] C:\> $Server = $ENV:ComputerName
[PS] C:\> Get-OWAVirtualDirectory –Server $Server | Set-
OWAVirtualDirectory –InternalURL "https://$FQDN/owa"
-ExternalURL "https://$FQDN/owa"
```

Note Instead of executing the individual commands, you can also use a PowerShell script to configure all virtual directories. On the Apress GitHub, you can find such a script called change_vdir_settings.ps1.

Mapi/Http is a protocol for Outlook clients that was introduced in Exchange 2013 SP1. Mapi/Http is enabled on an organizational level. In previous versions of Exchange, Mapi/Http was not enabled by default. If you are in this scenario, you can execute the following PowerShell command to enable it:

```
[PS] C:\> Set-OrganizationConfig -MapiHttpEnabled $true
```

If you are still running outdated and unsupported clients like Outlook 2007, you must configure Outlook Anywhere by entering the following PowerShell command:

```
[PS] C:\> Set-OutlookAnywhere -Identity "EXCH01\Rpc (Default
Web Site)" -ExternalHostname "webmail.proexchangeadmin.com" -Ex
ternalClientsRequireSsl:$true -ExternalClientAuthenticationMet
hod:NTLM -InternalHostname "webmail.proexchangeadmin.com" -In
ternalClientsRequireSsl:$true -InternalClientAuthenticationMe
thod:NTLM
```

If you do not use Outlook Anywhere, this configuration step can be omitted. When omitted, there is no need to configure Outlook Anywhere in the load balancer that is in front of the Exchange server.

Although not really a virtual directory, the Service Connection Point (SCP) for Autodiscover must be configured at this point as well. The SCP can only be configured using PowerShell; there is no GUI available for this. To configure the SCP, execute the following PowerShell command:

```
[PS] C:\> Set-ClientAccessService -identity EXCH01
-AutoDiscoverServiceInternalUri https://autodiscover.
proexchangeadmin.com/autodiscover/autodiscover.xml
```

It is also possible to configure the virtual directories in EAC. In EAC, navigate to Servers ➤ Virtual Directories and select the server you want to configure in the Select Server dropdown box. Select a virtual directory in the Details pane and use the wrench icon to configure it accordingly.

To configure Outlook Anywhere in EAC, navigate to Servers ➤ Servers and select the Exchange server you want to configure Outlook Anywhere for. In the toolbar click the pencil icon to edit the server's profile. In this navigation pane, select Outlook Anywhere and fill in the details over the internal and external hostnames and the authentication method.

Configure an SSL Certificate

By default, a self-signed certificate is installed on each Exchange server during installation of every Exchange server, regardless of its version. This self-signed certificate has the NetBIOS name of the server as its common name and the fully qualified domain name (FQDN) of the server configured in the Subject Alternative Name field of the certificate.

The self-signed certificate works fine for testing OWA and EAC, but should never be used for production purposes. Requesting a valid SSL certificate is the only option.

Request an SSL Certificate Using EMS

To use the Exchange Management Shell to request, install, and configure an SSL certificate is a bit more complex. To do this, use the following commands:

```
[PS] C:\> $Data = New-ExchangeCertificate -Server
EXCH01 -FriendlyName "ProExchangeAdmin SSL Certificate"
-GenerateRequest -SubjectName "c=US, o=ProExchangeAdmin,
cn=webmail.ProExchangeAdmin.com" -DomainName webmail.
ProExchangeAdmin.com,autodiscover.ProExchangeAdmin.com
-PrivateKeyExportable $true
[PS] C:\> Set-Content -path "C:\Install\SSLCertRequest.req"
-Value $Data
```

Note   Instead of using C:\Install to store the request file, it is also possible to use a UNC path to store the request file on a file share on a remote machine. The Universal Security Group Exchange Trusted Subsystem needs write permissions on this file share.

You can use the contents of the SSLCertRequest.req file to request an SSL certificate from a certificate authority (CA). This can be an Active Directory certificate authority or a third-party certificate authority like DigiCert or Comodo.

After ordering the certificate from your certificate authority, you store the new certificate on the same share and continue with the following commands:

```
[PS] C:\> Import-ExchangeCertificate -Server EXCH01 -FileData
([Byte[]]$(Get-Content -Path "\\fs01\install\certnew.cer"
-Encoding byte -ReadCount 0)) | Enable-ExchangeCertificate
-Server EXCH01 -Services IIS
```

This step consists of three commands:

1. The Import-ExchangeCertificate cmdlet, which imports the SSL certificate (the .cer file) that was returned from the CA into the local certificate store of the Exchange 2019 server.

2. The Get-Content cmdlet, which reads the certificate file from disk and sends it as byte data to the Import-ExchangeCertificate cmdlet.

3. The Enable-ExchangeCertificate cmdlet, which receives its input from the Import-ExchangeCertificate cmdlet. This cmdlet enables the newly imported SSL certificate to be used with the Internet Information Server.

In this example, only two domain names are used:

- webmail.proexchangeadmin.com

- autodiscover.proexchangeadmin.com

For a typical environment, this is sufficient.

Exporting an Existing SSL Certificate

When a new SSL certificate is created and installed on an Exchange server, it is recommended to export the certificate. This export can be stored somewhere safe, but it can also be used to import the certificate on other Exchange servers or on a load balancer, for example.

To export the SSL certificate on the Exchange server, you can use the following command:

```
[PS] C:\> Export-ExchangeCertificate -Thumbprint 3FE6DBADB43
36D796E6F27A9D723569BD37F331E -FileName "\\FS01\Install\webmail_
proexchangeadmin_com.pfx" -BinaryEncoded -Password (ConvertTo-
SecureString -String "P@ssw0rd01" -AsPlainText -Force)
```

The thumbprint value can be retrieved using the Get-ExchangeCertificate command. The password that is used for the exported certificate cannot be a plain-text password, hence the ConvertTo-SecureString function.

The file webmail_proexchangeadmin_com.pfx in the C:\Install directory can be copied to other Exchange servers for import or stored in a safe place for disaster recovery purposes.

Importing an Existing SSL Certificate

When you already have a valid SSL certificate, you can import that on an Exchange server as well. For example, if we want to install the SSL certificate from the Exchange 2019 server EXCH01 to another Exchange 2019 server called EXCH02, we can use the following command:

```
[PS] C:\> Import-ExchangeCertificate –Server EXCH02
-FileData ([Byte[]]$(Get-Content -Path "C:\install\webmail_
proexchangeadmin_com.pfx" -Encoding byte -ReadCount 0))
-Password:(Get-Credential).password | Enable-
ExchangeCertificate -Server EXCH01 -Services IIS
```

The -Password:(Get-Credential).password parameter shows a Windows popup in which you enter the password while importing the certificate. The output of the Import-ExchangeCertificate command is piped directly to the Enable-ExchangeCertificate command.

Note   In earlier versions of Exchange 2019, it was possible to process SSL certificates from the EAC, but from Exchange 2019 CU12 onward, all public certificate features were removed from EAC, and only a self-signed certificate can be created from the EAC.

Create a Send Connector

Out of the box, Exchange Server can receive messages on its Receive Connectors, but it cannot send messages to the external world because no default Send Connectors are created (unless you are deploying in an existing environment, of course).

When creating a new Send Connector, it needs a name, an address space, and a source transport server, that is, which server can use this connector to send email to the outside world. You can use the following PowerShell command to create a new Send Connector:

```
[PS] C:\> New-SendConnector -Internet -Name "Internet Send
Connector" -AddressSpaces "*" -SourceTransportServers "EXCH01.
proexchangeadmin.com"
```

It is also possible to use EAC to create a new Send Connector. To do this, open EAC and navigate to Mail Flow ➤ Send Connectors. Click the + icon and follow the wizard to create a new Send Connector:

- Give the Send Connector a name, select the Internet radio button, and click Next.

- Select the MX record associated with the recipient domain radio button and click Next.

- Under Address Space, click the + icon and enter * in the Fully Qualified Domain Name text box and click Save and then click Next.

- The Source Server is the server that is participating in the Send Connector. Use the + icon to add the newly created Exchange server and click Finish.

A new Send Connector that sends mail to the Internet using public MX records is now created.

Receive Connectors

Besides Send Connectors, Exchange 2019 also has Receive Connectors. There are default Receive Connectors for receiving messages from other SMTP hosts, and there are client Receive Connectors used so that authenticated clients can send SMTP messages. The latter may sound strange, but the Exchange 2019 server is receiving messages from the client and, when needed, routes those messages to the Internet.

A default Exchange 2019 server named EXCH01 has the following Receive Connectors:

- *Client Frontend EXCH01*: Listening on port 587, this Receive Connector is used by clients like Mozilla Thunderbird that want to use authenticated SMTP to send email. This port needs users to authenticate to use the service.

- *Client Proxy EXCH01*: Listening on port 465, this connector receives the client's messages from the Client Access services on the Exchange 2019 server or any other Exchange 2019 server in the same Active Directory site.

- *Default EXCH01*: Listening on port 2525, this is the SMTP service accepting messages from the Default Frontend Receive Connector on the Exchange 2019 server or any other Exchange 2019 server in the same Active Directory site. This connector is not scoped for regular clients to be used.

- *Default Frontend EXCH01*: Listening on port 25, this is the Receive Connector for regular inbound SMTP messages. Servers that connect to this port can be other SMTP servers, the Exchange 2010 Hub Transport service, other Exchange 2013/2016/2019 servers in the organization, or applications or devices that need to submit messages to mailboxes.

- *Outbound Proxy Frontend EXCH01*: This connector accepts messages from the Transport service on the Exchange server and relays the messages to external hosts. This only takes place on Send Connectors that have the front-end proxy option enabled.

These connectors are shown in Figure 2-8.

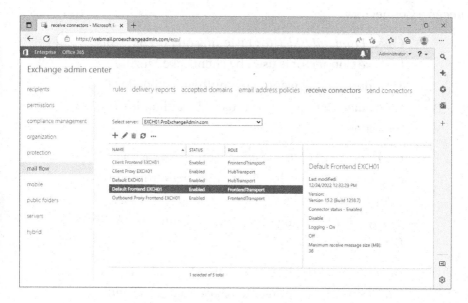

Figure 2-8. *Default Receive Connectors in Exchange 2019*

When installing Exchange 2019 out of the box, there is no need to configure anything on the Receive Connector; it just works. You configure your firewall to forward SMTP to TCP 25 on the Exchange 2019 server, and you are ready to go.

Accepted Domains

An accepted domain in Exchange Server is a domain used for email services that this specific Exchange environment will accept messages for. There are three types of accepted domains:

- *Authoritative domain*: This is a domain for which the Exchange environment is ultimately responsible, and when chaining email environments, this will be the final destination. There is no other mail environment after this. If a recipient does not exist in this environment, a non-delivery report (NDR) is generated and sent back to the original sender.

- *Internal relay*: This is a domain for which the Exchange environment might in part be responsible, but it is not the only environment accepting mail for this domain. If a recipient does not exist in this environment, the email will be forwarded to the other environment using a Send Connector containing this domain as the address space.

- *External relay*: This is a domain for which the Exchange environment will accept mail, but it does not have any recipient for this domain. It will also not try to look up recipients. All mail will be forwarded to another mail environment using a dedicated Send Connector.

By default, the first accepted domain in any Exchange environment is the Active Directory domain name. If the Active Directory domain name is exchange2019.local, the first accepted domain is also exchange2019.local. In this book the Active Directory name is proexchangeadmin.com, which is automatically the first authoritative accepted domain in the Exchange environment. The Exchange server will accept all mail for this domain, and if a recipient in the @proexchangeadmin.com address space is not found, an NDR is generated.

To create a new authoritative domain in Exchange with address space @proexchange2019.com, execute the New-AcceptedDomain command in PowerShell:

```
[PS] C:\> New-AcceptedDomain -Name "Pro Exchange 2019"
-DomainName ProExchange2019.com -DomainType Authoritative
```

Name	DomainName	DomainType	Default
Pro Exchange 2019	ProExchange2019.com	Authoritative	False

111

Note that for subdomains, you have the option to explicitly specify the subdomain as an accepted domain, or you can set the MatchSubdomains property of the accepted domain to $true. The MatchSubdomains option is not available in the New-AcceptedDomain command but must be set using the Set-AcceptedDomain command. This is useful in environments where Exchange is responsible for accepting inbound email to hand off to other systems responsible for subdomains, for example, list servers or Unix/Linux systems, which might be sending email using their hostname.

It is also possible to create a new AcceptedDomain using EAC. This can be achieved by opening EAC and navigating to Mail Flow ➤ Accepted Domains and clicking the + icon. Give the new accepted domain a name, enter the domain name, and select one of the radio buttons for the type of accepted domain.

Create an Email Address Policy

When an accepted domain is created, you can add email addresses manually to recipients. It is much more efficient to assign email addresses automatically. This is what an email address policy does. Email addresses are automatically applied to recipients based on certain criteria, such as the recipient type, a recipient container in Active Directory, or a certain attribute of the recipient. Also, the format of the email address is defined in an email address policy. An email address policy is applied on a recipient when the recipient is created, but an email address policy can also be generally applied. In this case all recipients that match a filter in the email address policy will have that policy applied.

An email address policy has

- A name

- An email address format

- A type of recipient

- A rule that defines how or where to find the recipients in Active Directory

In Exchange, there is always a default email address policy that is applied to all recipients in the Exchange organization; this email address policy uses the default accepted domain. An email address policy can only be created with an accepted domain in that Exchange organization. Multiple email address policies can be created.

To create a new additional email address policy that assigns an email address <alias>@ProExchange2019.com to all recipients that exist in the OU=Users,OU=Accounts in Active Directory, execute the New-EmailAddressPolicy command:

```
[PS] C:\> New-EmailAddressPolicy -Name ProExchange2019
-IncludedRecipients AllRecipients -RecipientContainer
"ProExchangeAdmin.com/ProExchange2019/users"
-EnabledEmailAddressTemplates "SMTP:%m@ProExchange2019.com"
```

Name	Priority	RecipientFilter
ProExchange2019	1	Alias -ne $null

This policy stamps an SMTP email address on each user that is within the reach of this policy with a format of %m@ProExchange2019.com, where %m means the user's alias in Exchange. To apply this newly created email address policy, you can use the following command:

```
[PS] C:\> Update-EmailAddressPolicy -Identity ProExchange2019
```

To create a new email address policy in EAC, navigate to Mail Flow ➤ Email Address Policies and click the + icon to start the new email address policy wizard.

Give the policy a unique and preferably an identifiable name and click the + icon to change the email address format. Here you can select the accepted domain that needs to be used, and you can select the format of the email address. Click Save to store this information and go back to the previous window. Scroll down and select the recipient type that must have this policy applied. Click the Add a rule button to create a rule to specify which recipients must have this policy applied.

When you click Save, the policy is stored, but it has not been applied yet. To apply the newly created policy, click the Apply option in the Details pane.

Relocate the Initial Mailbox Database (GUI Setup Only)

When performing an unattended installation of Exchange 2019, the initial mailbox database is defined as an option of the setup application. This includes the name of the mailbox database, but also the name and location of the mailbox database file and the transaction log files.

When performing an Exchange 2019 GUI setup, you cannot configure this during setup. Instead, a new mailbox database with a random name located in C:\Program Files\Microsoft\Exchange Server\V15\Mailbox\ Mailbox Database <number> is created. The name of this initial mailbox database is "Mailbox Database" followed by a random ten-digit number. This initial mailbox database is shown in Figure 2-9.

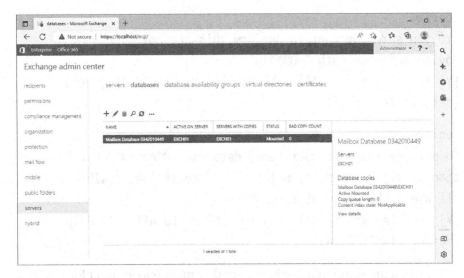

Figure 2-9. *The mailbox database that was created by the GUI setup*

It is possible to change the name of the default mailbox database by clicking the pencil icon. Change the name of the mailbox database, for example, to MDB2019 and click Save to store the new name in Active Directory.

You can also use PowerShell to change the name of the initial mailbox database using the Set-Mailbox Database command:

```
[PS] C:\> Set-Mailbox Database -Identity "Mailbox Database
0342010449" -Name MDB2019
```

Besides the name of the mailbox database, no other properties including the location of the mailbox database can be changed in EAC. To change the location of the mailbox database file and change the name of the actual mailbox database file (the .edb file) to, for example, MDB2019 located on drive F:\, you must use the Move-DatabasePath command in PowerShell:

```
[PS] C:\> Move-DatabasePath -Identity MDB2019 -EdbFilePath F:\
MDB2019\MDB2019.edb -LogFolderPath F:\MDB2019\LogFiles
```

115

```
Confirm
Are you sure you want to perform this action?
Moving database path "MDB2019".
[Y] Yes  [A] Yes to All  [N] No  [L] No to All  [?] Help
(default is "Y"): A

Confirm
To perform the move operation, database "MDB2019" must be
temporarily dismounted, which will make it inaccessible to
all users. Do you want to continue?
[Y] Yes  [A] Yes to All  [N] No  [L] No to All  [?] Help
(default is "Y"): A
```

When a mailbox database is renamed or moved to another location, it will automatically be dismounted. When dismounted, users are disconnected, so this must be done outside of business hours. Of course, this is not an issue when an empty (new) mailbox database is relocated. When executing this command, a warning message is shown on the console about the mailbox database dismount.

Relocate the SMTP Queue Database (Optional)

SMTP messages that are sent and received by an Exchange server are always queued and stored in a queue database. By default, this queue database is stored on the same disk as where the Exchange Server software is installed. Typically, this is the C:\Program Files\Microsoft\Exchange Server\V15\TransportRoles\data\Queue directory.

The queue database is used to temporarily store every message that is sent or received, and it can grow rapidly. You would not be the first administrator that faces an Exchange server that goes offline because of the C:\ drive filled up.

The recommendation is to relocate the queue database to another disk, preferably a dedicated disk with sufficient storage.

The configuration of the Transport service is in a configuration file called EdgeTransport.exe.config, which is stored in the C:\Program Files\ Microsoft\Exchange Server\V15\Bin of the Exchange server. It is possible to change the settings for the file locations manually, but there is also a PowerShell script available on the Exchange server that takes care of this. The Exchange server scripts directory has an alias $ExScripts. The following example uses a variable called $LogPath to make it a bit more easier to read and use:

```
[PS] C:\> CD $ExScripts
[PS] C:\> $LogPath = "D:\Program Files\Microsoft\Exchange
Server\V15\TransportRoles\data"
[PS] C:\> .\Move-TransportDatabase.ps1 -queueDatabasePath
"$LogPath\Queue" -queueDatabaseLoggingPath "$LogPath\
Queue" -iPFilterDatabasePath "$LogPath\IpFilter"
-iPFilterDatabaseLoggingPath "$LogPath\IpFilter"
-temporaryStoragePath "$LogPath\Temp"
```

The script will stop the MSExchangeTransport service, copy the queue database and accompanying files to the new location, and start the MSExchangeTransport service again. Because of the copy of the queue database, no messages will be lost during the move.

Note   This configuration is not stored in Active Directory. When a new Cumulative Update is installed and a new configuration file needs to be installed, the config file is overwritten. All changes are lost and need to be reapplied.

Relocate IIS Log Files (Optional)

Another component on an Exchange server that is notorious for using lots of disk space is the Internet Information Server (IIS), the web server hosting the Exchange Client Access Front End components. IIS logging takes place on

- C:\inetpub\logs\LogFiles\W3SVC1: Here are the Client Access Front End component log files located.

- C:\inetpub\logs\LogFiles\W3SVC2: Here are the Client Access Back End component log files located.

All HTTPS client requests of all clients are either direct or proxied and logged. Log files are clear text and take up a tremendous amount of disk space, with 10 GB per log file and multiple log files per day for a heavily loaded Exchange server.

Just with the SMTP queue database, IIS logging can fill up the default disk, and the Exchange server will come to a halt. I always recommend relocating the IIS log files to another disk. To achieve this, use the following PowerShell commands to relocate IIS log files to the D:\ drive:

```
PS C:\> Import-Module WebAdministration
PS C:\> $LogPath = "D:\Inetpub\Logs\LogFiles"
PS C:\> New-Item $LogPath -type directory
PS C:\> ForEach($site in (Dir iis:\sites\*)){Set-ItemProperty
IIS:\Sites\$($site.Name) -name logFile.directory -value
"$LogPath"}
```

Restart IIS for these changes to take effect.

Enter a Product Key

When the Exchange server is fully configured, a product key can be installed on the server. Without the product key, the Exchange server is running as an unlicensed server and is limited to only five mounted mailbox databases. More can be configured, but they cannot be mounted:

```
[PS] C:\> Set-ExchangeServer -Identity EXCH01 -ProductKey xxx-
xxx-xxx-xxx-xxx
```

After registering the product key, the Information Store needs to be restarted, but I always reboot the server before bringing the server into production.

At this point we have a fully configured and operational Exchange 2019 server that can be used by clients to send and receive email, use calendaring, etc. When the Exchange server is up and running, the high availability options like the Database Availability Group and protocol load balancing can be configured. That is discussed in the next section.

Add Additional Mailbox Databases

When the two Exchange servers were installed in the previous sections, two new mailbox databases were created:

- MDB01, located in C:\ExchDbs\MDB011 on EXCH01

- MDB02, located in C:\ExchDbs\MDB022 on EXCH02

Our Exchange 2019 servers have multiple database disks as discussed earlier in this chapter, so on the third and fourth disks, two additional mailbox databases can be created. To create another mailbox database

MDB03 on server EXCH01 and another mailbox database MDB04 on server EXCH02, you can use the New-MailboxDatabase command:

```
[PS] C:\> New-MailboxDatabase -Name MDB03 -Server EXCH01
-EdbFilePath C:\ExchDbs\MDB03\MDB03.edb -LogFolderPath C:\
ExchDbs\MDB03\LogFiles
```

```
Name               Server           Recovery         ReplicationType
----               ------           --------         ---------------
MDB03              EXCH01           False            None
WARNING: Please restart the Microsoft Exchange Information Store
service on server EXCH01 after adding new mailbox databases.
```

Repeat this step for the fourth mailbox database.

High Availability

When you have a single Exchange server, you have a single point of failure, or SPOF. When this server fails, it is not available anymore, and your users are without their messaging service until you have restored or rebuilt the Exchange server. Unfortunately, this can take a considerable amount of time.

To overcome this problem, you must implement a high availability solution; in short, that means implementing more servers offering the same service. In the case of Exchange, there are two distinct services affected:

- *Mailboxes*: To achieve high availability for mailboxes, a Database Availability Group or DAG must be implemented.

- *Client Access*: To achieve high availability for clients, multiple Exchange servers must be configured in a load-balanced array.

These will be discussed in the following sections.

Mailbox Service High Availability

A Database Availability Group or DAG is a logical grouping of a set of Exchange servers that can hold copies of each other's mailbox databases. So, when there are three Mailbox servers in a DAG, mailbox database MDB01 can be active on the first server in the DAG, but it can have a copy on the second and third servers in the DAG. When the first server in the DAG fails, the mailbox database copy on the second server becomes active and continues servicing the user requests with minimal downtime for the user.

Under the hood, a DAG is using components of Windows failover clustering, and as such we must discuss some of these components in more detail.

Cluster Nodes and the File Share Witness

A DAG consists of at least two Exchange Mailbox servers. It is possible to have a DAG with only one Exchange 2019 Mailbox server, but in this case there is no redundancy of course. Another server is involved in a DAG as well, and this is the Witness server.

Under the hood the DAG uses Windows failover clustering software, and there are two options to discuss here:

- *Dynamic quorum*: In Windows, the quorum majority is determined by the nodes that are active members of the cluster at a given time. This means that a cluster can dynamically change from an eight-node cluster to a seven- or six-node cluster, and in case of issues the majority changes accordingly. In theory it is possible to dynamically bring down a cluster to only one (1) cluster node, also referred to as the "last man standing."

Besides changing automatically, an administrator can also change a member manually by setting the cluster's NodeWeight property to 0. The official Exchange product team's best practice is to leave the dynamic quorum enabled, but not to take it into account when designing an Exchange environment.

- *Dynamic witness*: In Windows, when a cluster is configured with dynamic quorum, a new feature called dynamic witness becomes available. The witness vote with a dynamic witness is automatically adjusted, based on the status of the FSW. If it is offline and not available, its witness vote is automatically set to 0, thereby eliminating the chances of an unexpected shutdown of the cluster. Just as with dynamic quorum, the recommendation is to leave the dynamic witness enabled (by default). Exchange 2016 and 2019 are not aware of the dynamic witness, but can take advantage of this cluster behavior.

From an Exchange Server point of view, the failover clustering software and its features are fully transparent, so there is no need to start worrying about clusters, and there is no need to start managing the DAG with the failover cluster manager. All management of the DAG is performed using the Exchange Management Shell or the Exchange Admin Center. In fact, I strongly recommend not using the Windows failover cluster management tool in that case.

The Witness server and the file share witness (which is a shared directory on the Witness server) are used only when there is an even number of Mailbox servers in the DAG, but as explained before, it is automatically adjusted. Furthermore, the Witness server stores no mailbox information; it has only a cluster quorum role.

The following are the prerequisites for the Witness server:

- The Witness server cannot be a member of the DAG.

- The Witness server must be in the same Active Directory forest as the DAG.

- The Witness server must be running Windows Server 2008 or later.

- A single server can serve as a witness for multiple DAGs, but each DAG has its own witness directory.

Note   If your organization has two data centers with DAG members, the Witness server can be in either data center, but it can also be placed in a third data center or in Microsoft Azure.

The Witness server plays an important role when problems arise in the DAG—for example, when an Exchange server is not available anymore. The underlying principle is based on an N/2+1 number of servers in the DAG. This means that for a DAG to stay alive when disaster strikes, at least half the number of Mailbox servers plus one (which is the Witness server) need to be up and running. So, if you have a six-node DAG, the DAG can survive the loss of three Exchange servers and still keep a majority of "voters" in the DAG.

Microsoft recommends you use an Exchange server as a file share witness, which of course cannot be a Mailbox server that is part of the DAG. The reason for this is that an Exchange server is always managed by the Exchange administrators in the organization, and the Exchange Trusted Subsystem Universal Security Group has control over all Exchange servers in Active Directory.

In real life, it is more common to use another Windows server as the file share witness. The only prerequisite is that the Exchange Trusted Subsystem has full control over the Windows server, so the Exchange

Trusted Subsystem needs to be a member of the local Administrators security group of the Windows server. As Domain Controllers do not have local groups, it would be necessary to add the Exchange Trusted Subsystem to the Domain Administrators security group. However, this imposes a security risk, and it is therefore not recommended.

Note   There is no reason to configure the file share witness in its own high availability configuration such as on a file server cluster.

Exchange Server periodically checks for the file share witness—by default, every four hours—to see if the file share witness is still alive. If it is not available at that moment, the DAG continues to run without any issues. The only time the file share witness needs to be available is during DAG changes, when an Exchange server fails, or when Exchange servers are added to or deleted from the DAG.

A question that pops up on a regular basis is whether to store the file share witness on a DFS share, especially when the company is using a server with multiple locations. This is not a good idea.

Imagine this: There are two locations, A and B, and the Exchange location has three Exchange servers configured in one DAG. The file share witness is located on a DFS share and thus potentially available in both locations. Now, suppose the network connection between locations A and B fails for some reason. The DAG will notice the connection loss, and in both locations, Exchange will try to determine the number of available Mailbox servers and attempt to contact the file share witness. In location A, this will succeed, and the DAG will continue to run with four nodes (three Exchange servers plus the file share witness). In location B, the same will happen, so Exchange will try to contact the file share witness as well. Since the file share witness is available via the DFS share in location B also, the DAG will claim the file share witness in location B and continue to run as well. And Exchange in each location will assume that the DAG members in the other location have been shut down—which of course is not the case. This is called a split-brain scenario, a highly undesirable situation that will lead to unpredictable results, and it is a situation that is not supported at all.

Cluster Administrative Access Point

When a Windows failover cluster is created, an access point for the cluster is created as well. An access point is a combination of a name and an IP address. This IP address can be IPv4 or IPv6; it can be statically assigned or dynamically assigned using DHCP.

The first access point that gets created is the cluster administrative access point, sometimes also referred to as the cluster name and cluster IP address.

In Exchange 2019, this cluster administrative access point is the name of the DAG and its IP address. As the name implies, this is only used for management purposes. Important to note is that clients connect to the Exchange Client Access Front End and the Client Access Front End connects to a mailbox database where the mailbox resides.

Besides a cluster with an administrative access point, it is also possible to configure a cluster without an administrative access point, something that was introduced years ago in Windows Server 2012 R2. In Exchange Server, this means that you create a DAG with a name and without an IP address. Is this bad? No, not at all, since nothing connects to the cluster administrative access point, except for the failover cluster manager. But since all cluster management is performed using the Exchange Management Shell, this is not needed for Exchange. In the "DAG Creation" section, we will show how to create a DAG without an administrative access point.

Note   Be aware when using this. Even in 2023 there are still third-party solutions that require a regular (old-fashioned) administrative access point.

Replication

A Database Availability Group consists of several Exchange servers, and these Mailbox servers have multiple mailbox databases (see Figure 2-10). There is only one copy of a given mailbox database on a given Mailbox server in a DAG, so the total number of copies of a specific mailbox database can never exceed the number of Mailbox servers in the DAG.

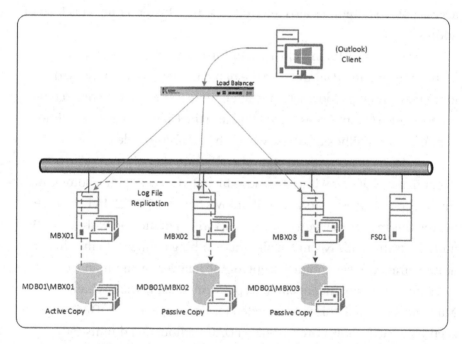

Figure 2-10. *Schematical overview of a Database Availability Group (DAG)*

The mailbox databases can be either active or passive copies. The active copy is where all the mailbox data processing takes place, and it is no different from a normal Exchange server that is not part of a DAG.

Now, another Exchange server in the DAG can host another copy of this same database; this is called a passive copy. A regular passive copy should be close to 100% identical to the active copy, and it is kept up to date by a technology called log shipping or log file replication.

There are two ways of replicating data from one Mailbox server to another:

- File mode replication
- Block mode replication

File Mode Replication

As explained earlier in this chapter, all transactions are logged in the transaction log files. When the Mailbox server has stored all the transactions in one log file, a new log file is generated, and the "old" log file is written to disk. At this moment, the log file is also copied to the second Mailbox server, where it is stored on disk. The log file is then inspected; if it is okay, the contents of the log file are replayed into the passive copy of the mailbox database. Since the log file on the passive copy is identical to the log file on the active copy, all contents are the same in both the active and the passive copies.

The process of copying transaction log files is called file mode replication since all log files are copied to the other Mailbox server.

Block Mode Replication

In block mode replication, the transactions are written into the active server's log buffer (before they are flushed into the active log file), and at the same time the transactions are copied to the passive server and written into that server's log buffer. When the log buffers are full, the information is flushed to the current log file, and a new log file is used. Both servers do this at the same time. When the Mailbox server is running block mode replication, the replication of individual log files is suspended; only individual transactions are copied between the Mailbox servers. The advantage of block mode replication is that the server holding the passive copy of the mailbox database is always 100% up to date and therefore failover times are greatly reduced.

The default process is block mode replication, but the Exchange server falls back to file mode replication when that server is too busy to cope with replicating individual transactions. If this happens, the Exchange server can replicate the individual transaction log files at its own pace and even queue some log files when there are not enough resources.

An active mailbox database copy can have multiple passive copies on multiple Mailbox servers (remember that one server can hold only one copy of a specific mailbox database, active or passive). The active copy of a mailbox database is where all the processing takes place, and all the replication, whether it is file mode or block mode, takes place from this active copy to all passive copies of the mailbox database. There is absolutely no possibility that one passive copy will replicate log files to another passive copy. The only exception to this is when a new copy of a mailbox database is created from another passive copy, but that is only the initial creation, which is seeding.

Seeding

Creating the passive copy of an active mailbox database is called seeding. In this process, the mailbox database is copied from one Mailbox server to another Mailbox server. When seeding, the complete mailbox database file (the actual edb file) is copied from the first Mailbox server hosting the active copy of this mailbox database to the second Mailbox server. This is not a simple NTFS file copy; the Information Store streams the file from one location to another.

Here is how it works: The Information Store reads the contents of the mailbox database page by page, automatically checking them. If there's an error on a particular page (i.e., a corrupt page), the process stops and the error is logged. This way, Exchange prevents copying a mailbox database to another location that has corrupted pages. When seeding, you can select which mailbox database acts as the source of the seeding. This can be the active mailbox database, but it can also be a passive mailbox database.

Since the pages of the mailbox database are copied from one Exchange server to another Exchange server, the passive copy is identical to the active copy. When the entire mailbox database is copied to the other Exchange server, the remaining log files are copied to the other Mailbox server as well. When a new mailbox database is seeded, the process takes only a couple of minutes because there is not too much data to copy. But imagine a mailbox database of 1 TB in a normal production environment. When that must be seeded, it can take hours. And not only is the timing an important factor but also the process puts additional load on the servers. The 1 TB of data needs to be read and checked, copied via the network, and written to disk on the other Mailbox server.

Replication (Copy) Queue and Replay Queue

In an ideal situation, transaction log files are replicated to another Exchange server directly after the log files are written to disk, and they are processed immediately after being received by the other Exchange server. Unfortunately, we do not live in an ideal world, so there might be some delay somewhere in the system.

When the Exchange servers are busy, it can happen that more transaction log files are generated than the replication process can handle and transmit. If this is the case, the log files are queued on the Exchange server holding the active copy of the mailbox database. This queue is called the replication queue. Queuing always happens, and it is normally not a reason for concern if the number of log files in the queue is low and the log files do not stay there too long. However, if there are thousands of messages waiting in line, it is time to do some further investigation.

When the transaction log files are received by the Exchange server holding the passive copy of the mailbox database, those transaction log files are stored in the replay queue. Queuing up in the replay queue happens as well and is also not reason for concern when the number of transaction log files is low. There can be spikes in the number of transaction log files in the replay queue, but when the number of transaction log files is constantly increasing, there is something wrong. It can happen that the disk holding the mailbox database is generating too many read-and-write operations. Or there may not be enough resources to flush the queue, and so the queue will grow. If the system can flush the queue in a reasonable time, and there are not thousands of messages in the queue, you should be fine.

Lagged Copies

Regarding the replay queue, there is one exception to note: lagged copies. If you have implemented lagged copies in your DAG, and you experience many log files in the replay queue, then there is nothing to worry about.

Lagged copies are passive copies of a mailbox database that are not kept up to date. This means that log files are replicated to the Exchange server holding the lagged copy, but the log files themselves are kept in the replay queue. This lag time between replication and writing to the server can be as little as 0 seconds (the log file is replayed immediately) or up to 14 days. A very long lag time will have a serious impact on scalability, of course. A full 14 days' worth of log files can mean a tremendous amount of data being stored in the replay queue; also, replaying the transaction log files of a lagged copy can take quite some time when longer timeframes are used.

Note   Lagged copies are not a high availability solution; rather, they are a disaster recovery solution.

Active Manager

The Active Manager is a component of Exchange, and it runs inside the Microsoft Exchange Replication services on all Exchange servers. The Active Manager is the component that is responsible for the high availability inside the Database Availability Group.

There are several types of Active Managers:

- *Primary Active Manager (PAM)*: The PAM is the role that decides which copy of a mailbox database is the active copy and which ones are the passive copies; as such, the PAM reacts to changes in the DAG, such as DAG member failures. The DAG member that holds the PAM role is always the server that also holds the quorum resource or the default cluster group.

- *Standby Active Manager (SAM)*: The SAM is responsible for providing DAG information—for example, which mailbox database is an active copy and which copies are passive copies—to other Exchange components like the Client Access service or the Hub Transport service. If the SAM detects a failure of a mailbox database, it requests a failover to the PAM. The PAM then decides which copy to activate.

- *Standalone Active Manager*: The Standalone Active Manager is responsible for mounting and dismounting databases on that particular server. This Active Manager is available only on Exchange servers that are not members of a DAG.

DAG Across (Active Directory) Sites

In the previous examples, the DAG has always been installed in one Active Directory site. However, there is no such boundary in the DAG, so it is possible to create a DAG that spans multiple Active Directory sites, even in different physical locations. For instance, it is possible to extend the DAG for anticipating two potential scenarios:

- *Database disaster recovery*: In this scenario, mailbox databases are replicated to another location exclusively for offsite storage. These databases are safe there, should disaster, like a fire or flood, strike at the primary location.

- *Site resiliency*: In this scenario, the DAG is (most likely) evenly distributed across two locations (see Figure 2-11). The second location, however, also has multiple Exchange servers with a full-blown Internet connection. When disaster strikes and the primary site is no longer available, the second site can take over all functions.

When using a GeoDNS solution, only one FQDN (i.e., webmail.proexchangeadmin.com) can be used. For example, in Figure 2-11, there are two Active Directory sites, one location in Amsterdam and another in London. When a user tries to contact webmail.proexchangeadmin.com when traveling in the United Kingdom, they are automatically connected to the London site.

When they try to access webmail.proexchangeadmin.com in the Netherlands, they are connected to the Amsterdam site. In either case, after authentication the client is automatically proxied to the correct Mailbox server to get the mailbox information.

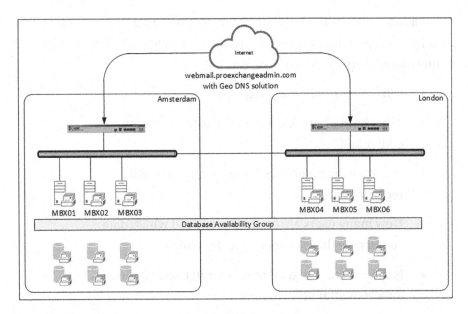

Figure 2-11. *A DAG stretched across two locations*

By default, a site failover is not an automated process. If a data center failover needs to happen, especially when the site holding the file share witness is involved, administrative action is required. However, it is possible to work around this limitation by placing the file share witness in a third Active Directory site.

It is possible to create an active/active scenario whereby both data centers are active, servicing users and processing mail data. In this case, two DAGs must be created; each DAG is active in one data center, and its passive copies are in the other data center. Note, however, that an Exchange server can be a member of only one DAG at a time. This could mean that you need more servers in an active/active scenario, a downside of having two DAGs.

Creating a site-resilient configuration with multiple DAGs requires careful planning, plus asking yourself a lot of questions, both technical and organizational. Typical questions are as follows:

- What level of service is required?

- What level of service is required when one data center fails?

- What are the objectives for recovery point and recovery time?

- How many users are on the system and which data centers are these users connecting to?

- Is the system designed to service all users when one data center fails?

- How are services moved back to the original data center?

- Are there any resources available (like IT staff) for these scenarios?

These are just basic planning questions to be answered before you even think about implementing a site-resilient configuration. And remember: The more requirements there are and the stricter they are, the more expensive the solution will be!

DAG Networks

A DAG uses one or more networks for client connectivity and for replication. Each DAG contains at least one network for client connectivity, which is created by default, and zero or more replication networks. In Exchange 2010, this default DAG network was called MAPI network. The MAPI protocol is no longer used in Exchange as a native client protocol, but the default DAG network is still called MapiDagNetwork.

For years Microsoft has been recommending the use of multiple networks to separate the client traffic from the replication traffic. With the current 10 Gb networks, separating client traffic from replication traffic is no longer an issue. Also, the use of a server blade infrastructure with its 10 Gb backbone separation of traffic was more a logical separation than a physical separation. Therefore, Microsoft moves away from the recommendation of separating network traffic, thereby simplifying the DAG network configuration.

When you still want to separate client traffic from replication traffic, you can do so in a supported manner. In Exchange, the network is automatically configured by the system. If additional networks need to be configured, you set the DAG to manual configuration and then create the additional DAG networks.

When using multiple networks, it is possible to designate a network for client connectivity and the other networks for replication traffic. When multiple networks are used for replication, Exchange automatically determines which network to use for replication traffic. When all the replication networks are offline or not available, Exchange automatically switches back to the MAPI network for the replication traffic.

Default gateways need to be considered when you are configuring multiple network interfaces in Windows Server. The only network that needs this configuring with a default gateway is the client connectivity network; all other networks should not be configured with a default gateway.

Other recommendations important for replication networks are the following:

- Disabling the DNS registration on the TCP/IP properties of the respective network interface

- Disabling the protocol bindings, such as client for Microsoft networks and file and printer sharing for Microsoft networks, on the properties of the network interface

- Rearranging the binding order of the network interfaces so that the client connectivity network is at the top of the connection order

When using an iSCSI storage solution, make sure that the iSCSI network is not used at all for replication purposes. Remove any iSCSI network connection from the replication networks list.

DAG Creation

Creating a Database Availability Group consists of several steps:

- Creating the DAG object

- Adding the Exchange servers to the DAG

- Creating additional Mailbox database copies

These are discussed in the following sections.

Creating the Database Availability Group Object

The first step in the process is to create the DAG object using the Exchange Management Shell. In this step, only an object in Active Directory is created. As explained earlier in this chapter, a Computer Name Object (CNO) and a cluster IP address are no longer needed in Exchange 2019. To create a new DAG object, you can use the New-DatabaseAvailabilityGroup command:

```
[PS] C:\> New-DatabaseAvailabilityGroup -Name DAG01
-WitnessServer FS01.proexchangeadmin.com -WitnessDirectory C:\
DAG01_FSW -DatabaseAvailabilityGroupIPAddresses ([System.Net.
IPAddress])::None
```

Name	Member Servers	Operational Servers
DAG01	{}	

Creating the DAG is straightforward—it is only an entry written in the configuration partition of Active Directory. If you want to check it, you can use ADSI Edit, open the Configuration partition and navigate to CN=Configuration, CN=Services, CN=Microsoft Exchange, CN=, CN=Administrative Groups, CN=Database Availability Groups, CN=DAG01.

This is shown in Figure 2-12.

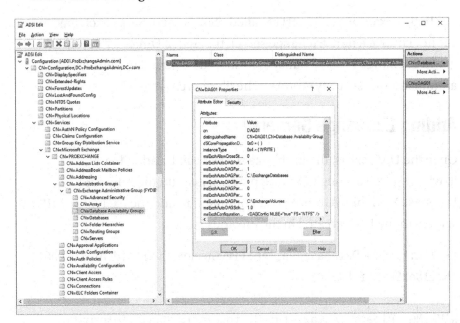

Figure 2-12. *The newly created DAG in Active Directory*

The information that's returned when running a Get-DatabaseAvailabilityGroup command is just a representation of this object in Active Directory, combined with information taken from the local registry (when using the -status parameter).

Note   Microsoft recommends that the file share witness best be another Exchange server. This Exchange server cannot be a member of the same DAG. However, it can be a member of another DAG or any other server in the same Active Directory site.

In this example, a file server called FS01 is used. Since Exchange cannot control a non-Exchange server, the Active Directory's security group Exchange Trusted Subsystem should be added to the local administrator's security group on the file share Witness server.

Adding Exchange Servers

Once the DAG exists, the Exchange servers can be added to it, which is also a straightforward process; just run the Add-DatabaseAvailabilityGroupServer command to add the Exchange 2019 servers to the DAG created in the previous step:

```
[PS] C:\> Add-DatabaseAvailabilityGroupServer -Identity DAG01
-MailboxServer EXCH01

WARNING: Please restart the Microsoft Exchange Information
Store service on server EXCH01
```

And of course, repeat this command for any subsequent Exchange 2019 servers.

When the Windows failover clustering components are not installed on the Mailbox server, the Add-DatabaseAvailabilityGroupServer cmdlet will install these automatically.

At this point, a DAG is created with two members using a file server as a Witness server.

Adding the Mailbox Database Copies

Now that the DAG is fully up and running, it is time for the last step: creating additional copies of the mailbox databases. Initially there's only one copy of the mailbox database, but you can create redundancy when you add multiple copies on other Mailbox servers in the DAG.

It is important to note that the location of the mailbox database is identical on all Mailbox servers holding a copy of a particular mailbox database. So, if you have a mailbox database C:\ExchDbs\Disk1\MDB01\MDB01.edb of server EXCH01, the copy of the mailbox database on server EXCH02 is on C:\ExchDbs\Disk1\MDB01\MDB01.edb as well. This might sound obvious, but every now and then, I talk to people who are not aware of this.

To create additional copies of a mailbox database in a DAG, you can use the Add-MailboxDatabaseCopy cmdlet, for example:

```
[PS] C:\> Add-MailboxDatabaseCopy -Identity MDB01
-MailboxServer EXCH02 -ActivationPreference 2

WARNING: Please restart the Microsoft Exchange Information
Store service on server EXCH02 after adding new mailbox
databases.
```

Just like with the previous step, repeat this command for any subsequent Mailbox database copies.

The activation preference is meant for administrative purposes and for planned switchovers. It is not used by an automatic failover. In case of an automatic failover, a process called the best copy selection on the Mailbox server is used to determine the optimal passive copy for activation.

Configuring the DAG Networks

In our example, the DAG is now configured with two Mailbox servers; by default, only one DAG network is configured, the default MapiDagNetwork. You can quickly see this in EAC, in the lower-right part of the DAG view, as shown in Figure 2-13.

Figure 2-13. *Only one network is configured by default in a DAG*

To add an additional DAG network (if the servers have multiple network interfaces, of course), the DAG itself should be set to manual configuration, as mentioned earlier. This can only be done using EMS with the following command:

```
[PS] C:\> Set-DatabaseAvailabilityGroup -Identity DAG01
-ManualDagNetworkConfiguration $true
```

To create a new additional network for replication purposes, you can use the following command:

```
[PS] C:\> New-DatabaseAvailabilityGroupNetwork
-DatabaseAvailabilityGroup DAG01 -Name "Replication Network"
-Subnets 192.168.0.0/24 -ReplicationEnabled:$true

Identity                    ReplicationEnabled  Subnets
--------                    ------------------  -------
DAG01\ Replication Network  True                {{192.168.0.0/24,
                                                Unknown}}
```

To designate this new network as a dedicated replication network, you must disable the replication feature of the regular MapiDagNetwork in the DAG. To disable this, you can use the following command:

```
[PS] C:\> Set-DatabaseAvailabilityGroupNetwork -Identity DAG01\
MapiDagNetwork -ReplicationEnabled:$false
```

After running these commands, you have created a separate network in the DAG specifically for replication traffic.

Exchange Transport

Exchange Transport is an integral part of any Exchange server, whether it be a Mailbox server or an Edge Transport server. Exchange Transport consists of several components that are responsible for

- Sending and receiving messages to and from the Internet

- Sending and receiving messages to and from other Exchange servers

- Picking up and delivering messages from and to mailboxes

141

- Relaying SMTP messages from other devices or applications

- Delivering message hygiene

- Providing redundancy in message delivery

To achieve this, any Exchange server has multiple services that are responsible for transport:

- Microsoft Exchange Transport

- Microsoft Exchange Transport Log Search

- Microsoft Exchange Front-End Transport

- Microsoft Exchange Mailbox Transport Submission

- Microsoft Exchange Mailbox Transport Delivery

- Microsoft Exchange Anti-spam Update

- Microsoft Exchange EdgeSync

These seven services combined make up Exchange Transport, and all are discussed in detail in this chapter.

Transport Pipeline

The complete, end-to-end mail delivery process, from accepting external SMTP messages on the Exchange server to delivering the actual message to the mailbox, is called the transport pipeline. The transport pipeline consists of several individual components:

1. *Front-End Transport service (FETS):* FETS is responsible for accepting SMTP messages from external SMTP hosts. FETS can also be configured as a front-end proxy on Send Connectors.

2. *Transport service*: The Transport service is
    responsible for processing all inbound and
    outbound SMTP messages. It receives messages
    on the Receive Connector from FETS, from the
    Transport server running on other Exchange
    servers, or from any down-level Hub Transport
    servers when running Exchange 2016 and Exchange
    2010 in coexistence. When the messages are
    received, they are queued in the submission queue.

3. *Submission queue*: The submission queue also
    receives messages from the pickup directory and
    from the replay directory. When messages are
    properly formatted (in an .EML format), you can
    drop them into the pickup directory, and they will
    be automatically processed.

4. *Categorizer*: From the submission queue, the
    messages are sent to the categorizer. This is the
    process whereby the Transport server determines
    whether the message must be delivered locally or
    remotely, whether it is on an internal Exchange
    server or an external server on the Internet. When
    categorized, the messages are delivered to a Send
    Connector. It is important to note that the Transport
    server never communicates directly with the
    mailbox databases.

5. *Mailbox Transport service*: The Mailbox Transport service, not to confuse with the Transport service, consists of two parts:

    Mailbox Transport Submission service: This is responsible for picking up messages from a user's drafts or outbox folder. Remote procedure call (RPC) is used to communicate with the Information Store to pick up messages, and then the SMTP is used to deliver messages to the local Transport server or to the Transport server running on other Exchange 2013 Mailbox servers in the organization.

    Mailbox Transport Delivery service: This is responsible for receiving messages from the Transport server and delivering those messages to the user's inbox or underlying folder. Messages are accepted from the local Transport server or from the Transport server running on other Exchange 2013 Mailbox servers in the organization. Next, RPC is used to communicate with the Information Store to deliver the messages to the inbox, and the SMTP is used to communicate with the Exchange 2013 Transport server.

The transport pipeline is shown in Figure 2-14.

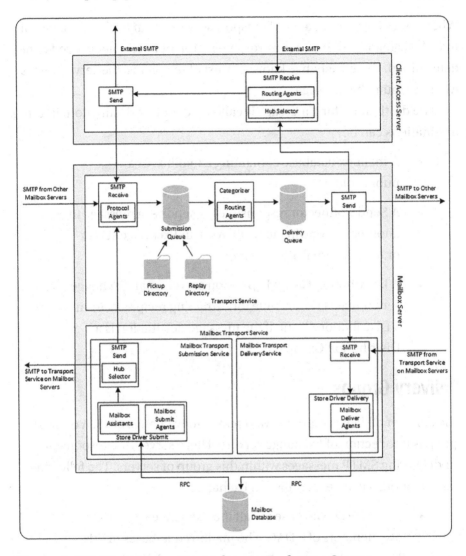

Figure 2-14. *The transport pipeline in Exchange Server*

Routing Destinations

When a message arrives at the Transport service on an Exchange server, it must be categorized. In other words, the recipient or recipients need to be determined. Once Exchange knows the list of recipients, the server knows where to route the message.

The destination for a message is called the routing destination. Routing destinations can be

- A mailbox database containing a mailbox or a public folder

- A Send Connector responsible for sending a message to another Active Directory site with an Exchange server or to an external SMTP server

- A Distribution Group Expansion server, or an Exchange server that is responsible for extracting recipients from a Distribution Group if the message destination is a Distribution Group

Delivery Groups

The concept of delivery groups was created in Exchange 2013. A delivery group is a collection of Exchange servers. These servers are responsible for delivering SMTP messages within this group of servers. The following delivery groups can be identified in Exchange:

- *Routable DAG*: These are all the Exchange servers that are members of a DAG. The mailbox databases in this DAG are the routing destinations of the delivery group. A message can be delivered to one Exchange server in a DAG, and this Exchange server is responsible for routing the message to the Exchange server that holds the active copy of the mailbox database in the

DAG. Since the DAG can span multiple Active Directory sites, the routing boundary for the routable DAG is the DAG itself, not the Active Directory site.

- *Mailbox delivery group*: This is a collection of Exchange servers in one Active Directory site that is not a member of a DAG. In a mailbox delivery group, the routing boundary is the Active Directory site itself.

- *Connector Source server*: This is a collection of Exchange servers that act as the source server for a particular Send Connector. These are only the source servers of a particular Send Connector; Exchange servers that are not defined as source servers of the Send Connector, but that are in the same Active Directory site, are not part of this delivery group.

- *Active Directory site*: This is an Active Directory site that is not the final Active Directory site, which means the message is in transit through this Active Directory site. For example, it can be a hub site or a connecting Active Directory site for an Exchange Edge Transport server. An Exchange server cannot contact an Edge Transport server that has an edge subscription in another Active Directory site, so the message must pass through this Active Directory site to be relayed to the Edge Transport server.

- *Server list*: This is one or more Exchange servers that are configured as Distribution Group Expansion servers.

Queues

In Exchange Server, a queue is a destination for a message, as well as a temporary storage location on the Exchange server. For every destination there is a queue, so there are queues for submissions, for message delivery to the mailbox, for routing to other Exchange servers in the organization, or for routing to an external destination.

When messages arrive at the Transport service, they are immediately stored on the local disk of the Exchange server. The storage technology used is the extensible storage engine (ESE), which is the same engine as used for the mailbox databases. By default, the mailqueue database and its accompanying log files and checkpoint file can be found on C:\Program Files\Microsoft\Exchange Server\V15\TransportRoles\data\Queue as shown in Figure 2-15. The ESE database has circular logging enabled. This means that log files no longer needed are automatically deleted and, as such, there is no recovery method, such as replay of log files.

Figure 2-15. *The mailqueue database is a normal ESE database*

It is possible to change some of the configuration options of the mailqueue database. When Exchange is installed in the default location, all configuration settings are stored in the EdgeTransport.exe.config file, which can be found in C:\Program Files\Microsoft\Exchange Server\ V15\bin. Most settings in this file can be left at their default values, but it is possible to change the location of all mailqueue-related files and directories to another disk. The advantage of doing this is that, if there's unexpected growth in these files, it will not affect the normal system and boot drives. If these fill up, there is always the possibility that the services running on this server will gradually stop working; worse, the entire server might stop working. This is an undesirable situation for any Exchange server.

If you open the EdgeTransport.exe.config file and browse through the file, you will see the following keys:

- QueueDatabasePath

- QueueDatabaseLoggingPath

- IPFilterDatabasePath

- IPFilterDatabaseLoggingPath

- TemporaryStoragePath

By default, these keys point to the location %ExchangeInstallPath% TransportRoles\data\, but by changing the values to, for example, D:\ TransportRoles\data\, another disk can be used. This is explained in the "Installing and Configuring Edge Transport Servers" section of this chapter.

Shadow Redundancy

There is one type of queue that always raises questions. At first look, there are always messages in this queue, and they do not seem to disappear quickly. Shadow queues, also referred to as shadow redundancy, are there for message redundancy: messages are stored in shadow queues until the next hop in the message path that moves toward delivering the message reports a successful delivery. Only then is the message deleted from the shadow queue.

Imagine an Exchange server in Portland (OR) that is sending messages to the Internet but has no Internet connection of its own. There are also two Exchange servers in Seattle (WA), and Seattle has its own Internet connection. A network connection exists between the two locations.

1.   The Exchange server in Portland sends an SMTP message to Exchange server (A) in Seattle, EXCH01. As soon as the message is delivered in Seattle, it is stored in the shadow queue on the server in Portland.

2.   Exchange server (A) in Seattle sends the message to server (B) in Seattle, EXCH02. As soon as the message is accepted, it is stored in the shadow queue on server (A).

3.   Server (A) knows the message was successfully delivered and reports back to the server in Portland. At this moment, the message can safely be deleted from the Portland shadow queue because there still is a backup message, but now it's on server (A).

4.   Server (B) sends the message to the Edge Transport server in the perimeter network, and when delivered, server (B) reports back to server (A), which can now delete the message from its shadow queue.

Sending a message from the Exchange server to the Internet is difficult, of course, because not all SMTP servers on the Internet support shadow queues. If not supported, the messages are automatically deleted from the sender's shadow queue after some time.

Shadow queue redundancy is built into Exchange 2019 for messages that are in transit. If one server fails, for whatever reason, and the server is no longer available, the previous Exchange server in the message path can retry delivering the message via a different available path.

Managing Queues

Most of the Exchange server queues exist for only a limited time. When the Transport server cannot deliver a message, the message stays in the queue until the server can successfully deliver the message (it keeps trying) or until the message expires; the default message expiration time is two days.

These queues can be managed by using the Queue Viewer, which is a graphic tool, or by using EMS. The Queue Viewer can be found in the toolbox, an MMC snap-in that is automatically installed during the installation of Exchange Server.

Open the Exchange toolbox and select "Queue Viewer" under Mail flow tools. The Queue Viewer shows the queues on the server currently operating, but if you select "Connect to Server" in the Actions pane, you can use it to view information on other Exchange servers as well as shown in Figure 2-16.

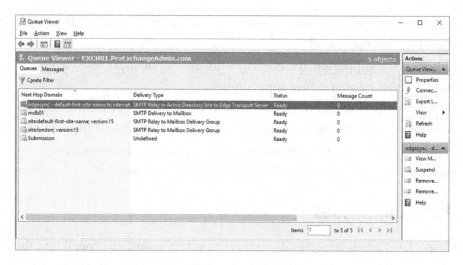

Figure 2-16. *Queue information using the Queue viewer*

The Queue Viewer is an incredibly valuable tool for troubleshooting purposes. It shows messages that are in a queue, of course, but if you open the message, it also shows the reason the message cannot be delivered. The tool also gives you the option of suspending a queue or removing messages from a queue, either with or without generating a non-delivery report (NDR).

It is also possible to manage the queues using EMS. This method is more complex, but it offers many more granular options. The basic command to get queue information is the Get-Queue cmdlet. The Get-Queue cmdlet will show the queues on the server where the cmdlet is executed. Using the identity of the queue, you can obtain more information by using the Get-Queue -Identity EXCH01\29 cmdlet, for example, where 29 is the number of the queue. The actual error is not shown when using this cmdlet, but you can use the Get-Queue -Identity EXCH01\29 | FL cmdlet for all information regarding the queue or the Get-Queue -Identity EXCH01\29 | select Identity, DeliveryType, Status, MessageCount, NexthopDomain, LastError to show the actual error message the Transport service is experiencing:

```
[PS] C:\> Get-Queue -Identity EXCH01\29 | select
Identity,DeliveryType,Status,MessageCount,NexthopDomain,LastError

Identity       : EXCH01\29
DeliveryType   : SmtpRelayWithinAdSiteToEdge
Status         : Connecting
MessageCount   : 1
NextHopDomain  : edgesync - default-first-site-name to internet
LastError      : [{LED=451 4.4.397 Error communicating with
                 target host. -> 421 4.2.1 Unable to connect ->
                 SocketTimedout: Socket error code 10060};{MSG=};
                 {FQDN=edgesync - default-first-site-name to
                 internet};{IP=10.83.4.124};{LRT=3/7/2023
                 6:11:57 PM}]
```

The Get-Queue cmdlet will only show results from the Exchange server where the cmdlet is executed. You can also use the Get-TransportService cmdlet to get a list of all Transport services running on all Exchange servers and pipe this output into the Get-Queue cmdlet: Get-TransportService | Get-Queue. This will show all queues on all Transport services in the organization.

When a message cannot be delivered, it will stay in the queue, and it can stay here for up to two days, which is the default wait time. When this happens, there is no need for any concern; Exchange will keep trying to deliver the message. Also, the number of messages in a queue can vary over time; for example, you could have 20–30 messages in a queue for an Internet Send Connector. But the messages must be delivered after some time, of course. If there is a steady increase in the number of messages in a queue or if many queues are created and the messages get stuck in there, then it's time to dig deeper into the cause of the excessive queuing.

Safety Net

Safety Net is a redundancy feature in Exchange 2019 for the Transport service. Safety Net stores messages in a queue that were successfully delivered to the mailboxes. Safety Net is redundant by itself; there's a primary Safety Net and a shadow Safety Net. The primary Safety Net exists on the Exchange server where the message originates, while the shadow Safety Net exists on the Exchange server where the message is delivered. As soon as the message is delivered, it is stored in the Safety Net queue. Messages are kept in the Safety Net queue for 48 hours, which is the default time.

Safety Net and shadow redundancy are complementary. That is, shadow redundancy is responsible for messages in transit, while Safety Net is responsible for messages that have been delivered to mailboxes. The cool thing is that Safety Net is a fully automated feature; there is no need for any manual action. All coordination is done by the Active Manager, who is also responsible for failover scenarios in the DAG.

When something happens on the Exchange server, the Active Manager requests a resubmission from Safety Net. For large organizations, these messages most likely exist on multiple Mailbox servers, so (a lot of) duplicate messages can occur. Exchange Server however has a mechanism that detects duplicate messages; it finds and eliminates those duplicate messages, preventing the recipient from receiving multiple copies. Unfortunately, resubmitted messages from Safety Net are also delivered to mail servers outside the Exchange organization. Since these servers do not have the duplicate message detection mechanism, external users can receive multiple identical messages.

When the primary Safety Net is not available, the Active Manager tries requesting a resubmit for 12 hours. If unsuccessful after this time, the Active Manager then contacts the other Mailbox servers and requests a resubmit of messages for the mailbox database.

Send and Receive Connectors

For sending and receiving SMTP messages, Exchange uses the concept of connectors:

- *Send Connector*: This is used to send messages. This can be to another SMTP host on the Internet, to an Edge Transport server, to an Exchange server in another Active Directory Site, or to Exchange Online Protection.

- *Receive Connector*: This is used to receive messages from other SMTP hosts, applications, multi-functional devices, or Exchange Online Protection.

A Receive Connector can also be used to relay SMTP messages from devices or applications. These messages can be delivered to mailboxes on Exchange, but also to the Internet. This requires some additional configuration and caution since it is easy to create an open relay to the Internet.

Send and Receive Connectors are discussed in the following sections.

Send Connectors

A Send Connector in Exchange is a connector that is responsible for sending SMTP messages. A well-known Send Connector is an Internet Send Connector, which will send messages to the Internet.

A Send Connector is known in the entire organization, so all Exchange servers in all Active Directory sites have knowledge about Send Connectors and can use them.

To create a new Send Connector to send messages from Exchange to the Internet, execute the following PowerShell command in EMS:

```
[PS] C:\> New-SendConnector -Name "To Internet" -Internet
-SourceTransportServer EXCH01 -AddressSpaces *
```

This will create a new Send Connector of type "Internet." The -SourceTransportServer option indicates which Exchange server can send mail via this connector. In this example it is only EXCH01, but it is a multivalued property, so your multiple servers can be added here. The address space value "*" means that all domains can be sent via this connector.

By default, MX routing is used for Send Connectors. It is also possible to use a smarthost for outbound email and have this smarthost deliver to the Internet. To create a Send Connector to send email to the Internet, but use a smarthost with FQDN smtphost.proexchangeadmin.com instead and use two Exchange servers, execute the following command in EMS:

```
[PS] C:\> New-SendConnector -Name "To Internet" -Internet
-SourceTransportServer EXCH01,EXCH02 -AddressSpaces
* -DNSRoutingEnabled $False -SmartHosts smtphost.
proexchangeadmin.com
```

A typical use case for sending email via a smarthost is when using a cloud-based message hygiene solution like Exchange Online Protection, Trend Micro Hosted Email Security, or Mimecast Email Security. The Send Connector will send out all email to the cloud provider, and they will deliver the email to its destination.

When using Exchange Online Protection in front of your Exchange 2019 servers, without a hybrid configuration, that is, you must use a command similar to the following:

```
[PS] C:\> New-SendConnector -Name "To Internet" -Internet
-SourceTransportServer EXCH01,EXCH02 -AddressSpaces *
-DNSRoutingEnabled $False -SmartHosts proexchangeadmin-com.
mail.protection.outlook.com
```

By default, a Send Connector can be used by all Exchange servers in the entire organization. A US-based Send Connector can be used by Exchange servers in Australia. To prevent this, it is possible to scope a Send

Connector to only the Active Directory where the source Transport servers are located using the -IsScopedConnector option. The default value of this option is $False, but when set to $True, only the local Exchange servers can use this Send Connector. For other Active Directory sites, dedicated Send Connectors need to be created in that Active Directory site.

It is also possible to create a Send Connector for specific domains and route messages for this domain via another path. For example, if we want to route messages for a domain @exchangelabs.nl not via the regular Internet Send Connector, but directly to the Edge Transport server for this domain, we can create such a Send Connector using the following command:

```
[PS] C:\> New-SendConnector -Name "Exchangelabs" -Partner
-SourceTransportServer EXCH01,EXCH02 -AddressSpaces
"*.exchangelabs.nl" -DNSRoutingEnabled $False -SmartHosts
Edge03.exchangelabs.nl
```

This is especially interesting if you want to route mail to a trusted partner and you want to secure this traffic using IPSEC or Mutual TLS.

The Send Connectors mentioned previously are all external connectors; this means that messages sent via these connectors have a destination outside of our Exchange organization. There is no need to worry about message routing between Exchange servers, not even if there are multiple Active Directory sites in the Exchange organization. For internal routing, an implicit connector called intra-organization Send Connector is automatically created in each Exchange organization. This intra-organization is invisible, requires no maintenance, and is automatically available.

For troubleshooting purposes, it can be useful to disable a Send Connector for some time. To achieve this, the Set-SendConnector command accepts the -Enabled option. By default, a Send Connector is

enabled; to disable it the -Enabled option must be set to false. To disable
the Send Connector that was previously created, execute the following
command in EMS:

```
[PS] C:\> Set-SendConnector -Identity "To Internet"
-Enabled $False
```

To re-enable the Send Connector, execute the command again with
the -Enabled option set to $True.

A Send Connector can log information to a protocol log file. This
logs quite some information, so it is disabled by default. The Microsoft
recommendation is to enable protocol logging only for troubleshooting
purposes.

To enable logging on the previously created Send Connector, execute
the following command in EMS:

```
[PS] C:\> Set-SendConnector -Identity "To Internet"
-ProtocolLoggingLevel Verbose
[PS] C:\> Restart-Service MSExchangeTransport
```

The default location for the transport protocol log files is C:\Program
Files\Microsoft\Exchange Server\V15\TransportRoles\Logs\Hub\
ProtocolLog\SMTPSend. Tons of information are written into these log
files, and it is easy to get lost. Several log files are created per day; the date
and time plus a sequence number is in the name of the log file. Be aware
that transport logging happens with UTC timestamp, so this can differ
several hours with your local time zone, depending on your location of
course. To prevent filling up the disk with protocol log files and causing the
server to halt, I always recommend placing the log files on a different disk.
This is a setting of the Transport service on the Exchange server.

To retrieve the current settings for the log files, execute the following command:

```
[PS] C:\> Get-Transportservice -Identity EXCH01 | Select *logpath*
```

```
ConnectivityLogPath          : C:\Program Files\Microsoft\
                               Exchange Server\V15\
                               TransportRoles\Logs\Hub\
                               Connectivity
MessageTrackingLogPath        : C:\Program Files\Microsoft\
                               Exchange Server\V15\
                               TransportRoles\Logs\
                               MessageTracking
IrmLogPath                    : C:\Program Files\Microsoft\
                               Exchange Server\V15\
                               Logging\IRMLogs
ActiveUserStatisticsLogPath : C:\Program Files\Microsoft\
                               Exchange Server\V15\
                               TransportRoles\Logs\Hub\
                               ActiveUsersStats
ServerStatisticsLogPath       : C:\Program Files\Microsoft\
                               Exchange Server\V15\
                               TransportRoles\Logs\Hub\
                               ServerStats
ReceiveProtocolLogPath        : C:\Program Files\Microsoft\Exchange
                               Server\V15\TransportRoles\Logs\
                               Hub\ProtocolLog\SmtpReceive
RoutingTableLogPath           : C:\Program Files\Microsoft\
                               Exchange Server\V15\
                               TransportRoles\Logs\Hub\Routing
SendProtocolLogPath           : C:\Program Files\Microsoft\
                               Exchange
```

```
                                      Server\V15\TransportRoles\Logs\
                                      Hub\ProtocolLog\SmtpSend
QueueLogPath                       : C:\Program Files\Microsoft\
                                      Exchange Server\V15\
                                      TransportRoles\Logs\Hub\
                                      QueueViewer
LatencyLogPath                     : C:\Program Files\Microsoft\
                                      Exchange Server\V15\
                                      TransportRoles\Logs\Hub\
                                      LatencyLog
GeneralLogPath                     : C:\Program Files\Microsoft\
                                      Exchange Server\V15\
                                      TransportRoles\Logs\Hub\
                                      GeneralLog
WlmLogPath                         : C:\Program Files\Microsoft\
                                      Exchange Server\V15\
                                      TransportRoles\Logs\WLM
AgentLogPath                       : C:\Program Files\Microsoft\
                                      Exchange Server\V15\
                                      TransportRoles\Logs\Hub\AgentLog
FlowControlLogPath                 :
ProcessingSchedulerLogPath         :
ResourceLogPath                    :
DnsLogPath                         :
JournalLogPath                     : C:\Program Files\Microsoft\
                                      Exchange Server\V15\
                                      TransportRoles\Logs\JournalLog
TransportMaintenanceLogPath        :
TransportHttpLogPath               : C:\Program Files\Microsoft\
                                      Exchange Server\V15\
                                      TransportRoles\Logs\Hub\
                                      TransportHttp
```

```
RequestBrokerLogPath          :
StorageRESTLogPath            :
AgentGrayExceptionLogPath     :
```

To relocate the log files, the Set-TransportService command must be used with the appropriate options. To relocate the log files for the Send Connector, execute the following command:

```
[PS] C:\> Set-TransportService -Identity EXCH01 -Send
ProtocolLogPath "D:\Program Files\Microsoft\ExchangeServer\V15\
TransportRoles\Logs\Hub\Connectivity\SMTPSend"
```

Changing one setting does not make much sense. When changing multiple settings, it makes sense to use a variable with the location of the log files, and if you want to change this for multiple servers, use another variable with the name of the Exchange server, for example:

```
[PS] C:\> $ServerName = "EXCH01"
[PS] C:\> $LogPath = "D:\Program Files\Microsoft\Exchange
Server\V15\TransportRoles\Logs"
[PS] C:\> Set-TransportService -Identity $ServerName -IrmLogPath
"$LogPath\IRMLogs" -ActiveUserStatisticsLogPath "$LogPath\
ActiveUsersStats" -ServerStatisticsLogPath "$LogPath\
ServerStats" -PickupDirectoryPath "$LogPath\Pickup" -Routing
TableLogPath "$LogPath\Routing" -PipelineTracingPath
"$LogPath\PipelineTracing" -ConnectivityLogPath "$LogPath\
Hub\Connectivity" -ReceiveProtocolLogPath "$LogPath\Hub\
ProtocolLog\SmtpReceive" -ReplayDirectoryPath "$LogPath\
Replay" -SendProtocolLogPath "$LogPath\Hub\ProtocolLog\
SmtpSend" -QueueLogPath "$LogPath\Hub\QueueViewer"
-WlmLogPath "$LogPath\WLM" -AgentLogPath "$LogPath\Hub\
AgentLog" -TransportHttpLogPath "$LogPath\Hub\TransportHttp"
-Confirm:$false
[PS] C:\> Restart-Service MSExchangeTransport
```

Note   Multiple Send Connectors write log files to the same location and write to the same log files. The name of the Send Connector is written to entries in the log files. Nevertheless, I recommend enabling logging only on one Send Connector at a time for troubleshooting purposes instead of enable logging on all Send Connectors. This will prevent you from drowning in all log files.

Receive Connectors

In contrast to Send Connectors that are created manually, Exchange also has Receive Connectors that are automatically created during installation. As the name implies, Receive Connectors are responsible for receiving messages. These can be internal messages between Exchange servers within the organization (which are automatically authenticated) and external messages from outside the organization. These are anonymous connections. Be aware that if you have a Cisco IronPort in front of your Exchange server, it is also treated as external mail and thus requires anonymous access.

During installation of Exchange server EXCH01, five Receive Connectors are created:

- *Client Frontend EXCH01*: Listening on port 587, this Receive Connector is used by clients like Mozilla Thunderbird that want to use authenticated SMTP to send email. This port needs users to authenticate to use the service.

- *Client Proxy EXCH01*: Listening on port 465, this connector receives the client's messages from the Client Access services on the Exchange 2019 server or any other Exchange 2019 server in the same Active Directory site.

- *Default EXCH01*: Listening on port 2525, this is the SMTP service accepting messages from the Default Frontend Receive Connector on the Exchange 2019 server or any other Exchange 2019 server in the same Active Directory site. This connector is not scoped for regular clients to be used.

- *Default Frontend EXCH01*: Listening on port 25, this is the Receive Connector for regular inbound SMTP messages. Servers that connect to this port can be other SMTP servers, the Exchange 2010 Hub Transport service, other Exchange 2013/2016/2019 servers in the organization, or applications or devices that need to submit messages to mailboxes.

- *Outbound Proxy Frontend EXCH01*: Listening on port 717, this connector accepts messages from the Transport service on the Exchange server and relays the messages to external hosts. This only takes place on Send Connectors that have the front-end proxy option enabled.

All SMTP servers, applications, devices, or appliances always connect to the Default Frontend Receive Connector on port 25. All messages delivered to this connector can be delivered to mailboxes anywhere in the Exchange organization.

So, if you have a multi-functional "scan to mail" device, it will scan a document and connect to this Default Frontend Receive Connector, and the mail will be delivered to a mailbox without a problem.

To demonstrate this, we can use Telnet from any computer in the network and set up a connection on port 25 to the Exchange server by running the following command from a command prompt:

```
C:> Telnet EXCH01.proexchangeadmin.com 25
```

And the Exchange server will return something like

```
220 EXCH01.ProExchangeAdmin.com Microsoft ESMTP MAIL Service
ready at Wed, 8 Mar 2023 16:37:37 +0100
```

This is an interactive session, so it is now possible to enter any SMTP command to mimic a sending SMTP server. To send an email from any sender to a recipient in Exchange, enter the following commands in the Telnet session:

```
HELO server.local
Mail from: sender@gmail.com
Rcpt to: s.summertown@proexchangeadmin.com
Data
Hello world
.
```

And the Exchange server will respond like this:

```
250 2.1.0 Sender OK
250 2.1.5 Recipient OK
354 Start mail input; end with <CRLF>.<CRLF>
250 2.6.0 <bbc83317-8b71-40ef-a3d0-68c6ee6d8c6f@EXCH01.
ProExchangeAdmin.com> [InternalId=3173980831776,
Hostname=PROX2016.ProExchangeAdmin.com] 1555 bytes in 0.137,
11.047 KB/sec Queued mail for delivery
```

This is the most basic form of sending an email using Telnet, and it will be delivered as well. The email will be delivered, but since it is not formatted well, it will not be a readable message in Outlook.

A better version would be something like this:

```
Set localecho
Set logfile c:\temp\telnet.txt
Open exch01.proexchangeadmin.com 25
```

```
HELO mytelnet.local
mail from: jaapwess@hotmail.com
rcpt to: s.summertown@proexchangeadmin.com
data
From: "Jaap Wesselius" <jaapwess@hotmail.com>
To: "Sarah Summertown" <S.Summertown@proexchangeadmin.com>
Date: Wed, 8 March 2023 16:41:00 +0200

Hi Professor,

welcome to Telnet magic

Kind regards
SMTP Admin Jaap

.
```

It is important to close with the dot; this is for the SMTP server to signal that the message has ended and that it can be delivered.

Using the Telnet command Set logfile c:\temp\telnet.txt, all information is automatically logged, so when opening the log file, we can see the following:

```
220 EXCH01.ProExchangeAdmin.com Microsoft ESMTP MAIL Service
ready at Wed, 8 Mar 2023 16:44:08 +0100
HELO mytelnet.local
250 EXCH01.ProExchangeAdmin.com Hello [10.83.4.121]
mail from: jaapwess@hotmail.com
250 2.1.0 Sender OK
rcpt to: s.summertown@proexchangeadmin.com
250 2.1.5 Recipient OK
data354 Start mail input; end with <CRLF>.<CRLF>
From: "Jaap Wesselius" <jaapwess@hotmail.com>
To: "Sarah Summertown" <S.Summertown@proexchangeadmin.com>
Date: Wed, 8 March 2023 16:41:00 +0200
```

```
Hi Professor,
Welcome to telnet magic
Kind Regards
Jaap
.
250 2.6.0 <6beffc8a-3bb9-4abd-a634-37d707e474b2@EXCH01.
ProExchangeAdmin.com> [In
ternalId=1644972474406, Hostname=EXCH02.ProExchangeAdmin.com]
1776 bytes in 54.3
14, 0.032 KB/sec Queued mail for delivery
```

The email is accepted by the Receive Connector and delivered to the mailbox. When checking the mailbox with Outlook, a readable message appears as shown in Figure 2-17.

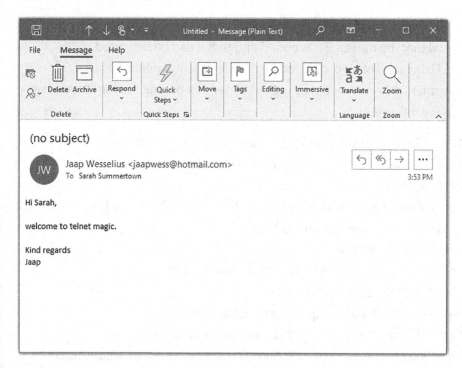

Figure 2-17. *A properly formatted email sent from the command line using Telnet*

Just like Send Connectors, Receive Connectors can perform protocol logging as well. Protocol logging should be used for troubleshooting purposes only since it generates a lot of information and can quickly fill up the local hard disk.

By default, the Default Receive Connector protocol log file is in C:\ Program Files\Microsoft\Exchange Server\V15\TransportRoles\Logs\ FrontEnd\ProtocolLog\SmtpReceive. Please note that these log files are in a very different location than the previously mentioned Send Connector log files. The Default Receive Connector is part of the Front-End Transport server. This is a completely different service and logs its information in another location.

To change the location of the protocol log files, the Set-FrontendTransportService command can be used with the -ReceiveProtocolLogPath option. To change the location of the log files to an additional disk D:\, execute the following commands:

```
[PS] C:\> Set-FrontEndTransportService -Identity EXCH01
-ReceiveProtocolPath D:\Program Files\Microsoft\Exchange
Server\V15\TransportRoles\Logs\FrontEnd\ProtocolLog\SmtpReceive
[PS] C:\> Restart-Service MSexchangeFrontendTransport
To change all FETS logging options in just one command, execute
the following commands in EMS:
[PS] C:\> $ServerName = "EXCH01"
[PS] C:\> $LogPath = "D:\Program Files\Microsoft\Exchange
Server\V15\TransportRoles\Logs\FrontEnd\"
[PS] C:\> Set-FrontendTransportService -Identity $ServerName
-AgentLogPath "$LogPath\ AgentLog" -ConnectivityLogPath
"$LogPath\ Connectivity" -ReceiveProtocolLogPath "$LogPath\
ProtocolLog\SmtpReceive" -SendProtocolLogPath "$LogPath\\
ProtocolLog\SmtpSend"
[PS] C:\> Restart-Service MSExchangeFrontEndTransport
```

SMTP Relay

When trying to relay SMTP messages to external hosts (e.g., on the Internet), you will receive an error message like Unable to relay or a more detailed 550 5.7.54 SMTP; Unable to relay recipient in non-accepted domain. Relaying to external is only possible for authenticated users or servers.

I always recommend to not configure the default Receive Connectors for relaying SMTP messages, but instead create a dedicated connector for SMTP relay purposes. The reason for this is when something happens, you can disable the relay connector and continue working with the default connector.

Creating an SMTP relay connector consists of the following steps:

1. Create a Receive Connector. This should be created on the Front-End Transport service.

2. Specify the IP addresses of hosts that are allowed to use the new Receive Connector.

3. Modify the permissions on the Receive Connector to allow anonymous relay.

Note   Sometimes I get the understandable question why a Receive Connector for relay purposes is used and not a Send Connector. It is all about accepting the message; Exchange must accept the message to relay it using the available Send Connector. Once accepted, Exchange will take care of delivering the message, internal or external.

Create a New Receive Connector

Creating a new Receive Connector is straightforward. To create a new Receive Connector for SMTP relay purposes, execute the following command in EMS:

```
[PS] C:\> New-ReceiveConnector -Name "SMTP Anonymous Relay"
-Server EXCH01 -TransportRole FrontendTransport -Custom
-Bindings 0.0.0.0:25 -RemoteIpRanges 127.0.0.1
```

This will create a new Receive Connector on the Front-End Transport service that listens on port 25, but only accepts connections from "localhost."

To make it identifiable when opening a connection, the banner can be changed. To do this, execute the following command in EMS:

```
[PS] C:\> Set-ReceiveConnector -Identity "EXCH01\SMTP Anonymous
Relay" -Banner "220 EXCH01 SMTP Relay Connector"
Note. The banner must always start with "220" followed by
a string.
To add more IP addresses that are allowed to use the Receive
Connector, execute the following commands in EMS:
[PS] C:\> $RemIPs = Get-ReceiveConnector "EXCH01\SMTP
Anonymous Relay"
[PS] C:\> $RemIPs.RemoteIPRanges += "10.38.96.235","10.38.96.23
6","10.38.96.225"
[PS] C:\> Set-ReceiveConnector "EXCH01\SMTP Anonymous Relay"
-RemoteIPRanges $RemIPs.RemoteIPRanges
```

An obvious mistake would be to use -RemoteIPRanges "10.38.96.235","1 0.38.96.225","10.38.96.226" in the previous example. While it does add the IP addresses to the RemoteIPRanges, it also overwrites existing IP addresses.

To remove an IP address, execute the following commands in EMS:

```
[PS] C:\> $RemIPs = Get-ReceiveConnector "EXCH01\SMTP
Anonymous Relay"
[PS] C:\> $RemIPs.RemoteIPRanges -= "127.0.0.1"
[PS] C:\> Set-ReceiveConnector "EXCH01\SMTP Anonymous Relay"
-RemoteIPRanges $RemIPs.RemoteIPRanges
```

Modify Permissions on the Receive Connector

For modifying permissions on the Receive Connector, two options are available:

1. Configure the connections as externally secured.

2. Configure the connections as anonymous.

When configured as "externally secured," the network hosts are considered as authenticated senders. Messages that are submitted bypass anti-spam features and message size limit checks. The sender's name must be resolved to a display name in Exchange. Permissions to submit messages are granted as if they originate from internal senders within the Exchange organization.

To configure the Receive Connector with externally secured, execute the following command in EMS:

```
[PS] C:\> Set-ReceiveConnector "EXCH01\SMTP Anonymous Relay"
-AuthMechanism ExternalAuthoritative -PermissionGroups
ExchangeServers
```

The advantage of this approach is that it is easy to configure, easier than the anonymous logon option as described in the following paragraph.

When configured as anonymous, the hosts are considered anonymous senders. Messages do not bypass anti-spam, and message size limits are applied. Permissions to NT AUTHORITY\ANONYMOUS

LOGON are granted to relay messages. Again, only IP addresses in the -RemoteIPRanges are allowed to submit messages and therefore relay messages.

To configure the Receive Connector as anonymous, execute the following commands in EMS:

```
[PS] C:\> Set-ReceiveConnector "EXCH01\SMTP Anonymous Relay"
-PermissionGroups AnonymousUsers
[PS] C:\> Get-ReceiveConnector "EXCH01\SMTP Anonymous Relay" |
Add-ADPermission -User "NT AUTHORITY\ANONYMOUS LOGON"
-ExtendedRights "Ms-Exch-SMTP-Accept-Any-Recipient"
```

The advantage of this second approach is that it grants the minimum required permissions to allow anonymous relay.

Is there an advantage of one way over another? The first one is easier to configure. A purist would say that the second is more secure. Since anti-spam and message limits are not bypassed, one can truly say it is more secure.

You can test the SMTP relay using Telnet. Open Telnet on port 25 and immediately you'll see the banner appear:

```
telnet localhost 25
220 EXCH01 SMTP Relay Connector
Helo Windows
Mail from
Rcpt to:
Data
Hello world

.
```

How does Exchange determine which Receive Connector to use? In this example, both the Default Receive Connector and the SMTP relay connector listen on the same IP address and the same port number. When a connection is set up with the Exchange server on port 25,

Exchange determines based on the source IP address which connector's RemoteIPRanges setting best matches. In our example, the source IP address is in the RemoteIPRanges property of the SMTP relay connector, and it will connect to this Receive Connector. If there is no match, the default Receive Connector is used.

Message Tracking

As an Exchange administrator, you are most likely familiar with users that complain they have never received a certain message or that they have sent an email, but it was never received by a recipient. Naturally, they blame Exchange for this behavior. Of course, this can be the case, but it also possible that the recipient deleted the message or that it was somehow lost in transit when the recipient is located elsewhere. This is impossible to trace, but it is possible to see that the message left the Exchange organization and thus is out of our reach.

To track sending, receiving, and delivering of messages, Exchange keeps track of all activity of the message flow in the Exchange transport pipeline. Message tracking can be used for troubleshooting purposes, for mail flow analysis, or for message forensics.

Message tracking log files are circular logging. Log files are deleted when

- They reach their maximum age; the default setting is 30 days.

- The message tracking log folder reaches its maximum size. Individual log files are 10 MB; the default log folder size is 1000 MB.

Note   Only metadata of messages are stored. The messages themselves are not kept.

Message tracking can be done using the Get-MessageTrackingLog command in the Exchange Management Shell. It accepts options like server, start and end date, sender and recipient, event ID, or subject of the message.

To find details of a message sent by Professor to Sara in the first week of February and list only information regarding sending or receiving, execute the following command in EMS:

```
[PS] C:\> Get-MessageTrackingLog -Server EXCH01 -Start
"02/01/2023" -End "02/07/2023" -Sender professor@
proexchangeadmin.com -Recipient sarah@proexchangeadmin.com
-EventID Send,Receive
```

If you are not interested in the event IDs, but are interested in getting information regarding a specific message, you can use the -MessageSubject option, for example:

```
[PS] C:\> Get-MessageTrackingLog -Server EXCH01 -Start
"02/01/2023" -End "02/07/2023" -Sender professor@
proexchangeadmin.com -MessageSubject Invoice
```

To get more detailed information when this message was delivered, use the -EventID Deliver option, and use the Format-List command, for example:

```
[PS] C:\> Get-MessageTrackingLog -Server EXCH01 -Start
"02/01/2023" -End "02/07/2023" -Sender professor@proexchange
admin.com -MessageSubject Invoice -EventID Deliver | Format-List
```

If there are multiple Exchange servers in your organization, it is not possible to predict which Exchange server is processing a message and in what order. To use message tracking across all Exchange servers, execute a command similar to this one in EMS:

```
[PS] C:\> Get-TransportService | Where{$_.Name -like "EXCH*"} |
Get-MessageTrackingLog
```

All Transport services will be retrieved with a server name starting with "EXCH"; in our example this includes all Exchange servers, but excludes the Edge Transport server.

Edge Transport Server

Microsoft introduced the Exchange Edge Transport server years ago, in Exchange 2007 to be precise, and it is still available in Exchange 2019. In the early days, the Edge Transport server was positioned as a message hygiene solution, especially when Microsoft Forefront Protection for Exchange was installed.

But Forefront Protection for Exchange was discontinued years ago, and in 2023, the only Microsoft solution for message hygiene is Exchange Online Protection. These days, the Exchange 2019 Edge Transport server is only installed in an organization perimeter network as an SMTP host between Exchange 2019 and Exchange Online, where the message hygiene functionality is achieved using Microsoft Exchange Online Protection.

Located in the perimeter network, the Edge Transport servers are not a member of the internal Active Directory domain. In fact, you can have multiple Edge Transport servers in your perimeter network. The positive side of this is that when the Edge Transport server gets compromised, the internal Active Directory is untouched. The downside, however, is that there is no shared configuration, and so you must configure all the Edge Transport servers manually, although there's an export and import utility to keep all the Edge Transport servers identical; the mechanism it uses is called cloning (more about this later in the chapter).

The Edge Transport servers need to have some knowledge of the Exchange configuration on the internal network, or else it would be hard to route messages to the correct Mailbox server on that internal network or to perform recipient filtering. Therefore, there exists a synchronization mechanism between the Mailbox servers on the internal network and the Edge Transport server on the perimeter network. This mechanism is called edge synchronization (EdgeSync). Using edge synchronization, the Mailbox servers push (limited) information to the Edge Transport servers on a regular basis. There is no pull mechanism, so the Edge Transport server never pulls information from the internal Exchange server. When it comes to firewalling, only port 50636 needs to be opened outbound. Naturally, port 25 for SMTP needs to be open in both directions.

So the Edge Transport servers act as your "man in the middle" when it comes to Simple Mail Transfer Protocol (SMTP) traffic, and all inbound and outbound messages are routed via your Edge Transport servers. The MX records in the public Domain Name Service (DNS) point to your Exchange Online Protection environment, and Exchange Online Protection will act as your smarthost.

A simple representation of a network of two Edge Transport servers and two Mailbox servers is shown in Figure 2-18.

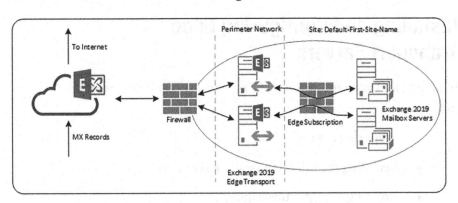

Figure 2-18. *The Edge Transport servers are located in the perimeter network*

Installation of Edge Transport servers is not bound to a particular site, but edge synchronization is bound to a particular site in Active Directory. So, if you have two Edge Transport servers at a site, as shown in Figure 2-18, the two Edge Transport servers are synchronized with the two

Mailbox servers at this site. If you have an additional (Active Directory) site, the Edge Transport servers will not send information directly to these Mailbox servers, but route messages via the Exchange 2019 Mailbox servers in the first site.

Note   Although this book is about Exchange 2019, the contents of this "Edge Transport Server" section also apply to Exchange 2016 and Exchange 2013 Edge Transport servers. They are 100% compatible, so an Exchange 2013 Edge Transport server can work perfectly with an Exchange 2019 Mailbox server. Looking at the support life cycle of Microsoft Exchange, I would not recommend using such an old version of Exchange Server.

Installing and Configuring Edge Transport Servers

Installing an Exchange 2019 Edge Transport server involves four main steps:

- Preparing the server

- Installing the Edge Transport server role

- Creating an edge subscription

- Starting edge synchronization

These steps are discussed in the following sections.

Prepare the Edge Transport Server

The Exchange Server 2019 Edge Transport server can only be installed on Windows Server 2019, and the recommendation is to use Windows Server 2019 Server Core, but the Desktop Experience version can be used as well. Please note that the Edge Transport server itself can only be managed using PowerShell; there is no EAC to manage the Edge Transport server.

The Edge Transport server is not a member of the internal Active Directory forest as it is typically installed in the perimeter network. It can be a member of a perimeter network Active Directory for management purposes.

The Edge Transport server needs an FQDN, and this FQDN must be configured before installing the Edge Transport server role. If the FQDN is changed after installing the Edge Transport role, the Exchange server will break beyond repair and needs to be rebuilt.

When using Windows Server 2022 Server Core, the server can be configured using the SCONFIG tool, including the server name. The DNS suffix however cannot be configured using SCONFIG and needs to be set in the registry of the server. Execute the following PowerShell command to set the correct DNS suffix of the Edge Transport server:

```
PS C:\> Set-ItemProperty -Path HKLM:\SYSTEM\CurrentControlSet\
Services\Tcpip\Parameters -Name 'NV Domain' -Value
"proexchangeadmin.com"
```

Reboot the server for the change to take effect.

Note   Do not forget to add an additional disk for the SMTP queue database.

When it comes to server features, only the Active Directory Lightweight Directory Server (ADLDS) needs to be installed. ADLDS is an LDAP server and is used to store specific information that the Edge Transport server needs for sending and receiving messages.

To install ADLDS, execute the following PowerShell command:

```
PS C:\> Install-WindowsFeature ADLDS, Telnet-Client
```

The following prerequisite software needs to be installed on the Edge Transport server role as well:

- Visual C++ Redistributable Package for Visual Studio 2012

Note   When using Windows 2019, you must install .NET Framework 4.8 as well.

Use the following PowerShell commands to download the software.

```
PS C:\> New-Item C:\Install -ItemType Directory
# .NET Framework 4.8 for Windows 2019
PS C:\> Start-BitsTransfer -Source "https://download.
visualstudio.microsoft.com/download/pr/7afca223-55d2-470a-
8edc-6a1739ae3252/abd170b4b0ec15ad0222a809b761a036/ndp48-x86-
x64-allos-enu.exe" -Destination C:\Install

# Visual C++ Redistributable package for Visual Studio 2012
PS C:\> Start-BitsTransfer -Source "https://download.microsoft.
com/download/1/6/B/16B06F60-3B20-4FF2-B699-5E9B7962F9AE/VSU_4/
vcredist_x64.exe" -Destination C:\Install
```

And use the following PowerShell commands to install the prerequisite software unattended:

```
PS C:\> Start-Process -FilePath "C:\Install\vcredist_x64.exe"
-ArgumentList "/q" -Wait
```

And when using Windows 2019:

```
PS C:\> Start-Process -FilePath "C:\Install\ndp48-x86-x64-
allos-enu.exe" -ArgumentList "/q" -Wait
```

When the server roles and prerequisite software are installed and the server is fully patched, the Exchange 2019 server Edge Transport server role can be installed.

Unattended Installation of the Edge Transport Server

The easiest way to install an Exchange Server 2019 Edge Transport server is using an unattended install. Compared with the Exchange Server 2019 Mailbox server unattended install as discussed earlier in the chapter, the unattended setup of an Edge Transport server only accepts one option, the /Mode option, which can take the value "install", "remove", or "upgrade".

To install an Exchange Server 2019 Edge Transport server in unattended mode, start a command prompt with elevated privileges, navigate to the installation media, and execute the following command:

```
PS Z:\> .\Setup.exe /Mode:Install /Roles:EdgeTransport /
IAcceptExchangeServerLicenseTerms_DiagnosticDataON

Microsoft Exchange Server 2019 Cumulative Update 13
Unattended Setup

Copying Files...
File copy complete. Setup will now collect additional
information needed for installation.

Languages
Management tools
Edge Transport Role
```

```
Performing Microsoft Exchange Server Prerequisite Check

    Configuring Prerequisites                    COMPLETED
    Prerequisite Analysis                        COMPLETED

Configuring Microsoft Exchange Server

    Preparing Setup                              COMPLETED
    Stopping Services                            COMPLETED
    Copying Exchange Files                       COMPLETED
    Language Files                               COMPLETED
    Restoring Services                           COMPLETED
    Language Configuration                       COMPLETED
    Exchange Management Tools                    COMPLETED
    Edge Transport Role                          COMPLETED
    Finalizing Setup                             COMPLETED

The Exchange Server setup operation completed successfully.
Setup has made changes to operating system settings that
require a reboot to take effect. Please reboot this server
prior to placing it into production.
PS Z:\>
```

Tip   You can add the /DoNotStartTransport switch when installing
the Edge Transport server. This will prevent the server from accepting
messages from outside and allow configuration first.

When the installation has finished, reboot the server.

Note   Make sure that the Edge Transport server can resolve the Exchange Server 2019 Mailbox servers on the internal network. This can be achieved by using DNS on the internal network (depending on your preferred server configuration, of course) or by using a HOSTS file where the FQDN and the IP addresses of the internal Exchange 2019 Mailbox servers are entered. The latter however is not the recommended way.

When the server is rebooted, change the location of the SMTP queue database from its default location to an additional disk. This is explained in the section "Configure Exchange 2019" earlier in this chapter.

The next step is to configure an edge subscription so that the Exchange Server 2019 Mailbox server can push configuration information to the Exchange Server 2019 Edge Transport server.

Create an Edge Subscription

When the Edge Transport server is installed, you can create the edge subscription. When the edge subscription is created, you can start the edge synchronization, which will push all needed information from the Mailbox server to the Edge Transport server.

Creating the edge subscription consists of the following steps:

1. Create an XML file on the Edge Transport server with the configuration information.

2. Copy the XML file to the Exchange 2019 Mailbox server.

3. Import the XML file into the Exchange 2019 Mailbox server.

4. Start the edge synchronization.

To create the configuration XML file on the Exchange Server 2019 Edge Transport server, execute the following PowerShell command on the Edge Transport server:

```
[PS] C:\> New-EdgeSubscription -FileName C:\Install\Edge01.xml
```

This will create an XML file with all information from the Edge Transport server that is needed by the Exchange Server 2019 Mailbox server. Copy the XML file to the Exchange 2019 Mailbox server, and on the Mailbox server, you execute the following PowerShell command:

```
[PS] C:\> [byte[]]$FileData = Get-Content -Path C:\Install\
edge01.xml -Encoding Byte -ReadCount 0
[PS] C:\> New-EdgeSubscription -FileData $FileData -Encoding
Byte -Site Default-First-Site-Name -CreateInternetSendConnector
$true -CreateInboundSendConnector $true
```

This will begin the edge subscription. Please note the -Site parameter that defines which Active Directory site the Edge Transport server will be bound to. In my experience it can take up to ten minutes before the edge subscription is fully active on the internal Exchange organization.

So, after ten minutes or so, execute the following PowerShell command on the Exchange Server 2019 Mailbox server:

```
[PS] C:\> Start-EdgeSynchronization
```

As mentioned before, for synchronization to work properly, you must make sure that the Exchange Server 2019 Mailbox server can resolve the Exchange Server 2019 Edge Transport server using DNS; this typically involves adding the Edge Transport server to the DNS on your internal network.

Another pitfall is a firewall between the Exchange Server 2019 Mailbox server and the Exchange Server 2019 Edge Transport server. The edge synchronization (EdgeSync) is using port 50636 (outbound) by default to push information to the Edge Transport server, so you must make sure that this port is open on the firewall to the perimeter network. This EdgeSync process runs on every Exchange server in the Active Directory site associated with the Edge Transport server. Needless to say, in addition to port 50636, port 25 should also be open between all Edge Transport servers and all the Exchange 2019 Mailbox servers in the Active Directory site those Edge Transport servers are subscribed to. Of course, port 25 should be open inbound and outbound.

Note   If for some reason you need to alter the default port used for EdgeSync, you can use the ConfigureAdam.ps1 script provided with Exchange. Modify the port on the Edge Transport server before you create the edge subscription.

That is all it takes to install the Exchange 2019 Edge Transport server, create an Edge Subscription, and start the edge synchronization. All relevant settings configured on the internal Exchange Server 2019 organization for proper functioning of the mail flow are synchronized at this point, including the accepted domains, connector information, and recipient information.

If you want to make changes to certain settings on the Edge Transport server, you must make these on the Exchange Server 2019 Mailbox server. For example, if you want to enable logging onto the Send Connector of the Exchange Server 2019 Edge Transport server, you must issue the command on the Exchange 2019 Mailbox server. To enable protocol logging, for example, you open the Exchange Management Shell on the Exchange Server 2019 Mailbox server and enter the following command:

```
[PS] C:\> Get-SendConnector <outbound connector> | Set-
SendConnector -ProtocolLoggingLevel Verbose
```

When it comes to making changes to the Exchange Server 2019 Edge Transport server, you always must be conscious of where you are making those changes. Changes related to message flow have to be made on the Exchange Server 2019 Mailbox server, but server-specific settings can be made on the Exchange Server 2019 Edge Transport server itself.

Note   Like the Exchange Server 2019 Mailbox server, the Exchange Server 2019 Edge Transport server is also configured with a self-signed certificate. This certificate is used for setting up an encrypted connection with other mail servers using TLS 1.2. This works fine for regular SMTP traffic, but there are situations where a regular third-party SSL certificate must be used.

After installing the Edge Transport server, the only configuration change that you can make is changing the location of the SMTP Transport databases. This is covered in the next topic.

Relocate the Transport Database

Like any Exchange server, the Transport database is installed on the same disk as where the Exchange binaries are installed; by default this is the C:\ drive. The Transport database is where all inbound and outbound messages are always stored.

When an Edge Transport server is used, all inbound and outbound messages are always routed via this Edge Transport server. As such, the Transport database can grow very rapidly. To prevent the disk filling up, it is recommended to use a separate disk for this Transport database.

When Exchange is installed, a script is automatically stored in the Exchange scripts directory that will relocate the Transport database. To move this database from the default C:\ drive to the D:\ drive, execute the following commands in EMS:

```
[PS] C:\> $LogPath = "D:\Program Files\Microsoft\Exchange
Server\V15\TransportRoles\data"
[PS] C:\> CD $ExScripts
[PS] C:\> .\Move-TransportDatabase.ps1 -queueDatabasePath
"$LogPath\Queue" -queueDatabaseLoggingPath "$LogPath\
Queue" -iPFilterDatabasePath "$LogPath\IpFilter"
-iPFilterDatabaseLoggingPath "$LogPath\IpFilter"
-temporaryStoragePath "$LogPath\Temp"
```

The script will stop the Transport service, move the database to another location, change the appropriate configuration files, and start the Transport service again.

Test the Edge Transport Server

The easiest way to test the installation of your Edge Transport server is to start sending email. You can also use the Remote Connectivity Analyzer (RCA) (`www.testexchangeconnectivity.com`) to test the environment. To use the analyzer, you open the RCA in your browser, select Exchange Server, and select Outbound SMTP Email. Then, you enter the IP address of the outbound SMTP server, select the options you want to check, and enter your email address, as shown in Figure 2-19.

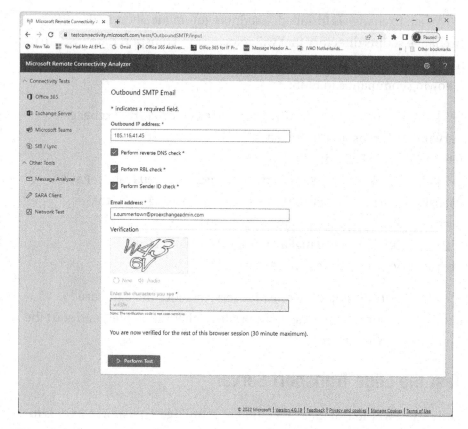

Figure 2-19. *Testing the outbound SMTP email configuration*

When all is well, you will see the results in seconds; all options should show the green balls with the white checkmark, as shown in Figure 2-20.

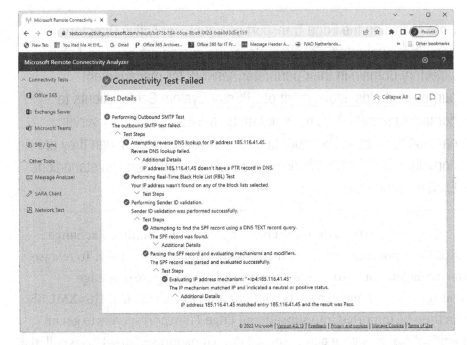

Figure 2-20. *Results that show the outbound SMTP test was successful*

In Figure 2-20, the first test fails. This is the reverse DNS check, which is not configured for the Edge Transport server in the ProExchangeAdmin environment.

Export and Import Edge Configuration

Exchange Mailbox servers are domain-joined, and almost all configuration is stored in Active Directory. This means that configuration information can be shared among multiple Exchange servers.

For example, information regarding transport rules on Exchange Mailbox servers is stored in Active Directory, and it is used by all Exchange Mailbox servers in the organization. The Exchange Edge Transport server, however, is not a member of the Active Directory domain, and therefore configuration information cannot be shared among multiple Edge Transport servers.

Note   Joining the Edge Transport servers to an Active Directory domain is supported. For example, some customers have an Active Directory domain in their perimeter network for management purposes; it aids deployment of GPOs or System Center clients to domain members. This does not mean the Edge Transport server can use this Active Directory domain, however. Even though they are domain-joined from a Windows point of view, they are still standalone Exchange servers.

As mentioned earlier in the chapter, if you have multiple Exchange Edge Transport servers, you must configure them individually. To release the management burden a bit, it is possible to configure one Edge Transport server and export its configuration to an XML file. This XML file can then be imported into subsequent Edge Transport servers to get an identical configuration across these Edge Transport servers. This is called a cloned configuration.

Note   Cloning works only when you're installing the Edge Transport servers. When making regular changes to the Edge Transport server during normal operation, these changes still must be made to the individual Edge Transport servers.

Microsoft has written a script that can be used for multiple installations, located in the $ExScripts directory on the Edge Transport server and called ExportEdgeConfig.ps1. To export the Edge Transport server configuration, you open the Exchange Management Shell, navigate to the $ExScripts directory, and enter the following command:

```
[PS] C:> .\ExportEdgeConfig.ps1 -CloneConfigData:"C:\Temp\
EdgeClonedConfig.xml"
```

This command will generate a configuration file that contains the individual settings of the Edge Transport server. You copy this XML file to another Edge Transport server. To do so, on the other Edge Transport server, you open the Exchange Management Shell and enter the following command:

```
[PS] C:\> .\ImportEdgeConfig.ps1 -CloneConfigData:"C:\Temp\
EdgeClonedConfig.xml" -IsImport $false -CloneConfigAnswer:"C:\
Temp\CloneAnswerFile.xml"
```

This command will run a trial import of the configuration file, and any settings that are not valid for this Edge Transport server are logged into the answer file. Any errors that are logged in the answer file can be edited in the clone answer file. When no changes are needed, the answer file will be empty!

To run a full import to the subsequent Edge Transport server, you can run the same command but change the value of the –IsImport parameter to $true, for example:

```
[PS] C:\> .\ImportEdgeConfig.ps1 -CloneConfigData:"C:\Temp\
EdgeClonedConfig.xml" -IsImport $true -CloneConfigAnswer:"C:\
Temp\CloneAnswerFile.xml"
```

Note   You cannot run the ImportEdgeConfig.ps1 script on an Edge Transport server that's subscribed to the internal Exchange servers; therefore, you must do this in advance of creating the edge subscription.

Protocol Logging

Like the Mailbox server role, the Edge Transport server role logs protocol information as well. When enabled, both the Send Connector and Receive Connector log information on the disk where the Exchange binaries are installed. The location of the protocol log files can be retrieved using the Get-TransportService command. To achieve this, execute the following command in EMS on the Edge Transport server:

```
[PS] C:\> Get-TransportService | select *ProtocolLogPath | fl

ReceiveProtocolLogPath : C:\Program Files\Microsoft\Exchange
Server\V15\TransportRoles\Logs\Edge\ProtocolLog\SmtpReceive

SendProtocolLogPath    : C:\Program Files\Microsoft\Exchange
Server\V15\TransportRoles\Logs\Edge\ProtocolLog\SmtpSend
```

To change the location of the protocol log files to (dedicated) drive D:\, execute the following commands in EMS:

```
[PS] C:\> $LogPath = "D:\Program Files\Microsoft\Exchange
Server\V15\TransportRoles\Logs\Edge\ProtocolLog"
[PS] C:\> Set-TransportService -Identity Edge01
-ReceiveProtocolLogPath "$LogPath\SmtpReceive"
[PS] C:\> Set-TransportService -Identity Edge01
-SendProtocolLogPath "$LogPath\SmtpSend"
[PS] C:\> Restart-Service MSExchangeTransport
```

SSL Certificates

For securing messages in transit, Exchange always tries to use TLS or Transport Layer Security. Exchange 2019 uses TLS 1.2 by default; older versions of TLS are disabled.

Note   TLS 1.3 is supported by Windows Server 2022 but is still not supported by Exchange 2019 CU13. Support for TLS 1.3 is expected in a future Cumulative Update.

As mentioned before, Exchange Transport supports opportunistic TLS. This way, Exchange Transport can use the default self-signed certificate or an expired certificate. The certificate is only used for encryption purposes and not for server validation purposes.

So you can safely use the default self-signed certificate, but you can also use a third-party SSL certificate on the Exchange server. When you do, this certificate can also be used for validation purposes and authentication purposes, which is mandatory when configuring cross-premises transport with Exchange Online.

To request a new certificate, execute the following commands in EMS on the Edge Transport server:

```
[PS] C:\> $RequestData = New-ExchangeCertificate
-GenerateRequest -Server EDGE01 -SubjectName "c=NL, S=Noord-
Holland, L=Amsterdam, O=ProExchangeAdmin, OU=RND, CN=Edge01.
Proexchangeadmin.com" -DomainName edge01.exchangelabs.nl
-PrivateKeyExportable $true
[PS] C:\> Set-Content -path C:\Install\ssl-request.req -value
$RequestData
```

The contents of the ssl-request.req file must be used with the certificate authority to request a new certificate. Once the certificate is issued downloaded to c:\install, execute the following commands in EMS on the Edge Transport server:

```
[PS] C:\> $Data = [Byte[]]$(Get-Content -Path "c:\install\
edge01_proexchangeadmin_com.p7b" -Encoding byte -ReadCount 0)
```

```
[PS] C:\> Import-ExchangeCertificate -Server EDGE01
-FileData $Data
[PS] C:\> Get-ExchangeCertificate -Thumbprint
94D3DEB2BC4F09430AEC7E20B822850F3A52F7C1 | Enable-
ExchangeCertificate -Services SMTP
```

A warning message appears, asking if you want to overwrite the default self-signed certificate. Choose No; do not overwrite the default certificate. This default certificate is used by the edge synchronization.

To check the certificate status on an Internet-facing Exchange server or any email server, I normally use the https://checktls.com site. CheckTLS can, as the name implies, check TLS possibilities of a mail server. Navigate to the site, enter the FQDN of the Edge Transport server, and check the results as partially shown in Figure 2-21.

```
[000.262]  We can use this server
[000.262]  TLS is an option on this server
[000.262] -->STARTTLS
[000.348] <--220 2.0.0 SMTP server ready
[000.348]  STARTTLS command works on this server
[000.535]  Connection converted to SSL
           SSLVersion in use: TLSv1_2
           Cipher in use: ECDHE-RSA-AES256-GCM-SHA384
           Perfect Forward Secrecy: yes
           Session Algorithm in use: Curve P-384 DHE(384 bits)
           Certificate #1 of 3 (sent by MX):
           Cert VALIDATED: ok
           Cert Hostname VERIFIED (edge01.proexchangeadmin.com = edge01.proexchangeadmin.com | DNS:edge01.proexchangeadmin.com)
           Not Valid Before: Mar 22 00:00:00 2022 GMT
           Not Valid After: Apr 22 23:59:59 2023 GMT
           subject: /CN=edge01.proexchangeadmin.com
           issuer: /C=US/O=DigiCert Inc/CN=GeoTrust TLS DV RSA Mixed SHA256 2020 CA-1
           Certificate #2 of 3 (sent by MX):
           Cert VALIDATED: ok
           Not Valid Before: Jul 16 12:21:44 2020 GMT
           Not Valid After: May 31 23:59:59 2023 GMT
           subject: /C=US/O=DigiCert Inc/CN=GeoTrust TLS DV RSA Mixed SHA256 2020 CA-1
           issuer: /C=US/O=DigiCert Inc/OU=www.digicert.com/CN=DigiCert Global Root CA
           Certificate #3 of 3 (added from CA Root Store):
           Cert VALIDATED: ok
           Not Valid Before: Nov 10 00:00:00 2006 GMT
           Not Valid After: Nov 10 00:00:00 2031 GMT
           subject: /C=US/O=DigiCert Inc/OU=www.digicert.com/CN=DigiCert Global Root CA
           issuer: /C=US/O=DigiCert Inc/OU=www.digicert.com/CN=DigiCert Global Root CA
[000.731] -->EHLO www12-azure.checktls.com
[000.818] <--250-EDGE01.ProExchangeAdmin.com Hello [40.76.159.115]
          250-SIZE 37748736
          250-PIPELINING
          250-DSN
          250-ENHANCEDSTATUSCODES
          250-X-EXPS NTLM
          250-8BITMIME
          250-BINARYMIME
          250-CHUNKING
          250-XEXCH50
          250-SMTPUTF8
          250 XSHADOW
[000.818]  TLS successfully started on this server
[000.819] -->MAIL FROM:<test@checktls.com>
[000.905] <--250 2.1.0 Sender OK
[000.905]  Sender is OK
[000.906] -->QUIT
[000.993] <--221 2.0.0 Service closing transmission channel
```

Figure 2-21. *CheckTLS.com for checking TLS options on your mail server*

Load-Balancing the Edge Transport Servers

When you have multiple Exchange Edge Transport servers, most likely you want to load-balance the SMTP traffic. The good thing is that you only must worry about load-balancing the incoming SMTP traffic; traffic between the Edge Transport servers and the internal Exchange Mailbox servers is automatically load-balanced.

An Edge Transport server is bound to an Active Directory site through the edge subscription. This means that all Exchange Mailbox servers will use this Edge Transport server. Going the other way, this one Edge

Transport server will use all the Exchange Mailbox servers so that SMTP traffic will be load-balanced across those Mailbox servers using a round robin mechanism.

If you have multiple Edge Transport servers in your perimeter network, then each Edge Transport server will have its own edge subscription. Of course, each Edge Transport server will automatically load-balance the inbound SMTP traffic across all available Exchange Mailbox servers. The Mailbox servers in turn automatically use all the edge subscriptions and therefore automatically load-balance their outbound SMTP traffic across the multiple Edge Transport servers.

Inbound SMTP traffic originating from external hosts (i.e., from the Internet) is a different story, though. If you have multiple Edge Transport servers, you will have multiple external IP addresses and multiple FQDNs, so you must distribute that inbound SMTP traffic across these servers. The easiest way to do this is to use multiple MX records in the public DNS. These MX records are used by sending SMTP hosts, and by using multiple MX records, the inbound connections are automatically distributed.

Another option is to use a (hardware) load balancer for inbound SMTP traffic. In the load balancer, you create a virtual IP (VIP), and this IP address is used in an MX record. This way, only one MX record is used and this MX record points to the load balancer.

In the load balancer, you can use layer-4 (L4) load balancing to distribute the incoming requests across all available Edge Transport servers. If for some reason one server fails, the load balancer will automatically disable this server so it is no longer used by the VIP in the load balancer.

So balancing the load to the Edge Transport servers is not a big deal and is relatively easy to implement.

Note   If you have multiple Edge Transport servers, you can also use Windows Network Load Balancing (NLB) as a load-balancing solution. However, the official Microsoft recommendation is to use a (hardware) load balancer for load-balancing your Exchange traffic.

Upgrading from Exchange 2013 or Exchange 2016

One of the design goals of Exchange 2019 was to make migrations from a previous version of Exchange as simple as possible. Compared with previous migrations, for example, from Exchange 2010 to Exchange 2016, a migration from Exchange 2013 or Exchange 2016 to Exchange 2019 is a piece of cake.

The front-end services between the three versions are 100% compatible, which means you install an Exchange 2019 Mailbox server in a load-balanced array of Exchange 2013 or Exchange 2016 servers. This will be completely transparent for users.

The Mailbox services in the back end are different; these are not compatible when it comes to mailbox database engines, and they cannot be matched and mixed in a DAG unfortunately. Also supported Windows versions are different between the Exchange versions.

In this chapter I will write Exchange 2013 to Exchange 2019 since it is a hot topic now that Exchange 2013 is end of life, but everything is the same for Exchange 2016. If there are major changes in moving from Exchange 2016 to Exchange 2019, I will make an additional note. But in the end, upgrading from Exchange 2013 to Exchange 2019 is not a daunting task.

Note   Although not much information is available about Exchange vNext (scheduled to be released in 2025), Microsoft already announced that Exchange vNext will support an in-place upgrade from Exchange 2019 and support side-by-side deployments of Exchange 2013, Exchange 2016, Exchange 2019, and Exchange vNext. This will make a migration even more simple!

Moving to Exchange 2019

Moving from Exchange 2013 is easy because Exchange 2019 is simply introduced into the current Exchange Server environment. A long story short, the only thing you must worry about is the storage.

From a protocol perspective, Exchange 2013, Exchange 2016, and Exchange 2019 are 100% compatible. In a mixed environment, if a client connects to Exchange 2013 and the client's mailbox is on Exchange 2016, the connection is proxied to the Exchange 2016 server. If their mailbox is on Exchange 2019, the connection is proxied to the Exchange 2019 server. Proxying means the client keeps the connection with Exchange 2013. This up-level proxy is scenario 1 with the solid line in Figure 2-22.

When the client connects to Exchange 2016 and the client's mailbox is on Exchange 2013, the connection is proxied to Exchange 2013 (down-level proxy). If the mailbox is on Exchange 2019, the connection is proxied to Exchange 2019 (up-level proxy). This is scenario 2 with the dashed line in Figure 2-22.

The last one is when the client connects to Exchange 2019. If the mailbox is on another (down-level) server, the connection is proxied to this server. This is scenario 3 with the dotted line in Figure 2-22.

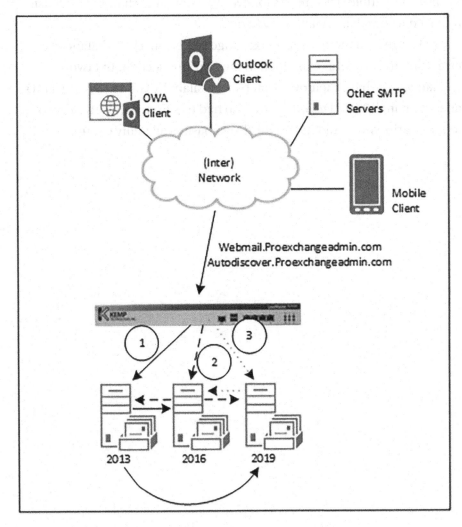

Figure 2-22. Protocol proxying in Exchange

In the back end, things are a bit less compatible. When upgrading from Exchange 2013 to Exchange 2019, you must build a new storage solution. From a mailbox database perspective, the different versions of Exchange are not compatible. This means for every version of Exchange, you must build a new Database Availability Group.

In Figure 2-23 there are four Exchange servers in a load-balanced array, and this works as explained in the previous section. But two Exchange 2013 have their own Database Availability Group (DAG1), and so does Exchange 2019 (DAG2). If you also had two Exchange 2016 servers in this scenario, you would have a third Database Availability Group.

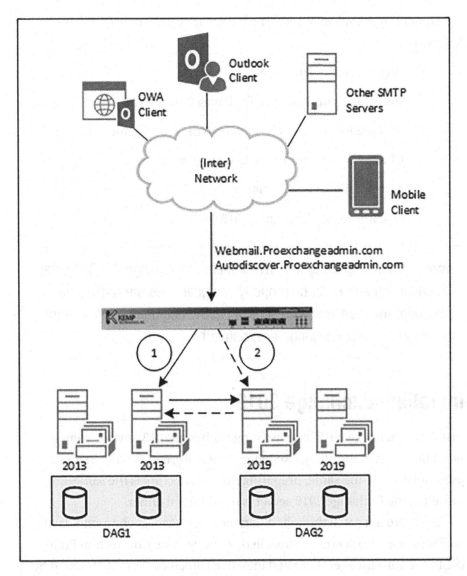

Figure 2-23. *Multiple DAGs in one Exchange environment*

After adding Exchange 2019 into the existing Exchange 2013
environment, you must move all mailboxes from DAG1 to DAG2 before
you can decommission Exchange 2013.

Upgrading from Exchange 2013 to Exchange 2019 consists of the following steps:

1. Prepare Active Directory.

2. Install and configure the Exchange 2019 servers.

3. Add the Exchange 2019 servers to the load balancer.

4. Change SMTP routing via Exchange 2019.

5. Move mailboxes to Exchange 2019.

6. Decommission Exchange 2013.

Note   When upgrading the environment to Exchange 2019, the new Exchange servers must be properly designed. Use the requirements calculator for Exchange as discussed in the beginning of this chapter to design the new Exchange environment.

Installing Exchange 2019

Installing Exchange 2019 in an existing Exchange 2013 environment is not different than installing Exchange 2019 in a green-field scenario. The prerequisites are the same, preparing Active Directory is the same, and installing the Exchange 2019 server is not different either.

But there is a catch though. When the Client Access components of an Exchange 2019 server are installed, a new Service Connection Point (SCP) for Autodiscover is created in Active Directory. This SCP is used by Outlook clients to find an Exchange server that can be used to retrieve Exchange and mailbox configuration, a process called "Autodiscover." When this SCP is created, it contains the URL of the Exchange server, for example, `https://exch11.proexchangeadmin.com/autodiscover/autodiscover.xml` where a more typical URL would be the autodiscover.

proexchangeadmin.com version. Another issue is that the Exchange server is configured with a self-signed certificate, not trusted by any client. So, when an Outlook client accidentally finds this local URL and tries to connect to it (which happens instantly!), it detects the self-signed certificate and generates a certificate warning as shown in Figure 2-24.

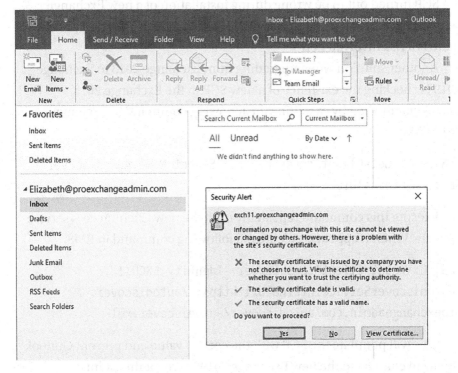

Figure 2-24. *A certificate warning in Outlook, caused by a self-signed certificate during installation*

This will generate helpdesk calls and frustrated users, something we would all like to avoid.

To avoid this, Microsoft recommends installing new Exchange servers in a separate Active Directory site. Outlook clients will find SCP records in their own site and not in such a dedicated installation site.

Another option is of course to install Exchange off business hours or to change the SCP to the normal value as soon as the installation of the new Exchange 2019 has finished and take the risk of Outlook clients finding this wrong SCP. Mind you, it can go wrong. I have faced such an issue in a large enterprise environment with 32 Exchange servers and 40,000 clients where the SCP turned out to be wrong during installation of a new Exchange server. This resulted in over 1,000 Outlook clients with a corrupt profile, so there is a risk involved here.

Another solution when upgrading from Exchange 2013 to Exchange 2019 is checking the existence of a new SCP in the Exchange 2013 Management Shell by executing the following command in Exchange 2013 EMS:

```
[PS] C:\> Get-ClientAccessServer | Select Name,Autodiscover
ServiceInternalUri
```

Execute this command repeatedly until the new Client Access service appears. When it appears, execute the following command in EMS:

```
[PS] C:\> Set-ClientAccessServer -Identity EXCH11
-AutodiscoverServiceInternalUri https://autodiscover.
proexchangeadmin.com/autodiscover/autodiscover.xml
```

This will populate the SCP with the correct value and prevent Outlook clients to connect to the new Exchange 2019 server at this point.

When running a mixed Exchange environment with server versions 2013 and higher, it is recommended to use the management interface of the newest version. So, after installing Exchange 2019 into an existing Exchange 2013 environment, use the Exchange Admin Center and Exchange Management Shell of Exchange 2019. To do this, move your administrative mailbox to an Exchange 2019 mailbox database.

Namespaces with Exchange

In a typical Exchange Server 2013 environment, three namespaces are used:

- webmail.proexchangeadmin.com: Used for all HTTPS-based services, including Outlook Anywhere

- autodiscover.proexchangeadmin.com: Used by external Outlook clients for discovering the internal Exchange configuration

- mail.proexchangeadmin.com: Used for SMTP mail purposes

As explained earlier in this chapter, nothing changes when installing an Exchange 2019 server into an Exchange 2013 environment from a Client Access perspective. The Client Access Front End services and the Front-End Transport service work seamlessly with the Exchange 2013 Client Access servers.

There are just a few settings you must take care of.

Virtual Directories

Since the Exchange 2019 Client Access Front End services are identical to the Exchange 2013 Client Access server, the virtual directories must be configured identical. When using the namespaces as mentioned in the previous section, the virtual directories in the new Exchange 2019 server must be configured as outlined in Table 2-5.

Table 2-5. *Virtual Directory Settings on the Exchange 2019 Server.*

Virtual Directory	InternalURL and ExternalURL
OWA Virtual Directory	`https://webmail.proexchangeadmin.com/owa`
ECP Virtual Directory	`https://webmail.proexchangeadmin.com/ecp`
ActiveSync Virtual Directory	`https://webmail.proexchangeadmin.com/` `Microsoft-Server-ActiveSync`
Webservices Virtual Directory	`https://webmail.proexchangeadmin.com/ews/` `exchange.asmx`
PowerShell Virtual Directory	`https://webmail.proexchangeadmin.com/` `Powershell`
Mapi Virtual Directory	`https://webmail.proexchangeadmin.com/Mapi`
Outlook Anywhere (internal and external hostname)	Webmail.proxexchangeadmin.com

Note   The Mapi Virtual Directory for Mapi/Http was introduced in Exchange 2016 and as such does not exist in Exchange 2013. When moving mailboxes, Outlook clients will automatically detect the new Mapi Virtual Directory and automatically switch from Outlook Anywhere to Mapi/Http.

SSL Certificates

Since the virtual directories on the Exchange 2019 server are configured identical to the virtual directories on Exchange 2013, the same SSL certificate can be used on Exchange 2019.

To use an existing SSL certificate from the Exchange 2013 Client Access server, you follow these steps:

1. On the Exchange 2013 Client Access server, execute the following command in EMS to export the SSL certificate to a .pfx file:

    ```
    C:\> Export-ExchangeCertificate -Thumbprint
    4952E8C42A8279D16999A85400CE9F3DD4EC7458 -FileName
    "\\FS01\Install\webmail_proexchangeadmin_com.pfx"
    -BinaryEncoded -Password (ConvertTo-SecureString
    -String "Pass1word" -AsPlainText -Force)
    ```

    The thumbprint value can be retrieved from the Exchange 2013 server using the Get-ExchangeCertificate command.

2. On the Exchange 2019 server, you open EMS and enter the following command to import the .pfx file:

    ```
    [PS] C:\> Import-ExchangeCertificate –Server EXCH11
    -FileData ([Byte[]]$(Get-Content -Path "\\FS01\Install\
    webmail_proexchangeadmin_com.pfx" -Encoding byte
    -ReadCount 0)) | Enable-ExchangeCertificate -Server
    EXCH11 -Services IIS
    ```

    The same SSL certificate is now ready for use on Exchange 2019.

SMTP Mail in a Coexistence Scenario

During the coexistence phase, SMTP mail flow is not changing dramatically. Exchange 2013 will gladly accept the new Exchange 2019 servers, and these servers will automatically take part in message routing.

For outbound messaging, the only thing you must do is add the new Exchange 2019 server to existing Send Connectors.

For inbound messaging, the firewall or anti-spam appliance needs to be changed so that inbound messages are also delivered to the Exchange 2019 server.

If you have any SMTP relay Receive Connectors, you must reconfigure these to use the Exchange 2019 server. Fellow MVP Thomas Stensitzki has written a PowerShell script that can copy a Receive Connector from one Exchange server to another Exchange server. This is extremely useful when upgrading from Exchange 2013 to Exchange 2019. You can find this script on https://bit.ly/CopyConnector.

Using an Edge Transport Server

As explained before, the Edge Transport server is typically used as an SMTP gateway located in the demilitarized zone of the network. As such, it exchanges mail between the Internet and the internal Exchange servers.

Just with the internal Mailbox servers, the Exchange 2013 Edge Transport server can work seamlessly with new Exchange 2019 Mailbox servers. Vice versa, the Exchange 2019 Edge Transport server with older Exchange 2013 servers works seamlessly as well.

During coexistence, there are two options:

- Continue with the Exchange 2013 Edge Transport server.

- Introduce a new Exchange 2019 Edge Transport server.

Continuing with the Previous Edge Transport Server

If you opt for the first option, using the Exchange 2013 Edge Transport server with the Exchange 2013 and Exchange 2019 servers in coexistence, it is just a matter of recreating the edge subscription. The Exchange 2013 Edge Transport server will continue working with both the Exchange 2013 and Exchange 2019 Mailbox servers. This is shown in Figure 2-25.

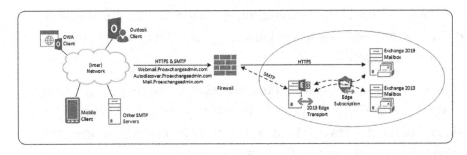

Figure 2-25. *The Exchange 2013 Edge Transport with Exchange 2013 and Exchange 2019 Mailbox servers*

When you opt for this scenario and you only have one Exchange 2013 Edge Transport server, this will cause some downtime for inbound and outbound mail flow.

The edge subscription must be removed from both the Exchange 2013 Edge Transport server and the Exchange 2013 Mailbox server. To remove the edge subscription, execute the following command in EMS on both servers:

```
[PS] C:\> Get-EdgeSubscription -Identity EXCH2013 | Remove-EdgeSubscription
```

At this stage you do not have any connection left between the Exchange 2013 Edge Transport server and the internal Exchange organization, so you must act quickly to minimize downtime.

To create a new edge subscription, execute the following command on the Exchange 2013 Edge Transport server:

```
[PS] C:\> New-EdgeSubscription -FileName C:\Temp\Edge2013.xml
```

A warning message is shown, saying the subscription file is valid for 1440 minutes (which equals 24 hours). If the subscription file is not processed within this timeframe, a new subscription must be created. Enter "Y" to confirm your knowledge of the warning message, and the subscription file will be created.

Copy the Edge2013.xml subscription file to a directory on the local disk of the 2019 Mailbox server. On this server, execute the following commands in EMS:

```
[PS] C:\> New-EdgeSubscription -FileData ([byte[]]$(Get-Content
-Path "C:\Temp\edge2013.xml" -Encoding Byte -ReadCount 0))
-Site "Default-First-Site-Name" -CreateInternetSendConnector
$true -CreateInboundSendConnector $true
[PS] C:\> Start-EdgeSynchronization
```

The first command is an instruction to read the contents of the subscription file, import it, and bind it to the Mailbox server in the Active Directory site. Also, an Internet Send Connector and an inbound Send Connector are created. The second command starts the edge synchronization process. It is as easy as that.

It can take some time before you can successfully run the Start-EdgeSynchronization command. If it fails directly after importing the edge subscription file, please wait a couple of minutes and try again.

Note   The Exchange 2013 Edge Transport server should be able to resolve the Exchange 2013 and the Exchange 2019 Mailbox server and vice versa. This can be achieved using DNS, but using a HOSTS file for resolving an Edge Transport server is quite common as well.

Introducing a New Exchange 2019 Edge Transport Server

The second option when working with Edge Transport servers is to introduce a new Exchange 2019 Edge Transport server next to the existing Edge Transport server.

You install a brand-new Windows 2019 server in the perimeter network and make sure you have Internet connectivity (at least on port 25) and that name resolution works fine, both to the Internet and to the internal network. Then you install the Exchange 2019 Edge Transport server role.

When the Exchange 2019 Edge Transport server is installed, you can create a new edge subscription. Log on to the Exchange 2019 Edge Transport server and execute the following command:

```
[PS] C:\> New-EdgeSubscription -FileName C:\Temp\Edge2019.xml
```

When the file is created, you copy it to the local hard disk of the Exchange 2019 Mailbox server. On this server, execute the following commands:

```
[PS] C:\> New-EdgeSubscription -FileData ([byte[]]$(Get-Content
-Path "C:\Temp\edge2019.xml" -Encoding Byte -ReadCount 0))
-Site "Default-First-Site-Name" -CreateInternetSendConnector
$true -CreateInboundSendConnector $true
[PS] C:\> Start-EdgeSynchronization
```

This will create the edge subscription between the Exchange 2019 Edge Transport server and the Exchange 2013 and Exchange 2019 Mailbox servers and initiate the synchronization process. You now have a situation as shown in Figure 2-26.

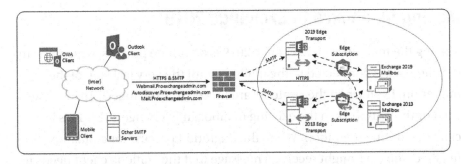

Figure 2-26. *Introducing a new Exchange 2016 Edge Transport server next to the down-level Edge Transport server*

To initiate proper communication between the "old" Exchange 2013 Edge Transport server and the internal Exchange 2013 and Exchange 2019 Mailbox servers, the edge subscription for this server should be replaced as well. You can use the procedure as described in the previous section.

After this, you will have two edge subscriptions in the internal Exchange organization, one for every Edge Transport server. At this point you can continue with two different Exchange Edge Transport servers, or you can choose to decommission the old Exchange 2013 Edge Transport server. But, before you can decommission the old Exchange 2013 Edge Transport server, do not forget to remove the edge subscription for this Edge Transport server. To do this, execute the following command on the Exchange 2019 Mailbox server

```
[PS] C:\> Get-EdgeSubscription -Identity <<Name>> | Remove-
EdgeSubscription
```

where <<Name>> is the NetBIOS name of the Exchange 2013 Edge Transport server.

Moving Resources to Exchange 2019

The most important step in the transition process is to move the mailboxes and other resources from Exchange 2013 to the new Exchange 2019 server.

Moving Mailboxes to Exchange 2019

Moving the mailboxes to Exchange 2019 is an online process, which means the client stays connected to the mailbox until the very last step of the migration. Even when the contents are moved to Exchange 2019, the user can continue to work in the existing mailbox in Exchange 2013. This is called an online migration. When the migration process for a mailbox is finished, the user might receive a message that the Outlook client needs to be restarted. At that point, the migration is finished, and the user connects to the Exchange 2019 Mailbox server.

The process responsible for moving the mailboxes is the Mailbox
Replication service (MRS), a service that is running on the Exchange 2019
server or, better, on every Exchange server as shown in Figure 2-27.

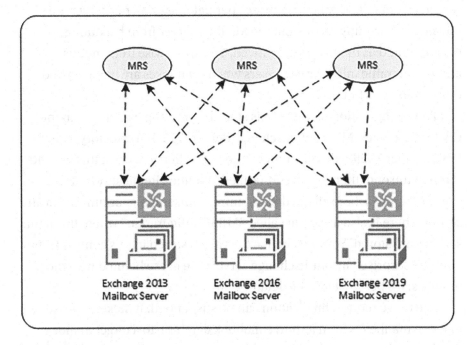

Figure 2-27. *The Mailbox Replication service (MRS)*

When a mailbox needs to be moved from one mailbox database to
another mailbox database, the actual mailbox move is initiated with a
move request. With a move request, a flag is set in the system mailbox of
the source mailbox database, and this flag is picked up by the MRS. The
MRS then creates a copy of that mailbox in the target mailbox database,
and it starts moving the mailbox data from the source to the target. This
is an online and fully transparent mechanism; the recipient can be online
and will not notice anything about moving data. When the MRS is about
to finish the migration of data, the source mailbox is closed, and all
remaining data is written into the target mailbox; the properties in Active
Directory are updated as well.

The MRS is running on every Exchange server, so if there are five Exchange servers, there are also five instances of MRS running in the Exchange environment. It is possible to tune the MRS on the Exchange server. By default, very few mailboxes per database and per server are moved concurrently, to prevent the Mailbox server from becoming overwhelmed as mailboxes are moved. This otherwise tremendous amount of traffic might impact users when mailboxes are being moved during business hours.

The configuration of the MRS is stored in a config file located in the C:\Program Files\Microsoft\Exchange Server\V15\Bin directory, called MSExchangeMailboxReplication.exe.config. When you open this file and scroll to the end, there is a section called "Mailbox Replication Service Configuration" where all the default, minimum, and maximum values are stored. There is also a section called "MRSConfiguration" where the actual settings are stored. You can change the values stored in this config file, but don't be surprised if your Exchange servers are overwhelmed with move requests; it's best to leave the default values.

The move request finalization can be suspended. It makes it possible to move mailboxes from a source mailbox database to a target mailbox database, but without finalizing the actual move. When the move is around 95% finished, the synchronization of mailbox data stops, and the source and the target are kept in sync. It is then possible to finalize the actual move later, for example, during off business hours. This way, the user does not receive the (disruptive) message about restarting the Outlook client at an inconvenient time.

Note   Moving mailboxes is a "pull" mechanism, so the move process is initiated from the Exchange 2019 server.

To initiate a mailbox move for a user called joe@proexchangeadmin. com, you log onto an Exchange 2019 server, open EMS, and execute the following command:

```
[PS] C:\> New-MoveRequest -Identity joe@proexchangeadmin.com -TargetDatabase MDB11
```

You can also get a list of mailboxes on the previous Exchange Mailbox server, for example, based on a mailbox database called MBX01, and use the pipeline feature to move all mailboxes to a mailbox database called MDB11. This will result in a command like

```
[PS] C:\> Get-Mailbox -Database "MBX01" | New-MoveRequest -TargetDatabase MDB11
```

You can monitor the move of the mailboxes with the Get-MoveRequest command. If needed you can add the Get-MoveRequestStatistics command, like this:

```
[PS] C:\> Get-MoveRequest | Get-MoveRequestStatistics
```

This will give you a quick overview of all move requests that are currently available and whether their status is queued, in progress, or completed. To get an overview of all move requests that are running at a particular moment, you can make a selection based on the status of the move request, like this:

```
[PS] C:\> Get-MoveRequest | Where {$_.Status -eq "InProgress"}
```

Exchange uses special system mailboxes, arbitration mailboxes, and the discovery search mailbox. I recommend migrating these first from Exchange 2013 to Exchange 2019. This way features like arbitration, eDiscovery, and audit logging become available on Exchange 2019.

To move these mailboxes, use the following commands:

```
[PS] C:\> Get-Mailbox -Arbitration | New-MoveRequest
-TargetDatabase MDB11
[PS] C:\> get-mailbox -Identity discovery* | New-MoveRequest -
TargetDatabase MDB11
```

Note   In Exchange the Offline Address Book is generated in an arbitration mailbox. By moving the arbitration mailbox to Exchange 2019, the Offline Address Book is automatically moved to Exchange 2019 as well.

If you do not specify a target database with the New-MoveRequest command, Exchange will select a mailbox database automatically, based on the availability of resources.

When the regular mailboxes, the discovery mailbox, and the system mailboxes are moved to Exchange 2019, then the mailbox databases on the previous version of Exchange Server should be empty and are ready for removal.

Address Lists in Exchange 2019

When all the mailboxes are moved to Exchange 2019, it is time to move the other resources. Regular address lists reside in Active Directory, so there is no need to "move" them to Exchange 2019. From a management perspective, address lists can be managed both from Exchange 2013 and Exchange 2019. There is no need to pay extra attention to address lists.

Decommissioning the Previous Exchange Server

When all resources have been moved or removed, you can decommission the Exchange 2013 server. This is not really a big deal at all, and it involves the following steps:

1. Make sure the Exchange 2013 server is not
    responsible anymore for any mail traffic. This not
    only includes SMTP from and to the Internet but
    also third-party appliances or (custom) applications
    that might have been using the Hub Transport
    server for receiving or relaying messages. Caution:
    You don't want to remove the Exchange 2013 server
    and find out that your multifunctional devices
    cannot send out messages anymore.

    To achieve this, you can enable SMTP logging on
    both the Receive Connector and the Send Connector
    and check the corresponding log files. By default,
    you can find these log files at the following locations:

- *SMTP receive*:
  C:\Program Files\Microsoft\Exchange Server\V15\
  TransportRoles\Logs\ ProtocolLog\SMTPReceive

- *SMTP send*:
  C:\Program Files\Microsoft\Exchange Server\V15\
  TransportRoles\Logs\ ProtocolLog\SMTPSend

2. Remove the mailbox databases from the Exchange
    2013 server. This can be achieved by using the
    Exchange Management Shell or Exchange Admin
    Center in both Exchange 2013 and Exchange 2019.

3. Uninstall the Exchange 2013 server. This can be done
    by opening the Control Panel on the Exchange 2013
    server and selecting "Uninstall Exchange Server."
    Uncheck the server roles and Exchange management
    tools option in the setup application. This will
    remove the Exchange 2013 server roles for this server.

Another option is to use the unattended setup by executing the following command from a command prompt with elevated privileges:

```
Z:\> Setup.exe /Mode:Uninstall /
Roles:Mailbox,ClientAccess /
IAcceptExchangeServerLicenseTerms
```

4. When uninstalled, the Windows server can be removed from the Active Directory domain and turned off.

When all these steps are successfully executed, the Exchange 2013 server is now fully removed, and only the Exchange 2019 servers remain in the Exchange organization.

(Important) Note   Decommissioning the previous version is not simply a matter of turning it off. This still happens in a virtualized server environment. It is tempting to turn off the virtual machines and just delete them, but this is wrong. When you do this, all information regarding previous versions of Exchange Server remains in Active Directory. From an Exchange point of view, "they" are still there (but not responding, of course). This can lead to erratic behavior. So fully uninstall the previous Exchange Server!

Summary

In this chapter I explained the basics of the Exchange 2019 infrastructure, how to design an Exchange infrastructure and how to build and configure an Exchange infrastructure.

In the first section of this chapter, I discussed designing and installing Exchange 2019 on Windows 2022, but Windows 2019 is also supported, followed by the high availability options in Exchange, protocol load balancing, and the Database Availability Group.

An important aspect is of course Exchange Transport, both in the Exchange 2019 Mailbox server and the Edge Transport server. Previously, the Edge Transport server used to be positioned for message hygiene purposes, but its main purpose these days is a gateway server between the internal Exchange 2019 Mailbox servers and Exchange Online, positioned in the company's demilitarized zone.

Exchange 2013 was introduced more than ten years ago, in January 2013 to be precise, and mainstream support ended in April 2018. Extended support ended in April 2023, so when this book is available, Exchange 2013 is at its end of life. Microsoft does not support Exchange 2013 any longer, and no more security updates are released. Looking at the vulnerabilities that are discovered on a monthly basis, keeping Exchange 2013 alive in your environment is a serious risk.

Upgrading from Exchange 2013 or Exchange 2016 to Exchange 2019 is a straightforward task. All three Exchange versions are very much compatible from a protocol perspective, and they integrate very well. Unfortunately, this is not the case for the back end services, so for Exchange 2019 a new storage solution must be built. In a typical environment, Exchange is always configured in a hybrid environment, where lots of mailboxes are migrated to Exchange Online, so the number of mailboxes that are left on Exchange 2019 is typically not too high and storage demand is therefore okay.

CHAPTER 3

Managing Exchange

In the previous chapter, we have discussed how to design, install, and configure the Exchange 2019 server.

This chapter will focus more on the next step, like managing the mailbox databases and managing the various kinds of recipients that are available in Exchange 2019:

- Mailboxes

- Distribution Groups

- Contacts

Besides managing these, in this chapter we will also focus on

- Cumulative Updates

- Security Updates

- Monitoring and reporting

The focus of this book is on hybrid environments, where recipients are both in Exchange Online and in Exchange 2019. This chapter will focus on the on-premises recipients; the online recipients will be discussed in Chapter 5.

© Jaap Wesselius and Michel de Rooij 2023
J. Wesselius and M. de Rooij, *Pro Exchange Administration*,
https://doi.org/10.1007/978-1-4842-9591-5_3

Managing Databases

When you install an Exchange server, its default behavior is to create a mailbox database on the system disk, typically in the directory C:\Program Files\Microsoft\Exchange Server\V15\Mailbox\. The name of the new mailbox database is "Mailbox Database," followed by a random number, so we get something like "Mailbox Database 0833106092."

Although this mailbox database can be used in a production environment, most likely it does not fit into your company's naming convention, and it is not stored in a proper location. Therefore, things you might want to do after the initial installation are the following:

1. Rename the mailbox database to match your company's naming convention.

2. Move the mailbox database and the accompanying log files to a more suitable location—for example, an external disk, whether it be direct attached storage (DAS) or some sort of SAN storage solution. Be aware that you can only do this before you create a DAG with additional mailbox database copies!

3. When you are using a DAG and following Exchange Native Data Protection, you can enable circular logging.

4. Change quotas for the mailbox database or change the retention times for deleted items.

5. Assign an Offline Address Book (OAB) to a mailbox database.

Rename a Mailbox Database

Renaming a mailbox database in Exchange Server 2019 is not a big deal; it's just a matter of one PowerShell command. To change a mailbox database name from Mailbox Database 0833106092 to MDB01, enter the following command in Exchange PowerShell:

```
[PS] C:\> Get-MailboxDatabase -Identity "Mailbox database
0833106092" | Set-MailboxDatabase -Name "MDB01"
```

Note   In the preceding example, the logical name of the mailbox database is renamed as it shows up in Exchange PowerShell or in the Admin Center. The actual EDB file or the directory on disk is not renamed. To rename these, you need to move the EDB file to another directory and give it a new filename.

Move a Mailbox Database

It is strongly recommended that you move mailbox databases to a separate location, preferably a dedicated disk. To move a mailbox database named MDB01 and its log files to a different location, just enter the following command in Exchange PowerShell:

```
[PS] C:\> Move-DatabasePath -Identity MDB01 -EdbFilePath C:\
ExchDbs\Mdb01\MDB01.edb -LogFolderPath C:\ExchDbs\Mdb01\LogFiles
```

```
Confirm
Are you sure you want to perform this action?
Moving database path "MDB01".
```

```
[Y] Yes  [A] Yes to All  [N] No  [L] No to All  [?] Help
(default is "Y"): y
```

Confirm
To perform the move operation, database "MDB01" must be temporarily dismounted, which will make it inaccessible to all users. Do you want to continue?
```
[Y] Yes  [A] Yes to All  [N] No  [L] No to All  [?] Help
(default is "Y"): y
```

You'll get two warning messages when running this command. The first warning is just a confirmation request; the second warning is about dismounting the database when moving it. Dismounting means it is temporarily not available for users. For both warnings, select "y" to continue.

An interesting option is the -ConfigurationOnly parameter. Normally when you use the Move-DatabasePath cmdlet, the mailbox database settings in Active Directory are changed, and the mailbox database and its log files are moved to the assigned location. When the -ConfigurationOnly parameter is used, the settings are changed in Active Directory, but the actual file move does not occur. This can be useful in a disaster recovery scenario, where a mailbox database is recovered in another location and the Mailbox server needs to use this mailbox database.

Circular Logging

Circular logging is a technique whereby only a very limited number of transaction log files are kept on the server. Normally, transaction log files are kept until a backup has successfully run, but when circular logging is enabled, the transaction log files are removed from the server once all the transactions have been successfully committed to the mailbox database and shipped to the passive copies of that mailbox database when using a DAG.

In a single-server scenario, circular logging is not recommended because of its lack of recovery options, but in a DAG environment, circular logging poses less risk of data loss. Recovery options are provided by the DAG itself, so if a mailbox database is lost, another server in the DAG takes over.

To enable circular logging on a mailbox database named MDB01, enter the following command in Exchange PowerShell:

```
[PS] C:\> Set-MailboxDatabase -Identity MDB01
-CircularLoggingEnabled:$TRUE
```

If you enable circular logging on a server that's not a DAG member, you'll get a warning message that the circular logging will become active only when the mailbox database is dismounted and mounted again. When the Mailbox server is a DAG member, the circular logging option is applied immediately, and there's no need for remounting the mailbox database.

To disable the circular logging, the -CircularLoggingEnabled option should be set to $FALSE.

Quota Settings

When a new mailbox database is installed, the default quotas are set on the mailbox database. Quotas are limits set on a mailbox; if they are not explicitly set on the mailbox itself, the mailbox database quotas are enforced on the mailboxes.

The following quota settings are set by default:

- *Issue Warning at 1.9 GB*: This value determines when Exchange starts sending warning messages to the user about the fact that they're reaching their mailbox limit. By default, this limit is 100 MB lower than the next limit, whereby the user cannot send email anymore.

- *Prohibit Send at 2.0 GB*: This value determines when the user cannot send email anymore.

- *Prohibit Send and Receive at 2.1 GB*: This value determines when the user cannot send email but at the same time cannot receive email either. By default, this value is 100 MB higher than the previous limit— the Prohibit Send quota. Some customers prefer to leave this quota setting open, especially on mailboxes that receive email from customers, so as to prevent bouncing back email to the customers.

While these settings are sufficient for most users, they can be extended to a very large level. In Exchange 2019, a mailbox of 100 GB is not a problem at all on a server level; the only thing you must be aware of is that the storage sizing must be able to accommodate these large mailboxes.

To change the default quota settings on a mailbox database called MDB01 to 19, 20, and 22 GB, you can use the following command in Exchange PowerShell:

```
[PS] C:\> Set-MailboxDatabase -Identity MDB01
-IssueWarningQuota 19GB -ProhibitSendQuota 20GB
-ProhibitSendReceiveQuota 22GB
```

Note   Having a 20 GB mailbox on an Exchange 2019 server is not a problem, but complications may arise when using Outlook in cached mode. Outlook will cache mailbox contents in an .OST file on the local hard disk. Outlook by default will cache only one year of data using "the slider" in the user's Outlook profile. When a larger time window is selected, the .OST file can grow dramatically.

Exchange periodically sends warning messages to users who have almost hit their quota (the Issue Warning) or who have hit their quota and cannot send (the Prohibit Send) or have hit their quota and cannot send and receive (the Prohibit Send and Receive limit). The frequency of these warning messages is set using the QuotaNotificationSchedule property on a mailbox database, which you can check using Exchange PowerShell:

```
[PS] C:\> Get-MailboxDatabase -Identity MBB01 | Format-List
Name,QuotaNotificationSchedule

Name                       : MDB01
QuotaNotificationSchedule : {Sun.1:00 AM-Sun.1:15 AM, Mon.1:00
AM-Mon.1:15 AM, Tue.1:00 AM-Tue.1:15 AM, Wed.1:00 AM-Wed.1:15
AM, Thu.1:00 AM-Thu.1:15 AM, Fri.1:00 AM-Fri.1:15 AM, Sat.1:00
AM-Sat.1:15 AM}
```

Mailboxes inherit their quotas from the mailbox database where they reside. It is possible to override these limits by setting the quotas directly on the mailbox. The quota can be higher or lower than the mailbox database setting.

To change the quota settings for Sarah Summertown to 29, 30, and 31 GB, execute the following command in Exchange PowerShell:

```
[PS] C:\> Set-Mailbox -identity S.Summertown
-UseDatabaseQuotaDefaults $False -IssueWarningQuota 29GB
-ProhibitSendQuota 30GB -ProhibitSendReceiveQuota 31GB
```

Assign an Offline Address Book

When a mailbox database is created, an Offline Address Book (OAB) is not assigned to it. In a typical environment, this is not needed, but there are situations where you can put one set of mailboxes in one mailbox database and another set of mailboxes in another mailbox database, and then you can assign a specific OAB to a specific mailbox database and thus to the mailboxes in this database.

You can use the following command in Exchange PowerShell to assign an Offline Address Book called Custom Department OAB to a mailbox database called MDB01:

```
[PS] C:\> Set-MailboxDatabase -Identity MDB01
-OfflineAddressBook "Custom Department OAB"
```

Create a New Mailbox Database

If you have a larger environment, then it's likely that you will need some additional mailbox databases besides the default mailbox database. When you have multiple mailbox databases, you can spread your mailboxes across these mailbox databases. Even better, when provisioning the mailbox, you do not assign a mailbox database; Exchange Server will look for a mailbox database to host this new mailbox.

To create a new mailbox database MDB02 hosted on server EXCH01, execute the following command in Exchange PowerShell:

```
[PS] C:\> New-MailboxDatabase -Name MDB02 -Server EXCH01
-EdbFilePath C:\ExchDbs\Disk2\MDB02.edb -LogFolderPath C:\
ExchDbs\Disk2\LogFiles
```

After creation of the mailbox database, you can mount it using the following command in Exchange PowerShell:

```
[PS] C:\> Mount-Database -Identity MDB02
```

Note   When you create a new mailbox database, this information is stored in Active Directory. The information needs to be replicated across all Domain Controllers. It can happen that, when creating a new mailbox database, this information is not replicated across all Domain Controllers when you enter the Mount-Database command. If that happens, the Mount-Database command fails, and an error is shown on the console. Nothing to worry about; just wait a couple of minutes and retry the Mount-Database command.

Delete a Mailbox Database

Before a mailbox database can be deleted, all the mailboxes in it need to be either deleted or moved to another mailbox database. When the mailbox database is empty, you can remove it. To remove a mailbox database, execute the following command in Exchange PowerShell:

```
[PS] C:\> Remove-MailboxDatabase -Identity MDB01 -Confirm:$false
```

When the mailbox database is deleted, it is only deleted from Active Directory. The files themselves still exist on the Exchange server and must be manually deleted. But one day you will run into the following issue: Suppose you've moved all the mailboxes to another mailbox database, and you want to delete the mailbox database. An error message says: "This mailbox database contains one or more mailboxes, mailbox plans, archive mailboxes, public folder mailboxes, or arbitration mailboxes."

When you check again, the mailbox database looks empty because nothing shows up in EAC and nothing is shown when you enter a Get-Mailbox -Database MDB01 command in EMS. This situation is caused by system mailboxes in this mailbox database, and these system mailboxes are not shown by default. They can only be shown in Exchange PowerShell by using the Get-Mailbox in combination with the following options:

- -Arbitration

- -Archive

- -AuditLog

- -AuxAuditLog

- -Migration

- -Monitoring

For example:

```
[PS] C:\> Get-Mailbox -Database MDB01 -Arbitration
[PS] C:\> Get-Mailbox -Database MDB01 -Archive
[PS] C:\> Get-Mailbox -Database MDB01 -Migration
```

To move these mailboxes to another mailbox database called MDB02, execute the following command in Exchange PowerShell:

```
[PS] C:\> Get-Mailbox -Database MDB01 -Arbitration |
New-MoveRequest -TargetDatabase MDB02
```

When these system mailboxes are moved and the mailbox database is empty, it is possible to remove the mailbox database.

Online Maintenance

Online maintenance is a broad term and describes several tasks. Discussed here are

- The deleted items retention settings

- The online maintenance

Deleted Items Retention

When items are removed from the mailbox database (messages, folders, mailboxes), they are not immediately deleted from the mailbox or the mailbox database; they are kept in the background for a particular amount of time called the retention time, and it is set by default to 14 days for individual mailbox items and 30 days for mailboxes.

The deleted items retention time and the mailbox retention time are properties of a mailbox database and can be retrieved using the following command in Exchange PowerShell:

```
[PS] C:\> Get-MailboxDatabase –Identity MDB01 | select Mailbox
Retention,DeletedItemRetention

MailboxRetention DeletedItemRetention
---------------- --------------------
30.00:00:00      14.00:00:00
```

The retention time is shown as a time span: dd.hh:mm:ss, where d=days, h=hours, m=minutes, and s=seconds.

To change the deleted items retention time to 90 days, for example, you use the following command:

```
[PS] C:\> Set-MailboxDatabase –Identity MDB01 –
DeletedItemRetention 90.00:00:00
```

When deleted items are past their retention time, they are permanently deleted from the mailbox database. When this happens, there's no way to get these items back.

There's an option in Exchange that only deletes these items permanently after they have been backed up. This option is called RetainDeletedItemsUntilBackup and is set to FALSE by default, so you must set it explicitly. To set this in combination with the 90-day deleted items retention time that was set in the previous example, you can use the following PowerShell command:

```
[PS] C:\> Set-MailboxDatabase -Identity MDB01
-DeletedItemsRetention 90.00:00:00 -
RetainDeletedItemsUntilBackup $TRUE
```

When a user deletes a message and purges it from the Deleted Items folder in their mailbox or when an administrator deletes a mailbox, it is moved to the Recoverable Items folder. This is a special location in the mailbox database, not visible for users, where items are stored for as long as stipulated by the retention time.

Online Maintenance

Online maintenance is a process in Exchange Server that maintains the internal structure of the mailbox database, and it consists of two parts:

1. *Content maintenance*: Responsible for purging deleted items, purging indexes, purging deleted mailboxes, and checking for orphaned messages. This part focuses on content maintenance—that is, it is responsible for purging old content and keeping the mailbox database as accurate as possible.

2. *ESE maintenance*: Keeps track of all database pages and indexes inside the mailbox database and performs checksum checks of all individual pages inside the database. Single-bit errors can be fixed on the fly by ESE maintenance. ESE maintenance also performs online defragmentation to optimize the internal structure of the mailbox database. Online defragmentation reads all pages and indexes in the database and reorganizes these pages. The idea is to free up pages inside the database so new items can be written in the free space inside the database, preventing unnecessary growth of the database.

Content maintenance can finish in a couple of hours, even on the largest mailbox databases. By default, content maintenance runs from 1 AM until 5 AM on the Mailbox server. This maintenance schedule is also a property of a mailbox database and can be retrieved using the following PowerShell command:

```
[PS] C:\> Get-MailboxDatabase -Identity MDB01 | Select
MaintenanceSchedule

MaintenanceSchedule
-------------------
{Sun.1:00 AM-Sun.5:00 AM, Mon.1:00 AM-Mon.5:00 AM, Tue.1:00
AM-Tue.5:00 AM, Wed.1:00 AM-Wed.5:00 AM, Thu.1:00 AM-Thu...
```

If you want to change this time span, you must use all different times as input for the Set-MailboxDatabase command using the -MaintenanceSchedule parameter, for example:

```
[PS] C:\> Set-MailboxDatabase -Identity MDB01 -MaintenanceSchedule
"Sun.00:00 AM-Sun.04:00 AM","Mon.00:00-Mon.04:00","Tue.00:00-
Tue.04:00","Wed.00:00-Wed.04:00","Thu.00:00-Thu.04:00",
"Fri.00:00-Fri.04:00","Sat.00:00-Sat.04:00"
```

WARNING: The parameter MaintenanceSchedule has been deprecated.

If you run this command, the time spans are set, but as shown in the preceding output, you are also presented a warning message that this parameter is being deprecated. The reason is understandable. For large mailbox databases, the timeframe for online maintenance was not sufficient; there was just not enough time to complete the online maintenance. It often conflicts with a backup schedule, ending up in an overloaded Exchange server in the middle of the night.

However, the warning saying it is deprecated was shown in Exchange Server 2013, and it is still shown in Exchange server 2019. It is unknown if this ever gets removed from Exchange.

The second part of online maintenance is the ESE maintenance. This is a 24/7 background process. It is enabled by default, and it is recommended that you leave this enabled. If for some reason you want to disable ESE maintenance, you can set the –BackgroundDatabaseMaintenance parameter to $FALSE by executing the following command in Exchange PowerShell:

```
[PS] C:\> Set-MailboxDatabase -Identity DB01 -
BackgroundDatabaseMaintenance $FALSE
```

WARNING: The BackgroundDatabaseMaintenance parameter change will not be applied on this database before it's remounted. Dismount and remount database "MDB01" to apply this parameter change.

Dismount and mount this database to effectuate this setting, but again, changing this setting is not recommended.

Managing Mailboxes

There are a couple of ways to create new user mailboxes in Exchange:

- Create a new mailbox in Exchange PowerShell or the Admin Center and have the accompanying user account in Active Directory created automatically.

- Mailbox-enable an existing user account.

We will discuss this in more detail.

Create a User Mailbox

It is possible to create a new user mailbox with the accompanying user account using the New-Mailbox command in Exchange PowerShell. To do this, execute the following command:

```
[PS] C:\> New-Mailbox -Name "David Honeychurch" -FirstName
David -LastName Honeychurch -Alias David -DisplayName "David
Honeychurch" -OrganizationalUnit "OU=Users,OU=Accounts,DC=Proe
xchangeadmin,DC=com" -Database MDB01 -UserPrincipalName david@
proexchangeadmin.com
```

```
WARNING: A script or application on the remote computer EXCH01.
LABS.LOCAL is sending a prompt request. When you are
prompted, enter sensitive information, such as credentials or
passwords, only if you trust the remote computer and the
application or script that is requesting the data.
```

```
cmdlet New-Mailbox at command pipeline position 1
Supply values for the following parameters:
Password: ********
```

Name	Alias	ServerName	ProhibitSendQuota
David Honeychurch	David	exch01	Unlimited

This command will create a new user account called "David Honeychurch" in the OU=Users Organizational Unit in the OU=Accounts Organizational Unit in Active Directory. The UserPrincipalName will be set to david@proexchangeadmin.com, and the mailbox will be created in the MDB01 mailbox database.

It is not possible to enter a password on the command line because passwords are only accepted as a secure string in Active Directory. Therefore, you are prompted for a new password for this user account.

To work around this, you can use the ConvertTo-SecureString function in PowerShell. This will convert a clear-text string like Pass1word into a secure string that will be accepted by PowerShell when creating a new user. The command for creating a new user with a mailbox and for setting the password will be something like this:

```
[PS] C:\> New-Mailbox -Name "Percy Blake" -OrganizationalUnit
"OU=Users,OU=Accounts,DC=Proexchangeadmin,DC=com" -Password
(ConvertTo-SecureString -String 'Pass1word' -AsPlainText
-Force) -Database MDB01 -FirstName Percy -LastName Blake
-DisplayName "Percy Blake" -UserPrincipalName percy@
proexchangeadmin.com
```

Name	Alias	ServerName	ProhibitSendQuota
Percy Blake	percy	exch01	Unlimited

In the preceding example, a mailbox database is explicitly set. It is also possible to omit the -Database option when creating a new mailbox. If you do this, the Mailbox server automatically determines the best location for the new mailbox.

The algorithm used here first determines which mailbox databases are available in Active Directory and are not excluded for provisioning. Then it looks at the number of mailboxes in each mailbox database and picks the mailbox database with the lowest number of mailboxes.

By default, when a mailbox is created, a new email address is assigned using an email address policy. It is also possible to bypass this using the -PrimarySmtpAddress option. When you use this option, the EmailAddressPolicyEnabled property of the new mailbox is set to false, and an email address policy is never applied. To do this, execute the following command in Exchange PowerShell:

```
[PS] C:\> New-Mailbox -Name "Jeronimo Ramirez" -FirstName
Jeronimo -LastName Ramirez -Alias Jeronimo -DisplayName
"Jeronimo Ramirez" -Password (ConvertTo-SecureString
-String 'Pass1word' -AsPlainText -Force) -Database
MDB01 -UserPrincipalName Jeronimo@proexchangeadmin.com
-PrimarySmtpAddress Jeronimo@proexchangeadmin.com
```

Note   The official name for a mailbox in Exchange is a mailbox-enabled user.

Mailbox-Enabling an Existing User Account

It is possible that an account in Active Directory already exists; it could have been created by the Active Directory team, for example. If so, you can mailbox-enable this user account. When mailbox-enabling an existing user account, a mailbox is added to it.

If you have an existing user account in Active Directory called "William Gray" and you want to assign a mailbox to him located in the mailbox database MDB02, you can execute the following command in Exchange PowerShell:

```
[PS] C:\> Enable-Mailbox -Identity "William Gray" -Alias
William -Database MDB02
```

Personally, I like to use a Get-User cmdlet first to see if it retrieves the correct user account from Active Directory. If it does, I repeat the command and pipe it into the Enable-Mailbox cmdlet:

```
[PS] C:\> Get-User -Identity "William Gray" | Enable-Mailbox
-Alias William -Database MDB02
```

The advantage of creating a user account in Active Directory in advance is that you can add a lot more properties using the New-ADuser command in PowerShell or in the Active Directory Users and Computers MMC snap-in. For Example, to create a new user account in Active Directory and populate additional properties, execute the following command in PowerShell:

```
[PS] C:\> New-ADUser -Name "Jessie Wingo" -SAMAccountName
Jessie -Server AD01 -UserPrincipalName Jessie@proexchangeadmin.
com -GivenName Jessie -Surname Wingo -DisplayName "Jessie
Wingo" -Path "OU=Users,OU=Accounts,DC=proexchangeadmin,
DC=com" -AccountPassword (ConvertTo-SecureString "Pass1word"
-AsPlainText -Force) -Company "Les Aventures" -StreetAddress
"1, Longway" -PostalCode "X3B 84W" -City London -Country "GB"
-OfficePhone "+44 123 456 789" -Title "Managing Consultant"
-HomePage "www.proexchangeadmin.com" -Fax "+44 123 456 789"
-MobilePhone "+44 123 456 789"  -Enabled:$TRUE
```

Note   You can visit the `https://countrycode.org/` site to find a complete list of all country codes.

Using variables in combination with the New-ADUser and Enable-Mailbox commands makes an IT admin life much easier.

Remove a Mailbox

Mailboxes need to be created, and at some point, mailboxes need to be removed as well. When it comes to removing mailboxes, there are two options:

1. The mailbox is disabled. In this case, the mailbox is deleted, and the values of the Exchange-related properties are removed from the user account. Important to note here is that the user account in Active Directory continues to exist, so the user can still log on to Windows and Active Directory and can continue to access other resources on the network. A resource mailbox has a disabled user account associated with it, and as such a resource mailbox cannot be disabled.

2. The mailbox is removed. In this case, the mailbox is deleted, including the user account, from Active Directory. An archive mailbox cannot be deleted; it can only be disabled.

When a mailbox is deleted, it remains in the mailbox database until the retention time for the deleted mailbox expires. Up until this point, this mailbox is referred to as a disconnected mailbox.

To disable a mailbox, the following command can be used:

```
[PS] C:\> Disable-Mailbox -Identity "Jessy Wingo"
```

When you perform this command, a confirmation is requested. You can avoid this question by adding the –Confirm:$false option to the Disable-Mailbox cmdlet.

Removing a mailbox is like disabling a mailbox. To remove a mailbox and its accompanying user account, you enter the following command:

```
[PS] C:\> Remove-Mailbox -Identity " Jeronimo Ramirez"
-Confirm:$false
```

To check if the mailbox has been deleted (or actually disconnected), you can run the following commands:

```
[PS] C:\> Get-MailboxDatabase | Get-MailboxStatistics |
?{$_.DisplayName -eq "Jessy Wingo" } | fl DisconnectReason,
DisconnectDate
```

When a mailbox is properly deleted, the DisconnectReason property will show "Disabled." Another value for the DisconnectReason is "SoftDeleted." A mailbox is soft-deleted when it is moved from one mailbox database to another mailbox database. Just as when removing a mailbox, the source mailbox is deleted in the source mailbox database, and it remains there until the retention period expires.

Tip   To avoid any issues with accidental removal of mailboxes or any Exchange recipient, I always recommend enabling the Active Directory recycle bin. When enabled and an object is accidentally deleted, you can always restore it easily from the recycle bin.

Managing Mailboxes

When the new mailbox is created and during normal operation, there are certain things you must do for managing the mailbox. Managing mailboxes can include the following:

- Set additional properties like Company or Department.

- Set quota settings on a mailbox.

- Set regional configuration properties.

- Assign a policy to the mailbox.

- Add an additional email address.

- Create an archive mailbox.

- Implement cmdlet extension agents.

- Move mailboxes.

- Import and export mailboxes to PST files.

Active Directory Properties

Properties like Company or Department are Active Directory properties and not Exchange-specific. Therefore, you cannot use the Set-Mailbox cmdlet to set these. Instead, you can use the Set-User cmdlet to set them, for example:

```
PS C:\> Set-User -Identity JBrown -Company "Bookworkx"
-Department "Sales"
```

Quota Settings

Earlier in this chapter, I explained that quota settings are put on a mailbox database. It is also possible to put quota settings on a mailbox, and these quota settings will override the mailbox database quotas. To change the quota settings for all users in, say, the BookWorkx Organizational Unit, you can use the following command:

```
[PS] C:\> Get-Mailbox -OrganizationalUnit "BookWorkx" |
Set-Mailbox -IssueWarningQuota 10GB -ProhibitSendQuota 11GB
-ProhibitSendReceiveQuota 15GB -UseDatabaseQuotaDefaults $false
```

It is important to set the -UseDatabaseQuotaDefaults property to $false. If you do not do this, the mailbox database quota settings are not overridden.

Regional Settings

The first time you log onto OWA, you are requested to set the time zone and to select a language. In a typical environment, these will be identical across all mailboxes. An exception could be if you are living in a dual-language country like Belgium. You would set the default time zone to "W. Europe Standard Time" and set the language to French or Dutch, depending on the location of the user. For example, for Brussels-based users, you would set it to

```
[PS] C:\> Set-MailboxRegionalConfiguration -Identity Pascal
-Language fr-FR -LocalizeDefaultFolderName  $TRUE -Timezone
"W. Europe Standard Time"
```

And for Antwerp-based users, you would set it to

```
[PS] C:\> Set-MailboxRegionalConfiguration -Identity Johan
-Language nl-NL -LocalizeDefaultFolderName  $TRUE -Timezone
"W. Europe Standard Time"
```

Tip   If you want to get the time zone you are currently in, you can use the TZUTIL utility. Run this in a command prompt, and it will show you the current time zone of the Windows machine you are logged onto.

Assign Address Book Policies

An Exchange-specific address book policy can be assigned to a mailbox using the Set-Mailbox cmdlet. If you have an address book policy called "BookWorkx ABP" and you want to assign it to the JBrown mailbox, you can use the following command:

```
[PS] C:\> Set-Mailbox -Identity JBrown -AddressBookPolicy
"BookWorkx ABP"
```

Adding Email Addresses

Adding email addresses to a mailbox is a little more difficult because the EmailAddress property of a mailbox is a multivalued property; that is, this particular property can have more than one value.

If you add a value to a property, the original value is overwritten, which is something to be avoided when using multivalued properties. To change a multivalued property, add an Add or Remove option to the value. For example, to add two additional email addresses to John's mailbox, you can use the following command:

```
[PS] C:\> Set-Mailbox -Identity JBrooks -EmailAddresses
@{Add="John.Brooks@proexchangeadmin.com", "John.A.Brooks@
proexchangeadmin.com"}
```

Removing a value from a multivalued property is similar:

```
[PS] C:\> Set-Mailbox -Identity JBrooks -EmailAddresses
@{Remove=John.A.Brooks@proexchangeadmin.com}
```

Archive Mailboxes

An archive mailbox is a secondary mailbox connected to a user's primary mailbox. To create an archive mailbox, you can use the Enable-Mailbox cmdlet with the –Archive option. For example, to enable the archive mailbox to John Brook's mailbox, you can use the following command:

```
[PS] C:\> Enable-Mailbox -Identity JBrooks -Archive
```

Exchange Server will automatically provision the archive mailbox in one of the available mailbox databases; it uses the same algorithm when creating a normal mailbox. If you want to set the mailbox database manually, you can use the –ArchiveDatabase option, for example:

```
[PS] C:\> Enable-Mailbox -Identity JBrooks -Archive -
ArchiveDatabase MDB10
```

Note   Archive mailboxes are explained in detail in Chapter 12.

Cmdlet Extension Agents

Not directly related to the creation of new mailboxes but interesting enough to discuss here are the cmdlet extension agents. Using cmdlet extensions, it is possible to expand the functionality of PowerShell cmdlets and tailor them to your organizational needs.

An example of such an extension could be the automatic creation of an archive mailbox whenever a normal user mailbox is created. The scripting agent configuration is stored in the file called ScriptingAgentConfig. xml, which is stored in a directory C:\Program Files\Microsoft\Exchange Server\V15\Bin\CmdletExtensionAgents on the Exchange server.

Note   There is a ScriptingAgentConfig.xml.sample file located in this directory that you can use as a reference. Be aware that this is strict XML and as such very sensitive for errors!

To create a cmdlet extension that is executed when the New-Mailbox cmdlet has finished ("onComplete") and create a new archive mailbox in the same mailbox database as the original user mailbox, you create a ScriptingAgentConfig.xml that contains the following code and store this file in the directory as mentioned previously:

```xml
<?xml version="1.0" encoding="utf-8" ?>
<Configuration version="1.0">
  <Feature Name="MailboxProvisioning" Cmdlets="New-Mailbox,
  Enable-Mailbox">
    <ApiCall Name="OnComplete">
    If($succeeded) {
      $Name= $provisioningHandler.UserSpecifiedParamete
      rs["Name"]
      If ((Get-Mailbox $Name).ArchiveDatabase -eq $null) {
        $ArchiveDatabase= (Get-Mailbox $Name).Database
        Enable-Mailbox $Name -Archive -ArchiveDatabase
        $ArchiveDatabase
        }
      }
    </ApiCall>
  </Feature>
</Configuration>
```

Another interesting example is to set the language and regional settings after a new mailbox is created or after an existing user is mailbox-enabled:

```
<?xml version="1.0" encoding="utf-8" ?>
<Configuration version="1.0">
<Feature Name="Mailboxes" Cmdlets="New-Mailbox, Enable-
Mailbox">
<ApiCall Name="OnComplete">
if($succeeded) {
$Name= $ProvisioningHandler.UserSpecifiedParameters["Name"]
Set-Mailbox $Name -Languages "en-US" -
LocalizeDefaultFolderName $TRUE
Set-MailboxRegionalConfiguration $Name -DateFormat "dd-MMM-yy"
-TimeZone "W. Europe Standard Time"
}
</ApiCall>
</Feature>
</Configuration>
```

To enable the cmdlet extension agent, you run the following PowerShell command on each Mailbox server:

```
[PS] C:\> Enable-CmdletExtensionAgent "Scripting Agent"
```

The actual provisioning of the mailbox and the archive mailbox takes place on the Mailbox server, so you must copy the XML files to all Exchange servers in your Exchange environment because you never know where a specific command is executed.

When you run the New-Mailbox or the Enable-Mailbox command, an archive mailbox is automatically created, the language is set, and the regional settings are set.

Mailbox Delegation

Another important item to be aware of is the mailbox delegation, a feature that is widely used in a manager and assistant scenario where the manager needs to grant their assistant access to their mailbox. There are three types of mailbox delegation in Exchange:

1. *Send As permission*: The assistant can send a message from the manager's mailbox. The recipient will see only the manager as the sender of the email message.

2. *Send on Behalf permission*: The assistant can send email on behalf of the manager. The recipient of the message will see that the message was sent on behalf of the manager, and the sender of the message will be shown as "Assistant on behalf of manager."

3. *Full Access permission*: The assistant has full access (read, write, edit, and delete) to all items in the manager's entire mailbox.

   For example, if Philip Mortimer is a manager at BookWorkx and Sarah Summertown is his assistant, you can follow these commands to set the different permissions:

   a. To grant Full Access permissions to user Sarah on Philip's mailbox using EMS, you can use the following command:

   ```
   [PS] C:\> Add-MailboxPermission -Identity Philip -User
   Sarah -AccessRights FullAccess -InheritanceType all
   ```

   b. To grant the Send As permission to user Sarah on Philip's mailbox using EMS, you can use the following command:

   ```
   [PS] C:\> Add-ADPermission -Identity Philip -User
   Sarah -ExtendedRights "Send As"
   ```

    c. To grant the Send on Behalf permission to user Sarah on Philip's mailbox using EMS, you can use the following command:

```
[PS] C:\> Set-Mailbox -Identity Philip
-GrantSendOnBehalfTo Sarah
```

When Sarah has Full Access on Philip's mailbox and opens her mailbox, Philip's mailbox will automatically appear as an additional mailbox in her Outlook. The process that is responsible for this automatic appearance is called "automapping" and is part of the Autodiscover process. Now Sarah can use her own mailbox, but when she sends an email, she can select her manager (i.e., Philip Mortimer) in the From field.

Note   When a user is only granted Full Access permission to a mailbox, this user cannot send email messages from the mailbox they have been granted permission to. To achieve this, the user must have Send As or Send on Behalf permission.

Instead of assigning permissions to a mailbox-enabled user directly, it is also possible to assign permissions to a security group. When a mailbox-enabled user or a mail-enabled user is added to the security group, the permissions are automatically assigned.

For example, suppose there is a shared mailbox for HR staff called "HR@Proexchangeadmin.com" and there is a security group called "All HR Employees" where all HR staff is a member of. To assign Full Access permissions to this security group, execute the following command:

```
[PS] C:\> Add-MailboxPermission -Identity HR -User "All HR
Employees" -AccessRights FullAccess -InheritanceType all
```

Now when user Peter is added to this security group, he automatically inherits the Full Access permission on the HR mailbox.

Note Automapping does not work when assigning permissions using security groups.

Moving Mailboxes

There are situations where you want to move mailboxes between Exchange servers. Moving mailboxes is an online process and has little or no impact on users.

Moving mailboxes is a process taken care of by the Mailbox Replication service or MRS, and MRS runs on every Exchange server. The name of the service is MSExchangeMailboxReplication.exe, not to be confused with the server MSExchangeRepl.exe, which is part of the Database Availability Group. This service has nothing to do with the Mailbox Replication service.

Moving mailboxes can be

- *Local mailbox moves*: Mailboxes are moved between mailbox databases in the same Exchange organization.

- *Cross-forest moves*: Mailboxes are moved between Exchange servers in different Exchange organizations in different Active Directory forests, often referred to as a cross-forest migration.

- *Remote mailbox moves*: Mailboxes are moved between on-premises mailbox databases and mailbox databases in Exchange Online. This kind of mailbox move is only available in an Exchange hybrid configuration.

Moving mailboxes using MRS can be across multiple Exchange versions as shown in Figure 3-1. Please note that this technique is similar in Exchange 2013, Exchange 2016, and Exchange 2019.

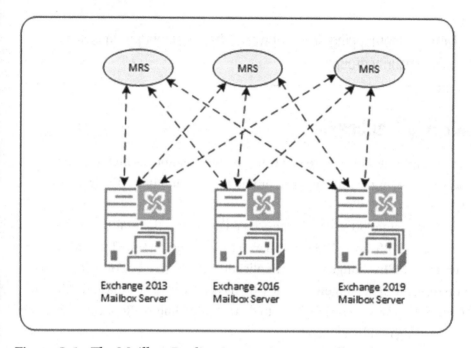

Figure 3-1. *The Mailbox Replication service across all Exchange versions*

Moving mailboxes is an asynchronous process. It is triggered by the New-MoveRequest command and is running in the background on an Exchange server in the organization. The New-MoveRequest command moves mailboxes individually. It is possible to create batches with move requests, making it possible to process large amounts of mailbox moves in just one batch.

When a New-MoveRequest command is executed, a move request is registered in the system mailbox of the active copy of the mailbox database. MRS periodically scans this system mailbox, and when found, MRS starts moving the mailbox. When the move request has not been picked up by MRS, it shows the status "queued" when executing the Get-MoveRequest command.

While the move requests are registered in the system mailbox of the source mailbox database, MRS itself writes status information to the Migration system mailbox (Migration.8f3e7716-2011-43e4-96b1-aba62d229136, found in every Exchange organization) to keep track of all mailbox moves, even when the original source mailbox database has been deleted.

MRS copies the mailbox content from the source database to the target database. As such, the user can continue to work with the mailbox in the source database. This is extremely useful when moving mailboxes of several gigabytes in size.

When the move reaches 95%, MRS locks the mailbox and checks the mailbox for any changes like new messages or changed messages. If any changes are found, they are copied to the new location. MRS changes the Active Directory attributes and deletes the mailbox in the source database, and Outlook continues to work with the mailbox in the new mailbox database.

Finalizing the mailbox move can be fully automatic, but it can also be scheduled using the -CompleteAfter option when executing a New-MoveRequest command. What I normally recommend is moving mailboxes during office hours but finalize the moves off-business hours. This way the move is finalized overnight, Active Directory replication can take place, and the next morning when the user logs on, Outlook automatically connects to the "new" mailbox.

To move the mailbox of user Glenn from mailbox database MDB01 to mailbox database MDB04 on another Exchange server and finalize it overnight, execute the following command:

```
[PS] C:\> New-MoveRequest -Identity "Glenn Kendall"
-TargetDatabase MDB04 -AllowLargeItems -BadItemLimit 10
-CompleteAfter "03/21/2023 02:00 AM"

WARNING: When an item can't be read from the source database
or it can't be written to the destination database, it will be
considered corrupted. By specifying a non-zero BadItemLimit,
you are requesting Exchange not copy such items to the
destination mailbox. At move completion, these corrupted items
will not be available at the destination mailbox.
```

What happens is that when MRS finds a corrupt message, it will stop moving the mailbox. When using the -BadItemLimit option, MRS will skip corrupted messages and continue moving the mailbox. But when the threshold is reached and another corrupt item is found, it will stop moving mailboxes.

To view the status of a move request, you can use the Get-MoveRequest and Get-MoveRequestStatistics commands. When combining with the select command, it is possible to retrieve only specific values, for example:

```
[PS] C:\> Get-MoveRequest | Get-MoveRequestStatistics | select
DisplayName, status, BadItemsEncountered, BytesTransferred,
PercentComplete
```

This will retrieve only the name of the mailbox being moved, the status of the move, the number of corrupt items that have been encountered, the number of bytes that have been moved, and the percentage of the move.

When moving mailboxes, both the primary mailbox and the archive mailbox are moved to the target database. It is possible to move the archive mailbox only using the -ArchiveOnly option. The -ArchiveTargetDatabase option can be used to locate the archive mailbox on a different mailbox database.

Note   The Exchange Admin Center does not work with individual mailbox moves. Instead, migration batches are used. So the previous example of moving one mailbox using the New-MoveRequest command does not show up in EAC.

In Exchange 2019, migration batches are used. A migration batch is a batch of move requests that are managed as a whole. You can create a CSV file containing the individual mailboxes that must be moved and start and stop the batch with just one command. Also, the migration batch can send out notification messages with detailed information regarding the moves.

The CSV file can contain one or two columns. The first column indicates the mailbox that must be moved; the second column indicates the mailbox type. A typical CSV file can look like this:

```
EmailAddress,MailboxType
user1@proexchangeadmin.com,Primary
user2@proexchangeadmin.com,Archive
user3@proexchangeadmin.com,PrimaryAndArchive
user4@proexchangeadmin.com,PrimaryAndArchive
```

To create and start a new migration batch that will read a CSV file, send notification messages to the administrator, and move the mailboxes to either mailbox database MDB03 or MDB04, execute the following commands in EMS:

```
[PS] C:\> New-MigrationBatch -local -Name "Move user mailboxes"
-CSVData ([System.IO.File]::ReadAllBytes("C:\Scripts\Mailboxes.
csv")) -NotificationEmails "admin@proexchangeadmin.com"
-TargetDatabases MDB03,MDB04
[PS] C:\> Start-MigrationBatch -Name "Move user mailboxes"
```

The replication service will send out status request messages to the recipients mentioned in the -NotificationEmails option. This notification message will show how long the batch is running, the number of mailboxes, and a CSV file containing details about the status of the individual mailboxes being moved.

The migration batch will trigger individual move requests, so you can check the status of the migration batch using the Get-MigrationBatch command, and you can check the individual moves using the Get-MoveRequest command. You can finalize the migration batch using the Complete-MigrationBatch command, which completes the entire batch, but you can also finalize individual move requests using the Resume-MoveRequest command.

To finalize the entire migration batch, execute the following command in Exchange PowerShell:

```
[PS] C:\> Complete-MoveRequest -Identity "Move user mailboxes"
-Confirm:$false
```

To finalize an individual move request as part of a migration batch, use the Get-MoveRequest command to check the move you want to finalize and execute the following command in Exchange PowerShell:

```
[PS] C:\> Resume-MoveRequest -identity "Percy Blake"
-confirm:$false
```

Note   The -confirm:$false option is to suppress the "Are you sure you want to perform this action?" message when executing the command.

Importing and Exporting Mailboxes to PST Files

Importing and exporting mailboxes is like moving mailboxes, except that a PST is involved instead of a mailbox. Importing and exporting PST files is an asynchronous process, also carried out by the Mailbox Replication service.

By default, no one can import or export mailboxes in Exchange; these permissions have not been granted. To grant this permission, the management role "Mailbox Import Export" needs to be assigned to a user. To do this for the administrator, execute the following command in EMS:

```
[PS] C:\> New-ManagementRoleAssignment –Role "Mailbox Import
Export" –User "Administrator"
```

To effectuate this new permission, you must log off and log on again.

When exporting mailboxes to a PST file, the PST file needs to be stored on a file share. The Universal Security Group "Exchange Trusted Subsystem" needs permissions on this file share. To export a mailbox to this file share, this group must have Read/Write permission; to import a PST from this file share, this group must have Read permission.

To export a mailbox to the file share, execute the following command in EMS:

```
[PS] C:\> New-MailboxExportRequest -Mailbox S.Summertown
-FilePath \\FS01\PSTFiles\Summertown.pst
```

The New-MailboxExportRequest command accepts the -BadItemLimit and -LargeItemItemLimit options, like moving mailboxes to prevent halting the export when corrupt items or large items are encountered.

An interesting option when exporting mailboxes to a PST file is the -ContentFilter option. This option uses an OPATH filter to filter out content and thus export only a specific subset of the mailbox. An example of an export where only Exchange 2016 and author information before January 1, 2018, is filtered could be

```
[PS] C:\> New-MailboxExportRequest -Mailbox S.Summertown
-ContentFilter "(Body -like 'Exchange 2019') -and (body -like
'author') -and (Received -lt '04/01/2023')" -FilePath \\FS01\
PSTFiles\Summertown-Exchange2019.pst
```

To export an archive mailbox to a PST file, the -IsArchive option can be used.

To import a PST file in a mailbox, the New-MailboxImportRequest command can be used. Like exporting a mailbox and moving a mailbox, this is also functionality that is performed by the Mailbox Replication service. To import a PST file from a file share, execute the following command in EMS:

```
[PS] C:\> New-MailboxImportRequest -Mailbox S.Summertown
-FilePath \\FS01\PSTFiles\Summertown.pst
```

It is possible to monitor the progress of a mailbox import or export by using the Get-MailboxImportRequestStatistics or Get-MailboxExportRequestStatistics command. By default, it does not reveal much information, but when using the Format-List command, all parameters are returned on the console. A subset of this can be returned by using the -Select option. To request the statistics of the previous mailbox import request, execute a command similar to

```
[PS] C:\>Get-MailboxImportRequest | Get-
MailboxImportRequestStatistics | select TargetAlias, status,
BadItemsEncountered, BytesTransferred, PercentComplete
```

Importing, exporting, and moving mailboxes are limited by the hardware resources available to Exchange. When there are not enough resources available, the import, export, or move is stalled, and a status detail is shown when executing a statistics command. Most common status details are

- StalledDueToTarget_Processor

- StalledDueToTarget_DiskLatency

- StalledDueToTarget_ContentIndexing

- StalledDueToTarget_MdbReplication

While annoying and not good for performance, this is not something to worry about immediately. When resources become available again, MRS will automatically resume where it was halted.

Resource Mailboxes

A resource mailbox is a normal mailbox with the exception that it does not belong to a normal user; instead, it belongs to a resource. In Exchange, there are two types of resource mailboxes:

- *Room mailbox*: Represents a (conference) room in your office

- *Equipment mailbox*: Represents some sort of equipment, like a beamer, that's not tied to a conference room

A resource mailbox represents something that can be booked by regular users when scheduling meetings. Since these resources cannot log onto the mailbox, the accompanying user account in Active Directory is disabled. They also do not require any user license.

However, they are quite useful. It is possible to use a resource mailbox to schedule meetings, such as a conference room, thereby indicating when this resource is available. Like a regular email, this meeting request is sent to the resource mailbox, but in contrast, the request is automatically accepted when the resource is available. The response, whether the meeting is accepted or not, is sent back to the sender to confirm that availability. To create this type of room mailbox—say, with a capacity of 20 persons—you use the following command:

```
[PS] C:\> New-Mailbox -Room -UserPrincipalName ConfRoom2ndFloor@
Proexchangeadmin.com -Alias ConfRoom2ndFloor -Name "Conference
Room 2nd Floor" -ResourceCapacity 20 -Database "MDB01"
-ResetPasswordOnNextLogon $true -Password (ConvertTo-
SecureString -String 'P@$$w0rd1' -AsPlainText -Force)
```

Creating an equipment mailbox is similar; the only difference is that there is less to configure. There is no location, no phone number, and no capacity to enter, but otherwise the process is the same. To create an equipment mailbox for a Sony Beamer, you can use the following command:

```
[PS] C:\> New-Mailbox -Equipment -UserPrincipalName SonyBeamer@
Proexchangeadmin.com -Alias SonyBeamer -Name "Sony Beamer"
-Database "MDB01" -ResetPasswordOnNextLogon $true -Password
(ConvertTo-SecureString -String 'P@$$w0rd1' -AsPlainText -Force)
```

Resource mailboxes do not show up in the Exchange Admin Center under the regular mailboxes. Instead, select the Resources tab to view all resource mailboxes.

Shared Mailboxes

A shared mailbox is a mailbox that has a user account, but the user account is disabled. As such, a user cannot log onto a shared mailbox directly. To access a shared mailbox, a user must have appropriate permission (Full Access or Send As) to use this mailbox. Once the user has Full Access, they can log onto their own mailbox and open the shared mailbox as a secondary mailbox.

A shared mailbox for the BookWorkx Sales Department could be created using the following command:

```
[PS] C:\> New-Mailbox -Shared -UserPrincipalName Sales@
Proexchangeadmin.com -Alias Sales -Name "Sales"
-DisplayName "BookWorkx Sales Department" -Database "MDB01"
-OrganizationalUnit "OU=Functional Accounts, OU=Accounts,
DC=ProExchangeAdmin, DC=COM" -ResetPasswordOnNextLogon
$true -Password (ConvertTo-SecureString -String 'P@$$w0rd1'
-AsPlainText -Force)
```

To grant all users in the "Functional Accounts" Organizational Unit Full Access permission for this shared mailbox, you could use the following command:

```
[PS] C:\> Get-Mailbox –OrganizationalUnit "Functional Accounts"
| ForEach {Add-MailboxPermission -Identity Sales –User
$_.Identity -AccessRights FullAccess -InheritanceType all}
```

To grant all users in the "Functional Accounts" Organizational Unit Send As permission for this shared mailbox, you could use the following command:

```
[PS] C:\> Get-Mailbox -OrganizationalUnit "Functional Accounts"
| ForEach {Add-ADPermission -Identity Sales -User $_.Identity
-ExtendedRights "Send As"}
```

To check if this command was successful, you can use the following command:

```
[PS] C:\> Get-Mailbox -Identity Sales | Get-MailboxPermission |
Select Identity, User, AccessRights
```

This command will show a list of all users who have permission on this mailbox.

Linked Mailboxes

A linked mailbox differs from a regular mailbox in that it does not have an active user account in Active Directory. Instead, it is used by a normal user, and that user is created in another Active Directory forest. There is a forest trust between the forest holding the user account and the forest holding the mailbox. Thus, the user account is linked to the mailbox. The forest that holds the Exchange servers, and thus the mailboxes, is sometimes also referred to as the resource forest. The other forest is referred to as the account forest.

A regular mailbox always has an accompanying user account, but when a linked mailbox is used, this accompanying user account is disabled. For this scenario, you need some sort of provisioning process. This is how the user account in forest A and the mailbox in forest B are linked, as can be seen in Figure 3-2. Note that the Active Directory forest A does not have any Exchange servers installed, and thus the user accounts do not have any Exchange-related properties. Since there is a trust relationship, users in forest A can log on and seamlessly access their mailboxes in forest B.

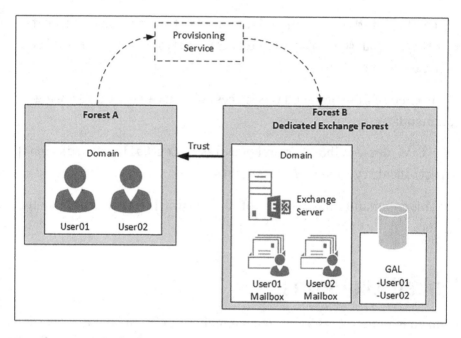

Figure 3-2. *A linked mailbox scenario consists of an account forest A and an Exchange forest B*

The advantage of this arrangement is that it makes it possible to have multiple, fully separated Active Directory forests where the user accounts reside but have only one Exchange forest with all the mailboxes of all the (trusted) Active Directory accounts.

You may want to implement linked mailboxes if you have multiple Active Directory forests holding user accounts governed by strict security policies that do not allow multiple departments in one Active Directory forest. Using linked mailboxes makes it possible to create one Exchange environment for multiple, fully separated departments. While this might seem strange from an Active Directory point of view, when viewed from an Exchange perspective, it is a fully supported scenario.

Provisioning linked mailboxes is a bit more work since it involves creating a user account in the account forest and a user account and mailbox in the resource forest.

In the following PowerShell examples, which are run from an Exchange 2019 server in the resource forest, a new resource mailbox is created for user John Smith. The account forest is "accounts.local" and the resource forest where Exchange 2019 is installed is "resources.local." The name of the Domain Controller is DC1.accounts.local:

```
[PS] C:\> $AccCred = Get-Credential accounts\administrator
[PS] C:\> New-ADUser -Name "John Smith" -SAMAccountName
JohnS -Server DC1.accounts.local -Credential $AccCred
-UserPrincipalName Johns@proexchangeadmin.com -GivenName John
-Surname Smith -DisplayName "John Smith" -Path "OU=Accounts,
DC=accounts,DC=com" -AccountPassword $SecurePassword
```

When the user account is created, the mailbox in the resource forest can be created. The LinkedMasterAccount property links the new mailbox in the resource forest to the user account in the account forest:

```
[PS] C:\> $AccCred = Get-Credential resources\administrator
[PS] C:\> New-Mailbox -Name "John Smith"
-LinkedDomainController DC1.accounts.local -LinkedMasterAccount
"John Smith" -OrganizationalUnit "OU=Accounts,DC=resources,
DC=local" -UserPrincipalName johns@resources.local
-LinkedCredential $AccCred -DisplayName "John Smith"
-FirstName John -LastName Smith -PrimarySmtpAddress
Johns@proexchangeadmin.com
```

Note   These procedures have not been changed since Exchange 2010 and can still be used in Exchange 2019.

Managing Groups

In Active Directory, there are two types of groups:

- *Security group*: Used for granting permissions to users or other groups that are members of this group.

- *Distribution Group*: Used for distributing email to users or other groups that are members of this group.

Before Exchange 2019 can use these groups, the groups must be mail-enabled. When a group is mail-enabled, all Exchange-related properties are set, and you can start using the group for distributing email messages.

Note   Both a security group and a Distribution Group can be mail-enabled. As such, you can use a security group for mail-related purposes. On the other hand, a Distribution Group cannot be used for granting permission to resources, as you can with a security group. If you want to grant permission to a Distribution Group, you must first convert it to a security group using PowerShell or the Active Directory Users and Computers (ADUC) MMC snap-in.

In Exchange, it is possible to create a new Distribution Group, as well as to mail-enable a Distribution Group or security group that exists in Active Directory.

In Active Directory, there are three types of groups:

- Domain local groups

- Global groups

- Universal groups

When it comes to Exchange, only universal groups are used. The primary subject of this section is the universal Distribution Group.

Create a New Distribution Group

To create a new Distribution Group in Active Directory and automatically mail-enable it, you can use the following command:

```
[PS] C:\> New-DistributionGroup -Name "Management"
-OrganizationalUnit Groups
```

To create a new security group in Active Directory and automatically mail-enable it, you can add the -Type Security option to the previous command:

```
[PS] C:\> New-DistributionGroup -Name "Management"
-OrganizationalUnit Groups -Type Security
```

Mail-Enable an Existing Group

An existing group in Active Directory (either Distribution Group or security group) can be mail-enabled as well. To do this, you can use the following command:

```
[PS] C:\> Enable-DistributionGroup -Identity AllEmployees
-Alias AllEmployees
```

If the existing group in Active Directory has a non-universal group scope, an error message is displayed saying, "You can't mail-enable this group because it isn't a universal group. Only a universal group can be mail-enabled."

So, before an existing group can be mail-enabled, its group scope needs to be converted to universal. This can be achieved using the following command:

```
[PS] C:\> Set-ADGroup -Identity AllEmployees -GroupScope
Universal
```

Once converted, the group can be mail-enabled.

Manage Group Membership

Adding or removing a member to or from a Distribution Group is straightforward. To add a member to a Distribution Group, just enter the following command:

```
[PS] C:\> Add-DistributionGroupMember -Identity AllEmployees
-Member "Colonel Olrik"
```

Removing a member from a Distribution Group is similar:

```
[PS] C:\> Remove-DistributionGroupMember -Identity AllEmployees
-Member "Colonel Olrik"
```

Instead of adding mailboxes as members of a Distribution Group, it is possible to add other Distribution Groups as a member, a process called nesting. The commands are identical. To add a Distribution Group called HR to the AllEmployees Distribution Group, you can use the following command:

```
[PS] C:\> Add-DistributionGroupMember -Identity AllEmployees -
Member "HR"
```

Group Membership Approval

Users can decide whether they are members of a Distribution Group. This can be useful for special-interest groups, but not for company-wide Distribution Groups. You do not want users to leave a Distribution Group like "All Employees" or to join certain Distribution Groups like "HR," for example.

Distribution Group membership approval has the following options:

- *Open*: Anyone can join or leave the Distribution Group without approval of the group manager.

- *Closed*: No one can leave or join the group. All requests will automatically be rejected.

- *Owner Approval*: The group manager must approve a request to join the group. This option is for joining only, needless to say, but the owner property on the group must be set for this to work.

Note   Mail-enabled security groups are closed.

The New-DistributionGroup cmdlet has the –MemberJoinRestriction and –MemberDepartRestriction options to control group membership behavior. To create a new Distribution Group called "All Employees" where no users can automatically join or leave, you can use the following command:

```
[PS] C:\> New-DistributionGroup -Name "All Employees"
-OrganizationalUnit Groups -MemberDepartRestriction Closed
-MemberJoinRestriction Closed
```

An interesting option is the ApprovalRequired. When this is used and a user wants to join the Distribution Group, a request message is sent to the manager or owner of the Distribution Group. For example, suppose we create a Distribution Group called "Exchange Authoring," with the ApprovalRequired set for the join restriction:

```
[PS] C:\> New-DistributionGroup -Name "Exchange Authoring"
-OrganizationalUnit Groups -MemberDepartRestriction
Closed -MemberJoinRestriction ApprovalRequired -ManagedBy
proexchange\sarah
```

Now, when user Professor Labrousse wants to join this Distribution Group, a message is sent to the manager of the group, and the manager (Sarah in this example) must approve the membership request as shown in Figure 3-3.

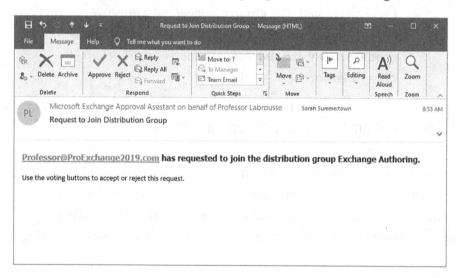

Figure 3-3. *A request is sent to the owner of the Distribution Group*

Group membership for a regular Distribution Group is static: you must manually add or remove members. For large organizations, this can be quite some administrative work. Instead of using regular Distribution Groups, you can use dynamic Distribution Groups (DDGs).

Dynamic Distribution Groups

A dynamic Distribution Group is like a regular Distribution Group, but group membership is dynamically determined, based on certain properties of the mailboxes.

For example, you can create a dynamic Distribution Group called "All Employees" that contains all recipients (i.e., mailboxes, public folders, contacts, and other Distribution Groups) that have the value "ProExchangeAdmin" in their company attribute.

When the New-DynamicDistributionGroup is used, you cannot set the -ManagedBy option, although this option is shown on the console when the group is created. You must use the Set-DynamicDistributionGroup cmdlet to set this option.

To create a new dynamic Distribution Group and set the ManagedBy option, execute the following commands in Exchange PowerShell:

```
[PS] C:\> New-DynamicDistributionGroup -Name "All Employees"
-IncludedRecipients AllRecipients -OrganizationalUnit Groups
-ConditionalCompany "ProExchangeAdmin"
[PS] C:\> Set-DynamicDistributionGroup -Identity "All
Employees" -ManagedBy ProExchange\Sarah
```

It is possible to include fewer recipients by using only the mailbox users in the -IncludedRecipients option and using the department filter instead of the company filter, for example:

```
[PS] C:\> New-DynamicDistributionGroup -Name "HR Employees"
-IncludedRecipients MailboxUsers -ConditionalDepartment "HR"
[PS] C:\> Set-DynamicDistributionGroup -Identity "HR Employees"
-ManagedBy Proexchange\Sarah
```

More granularities can be achieved by filtering on the custom attributes. In a migration scenario, you can stamp CustomAttribute1 with a value "Migrated" after a successful mailbox migration to Exchange 2019.

To create a dynamic Distribution Group that contains only mailboxes that are migrated to Exchange 2019, you can use something like this:

```
[PS] C:\> New-DynamicDistributionGroup -Name "Migrated
Mailboxes" -IncludedRecipients MailboxUsers
- ConditionalCustomAttribute1 "Migrated"
[PS] C:\> Set-DynamicDistributionGroup -Identity "Migrated
Mailboxes" -ManagedBy Administrator
```

To check which mailboxes are members of a dynamic Distribution Group, you must use the recipient filter functionality. Load the group into a variable and retrieve the recipients by using the filter, like this:

```
[PS] C:\> $HREmployees = Get-DynamicDistributionGroup "HR
Employees"
[PS] C:\> Get-Recipient -RecipientPreviewFilter $HREmployees.
RecipientFilter
```

This will provide a list of all recipients who are members of this dynamic Distribution Group.

Moderated Distribution Group

A moderated Distribution Group is a Distribution Group where messages that are intended for this group are first sent to a moderator and the moderator approves or rejects the message. After approval, the message is sent to all members of the Distribution Group.

To use the moderation function, the Distribution Group must be enabled for moderation by using the –ModerationEnabled option and using the –ModeratedBy option to set the moderator. These options are available on the New-DistributionGroup and the Set-DistributionGroup.

To enable moderation on a Distribution Group called "Finance" and set user Sarah Summertown as the moderator, you can use the following command:

```
[PS] C:\> Set-DistributionGroup -Identity Finance
-ModerationEnabled:$TRUE -ModeratedBy S.Summertown@
proexchangeadmin.com
```

When a user named Professor Labrousse, who is a member of the Finance Distribution Group, tries to send a message to members of this Distribution Group, a mail tip appears indicating the moderation of this Distribution Group, as shown in Figure 3-4.

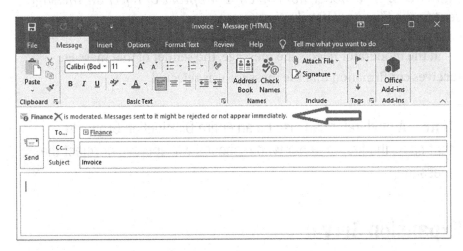

Figure 3-4. *A mail tip is shown, indicating moderation of the message*

When the professor sends the message, a confirmation message is first sent to the moderator, that is, Sarah Summertown, who finds an approval request when she logs onto her mailbox, as shown in Figure 3-5. When Sarah approves the message, it is delivered to members of this Distribution Group.

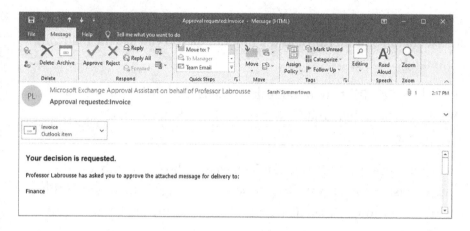

Figure 3-5. *The moderator can either approve or reject the message sent to the Finance Distribution Group*

If the moderator rejects the message, the sender of that message receives confirmation that the message was rejected.

Note   A moderator can also be an entire Distribution Group. In that case, the first member who responds will approve or reject the message.

Expansion Server

When a message is sent initially to a Distribution Group, it has only one recipient, the Distribution Group itself. The Transport service running on an Exchange server must determine the individual that message must be forwarded to. This process is known as expansion.

Distribution Group membership is static, based on the memberOf property of the mailboxes. Since a dynamic Distribution Group has no membership the way a regular Distribution Group has, and thus there are no properties set, an Active Directory query is used for retrieving the members of a dynamic Distribution Group.

An Expansion server is an Exchange 2019 Mailbox server that is responsible for expanding the Distribution Groups when it is processing messages. By default, no Expansion server is set for a Distribution Group, so any Mailbox server to which an email is delivered can perform the expansion.

Setting a dedicated Expansion server on a Distribution Group can be useful in a multi-site environment. Suppose ProExchangeAdmin.com has a Distribution Group in the United Kingdom with lots of members; it would make sense to use a Mailbox server at the local site for expansion purposes. This way, a message sent to this Distribution Group is dispatched to the UK Mailbox server before being expanded.

If the Expansion server is set, the Mailbox server accepting the message does not do any processing; it just routes the message to the Expansion server. If this server is, for some reason, not available, the message will not be delivered until the Expansion server again becomes available.

You can set the ExpansionServer property on a Distribution Group to an Exchange server in the United Kingdom called EXCH04 by using the following command:

```
[PS] C:\> Set-DistributionGroup -Identity "All Employees"
-ExpansionServer EXCH04
```

Note   This command can be used for both Distribution Groups and dynamic Distribution Groups.

Remove a Distribution Group

A Distribution Group can be removed as well as disabled. As with disabling mailboxes, disabling a Distribution Group retains the group in Active Directory but removes all Exchange properties, whereas removing a Distribution Group deletes the group from Active Directory as well.

To disable a Distribution Group, you can use the following command:

```
[PS] C:\> Disable-DistributionGroup -Identity "All Employees"
-Confirm:$FALSE
```

To remove a Distribution Group, you can use the following command:

```
[PS] C:\> Remove-DistributionGroup -Identity "All Employees"
-Confirm:$FALSE
```

Managing Contacts

In Exchange 2019 there are mail-enabled contacts and mail-enabled users. They are somewhat related, and in the Admin Console they are both listed under the Contacts tab. In the following two sections, we'll discuss the differences.

Mail-Enabled Contacts

A contact in Active Directory is not a security principal, as is a user account. It cannot be used to log on to the network and access network resources, as you can with a normal user account. Instead, a contact in Active Directory can be compared to a business card in a Rolodex: you can use it to store contact information.

In Exchange, a contact can also be mail-enabled, and as such it becomes a recipient. However, a mail-enabled contact in Exchange does not have a mailbox; it does have an external email address. For internal purposes, it might also have a local address, but when messages are sent to this local address, they are routed to the contact's external address.

A mail-enabled contact also appears in the Exchange address lists, and thus it can be selected as a recipient by clients.

To create a mail-enabled contact, you can use the following command:

```
[PS] C:\> New-MailContact -ExternalEmailAddress John@hotmail.
com -Name "John Smith" -OrganizationalUnit "OU=Contacts,
OU=Accounts, DC=ProExchangeAdmin, DC=COM" -FirstName John
-LastName Smith
```

When a contact already exists in Active Directory, it can be mail-enabled using the following command:

```
[PS] C:\> Enable-MailContact -Identity "Greg McGain"
-ExternalEmailAddress Greg@hotmail.com
```

When a user checks the "All Contacts" address list, all mail-enabled contacts show up. The contact can be selected for receiving an email message or for scheduling a meeting with the person, depending on the icon selected.

Mail-enabled contacts can be removed or disabled. When removed, the accompanying contact in Active Directory is deleted as well; when just disabled, the accompanying contact in Active Directory is preserved.

To disable a mail-enabled contact and keep the contact in Active Directory, you can use the following command:

```
[PS] C:\> Disable-MailContact -Identity "John Smith"
-Confirm:$FALSE
```

To remove a mail-enabled contact and remove the accompanying contact from Active Directory as well, you can use the following command:

```
[PS] C:\> Remove-MailContact -Identity "Greg McGain"
-Confirm:$FALSE
```

Mail-Enabled Users

In Exchange the concept of mail-enabled users (MEUs) is also known. A MEU is a regular user account in Active Directory with regular permissions that can log onto the network and access company resources. It does not have a mailbox in Exchange, but it has an external email address. With this external email address, it is a recipient in Exchange, and it also shows up in the address lists of Exchange.

A use case of a MEU is an external (financial) auditor that needs access to company resources to do their auditing work. The MEU is also visible in the address book and can be reached using a regular company SMTP address. When a message is sent to a MEU, it is forwarded to their external email address.

Note   When running Exchange hybrid, a remote mailbox is a MEU. It is a user account in Active Directory, but an external mailbox in Office 365.

A mail-enabled user can be created directly in Exchange using the New-MailUser command, or an existing account in Active Directory can be mail-enabled using the Enable-MailUser command.

To create a new mail-enabled user, execute the following command in EMS:

```
[PS] C:\> New-MailUser -Name "External Auditor"
-ExternalEmailAddress ExternalAuditor@gmail.com
-PrimarySMTPAddress ExternalAuditor@proexchangeadmin.com
-DisplayName "External Auditor" -FirstName External -LastName
Auditor -OrganizationalUnit "OU=Functional Accounts,
OU=Accounts, DC=ProExchangeAdmin, DC=COM" -Password (ConvertTo-
SecureString -String 'P@$$w0rd1' -AsPlainText -Force)
```

To mail-enable an existing Active Directory account, execute the following command in EMS:

```
[PS] C:\> Enable-MailUser -Identity "Financial Auditor"
-ExternalEmailAddress FinancalAuditor@gmail.com
-PrimarySMTPAddress FinancialAuditor@proexchangeadmin.com
```

Once created, the mail-enabled accounts appear in the Exchange address book.

Cumulative Updates and Security Updates

Every administrator knows they must patch their servers, and this is of course not different for an Exchange Server 2019 server. Windows Server 2019 is patched using Windows Update, WSUS, or maybe even SCCM. For the Exchange server, it is a bit different. Updates are released on a regular basis and called Cumulative Updates (CUs). CUs are not released through Windows Update but are only available as a separate download and need to be installed manually.

Microsoft also releases Security Updates (SUs) for Exchange 2019. These SUs contain fixes for vulnerabilities found in Exchange. On rare occasions Microsoft also releases new security features in a SU. SUs are released on an ad hoc basis. There's no cadence, but they are released when new vulnerabilities are found. In contrast to CUs, SUs are released through Windows Update (and thus WSUS) but are also available as a manual download.

CUs and SUs are discussed in the following sections.

Cumulative Updates

Microsoft releases Cumulative Updates for Exchange Server versions that are in standard support twice a year. This used to be four times a year, but due to customer complaints, the cadence is lowered to two times per year. This makes it easier to keep up to date for companies with large numbers of Exchange servers. When a version of Exchange Server is in extended support, like Exchange 2016, Cumulative Updates are no longer released, but only Security Updates when updates are marked as critical. Exchange 2013 is not supported at all as of April 2023, and no more SUs are released for Exchange 2013.

As the name implies, Cumulative Updates contain the current updates, but also all previously released updates. As such, every Cumulative Update is a full version of Exchange Server and can be used for a new or recovery installation of Exchange Server as well.

A Cumulative Update supports an in-place upgrade of Exchange Server, but only for that version of Exchange. It is not possible to perform an in-place upgrade of Exchange Server 2016 to Exchange Server 2019.

Note   Microsoft announced during Ignite in 2020 that the next version of Exchange Server (vNext) is going to support in-place upgrades from Exchange 2019, for a period of approximately two years following the release of vNext. The release of Exchange vNext is currently planned for October 2025.

Exchange Server 2019 is a .NET application, and Exchange 2019 only supports .NET Framework 4.8. Windows Server 2022 comes with .NET Framework 4.8 by default. Windows Server 2019 comes with .NET Framework 4.7.2, so for Windows Server 2019, .NET Framework 4.8 is a sperate install.

Although not specific for Exchange 2019, fellow MVP Michel de Rooij wrote an interesting blog post about Exchange Server CU upgrades and .NET dependencies. You can find this blog post on `https://eightwone.com/2017/12/21/upgrade-paths-for-cus-net/`.

As explained earlier in this book, you must prepare Active Directory before installing an Exchange server. Some Cumulative Updates for Exchange Server come with schema changes and configuration changes. It does not happen that often anymore, but especially when upgrading from a very old Cumulative Update, there is a chance the schema or configuration partition must be upgraded.

When needed, you can prepare Active Directory using the following commands:

```
Z:\> Setup.exe /PrepareSchema /IAcceptExchange
ServerLicenseTerms
Z:\> Setup.exe /PrepareAD /IAcceptExchangeServerLicenseTerms
Z:\> Setup.exe /PrepareDomain /IAcceptExchange
ServerLicenseTerms
```

In earlier versions of Exchange Server, it was important to install Exchange Server and updates in the following order:

- Internet-facing sites first

- Followed by non-Internet-facing sites

- Edge Transport server last

Although Exchange Server versions are getting more and more compatible with each other, the preceding list is still the recommended approach.

Installing a Cumulative Update on an Exchange server is straightforward. Use the setup application with the /Mode:Upgrade switch as shown in the following console output:

```
PS Z:\> .\Setup.EXE /Mode:Upgrade /IAcceptExchange
ServerLicenseTerms_DiagnosticDataOn

Microsoft Exchange Server 2019 Cumulative Update 13
Unattended Setup

Copying Files...
File copy complete. Setup will now collect additional
information needed for installation.

Languages
Management tools
Mailbox role: Transport service
Mailbox role: Client Access service
Mailbox role: Mailbox service
Mailbox role: Front End Transport service
Mailbox role: Client Access Front End service

Performing Microsoft Exchange Server Prerequisite Check

    Configuring Prerequisites                      COMPLETED
    Prerequisite Analysis                          COMPLETED

Configuring Microsoft Exchange Server

    Language Files                                 COMPLETED
    Restoring Services                             COMPLETED
    Language Configuration                         COMPLETED
    Exchange Management Tools                      COMPLETED
    Mailbox role: Transport service               COMPLETED
    Mailbox role: Client Access service           COMPLETED
```

```
Mailbox role: Mailbox service                    COMPLETED
Mailbox role: Front End Transport service        COMPLETED
Mailbox role: Client Access Front End service    COMPLETED
Finalizing Setup                                 COMPLETED
```

The Exchange Server setup operation completed successfully.

Exchange Setup preserved the required configurations during upgrade. More details can be found in Exchangesetup.log located in <SystemDrive>:\ExchangeSetupLogs folder. For more information, visit: https://aka.ms/PreserveExchangeConfig2019.

New in Exchange 2019 CU13 is the preservation of configuration files during installation of a new CU, a feature that was requested since the early days of Exchange.

Upgrading a single Exchange server with the latest Cumulative Update is straightforward; installing a Cumulative Update on members of a Database Availability Group (DAG) involves a bit more work. In a DAG, the workload is distributed dynamically, and you do not want any changes in workload during an upgrade to a newer Cumulative Update. To prevent this, members in a DAG need to be in maintenance mode during installation of a Cumulative Update, so a failover to an updated DAG member will not occur. Also, SMTP processing is suspended when in maintenance mode, so no activity will take place.

To place an Exchange Server 2019 Mailbox server in a DAG in maintenance mode, the following Exchange PowerShell commands can be used:

```
[PS] C:\> $Computer = $ENV:ComputerName
[PS] C:\> Set-ServerComponentState $Computer -Component
HubTransport -State Draining -Requester Maintenance
```

```
[PS] C:\> Redirect-Message -Server $Computer -Target <other
Exchange Server> -Confirm:$False
 # Prevent DAG member becoming PAM
[PS] C:\> Suspend-ClusterNode $Computer
 # Move all Mailbox Databases and prevent hosting copies on
current server
[PS] C:\> Set-MailboxServer $Computer
-DatabaseCopyActivationDisabledAndMoveNow $True
[PS] C:\> Set-MailboxServer $Computer
-DatabaseCopyAutoActivationPolicy Blocked

# Put the Exchange server in Maintenance Mode:
[PS] C:\> Set-ServerComponentState $Computer -Component
ServerWideOffline -State Inactive -Requester Maintenance
```

To check if a server is in suspended mode, the following Exchange
PowerShell command can be used as can be seen in the following
console output:

```
[PS] C:\> Get-ServerComponentState $Computer | ft
Component,State -Autosize
Component                 State
---------                 -----
ServerWideOffline         Inactive
HubTransport              Inactive
FrontendTransport         Inactive
Monitoring                  Active
RecoveryActionsEnabled      Active
AutoDiscoverProxy         Inactive
ActiveSyncProxy           Inactive
EcpProxy                  Inactive
EwsProxy                  Inactive
ImapProxy                 Inactive
```

OabProxy	Inactive
OwaProxy	Inactive
PopProxy	Inactive
PushNotificationsProxy	Inactive
RpsProxy	Inactive
RwsProxy	Inactive
RpcProxy	Inactive
XropProxy	Inactive
HttpProxyAvailabilityGroup	Inactive
ForwardSyncDaemon	Inactive
ProvisioningRps	Inactive
MapiProxy	Inactive
EdgeTransport	Inactive
HighAvailability	Inactive
SharedCache	Inactive
MailboxDeliveryProxy	Inactive
RoutingUpdates	Inactive
RestProxy	Inactive
DefaultProxy	Inactive
Lsass	Inactive
RoutingService	Inactive
E4EProxy	Inactive
CafeLAMv2	Inactive
LogExportProvider	Inactive

When the DAG members are in maintenance mode, the Cumulative Update can be installed. This is for a DAG member not different than for a single Exchange server.

After installation and reboot, the DAG members can be resumed using the following Exchange PowerShell commands:

```
[PS] C:\> $Computer = $ENV:ComputerName
[PS] C:\> Set-ServerComponentState $Computer -Component
ServerWideOffline -State Active -Requester Maintenance
[PS] C:\> Resume-ClusterNode $Computer
[PS] C:\> Set-MailboxServer $Computer
-DatabaseCopyActivationDisabledAndMoveNow $False
[PS] C:\> Set-MailboxServer $Computer
-DatabaseCopyAutoActivationPolicy Unrestricted
[PS] C:\> Set-ServerComponentState $Computer -Component
HubTransport -State Active -Requester Maintenance
[PS] C:\> Restart-Service MSExchangeTransport
[PS] C:\> Restart-Service MSExchangeFrontEndTransport
```

To verify all Exchange components are available again, the following Exchange PowerShell command can be used:

```
[PS] C:\> Get-ServerComponentState $Computer | ft
Component,State -Autosize

Component                State
---------                -----
ServerWideOffline        Active
HubTransport             Active
FrontendTransport        Active
Monitoring               Active
RecoveryActionsEnabled   Active
AutoDiscoverProxy        Active
ActiveSyncProxy          Active
EcpProxy                 Active
```

```
EwsProxy                        Active
ImapProxy                       Active
OabProxy                        Active
OwaProxy                        Active
PopProxy                        Active
PushNotificationsProxy          Active
RpsProxy                        Active
RwsProxy                        Active
RpcProxy                        Active
XropProxy                       Active
HttpProxyAvailabilityGroup      Active
ForwardSyncDaemon               Inactive
ProvisioningRps                 Inactive
MapiProxy                       Active
EdgeTransport                   Active
HighAvailability                Active
SharedCache                     Active
MailboxDeliveryProxy            Active
RoutingUpdates                  Active
RestProxy                       Active
DefaultProxy                    Active
Lsass                           Active
RoutingService                  Active
E4EProxy                        Active
CafeLAMv2                       Active
LogExportProvider               Active
```

When installing Exchange Cumulative Updates, the following tips or best practices can be used:

- Test a new CU before bringing it in production. This sounds logical, but there are a lot of customers still installing a new CU in their production environment without testing. Especially when using third-party solutions like backup and anti-virus, it is recommended to deploy in test first.

- Keep the Exchange servers up to date. Running the last or one last Cumulative Update is not a problem, but try to avoid running a Cumulative Version that is eight versions old.

- Always install the latest CU when installing a new server.

- Reboot the server before updating. Before rebooting, dismount the mailbox databases manually first. This will speed up the shutdown process of a reboot.

- Back up any customizations! Customizations like OWA branding are overwritten when installing a new Cumulative Update.

- Use an elevated command prompt when starting the upgrade.

- Disable any anti-virus product, including Windows Defender running on the Exchange server.

- Not mentioned when the upgrade is finished, but reboot the Exchange server after installing a Cumulative Update.

Security Updates

Security Updates (SUs) are released on an ad hoc basis, but only when a vulnerability is found and fixed. SUs are released through Windows Update, but they are also available as a separate download. Be careful; a SU is specific for a CU, so multiple versions of a SU are released. But SUs are only released for CUs that are supported, which are the current version and the previous version.

In 2022, Microsoft finally made some changes to the way SUs must be installed. In the past, SUs must be installed using elevated privileges, but this is no longer the case. You can just start the installation of a SU directly. This is shown in Figure 3-6.

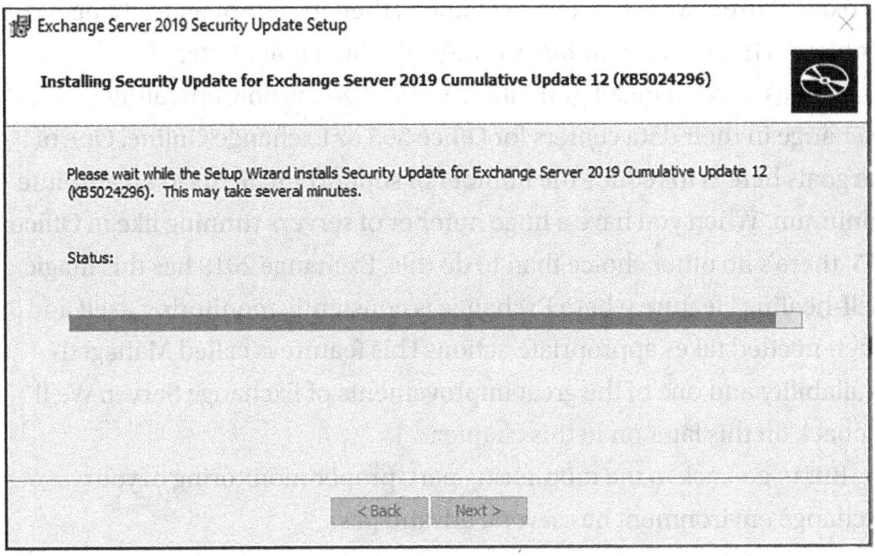

Figure 3-6. *Installing a Security Update on Exchange Server 2019 CU12*

Monitoring and Reporting

Monitoring your Exchange Server 2019 environment is a very important part of managing your Exchange Server environment. Monitoring the environment gives you an idea how the service is running, and if monitored properly, it can give you an indication of upcoming issues or bottlenecks. Unfortunately, most Exchange administrators start monitoring their environment when it's too late, that is, when end users start to complain or when they raise a support call at Microsoft.

In the early days, monitoring an Exchange server was nothing more than checking if a particular service was running, for example, the Information Store. If it was running, then everything was supposed to be okay. If users were not able to connect, then it was not an Exchange problem. The service running was the only thing that mattered.

Things have changed dramatically. Microsoft is now operating Exchange in their data centers for Office 365 or Exchange Online. One of the goals here is to reduce the number of support incidents to an absolute minimum. When you have a huge number of servers running like in Office 365, there's no other choice than to do this. Exchange 2019 has this magic "self-healing" feature where Exchange is constantly monitoring itself and when needed takes appropriate action. This feature is called Managed Availability and one of the great improvements of Exchange Server. We'll get back on this later on in this chapter.

But to go back to the monitoring part, proper monitoring of your Exchange environment has several advantages:

- As mentioned earlier, monitoring gives you a good insight into the functioning of your Exchange environment. If you monitor on a regular interval, you can also create a baseline that you can use as a comparison in case of issues.

- It is possible to perform trend analysis, which you can use to timely identify capacity issues for capacity management purposes. For example, when monitoring disk space on your Exchange servers, it is possible to identify mailbox growth and predict when you need additional disk space. You'll get a much better story when you go to management about additional disk space 12 months in advance. This is a much better story than going to management yelling, "I need additional disks and I need them now."

Monitoring your Exchange Server 2019 environment consists of a number of manual tools like the event log, Performance Monitor, or Exchange Management Shell, plus a number of automated tools like the new Managed Availability service, maybe combined with System Center Operations Manager.

Monitoring Tools

There are tools available for monitoring your Exchange environment on an ad hoc basis like the Event Viewer, the Performance Monitor MMC snap-in, or the Queue Viewer.

Besides giving an inside view on the behavior of the Exchange 2019 servers, these tools are also the beginning of troubleshooting your Exchange 2019 servers.

Event Viewer

The Event Viewer is available as long as Microsoft Windows is available. The Event Viewer is an MMC snap-in used to view the event logs that are available on every server.

Event logs can be separated into multiple different log categories:

- *Windows logs*: These are the default logs that are used by Windows and applications running on top of Windows. The Windows logs contain four separate logs:

- *Application log*: This is the log file where applications can store application-specific messages. These can be informational messages, warning messages, error messages, or critical messages. Exchange Server 2019 is an application that uses the Application event log extensively, and as such it is a very informative source of information.

- *Security log*: This log file is used by Windows to store security-related events like successful logon of accounts.

- *Setup log*: This log file is used by the setup application for various applications to store information regarding the installation of these applications. Installation of Windows roles or features is also logged in the setup log.

- *System log*: This log file is used by Windows to log all system-related events. These can be events from services running on the server.

- *Forwarded events*: Out of the box this is empty, but it can be configured to accept events from other servers to create an aggregate view of multiple Windows servers.

- *Applications and Services logs*: The Applications and Services logs is an interesting feature. It contains additional logs from hardware or applications and services like Internet Explorer, MSExchange Management, and Windows PowerShell, that is, applications and services that have a very close relationship with the operating system.

- *Exchange Management Shell*: The Exchange Management Shell (EMS) is running on top of Windows PowerShell. All commands that are run in EMS are logged in the MSExchange Management log. This can be very valuable to find if any issues or problems are available that prevent EMS from running properly.

- *Windows PowerShell*: PowerShell commands that are executed on the Windows server are logged in the Windows PowerShell log.

- *Microsoft*: This event log is known as the crimson event channel, an event channel on which Exchange Server 2019 relies very heavily. This will be explained later in this chapter.

The Application event log contains a lot of interesting information when it comes to Exchange. This is not only true for Exchange Server 2019, but all versions of Exchange Server have always written their events in the Application event log.

Informational events are general events that are written to the Application event log to log general information about the well-being of the Exchange server. As an example, Exchange Server 2019 regularly logs information about the Active Directory environment, specifically the Domain Controllers the Exchange server has access to. As we've seen in Chapter 1, Exchange Server relies heavily on Active Directory, so proper access to a Domain Controller is crucial for an Exchange server. This is logged in the Application event log as follows:

```
Log Name:       Application
Source:         MSExchange ADAccess
Date:           4/5/2023 9:53:18 PM
Event ID:       2080
Task Category:  Topology
Level:          Information
Keywords:       Classic
User:           N/A
Computer:       EXCH02.ProExchangeAdmin.com
Description:
        Process Microsoft.Exchange.Directory.TopologyService.exe
(PID=5792). Exchange Active Directory Provider has discovered
the following servers with the following characteristics:
 (Server name | Roles | Enabled | Reachability | Synchronized | GC
capable | PDC | SACL right | Critical Data | Netlogon | OS Version)
In-site:
DC01.ProExchangeAdmin.com     CDG 1 7 7 1 0 1 1 7 1
DC02.ProExchangeAdmin.com     CDG 1 7 7 1 0 1 1 7 1
DC03.ProExchangeAdmin.com     CDG 1 7 7 1 0 1 1 7 1
```

What does this entry specifically tell us? The Topology service that's running on the Exchange server has discovered three Domain Controllers in this environment:

- DC01.ProExchangeAdmin.com: This Domain Controller is in the same Active Directory site as where the Exchange server resides.

- DC02.ProExchangeAdmin.com: This Domain Controller is in the same Active Directory site as where the Exchange server resides.

- DC03.ProExchangeAdmin.com: This Domain Controller is in the same Active Directory site as where the Exchange server resides.

Each Domain Controller has its own view on Active Directory, which is described by the string right after the name of the Domain Controller, in this example CDG 1 7 7 1 0 1 1 7 1.

Quite cryptic, but a description of each entry is given in the same entry where it says: Server name | Roles | Enabled | Reachability | Synchronized | GC capable | PDC | SACL right | Critical Data | Netlogon | OS Version. Some of the characteristics speak for themselves, but I'd like to give a brief explanation here:

- *Server name*: The name of the Domain Controller being discovered.

- *Roles*: The roles a Domain Controller can have, which are Configuration Domain Controller (C), Regular Domain Controller (D), or Global Catalog server (G). When a hyphen (-) appears, it means that one particular role cannot be found on this Domain Controller.

- *Reachability*: This means how the Exchange server can reach the Domain Controller over the network via a regular TCP port:

  - 0x1 means the server is reachable as a Global Catalog server (via port 3268).

  - 0x2 means it is reachable as a Domain Controller (via port 389).

  - 0x4 means it is reachable as a Configuration Domain Controller (via also port 389).

Multiple functions are added so that a Domain Controller is reachable on all three roles; the end result will be 7 (1 + 2 + 4). An Exchange server should typically see and reach all roles of a Domain Controller. Since a firewall is not supported between an Exchange 2013 server and a Domain Controller, a value of 7 should be expected here.

- *Synchronized*: This value shows if the role is synchronized with other Domain Controllers in the network. It follows the Reachability column, and therefore a value of 7 should be considered normal as well.

- *GC capable*: Tells us if this server is a Global Catalog server or not.

- *PDC*: Tells us if this Domain Controller holds the PDC Emulator role (value 0x1) or not (value 0x0). There is only one Domain Controller in the entire organization holding the PDC Emulator role.

- *SACL right*: This column tells us whether DSAccess has the correct permissions to read the SACL (part of nTSecurityDescriptor) against that directory service.

- *Critical Data*: Tells us whether this server found its own computer object in the Configuration container of the Domain Controller listed in the Server name column. If you find a zero here, you most likely face an Active Directory replication issue.

- *Netlogon Check*: Shows whether DSAccess successfully connected to a Domain Controller's Net Logon service.

- *OS Version*: This column tells us if the correct version (minimal version) of the operating system is used at the Domain Controller. If it's Windows 2003 SP1 or higher, it lists 0x1 here; otherwise, it will list 0x0. Therefore, it should read 0x1 here.

Plenty of other entries are logged in the Application event log as well and are there for informational purposes. Warning messages, shown with a yellow exclamation mark icon, show potential issues that need attention, but sometimes Exchange 2019 is able to solve these issues automatically.

Error messages are shown with a red exclamation mark and do need attention and should be resolved, although immediate action is not always needed.

For example, when Exchange 2019 is not licensed, whether you have a trial license or are still in the 120-day grace period, event ID 8198 is logged as an error message:

```
Log Name:       Application
Source:         Microsoft-Windows-Security-SPP
Date:           4/5/2023 4:06:17 PM
Event ID:       8198
Task Category:  None
Level:          Error
Keywords:       Classic
User:           N/A
Computer:       EXCH02.ProExchangeAdmin.com
Description:
License Activation (slui.exe) failed with the following
error code:
hr=0x8007232B
```

Exchange Server 2019 continuously logs information in the Application event log. Checking this event log will give you more information regarding the functioning of your server, or you'll notice if there are any emerging issues.

Note   In all my years as an Exchange consultant, I've never seen an Exchange server that was completely free of warning messages and error messages in the Application event log. Even worse, if you start investigating issues using Google or Bing, you'll encounter official Microsoft knowledge base articles saying things like "This error message can be safely ignored." It's up to your troubleshooting skills of course, but there's no such thing as an "errorless Exchange server," and Exchange will happily survive error messages in the Application event log.

Crimson Channel

In Windows Server 2008, a new type of event log was introduced, the crimson channel event log. The crimson channel is a special event log where applications like Exchange can write certain types of events. At the same time, other services running on the same server can subscribe to a crimson channel to consume entries in this particular crimson channel.

The crimson channel can be found in the Event Viewer tool in the Applications and Services logs in the Microsoft/Exchange folder (see Figure 3-7).

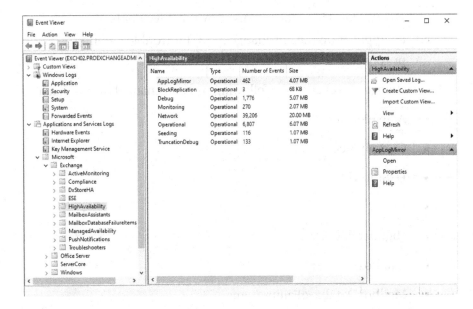

Figure 3-7. *The crimson channel for Exchange Server 2019*

Using a solution like the crimson channel, it is possible for one service or application to log a certain event, while another server reacts to this event. The Managed Availability service in Exchange 2019 is working according to these principles.

The Applications and Services logs category includes four subtypes:

- *Admin logs*: Events in the Admin logs are interesting for troubleshooting purposes.

- *Operational logs*: These events are for the more experienced system administrator since they require (a lot) more interpretation.

- *Analytic logs*: These logs are hidden and disabled by default, but events are stored here that trace an issue. Normally lots of events are written in these logs.

- *Debug logs*: These logs are used by the developers of an application (i.e., Exchange 2013) for troubleshooting purposes.

For Exchange Server 2019, the following crimson channels are available:

- ActiveMonitoring
- Compliance
- DxStoreHA
- ESE
- HighAvailability
- MailboxAssistant
- MailboxDatabaseFailureItems
- ManagedAvailability
- PushNotifications
- Troubleshooters

The HighAvailability channel contains information that is related to the startup and shutdown of the Microsoft Exchange Replication service and the components that run inside the Exchange Replication service such as the Active Manager and the Volume Shadow Copy Service (VSS) writer. This channel is also used by the Active Manager to log events related to the role monitoring and database actions such as mounting and dismounting of mailbox databases or the truncations of transaction log files. Also, events coming from the underlying failover clustering software are written in this channel.

For example, the AppLogMirror log in the HighAvailability channel shows all kinds of interesting information regarding the redundancy of mailbox databases within a Database Availability Group (DAG). Exchange is constantly monitoring the redundancy of its mailbox databases, and the results are written in this crimson channel. When all is well, Event ID 1104 is written, which is shown in Figure 3-8.

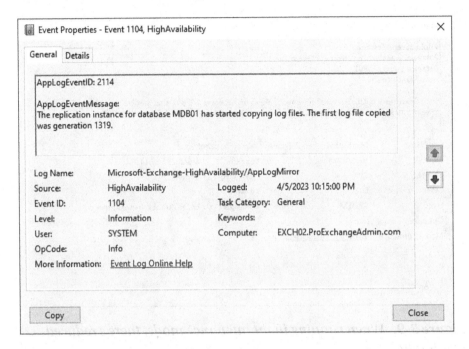

Figure 3-8. *Mailbox database redundancy written in the crimson channel*

Not visible in Figure 3-8, but there's a lot more information regarding the mailbox database copies when you scroll down, like the lowest available log file present, volume information where the mailbox database copies are stored, (free) disk space information, backup information, and content index information to name a few.

When running in maintenance mode, for example, when installing a new Cumulative Update, the server is not operating a passive copy, and the DAG and thus the availability are running in a degraded state. If this is the case, Event ID 1106 is logged in the AppLogMirror log in the HighAvailability crimson channel saying the database availability health check failed and that the availability is reduced as shown in Figure 3-9.

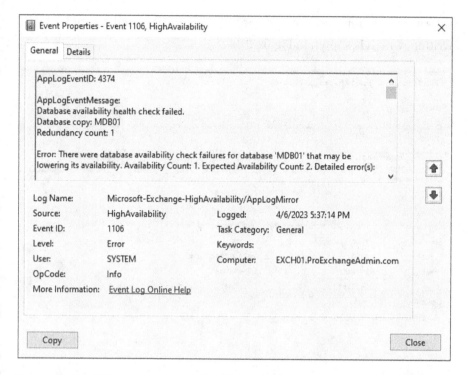

Figure 3-9. *When running in maintenance mode, there's reduced availability*

We'll see more of the crimson channel in the "Managed Availability" section of this chapter.

Performance Monitoring

When end users start calling your help desk about performance issues, you most likely are getting into trouble. But how do you know the server is experiencing performance issues? When you log on to the console of the Exchange server and it is responding sluggishly, you know there's something wrong, but a sluggish response is not exactly something that can be precisely monitored.

Task Manager

The Task Manager of Windows will give you a good first glance of the performance of an Exchange server. To open the Task Manager, right-click the task bar and select Task Manager.

When you select the Performance tab, there are multiple options available:

- *CPU*: This will give a quick overview of the CPU utilization of the server. Don't be alarmed when it spikes to 80%, but when the CPU utilization is constantly over 80%, this is a good indication the server is suffering from performance issues.

- *Memory*: Selecting this option will show the amount of memory being used by the server. The total amount of memory will be shown as well as the amount of memory in use and available. Please note that the committed bytes of memory can be larger than the physical amount of memory; this is because of virtual memory, which can be temporarily stored on disk when it is not needed.

- *Ethernet*: For every network card (NIC) that's available in your Exchange server, an additional NIC option is shown. Network speeds for Send and Receive are shown, including the adapter name, the connection type, and the IPv4 and IPv6 addresses.

Again, this will give you a quick overview of the performance of your Exchange server. Also available in the Task Manager is the Resource Monitor, which will give you more information. To open it just click Open Resource Monitor at the bottom of the Task Manager.

The Resource Monitor, shown in Figure 3-10, will also give a brief overview of what's happening in your Exchange server, but the Resource Monitor also includes the hard disk, something that's not available in the Task Manager. Interesting to see is the separation into the various processes on the server, so you'll see immediately which process is consuming the most resources. The Overview tab gives a brief overview of all different subjects. The tabs for CPU, Memory, Disk, and Network give an overview of these components.

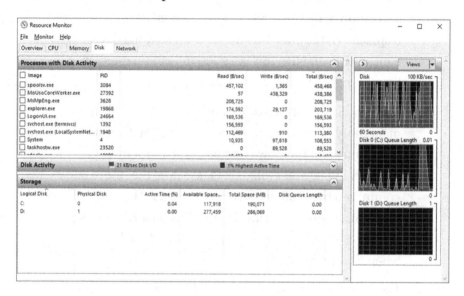

Figure 3-10.   *The resource monitoring of an Exchange 2019 server*

Memory and disk have a close relationship in an Exchange server. The more memory an Exchange server has, the more mailbox data it can keep in memory. As a result you'll see fewer disk I/O (Input/Output) operations when there's sufficient memory. The other way around, if the server lacks enough memory, you'll see a dramatic increase in disk I/O. If this is the case, most likely you'll see an increase in CPU usage as well because the CPU needs to coordinate all traffic flowing through the Exchange server.

Performance Monitor Tool

All objects, including the Exchange 2019 object, have performance monitor counters that can be used for usage monitoring. The tool that can be used to monitor these counters is called the Performance Monitor or Perfmon. The Performance Monitor tool can display data in real time, and it can log data for longer-term monitoring.

Real-Time Monitoring

The Performance Monitor can be used to view performance data in real time, which means you can open the tool, select some counters, and monitor the performance on the spot.

You can open the Performance Monitor by typing perfmon.msc in the Start menu. Once open you'll see the following sections, shown in Figure 3-11, in the navigation pane on the left-hand side:

- *Monitoring Tools*: This section of the Performance Monitor shows the real-time results.

- *Data Collector Sets*: This section contains the logging option where you can create custom sets of objects that need to be monitored.

- *Reports*: Reports are constantly generated and stored on the local hard disk of the Exchange 2013 server

in C:\Program Files\Microsoft\Exchange Server\
V15\Logging\Diagnostics \DailyPerformanceLogs.
From there these log files are used by the Managed
Availability service for constant checking of the server's
performance.

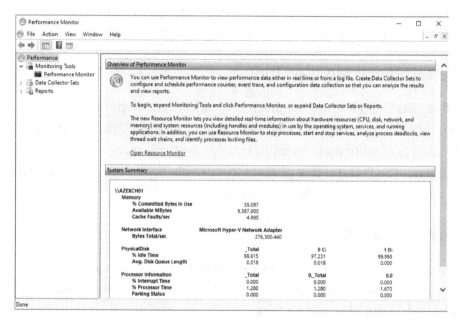

Figure 3-11. *Initial screen of the Performance Monitor tool*

To start monitoring, select Performance Monitor in the navigation
pane and click the + icon in the results pane. A new window is shown
where you can select the server that you want to monitor. This can be the
local computer you're logged onto, but it can also be a remote Exchange
server. In the scroll-down box below the computer name, you can select
the object that you want to monitor. I haven't counted them, but on a
typical Exchange 2019 server, there are hundreds of objects that can be
selected.

Each object on a Windows server and thus on an Exchange server can be monitored. Interesting objects to monitor can be

- Logical Disk

- Memory

- MSExchange Active Manager

- MSExchange Database

- MSExchange Replication Server

- MSExchangeFrontEndTransport SmtpReceive

- Network Adapter

- Physical Disk

- Processor

An object can have one or multiple instances that can be monitored. For example, the "MSExchangeFrontEndTransport SmtpReceive" object has the following available instance options, also shown in Figure 3-12:

- _total

- <All instances>

- Client frontend ams-exch02

- Default frontend ams-exch02

- Outbound proxy frontend ams-exch02

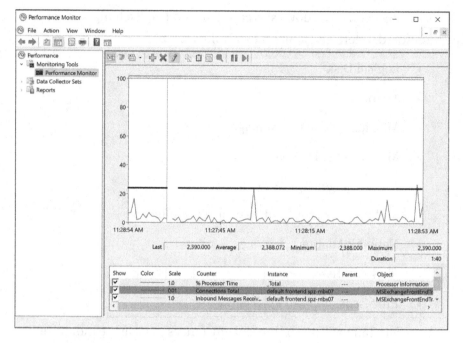

Figure 3-12. *Monitoring the Default Receive Connector on an Exchange 2019 server*

"What are interesting objects to monitor?" one might ask. Personally, I always start monitoring the Physical Disk object, just to see how the disk is performing, especially when there are performance complaints. A disk that cannot keep up with the demand will always result in a slow responding server and complaining users. Counters of a Physical Disk object that can be monitored are

- *% Disk Time*: The "% Disk Time" counter is nothing more than the "Avg. Disk Queue Length" counter multiplied by 100. It is the same value displayed in a different scale.

- *Disk Reads/sec*: An average disk is capable of handling 100 I/O operations per second at maximum, so this value should give you a quick overview how busy a particular disk is.

- *Disk Writes/sec*: The same applies as with the previous bullet.

- *Average Disk sec/Read*: This value should be below 20 milliseconds. It is allowed to show spikes to a higher value, but on average it should be below 20 msec.

- *Average Disk sec/Write*: The same applies as with the previous bullet.

- *Average Disk Read Queue Length*: This value shows how many read actions are queued for the disk to process. On average it should be below 2 per spindle. If you're using a JBOD solution, then it should be below 2, but if you're using a RAID set, it can be higher. A RAID-10 set, for example, with ten disks (five disks in a mirror) should show a maximum value of 10 for this counter. The disk controller on the other hand has a serious impact here as well. For detailed information, please consult your hardware vendor.

- *Average Disk Write Queue Length*: The same applies as the previous bullet.

Note   In Performance Monitor there are two disk objects, the Physical Disk and the Logical Disk. The physical is a representation of the actual physical spindle. A Logical Disk object is a representation of a drive letter. A disk in a server can hold multiple volumes, each representing a Logical Disk object in Performance Monitor.

Another interesting counter to have a look at is the "MSExchangeTransport SMTPReceive" and then specifically the Default Receive Connector. This counter shows you all kinds of detailed information regarding messages received on the Default Receive Connector on this Exchange 2019 server. Counters to have a look at are Messages Received/sec, Message Byte Received/sec, Average Bytes/message, and Bytes Received/sec. This counter will give you a good estimate on the load that is generated on your server by incoming SMTP messages.

The topics mentioned previously are for real-time monitoring. While this is interesting to see at that particular moment, it does not give you any insight into longer-term monitoring.

Performance Monitor Logging

Real-time monitoring performance data is good for a quick overview of how the Exchange 2013 server is doing when it comes to performance, but if you have nothing else to do, then watching a console logging performance data might be a better solution.

You can use the Performance Monitor tool to capture and log performance data to a log file on disk. This log file can be read at a later moment, and you can select a particular timeframe when monitoring.

To achieve this you have to create a User-Defined Data Collector Set. To create one, you can follow these steps:

1. Log onto an Exchange 2019 server and start the Performance Monitor tool. In the navigation pane, expand Data Collector Sets, right-click User Defined, select New, and select Data Collector Set.

2. In the Create New Data Collector Set, enter a descriptive name like My Exchange 2019 Logging and select the Create manually (Advanced) radio button. Click Next to continue.

3. In the next window, check the Performance counter checkbox and click Next to continue.

4. In the next window, you can add the performance counters you want to log. It depends per situation and requirements, but for informational logging, the following counters are good candidates:

   - MSExchange Database
   - MSExchange Autodiscover
   - MSExchange ActiveSync
   - MSExchange OWA
   - MSExchange EWS
   - MSExchange Transport Receive Connector
   - MSExchange Transport Send Connector
   - Physical Disk
   - Processor
   - RPC/HTTP Proxy

5. Change the sample interval to something useful for a longer term-logging. A 15-second interval gives you much information, but when logging for 24 hours, 48 hours, or maybe a week, the log file size will be horrible. Personally, I use a one- or two-minute interval for logging. Click Next to continue.

6. By default the log files will be stored on the system drive with the Data Collector Set name appended. In this example this would be %systemdrive%\ PerfLogs\Admin\My Exchange 2019 Logging. Click Next to continue.

7. The last window is to set the permissions under which the data is logged. You can leave this <default> and click Finish to create a Data Collector Set and close the wizard.

The new Data Collector Set will now show up in the User Defined section. Right-click the Data Collector Set and select Start to start the actual logging. Logging is a background process, so it's safe to log off and log on back to the server when you want to check your logging after 24 or 48 hours.

When logging has been stopped after enough time, you can use the Performance Monitor again, but instead of using real-time data, import the data from the log file that was collected earlier. At the same time, you can use the slider to set the timeframe of the data you want to analyze.

Note   If you are not sure which counters you should log, you can always decide to open the predefined Performance Monitor log files ExchangeDiagnosticsDailyPerformanceLogs and ExchangeDiagnosticsPerformanceLog that are created by the Exchange Diagnostics Service. You can find these in the Performance Monitor tool in the User Defined section of Data Collector Sets. These are also shown in Figure 3-11 earlier in this chapter.

It's a good practice to monitor your Exchange servers this way on a regular basis to get a good overview of the performance of your Exchange servers and establish a performance baseline. When performance issues arise later on, you always have a good reference of how performance should be. At the same time, this way of logging and analyzing performance data can help you in your capacity management.

Managed Availability

Managed Availability is one of the most underestimated features in Exchange 2019, but at the same time one of the most valuable features. Introduced in Exchange 2013, Managed Availability is a built-in end-to-end monitoring solution that can take preventive actions when needed.

End-to-End Monitoring

Managed Availability is a service in Exchange 2019 that monitors the Exchange servers constantly and takes appropriate action when needed, without any system administrator intervention. Managed Availability not only monitors the various services within an Exchange server for their availability, but it's also a monitoring solution that does end-to-end monitoring from a user's perspective.

So it not only monitors if the Information Store is running and the mailbox database is mounted; at the same time, it monitors if the mailbox itself is available as well. Another example is monitoring the Outlook Web App (OWA) functionality. Managed Availability not only monitors if the Internet Information Server (IIS) is running and offering OWA functionality; it also tries to log into a mailbox to see if the OWA service is actually available. This is a huge difference from the past versions of Exchange Server and their monitoring solutions where the only monitoring was if the web server functionality was up and running. If a logon page was shown, OWA was supposed to be running fine. SMTP monitoring in the past is also a good example. If you could set up a Telnet session on port 25 and a banner was shown, the service was supposed to be up and running; if a message could actually be delivered was not monitored.

Managed Availability has the following characteristics:

- *Cloud trained*: Microsoft has developed Managed Availability in Exchange Online, sometimes referred to as "the service," and brought it back to the on-premises Exchange installations.

- Multiple years of running as a service allows for the incorporation of learnings and best practices from operations in a large environment and a very diverse client base from all over the world, running 24/7.

- In Exchange Online, developers were responsible for building, maintaining, and improving Managed Availability. Developers also handled escalations in Exchange Online, which allowed the developers to take feedback, not only for the software they were coding but also for improvements in the monitoring process itself. Developers were paged in the middle of the night when issues were escalated, so these developers were very focused on improving Managed Availability.

- It is included in the product and installed out of the box by default; any additional configuration is not needed. At the same time, this means that Microsoft has the ability to make changes and improvements to Managed Availability every time a new Cumulative Update is released.

- *User focused*: Managed Availability is based on an end user experience. Listening on port 443 for OWA or on port 25 for SMTP does not guarantee successful message delivery.

- Monitoring checks for

  - *Availability*: Is the service being monitored accessible and available?

  - *Latency*: Is the service working with an acceptable degree of latency?

  - *Error*: When accessing the service, are there any errors logged?

- These bullets result in a customer touch point, a test on a service that ensures the availability of the service that responds at or below an acceptable latency and returns no error when performing operations.

- *Recovery oriented*: Managed Availability protects the user experience through a series of recovery actions. It's basically the recognition that issues may arise, but the user experience should not be impacted. Here's an example for Managed Availability monitoring OWA:

  - The monitor attempts to submit a message via OWA, and an error is returned.

  - The responder is notified and tries to restart the OWA application pool.

  - The monitor attempts to verify OWA and checks if its healthy. When healthy, the monitor again attempts to submit a message, and again an error is returned.

  - The responder now moves the active mailbox database to another Mailbox server.

  - The monitor attempts to verify OWA and checks for a health status. When healthy the monitor attempts to submit a message and now receives a success.

Managed Availability is implemented through the Microsoft Exchange Health Manager Service running on the Exchange 2019 server. How does the Health Manager Service get its information? Through a series of new crimson event channels. As outlined in the previous section, a crimson event channel is a channel where applications can store certain events, events that can be consumed by other applications or services. In this case various Exchange components write events to a crimson event channel, and the Health Manager Service consumes these events to monitor the service and take appropriate actions.

The configuration files that are used by Managed Availability are XML files supplied by Microsoft and stored on the local hard drive on C:\Program Files\Microsoft\Exchange Server\V15\Bin\Monitoring\ Config. Early 2023, a newly installed Exchange 2019 server comes with 257 different XML files for the Managed Availability configuration.

Note   While it is interesting to check out these XML files, it's not a good idea to modify these, not even when you know for 120% what you're doing. You will most likely see unexpected results and see Managed Availability do things you don't want it to do like rebooting servers that have no issues, only because you changed some configuration file the wrong way.

You must be careful anyways. When you look at the SmtpProbes_Hub. xml, for example, you'll see the following in the WorkContext of the HubAvailabilityProbe:

```
<WorkContext>
<SmtpServer>127.0.0.1</SmtpServer>
<Port>25</Port>
<ExpectedReponseOnConnect>220</ExpectedResponseOnConnect>
<ExpectedResponseOnHelo>250</ExpectedResponseOnHelo>
```

```
<ExpectedConnectionLostPoint>None</ExpectedConnectionLostPoint>
</WorkContext>
```

Above all this tells us that the Health Manager Service is using port 25 on IP address 127.0.0.1 to check for the SMTP functionality, and it defines the expected SMTP responses. As an example, if you edit this information, you know for sure Managed Availability will take unpredictable actions.

Managed Availability Architecture

Managed Availability consists of three different components (illustrated in Figure 3-13):

- Probe engine

- Monitor

- Responder engine

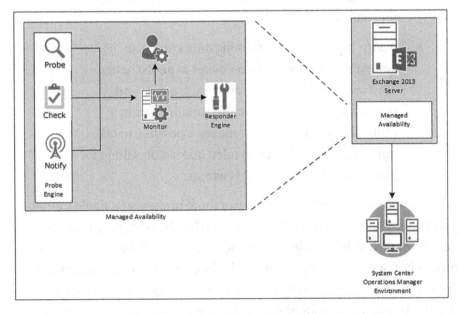

Figure 3-13. *Architectural overview of Managed Availability*

The probe engine consists of three different components:

- *Probe*: A probe determines the success of a particular service or component from an end user perspective. A probe performs and end-to-end test also known as a synthetic transaction. A probe may perform a portion of a stack like checking if a web service is actually running, while other probes may test the full stack, that is, a check if any successful data is returned. Each component team in the Exchange product group is responsible for building its own probe.

- *Check*: A check monitors end user activity and is looking for trends within the Exchange server that might indicate (known) issues. A check is implemented against performance counters where thresholds can be monitored. A check is a passive monitoring mechanism.

- *Notify*: Notify processes notifications from the system that are known to be issues in an Exchange 2013 server. These are general notifications and do not automatically mean they originate from a probe though. The notifier makes it possible to take immediate action when needed instead of waiting for a probe to signal something is wrong.

A monitor receives data from one or more probes, so a single monitor may collect data from multiple probes. The feedback from a probe determines if a monitor is healthy or not. If a monitor is using multiple probes but one probe returns unhealthy feedback, the entire monitor is unhealthy. Based on the frequency of the probe feedback, the monitor decides whether a responder should be triggered.

In Figure 3-14 it is clear that a monitor works at different levels.

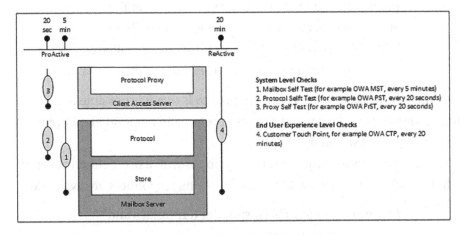

Figure 3-14. *Monitoring occurs at different layers*

The levels illustrated in the figure include

1. *Mailbox self test (MST)*: This first check makes sure
   the mailbox database is accessible. The mailbox self
   test runs every five minutes.

2. *Protocol self test (PST)*: The second test is about
   testing the protocol used to access the mailbox
   database is functioning correctly. The protocol self
   test runs every 20 seconds.

3. *Proxy self test (PrST)*: The third test is actually
   running on the Exchange 2013 CAS server to make
   sure that the requests are proxied correctly to the
   Mailbox server. Like the protocol self test, this proxy
   self test runs also every 20 seconds.

4. *Customer touch point (CTP)*: The customer touch point is an end-to-end test that validates the entire accessibility of the mailbox, starting at the Exchange 2019 Client Access components to the actual mailbox. The customer touch point runs every 20 minutes.

The advantage of a multi-layer approach is that it is possible to check for various components using different probes and respond in different ways using the responder.

A responder is a component that responds with a pre-defined account when a monitor turns unhealthy. The following responders are available:

- *Restart responder*: This responder terminates and recycles a particular service.

- *Reset AppPool responder*: This responder can recycle the IIS application pool.

- *Failover responder*: This responder can take an Exchange 2013 Mailbox server out of service by failing over all mailbox databases on this Mailbox server to other Mailbox servers.

- *Bugcheck responder*: This responder can bugcheck a particular server, that is, it will restart with a "blue screen."

- *Offline responder*: This responder can take a protocol running on an Exchange 2013 server out of service. Especially when using a load balancer, this is important. When the Offline responder kicks in, a protocol component is shut down, and the load balancer will notice and disable the Exchange 2013 CAS (or this particular protocol) so it stops servicing client requests.

- *Escalate responder:* This responder can escalate an issue to another application like System Center 2012 Operations Manager. This indicates human intervention is required.

The responder sequence is stopped when the associated monitor becomes healthy again. Responders can also be throttled. Imagine you have three Exchange 2019 servers in a DAG. You don't want two different responders (each on a Mailbox server) to bugcheck these particular Mailbox servers since it will result in a complete outage of the DAG. When two Mailbox servers are bugchecked, then the remaining Mailbox server loses quorum and therefore shuts down the DAG, which of course will result in downtime for all users.

Exchange 2013 CAS and Managed Availability

So in theory this is nice, but how does it work in a production environment? When looking at the Exchange 2013 Client Access protocols, Managed Availability dynamically generates a file called healthcheck.htm. Since this file is dynamically generated to test a particular protocol, you will not find it anywhere on the Exchange server's hard disk.

This is a very basic HTML file, and the only thing it does is returning a 200 OK code plus the name of the server. You can easily open this file using a browser. It doesn't reveal much information, but when it returns the information as shown in Figure 3-15, you know your server is fine from an OWA protocol perspective.

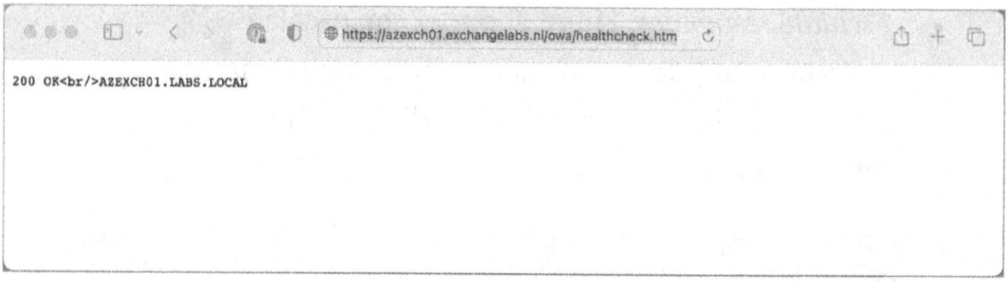

```
200 OK<br/>AZEXCH01.LABS.LOCAL
```

Figure 3-15. *A dynamically generated file for health checking by a probe*

All other protocols like ECP, EWS, Autodiscover, and Outlook Anywhere have their own healthcheck.htm files when the server is running fine. A (hardware) load balancer can use this information as well. The load balancer checks for this file, and when a "200 OK" is returned, the load balancer knows that the respective protocol is doing fine. If an error is returned, the load balancer knows there's something wrong and it should take this protocol out of service.

Note   This is only a protocol check and doesn't say anything if a user can actually log in or not.

What can you do with this? The Offline responder, for example, can be invoked to place a node in maintenance mode, for example, when you're patching your server or updating it to the latest Cumulative Update. To accomplish this, you must change the server component state of an Exchange server.

Note   All server components change their status immediately except for the Hub Transport and the Front-End Transport components. When these components are disabled in PowerShell, they continue to run until the service is restarted. This can be confusing when you are not aware of this; you think you disabled the component (actually you did!), but it continues working. However, Managed Availability will notice this inconsistency and force a restart of this service after some time.

The component state is stored in two places:

- *Active Directory*: In Active Directory they are stored in a property of the Exchange server object in the configuration partition. You can find this server object in

  CN=Configuration, CN=Services, CN=Microsoft Exchange, CN=, CN=Administrative Groups, CN=Exchange Administrative Group (FYDIBOHF23SPDLT), CN=Servers.

  The value in Active Directory is used when performing Set-ServerComponentState commands against a remote server.

- *Local registry*: When checking the registry, you have to check

  HKEY_LOCAL_MACHINE\Software\Microsoft\ExchangeServer\v15\ServerComponentStates and then the component you want to check.

When the work on the Exchange 2019 server is finished, the components can be activated again in PowerShell.

Monitoring Using the Exchange Management Shell

Besides all kinds of manual tools you can use to monitor your Exchange environment, the Exchange Management Shell (EMS) can also be very helpful.

Server Health

As we've seen in the previous section, Managed Availability constantly monitors the health of the Exchange server and when needed takes appropriate action. However, not all parts of the Exchange server can be fixed automatically.

To get an overview of the health of components in the Exchange server, you can use the Get-ServerHealth and Get-HealthReport commands in Exchange PowerShell.

The Get-HealthReport command presents a complete list of all components on the Exchange server, and if all goes well, all components will show "Healthy" as can be seen in a snippet of the console output:

```
[PS] C:\>Get-HealthReport -Identity EXCH01
```

Server	State	HealthSet	AlertValue	LastTransitionTime
	MonitorCount			
------	-----	---------	----------	------------------

EXCH01	NotApplicable	O365Griffin	Healthy	3/21/2023 9:27:12 AM
160				
EXCH01	Online	HubTransport	Healthy	3/16/2023 3:01:33 PM
67				
EXCH01	NotApplicable	Ecosystem_Connectors	Healthy	3/16/2023 2:14:28 PM
35				
EXCH01	NotApplicable	EDS	Healthy	3/21/2023 9:28:39 AM
42				
EXCH01	Online	FrontendTransport	Healthy	3/16/2023 2:24:14 PM
20				
EXCH01	NotApplicable	Search	Healthy	3/21/2023 9:29:35 AM
31				
EXCH01	NotApplicable	Mars	Healthy	3/16/2023 2:14:21 PM
10				

```
EXCH01 NotApplicable HxService          Healthy   3/16/2023 2:14:19 PM
116
EXCH01 NotApplicable Xrm                Healthy   3/16/2023 2:09:34 PM
50
EXCH01 NotApplicable StreamingOptics    Healthy   3/24/2023 12:12:19 PM
9
EXCH01 NotApplicable PublicFolders      Healthy   3/16/2023 2:23:20 PM
7
EXCH01 NotApplicable DataProtection     Healthy   4/7/2023 11:18:21 AM
68
EXCH01 NotApplicable Store              Healthy   4/5/2023 10:59:39 PM
50
EXCH01 NotApplicable OWA                Healthy   3/16/2023 2:31:05 PM
31
EXCH01 NotApplicable EAS                Healthy   3/21/2023 9:30:37 AM
2
EXCH01 NotApplicable AntiSpam           Healthy   3/16/2023 2:22:18 PM
26
EXCH01 NotApplicable OWA.Attachments    Healthy   3/16/2023 2:09:33 PM
26
EXCH01 NotApplicable ActiveSync.Protocol Healthy  4/5/2023 10:31:05 PM
7
EXCH01 NotApplicable TokenIssuerService Healthy   3/16/2023 2:14:27 PM
10
EXCH01 Online        OutlookMapiHttp.P... Healthy 4/5/2023 10:30:23 PM
6
```

It is also possible to drill down into the health of a component using the Get-ServerHealth command, and this command takes the -HealthSet as a parameter. To drill down into the health of OWA, for example, you can use the following command:

```
[PS] C:\>Get-ServerHealth -Identity EXCH01 -HealthSet OWA.Proxy
```

These commands are nice for informational purposes but can show their real value when you have to troubleshoot components as will be discussed in the next chapter.

Queue Monitoring

The SMTP queues should be monitored on a regular basis as well. The Transport service running on the Exchange server uses SMTP queues, both inbound and outbound, to store messages temporarily before they are delivered. Delivery can be in a local mailbox or to another SMTP server, either internal or external.

To have a look at the SMTP queues, the Queue Viewer can be used. The Queue Viewer can be found in the Exchange toolbox from the Windows Start menu.

It is a good practice to open the Queue Viewer every now and then and see how the queues are actually behaving. During normal operations you'll see queues increasing and decreasing, and that's okay. An SMTP queue can show a serious number of messages in the queue, for example, when the remote server is not available because of maintenance or when an Internet connection is not available. As long as queues also decrease after some time, that is not a big deal. What also happens is that an Exchange server receives spam for nonexisting users. This will result in an NDR (non-delivery report) typically to a nonexisting domain. These NDRs typically end up in the queue for 48 hours before they are deleted. The 48-hour hold time is configurable using the Set-TransportService command. To change the 48 hours to 72 hours, you can use the following command:

```
[PS] C:\> Set-TransportService -MessageExpirationTimeout
3.00:00:00
```

In the preceding example, the timeout is configured as days. hours:minutes:seconds; 72 hours equals 3 days.

It is also possible to use Exchange PowerShell to retrieve queue information from the Transport service using the Get-Queue command:

```
[PS] C:\>get-queue
```

```
Identity          DeliveryType         Status MessageCount Velocity RiskLevel
OutboundIPPool NextHopDomain
--------          ------------         ------ ------------ -------- ---------
-------------- --------------
EXCH01\Submission Undefined            Ready  0                  0      Normal
0                 Submission
EXCH01\Shadow\3   ShadowRedundancy Ready  1                  0      Normal
0              exch02.proexchangeadmin.com
```

This will show all queues at a given moment on this particular server. You can use the -Server option to check the queues on a different server, for example:

```
[PS] C:\>get-queue -server exch02

Identity          DeliveryType                     Status MessageCount Velocity
RiskLevel OutboundIPPool NextHopDomain
--------          ------------                     ------ ------------ --------
--------- -------------- -------------
EXCH02\3          SmtpRelayWithinAdSiteToEdge Ready  0                  0
Normal    0                 edgesync - defau...
EXCH02\Submission Undefined                        Ready  1                  0
Normal    0                 Submission
```

To have a closer look at a particular queue, for example, the EXCH02\3 queue, you can use the -Identity option and, if needed, use the Format-List command:

```
[PS] C:\>get-queue -identity exch02\03 | fl
```

```
RunspaceId                    : 3ae68604-10fb-45d6-
                                b6f6-7bb1ec9f63f2

DeliveryType                  : SmtpRelayWithinAdSiteToEdge
NextHopDomain                 : edgesync - default-first-
                                site-name to internet

TlsDomain                     :
NextHopConnector              : 7b3d1502-28a1-49aa-8030
                                -34c000112398
```

```
Status                               : Ready
MessageCount                         : 0
LastError                            :
RetryCount                           : 0
LastRetryTime                        : 4/10/2023 12:46:05 PM
NextRetryTime                        :
FirstRetryTime                       :
DeferredMessageCount                 : 0
LockedMessageCount                   : 0
LockedScopes                         :
MessageCountsPerPriority             : {0, 0, 0, 0}
IncludeInSlaCount                    : 0
DeferredMessageCountsPerPriority     : {0, 0, 0, 0}
RiskLevel                            : Normal
OutboundIPPool                       : 0
NextHopCategory                      : Internal
IncomingRate                         : 0
OutgoingRate                         : 0
Velocity                             : 0
OverrideSource                       :
QueueIdentity                        : EXCH02\3
PriorityDescriptions                 : {High, Normal, Low, None}
Identity                             : EXCH02\3
IsValid                              : True
ObjectState                          : New
```

This can be very useful when troubleshooting mail delivery issues in your Exchange environment.

It is possible to use one Exchange PowerShell command and "pipe" this output to another Exchange PowerShell command, for example:

```
[PS] C:\> Get-TransportService | Get-Queue
```

or

```
[PS] C:\> Get-TransportService| Get-Queue | Select Identity,
Status, MessageCount, NextHopDomain, LastRetryTime,
NextRetryTime
```

This command will list all Transport services on all Exchange 2019 servers in the organization and use this as an input for the Get-Queue command. In turn this will return all queues on these servers, but show only their identity, the status, the number of messages in the queue, the next domain the queue is destined for, and the times the queue has been trying to deliver or will try to deliver.

Mailbox Database Replication

Mailbox database replication is another key example of a service that's a good indication if the servers are performing as expecting. When the performance of an Exchange 2019 server or related service like the network degrades, you'll see the replication queues start growing.

There are two types of queues available for mailbox database replication:

- *Copy queue*: This is the queue where transaction log files reside before they are replicated (over the network) to other Mailbox servers holding a passive copy of a mailbox database.

- *Replay queue*: This queue resides on the Mailbox server holding a passive copy of a mailbox database. This queue holds transaction log files that are received from the active mailbox database copy but haven't replayed into the passive mailbox database copy yet.

Both queues fluctuate constantly, and it is no big deal when they are momentarily increasing, as long as they are decreasing in minutes.

Note   When you have lagged copies in your DAG, especially when the lag time is long, you can expect many items in the replay queues. If you have, there's no need to worry since this is expected behavior.

You can monitor the replication queues in EMS using the Get-MailboxDatabaseCopyStatus command:

- To monitor all copies of a particular mailbox database, you can use the following command:

  ```
  [PS] C:\> Get-MailboxDatabaseCopyStatus -Identity
  MDB1 | Format-List
  ```

- To monitor all mailbox database copies on a given server, you can use the following command:

  ```
  [PS] C:\> Get-MailboxDatabaseCopyStatus
  -Server EXCH01 | Format-List
  ```

- To monitor status and network information for a given mailbox database on a given server, you can use the following command:

  ```
  [PS] C:\> Get-MailboxDatabaseCopyStatus -Identity
  MDB3\EXCH03 -ConnectionStatus | Format-List
  ```

Note   The syntax of the identity of the mailbox database copy looks a bit odd, but it is the name of the mailbox database located on the Mailbox server holding the passive copy. In this case it is mailbox database MDB3 located on Mailbox server EXCH03, thus MDB3\EXCH03.

- To monitor the copy status of a given mailbox database on a given server, you can use the following command:

```
[PS] C:\> Get-MailboxDatabaseCopyStatus
-Identity MDB1\EXCH02 | Format-List
```

Personally, I often combine the Get-MailboxDatabaseCopyStatus command with the Get-MailboxDatabase command to get a quick overview of all mailbox databases, their passive copies, and the status of the replication queues. To do this the following command can be used:

```
[PS] C:\> Get-MailboxDatabase | Get-MailboxDatabaseCopyStatus
```

Name	Status	CopyQueue Length	ReplayQueue Length	LastInspectedLogTime
MDB02\EXCH02	Mounted	0	0	
MDB02\EXCH01	Healthy	0	0	3/31/2023 1:25:25 PM
MDB01\EXCH01	Mounted	0	0	
MDB01\EXCH02	Healthy	0	2	3/31/2023 1:59:01 PM

Another way in Exchange PowerShell to check for mailbox replication is the Test-ReplicationHealth command. This command tests the continuous replication, the availability of the Active Manager, the status of the underlying failover cluster components, the cluster quorum, and the underlying network infrastructure. To use this command against server EXCH01, you can use the following command:

```
[PS] C:\> Test-ReplicationHealth -Identity EXCH01
```

Server	Check	Result	Error
EXCH01	ClusterService	Passed	
EXCH01	ReplayService	Passed	
EXCH01	ActiveManager	Passed	
EXCH01	TasksRpcListener	Passed	
EXCH01	TcpListener	Passed	

EXCH01	ServerLocatorService	Passed
EXCH01	DagMembersUp	Passed
EXCH01	MonitoringService	Passed
EXCH01	ClusterNetwork	Passed
EXCH01	QuorumGroup	Passed
EXCH01	FileShareQuorum	Passed
EXCH01	DatabaseRedundancy	Passed
EXCH01	DatabaseAvailability	Passed
EXCH01	DBCopySuspended	Passed
EXCH01	DBCopyFailed	Passed
EXCH01	DBInitializing	Passed
EXCH01	DBDisconnected	Passed
EXCH01	DBLogCopyKeepingUp	Passed
EXCH01	DBLogReplayKeepingUp	Passed

Microsoft has written two health metric scripts, which are in the C:\ Program Files\Microsoft\Exchange Server\v15\Scripts directory, that gather information about mailbox databases in a DAG. These scripts are

- CollectOverMetrics.ps1

- CollectReplicationMetrics.ps1

The CollectOverMetrics.ps1 script reads DAG member event logs to gather information regarding mailbox database operations over a specific timeframe. Database operations can be mounting, dismounting, database moves, or failovers. The script can generate an HTML file as well as a CSV file for later processing in Microsoft Excel, for example.

To show information in a DAG called DAG01 and all mailbox databases in this DAG, you can navigate to the scripts directory and use a command similar to the following:

```
[PS] C:\> .\CollectOverMetrics.ps1 -DatabaseAvailabilityGroup
DAG01 -Database:"DB*" -GenerateHTMLReport -ShowHTMLReport
```

The CollectReplicationMetrics.ps1 script is a more advanced script since it gathers information in real time while the script is running and it gathers information from performance monitor counters related to mailbox database replication. The script can be run to

- Collect data and generate a report (CollectAndReport, the default setting).

- Collect data and store it (CollectOnly).

- Generate a report from earlier stored data (ProcessOnly).

The scripts start PowerShell jobs that gather all information, and as such it is a time- and resource-consuming task. The final stage of the script when all data is processed to generate a report can also be time- and resource-intensive.

To gather one hour of performance data from a DAG using a one-minute interval and generate a report, the following command can be used:

```
[PS] C:\> .\CollectReplicationMetrics.ps1 -DagName DAG1 -Duration
"01:00:00" -Frequency "00:01:00"
```

To read data from all files called CounterData* and generate a report, the following command can be used:

```
[PS] C:\> .\CollectReplicationMetrics.ps1 -SummariseFiles
(dir CounterData*) -Mode ProcessOnly -ReportPath
```

Note   Do not forget to navigate to the scripts directory before entering this command.

Not directly related to monitoring an Exchange server is the RedistributeActiveDatabases.ps1 script. It can happen, especially after a failover, that the mailbox databases are not properly distributed among the Mailbox servers. For example, in such a scenario, it can happen that one Mailbox server is hosting only active copies of mailbox databases, while another Mailbox server is hosting only passive copies of mailbox databases. To redistribute the mailbox database copies over the available Mailbox servers, you can use the following command:

```
[PS] C:\> .\RedistributeActiveDatabases.ps1
-DagName DAG1 -BalanceDbsByActivationPreference
-ShowFinalDatabaseDistribution
```

This will distribute all mailbox databases by their activation preference that was set during creation of the mailbox database copies. If you have a multi-site DAG, you can use the -BalanceDbsBySiteAndActivationPreference parameter. This will balance the mailbox databases to their most preferred copy, but also try to balance mailbox databases within each Active Directory site.

Note   Exchange 2019 will redistribute the mailbox databases on a regular basis.

Workload Management

An Exchange workload is an Exchange Server feature, protocol, or service within an Exchange server that has been explicitly defined for the purpose of Exchange system resource management.

Examples of Exchange workloads are

- Outlook Web App

- Exchange ActiveSync

- Outlook Anywhere

- Moving mailboxes

- Mailbox assistants

Basically, anything that consumes system resources on an Exchange server is an Exchange workload and can be somehow managed. There are two ways to manage Exchange workloads:

- *Monitoring the health of system resources*: This is what we have been discussing earlier in this chapter.

- *Controlling how resources are consumed*: In Exchange Server 2010, this was referred to as throttling. This feature has been expanded in Exchange Server 2013.

Managing Workloads by Monitoring System Resources

When you manage Exchange workloads by monitoring the Exchange system resources, you are able to optimize resource utilization and thus hopefully manage user expectations when it comes to performance of the Exchange environment.

Workloads and Performance

When an Exchange server starts to suffer due to high load, Exchange will start to slow down low-priority tasks or workloads on the server. This way Exchange can spread the load across multiple services within the server and bring back the resources to a healthy state without negatively impacting the user's experience.

Exchange constantly monitors the following resources within the server:

- CPU usage

- Mailbox database RPC latency

- Mailbox database replication health

- Content indexing age as of last notification

- Content indexing retry queue size

Besides regular services, Exchange workloads can also include background services or asynchronous services like the Exchange Mailbox Replication service, the Calendar Synchronization workload, or the Exchange Mailbox Assistance service.

By monitoring the resources in an Exchange server, it is also possible to throttle these resources. When an Exchange service performance starts to degrade, the Exchange workloads that rely on this specific service are throttled down so Exchange can work on a backlog efficiently (if one exists of course) and get back to a healthy state. This way of throttling allows a user to work with an Exchange server without noticing any performance degradation. This way of throttling is sometimes referred to as "shaving the peaks" in Exchange performance. The other way around is also possible. When performance permits, workloads are allowed to speed up in resource usage. This is sometimes referred to as "fill the valleys" in Exchange performance.

Workload Classifications

Exchange workloads are assigned a classification, and the following classifications can be assigned to a workload:

- Urgent

- Customer Expectation

- Internal Maintenance

- Discretionary

When resource health shows signs of performance degradation, a workload in a higher classification is given preference over a workload with a lower classification. Take a look at the local Exchange server CPU. When it is running at high usages, workloads classified as Internal Maintenance can continue to run, while workloads classified as Discretionary can be temporarily stopped. Table 3-1 shows all Exchange server workloads, a description of the workloads, and their default classification.

Now why is this good to know? The various workload policies give you a good overview of their classification and which classifications have a higher preference. For example, Exchange ActiveSync (EAS) in Table 3-1 has a classification of Customer Expectation, while Exchange Web Services (EWS) and MOMT (RPC Client Access) have a classification of Internal Maintenance. This indicates that when an Exchange server is under pressure, it will assign more system resources to EAS, in preference of EWS and MOMT. EAS in this case will continue to run better than EWS and MOMT.

Table 3-1. *Exchange Workloads and Their Classification*

Workload Policy Name	Description	Workload Classification
MailboxReplicationservice highpriority	Mailbox Replication service high priority	Urgent
EAS	Exchange ActiveSync	Customer Expectation
JunkEmailOptionsCommitter-Assistant	Junk email	Customer Expectation
PowerShellBackSync	Windows PowerShell BackSync operations	Customer Expectation
PowerShellForwardSync	Windows PowerShell FwdSync operations	Customer Expectation
PublicFolderMailboxSync	Public folder mailbox synchronization	Customer Expectation
TeamMailboxSync	Site mailbox synchronization	Customer Expectation

(*continued*)

Table 3-1. (*continued*)

Workload Policy Name	Description	Workload Classification
Transport	Transport mail flow	Customer Expectation
CalendarRepairAssistant	Calendar Repair Assistant	Internal Maintenance
CalendarSyncAssistant	Calendar Synchronization Assistant	Internal Maintenance
ContactLinkingAssistant	Contact Linking Assistant	Internal Maintenance
DirectoryProcessorAssistant	Directory Processor Assistant	Internal Maintenance
Domt	Address book	Internal Maintenance
ELCAssistant	Managed Folder Assistant	Internal Maintenance
EWS	Exchange Web Services	Internal Maintenance
IMAP	IMAP4	Internal Maintenance
MOMT	RPC Client Access	Internal Maintenance
OABGeneratorAssistant	Offline Address Book generation assistant	Internal Maintenance
OrgContactsSyncAssistant	Organizational Contacts Synchronization Assistant	Internal Maintenance
OWA	Outlook Web App	Internal Maintenance

(*continued*)

Table 3-1. (*continued*)

Workload Policy Name	Description	Workload Classification
OWAVoice	Outlook Web App voice access	Internal Maintenance
PeopleRelevanceAssistant	People Relevance Assistant	Internal Maintenance
POP	POP3	Internal Maintenance
PowerShell	PowerShell work not included in other workloads	Internal Maintenance
PowerShellGalSync	PowerShell work for GAL synchronization	Internal Maintenance
PowerShellLowPriority WorkFlow	Non-time-sensitive PowerShell work	Internal Maintenance
PushNotificationService	Push Notification service	Internal Maintenance
SharingPolicyAssistant	Sharing Policy Assistant	Internal Maintenance
SiteMailboxAssistant	Site Mailbox Assistant	Internal Maintenance
StoreMaintenanceAssistant	Store Maintenance Assistant	Internal Maintenance
TopNAssistant	Top N Words Assistant	Internal Maintenance
TransportSync	Transport synchronization	Internal Maintenance
UMReportingAssistant	Unified Messaging Reporting Assistant	Internal Maintenance

(*continued*)

Table 3-1. (*continued*)

Workload Policy Name	Description	Workload Classification
InferenceDataCollection Assistant	Inference Data Collection Assistant	Discretionary
InferenceTrainingAssistant	Inference Training Assistant	Discretionary
MailboxReplicationService	Mailbox Replication service	Discretionary
PowerShellDiscretionary WorkFlow	Non-time-sensitive PowerShell work	Discretionary
PublicFolderAssistant	Public Folder Assistant	Discretionary

Policies, classifications, and monitoring are nice to do, but you need certain predefined values to compare against. Thresholds are values when monitoring that define the state of a particular resource. For example, a particular service is using CPU resources, which can be between 0% and 100%. A threshold can be set on 80% to avoid the service to consume too many CPU resources. This means that when this service peaks over its threshold, that is, 80%, certain action needs to be taken, like throttling the service so it doesn't consume more than 80% of the available CPU resources.

Workloads have similar thresholds, and these thresholds define the state of a particular resource. For example, a workload can have a state of "Critical" when it is consuming way too much resources and it needs to be stopped in favor of server health.

The following thresholds are available for Exchange workloads:

- *Critical*: Workloads using a resource must be stopped when they are above this threshold.

- *Overloaded*: Workloads using a resource must be throttled ("shaving the peak") when they are above this threshold.

- *Underloaded*: Workloads using a resource can be sped up ("fill the valleys") when they are below this threshold.

Note   When a workload is above Underloaded and below Overloaded, then performance isn't throttled.

Workload Management Policy Settings

Out of the box, Exchange 2019 comes with a default set of workload management policy settings, which are sufficient in most scenarios. It is possible though to change these default workload management policy settings, which can be done for the entire Exchange organization or on a per-server basis.

To make workload management policy changes for the entire organization, you have to create a new workload management policy and apply it to the GlobalOverrideWorkloadManagementPolicy policy. Using the GlobalOverrideWorkloadManagementPolicy, all settings in the default policy will be overridden. For example, to create a new workload management policy for ActiveSync with a classification of

Discretionary (useful when iPhone and iPad users bring too much load on your Exchange servers) that overrides the default policy, you can use the following command in EMS:

```
[PS] C:\> New-WorkloadPolicy OrgActiveSyncWorkloadPolicy
-Workload EAS -WorkloadClassification
Discretionary -WorkloadManagementPolicy
GlobalOverrideWorkloadManagementPolicy
```

If you want to check whether this workload policy is actually created, you can use the Get-WorkloadPolicy and filter on the name of the new workload policy, like this:

```
[PS] C:\> Get-WorkloadPolicy | where {$_.Name -like "*ActiveSync*"}
```

Creating a new workload policy on a per-server basis is a little bit more work and consists of the following steps:

1. Create a new workload management policy for a specific server.

2. Create a new workload policy that defines the workload type and its classification and assign it to the workload management policy that was created in the previous step.

3. Apply the new workload management policy to a specific server.

Managing Workloads for Individual Users

In Exchange 2019 it is also possible to throttle performance on an individual basis. This makes it possible to control resource usage per individual user and prevents that one user from negatively affecting server performance.

User throttling in Exchange Server 2019 allows users to increase resource usage for small amounts of time. On the other hand, a lockout of users who use very large amounts of system resources is very infrequent as well. Instead of locking out users and therefore denying them access to the Exchange services, their usage is throttled, and processes are delayed only for a small amount of time.

Users are assigned a "usage budget" that contains a certain amount of system resource usage. When users are using system resources, this usage is subtracted from their budget. When their budget is empty, the users are temporarily locked out, and their budget can recharge.

The following characteristics of the way Exchange controls resources for individual users are as follows:

- *Maximum usage*: When a user consumes a large amount of system resources and they hit their threshold, they will be temporarily locked out from using system resources. If this happens, the user can start using system resources again when their budget is recharged. This happens very infrequently though.

- *Traffic shaping*: When users' usage reaches their threshold over a period of time, their usage is delayed for a very short period of time. This happens well in advance of causing any performance impact on the Exchange server. Traffic shaping has less impact than a lockout of course since the usage is only limited.

- *Recharge rate*: The recharge rate manages the users' resource consumption by using a budget system, and the rate at which the budget is recharged again can be set. A value of 600,000 milliseconds implies that the budget is recharged with 10 minutes per hour of usage.

- *Burst allowance*: Users can use large amounts of resources, but only for a very limited amount of time without experiencing any throttling.

Out of the box there's only one throttling policy available in an Exchange organization, and most of the time this throttling policy is sufficient. You can check the default throttling policy using the Get-ThrottlingPolicy command in Exchange PowerShell. To display all throttling policy settings related to Exchange ActiveSync (EAS), you can use the following command in Exchange PowerShell:

```
[PS] C:\> Get-ThrottlingPolicy | select name,*EAS*

Name                                     : GlobalThrottlingPolicy_
                                           16017db3-ec90-41a8-a4fc-
                                           ed1ecdebf6f6
EasMaxConcurrency                        : 10
EasMaxBurst                              : 480000
EasRechargeRate                          : 1800000
EasCutoffBalance                         : 600000
EasMaxDevices                            : 100
EasMaxDeviceDeletesPerMonth              : Unlimited
EasMaxInactivityForDeviceCleanup         : Unlimited

Name                                     : OrgInPlaceDiscoveryPolicy
EasMaxConcurrency                        : 10
EasMaxBurst                              : 480000
EasRechargeRate                          : 1800000
EasCutoffBalance                         : 600000
EasMaxDevices                            : 100
EasMaxDeviceDeletesPerMonth              : Unlimited
EasMaxInactivityForDeviceCleanup         : Unlimited
```

When using this command, the default throttling policy is read from the Exchange organization, but only the settings related to Exchange ActiveSync are shown.

Exchange 2019 also has the concept of scoping when using throttling policies. The default throttling policy has a Global scope, hence its name GlobalThrottlingPolicy_<< GUID>>. This Global throttling policy can be seen as a baseline when it comes to user throttling, and there's no need to change this. Since the default throttling policy has a Global scope, Microsoft recommends not to change this default throttling policy.

Instead of changing the default throttling policy, you can create a new throttling policy with a scope of Organization or Regular. This way the default throttling policy will always remain intact, but it also prevents a customized default throttling policy to be overwritten when upgrading to a new Cumulative Update in the future.

When creating a new throttling policy with an Organization scope, you only must set the new throttling settings that are different from those in the default throttling policy. The Organization throttling policy is also applied to all mailboxes in the Exchange organization.

If you want to create a throttling policy for specific users, you can create a new throttling policy with a Regular scope. Only the changes must be set in this Regular throttling policy; all other settings will be inherited from the default throttling policy or the Organization throttling policy.

By default, all throttling policy settings related to PowerShell are set to UNLIMITED, except for the number of concurrent sessions, which is set to 18. To create a new Regular policy that can be set to, for example, help desk staff that have a throttled amount of PowerShell sessions, you can use the following command in Exchange PowerShell:

```
[PS] C:\> New-ThrottlingPolicy -Name
ITStaffPowerShell -PowerShellMaxDestructiveCmdlets
10 -PowerShellMaxDestructiveCmdletsTimePeriod 60
-PowerShellMaxConcurrency 6 -PowerShellMaxCmdletQueueDepth 12
-ThrottlingPolicyScope Regular
```

```
Name                 ThrottlingPolicyScope IsServiceAccount
----                 --------------------- ----------------
ITStaffPowerShell Regular                   False
```

To assign this throttling policy to a help desk employee called Beau, you can use the following command in Exchange PowerShell:

```
[PS] C:\> Get-Mailbox -Identity S.Summertown | Set-Mailbox
-ThrottlingPolicy ITStaffPowerShell
```

Remember that only the PowerShell settings come from the Regular throttling policy; all other settings are inherited from the default throttling policy.

Summary

When the Exchange servers are installed, configured, and up and running, they must be managed as well.

We have been discussing how to manage mailbox databases on your Exchange 2019 servers, create new mailbox databases, configure the most important settings, and, when needed, remove mailbox databases.

A second important aspect in any Exchange environment is to manage recipients. Create new mailboxes, configure mailboxes, and automatically configure additional settings when creating new mailboxes using cmdlet extension agents. Cmdlet extension agents are not used often, but they can be a very interesting add-on when managing recipients.

The last part of this chapter is something that's often underutilized by Exchange administrators, and that's monitoring the Exchange servers. Using proper (pro-active) monitoring, you can prevent a lot of nasty issues. And by preventing these, you can keep your users happy.

PART II

Office 365 Integration

CHAPTER 4

Azure AD Identities

While there are companies out there still running Exchange Server on-premises as part of a standalone email infrastructure, an increasing number of customers operate Exchange Server complementary to Exchange Online, the email infrastructure that is part of Microsoft 365. Microsoft 365 and thus Exchange Online are subscription-based offerings built around Office and Windows-related software and services.

While many consider today's Microsoft 365 and Exchange Online offerings well established, they were officially launched around June 2011. Microsoft 365, which is the branding for Office 365 with the addition of Windows and security products, is the successor of Business Productivity Online Suite (BPOS). BPOS was launched in 2008 as a package of individually hosted Microsoft products, such as Exchange and Live Meeting.

Microsoft 365 offers software and cloud-based services, which are founded on workloads or workload integrations, such as

- Microsoft Exchange Online for email, with Exchange Online Protection and Defender for cloud-based email filtering

- Microsoft Teams for communications and conferencing

- Microsoft SharePoint for social networking and collaboration

© Jaap Wesselius and Michel de Rooij 2023
J. Wesselius and M. de Rooij, *Pro Exchange Administration*,
https://doi.org/10.1007/978-1-4842-9591-5_4

- OneDrive for cloud file storage

- Power Apps and Power Automate for workflow and process automation

What products and services are available to your organization depend on your subscription plan. The Microsoft 365 subscriptions and packages change quite frequently; current plans for small businesses can be compared at **https://bit.ly/M365Bplans** and enterprise plans at **https://bit.ly/M365Eplans**. This is also the location to start your Microsoft 365 journey by selecting one of the subscription plans. Most plans offer trial options, where you can try out their features.

Note   Since Office 365 is also available as a subscription plan, without the addition of Windows or Enterprise Mobility + Security (EMS), we will refer to **Office 365**. Statements made with regard to Office 365 will also apply to Microsoft 365, unless noted otherwise.

Since 2014, Microsoft in essence has adopted a cloud-first strategy. This means that changes and new features will be introduced in Office 365 first. Contrary to customer environments, the high level of standardization in the Office 365 service enables introduction or rolling back of small, gradual changes. When they are deemed suitable for on-premises usage, changes get ported to and validated for the on-premises Exchange Server product in the form of a Cumulative Update or Security Update. Do note that historically, updates for Exchange on-premises were ports of changes to the Exchange Online code. Per Exchange 2019, the codebase between Exchange on-premises and Exchange Online has been separated to avoid issues caused by dependencies only available in Office 365.

However, owing to scale and dependencies, some workloads never make it to the on-premises world, such as Microsoft Teams. Where Teams' predecessor Skype for Business still is available as an on-premises deployable product, Teams could never run on-premises due to its architecture, depending on Exchange for user and group mailboxes, SharePoint for sites and file storage, (Azure) Active Directory, Enterprise Voice, and integration with Power Platform to name a few.

Because of the nature of Outlook Web App and the Outlook client, this cloud-first strategy also means feature changes usually become available in Outlook Web App first. Web apps are closely followed by Microsoft 365 Apps for Enterprise, formerly known as Office 365 Pro Plus, the Click-to-Run (C2R) version of the Microsoft Office desktop product. The standalone Office 2019 product (MSI) will require a hotfix or service pack for every new or changed feature. In some cases, the MSI will not even receive the same features as the C2R version, such as support for more than 500 folders per mailbox.

When considering moving to Office 365, hybrid or all-in, organizations need to be aware of the consequences and potential impact of this switch. For example, while you can configure aspects of your cloud-based tenant, some limitations are set in stone by the provider, such as the maximum item retention.

Caution   Organizations using Office 365 services, in full or partially like with Exchange hybrid deployments, will need to keep track of changes in the cloud service, as changes might affect businesses. Examples of such changes were the deprecation of basic authentication or supportability of TLS v1.3. A good place to start monitoring for changes is the Message Center in the Office 365 portal, which contains announcements tailored to your organization. You can also configure to receive a digest per email.

This chapter will focus mainly on the identity models that are concerned when it comes to Office 365:

- Cloud Identities

- Synchronized Identities

- Federated Identities

The following sections will describe each model. Core of each model is Azure Active Directory, which is now part of the Microsoft Entra family of products. After that we will go into detail on deploying the identity model most utilized with Exchange hybrid deployments, Synchronized Identities.

Note   Entra is the family of products related to identity. Apart from Azure Active Directory, which we will discuss in this chapter, it consists of other products, such as Entra Identity Governance. More on Entra at **https://aka.ms/entra**.

Cloud Identities

While the other Synchronized and Federated identity models are the most common, it is still useful to mention Cloud Identities. In this model, depicted in Figure 4-1, the identity is stored in Azure Active Directory and Azure Active Directory only. Authentication is performed against Azure Active Directory as well. There is no relationship with Active Directory on-premises. Even when the Synchronized or Federated identity model is used, organizations can still if needed create Cloud Identities. This can be explicit, for example, by creating a cloud-only user directly in Azure Active Directory with a license for Exchange Online or creating a cloud-only dynamic Distribution Group. Implicit identities can be created via, for example, Microsoft Teams with a Microsoft 365 Group and assigned email address underneath.

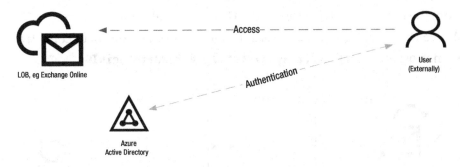

Figure 4-1. *Cloud Identities*

When using Synchronized or Federated Identities with Cloud Identities, when the latter are independent of Active Directory on-premises, there is a chance of conflicts. For example, you might have a cloud-only Distribution Group with an email address that you also want to assign to a newly created (synchronized) Distribution Group. The synchronization process will detect the conflict, and you need to manually resolve the situation. To make sure these cloud-originating identities also become known on-premises, the synchronization process can use write-back functionality. More on that in the "Azure AD Connect" section later in this chapter.

Synchronized Identities

With Synchronized Identities, Azure Active Directory, holding security principles such as users and groups, is kept in sync with identities originating from the local Active Directory. This synchronization process can be tailored to meet the needs of the organization. For example, it is possible to filter identities based on attribute characteristics or the Organizational Unit where the object is located. It is also possible to perform attribute translation. For example, when you are using non-routable User Principal Names on-premises such as james@contoso.local, which cannot be synchronized to Azure Active Directory because .local is a non-routable email domain, you can synchronize a different attribute from the local Active Directory to the User Principal Name in Azure Active Directory. This principle is, for example, used in Alternate Login ID scenarios; more on that at **https://bit.ly/AlternateLoginID**.

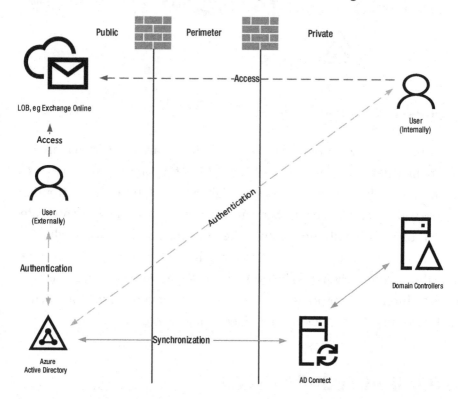

Figure 4-2. *Synchronized Identities*

In this model, depicted in Figure 4-2, the identity is stored in Azure Active Directory, and authentication is performed against Azure Active Directory as well. Authentication leverages the synchronized password hashes (Password Hash Synchronization or PHS), or when organizations do not desire this, authentication can be relayed from Office 365 to Active Directory using agent technology (Pass-Through Authentication or PTA). Identities authenticating this way are known as managed identities; this is configured on the domain level.

There are two types of deployments when considering Synchronized Identities:

- **Azure AD Connect** is the de facto topology for Exchange hybrid and requires installing one or more synchronization servers in your local infrastructure (AD Connect). Multiple AD Connect servers can be used for availability, with one being the designated main server propagating changes and others functioning as staging servers. During long outages or maintenance, staging servers can be promoted to become main servers. More on deploying AD Connect later in this chapter.

- **Azure AD Connect Cloud Sync** differs from AD Connect in that it does not require deploying additional infrastructure. Synchronization of objects is achieved by deploying agents in your local infrastructure, which can be existing servers. Availability can be increased by deploying multiple agents. However, some features are lacking when deploying Azure AD Connect Cloud Sync at this moment, which is why this deployment is not supported for Exchange hybrid.

Federated Identities

In this model, the identity is synchronized to Azure Active Directory via Azure AD Connect, but the actual authentication is performed by solutions such as Active Directory Federation Services or AD FS. This solution will perform authentication against the local Active Directory, as depicted in Figure 4-3. Identities authenticating this way are known as Federated Identities. This is configured on the domain level.

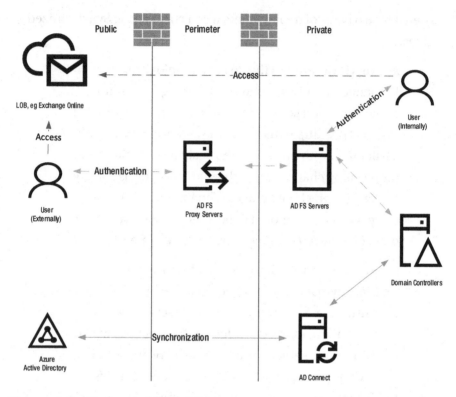

Figure 4-3. *Federated Identities*

Deployments using AD FS are becoming rare and usually are more complex as other services are usually bolted on to perform additional third-party services, such as third-party multifactor authentication.

AD FS is complementary to Synchronized Identities, where AD FS provides authentication services; it does not populate identities. For this reason, the book will focus on cloud authentication.

Note that Microsoft is actively deemphasizing AD FS in favor of Azure Active Directory. New security-related developments, such as Modern Authentication enhancements or Conditional Access-related, are all Azure Active Directory based.

Writing on migrating from AD FS to Azure AD can be a book in itself. If your organization is still using AD FS, a good starting point for planning and migrating from AD FS to Azure AD can be found at **https://bit.ly/ADFStoAzureAD**.

Azure AD Connect

The infrastructure component synchronizing identities to Azure Active Directory, and optionally properties such as password hashes for cloud authentication, is the directory synchronization server, or Azure AD Connect. Originally named DirSync, and still commonly referred to by this name, AD Connect is a software component that needs to be installed in the local infrastructure. It periodically updates its database, the metaverse, with information from Active Directory and Azure Active Directory. Based on this information, it will determine which changes it needs to propagate to the other end, resulting in Active Directory changes ending up in Azure Active Directory and vice versa.

Synchronized objects need to be made in scope of the synchronization process, and during deployment you need to configure that it will also synchronize Exchange-related attributes such as email addresses. Synchronization is in principle one way for most attributes; some attributes like publicDelegates can be written back when write-back is specifically configured. Implication of this model is that management of those synchronized objects and attributes, such as mailboxes and Distribution Groups, in principle is performed on-premises (source of authority).

Note   Before you implement AD Connect, it is recommended you use a tool called IdFix to identify erroneous objects that may exist in your Active Directory and that could lead to synchronization problems. You can download the IdFix tool at **https://microsoft.github. io/idfix**.

AD Connect can also be configured to synchronize password hashes (Password Hash Synchronization or PHS). This means the hash of your on-premises user is synchronized to Azure Active Directory, so that you can use the same credentials on-premises as well when accessing Office 365 applications. This creates a same sign-on experience. This can also function as a fallback authentication mechanism when AD FS is unavailable. AD Connect can also be configured to sync password hashes back as well, for example, to accommodate changing your password in Azure Active Directory instead of the local Active Directory.

AD Connect can selectively synchronize objects, for domains, OU, groups, or attribute filters. Do note that some functionality may require synchronizing all mail-related objects, such as Global Address List generation in Exchange Online or population of dynamic Distribution Groups (DDGs). Not synchronizing a potential member of a dynamic Distribution Group to Azure Active Directory means that mail sent to that recipient may never get delivered, as the DDG will not include the non-synchronized recipients, even when they match the DDG's filter.

Tip   AD Connect can synchronize objects from one or more local Active Directories to Azure Active Directory. For an overview of supported Azure AD Connect topologies, see **https://bit.ly/ ADConnectTopologies**.

When deploying AD Connect for Exchange hybrid, a local Exchange server can still be required for managing synchronized objects and handling mail routing. Changing attributes directly or using third-party tools is not supported. Also, changing attributes of synchronized objects is actively blocked in Office 365.

Note   *Exchange Hybrid Server* is a term frequently used for Exchange servers that are used in hybrid deployments. However, they are "just Exchange servers" that are functionally identical to any Exchange server.

In the past, organizations that wanted to go all-in on Office 365, moving all of their mailboxes and related configuration to Exchange Online, were often surprised to discover they still had to keep a minimal Exchange on-premises infrastructure for management. Per Exchange 2019 Cumulative Update 12, released in April 2022, organizations have the option to get rid of those last Exchange "hybrid" servers running on-premises, if all of the following are true:

- The organization is running Exchange 2019 CU12 or later in hybrid.

- There are no mailboxes or public folders hosted on-premises.

- They are not using Exchange servers to handle email traffic or additional email processing, for example, relaying mail from multi-functional devices or adding disclaimers.

Caution   When using AD Connect, the source of authority for objects is on-premises. These objects need to be managed using Exchange on-premises, even when you have migrated all mailboxes to Exchange Online. Exchange 2019 CU12 or later introduced Exchange server-less recipient management, under certain conditions. More on that in Chapter 5.

Something to also be aware of when working with identities and Exchange Online is that Exchange Online does not talk directly to Azure Active Directory. Exchange Online has its own directory, called EXODS (Exchange Directory Services). EXODS is a different directory from Azure Active Directory and contains Exchange-related objects and information. A background process (backsync) synchronizes objects and attributes between Azure Active Directory and EXODS. This process is something to be aware of, as it could happen that changes in Azure Active Directory are not instantly visible in Exchange Online.

AD Connect Deployment

Download the AD Connect package via the **Azure AD portal ➤ Azure AD Connect**, or go to **https://bit.ly/ADConnectDownload**. During installation, the AD Connect setup will ask a few questions regarding your deployment. Note that you can choose **Express** or **Custom** setup. Express setup is meant for organizations running a single Active Directory forest that are going to use Password Hash Synchronization. In other scenarios or when you want full control over the configuration, select Custom setup. Note that AD Connect setup will fetch required dependencies such as SQL Server Express during setup.

Tip   During Custom setup, AD Connect contains an option to **Import synchronization settings**. This allows you to quickly deploy additional AD Connect staging servers, after exporting settings from an existing AD Connect server, or replicate configuration from or to a test environment.

During setup, you can configure AD Connect to use a global Managed Service Account (gMSA) for running its services, by selecting Use an existing service account and specifying a pre-created gMSA. The benefit of using a gMSA over a regular Active Directory service account is that Active Directory will manage the account, including periodically changing the password. During setup specify which type of account is going to be used. Once decided, switching is not possible; you need to deploy a new AD Connect server in staging mode, promote it, and decommission the old AD Connect server. More background on Managed Service Accounts can be seen at **https://bit.ly/ADConnectMSA**.

After installing AD Connect and its services, Custom setup will proceed with its initial configuration by starting to ask what sign-on method it needs to configure. Enable single sign-on when you want users to have a single sign-on experience working with Office 365 services. Note that this only works when AD Connect is configured to use PHS or Pass-Through Authentication (PTA). More about PHS, PTA, and federation using Active Directory Federation Services (AD FS) and their differences at **https://bit.ly/ADConnectSingleSignOn**.

Next, provide the account to connect to your Office 365 tenant. Setup will verify connection to your tenant. Setup will create the account (prefixed ...) in your tenant, which will be used for its synchronization process. Proceed by specifying which Active Directories it needs to synchronize with. Select the UPN suffix it needs to use to synchronize identities for (only suffixes that match verified domains in your tenant can be selected), and pick the attribute which needs to be synchronized as User Principal Name to your tenant. This then also becomes the account that users need to log onto Office 365 services, except when using federation as authentication, in which case they need to use their on-premises identity.

Caution   When installing AD Connect, setup will ask about **SourceAnchor**, the attribute to uniquely identify users from your organization. By default, this will be objectGuid, which is fine for small, single-forest organizations. However, when you have multiple forests, there is a slight chance objectGuids might overlap. Select msDS-ConsistencyGuid to prevent this issue and conform with best practices. The mSDS-ConsistencyGuid attribute needs to be populated to sync, and your provisioning process or Identity Management solution needs to provision it with something unique. AD Connect will translate your on-premises msDS-ConsistencyGuid (Byte Array) back and forth to ImmutableId in your tenant. To do this manually, use something like

msDS-ConsistencyGuid to ImmutableId

```
$Guid= [GUID]((Get-ADUser -Identity UserA -Properties
MS-DS-ConsistencyGuid).'ms-DS-ConsistencyGuid')
$ImmutableId= [system.convert]::ToBase64String
( $Guid.ToByteArray())
```

ImmutableId to msDS-ConsistencyGuid:

```
[GUID]([System.Convert]::FromBase64String
((Get-AzureADUser -ObjectId UserA).ImmutableID))
```

In the next screens during AD Connect setup, you can select to synchronize objects from all domains and Organizations Units or narrow down the selection to specific domains, Organizational Units, or other filtering options such as groups. The Optional Features screen shows an option that is important for Exchange hybrid, which is **Exchange hybrid deployment.** Enabling it allows AD Connect to sync back the attributes mentioned in Figure 4-4 from your tenant to Active Directory.

Attribute	Description
msDS-ExternalDirectoryObjectId	This attribute correlates to the object in Azure Active Directory.
msExchArchiveStatus	Personal archive status for users using cloud-based personal archives — i.e., Exchange Online Archiving.
msExchUserHoldPolicies	In-place hold status of mailboxes.
ProxyAddresses	The legacyExchangeDN of the User, Contact or Group in Exchange Online is added as X500 address to the proxyAddresses attribute in the local Active Directory. This makes sure replies or cached name entries still work after migrating mailboxes to Exchange Online.
SafeSendersHash BlockedSendersHash SafeRecipientHash	Filtering and online safe and blocked sender information.
msExchUCVoiceMailSettings	Voice-mail status for users having cloud-based voice mail configured.
publicDelegates	Allows mailboxes in Exchange Online to be granted SendOnBehalfTo permissions to mailboxes in Exchange on-premises.

Figure 4-4. *Exchange hybrid deployment attribute write-back*

To see the current list of which attributes get synchronized or synchronized back, see **https://bit.ly/ADConnectAttributes**.

Tip   To prevent non-delivery reports when replying to old email messages after offboarding mailboxes, AD Connect will write back the legacyExchangeDN address as an X500 address to on-premises recipients.

After deployment, depending on your environment, your AD Connect server is set to automatically perform upgrades. The default synchronization schedule will be set to run every 30 minutes. You can view these settings by opening a local PowerShell session on the AD Connect server and running Get-ADSyncAutoUpgrade or Get-ADSyncScheduler, respectively. The results can be seen in Figure in 4-5.

```
PS C:\Users\Administrator> Get-ADSyncAutoUpgrade
Enabled
PS C:\Users\Administrator> Get-ADSyncScheduler


AllowedSyncCycleInterval        : 00:30:00
CurrentlyEffectiveSyncCycleInterval : 01:00:00
CustomizedSyncCycleInterval     : 01:00:00
NextSyncCyclePolicyType         : Delta
NextSyncCycleStartTimeInUTC     : 2/6/2023 12:44:58 AM
PurgeRunHistoryInterval         : 7.00:00:00
SyncCycleEnabled        : True
MaintenanceEnabled        : True
StagingModeEnabled        : False
SchedulerSuspended        : False
SyncCycleInProgress        : False
```

Figure 4-5. *Default AD Connect AutoUpgrade and Scheduler settings*

Disabling AutoUpgrade is generally not recommended, but if the need occurs, you can adjust this setting using Set-ADSyncAutoUpgrade Enabled or Set-ADSyncAutoUpgrade Disabled. You might also discover that AD Connect will not perform automatic upgrade for major updates. In that case, you might need to perform a manual upgrade by downloading and running the latest version of AD Connect installation files.

Depending on your requirements and number of objects, you might wish to adjust the default synchronization schedule of 30 minutes. To accomplish this, from PowerShell on the server where AD Connect is installed, run the Set-ADSyncScheduler -CustomizedSyncCycleInterval hh:mm:ss, where hh:mm:ss is the interval in hours, minutes, and seconds. Note that you cannot use an interval less than 30 minutes.

Tip   Per version 2.0.3.0 of AD Connect, a new endpoint (v2) is used, which performs better and supports groups with up to 250,000 members. Version 1 of AD Connect has been retired on August 31, 2022, due to its dependency on SQL Server 2012, which is end of life. AD Connect v2 builds will be supported up to 12 months after a newer build has been released. You can find the AD Connect release notes at **https://bit.ly/ADConnectReleaseNotes**.

AD Connect Health

After deploying and configuring AD Connect, unless you are utilizing another method of monitoring Azure AD Connect's status, it is recommended to deploy the Azure AD Connect Health agents. This will monitor your AD Connect server as well as optionally AD FS and Active Directory Domain Services after deploying Azure AD Connect Health agents within your local infrastructure.

The collected data is pushed to Azure Active Directory and presented in the Azure AD Connect Health portal. You can then use the Azure AD Connect Health portal to view alerts, identify synchronization issues, and monitor performance, usage analytics, and other information. Azure AD Connect Health enables a single pane of view of health for your key identity components in a single location.

You can download the Azure AD Connect Health agents from the portal at **https://aka.ms/aadconnecthealth**.

CHAPTER 5

Exchange Online

"Why a chapter on Exchange Online in a book on Exchange Server?" you might ask. The answer is simple: While there are companies still running Exchange Server on-premises, a large part of Exchange customers run Exchange Server complementary to Exchange Online, the email platform that is part of Microsoft 365, a subscription-based offering built around Office and Windows-related software and services. This warrants a look on Exchange Online, especially where it meets Exchange Server.

Microsoft 365 and Exchange Online are a well-established service offering nowadays, being over ten years since their official rebranding with Windows 10 and Office 365 in June 2011 and even longer if you take into account the initial offering named Business Productivity Online Suite (BPOS). BPOS was launched in 2008 as a package of individually hosted Microsoft products, such as Exchange and Live Meeting. The platform has come a long way.

At the time of writing, Microsoft 365 offers software and cloud-based services founded on workloads such as

- Azure Active Directory for authentication and authorization

- Microsoft Exchange Online for email, with Exchange Online Protection and Defender for Office for cloud-based email hygiene

- Microsoft Teams for communications and conferencing

© Jaap Wesselius and Michel de Rooij 2023
J. Wesselius and M. de Rooij, *Pro Exchange Administration*,
https://doi.org/10.1007/978-1-4842-9591-5_5

- Microsoft SharePoint Online for document storage and collaboration

- Microsoft Office Web Apps as the online Microsoft Office Suite

- OneDrive for Business for cloud-based file storage

- Power Automate for workflow and process automation

- Power BI for analytics and data visualization

- Microsoft Windows and Microsoft Office desktop application licenses

What products and services are available to your organization depend on your subscription plan. The Microsoft 365 subscriptions and packages change quite frequently; current subscriptions for businesses can be compared at **https://bit.ly/M365Bplans** and enterprise plans at **https://bit.ly/M365Eplans**. This is also the location to start your Microsoft 365 journey by selecting one of the subscription plans. Most plans offer the option of a trial, where you can try out their features.

Note   Since Office 365 is also available as a subscription plan, without the addition of Windows 10 or Enterprise Mobility + Security (EMS), we will refer to **Office 365**. Statements made with regard to Office 365 will also apply to Microsoft 365, unless noted otherwise. Also, with **Exchange Online** (EXO), we will refer to the Exchange Online environment that is part of Office 365, as Exchange Online also happens to be the name given to a specific Office 365 business plan offering hosted Exchange email services.

In 2014, Microsoft started adopting a cloud-first strategy. This means that changes and new features will be introduced in Office 365 first. Contrary to customer environments, the high level of standardization in the Office 365 service enables introduction or rolling back of small, gradual changes. The Exchange Server product is no longer a fork of the Exchange Online product and stands on its own. When changes in Exchange Online are deemed suitable for on-premises usage, they might get propagated to the Exchange Server product, which might lead to a new Security Update or when accumulated a new Cumulative Update.

However, owing to scale, some applications never make it to the on-premises world, such as Microsoft Teams. Where Teams' predecessor Skype for Business is (still) available as an on-premises deployable product, Teams could never run on-premises due to its architecture, depending on Exchange for user and group mailboxes, SharePoint for sites and file storage, (Azure) Active Directory, Enterprise Voice, and integration with Power Platform to name a few.

Because of the nature of Outlook Web App and the Outlook client, this cloud-first strategy also means changes become available for Outlook Web App first. This is also true for the Microsoft 365 Apps for Enterprise, previously known as Office 365 Pro Plus. This Click-to-Run version of Microsoft Office contains some features that Microsoft said will not get propagated to the standalone installable .MSI version of Microsoft Office, despite it receiving periodic functionality or Security Updates. One of these features is the support for more than 500 folders per mailbox, which can happen easily with nowadays large mailboxes.

Things will take a bigger turn with the introduction of the new Outlook for Windows client, which is currently in preview for Exchange-backed Microsoft 365 work or school accounts. The goal of this new Outlook Preview client is not to offer a complete replacement, but instead to be a more than acceptable replacement for Outlook Desktop when suited. Being a web application, it can self-update similar to the Teams client, offers some offline access and multi-account support, but lacks features simply because of the platform, such as lack of Outlook add-in support. This also can be a good thing, as these need to be maintained and can be a headache topic with every major Outlook upgrade.

Eligible users can switch the "Try the New Outlook" toggle in Outlook on the Web view to install the web application and have a look, provided administrators did not disable access to it.

When considering moving to Office 365, cloud-only or hybrid, organizations need to be aware of the consequences and potential impact of this switch, as it also means you will be bound to usage and limitations as defined by the cloud provider. For example, while you can configure aspects of your cloud-based tenant, such as the message size limit, which can be changed within the boundaries offered by your provider, some are simply set in stone, such as the maximum mailbox size, which depends on the type of mailbox and effective license.

Caution   Organizations using Office 365 services need to keep track of changes in the cloud services, as they might affect their business operation. An example is the recent disabling of basic authentication as the authentication method for all non-SMTP protocols. Announcements targeted at your tenant are published in the Message Center, at **https://admin.microsoft.com/ Adminportal/Home#/MessageCenter.**

In the previous chapters, we discussed the Exchange infrastructure, how to deploy Exchange Server, and what identity models are available when integrating your on-premises environment with Office 365. In this chapter, after briefly talking about moving to Exchange Online, we will continue focusing on the deployment of Exchange hybrid, where companies integrate their on-premises Exchange infrastructure with Exchange Online. This is the most common setup found in enterprise environments, which often have a technical or legal requirement preventing them from moving completely to Exchange Online. Examples of this are legacy applications that cannot interact with Exchange Online, applications that cannot use Exchange Online to send bulk email, or requirements to send outbound messages through on-premises infrastructure.

Exchange Hybrid Topologies

One of the steps when configuring Exchange hybrid is to decide regarding the Exchange hybrid topology your organization wants to deploy. The greatest drivers that we see will determine this choice will be

- *Timelines*: Is the primary goal of your organization to move mailboxes to Exchange Online as soon as possible, or does it require a more phased planning, creating a need to arrange for proper coexistence during the overall migration process?

- *Coexistence*: If the migration takes place over a longer period of time or without a fixed end date, it is better from a user experience to deploy Exchange hybrid with the best possible experience, independent of whether a mailbox is migrated or not. Think of functionality such as Full Access to shared mailboxes, Send As another mailbox, or Free/Busy lookup.

- *Anticipated support for migrated users, which is in principle a logistical component of adoption*: For example, if your organization lock-steps mailbox migration with rollout of new modern workplace, including new devices that need enrolling, you may find other elements of the migration becoming a bottleneck. Consequently, while you could in theory migrate 100 mailboxes just as easy as 1,000, you may need to slow down the pace.

So what are the options for deploying Exchange hybrid? The first choice when deploying Exchange hybrid, as shown in Figure 5-1, is in regard to Classic or Modern topology:

- **Classic topology** will require more configuration, is more feature-rich, and requires publishing of Exchange on-premises to the outside world.

- **Modern topology** uses one or more Hybrid Agents that need to be deployed. These agents will manage mailbox migrations (MRS) and Free/Busy requests. It will utilize an Azure App Proxy for these tasks and therefore only requires outbound connections to the Internet for this functionality.

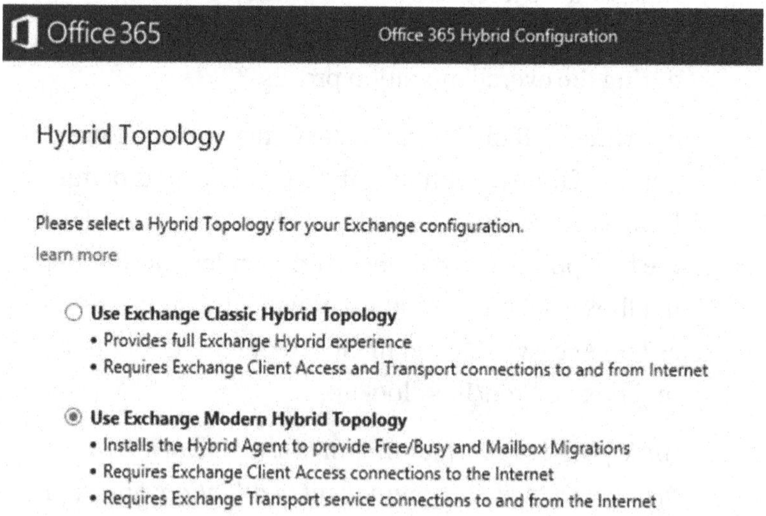

Figure 5-1. *Exchange hybrid topology*

Note   You can switch from Modern to Classic topology. This is useful when it turns out migration executing takes longer than expected and lack of cross-premises functionality becomes a problem. To switch, select the Classic topology when running the Hybrid Configuration Wizard to reconfigure, after making any required additional configuration changes, such as publishing Exchange. Switching from Classic to Modern is also possible, provided you wipe the current Hybrid Configuration state and pretend to start from scratch.

The second choice is related to deploying a Full or Minimal configuration:

- *Full hybrid*: Best fit for large organizations, which require integration between Exchange on-premises and Exchange Online during the migration period. This option is also the most flexible, offering migrating mailboxes back on-premises, exchange of Free/Busy information, and additional mail flow controls.

- *Minimal hybrid*: Best suited for small- to medium-sized organizations that are more time-constraint and do not require cross-premises integration during the migration. Additionally, this option requires the least configuration and resources.

It might be helpful to understand what the exact technical differences are between Classic and Modern and Full and Minimal. To this purpose, Table 5-1 contains an overview of all technical requirements needed for these topologies and modes.

Table 5-1. *Exchange Hybrid Topology: Classic vs. Modern, Full vs. Minimal*

	Classic		Modern	
	Minimal	Full	Minimal	Full
Feature				
Cross-premises Free/Busy	No	Yes	No	Yes
Organization Configuration Transfer (OCT)	Yes	Yes	Yes	Yes
Hybrid Modern Auth Support	No	Yes	No	No
Cross-Premises Feature				
eDiscovery	No	Yes	No	No
Message tracking	No	Yes	No	No
Delegates	No	Yes	No	Yes
Folder access	No	Yes	No	No
Retention to Archive (EXO)	No	Yes	No	Yes
Required Configuration				
Send/Receive Connectors	No	Yes	No	Yes
Federation trust	No	Yes	No	Yes
Organizational relationship	No	Yes	No	Yes
OAuth	No	Yes	No	Yes
Autodiscover + certificate	Yes	Yes	Yes	Yes
SMTP certificate	No	Yes	No	Yes
EWS certificate	Yes	Yes	No	No

(*continued*)

Table 5-1. (*continued*)

	Classic		Modern	
	Minimal	Full	Minimal	Full
Publishing				
TCP/443 Internet > Exchange	Yes	Yes	Yes[1]	Yes[1]
TCP/443 Exchange > EXO + Office 365 Common[2]	Yes	Yes	Yes[3]	Yes[2]
TCP/25 EXO > Exchange	No	Yes	No	Yes
TCP/25 Exchange > EXO	No	Yes	No	Yes
TCP/80 Exchange > Internet (Certificate CRL)	Yes	Yes	Yes	Yes
TCP/5985 Hybrid Agent > Exchange	N/A	N/A	Yes	Yes
TCP/5986 Hybrid Agent > Exchange	N/A	N/A	Yes	Yes

Note   Many vendors offer features to automatically configure services to allow connecting to or from Office 365 services. Note that other (e.g., inbound) connections are listed at a different page, at `https://bit.ly/O365OtherUrlsIps`.

[1] Only when required for Autodiscover, not required for Hybrid Agent.
[2] Common Office 365 services, published at `https://bit.ly/O365UrlsIps`.
[3] Includes Hybrid Agent for *.msappproxy.net.

The remainder of this chapter will focus on the Exchange Full hybrid/Classic deployment, which is what most organizations choose. It is also the deployment that offers the best coexistence options and flexibility and is usually the end situation after onboarding of mailboxes has been completed—in full or partial because of various legitimate reasons. Where appropriate, specific details on those other scenarios will be highlighted.

Note   To help organizations make a choice for their migration path, the Exchange deployment assistant might prove useful. After answering a few basic questions, such as what version of Exchange is currently used and what requirements you have, the tool generates step-by-step instructions. The Exchange deployment assistant can be found at **http://bit.ly/exchangeda**.

Deploying Exchange Hybrid

For Exchange hybrid, you integrate your on-premises Exchange infrastructure with Exchange Online. This needs to occur after setting up hybrid identity, as discussed in the previous chapter. Configuring Exchange hybrid consists of validating domains you want to use and configuring secure mail flow, domains, connectors, interoperability for Free/Busy, etc. There used to be around 50 manual steps involved in setting up Exchange hybrid before the Hybrid Configuration Wizard became available in 2015. While many administrators are only familiar with the HCW process, during troubleshooting you may have to dive into the setup itself, at which point knowing what gets configured can be very helpful.

Caution   The HCW must run successfully for your Exchange hybrid deployment to be supported. Also, after upgrading your Exchange version, you officially need to rerun the HCW to anticipate any changes in the Exchange on-premises version. Gentle reminder that in order to stay supported with Exchange hybrid, your Exchange servers on-premises need to stay current, trailing one Cumulative Update version at most.

Hybrid Configuration Wizard

When we talk about running the Hybrid Configuration Wizard (HCW), we talk about the web application that can be run to assist in configuring or reconfiguring your Exchange hybrid deployment. While this book focuses on Exchange Server 2019, it is possible to deploy Exchange Server 2019 in front of Exchange Server 2016 and let it down-level proxy hybrid or client traffic. This deployment is sometimes referred to as deploying "Hybrid Server," which is nothing more than an ordinary Exchange server handling traffic related to the hybrid configuration.

The Hybrid Configuration Wizard, or HCW, is an app that you run via the **Exchange Admin Center ➤ Hybrid** or via `https://aka.ms/ HybridWizard`. The app will download the latest app (**Microsoft.Online. CSE.Hybrid.Client.application**) from `https://shcwreleaseprod.blob. core.windows.net/shcw/`, so this URL needs to be accessible. Being a web app, you are always guaranteed to run the latest version when (re) configuring your Exchange hybrid setup. The HCW has become a fully evolved tool to set things up, and configuring Exchange hybrid using the HCW is the only supported procedure. Note that while the HCW is web app based, it runs Exchange Management Shell commands against your local Exchange infrastructure and Exchange Online as well.

Note   The HCW does not configure your public DNS MX records. If at some point in your migration project, you want to start routing inbound messages through Exchange Online Protection, you need to reconfigure the MX record, pointing it to <domain-extension>.mail. protection.outlook.com, for example, **contoso-com.mail.protection. outlook.com**.

After installing the HCW, you will be presented with a dialog similar to the dialog shown in Figure 5-2.

Figure 5-2. Hybrid Configuration Wizard

Tip   When you press F12 in the HCW, you will get a small menu with shortcuts to certain functions, such as opening the log file or the folder with the HCW logs. This can be helpful during troubleshooting.

To start, it is good to understand what the global process looks like when running the HCW. Configuring Exchange hybrid using Classic Full topology using the HCW follows these global steps:

1. Using the HCW, you define the desired state. Part of the process is proving ownership of the domain names you want to enable for integration by creating TXT records in the public DNS containing secrets. So be prepared to make changes in the public DNS when running the HCW, or provide network administrators with the information they need to register. Some steps, such as what to provide as proof of ownership, are only presented when running the HCW, so be prepared that the overall process might take some time.

2. Behind the scenes, the desired hybrid configuration is then stored in Active Directory using the cmdlet Set-HybridConfiguration. The location of the information is below the Configuration container at **CN=Services ➤ CN=Microsoft Exchange ➤ CN=<Exchange Organization Name> ➤ CN=Hybrid Configuration**.

3. At the completion of the HCW, Update-HybridConfiguration is called, which triggers the hybrid configuration engine.

4. The engine reads the desired state.

5. The engine collects the current Exchange on-premises and Exchange Online configuration.

6. Based on the desired state and the current state, the engine determines the delta and tasks that need to execute. Depending on the delta, these tasks may include

    a. Managing accepted domains for mail flow and Autodiscover requests. Your Office 365 tenant will have a domain in the form of **<domain name>.onmicrosoft.com**. This address space, also called Microsoft Online Email Routing Address (MOERA), is added to the default email address policy. Secondary email addresses are stamped with this address for internal routing between on-premises and Exchange Online.

    b. Picking and configuring an on-premises certificate for secure mail flow between Exchange on-premises and Exchange Online using TLS.

    c. Configuring federation and defining the organizational relationships between the Exchange on-premises and Exchange Online and vice versa.

    d. Configuring secure mail flow between Exchange on-premises Mailbox servers, via Edge servers when available and desired, and Exchange Online Protection (EOP). Here, you also have the option to always route outbound messages through your on-premises organization using the Centralized Mail Transport (CMT) option. There's more on mail flow later in this chapter.

e. Configuring Open Authorization (OAuth). This
    enables cross-premises functionality, such as
    full mailbox access, folder-level delegations, etc.

Note   The HCW supports configuring hybrid for Exchange on-premises to up to five tenants simultaneously. This requires AD synchronization to not overlap synchronizing the same object and requires every tenant to use its own namespace for routing and authentication and separate certificates to secure mail flow and proper attribution of messages.

As examples sometimes give a better impression of what needs to happen, we will now provide a quick run-through of the HCW. Requirements for running the HCW are a supported browser, meaning Microsoft Edge, Firefox, or Chrome. Also, TLS 1.2 needs to be supported and enabled by the operating system you run the HCW on. Finally, Exchange management tools need to be present on the system when using a member workstation or server. This does not apply of course when running the HCW from an Exchange server itself.

1. To run the HCW, using a browser on one of your
    Exchange servers or a member server with Exchange
    management tools installed, navigate to **aka.ms/
    HybridWizard**, and install the app from **Microsoft
    Office 365 Hybrid Configuration Wizard**.

2. After clicking **Next**, the HCW will check your
    Exchange on-premises environment and try to
    detect one of your on-premises Exchange servers
    suitable for configuring Exchange hybrid. This is
    determined by things like the requirement to set
    up an Exchange Management Shell session from
    where you run the HCW to this Exchange server,

so PowerShell ports (WinRM, 5985, and 5986 by default) to this server need to be open. Alternatively, you can pick a server yourself by specifying its FQDN. You can select where your tenant is hosted, which is Office 365 Worldwide for most organizations.

3. Next, you are asked to specify your Exchange on-premises administrator credentials, as well as credentials for Exchange Online.

4. After successful authentication, the HCW will start collecting information from your Exchange on-premises environment, as well as your Exchange Online environment.

5. Next, the question is asked which Exchange hybrid model you wish to deploy. As mentioned in the beginning of this chapter, possible options are **Minimal** or **Full hybrid configuration**. We will select the **Full** option as an example, which involves the most configuration. Optionally, you can check Organization Configuration Transfer (OCT) here. The purpose of OCT is to port certain settings from your Exchange on-premises environment to Exchange Online. The policies and configuration elements that are covered are shown in Table 5-2. Note that OCT is a one-time transfer; it does not synchronize existing configuration elements.

Note   At the time of writing, the HCW has some dependencies on remote PowerShell. Remote PowerShell will get deprecated in September 2023. An update for the HCW is being worked on that will remove this dependency.

Table 5-2. *Organization Configuration Transfer*

Policy or Attributes Transferred by OCT

Active Sync Device Access Rule	DLP Policy	OWA Mailbox Policy	Retention Policy Tags
Active Sync Mailbox Policy	Malware Filter Policy	Policy Tip Config	Sharing Policy
Active Sync Organization Settings	Mobile Device Mailbox Policy	Remote Domains	S/MIME Config
Address List	Organization Config	Retention Policy	Transport Config

6. Then, you need to specify which domains you want to include in the hybrid deployment at the Hybrid Domains step. When you have a single accepted domain configured, this step is skipped, and the domain will be used for configuration.

7. The HCW will then ask about configuring secure mail flow between your Exchange on-premises environment and Exchange Online. When you have no Edge Transport servers, choose the Mailbox server(s) to configure. When you are using

Edge Transport servers in your organization, you can select that option, after which the HCW will configure the necessary connectors through the Edge Transport subscription. Clicking **Advanced** will display an option to configure Centralized Mail Transport. More on that later in this chapter.

8. You then need to specify which Exchange servers are going to host inbound connections. Click the dropdown box and check the Mailbox servers that should get the Receive Connector configured.

9. Now you are asked to specify which Exchange servers are going to be allowed to send mail to Exchange Online through an outbound Send Connector, to be configured by the HCW. Click the dropdown box and check the Mailbox servers that should become eligible.

10. One of the last steps is selecting the certificate that should be used to secure mail flow. This certificate should be installed on the Exchange servers selected for inbound and outbound mail flow, prior to running the HCW.

11. Enter the FQDN that should be configured on the outbound connector in Exchange Online to access your Exchange on-premises environment, for example, mail.contoso.com.

12. Now the HCW has collected all the information it needs to know to (re)configure your Exchange hybrid deployment.

Caution   As of March 2023, the first inbound connector of type **OnPremises** in Exchange Online will be created in disabled state. You may see a notice in the HCW, *"Inbound Connectors created by HCW are in disabled state"* or a similar message if you create an inbound OnPremises connector manually. This is to prevent malicious actors abusing new trial tenants just for the purpose of sending spam. Contact Microsoft Support—providing a business justification—to have it enabled.

Once the HCW finishes successfully and depending on your deployment, whether you contacted support to enable the inbound OnPremises-type connector in Exchange Online, your Exchange hybrid deployment should be ready. Should issues occur, the Hybrid Configuration Wizard log is an invaluable source of information mentioning the configuration steps that have been performed against your Exchange on-premises and Exchange Online environments. It will also show you potentially what went wrong or provide clues thereabout.

By default, the name of the HCW log file is the timestamp of starting the HCW (YYYYMMDD_HHMMSS.log), and the file is stored in the **%APPDATA%\Microsoft\Exchange Hybrid Configuration** folder, located on the Exchange server that was hosting the HCW session. In addition to the HCW log, you can also use the Remote Connectivity Analyzer (RCA) to troubleshoot connectivity issues that might be preventing you from successfully setting up Exchange hybrid. You can find the RCA at `http://exrca.com`.

Tip   To track log entries as they are produced while running the HCW, open a PowerShell session with the HCW open, navigate to the log folder—use the F12 trick to open the folder and get its name—and enter `Get-Content <LogFile.log> -Wait`. This will display lines as they are added to the log, like `tail -f` in Linux.

PowerShell: Connecting to Office 365

While PowerShell is really powerful for management of Exchange environments, on-premises and online, most administrators still use the Exchange Admin Center when administering Office 365 workloads for one-off tasks. But, as with on-premises Exchange, using PowerShell often is the preferred option, especially when repetitive tasks become tedious when performed through EAC. In some situations, using PowerShell might even be required, as some settings are not available from EAC.

Knowing how to connect to Exchange Online, Azure Active Directory, or one of the other workloads using PowerShell is crucial. Unfortunately, every workload, being it Exchange Online or Azure Active Directory or Teams, requires its own module. That would not be a problem, if every workload was consistent in the way to connect. Unfortunately, that is not yet always the case. Apart from workloads often having their own PowerShell module, which needs to be installed and needs to be updated, modules can have small deviations in how they operate or elementary things such as inconsequent naming of parameters.

As this chapter is about Exchange Online, we will now tell you how to set up PowerShell sessions to Exchange Online and Azure Active Directory.

Connecting to Exchange Online

When you connect to Exchange Online using PowerShell, you need to be aware of the fact that the session you will create will be subject to Role-Based Access Controls (RBACs). These controls determine what cmdlets and parameters you will have at your disposal and which ones you do not. For example, by default Exchange administrators cannot use the New-MailboxImportRequest cmdlet. More on RBAC in Chapter 10.

After connecting to Exchange Online, you will notice majority of the cmdlets are similar to their Exchange on-premises counterparts. Cmdlets might carry a different name, such as Get-OutboundConnector instead of Get-SendConnector or Get-MessageTrace instead of Get-MessageTracking. Cmdlets might also be absent, such as Get-MailboxDatabase, or are missing parameters, such as Server or ADSite, as these do not make a lot of sense in a cloud service. Output might also differ, as internal information might be omitted from output, such as server names.

Connecting to Exchange Online using PowerShell is performed using the Exchange Online Management module. At the time of writing, the legacy method of using remote PowerShell is still an option for existing tenants, but this will completely stop functioning in September 2023, including tenants that have requested postponement of this measure for their tenant. New tenants since April 2023 already have RPS disabled, and organizations should be using the Exchange Online Management v3 module. This module contains REST-based or REST-backed cmdlets matching all original Exchange cmdlets, together with its robustness and resilience to temporary issues and support for certificate-based authentication for automation.

The module is available from the PowerShell Gallery, a public repository for PowerShell modules. Installation is straightforward:

1. Open a PowerShell session in elevated mode.

2. Run Install-Module ExchangeOnlineManagement to install the module; by default it will be installed in the user scope, not machine-wide.

3. Use Import-Module ExchangeOnlineManagement to explicitly load the module.

4. Run Connect-ExchangeOnline to initiate connection to Exchange Online.

After connecting, your session is set up. You will have received an authentication token that has a certain lifetime. This locally cached token can be reused in your current security context during reconnection or when you use the same UPN at a later point, for example:

```
Connect-ExchangeOnline -UserPrincipalName admin@contoso.com
```

When connected successfully, you will be greeted with a banner informing you there is a new module, despite you already using that module, as shown in Figure 5-3.

```
[PS] >Connect-ExchangeOnline -UserPrincipalName admin@contoso.onmicrosoft.com
Connecting to Exchange Online with specified Modern Authentication method ..

--------------------------------------------------------------------------------

This V3 EXO PowerShell module contains new REST API backed Exchange Online cmdlets which doesn't require
WinRM for Client-Server communication. You can now run these cmdlets after turning off WinRM Basic Auth in your
client machine thus making it more secure.

Unlike the EXO* prefixed cmdlets, the cmdlets in this module support full functional parity with the RPS (V1) cmdlets.

V3 cmdlets in the downloaded module are resilient to transient failures, handling retries and throttling errors
inherently.

However, REST backed EOP and SCC cmdlets are not available yet. To use those, you will need to enable WinRM Basic
Auth.

For more information check https://aka.ms/exov3-module
--------------------------------------------------------------------------------
```

Figure 5-3. *Connect using Exchange Online Management*

Beyond the scope of this book but interesting to note is that the Exchange Online Management module contains nine cmdlets that use Graph API (REST-based) to query Office 365, instead of the "regular" REST-backed cmdlets. These REST-based cmdlets can be identified using their EXO noun-prefix, such as Get-EXOMailbox. To list them, use Get-Command -Module ExchangeOnlineManagement -Noun EXO*.

The difference between REST-based and REST-backed cmdlets is that REST-backed cmdlets leverage Microsoft Graph API to interact with Exchange Online resources. They are built on top of the underlying REST (Representational State Transfer) architecture. REST-backed cmdlets act as a wrapper around the REST API calls, providing the familiar PowerShell syntax.

REST-based cmdlets are cmdlets that directly use the underlying REST API calls to interact with Exchange Online resources. Unlike REST-backed cmdlets, they are not a wrapper and are typically used when more advanced or specific functionality is required that is not available through the REST-backed cmdlets. Also, the REST-based EXO cmdlets have a performance benefit, as they are optimized for speed.

REST-based cmdlets also have some peculiarities because of this architecture, such as the requirement to explicitly specify properties or property sets to return. This is one of the reasons they cannot be interchanged one on one with their non–Graph API counterparts, without checking first. In other words, if your script contains Get-Mailbox, you cannot simply replace it with Get-EXOMailbox to enjoy a performance benefit.

The Connect-ExchangeOnline cmdlet contains an optional Prefix parameter, which can be used to prefix nouns of imported cmdlets. For example, Connect-ExchangeOnline -Prefix Cloud will result in Get-Recipient being imported as Get-CloudRecipient. Note that "Cloud" can be any textual label. While -Prefix Super will work, Get-SuperMailbox does not make a lot of sense. So referring to the context is recommended. These prefixes are ideal when working with multiple Exchange environments, for example, Exchange on-premises and Exchange Online or the Exchange on-premises environment of a remote organization. It allows you to identify which environment you are addressing, the local Exchange on-premises without prefix, "cloud" for Exchange Online, or "partner" for a subsidiary. The only thing to keep in mind is that when used in scripts or procedures, you need to make sure you are connected to the proper environment using the proper prefix.

Tip   When you cannot download or install required PowerShell modules, you can export the module files using another workstation with access and copy the files. Then, you can import the module directly from the copied file set. In short, `Save-Module -Name ExchangeOnlineManagement -Path C:\PSModules -Repository PSGallery`. Then, after copying the exported module from C:\PSModules, import the module using the explicit path, `Import-Module -Name C:\PSModules\ExchangeOnlineManagement`.

Connecting to Azure Active Directory

Connecting to Azure Active Directory using PowerShell used to require installing the MSOnline or AzureAD/AzureADPreview module from the PowerShell Gallery. However, these modules are going to be retired at some point, in favor of the PowerShell Graph SDK module (MgGraph). As we speak, the MSOnline and AzureAD modules just got extended again to March 2024, due to some feature parity issues. Covering these gaps is essential when updating procedures and scripts, which is why Microsoft probably extended the retirement date. The licensing-related cmdlets are already unsupported, and organizations need to use the PowerShell Graph SDK for this.

Tip   Many code samples and scripts still depend on the MSOnline or AzureAD module. To assist organizations with refactoring those, there are a few websites and tools available:

- Documentation to help with the process at **https:// bit.ly/MigrateAzureADMSGraph**

- For one-off and assisted translation, Graph PowerShell Conversion Analyzer at **https://graphpowershell. merill.net/**

- Bulk conversion at **https://github.com/ FriedrichWeinmann/PSAzureMigrationAdvisor**

---

1) Open a PowerShell session in elevated mode.

2) Run `Install-Module MSGraph` to install the module in the user scope.

3) Run `Connect-MSGraph` to initiate connection to Graph. After connecting, your session is set up, with the default authentication scope.

Be advised that, unlike MSOnline and AzureAD, Graph has a more strict permissions model, where you need to authenticate specifying the scopes (permissions) you require, for example, `Connect-MgGraph -Scopes 'User.ReadWrite.All','Group.ReadWrite.All'`. To explore which permissions are required to make a certain call, you can use the websites mentioned in the preceding tip.

Note   The Microsoft Graph API is a unified method to access Microsoft 365 resources such as Azure Active Directory, Exchange Online, and Enterprise Mobility and Security services. To get an idea of all things Graph can do, have a look at Graph Explorer, at **https:// developer.microsoft.com/graph/graph-explorer**.

OAuth

One of the last steps when running the HCW is the configuration of OAuth. OAuth is an authentication protocol that provides applications or services a secure way to delegate access to their resources. For Exchange 2019, this means allowing applications such as Exchange Online or Microsoft Teams to authenticate to Exchange on-premises or vice versa.

For this purpose, applications or the services that they represent are configured as partner applications. Here are some of the benefits of having a proper OAuth configuration:

- Exchange delegation, honoring full mailbox access or configured folder permissions instead of being bound by the organization sharing configuration

- In-place eDiscovery of messages stored in both Exchange on-premises and Exchange Online locations

- Cross-premises message tracking to track messages flowing through Exchange on-premises and Exchange Online

- Retention policies on mailboxes hosted in Exchange on-premises archiving directly to Exchange Online Archives

- Microsoft Teams integrating with mailboxes hosted in Exchange on-premises for calendar integration

After the HCW set up OAuth, you can test it from the on-premises environment to Exchange Online and vice versa by using Test-OAuthConnectivity, specifying the mailbox you want to use for testing. This mailbox needs to reside in the location you are testing from, that is, if you are testing OAuth from Exchange Online to Exchange on-premises, you need to specify a mailbox hosted in Exchange Online.

You also need to specify the application or protocol to test, using TargetUri to specify the endpoint. Services supported for the Test cmdlet are

- EWS for Exchange Web Services

- AutoD for Autodiscover

- Generic

So, for example, to test OAuth from on-premises to Exchange Online with EWS:

```
Test-OAuthConnectivity -Service EWS -TargetUri https://outlook.
office365.com/EWS/Exchange.asmx
  -Mailbox <onpremmailbox@contoso.com>
```

To test OAuth from Exchange Online to Exchange on-premises for Autodiscover:

```
Test-OAuthConnectivity -Service AutoD -TargetUri https://
autodiscover.contoso.com/Autodiscover/Autodiscover.svc/
WSSecurity
 -Mailbox <cloudmailbox@contoso.com>
```

When successful, the command will return ResultType Success for Task "Checking EWS API Call Under Oauth". When not successful, you need to investigate the issue. In that case, perform the same command but pipe the output to fl. It will show detailed output on the calls performed and the results. For example, make sure the account you use is synchronized; otherwise, you may encounter 401 Unauthorized errors. Note that when you want to manually check the configuration, the manual OAuth setup process mentioned earlier can provide helpful guidance.

With OAuth configured, in organizations that have configured relationships with other organizations or between Exchange on-premises and Exchange Online, Exchange will first try OAuth before trying Delegated Authentication (DAuth). That is, if there is a definition of a possible OAuth-enabled relationship, this is where the **Intra-Organization Connector** (IOC) and **Intra-Organization Configuration** come into play. Configuration-wise, the IOC looks similar to organizational relationships: it defines the domains to use with the IOC, what the discovery endpoint is (Autodiscover), etc.

The Intra-Organization Configuration contains the IOC details of the current environment, so the information in Exchange on-premises differs from Exchange Online, also with Exchange hybrid configured. Details of the IOC should match the IOC configuration of the partner organization. For example, the discovery endpoint of the IOC in Exchange Online pointing to on-premises should match the IOC discovery endpoint attribute of Exchange on-premises.

```
[PS] >Get-IntraOrganizationConfiguration
WARNING: Please check that the Autodiscover endpoint of
"https://mail.contoso.com/autodiscover/autodiscover.svc"
 is correct and can be accessed externally. If it's incorrect or can't be accessed externally, use an existing
Autodiscover endpoint that can be accessed externally for the configuration of the intra-organization connector.

OnlineDiscoveryEndpoint           :
OnlineTargetAddress               :
OnPremiseTargetAddresses          : {}
OnPremiseDiscoveryEndpoint            : https://mail.contoso.com/autodiscover/autodiscover.svc
OnPremiseWebServiceEndpoint           : https://mail.contoso.com/ews/exchange.asmx
DeploymentIsCompleteIOCReady          : True
HasNonIOCReadyExchangeCASServerVersions    : False
HasNonIOCReadyExchangeMailboxServerVersions : False
```

Figure 5-4. *Intra-Organization Configuration*

Figure 5-4 shows the output of Get-IntraOrganizationConfiguration
when run in Exchange on-premises. This is why it only shows values
for the on-premises attributes. When you run it in Exchange Online, it
will show values for the other attributes. The IOC configuration is not
configurable; values are determined when setting up Exchange hybrid.
Also note the warning, indicating that the on-premises endpoints need to
be accessible externally. Now let us have a look at the details of the IOC
configuration:

- **OnlineDiscoveryEndpoint** is the Exchange Online
  Autodiscover endpoint. When run in Exchange Online,
  this attribute is set to **https://autodiscover-s.
  outlook.com/autodiscover/autodiscover.svc**.

- **OnlineTargetAddress** is the Exchange Online default
  address space. In Exchange Online, this attribute is the
  default mail routing address associated with Exchange
  Online, for example, **contoso.mail.onmicrosoft.com**.

- **OnPremiseTargetAddresses** are the email domains
  associated with the on-premises environment, for
  example, **contoso.com**.

– **OnPremiseDiscoveryEndpoint** is the Exchange on-premises Autodiscover URI. In Exchange Online, this attribute is not set.

– **OnPremiseWebServiceEndpoint** is the Exchange on-premises EWS URI. In Exchange Online, this attribute is not set.

Tip   If you ever run into the problem of having on-premises organization configuration lingering in your tenant, you can view currently configured on-premises organizations in your tenant using Get-OnPremisesOrganization. When needed, you can use Remove-OnPremisesOrganization -Identity <Guid> to remove the orphaned configuration object of the organization identified by Guid.

To watch the configuration of IOCs, use Get-IntraOrganization Connector, for example (excerpt):

```
[PS] >Get-IntraOrganizationConnector | fl

TargetAddressDomains : {contoso.mail.onmicrosoft.com}
DiscoveryEndpoint    : https://autodiscover-s.outlook.com/
                       autodiscover/autodiscover.svc
Enabled              : True
Identity             : HybridIOC - a46fac84-50d1-4953-8e4c-
                       c924f33dfa5b
```

IOCs are configurable, but in principle should be left under management of the HCW. They do provide the actual endpoints and domain names that apply, so can be used to validate theoretical federation path during troubleshooting:

- **TargetAddressDomains** are the email domains associated with the remote organization. In this case, we are
  running the cmdlet on-premises, so we see the default
  email routing domain associated with Exchange Online.

- **DiscoveryEndpoint** is the Autodiscover endpoint of
  the remote organization. We ran this on-premises, so it
  contains the Exchange Online Autodiscover URI. When
  running in Exchange Online, we will see the
  Autodiscover URI for on-premises here.

- **TargetSharingEpr** is the EWS endpoint. This is only
  available in Exchange Online and can be used to
  override the EWS endpoint. When not set, the endpoint
  is determined through Autodiscover.

Autodiscover in Exchange Hybrid

Autodiscover is an Exchange feature that simplifies the configuration
of email clients such as Microsoft Outlook, by providing the necessary
settings for connecting to an Exchange server. Depending on the client
configuration, it allows the client to self-configure connecting to Exchange
on-premises or Exchange Online, with minimal to no manual user input.

Chapter 6 will talk more extensively about the Autodiscover process
and how this works for Exchange on-premises. For Exchange hybrid, the
process depends on the Outlook client used. Outlook that is part of the
Microsoft 365 Apps suite (Click-to-Run or C2R) follows an iteration of
Autodiscover, Autodiscover V2. Autodiscover V2 will first check Exchange
Online to see if there is any mailbox present for the logged-on user. While
helpful, it may lead to unexpected situations when, for example, users
with a mailbox on-premises erroneously receive an additional mailbox
in Exchange Online. Outlook may start to connect to the mailbox in

Exchange Online instead, despite the mailbox still being on-premises and Autodiscover still pointing to Exchange on-premises. In those cases, solutions are usually found in AD Connect synchronization or inadvertent licensing. The lookup for a mailbox in Exchange Online can be skipped by Outlook C2R using a registry key, where **<version>** should be replaced with **16.0** for Outlook 2019:

```
Key: HKEY_CURRENT_USER:\Software\Microsoft\Office\<version>\
Outlook\AutoDiscover
Name: ExcludeExplicitO365Endpoint
Value: 1 (REG_DWORD)
```

This key does not work for Outlook (standalone or MSI), which will just follow the Autodiscover V1 process mentioned in Chapter 6.

During mailbox migrations, when mailboxes exist in Exchange on-premises as well as in Exchange Online, your Autodiscover record can stay pointing to the Exchange on-premises environment. But when all user mailboxes have finished migrating to Exchange Online, the question arises if you perhaps switch it to point to Exchange Online. The answer to this question depends on if you want to keep configuring clients for mailboxes that are still hosted on-premises or not. If not, and all user mailboxes have moved to Exchange Online, you can replace the current Autodiscover record with a CNAME record pointing to Exchange Online, for example:

```
Name: autodiscover.contoso.com
Type: CNAME
Value: autodiscover.outlook.com
```

If you still have application mailboxes residing on-premises for which you may want to perform Free/Busy lookups, you can reconfigure the organizational relationship, so that it does not use Autodiscover (which you changed to autodiscover.outlook.com), but points directly to your Exchange environment, for example, mail.contoso.com. More on that later in this chapter. Note that Microsoft Teams follows its own plan and will always consult the Autodiscover endpoint, regardless of any Exchange Online configuration setting.

For mailboxes that have been migrated, the Mailbox Replication service (MRS) will leave behind a mail-enabled user (MEU), also known as a remote mailbox object, in the on-premises environment. This way, the on-premises Global Address List will still contain those entries, and mail will still route properly as your legacyExchangeDN, the addressing scheme used by Exchange internally, will be retained and stamped on your migrated mailbox. The targetAddress property of the MEU however will be pointing to the MOERA configured on the MEU and mailbox. This address will be in the format <alias>@<tenant>.mail.onmicrosoft.com and gets stamped by the default email address policy, which will be modified by the Hybrid Configuration Wizard for this purpose.

Note   RemoteRoutingAddress in remote mailboxes is what ExternalEmailAddress is to mail users and what targetAddress is to Active Directory user objects.

With targetAddress pointing to <alias>@<tenant>.mail.onmicrosoft. com, continuation of mail flow is covered, as mail gets rerouted to Exchange Online. Important for Autodiscover is that Exchange on-premises supports Autodiscover redirection. When Exchange is asked to perform an Autodiscover lookup and the targetAddress is set, its value will be used for redirection. Instead of endpoint configuration, clients or services will receive response similar to the following excerpt:

```
<Account>
    <Action>redirectAddr</Action>
    <RedirectAddr>alias@tenant.mail.contoso.com</RedirectAddr>
</Account>
```

Note that the opposite is also true, which you might or might not have noticed when configuring AD Connect and synchronizing user objects. For mailboxes that are located on-premises, AD Connect will provision MEUs in your tenant. Their "targetAddress" will point to their regular email address, as that still resolves to the Exchange on-premises endpoint for Autodiscover and mail flow. A visual example of this setup is shown in Figure 5-5.

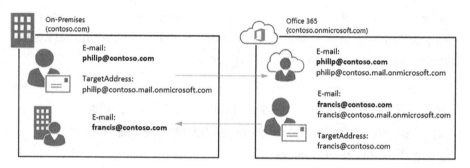

Figure 5-5. *Autodiscover redirection*

In this figure, Philip is a user with a mailbox in Office 365. His email address is philip@contoso.com. When Outlook does an Autodiscover lookup, it contacts contoso.com for Autodiscover information. That request is processed by the Exchange on-premises infrastructure, which finds a mail-enabled user object with that address. It also discovers that its target address is configured as philip@contoso.mail.onmicrosoft.com, and it will return that value to the client in a redirect response. The client will now try to use this redirect address philip@contoso.mail.onmicrosoft.com for Autodiscover, which can be successfully processed by Exchange Online.

Be advised clients such as Outlook or Teams may perform an Autodiscover V2 lookup. In those cases, REST calls are performed initially against Office 365 to determine endpoints. Apart from the email address of the target, the requestor also needs to specify the protocol or service as well, such as Autodiscover V1 or EWS. The goal is to increase performance of the lookup process for onboarded users, but be aware it may interfere with the expected process as it may take some shortcuts.

Here's an example of a REST Autodiscover V2 call for EWS services and returned output:

```
$endpoint= 'https://autodiscover-s.outlook.com/autodiscover/
autodiscover.json'
$mail= 'michel@contoso.com'
$protocol= 'Ews'
$uri= '{0}?{1}&{2}' -f $endpoint, $mail, $protocol
Invoke-RestMethod $uri

Protocol Url
-------- ---
Ews      https://outlook.office365.com/EWS/Exchange.asmx
```

As shown, the endpoint for EWS is located in Office 365. If the recipient was found in Office 365 and had a MEU pointing on-premises, the returned endpoint location would be the on-premises endpoint for EWS.

Mailbox Migration

Now that we have set up Exchange hybrid, we can talk about moving mailboxes to Exchange Online. AD Connect should have taken care of provisioning mail-enabled users (MEUs) in your tenant, provided there are no synchronization issues and objects are in scope of the synchronization process. Now, how to get mailboxes moved to Exchange Online, often referred to as onboarding.

Caution Before you can start using mailboxes in Exchange Online, make sure you have applied a license including an Exchange Online plan. If not, mailboxes will be inaccessible. Unlicensed mailboxes will have a 30-day grace period in Exchange Online. After this grace period, mailbox data will be removed—permanently.

To move mailboxes, a process is followed, which is somewhat similar to cross-forest mailbox moves performed on-premises. It is shown in Figure 5-6. The target MEU has already been provisioned by AD Connect.

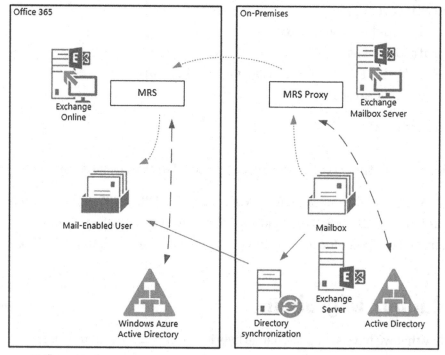

Mailbox contents
Validation, updating of properties to convert from MEU to Mailbox and vice-versa
Synchronization of objects and attributes

Figure 5-6. *Onboarding mailboxes to Exchange Online*

When you perform regular mailbox moves within the Exchange on-premises organization, a service called Microsoft Exchange Mailbox Replication service (MRS) will coordinate the move. When you are performing cross-forest moves or moves between Exchange on-premises and Exchange Online (also known as remote moves), something called the MRS proxy will proxy the traffic related to the move, acting as the counterpart to the MRS. Both MRS and the MRS proxy update the Active Directory in their respective environments with information, such as the database hosting the mailbox. Eventually, MRS will convert the mailbox user objects to mail-enabled user objects when the migration is complete and convert the MEU to a mailbox object in the destination.

By default, the MRS proxy functionality is disabled. So, before you can perform any remote moves, you need to enable the MRS proxy yourself. This can be performed via the EAC (**Servers ➤ Virtual Directories ➤ EWS (default website)** entries), or you can use EMS for specific Exchange servers:

```
Get-WebServicesVirtualDirectory -Server ex1 | Set-
WebServicesVirtualDirectory -MRSProxyEnabled $true
```

Note   The HCW should enable the MRS proxy setting on the Exchange Web Services virtual directories for you, but if you encounter migration problems, this is something you could check using `Get-WebServicesVirtualDirectory | Select Identity,MRSProxyEnabled`.

Remote moves can be initiated from the source or the target environment, effecting a push or pull mailbox move. Depending on the origin of the move request, the MRS proxy is used on the remote end as the source Exchange servers (pull) or the target Exchange servers (push). When you are moving mailboxes between Exchange on-premises and

Exchange Online, the move is always initiated from Exchange Online. For this reason, you always need to enable the MRS proxy in Exchange on-premises.

Note   Today, mailbox moves are an online process, where at most users need to restart clients in order to pick up administrative changes. Because the move is performed natively by Exchange, the mailbox signature is preserved, which has the benefit of OST offline cache files remaining valid, so these do not require any full synchronization.

Now let us briefly introduce some terms that are related to onboarding (and offboarding) mailboxes to Exchange Online:

- A **Migration Endpoint** defines the FQDN to be used for migration, together with credentials for authentication and tuning information such as how many moves and mailbox syncs can be performed in parallel. Note that when modifying these last parameters, your environment including any network components needs to be able to handle the load. In general, it is best to use the defaults as a starting point. When needed, organizations can introduce additional Migration Endpoints via additional Internet breakouts to improve overall throughput.

- A **migration batch** is a batch of identities indicating mailboxes that need to be migrated. You configure it with the identities of the users, handpicked or provided using a CSV file, together with the Migration Endpoint. You also configure it to automatically complete after finishing or not (after which you can complete them at a later date, while content is kept in sync) and what email domain should be used to pick the address to stamp as targetAddress on the mailbox on-premises after it gets converted to a MEU after completion. A recipient needs to be selected, which will receive mail reports on the progress of the migration.

- A **migration user** is an entity representing the mailbox being moved. Note that for mailboxes with online archives, there will be migration user objects for the mailbox and the archive as well. Parameters are taken from the attached migration batch; you cannot create a separate "migration user."

- A **move request** is the underlying job for MRS that moves mailbox contents from location to location. It inherits its settings from the migration user object.

To verify if requirements for a successful migration are in place, you can use the Test-MigrationServerAvailability cmdlet. You can optionally add the -Verbose switch to add extra information to the output, which might prove useful when you are troubleshooting:

```
[PS] >Test-MigrationServerAvailability -ExchangeRemoteMove
-EmailAddress henk@contoso.com -Autodiscover -Credentials
(Get-Credential)

Result            : Success
Message           :
SupportsCutover   : False
ErrorDetail       :
TestedEndpoint    : mail.contoso.com
IsValid           : True
Identity          :
ObjectState       : New
```

399

Or if you created a separate endpoint for migration, you therefore need to explicitly specify it, bypassing Autodiscover:

```
[PS] >Test-MigrationServerAvailability -ExchangeRemoteMove
-Credentials (Get-Credential)
-RemoteServer mail.contoso.com

Result          : Success
Message         :
SupportsCutover : False
ErrorDetail     :
TestedEndpoint  : mail.contoso.com
IsValid         : True
Identity        :
ObjectState     : New
```

Caution   Migration Endpoints are authenticated against using basic authentication. If you disable basic authentication or underlying authentication methods such as NTLM, mailbox moves cannot be performed successfully.

During setup of Exchange hybrid using the HCW, a Migration Endpoint should already be configured in your Exchange Online organization pointing to Exchange on-premises. To inspect it, open its EAC, and navigate to **Recipients ➤ Migration ➤ ... ➤ Migration Endpoints**, or just use Get-MigrationEndpoint in an Exchange Online Management shell session:

```
> Get-MigrationEndpoint

Identity          EndpointType        RemoteServer
--------          ------------        ------------
mail.contoso.com  ExchangeRemoteMove  mail.contoso.com
```

With the Migration Endpoint in place, you are ready to start onboarding mailboxes. How is mainly dictated by frequency and scale. For ad hoc moves, EAC will suffice. It's easy and rather self-explaining:

1) In EAC from Exchange Online, navigate to **Recipients ➤ Migration**. Click the + sign, and you will have the option to migrate to or from Exchange Online.

2) After selecting **Migrate to Exchange Online**, you can start defining the parameters of your migration batch. You are asked what type of move you want to perform. Since the source is Exchange, pick **Remote Move Migration**.

3) The next screen allows you to pick the identities of the mailboxes you would like to move. You can pick them manually with + or provide a CSV file containing a column **EmailAddress** and the identities of the mailboxes to move.

4) Next, you need to pick the **Migration Endpoint** to use for this move.

5) You are then asked to provide a name for the migration job, as well as provide the target delivery domain. This is the email domain name that is going to be used to configure the targetAddress on the MEU after migration completes, effectively forwarding mail and routing requests like Free/Busy. By default this is set to the OnlineTargetAddress of the IOC configuration, for example, **contoso.mail.onmicrosoft.com**. If needed, you can move the primary mailboxes and

any archives together or only move the archives of those mailboxes. This can be useful when you want to move to an Exchange Online Archiving plan, for example.

6) The last screen will ask a few things. First, you can set the recipient who will receive mail on the progress of the migration job. You also can specify when the job needs to start and when the job needs to finish. Note that you can choose to manually complete the migration. The benefit of this mechanism is that you can stage mailbox contents early and complete the migration at a later point. In the meantime, Exchange will incrementally synchronize mailbox contents every 24 hours, so that the delta of changes when completion is required is minimal.

7) Click **New** to create the migration batch.

The migration page should now contain your newly created migration batch. You can check its progress, inspecting per-mailbox progress, or issues, clicking mailbox status. This is also where you need to click Complete when you have configured the job for manual completion as opposed to AutoComplete.

To successfully migrate mailboxes, the secondary email addresses of that mailbox need to contain an entry using the domain specified at step 5. If not, MRS cannot set the targetAddress post-migration, and the operation for that mailbox will fail. Validation performed during the migration will point this out to you, and you need to resolve this first. Also, addresses with domains not configured as accepted domains in Exchange Online need to be removed first.

Caution   When migrating mailboxes using manual completion, be advised that those staged mailboxes are subject to mailbox deletion retention time, which is 30 days. After this period, mailboxes for which the move has not been completed will be removed. When a mailbox is removed, it is recreated when the move is resumed. In this case, all items that were already transferred need to be copied again.

When the move is successful, you might be prompted to restart the Outlook client ("The administrator made a change..."), depending on the authentication methods used and single sign-on configuration. You may also be required to enter your credentials when you were not using Modern Authentication. The reason for this is that your (on-premises) credentials might be saved but are useless against Exchange Online, which uses Modern Authentication, which is token-based, and you might not have this token (yet). If this token was issued by AD FS, when you use this for authentication, you might not need to reauthenticate.

In addition to moving mailboxes using EAC, you can also use an Exchange Online Management shell to create and manage migration batches and users. To perform a migration using **New-MigrationBatch**, the following parameters are relevant:

- **Name** is the name of the migration batch. Note that underlying MigrationUser and MoveRequests jobs created from MigrationBatch will carry this name as well, for easy reference and selection. The MoveRequest BatchName property will get prefixed with "MigrationService:", as will be shown later.

- **SourceEndpoint** is the identity of the Migration Endpoint to use.

- **TargetDeliveryDomain** is the email domain that will determine which secondary email address will be stamped as targetAddress post-migration.

- **AutoComplete** determines if the mailbox move should automatically complete (**$true**) or not (**$false**). Alternatively, CompleteAfter can be used to specify a timestamp to start move completion, like the options provided in EAC.

- **AutoStart** determines if the mailbox move should start immediately. When AutoComplete is set to $false, setting this to $true will start validation and staging immediately.

- **CSVData** contains the contents of the CSV of the mailboxes to migrate. Use [System. IO.File]::ReadAllBytes($Filename) to import its contents.

- If identities are not provided via a CSV file, you can use the **Users** parameter to specify one or more identities.

- **NotificationEmails** can be used to specify one or more recipients who will receive periodic move reports.

For example, assume we have a CSV file "Users.csv" containing identities of mailboxes we are going to move. Note that the following example uses a splatting technique, which improves readability when using multiple parameters by offering them as a hash table:

```
$UsersFile= '.\Users.csv'
$BatchParam= @{
    Name= 'TestBatch'
    SourceEndpoint= 'mail.contoso.com'
    TargetDeliveryDomain= 'contoso.mail.onmicrosoft.com'
```

```
    AutoComplete= $false
    AutoStart= $true
    CSVData= [System.IO.File]::ReadAllBytes( $UsersFile)
    NotificationEmails= 'blake@consoto.com'
}
New-MigrationBatch @BatchParam
```

Tip   Exchange Online mailbox moves are throttled. When planning
mailbox moves, calculate with an average of 0.3–1 GB/hour rate
per mailbox. An exact number is impossible to determine, owing to
the many variables such as hardware, bandwidth, and latencies,
but also number of items in those mailboxes (migrating less larger
items is faster than more smaller items due to overhead). The
best way is to start staging mailbox contents early by disabling
AutoComplete and completing those jobs at a later date. To make
a calculated estimation, perform trial migrations and analyze those
throughput rates.

Your migration batch should now be submitted and also be visible in
EAC, for example. Note that there is a limit of 100 migration batch jobs, so
when you are reaching the limit, make room by clearing up old, finished
migration batches. You can view current migration batches using **Get-
MigrationBatch**; to view migration, use **Get-MigrationUser**, optionally
specifying the batch name. Also interesting to know is that you can use
Get-MigrationUserStatistics to retrieve statistics related to individual
mailbox moves, as shown in Figure 5-7.

```
[PS] >Get-MigrationBatch

Identity    Status      Type                    TotalCount
--------    ------      ----                    ----------
TestBatch  Completed  ExchangeRemoteMove  2

[PS] >Get-MigrationUser -BatchId TestBatch

Identity                Batch        Status      LastSyncTime
--------                ------       -----       ------------
francis@contoso.com  TestBatch  Completed  6/22/2023 00:45:00

[PS] >Get-MigrationUser -BatchId TestBatch | Get-MigrationUserStatistics

Identity                Batch        Status      Items Synced  Items Skipped
--------                -----        ------      ------------  -------------
francis@contoso.com  TestBatch  Completed  24            0
```

Figure 5-7. *Monitoring migration batches using PowerShell*

During migration, a Data Consistency Score grade is awarded to the migration job. There are four possible grades:

- **Perfect** means no inconsistencies were encountered.

- **Good** means at least one inconsistency was found, but potential data loss was not found to be impactful. This can happen when permissions could not be matched in Exchange Online due to missing security principals, for example.

- **Investigate** means a small amount of significant data loss was detected, due to inconsistencies.

- **Poor** means major data loss was detected. Migration cannot complete without contacting Microsoft Support.

If a migration job encounters too many corrupt items, such as old calendar items missing essential properties, or too many large items (default maximum item size is ~25 MB) and your job is graded Investigate, you need to approve of the skipped items through the menu option shown in EAC or using an Exchange Online Management shell. This approval can be done for the whole batch or for an individual migration user. To accomplish this, run

```
Set-MigrationBatch -Identity TestBatch -ApproveSkippedItems
Set-MigrationUser -Identity <ID> -ApproveSkippedItems
```

Tip   When issues arise during mailbox moves, use the command `Get-MigrationUser <ID> | Get-MigrationUserStatistics -Report | fl Report` to retrieve a detailed mailbox synchronization report.

Should the need arise to offboard mailboxes, the process is similar. In EAC, select **Migrate from Exchange Online**. The dialogs that follow are identical, except for the following differences:

– **TargetDeliveryDomain** should be the on-premises email domain, for example, contoso.com. This will be used to select an entry from the secondary addresses and stamp it as targetAddress on the MEU in Exchange Online after completing offboarding.

– **RemoteTargetDatabase** is the mailbox database(s) where the mailboxes need to be migrated to on-premises. You can enter multiple database names, separated by a comma. Mailbox requests created will be spread by MRS over these databases.

– **RemoteArchiveTargetDatabase** (optional) is to specify the name of the mailbox database to migrate personal archives to, when applicable.

Managing Remote Mailboxes

Mail-enabled users (MEUs) left behind after onboarding mailboxes are visible in Exchange on-premises as remote mailboxes, to indicate they have been moved. As such, you will also have more management options available to you as opposed to managing ordinary mail users. Do note that remote mailboxes cannot be managed using *-MailUser cmdlets, as they will result in a possibly confusing "User not found" message. Instead, they need to be managed using *-RemoteMailbox cmdlets instead. This applies to remote mailboxes of type User, Shared, Room, or Equipment.

Another benefit is that these remote mailboxes are visible in EAC in the same view as regular mailboxes, as shown in Figure 5-8.

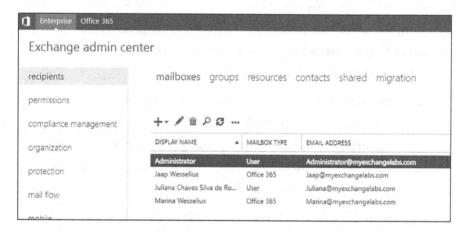

Figure 5-8. *Mixed view of mailboxes and remote mailboxes*

With Active Directory, Exchange, and Exchange Online having their own management options, it can be confusing sometimes. It becomes complex when commands use different parameters for the same attribute. With regard to remote mailboxes, RemoteRoutingAddress is used to redirect messages and federation traffic. In Exchange Online, for mail-enabled users, this is ExternalEmailAddress. In Active Directory, this is targetAddress. When used, all three in principle configure the same underlying attribute.

When Exchange hybrid is deployed, creating a new remote mailbox is a phased process:

1) Create a new on-premises user with the required email properties, such as primary SMTP address and User Principal Name, and provide an initial password, which they need to reset at first logon, for example:

```
[PS] >New-RemoteMailbox -Name Xavier
-PrimarySmtpAddress xavier@contoso.com
-UserPrincipalName xavier@contoso.com
-ResetPasswordOnNextLogon $True

cmdlet New-RemoteMailbox at command pipeline
position 1
Supply values for the following parameters:
Password: **********

Name      RecipientTypeDetails    RemoteRecipientType
----      --------------------    -------------------
Xavier    RemoteUserMailbox       ProvisionMailbox
```

2) Wait for AD Connect to provision the user in Azure Active Directory.

3) Depending on if you have enabled group-based licensing, the user synchronized to Azure Active Directory might already get assigned an Exchange Online license. If not, assign one using the Azure portal, or use the PowerShell Graph SDK:

```
Connect-MgGraph -Scopes User.ReadWrite.All,
Organization.Read.All
Update-MgUser -UserId xavier@contos.com
-UsageLocation US
```

```
$SKU = Get-MgSubscribedSku | Where
{ $_.SkuPartNumber -eq 'ENTERPRISEPACK'}
Set-MgUserLicense -UserId xavier -AddLicenses
@{SkuId = $SKU} -RemoveLicenses @()
```

4) After the license has been assigned, and provided
   there are sufficient licenses available, a mailbox
   will get provisioned in Exchange Online, and after a
   short while, the user can log into the mailbox.

5) Any changes to this user need to be performed on-
   premises, as the source of authority with Exchange
   hybrid is on-premises (Active Directory), and Azure
   AD Connect will propagate changes to Azure Active
   Directory.

Federation with Azure Active Directory

Another configuration element to mention is federation of Exchange on-
premises with Azure Active Directory. At some point, your organization
and users might wish to exchange information with other organizations.
For example, companies agreeing to a form of partnership or preparing for
an upcoming merger might want to share their calendaring information.
Another example is organizations with meeting room mailboxes wanting
to share their Free/Busy information with the organizations using those
locations.

Federation allows the secure sharing of information between Exchange
organizations, and the mechanism is displayed in Figure 5-4. After
configuration, which the HCW will do for you, your Exchange on-premises
organization will have a federation trust with the Azure Active Directory
Federation Gateway. You can view the current federation trust configured
for Exchange on-premises using

```
[PS] >Get-FederationTrust | fl Name,TokenIssuerUri,
TokenIssuerMetadataEpr
```

```
Name                     : Microsoft Federation Gateway
TokenIssuerUri           : urn:federation:MicrosoftOnline
TokenIssuerMetadataEpr : https://nexus.microsoftonline-p.com/
FederationMetadata/2006-12/FederationMetadata.xml
```

Should you run this cmdlet in Exchange Online Management shell, you will see a similar entry:

```
[PS] >Get-FederationTrust | fl Name,TokenIssuerUri,TokenIssuerM
etadataEpr
```

```
Name                     : MicrosoftOnline
TokenIssuerUri           : urn:federation:MicrosoftOnline
TokenIssuerMetadataEpr : https://nexus.microsoftonline-p.com/
federationmetadata/2006-12/federationmetadata.xml
```

Note   The **nexus.microsoftonline-p.com** URI should be accessible from the system running the HCW. It is sometimes blocked, resulting in the inability to configure hybrid.

Other organizations can also have a federation trust with the Azure Active Directory Federation Gateway. Azure Active Directory will then function as an online trust broker for authentication and authorization, as depicted in Figure 5-9. If you trust Azure Active Directory and you have registered and verified your domains in Office 365, you are good to go. Sharing of information between Exchange Online and Exchange on-premises in Exchange hybrid is configured by default. It is up to the organization to configure sharing of information with other organizations. More on configuring organization-level sharing of information later in this chapter.

411

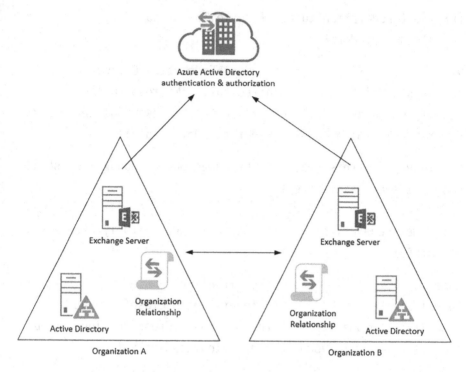

Figure 5-9. *Federation with Azure Active Directory*

Note   The federation trust with Azure Active Directory should not be confused with Active Directory Federation Services or AD FS, which is an identity provider.

Normally, Exchange is very capable of managing the certificates related to the federation trust and providing a proper rollover when the certificate is about to expire. If you encounter issues with cross-organization sharing, one of the things to check is the federation trust using Test-FederationTrust, providing a valid account as shown in Figure 5-10.

```
[PS] >Test-FederationTrust -UserIdentity michel@contoso.com

Begin process.
STEP 1 of 6: Getting ADUser information for michel@contoso.com...
RESULT: Success.

STEP 2 of 6: Getting FederationTrust object for michel@contoso.com...
RESULT: Success.

STEP 3 of 6: Validating that the FederationTrust has the same STS certificates as the actual certificates published by
the STS in the federation metadata.
RESULT: Success.

STEP 4 of 6: Getting STS and Organization certificates from the federation trust object...
RESULT: Success.

Validating current configuration for FYDIBOHF25SPDLT.contoso.com...

Validation successful.

STEP 5 of 6: Requesting delegation token...
RESULT: Success. Token retrieved.

STEP 6 of 6: Validating delegation token...
RESULT: Success.

Closing Test-FederationTrust...

RunspaceId : a192e8b9-2620-4296-a584-75e96133a493
Id         : FederationTrustConfiguration
Type       : Success
Message    : FederationTrust object in ActiveDirectory is valid.

RunspaceId : a192e8b9-2620-4296-a584-75e96133a493
Id         : FederationMetadata
Type       : Success
Message    : The federation trust contains the same certificates published by the security token service in its
              federation metadata.

RunspaceId : a192e8b9-2620-4296-a584-75e96133a493
Id         : StsCertificate
Type       : Success
Message    : Valid certificate referenced by property TokenIssuerCertificate in the FederationTrust object.

RunspaceId : a192e8b9-2620-4296-a584-75e96133a493
Id         : StsPreviousCertificate
Type       : Success
Message    : Valid certificate referenced by property TokenIssuerPrevCertificate in the FederationTrust object.

RunspaceId : a192e8b9-2620-4296-a584-75e96133a493
Id         : OrganizationCertificate
Type       : Success
Message    : Valid certificate referenced by property OrgPrivCertificate in the FederationTrust object.

RunspaceId : a192e8b9-2620-4296-a584-75e96133a493
Id         : TokenRequest
Type       : Success
Message    : Request for delegation token succeeded.

RunspaceId : a192e8b9-2620-4296-a584-75e96133a493
Id         : TokenValidation
Type       : Success
Message    : Requested delegation token is valid.
```

Figure 5-10. *Testing federation trust*

413

Should the output display errors such as **Failed to validate delegation token**, it might help to refresh the federation configuration and certificate. To accomplish this, run

```
Get-FederationTrust | Set-FederationTrust -RefreshMetadata
```

Sharing of Information

Sharing information with other organizations is possible on two levels in Exchange and Exchange Online:

- **Organizational relationships**, or organizational sharing as it is named in Exchange Online, allow federated organizations to share calendar information with other federated organizations.

- **Sharing policies** allow user-level sharing of calendar information, within the boundaries of these policies.

An organizational relationship is tied to a namespace. For Exchange on-premises, this is usually the regular domain, for example, contoso. com. For Exchange Online, this is the routing email domain, for example, contoso.mail.onmicrosoft.com. With Autodiscover pointing to Exchange on-premises, requests for contoso.com will get a redirection instruction to Exchange Online via the targetAddress attribute set on migrated mailboxes.

Caution   Federation for on-premises Exchange with other organizations running Exchange hybrid does not work for cloud-based mailboxes. Because the Exchange server on-premises performing the availability lookup has an organizational relationship with the on-premises Exchange organization of the partner, it will not proxy the request to Office 365 after receiving the `targetAddress` redirect to the `@<tenant>.mail.onmicrosoft.com` address. A trick is to create an organizational relationship with `<tenant>.mail.onmicrosoft.com` for partners. Ideally, those routing addresses are set as `targetAddress` on locally stored contacts, which makes the lookup more efficient, but is far from ideal as it requires you to know which partner mailboxes are cloud-based and which are not. A tool providing "GALSync" functionality might help in those scenarios. For tenants with cloud-only mailboxes, this can be accomplished by a Microsoft Entra feature named Cross-Tenant Synchronization; see **https://bit.ly/CrossTenantSync**.

Because Exchange on-premises is a different organization than your Exchange Online tenant, you will have two locations where organizational relationships and sharing policies are defined. The Organization Configuration Transfer option in the Hybrid Configuration Wizard can assist in creating the initial sharing policies in Exchange Online using the definitions found in Exchange on-premises. However, it cannot be used to maintain settings by propagating changes.

You can inspect and configure the current sharing policy by using EAC, navigating to **Organization ➤ Sharing**, as shown in Figure 5-11.

Note   If your organization has not been enabled for federation yet, EAC will notify you and give you the option to perform this step at this point.

Figure 5-11. *Organization Sharing and Individual Sharing options in EAC*

Visible in Figure 5-11 is the HCW has created an organizational relationship in Exchange on-premises **On-premises to O365 - <GUID>** for the domain ending in mail.onmicrosoft.com. The GUID in the name is the GUID of your tenant organization, as can be found using (Get-OrganizationConfig).Guid in an Exchange Online Management shell.

Organizational Relationships

Federating information with other organizations is configured through so-called organizational relationships. You can view the configured organizational relationship by using the cmdlet **Get-OrganizationRelationship**. If you run this cmdlet in an Exchange Online Management shell, you will see the organizational relationship created by the HCW. This is the counterpart of the organizational relationship created on-premises, making the relationship two-way.

Caution   Important to note is that organizational relationships use the Delegated Authentication (DAuth) model. DAuth uses a broker (Azure AD) to authenticate users and allows the broker to act on behalf of users to other services, such as User A requesting Free/Busy of User B and the Exchange environment of User A requesting this information from organization B on behalf of User A.

Now, in organizations running Exchange 2019, there are no more Exchange 2010 servers, and token-based Open Authorization (OAuth) is the default instead, also opening up other functionality such as cross-premises. You will notice this as in the HCW as it will skip steps to configure federation and organizational relationships lacking information such as the TargetAutodiscoverEpr. However, when federating with other organizations, implementation of organizational relationships using DAuth might still be required.

```
[PS] >Get-OrganizationRelationship | fl

PSComputerName       : ex1.ad.contoso.com
RunspaceId           : a192e8b9-2620-4296-a584-75e96133a493
PSShowComputerName   : False
DomainNames          : {contoso.mail.onmicrosoft.com}
FreeBusyAccessEnabled : True
FreeBusyAccessLevel  : LimitedDetails
FreeBusyAccessScope  :
MailboxMoveEnabled   : True
MailboxMoveDirection : None
DeliveryReportEnabled : True
MailTipsAccessEnabled : True
MailTipsAccessLevel  : All
MailTipsAccessScope  :
PhotosEnabled        : True
TargetApplicationUri :
TargetSharingEpr     :
TargetOwaURL         : http://outlook.com/owa/contoso.com
TargetAutodiscoverEpr :
OrganizationContact  :
Enabled              : True
ArchiveAccessEnabled : True
AdminDisplayName     :
ExchangeVersion      : 0.10 (14.0.100.0)
Name                 : On-premises to O365 - a46fac84-50d1-4953-8e4c-c924f33dea5b
DistinguishedName    : CN=On-premises to O365 -
                       a46fac84-50d1-4953-8e4c-c924f33dfa5b,CN=Federation,CN=Contoso,CN=Microsoft
                       Exchange,CN=Services,CN=Configuration,DC=ad,DC=contoso,DC=com
Identity             : On-premises to O365 - a46fac84-50d1-4953-8e4c-c924f33dfa5b
Guid                 : fb70bccc-9838-45c9-a58e-4f4d56f59bfd
ObjectCategory       : ad.contoso.com/Configuration/Schema/ms-Exch-Fed-Sharing-Relationship
ObjectClass          : {top, msExchFedSharingRelationship}
WhenChanged          : 7/1/2021 4:14:26 PM
WhenCreated          : 7/1/2021 4:14:25 PM
WhenChangedUTC       : 7/1/2021 2:14:26 PM
WhenCreatedUTC       : 7/1/2021 2:14:25 PM
OrganizationId       :
Id                   : On-premises to O365 - a46fac84-50d1-4953-8e4c-c924f33dea5b
OriginatingServer    : dc1.ad.contoso.com
IsValid              : True
ObjectState          : Unchanged
```

Figure 5-12. *Organizational relationship*

In Figure 5-12, you can see that from an Exchange on-premises
viewpoint, sharing information with the contoso.mail.onmicrosoft.com
address space has been defined. This information exchange for address
spaces mentioned in DomainNames is defined by the following properties:

- `FreeBusyAccessEnabled` defines if the organization allows sharing Free/Busy information with the other organization.

- `FreeBusyAccessLevel` sets the amount of detail that is shared. Options are

  - *None* when no Free/Busy information is to be shared

  - *AvailabilityOnly* when only availability is shared

  - *LimitedDetails* when Free/Busy is shared with time, subject, and location information

- `FreeBusyAccessScope` can be used to limit the information sharing to a certain security group. When this is not set, the Free/Busy settings in the organizational relationship apply to the whole organization.

- `MailboxMoveEnabled` defines if mailboxes can be moved to the external organization.

- `DeliveryReportEnabled` defines if the organization wants to return delivery report information. This needs to be enabled in both organizations when they want to perform cross-organization message tracking.

- `ArchiveAccessEnabled` defines whether the organization has been configured to provide access to remote personal archives. This needs to be enabled in your on-premises organizational relationship setting when using Exchange Online Archiving (EOA), for example.

419

- `MailTipsAccessEnabled` defines if mail tips information is provided to the external organization.

- `MailTipsAccessLevel` sets the level of mail tips provided to the external organization. Options are

  - *None* when no mail tips information is to be provided.

  - *Limited* when only mail tips are to be provided that can prevent non-delivery reports (NDRs) or automatic replies such as out-of-office (OOF) notifications. Other mail tips such as large audience are not returned.

  - *All* when all mail tips are to be provided.

- `MailTipsAccessScope` can be used to return mail tips only for certain security groups. When this is not set, the mail tips settings in the organizational relationship are applied to the whole organization.

- `PhotosEnabled` defines if photo data is returned to the external organization.

When running this from an Exchange Online Management shell, you will get similar results, only having other domains specified with DomainNames and URIs pointing to Exchange on-premises endpoints such as **https://mail.contoso.com/autodiscover/autodiscover.svc/wssecurity**.

To customize organizational relationships, use `Set-OrganizationRelationship`. To manually create one, use `New-OrganizationRelationship`, or use the option from EAC.

Caution   Before you can customize specific sharing details in your tenant, you might be required to enable tenant customization. To accomplish this, run `Enable-OrganizationCustomization` in an Exchange Online Management shell. You will be notified when you need to perform this step.

Note that when you modify an existing organizational relationship, you will have additional configuration options, for Application Uri and Autodiscover endpoint. These settings and an additional one, which you should be aware of, are also available as parameters to `New-OrganizationRelationship` and `Set-OrganizationRelationship`. These parameters and their usage are as follows:

- **TargetAutodiscoverEpr**, when set, defines the Autodiscover endpoint to use to look up endpoints for resources defined by the domains specified in DomainNames, for example, **https://autodiscover. contoso.com/autodiscover/autodiscover.svc/ wssecurity**. When not set, public DNS is used.

- **TargetOWAURL**, when set, defines the URL used for OWA redirection after logging into a migrated mailbox. This is not a silent redirection, just a link presentation.

- **TargetSharingEpr**, when set, overrides the Exchange Web Services endpoint to use for resources defined by the domains in DomainNames, for example, **https:// mail.contoso.com/EWS/exchange.asmx/wssecurity**. When not set, the endpoint for EWS provided by the Autodiscover process will be used for directing availability lookups.

Tip   If your organization does not like the default OWA redirection URL **https://outlook.com/OWA/contoso.com**, you can use a CNAME record to perform the redirection. First, create a CNAME in public DNS pointing to **outlook.com**. Second, reconfigure the **TargetOWAUrl**, pointing it to the CNAME followed by **/owa**. For example, when a CNAME has been defined named **cloudmail.contoso.com**, redefine the **TargetOWAUrl** using Set-OrganizationRelationship -Identity 'On-premises to O365 - <GUID>' -TargetOwaUrl http://cloudmail.contoso.com/owa.

If at any point you want to validate your organizational relationships, use Test-OrganizationRelationship, specifying the name of the organizational relationship object as identity and the mailbox to initiate the test request, for example: Test-OrganizationRelationship -UserIdentity francis@contoso.com -Identity 'On-premises to O365 - <GUID>'.

Tip   If your Free/Busy lookups stop working at some point, check if the federation trust is still in working order by using **Test-FederationTrust**. If it reports "Failed to validate delegation token", try to refresh the metadata of the on-premises federation trust by using Get-FederationTrust | Set-FederationTrust -RefreshMetaData:$true.

Sharing Policies

Whereas organizational relationships define how information is shared on the organization level, sharing policies, or individual sharing as it is called in EAC, define the user-level calendar sharing options. This includes sharing calendar or contact information with users of both federated organizations and non-federated organizations. In the latter case, Internet publishing is used to publish the information.

The sharing policies define what users are allowed to share. The action of sharing that information is initiated by the user. When you want to manage the sharing policies through EAC, you navigate to **Organization ➤ Sharing**. In the bottom section named "Individual Sharing," you will find the currently configured sharing policies, as shown earlier in Figure 5-11.

When using an Exchange Online Management session, you can retrieve the list of current sharing policies by using the SharingPolicy cmdlets. You will see that by default one sharing policy is already configured: the default sharing policy. To inspect this policy, use Get-SharingPolicy | fl Name, Domains, Enabled as shown in Figure 5-13.

```
[PS] >Get-SharingPolicy | fl Name,Domains,Enabled

Name    : Default Sharing Policy
Domains : {Anonymous:CalendarSharingFreeBusyReviewer, *:CalendarSharingFreeBusySimple}
Enabled : True
```

Figure 5-13. *Default sharing policy*

As visible in Figure 5-13, you can see that there are two entries configured in the default sharing policy: **Anonymous:CalendarSharing FreeBusyReviewer** and ***:CalendarSharingFreeBusySimple**. The format of these entries is **Domain:Action[,Action]**, whereby

- The domain "**Anonymous**" applies to everyone outside your organization.

- The domain "*****" represents everyone inside your organization.

- Action can be one of the following values:

  - `CalendarSharingFreeBusySimple` enables sharing of Free/Busy hours only.

  - `CalendarSharingFreeBusyDetail` enables sharing of Free/Busy hours, subject, and location.

  - `CalendarSharingFreeBusyReviewer` enables sharing of Free/Busy hours, subject, location, and the body of the message or calendar item.

  - `ContactsSharing` enables sharing of contacts.

So the default policy is configured to allow users to individually share Free/Busy hours, subject, location, and the body of the message or calendar item with external users and to share Free/Busy hours with any internal domain.

Caution   For anonymous calendar and contact sharing features to work, verify that `AnonymousFeaturesEnabled` is set to `$True` on the OWA Virtual Directory.

Let us create a new sharing policy named "Custom Sharing Policy" and allow users to share `CalendarSharingFreeBusyReviewer` and contact information with the domain litware.com. For this you need to run

```
New-SharingPolicy -Name 'Custom Sharing Policy'
 -Domains 'litware.com:CalendarSharingFreeBusyReviewer,
 ContactsSharing'
```

Now, suppose you want to allow `CalendarSharingFreeBusySimple` sharing with all other external domains as well. You need to run `Set-SharingPolicy` adding this configuration to the Domains attribute:

```
Set-SharingPolicy -Identity 'Custom Sharing Policy'
 -Domains @{Add='Anonymous:CalendarSharingFreeBusySimple'}
```

The instruction **Add** makes sure the entry gets added to any existing entries on the Domains attribute. Now what is left is configuring this sharing policy on mailboxes that are allowed this new policy. Each mailbox is assigned one sharing policy. This will be the default sharing policy. To assign a mailbox a different sharing policy, use Set-Mailbox with the SharingPolicy parameter:`Set-Mailbox -Identity francis@contoso.com -SharingPolicy 'Custom Sharing Policy'`.

Now, if this user wants to share their calendar or contacts folder, they can use the Share Calendar or Share Contacts Folder option from Outlook. For calendar sharing, they may choose a lower level of detail than set by the policy. Note that Outlook is unaware of the sharing policy settings; when the user tries to share more details than permitted, they will receive an error message as soon as they try to send the email with the sharing link. Also, when the intended recipient is not part of a federated organization, the user is notified, and they will need to use Internet Calendar Publishing instead.

Note   The link sent to recipients to access the calendar or contacts is obfuscated, but it is not password protected.

Internet Calendar Publishing

To share calendar information with non-federated or non-Exchange recipients, users can be allowed to publish their calendar online, depending on the effective sharing policy configuration. This requires external publishing of OWA, as well as calendar publishing, which is enabled by default. You can inspect current configuration using `Get-OWAVirtualDirectory | Select Identity,ExternalUrl, CalendarEnabled`.

When allowed and configured, users can publish their calendar. The location will be based on OWA's ExternalURL configuration. The calendar is published as an iCalendar .ics file and as an HTML page. Apart from the publication window and detail level, users can also pick the access level when publishing.

Mail Transport

Mail transport describes how email is routed within an organization, including Exchange on-premises and Exchange Online, and between the organization and external destinations, such as the Internet or partners. With Exchange hybrid, there will be messages routed between your organization and Exchange Online, where mailboxes can reside on-premises as well as in Exchange Online, and depending on routing preferences, inbound external messages can enter through Exchange Online, Exchange on-premises, or any SaaS for mail hygiene that sits in between public and your organization.

Chapter 2 touched on mail transport and how to configure it for Exchange on-premises deployments. In Exchange Online, you also can define connectors. There you will need the **New/Set/Remove-OutboundConnector** and **New/Set/Remove-InboundConnector** cmdlets for managing connectors, as opposed to **New/Set/Remove-SendConnector** and **New/Set/Remove-ReceiverConnector** with Exchange on-premises. Also, an **InboundConnector** applies to your whole Exchange Online organization, where **ReceiveConnector** is configured per Exchange server.

The HCW will take care of configuring secure mail flow between Exchange on-premises and Exchange Online, also when you have Edge Transport servers deployed. What it does not do is reconfiguring your public MX record, which determines if inbound messages will land on-premises or in Exchange Online. However, both inbound mail flow options will work, as both environments are set up to accept the same managed domain name and the connectors are configured to transport mail between the on-premises and the Exchange Online organization.

Note that issues in mail delivery might arise when, for example, you have inbound mail delivered to Exchange Online (MX points to Exchange Online) and you do not fully synchronize all mail-enabled recipients to Exchange Online. This can easily occur when you have dynamic Distribution Groups, for example, which are not synchronized by AD Connect. By default, the accepted domain is configured as authoritative, which means any recipients not found in Exchange Online will result in a non-delivery.

A solution is then to either set the domain in Exchange Online to InternalRelay, after which messages not delivered in Exchange Online will get handed off to Exchange on-premises. The downside is that messages will bounce a few times when the specified recipient does not exist, leading to a *Hop Count Exceeded* message instead of *Non-Delivery Report*. This situation can happen easily because of a simple typo. Alternatively, for dynamic Distribution Groups, you can create placeholders in Exchange Online forwarding messages to the on-premises group.

The same issue will occur when you do not synchronize mail-enabled public folders, for instance, for which you periodically need to run a script called Sync-ModernMailPublicFolders.ps1, which will create MEUs in Exchange Online for this purpose. More on this at **https://bit.ly/ SyncModernMailPublicFolders**.

Inbound Mail

Exchange Online depends on the mail-enabled users in Exchange on-premises in conjunction with the accepted domain configuration of **authoritative** or **internal relay** to determine where to redirect the email to the coexistence domain, as shown in Figure 5-14.

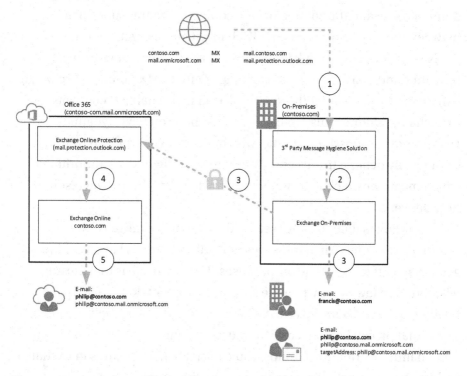

Figure 5-14. *Inbound mail flow routed via on-premises*

A quick walkthrough for when Exchange hybrid is configured, and inbound mail flow keeps landing on the on-premises organization. In this example, the sender is contoso.com, and the recipient is either philip @contoso.com, who has his mailbox in Exchange Online, or francis @contoso.com, who has his mailbox on-premises:

1) The mail transfer agent that wants to deliver the mail looks up the **MX** record for contoso.com. This points to mail.contoso.com, so it hands it off to the on-premises third-party gateway.

2) This third-party gateway processes the message and delivers it to Exchange on-premises.

3) Exchange on-premises accepts mail for contoso.com. It also has a matching recipient for francis@contoso.com and delivers the message to the mailbox. For philip@contoso.com, it finds a matching **MEU** (remote mailbox). This MEU has a **targetAddress** directing the message to **philip@contoso.mail.onmicrosoft.com**. For this domain, an address space is present on a Send Connector, **Outbound to Office 365 - <Guid>**, which has been set up by the HCW, and is configured to securely deliver messages. Exchange looks up the MX record for contoso.mail.onmicrosoft.com, which points to **contoso-mail-onmicrosoft-com.mail.protection.outlook.com** (Exchange Online Protection), where it delivers the message.

4) Exchange Online Protection uses an internal connector for the internal address space contoso.mail.onmicrosoft.com domain and hands off the message to Exchange Online.

5) The message is delivered to **philip@contoso.mail.onmicrosoft.com**, which is **philip@contoso.com**.

Caution   Third-party gateways between Exchange Online and Exchange on-premises are not supported, only in front of either one, sitting between public and your organization email infrastructure.

Centralized Mail Transport

Centralized Mail Transport (CMT) is an option presented when running the HCW, which is also the easiest method to configure this mail transport option. It will configure mail transport so that every message will be routed through Exchange on-premises. This can be required because of various reasons. Some examples are as follows:

- Legal reasons require you to use DNSSEC and DANE, and those options are at this moment only partially available. Using CMT creates a single mail path, where you can have a fully compliant solution between Exchange on-premises and the public network.

- You have specific Exchange Transport Rules on-premises, which you cannot port to Exchange Online.

- You might have a closed network with secure partners that is only available through on-premises (e.g., site-to-site VPN or secure email relay network). Sending or receiving those messages directly to or from Exchange Online is not an option.

- When you have certain third-party agents running on Exchange on-premises, such as signatures. By forcing traffic to flow through your on-premises organization, you create a single point of administration as all external messages in principle will pass Exchange on-premises.

Perhaps needless to say that CMT also creates a dependency on the Exchange on-premises infrastructure, so it needs the proper measures for improved availability and resilience, such as running multiple Exchange servers and having load balancing.

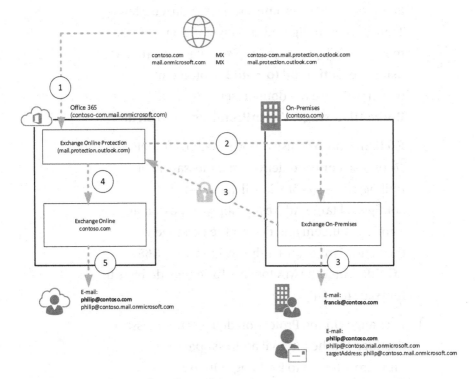

Figure 5-15. *Centralized Mail Transport*

When the MX record is configured to deliver inbound mail to Exchange Online Protection, the following occurs:

1) The mail transfer agent that wants to deliver the mail looks up the MX record for contoso.com. This points to contoso-com.mail.protection.outlook.com (EOP) and so hands it off to EOP.

2) Had Centralized Mail Transport not been configured, the message for philip@contoso.com would have been delivered to his mailbox, and the mail to francis@contoso.com would have been routed to on-premises. If Centralized Mail Transport is configured as shown in Figure 5-15, messages will get routed to Exchange on-premises using the **Outbound to <Guid>** connector, which will have the domain set to "*" and **RouteAllMessagesViaOnPremises** set to **$true**.

3) Exchange on-premises knows mailbox francis @contoso.com and delivers the message. For philip@contoso.com, it will again use the configured targetAddress philip@contoso.mail. onmicrosoft.com and deliver the message via the Send Connector **Outbound to Office 365 - <Guid>**. After the MX lookup, Exchange delivers the message to EOP.

4) Exchange Online Protection delivers the message destined for the internal address space mail. onmicrosoft.com to Exchange Online.

5) The message is delivered to philip@contoso.mail. onmicrosoft.com or philip@contoso.com.

Tip   In the HCW, the **Centralized Mail Transport** option is hidden from view. You need to make it visible by selecting **More Options**.

Outbound Mail

Regarding outbound mail flow from Exchange Online, the route again depends on if your organization has configured Centralized Mail Transport.

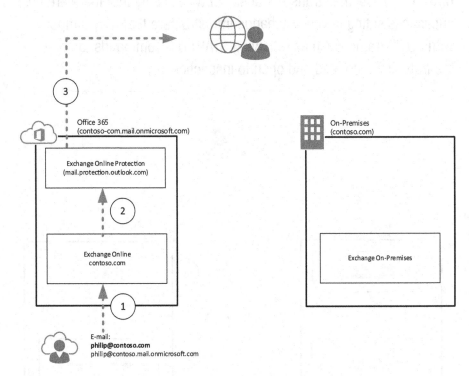

Figure 5-16. *Exchange Online, outbound mail flow*

When your Exchange hybrid is configured to not use Centralized Mail Transport, the following as shown in Figure 5-16 will happen:

1) The user philip@contoso.com submits a message to joe@fabrikam.com in Exchange Online.

2) Exchange Online sees that it is not authorized for fabrikam.com and routes the message to Exchange Online Protection for delivery.

433

3) Exchange Online Protection determines that
    fabrikam.com is external, does an MX lookup, and
    delivers the message to the configured host.

Caution   If the mail transport does not work, verify that there are no
appliances sitting in your Exchange infrastructure that may tamper
with SMTP traffic, such as removing STARTTLS commands to keep
the traffic unencrypted and open to inspection.

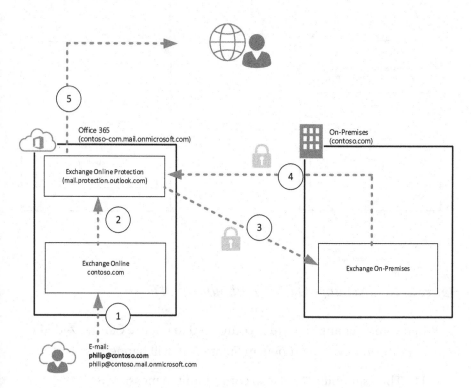

Figure 5-17.   Exchange Online, outbound mail flow with CMT

When your Exchange hybrid deployment is configured to use Centralized Mail Transport, the following occurs as shown in Figure 5-17:

1) The user philip@contoso.com submits a message to joe@fabrikam.com in Exchange Online.

2) Exchange Online sees it is not authorized for fabrikam.com and hands off the message to Exchange Online Protection for delivery.

3) Exchange Online Protection finds a matching connector Outbound to <Guid>, which is configured to always route all messages (RouteAllMessagesViaOnPremises) to mail. contoso.com.

4) Assuming you have configured outbound email to be delivered to Exchange Online Protection and there is no connector for fabrikam.com, the message is delivered to Exchange Online Protection.

5) Exchange Online Protection determines fabrikam. com is external, does an MX lookup, and delivers the message.

Enhanced Filtering

When you route messages destined to Exchange Online through a third-party service, the external IP address of this service will be taken into account by Exchange Online. What would be better for Defender for Office 365 or Exchange Online Protection is to take into account the original IP address of the sender, instead of the address of the intermediate sending third-party service. To facilitate this, Enhanced Filtering can be used, which is also known as Skip Listing, as it will skip last hosts in the sending path for message classification.

In short: When the inbound mail path looks like ClientIP ➤ ServiceIP ➤ Exchange Online, without Enhanced Filtering MDO will look at ServiceIP, and with Enhanced Filtering it will look at ClientIP.

To use Enhanced Filtering in Exchange Online, proceed as follows:

1) Navigate to the Defender for Office 365 portal, for example, **https://security.microsoft.com**.

2) Open the **Policies & Rules** pane, and select **Enhanced Filtering**.

3) Select the inbound connector to which you want to apply Enhanced Filtering, for example, **Inbound from <Guid>**.

4) Double-click it and configure the specific connector. You have per connector three options:

   a. **Disable Enhanced Filtering for Connectors**, which is the default.

   b. **Automatically detect and skip the last IP address**, which does exactly what the label says.

   c. Select **Skip these IP addresses**..., and manually enter the IP addresses of your third-party gateway.

Note   Entering private IP addresses (10.0.0.0/8, 172.16.0.0/12, or 192.168.0.0/16) is not supported. Also, Enhanced Filtering automatically detects and skips private IP addresses.

---

5) When you select either automatic or manual IP addresses, you need to select if you want to apply the filter to every recipient in your organization or specific recipients, which can be users or groups. This allows you to further restrict the filter to only ignore hosts in the transport path when messages are sent to specific recipients.

Enhanced Filtering is highly recommended when you have a third-party email hygiene SaaS service sitting in front of your inbound email traffic. Also, Enhanced Filtering can be used for inbound connectors of the type Partner, as the partner "source" addresses are in principle always identical and you want to have a look at the original source instead.

Note   You only need to include the third-party service host(s) in your SPF record if your organization sends outbound mail through these hosts, as this service becomes the source of these mail messages.

Exchange Online Archiving

With the potential mix of on-premises mailboxes and mailboxes in Office 365 comes the flexibility for organizations to find cost-effective business solutions. The *in-place archive* adds to that flexibility, as an organization can choose to host its mailboxes on-premises while hosting those in-place archives in Exchange Online, as depicted in Figure 5-18. Some of the Exchange Online plans and enterprise plans offer in-place archives. As an alternative, organizations can add the standalone Exchange Online Archiving plan, to complement their subscription.

Caution   Auto-expanding archiving (AutoExpandingArchive), often advertised as "unlimited storage" (which in practice translates to 1.5 TB, granted in chunks of 100 GB), is only supported for individual mailboxes or shared mailboxes growing with 1 GB/day at most. Journaling, using transport rules, or auto-forwarding to move messages to an auto-expanding archive is not permitted. Also, additional storage space in auto-expanding archives may take up to 30 days to get provisioned.

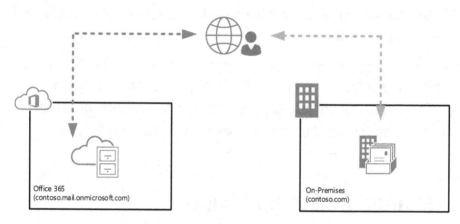

Figure 5-18.   *Exchange Online Archiving*

To use Exchange Online Archiving, you need to deploy Exchange hybrid. By enabling Exchange hybrid in AD Connect, several attributes are written back to the on-premises environment. One of those attributes is **msExchArchiveStatus**. When an on-premises mailbox user has msExchArchiveStatus set to **1**, that is an indication there is an in-place archive configured in Exchange Online.

Creating an Exchange Online Archive is a two-stage process. First, the on-premises mailbox gets enabled for an Exchange Online Archive. This is made effective in the next AD Connect cycle, which picks up the on-premises configuration change and provisions an in-place archive in Exchange Online. This archive is not immediately provisioned, but when it has been created, the **msExchArchiveStatus** gets set. In the next AD Connect cycle, that attribute is written back to the on-premises Active Directory, and users are able to access their in-place archives.

To enable an in-place archive in Exchange on-premises, you can use EAC or use **Enable-Mailbox** in conjunction with **RemoteArchive** from the Exchange Management Shell. You also need to specify **ArchiveDomain**, which functions similar to **TargetDeliveryDomain** when migrating mailboxes. ArchiveDomain points to the environment hosting the archive and can be the MOERA, for example, contoso.mail.onmicrosoft.com.

The following cmdlet will trigger creation of a remote archive for user Francis:

```
[PS] >Enable-Mailbox Francis -RemoteArchive -ArchiveDomain
contoso.mail.onmicrosoft.com
```

Name	Alias	ServerName	ProhibitSendQuota
Francis	Fran	ex1	Unlimited

Now, you wait for the AD Connect synchronization or manually run it to trigger creation of the in-place archive. When you consult the archive-related properties of the mailbox, you will see that the **archive status** has changed from **None** to **Hosted Pending**, indicating that **msExchArchiveStatus** is still not set:

```
[PS] >Get-Mailbox Francis | fl DisplayName, ArchiveStatus,
ArchiveState

DisplayName   : Francis
ArchiveStatus : None
ArchiveState  : HostedPending
```

After the second AD Connect synchronization cycle, the on-premises msExchArchiveStatus becomes 1. You can take a peek at the AD Connect services. On the Operations pane, wait for the last **Active Directory Connector | Export** log entry and check if there have been **updates** in the **Export Statistics** pane. Or simply check the local Active Directory object:

```
[PS] >Get-Mailbox Francis | fl ArchiveGuid, ArchiveStatus,
ArchiveDomain, ArchiveState

ArchiveGuid    : 5e739e26-b705-4da9-bffc-f34bef3c811e
ArchiveStatus : Active
ArchiveDomain : contoso.mail.onmicrosoft.com
ArchiveState  : HostedProvisioned

[PS] >Get-ADUser (Get-Mailbox Francis).distinguishedName
-Properties msExchArchiveStatus | fl Name, msExchArchiveStatus

Name                : Francis
msExchArchiveStatus : 1
```

The user with an Exchange Online Archive will notice that, if the Outlook Connection Status window is opened, it will show that their Outlook client is connected to their on-premises Exchange environment, as well as to Exchange Online. To make the user experience seamless, it is recommended you have the same sign-on or single sign-on.

Message Tracking

In Exchange on-premises, you can use the **Get-MessageTrackingLog** cmdlet to track messages passing through your local Exchange infrastructure. Of course, in Exchange Online, your tenant is part of a shared infrastructure, and therefore tracking with the details normally available using Exchange on-premises could raise privacy issues.

This is where the commands **Get-MessageTrace** and **Get-MessageTraceDetail** come into play. Get-MessageTrace is to be used for message tracking in Exchange Online and functions similar to Get-MessageTrackingLog, obfuscating certain elements of the shared infrastructure.

Here is a short list of the parameters you can use with Get-MessageTrace and how they work in comparison with Get-MessageTrackingLog:

- **StartDate** and **EndDate** work identically; they enable you to restrict the results to a specific date range.

- **RecipientAddress** filters results on recipient email address. You can specify multiple values using a comma, and you can use wildcards such as *@con-toso.com.

- **SenderAddress** is similar to RecipientAddress, but filters on sender email address instead. Like RecipientAddress, you can use wildcards.

- **FromIP** allows you to filter on the source IP address for inbound messages, which normally is the public IP address of the SMTP server that delivered the message.

- **MessageTraceID** can be used in combination with RecipientAddress to uniquely identify a message trace and obtain more details. A message trace ID is generated for every message processed.

- **MessageId** filters works identical and filters on the message ID header field of the message.

- **Status** filters on the delivery status of the message. Options are None, Failed, Pending, Delivered, or Expanded. This is similar to Get-MessageTrackingLog's EventId parameter. It is not identical, as internal routing of messages will be hidden.

- **ToIP** can be used to filter on the public IP address of the destination server for outbound messages.

Caution   You can only trace messages from the last 30 days.

For example, to retrieve all message traces of messages received between June 1, 2023, and June 2, 2023, sent to michel@contoso.com, you would use something like

```
[PS] >Get-MessageTrace -StartDate 6/1/2023 -EndDate 6/2/2023
-Recipient michel@contoso.com | Format-Table -AutoSize
Received, SenderAddress, RecipientAddress, Subject
```

To see all the message traces of email coming from an email domain named "microsoft.com" in the past seven days, showing only the last ten trace events, you would use

```
[PS] >Get-MessageTrace -StartDate (Get-Date).AddDays(-7)
-EndDate (Get-Date) -SenderAddress '*@microsoft.com' |
Select Received, MessageId, Status | Sort-Object Received
-Descending | Select -First 10 | Format-Table -AutoSize
```

Finally, if the level of detail provided with Get-MessageTrace is not sufficient, you can retrieve more details per message trace using Get-MessageTraceDetail. For example, to get the details of the last message delivered, use

```
[PS] >Get-MessageTrace -Status Delivered -PageSize 1 |
Get-MessageTraceDetail
Date                    Event             Detail
----                    -----             ------
21-6-2023 09:07:59      Receive           Message received
by: AM7PRO5MB6727.eurprd05.prod.outlook.com using TLS1.2 ...
21-6-2023 09:08:03      Deliver           The message was
successfully delivered.
```

You might need to expand the output for all properties to become visible, for example:

```
[PS] >Get-MessageTrace -Status Delivered -PageSize 1 |
Get-MessageTraceDetail | fl *
```

```
Organization    : contoso.onmicrosoft.com
MessageId       : <03de1806-0d72-40f9-80a5-6a49daf5ed73@
                  az.westeurope.unknown.microsoft.com>
MessageTraceId  : 4b29efeb-10c4-4e41-4562-08db72370213
Date            : 21-6-2023 09:07:59
Event           : Receive
Action          :
Detail          : Message received by: AM7PRO5MB6717.eurprd05.
                  prod.outlook.com using TLS1.2 with AES256
Data            : <root><MEP Name="ConnectorId" String=
                  "AM7PRO5MB6727\Default AM7PRO5MB6727"/>
                  <MEP Name="ClientIP" String="2603:10a6:10:
                  4f9::22"/><MEP Name="ServerHostName" String=
                  "AM7PRO5MB6727.eurprd05.prod.outlook.com"/>
                  <MEP Name="FirstForestHop" String=
                  "AM7PRO5MB6727.eurprd05.prod.outlook.com"/>
                  <MEP Name="DeliveryPriority" String=
                  "Normal"/><MEP Name="ReturnPath" String=
```

"azure-noreply@microsoft.com"/><MEP Name=
"CustomData" Blob="S:ProxyHop1=DB5EURO2FT066
.mail.protection.outlook.com(10.13.59.11);
S:ProxyHop2=DUZP191CA0003.outlook.office365.
com(2603:10a6:10:4f9::22);S:tlsversion=
SP_PROT_TLS1_2_SERVER;S:tlscipher=CALG_
AES_256"/><ME P Name="SequenceNumber"
Long="0"/><MEP Name="RecipientReference"
String=""/></root>

```
SenderAddress      :
RecipientAddress   :
StartDate          : 1-1-0001 00:00:00
EndDate            : 1-1-0001 00:00:00
Index              : 0

Organization       : contoso.onmicrosoft.com
MessageId          : <03de1806-0d72-40f9-80a5-6a49daf5ed73@az.
                     westeurope.unknown.mi
                     crosoft.com>
MessageTraceId     : 4b29efeb-10c4-4e41-4562-08db72370213
Date               : 21-6-2023 09:08:03
Event              : Deliver
Action             :
Detail             : The message was successfully delivered.
Data               : <root><MEP Name="SourceContext" String="08
                     DB71F102D8120B;2023-06-21T09:08:01.827Z;
                     ClientSubmitTime:"/><MEP Name="Mailbox
                     Server" String="AMOPRO5MB5043.eurprd05.
                     prod.outlook.com"/><MEP Name="Delivery
                     Priority" String="Normal"/><MEP Name=
                     "TotalLatency" Integer="5"/><MEP Name=
                     "ReturnPath" String="azure-noreply@
```

```
microsoft.com"/><MEP Name="ClientName"
String="AM7PRO5MB6727.eurpizationReason=
EnvelopePriority"/><MEP Name="Sequence
Number" Long="0"/><MEP Name="Recipient
Reference" String=""/></root>
SenderAddress    :
RecipientAddress :
StartDate        : 1-1-0001 00:00:00
EndDate          : 1-1-0001 00:00:00
Index            : 0
```

Recipient Management Only

We talked about keeping Exchange servers around for managing recipients and offering mail relay functionality. But what if you have no need to keep an Exchange server around for relaying mail on-premises and you only need it for recipient management as you have moved all of your mailboxes to Exchange Online? The official support stance was that you needed to keep Exchange server around for recipient management as well, and using ADSI Edit or other tools for direct Active Directory attribute manipulation was not supported.

Fortunately, per Exchange Server 2019 CU12 (or later), you can now run an Exchange server-less environment on-premises, if that is the only requirement for keeping Exchange server around on-premises. Yes, you are able to get rid of that "last Exchange server."

The Exchange management tools that come with Exchange Server 2019 CU12 or later allow for Exchange server-less recipient management if

- You migrated all mailboxes and public folders to Exchange Online.

- You use AD Connect or AD Cloud Sync for synchronization.

- You do not require Role-Based Access Controls on-premises.

- You do not require logging or auditing of recipient management activities.

- You have no need to keep Exchange Server on-premises for relaying email messages to Exchange Online.

Be advised that when going this route, you will have limited cmdlets at your disposal. This will only be the Exchange recipients used for recipient management tasks, such as Set-MailUser, New-RemoteMailbox, Add-DistributionGroupMember, or Set-User.

After making sure you have no mailbox in Exchange on-premises, proceed as follows:

1) In the Exchange Management Shell, verify there are no mailboxes left on-premises:

```
[PS] >Set-AdServerSettings -ViewEntireForest $true
[PS] >Get-Mailbox
```

Note that admin mailboxes are by default not synced, and you may need to disable these using Disable-Mailbox.

2) Check there are no messages being routed
    through Exchange Server on-premises, using **Get-
    MessageTrackingLog**, for example. If you have still
    multiple Exchange servers, note that these might
    send messages to each other to check availability
    and create shadow redundant messages for
    availability purposes.

3) Verify the coexistence domain (MOERA) is
    configured as the target delivery domain:

    ```
    [PS] >Get-RemoteDomain Hybrid* | Format-List Do
    mainName,TargetDeliveryDomain
    ```

4) If you have not already done so, install the Exchange
    management tools using the Exchange Server 2019
    CU12 or later installation set. The updated tools
    can be installed on any domain-joined computer in
    an Exchange organization running Exchange 2013
    or later.

5) Install the Windows Remote Server Administration
    Tools, for example, on Windows Server from an
    elevated PowerShell prompt:

    ```
    [PS] >Install-WindowsFeature RSAT
    ```

6) Run the following with Exchange 2019 CU12
    (or later) provided scripts to create the Recipient
    Management EMT security group. This group grants
    users without domain admin rights the right to
    manage recipients:

    ```
    [PS] >Add-PSSnapin *RecipientManagement
    [PS] >. $env:exscripts\Add-PermissionForEMT.ps1
    ```

7) Relog using an account that is part of the Recipient Management EMT group, and validate the recipient management cmdlets are functioning after loading the Recipient Management snap-in using **Add-PSSnapIn *RecipientManagement**.

8) Shut down your Exchange server(s), and repeat step 6 to validate everything is still functional.

Caution   Under any circumstance, DO NOT uninstall your last Exchange server. This will remove all Exchange configuration elements from Active Directory, which is not what you want as management of recipients still originates from on-premises through Azure AD Connect synchronization.

Now, if you verified everything and you want to permanently remove Exchange Server for recipient management from your environment, perform the following steps to remover Exchange and Exchange hybrid-related elements from your environment:

1) Turn on that last Exchange server again.

2) Clean up Autodiscover SCP records and hybrid configuration:

```
[PS] >Get-ClientAccessService | Set-ClientAccess
Service -AutoDiscoverServiceInternalUri $Null
[PS] >Remove-HybridConfiguration
```

3) Remove (or disable first if you prefer) the Intra-Organization Connector from an Exchange Management Online shell to Exchange on-premises and vice versa:

```
[PS] >Get-IntraorganizationConnector -Identity
HybridIOC* | Remove-IntraOrganizationConnector
```

4) Remove (or disable first) the inbound and outbound connectors from Exchange Online:

```
[PS] >Get-OutboundConnector | Where {$_.Connector
Type -eq 'OnPremises'} | Remove-OutboundConnector
[PS] >Get-InboundConnector | Where {$_.Connector
Type -eq 'OnPremises'} | Remove-InboundConnector
```

5) Remove any organizational relationship from an Exchange Online Management shell to Exchange Online and vice versa:

```
[PS] >Get-OrganizationRelationship | Remove-
OrganizationRelationship
```

6) In Azure AD Connect or AD Cloud Sync, leave the Hybrid Exchange feature enabled.

7) Shut down and destroy Exchange Server(s).

Tip   Since many administrators still prefer a graphical tool over command-line instructions for management, Microsoft MVP Steve Goodman created a tool called Exchange Recipient Admin Center, which is a client/server-type application with an EAC-like GUI for simple recipient administrative tasks. It leverages the Exchange Recipient Management module and therefore is a valid way to manage recipients. You can find the tool on GitHub at **https://github.com/spgoodman/ExchangeRecipientAdmin**.

Summary

In this chapter on Exchange Online, we covered various important topics. We began by discussing the significance of identity and the available Exchange hybrid topologies, highlighting their key differences. We then explored the configuration of Exchange hybrid using the Hybrid Configuration Wizard.

Next, we delved into connecting to Exchange Online using the Exchange Online Management module and the PowerShell Graph SDK for managing Azure Active Directory objects through cmdlets. We emphasized the value of OAuth, which is configured by the Hybrid Configuration Wizard, especially during migration and long-term coexistence scenarios in Exchange hybrid environments.

Autodiscover was another topic we addressed, explaining its role in Exchange hybrid deployments when mailboxes are moved. We also covered onboarding and offboarding mailboxes, emphasizing the management of remote mailbox objects left after migration and their utilization for creating new mailboxes in Exchange Online.

We further discussed federation between Exchange on-premises and Exchange Online, along with partnership options with other organizations, which are particularly relevant in merger and acquisition scenarios. We dedicated a significant portion of the chapter to mail transport in Exchange hybrid deployments, including an explanation of Centralized Mail Transport and its associated requirements.

Additionally, we explored Exchange Online Archiving, which involves hosting the in-place archive in Exchange Online while the mailbox resides in Exchange on-premises. We provided guidance on easily tracking messages in Exchange Online. Lastly, we addressed the circumstances that warrant the removal of the last Exchange server, enabling the management of Exchange recipients without an on-premises server, which is now a viable option.

PART III

Security

CHAPTER 6

Publishing Exchange Server

Part of configuring Exchange Server is making the Exchange services available to clients or handling mail transport. Every Exchange 2019 server handles two types of protocols:

- The part of Exchange Server that is responsible for handling HTTP requests is the Client Access Front End (CAFE). This service authenticates client requests and proxies requests to the relevant Mailbox service, for example, the Mailbox server that is hosting the mailbox. This service sits on top of the Internet Information Server (IIS).

- The Front-End Transport service (FETS) is responsible for accepting inbound SMTP messages from other mail servers, clients, or devices. Optionally, the Front-End Transport service is also responsible for routing messages outbound.

In a typical deployment, clients connect to the Exchange infrastructure through a load balancer or application delivery controller. This load balancer can accept these protocols on behalf of the Exchange servers behind it and optionally add functionality such as pre-authenticating clients.

© Jaap Wesselius and Michel de Rooij 2023
J. Wesselius and M. de Rooij, *Pro Exchange Administration*,
https://doi.org/10.1007/978-1-4842-9591-5_6

Most common load balancers also have a way to intelligently distribute client traffic over Exchange servers sitting behind them, for example, to distribute load but also to avoid sending client traffic to an Exchange server when it has been placed in maintenance mode. Thus, by putting more than one Exchange server behind the load balancer, organizations can increase the availability of Exchange services.

This is shown in Figure 6-1, where clients connect to CAFE on server EXCH01, but the mailbox is on server EXCH02.

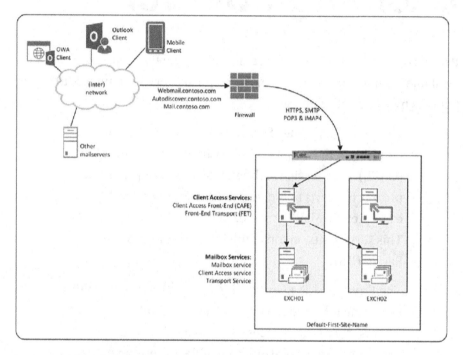

Figure 6-1.   Exchange Client Access service

When going into more detail, clients actually connect to the Internet Information Server (IIS) component, which is part of the CAFE server. Then, after authenticating to IIS, the request is proxied to the Mailbox server in the back end where the user's mailbox is hosted. This back-end service is also part of the IIS configuration. Where CAFE listens on port 443, the back-end service listens on 444, respectively[1]. This configuration is also visible when opening Internet Information Server Manager, as shown in Figure 6-2.

Figure 6-2. *Front-end and back-end configuration in IIS Admin*

POP3 and IMAP4 have their own services running on both CAFE and the Mailbox server. Again, after authentication to the POP3 or IMAP4 service, CAFE determines where the user mailbox is hosted and proxies the request to this Mailbox server.

SMTP works similar. When an email is sent to an Exchange server, the Front-End Transport service accepts the connection. It determines which server hosts the mailbox and proxies the SMTP connection to the Transport services running on this server for delivery to the mailbox. The protocol handling is shown in Figure 6-3.

---

[1] For completeness, IIS also serves unencrypted HTTP on port 80 on the front end, as well as port 81 on the back end.

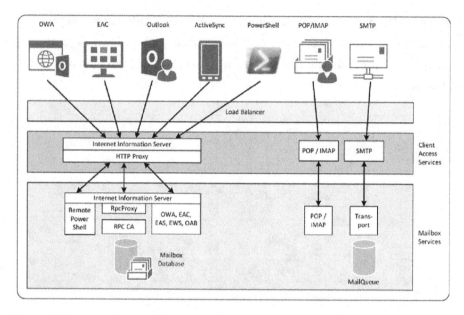

Figure 6-3. *Exchange Server 2019 protocol handling*

To avoid conflicts on an Exchange server, which serves both CAFE and Mailbox services, the front-end part and back-end part in IIS use different ports, 443 and 444, respectively, as mentioned earlier.

POP3 clients connect using port 110 (unencrypted) or port 995 (encrypted) to CAFE. After authentication, the request is proxied to the Mailbox server hosting the mailbox. The POP3 service here is using port 1995.

For IMAP4, ports 143 (unencrypted) and 995 (encrypted) are used at CAFE; the Mailbox server is using port 1995 for IMAP4.

For SMTP, multiple ports are used. The default front-end connector as part of FETS is listening on port 25. This is the port where all SMTP clients by default connect to. This traffic is unauthenticated (anonymous) and in principle regular SMTP traffic from the Internet or internal SMTP clients that need to deliver messages to mailboxes. Being anonymous, it is also the port used when relaying messages from other email infrastructure, such as applications or scan-to-mail devices.

Note   Information about the mail hygiene parts that are involved in handling SMTP messages is discussed in Chapter 8.

After accepting the message, FETS determines the Mailbox server hosting the user mailbox and forwards the message to the Transport service running on that Mailbox server. This Transport service uses port 2525 for connections from FETS.

Authenticated SMTP, sometimes referred to as SMTP Submit, uses port 587. This is used by mail clients such as Windows Mail and Mozilla Thunderbird or applications that cannot submit messages using SMTP on port 25. After authentication, the submitted SMTP message follows the regular path for either delivery to a recipient or the Internet.

An odd port used by SMTP is port 717. Normally, the Transport service will try to deliver outbound messages directly from the Mailbox server, based on configured Send Connectors. A Send Connector with FrontendProxyEnabled enabled forces the Transport service on Mailbox servers to talk through FETS when delivering those messages. In this communication, this port is used for outbound SMTP traffic from a Send Connector that is configured to use an outbound front-end proxy, which is delivered by FETS.

Table 6-1 presents an overview of all ports used by the Client Access service and the Transport service.

Table 6-1. *Ports Used by CAFE and FETS*

Protocol	Front End	Back End
HTTPS	443	444
POP3	110 or 995 (POP3S)	1995
IMAP4	143 or 993 (IMAP4S)	1993
SMTP	25	2525
SMTP Submit	587	465
Outbound SMTP Proxy	717	N/A

Virtual Directories

Exchange Server makes heavy use of HTTPS for various types of services. Those services have front-end and back-end components, as displayed in Figure 6-2 earlier. To manage each service, Exchange has the concept of virtual directories, which as the name implies are hosted through a folder in IIS, and each can be configured and monitored independently.

Exchange by default configures the following virtual directories:

- **Autodiscover** (/Autodiscover) is used by clients to discover the configuration including the endpoints it needs to use when accessing a mailbox.

- **Outlook Web App** (/OWA), used for Outlook on the Web, also known by its older name, Outlook Web Access (OWA).

- **Exchange Admin Console** (/ECP), used for the Exchange Admin Center as well as Control Panel for configuring mailbox settings for mailbox users. It is still named after the original Exchange Control Panel.

- **Exchange Web Services** (/EWS), used for Exchange Web Services such as Free/Busy requests, mail tips, or out-of-office settings. It is also used by the Mailbox Replication service to move mailboxes between Exchange servers, as well as Exchange in hybrid deployments when on- or offboarding mailboxes.

- **Exchange ActiveSync** (/Microsoft-Server-ActiveSync), used for mobile clients.

- **Offline Address Book** (/OAB), used by clients to download the Offline Address Book.

- **(Remote) PowerShell** (/PowerShell) is used by PowerShell, which covers Exchange Management Shell access.

- **RPC Client Access** (/RPC) is used by older Outlook clients using Outlook Anywhere (RPC over HTTP) to connect to Exchange. Note that this protocol is superseded by MAPI over HTTP.

- **MAPI** (/Mapi), used by Outlook clients to connect to Exchange. Also known as MAPI over HTTP.

While the associated folder for every virtual directory is also visible in IIS Admin, management needs to take place using the corresponding virtual directory cmdlets from the Exchange Management Shell or the Exchange Admin Center.

The configuration of each virtual directory has two URL properties: one for internal usage, InternalURL, and one for external usage, ExternalURL. Clients use these properties to determine which endpoint to use when connecting to Exchange, depending on the location of the client; that decision is up to the client.

For example, Outlook will use a process called Autodiscover to determine which endpoint it should use to connect to Exchange for the various protocols and services. It does this by sending an Autodiscover request specifying the email address of the desired mailbox. Among the information returned are InternalURL and ExternalURL properties for Exchange Web Services, for example. It is up to Outlook to determine based on the network settings which URL is used to connect. First, it will try to connect using the InternalURL, and if that fails it will try to connect using the ExternalURL property. If that fails as well, Outlook determines it cannot connect to the Exchange server, and it will stay in a disconnected state.

Initially, after installing a new Exchange server, the InternalURL properties of all virtual directories will be set to a path using the hostname of the server, while the ExternalURL property is empty.

When requesting the properties of the MAPI virtual directories, for example, it returns the following output:

```
[PS] C:\>Get-MapiVirtualDirectory -Server EXCH01 | select
*ternal* | fl
InternalUrl : https://exch01.proexchange2019.com/mapi
InternalAuthenticationMethods : {Ntlm, OAuth, Negotiate}
ExternalUrl :
ExternalAuthenticationMethods : {Ntlm, OAuth, Negotiate}
```

And when requesting the properties of Outlook Anywhere, it returns the following information:

```
[PS] C:\>Get-OutlookAnywhere -Server EXCH01 | select *ternal*
ExternalHostname :
InternalHostname : exch01.proexchange2019.com
ExternalClientAuthenticationMethod : Negotiate
InternalClientAuthenticationMethod : Ntlm
ExternalClientsRequireSsl : False
InternalClientsRequireSsl : False
```

Visible in this example is that a virtual directory has its own authentication method, which is configured independently of other virtual directories. The allowed authentication methods can be different for internal as well as external clients.

Exchange Server can use multiple authentication methods. The defaults that are used when installing Exchange are sufficient for most scenarios. For large and complex organizations or when working with previous versions of Exchange such as Exchange 2010, authentication methods become more important as they need to be aligned and compatible. Also, after being authenticated by CAFE, requests are likely proxied to another Exchange server, and the credential is passed to the server where the connection is proxied to.

The following authentication methods are available in typical Exchange deployments; note that not every virtual directory supports all authentication methods:

- **Form-based authentication** (FBA) is the authentication method used when logging onto Outlook on the Web or the Exchange Admin Center. The user enters the credentials, which are encrypted and sent to the Exchange server.

- **Basic authentication** is typically identified by a small pop-up window requesting the credentials. Credentials are sent across the wire unencrypted, so basic authentication must always be used in combination with SSL. Also note that basic authentication is no longer recommended, in favor of Modern Authentication. Modern Authentication is more secure and, for example, less vulnerable to password spray attacks, which are a method of trying weak, common (Password123), or leaked credentials across an organization to gain access. Modern Authentication requires an additional authentication factor. This factor can be a token, sign-in confirmation through a mobile device, or a network location, for example, on-site network.

Tip   To see if your email address and possibly password used at a website were leaked, have a look at `https://haveibeenpwned.com`.

- **Kerberos authentication** is the native Windows client-server authentication method. Originally developed by the Massachusetts Institute of Technology (MIT) and later incorporated in Active Directory in Windows 2000, Kerberos allows secure network authentication, but a connection to the Key Distribution Center (KDC) running on a Domain Controller needs to be always available. This works fine on the internal network, but not for clients on the Internet, non-domain-joined clients, or non-Windows clients such as Mac or Linux clients. Once a client has a valid Kerberos token, it can use this token to access other resources on the internal network.

- **NTLM** stands for New Technology LAN Manager. Despite the name, it is an older Microsoft technology. It uses a challenge/response system, sending credentials across the wire. However, it can easily be compromised using modern brute-force techniques. It can still be used on isolated networks within the enterprise boundaries, for example.

- **Windows Integrated Authentication** (WIA) is the native client-server authentication method used by IIS, and it can use both NTLM and Kerberos authentication when enabled.

- **OAuth** or Modern Authentication is the method used with Exchange hybrid or Exchange with hybrid Modern Authentication. This method leverages Azure Active Directory integration to hand off authentication, where Azure Active Directory can be configured to set authentication requirements to the client such as application, location, or multi-factor authentication. More on this in Chapter 9.

- **Negotiate** allows the client and server to agree on the authentication method to use, based on what they both support. While it sounds convenient, not all clients nor virtual directories support Negotiate. For example, Outlook Anywhere supports Negotiate, supporting basic as well as NTLM. Exchange Web Services does not support Negotiate.

- **WSSecurity** is the WS-Security (Web Services Security) authentication method, an extension to the underlying Simple Object Access Protocol (SOAP) to secure those messages between client and server by setting up a secure channel. It can be used to secure Autodiscover or Exchange Web Services, for example.

As mentioned earlier, each virtual directory has an InternalURL and ExternalURL property, used by clients to determine which endpoint to use based on their location. For OWA and EAC, you can use any URL to access OWA as long as the name is resolved to the IP address of the Exchange server. You will see a certificate warning when the name in the request does not match the name on the certificate, but other than that, you can access the service fine. This usually also happens when you open the Exchange Admin Center shortcut installed on every Exchange server, which opens the EAC web page.

For Outlook and mobile clients, it is different because these clients get their Exchange configuration via Autodiscover, and if something is configured incorrectly, the wrong data is returned to the client, and the client in turn cannot connect to the various services or starts complaining about certificate mismatches. So that bears the question how to configure the virtual directories and what URL you should use.

When only one Exchange server is used, the default setting of the local FQDN of the Exchange server can be used if it is configured with a valid certificate, which can be validated by the client. With one server, the same FQDN can be used for the ExternalURL as well, if the FQDN is publicly resolvable, but this is rarely the same as the internal name.

When multiple Exchange servers are used, things become a bit more complicated when load balancers are put in front of the Exchange server. Typically, a general server name like webmail is used, and the FQDN will be something like webmail.contoso.com. This FQDN should resolve to the virtual service or VIP on the load balancer, and the request will be forwarded from the load balancer to one of the Exchange servers.

Tip   Virtual directories support HealthCheck.htm pages, which allow load balancers to determine if services are healthy and servers are not put in maintenance mode. For example, `https://exch01.proexchange2019.com/EWS/Healthcheck.htm` will return a 200 HTTP status code if the EWS service on the exch01 is available and healthy. This allows load balancers to forward requests only to healthy Exchange servers, increasing the overall experience in 24/7 operations as load balancers can detect failing servers and void them, as well as simplifying maintenance windows as admins do not have to manually manage traffic.

The recommendation is to use split DNS, so webmail. proexchangeadmin.com will resolve to the external address when on the Internet and resolve to the internal address when used on the internal network. This way, both the InternalURL and ExternalURL can be configured with the same endpoint value, for example, webmail. proexchangeadmin.com.

When managing virtual directories, each virtual directory has its own cmdlets for viewing and configuring, such as Get-OWAVirtualDirectory and Set-OWAVirtualDirectory or Get-WebServicesVirtualDirectory and Set-WebServicesVirtualDirectory.

To change all virtual directories of Exchange server EXCH01 to webmail.proexchangeadmin.com for both the InternalURL and ExternalURL, execute the following commands in EMS:

```
[PS] C:\> Set-OWAVirtualDirectory -Identity "EXCH01\OWA
(Default Web Site)"
-ExternalURL https://webmail.proexchangeadmin.com/
owa -InternalURL https://
webmail.proexchangeadmin.com/owa
[PS] C:\> Set-ECPVirtualDirectory -Identity "EXCH01\ECP
(default web
site)"-ExternalURL https://webmail.proexchangeadmin.com/
ecp -InternalURL
https://webmail.proexchangeadmin.com/ecp
[PS] C:\> Set-ActiveSyncVirtualDirectory -Identity "EXCH01\
Microsoft-
Server-ActiveSync (Default Web Site)" -ExternalURL https://
webmail.
proexchangeadmin.com/Microsoft-Server-ActiveSync -InternalURL
https://
webmail.proexchangeadmin.com/Microsoft-Server-ActiveSync
```

```
[PS] C:\> Set-WebServicesVirtualDirectory -Identity "EXCH01\EWS
(Default
Web Site)" -ExternalURL https://webmail.proexchangeadmin.com/
ews/Exchange.
asmx -InternalURL https://webmail.proexchangeadmin.com/ews/
Exchange.asmx
[PS] C:\> Set-OABVirtualDirectory -Identity "EXCH01\OAB
(Default Web Site)"
-ExternalURL https://webmail.proexchangeadmin.com/
OAB -InternalURL https://
webmail.proexchangeadmin.com/OAB
[PS] C:\> Set-PowershellVirtualDirectory -Identity
"EXCH01\PowerShell
(Default Web Site)" -ExternalURL https://webmail.
proexchangeadmin.com/
Powershell -InternalURL https://webmail.proexchangeadmin.com/
Powershell
[PS] C:\> Set-MAPIVirtualDirectory -Identity "EXCH01\Mapi
(Default Web
Site)" -ExternalURL https://webmail.proexchangeadmin.com/
mapi -InternalURL
https://webmail.proexchangeadmin.com/mapi
```

Note that the RPC Virtual Directory is not configured this way, and there is no *-RpcVirtualDirectory command available. The RPC Virtual Directory is part of Outlook Anywhere, which is configured using the Set-OutlookAnywhere command in EMS.

Also, while the Autodiscover Virtual Directory also has the InternalURL and ExternalURL properties, they are not used. Therefore, there is no need to configure them, and they can stay undefined ($null). More on Autodiscover later in this chapter.

When configuring multiple Exchange servers, pay attention when configuring the virtual directories, as any misalignment may cause inconsistent behavior, especially when these Exchange servers sit behind a load balancer. These inconsistencies will pop up occasionally when you happen to hit the misconfigured server, and it will be toughest to troubleshoot. We have seen this happening in a large environment with 32 Exchange servers in a load balancer where two new Exchange servers were configured incorrectly. This resulted in a considerable number of Outlook clients ending up with misconfigured profiles and thus tickets and unhappy users.

Since all HTTPS communication goes through IIS on the Exchange server, a lot of logging is already generated on the IIS level. The default location of IIS log files is C:\inetpub\logs\LogFiles\W3SVC1. For a typical busy Exchange server, it is not unusual to generate hundreds of megabytes of logging data on a daily basis.

This amount of data can quickly fill up the system disk of your Exchange server if you have not relocated IIS logging. A solution to this is to run a scheduled task that periodically cleans up the IIS logging folder. An example of managing IIS log files running a simple PowerShell script as a scheduled task can be found at **https://bit.ly/CleanupIISLogs**.

Namespaces

Namespaces play an increasingly important role in Exchange Server; this started with the introduction of Autodiscover and its namespace back in the days of Exchange Server 2007. A namespace is a domain name used by clients to access the Exchange environment. An example of a namespace is webmail.proexchangeadmin.com. Browsers can use webmail. proexchangeadmin.com/owa to access Outlook on the Web for their mailbox, and Outlook can use webmail.proexchangeadmin.com/MAPI to interact with the mailbox.

An additional namespace being used in an Exchange server environment is autodiscover.proexchangeadmin.com. This is used by Outlook clients to send the Autodiscover requests to the Exchange server to retrieve information on where to find and how to access a mailbox. The minimum number of namespaces in a typical Exchange environment is two: the protocol namespace and the Autodiscover namespace. However, it is theoretically possible to host everything on autodiscover. proexchangeadmin.com but is not recommended for reasons of security and traffic segmentation.

Apart from Autodiscover and a common namespace, it is possible to use service-specific namespaces. For example, we have seen customers use smtp.proexchangeadmin.com for mail delivery, imap. proexchangeadmin.com for IMAP, or eas.proexchangeadmin.com for ActiveSync.

One of the advantages of the loosely coupled architecture of Exchange Server is its unified namespace. It is possible to use only one namespace for the entire Exchange organization, as opposed to having different namespaces for different geographical regions, such as webmail.emea. proexchangeadmin.com and webmail.apac.proexchangeadmin.com. Using Geo-DNS solutions, it is possible to leverage the same external namespace for different regions and have local DNS resolvers point to the most local Exchange environment. This might however require sufficient WAN bandwidth between data centers, as requests might come in from any geographical region. An example is displayed in Figure 6-4.

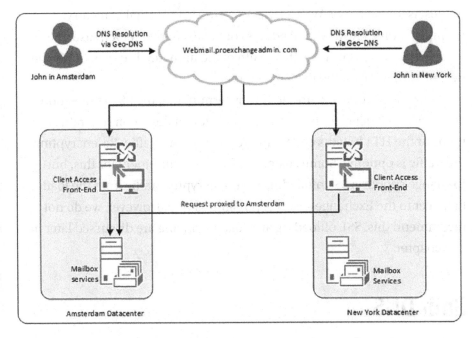

Figure 6-4. *Exchange unified namespace and Geo-DNS*

In the example, John logs onto webmail.proexchangeadmin.com when he is in Amsterdam. This is where his mailbox is located. He is authenticated by the Exchange infrastructure in the Amsterdam region, and his request is proxied to the appropriate Mailbox server, also located in the Amsterdam region. When John travels to New York, he still can use webmail.proexchangeadmin. The Geo-DNS solution resolves to the Exchange infrastructure in New York, where his request is authenticated. The Exchange server detects that John's mailbox is in the Amsterdam data center and proxies the request to the Exchange Mailbox servers in the Amsterdam region using the internal network.

From a load balancing perspective as well, namespaces are an important factor to consider. A layer-4 load balancer cannot perform content inspection and therefore cannot determine which protocol is used in a specific request. This means the load balancer does not know if the request is for Exchange Web Services or the MAPI Virtual Directory, for example. It only knows the IP address of the Exchange server. Also, the load balancer cannot check the health of the individual services, only the overall availability of the Exchange server.

It is possible to work around this by terminating the SSL connection at the load balancer, do the content inspection of the incoming traffic to monitor the HTTP status codes, and re-encrypt the traffic. Re-encrypting the traffic is optional. Some customers have a requirement for this, but Exchange supports SSL offloading, so unencrypted traffic from the load balancer to the Exchange server is possible as well. However, we do not recommend this. SSL offloading and load balancing are discussed later in this chapter.

Split DNS

We briefly talked about namespaces, but these were external namespaces, that is, namespaces used by clients that do not reside on the internal network. Internal clients usually need to connect to Exchange as well, so namespaces are also used on the internal network.

When an Exchange server is installed, it is typically accessed using its fully qualified domain name (FQDN), which can be something like `https://exch01.proexchangeadmin.com`.

While these are all valid names and can be safely used, it makes life much easier if the same namespace is used on the internal as on the external network, such as webmail.proexchangeadmin.com. Using one namespace is not only clearer; there is also no need to use additional names on an SSL certificate.

When webmail.proexchangeadmin.com is used from the Internet, the external IP address of the load balancer publishing Exchange is resolved, that is, 178.251.192.3. When webmail.proexchangeadmin.com is used on the internal network, the IP address of the internal virtual server is resolved, that is, 10.38.96.233. This configuration is called a split DNS configuration and is the recommended approach for namespace planning.

Certificates

Certificates are used to encrypt traffic between Exchange servers. When an Exchange server is installed, a self-signed SSL certificate is automatically assigned to HTTPS as well as SMTP for encrypting traffic. This self-signed certificate contains only the NetBIOS name of the server as Subject and Subject Alternative Name. The FQDN of the server is also present in the Subject Alternative Name field. Since the issuer of this certificate is the Exchange server, which is not trusted by other Exchange servers, it cannot be used for server authentication.

Exception to this is the default SMTP certificate used when creating subscriptions to Exchange Edge Transport servers. When the edge subscription is created, the thumbprint of the certificate is copied from the Exchange Edge Transport server to the Exchange server.

Certificates issued by known third-party certificate authorities are trusted by Exchange servers and clients on common operating systems. These certificate authorities, such as DigiCert or Verisign, can provide the necessary certificate that can be assigned to Exchange services and be trusted by clients based on the namespace they are accessing, the names on the certificate, as well as validating the expiration date and issuer.

When requesting SSL certificates with third-party certificate authorities, having more namespaces means more domain names on your SSL certificate, unless wildcard certificates are used. In a typical environment, webmail.proexchangeadmin.com and autodiscover. proexchangeadmin.com namespaces are used and therefore are the names that need to be present on the SSL certificate. This means that you need to request multi-domain certificates, which support Subject

471

Alternative Names (SANs). Then, the common name webmail is usually entered as Subject (CN), and all additional namespaces such as Autodiscover are specified as Subject Alternative Name (SAN). Again, wildcard certificates can be used, but from a security perspective less favorable due to their blanket namespace coverage.

Of course, you can also use an internal certificate authority to generate certificates for Exchange. But this certificate will by default not be trusted by non-domain-joined systems or mobile devices. If you want to use this construction, you need to distribute the certificate authority issuing certificates to these devices for its certificates to be trusted. It is however an option, but be aware that using your own certificates involves additional management.

Requesting Certificates

To request a new SSL certificate, log onto the Exchange server as an Exchange administrator, and use the following cmdlets, replacing EXCH01 with your Exchange Server name and SubjectName and DomainName with the proper values for your deployment:

```
[PS] C:\> $Data= New-ExchangeCertificate -Server EXCH01
-FriendlyName "Exchange Certificate" -GenerateRequest
-SubjectName "cn=webmail.contoso.com" -DomainName "webmail
.contoso.com","autodiscover.contoso.com" -PrivateKeyExportable
$true
[PS] C:\> Set-Content -path "C:\Cert\SSLCertRequest.req" -Value
$Data
```

The parameters are self-explanatory. **PrivateKeyExportable** makes sure that the certificate we are going to receive after our request gets processed can be exported. The private part of the certificate, needed for encryption, is only available on the server generating the request. Making this part exportable as part of the certificate allows us to import and use the certificate on other Exchange servers as well.

After the certificate is generated by the certificate authority, it is important that you finish the certificate request on the Exchange server used to generate the initial request. Using EMS, use a command like the following to complete the request, and assign it to IIS, that is, all HTTPS-based services:

```
[PS] C:\> Import-ExchangeCertificate –Server EXCH01 -FileData
([Byte[]]$(Get-Content -Path C:\Cert\CertNew.p7b" -Encoding
byte -ReadCount 0))
[PS] C:\> Get-ExchangeCertificate -DomainName webmail.contoso.
com | Enable-ExchangeCertificate -Server EXCH01 -Services IIS
```

If you want to use this certificate also for POP3 and IMAP4 services, you can specify IMAP or POP with -Services.

You can also use this certificate for SMTP by specifying SMTP with -Services. Note that with SMTP you will be asked if you would like to overwrite the default certificate that is used for SMTP. This means that the Transport service will use this certificate for any SMTP communication, which needs to be encrypted and for which no matching certificate can be found for the SMTP connector's fqdn property.

Exporting Certificates

When the certificate is installed and configured correctly, you can use the Export-ExchangeCertificate command to create a copy of it. This copy can be used as backup, storing it in a safe location, but it can also be used to import on other Exchange servers.

To create an export file of the SSL certificate, you first have to find out the thumbprint of the SSL certificate. This thumbprint is the unique identifier of the SSL certificate. The thumbprint of the SSL certificate is shown when executing a Get-ExchangeCertificate command in EMS:

```
[PS] C:\> Get-ExchangeCertificate -Server EXCH01
Thumbprint                                Services Subject
----------                                -------- -------
D4FA1A0243A929AEEBF4D77DE93D50B691DB0A79 IP.WS..  CN=EXCH01
EB3A32C2079C31B281736FDB065310516E69C17A .......  CN=WMSvc-SHA2-EXCH01
C7DDAE9409B27CD08C9E5863A4906B1D75B3A617 ....S..  CN=Microsoft Exchange
                                                  Server Auth Certificate
54C1DF64138E27A56CBB4E8ABE1C2AE0EB430BF7 ...W...  CN=webmail.proexchange
                                                  admin.com
```

To extract attributes of a specific certificate, you can use its thumbprint:

```
[PS] C:\> Get-ExchangeCertificate -Server EXCH01 -Thumbprint
54C1DF64138E27A56CBB4E8ABE1C2AE0EB430BF7 | fl Subject,
CertificateDomains, PublicKeySize, HasPrivateKey, Issuer,
NotAfter, Services
Subject            : CN=webmail.proexchangeadmin.com
CertificateDomains : {webmail.proexchangeadmin.com,
                     autodiscover.proexchangeadmin.com}
PublicKeySize      : 2048
HasPrivateKey      : True
Issuer             : CN=GeoTrust TLS DV RSA Mixed SHA256 2020
                     CA-1,O=DigiCert Inc, C=US
NotAfter           : 3/8/2022 12:59:59 AM
Services           : IIS
```

To export the certificate into a .pfx file, which is a format that includes the private key, you first must collect an export of the SSL certificate, protected with a password since it contains the private key, after which you can write the contents to disk. To do this, execute the following commands in EMS:

```
$PW= (Get-Credential).Password
$ExportFile = Export-ExchangeCertificate -Server EXCH01
-Thumbprint
54C1DF64138E27A56CBB4E8ABE1C2AE0EB430BF7 -binaryencoded:$true
-password $Pw
Set-Content -Path C:\Cert\webmail_proexchangeadmin_com.pfx
-Value $ExportFile.FileData -Encoding Byte
```

Note that only the password is used for the credential you enter, so you can leave the username blank. Another option is to convert text to a secure string, the format in which a password needs to be provided, for example:

```
$PW= ConvertTo-SecureString -String 'P@ssw0rd' -AsPlainText
-Force
```

Importing Certificates

When you have an export of an SSL certificate, you can use PowerShell to import this SSL certificate on additional Exchange servers. To do this, you can use commands such as the following in EMS:

```
Import-ExchangeCertificate -Server EXCH02 -FileData ([Byte[]]
$(Get-Content -Path C:\Cert\webmail_proexchangeadmin_com.
pfx -Encoding byte -ReadCount 0)) -Password:(Get-Credential).
password | Enable-ExchangeCertificate -Server EXCH02
-Services IIS,IMAP4
```

Note   When using multiple Exchange servers behind a load balancer, use the same certificate on every server. Also, if your load balancer is layer 7 (content switching), do not forget to update the certificate used on your virtual server as well.

Autodiscover

Autodiscover was introduced in Exchange 2007 to support Outlook 2007, and it has evolved into one of the most important parts of any Exchange environment. It is used extensively in Exchange on-premises, Exchange Online, and Exchange hybrid scenarios. If you do not have a proper Autodiscover configuration, you will experience all kinds of issues, ranging from not being able to check Free/Busy information when scheduling a meeting to not being able to download an Offline Address Book, not being able to set the out-of-office message using the Outlook client, or not being able to connect at all.

Autodiscover is most noticeable for end users when they set up their Outlook client. When setting up Outlook, in its simplest form, a user has only to enter their email address and password, and the Outlook client will configure itself automatically. It discovers all the parameters it needs to use and uses this information to configure an Outlook profile.

But not only does it do this on the initial setup. Clients such as Outlook also perform this action on a regular basis to check for any changes in the Exchange environment, such as changes in endpoints, but also information regarding additional mailboxes to which one has been granted Full Access with automapping or online archives is published through Autodiscover.

Autodiscover works by sending a SOAP request to the Exchange infrastructure. Exchange checks Active Directory for the location of the user's mailbox and, when needed, proxies the request to the Exchange server hosting the mailbox. The Autodiscover process on this Exchange server processes the request, collects all information, and returns the information in XML format to the client. The client in turn configures the Outlook profile. The process is shown in Figure 6-5.

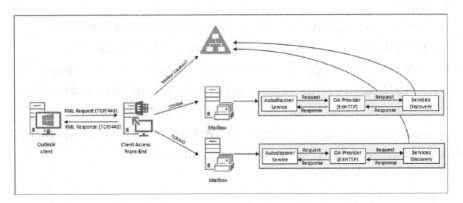

Figure 6-5. *Autodiscover process*

How does the Outlook client discover which Exchange server to send its request to? The answer is twofold:

- Domain-joined clients with Outlook on which one is logged onto Active Directory retrieve this information directly from Active Directory.

- Non-domain-joined clients with Outlook, or domain-joined clients who cannot access Active Directory (e.g., when working remotely), build the Autodiscover URL based on the user's SMTP address.

Both scenarios are covered in the next sections.

Domain-Joined Clients

When an Exchange server is installed, a computer object is created in the configuration partition of Active Directory. Besides this computer object, a Service Connection Point (SCP) is also created in Active Directory. For every Exchange server that is installed, a corresponding SCP is created. So, if you have six Exchange servers, you also have six SCP objects in Active Directory.

An SCP has a well-known GUID (Global Unique Identifier) that is unique for the type of application that is using the SCP. In the case of Exchange Server, this application is Outlook. All Service Connection Points created by Exchange setup have the same well-known GUID, and Outlook clients query Active Directory for this GUID. This GUID is stored in the keywords attribute together with the Active Directory site name where the Exchange server is installed, as shown in Figure 6-6.

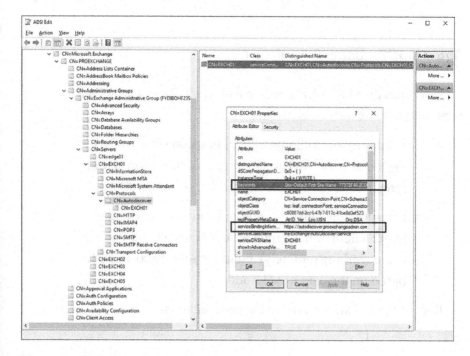

Figure 6-6. *Service Connection Point*

Once located, the serviceBindingInformation attribute is fetched, and this value should contain the Autodiscover FQDN of the Exchange environment, for example, `https://autodiscover.proexchangeadmin.com/autodiscover/autodiscover.xml`. If there are multiple Exchange servers in the Active Directory site of the Exchange environment, a virtual server on the load balancer should be created that should resolve for autodiscover.proexchangeadmin.com, with all real Exchange servers sitting behind it.

After Outlook retrieves the Autodiscover FQDN from Active Directory, it sends an HTTP POST command to this URL. The Exchange server then accepts the request and proxies it to the Exchange server hosting the user's mailbox. This Mailbox server collects all the required information and returns this as an XML package to the Outlook client. The Outlook client uses this package to configure a new profile (new setup) or reconfigure the profile.

This process is continuous and not only during Outlook setup. By default, the request is sent once every hour to see if reconfiguration is needed. Since it is an HTTP request that must be secured, the SSL certificates come into play, and autodiscover.proexchangeadmin. com needs to be covered by the certificate as well, next to the webmail. proexchangeadmin.com name. The Autodiscover URL is configurable only by using the Exchange Management Shell. To configure this, use EMS:

```
[PS] C:\> Set-ClientAccessService -Server EXCH01 -AutoDiscover
ServiceInternalUri https://autodiscover.proexchangeadmin.com/
autodiscover/autodiscover.xml
```

To reconfigure all SCP objects for all Exchange servers, use the following:

```
[PS] C:\> Get-ClientAccessService | Set-ClientAccessService
-AutoDiscoverServiceInternalUri https://autodiscover.
proexchangeadmin.com/autodiscover/autodiscover.xml
```

Tip   Change the SCP record using the Set-ClientAccessService command directly after installing a new Exchange server, to prevent Outlook clients accidentally retrieving wrong information from the newly installed Exchange server. This information contains the server, which will result in certificate mismatch messages on Outlook.

Alternatively, you can create a dedicated Active Directory site with a Domain Controller and its own IP range, where you can deploy Exchange without the possibility of disturbing clients. After configuration, you can relocate the new Exchange server by changing its IP address and restart, and all will be well.

It is possible to verify the Autodiscover functionality from within Outlook. With Outlook running, check the system tray for the Outlook icon. Press **Ctrl** and right-click the Outlook icon, and select **Test Email AutoConfiguration**. This will open a dialog where you need to enter your email address and optionally password to be used for testing purposes. If you do not specify the password, your current credentials are used. Deselect the Guessmart checkboxes, and click Test to start the Autodiscover process. A sample output is shown in Figure 6-7.

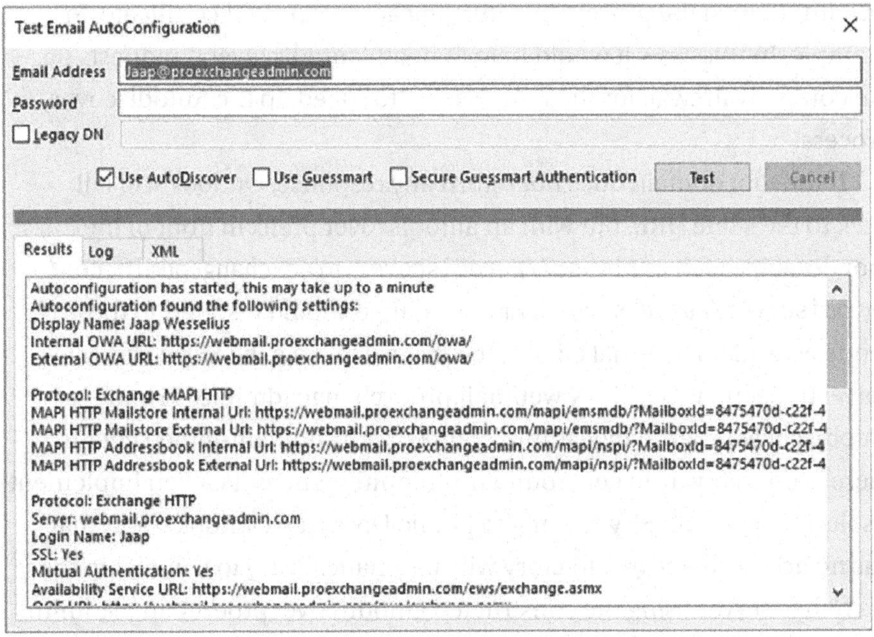

Figure 6-7. *Test Email AutoConfiguration*

Results give an overview of the information returned. If you are interested in the process, consult the Log tab, or click XML to view the raw XML that has been retrieved.

Non-Domain-Joined Clients

Non-domain-joined clients, or domain-joined clients who do not have access to Active Directory, use a different approach for getting Autodiscover information. In this process, which is DNS-based, Outlook will construct an FQDN based on the domain part of the email address. So, if the user's email address is john@proexchangeadmin.com, Outlook will first try connecting to `https://proexchangeadmin.com/autodiscover/autodiscover.xml`. Often, this causes issues, since the root domain proexchangeadmin.com usually contains the company website and may interfere in the process by returning an unexpected certificate, for example. In this case, it would help to deny /autodiscover/* requests on the company firewall for the root website to speed up the Autodiscover process.

If the root domain does not return any response, Outlook will fall back to the same URL, but with an autodiscover prefix in front of the root domain, such as `https://autodiscover.proexchangeadmin.com/autodiscover/autodiscover.xml`. Exchange should respond to these requests, and for external clients, it is crucial to have the SSL certificate correctly set up with FQDN webmail.proexchangeadmin.com and autodiscover.proexchangeadmin.com. For non-domain-joined clients, there is no easy way to get around this requirement, unless you implement a solution based on SRV records in public DNS. Any Outlook client that has no access to Active Directory will automatically try to connect to the Exchange server using the constructed autodiscover.proexchangeadmin. com endpoint. This is hard-coded in the Outlook application!

The built-in Outlook test function, as shown in Figure 6-7, also works when Outlook is operating outside the corporate network. An alternative is Microsoft's remote test tool that is part of the Remote Connectivity Analyzer (RCA) website, accessible through `https://aka.ms/exrca`.

When opening the website and selecting the Exchange Server option, you have the option to have it test **Outlook Connectivity**. After clicking, you are requested to provide email and credentials and confirm that you are using a test account.

You can click the Verify button or proceed to the Perform Test button directly as this will start the verification process. There are multiple methods for retrieving Autodiscover information, and these are shown as a red circle with a white cross in it, a green circle with a white checkbox in it, or an orange triangle with an exclamation mark. When one method fails, Outlook (and thus also RCA) will continue with the next alterative option.

There is no need to panic when you see a red circle; only when you see only red circles and no green ones is time to start troubleshooting. Figure 6-8 shows sample output of RCA. The MAPI over HTTP tests are all successful, but the Outlook Anywhere tests show a warning. You can expand each step to drill down in the process and investigate what was tested and what was the result. In this test, it was just a warning about RPC encryption, so no need to worry.

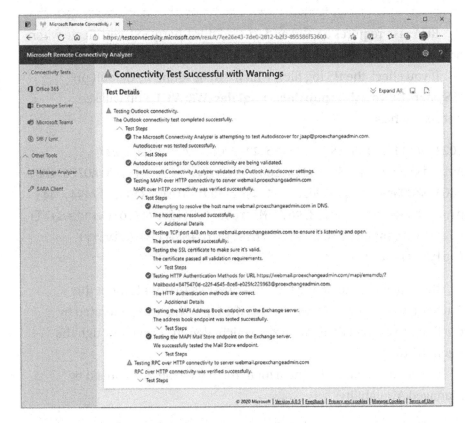

Figure 6-8. *Remote Connectivity Analyzer*

Note   The Remote Connectivity Analyzer is a publicly available portal
from Microsoft to test connectivity to your Exchange environment.
Since it must access your Exchange environment from the Internet,
your Exchange server needs to be accessible from the Internet. If
your Exchange environment is only available after setting up a VPN
tunnel, for example, RCA cannot perform its tests.

RCA also requires a valid and trusted third-party SSL certificate when
accessing your environment. It does not work with self-signed certificates.

If you check the IIS log files, which can be found by default on
%SystemDrive%\inetpub\logs\LogFiles\W3SVC1, you will see
entries such as

```
2023-04-11 19:58:05 10.38.96.223 POST /Autodiscover/
Autodiscover.xml &CorrelationID=<empty>;&ClientId=XYAOZEOJEMDY
FBGAVSKQQ&cafeReqId=dd1847b5-45e2-4e01-9fe1-43a9ac7f7494; 443
proexchange\jaap 10.38.96.9 Microsoft+Office/15.0+(Windows+NT+
6.2;+Microsoft+Outlook+15.0.4615;+Pro;+MS+Connectivity+
Analyzer)- 200 0 0 46
```

By inspecting the IIS log files, it is possible to troubleshoot the
Autodiscover process. Shown here is the entry that was generated by
the Remote Connectivity Analyzer, which identifies itself through the
Agent field.

Other entries you will find a lot in the IIS log files are caused by
Managed Availability:

```
2023-04-13 08:41:03 ::1 GET /AutoDiscover/ &CorrelationID=
<empty>; &cafeReqId=8c0af66b-3865-47c7-b221-7a4525d32a49; 443
PROEXCHANGE\HealthMailbox39af3e9 ::1 AMProbe/Local/
ClientAccess - 200 0 0 6
```

Managed Availability is a service in every Exchange server that tests connectivity between your Exchange servers, for example, to see if proxying is possible.

Autodiscover Redirect

In the previous section, we learned that Outlook creates an Autodiscover FQDN based on the user's email address and this FQDN must be present on the SSL certificate used for publishing Exchange. This setup works well if there is only one or two primary SMTP domains in the Exchange organization, but it can be challenging when there are numerous SMTP domains.

For example, when an organization acquired multiple smaller organizations over time or spawns of business operating under their own domain, FQDNs for all these domains in principle need to be present on the certificate. This can be difficult to manage and can become costly due to the validation process becoming more extensive to validate all the domains. Also, many certificate authorities have a hard limit on the number of domain names that can be issued per certificate, in the order of 25.

Now suppose there is another SMTP domain hosted by your organization, named inframan.nl, and suppose the SSL certificate only contains the webmail.proexchangeadmin.com and autodiscover. proexchangeadmin.com names. In this scenario, Autodiscover Redirect might be an option.

To implement this option, Exchange servers have an additional website on port 80 with an FQDN called autodiscoverredirect.proexchangeadmin. com. Requests for this site are automatically redirected to autodiscover. proexchangeadmin.com internally in IIS. The additional domain inframan. nl has an Autodiscover record in public DNS, which is a CNAME record that refers to autodiscoverredirect.proexchangeadmin.com located on the Exchange server. When an external user with an email address m.jones @inframan.nl opens Outlook, Outlook tries to connect to autodiscover. inframan.nl automatically. However, this attempt fails because the Exchange server responds with an SSL warning message. In the next step, Outlook checks for an HTTP redirect option by accessing the Exchange server and looking for an HTTP/302 redirect. If a redirect is returned, Outlook continues with the Autodiscover process using the website found in the redirect string.

From this point on, the process is the same. Outlook sends an HTTP POST command to the Exchange server, and the Autodiscover service running on the Exchange server gathers all the necessary information and sends it back to the Outlook client as an XML file. The Autodiscover process with the HTTP/302 redirect can be seen in Figure 6-9 as part of the RCA testing outcome.

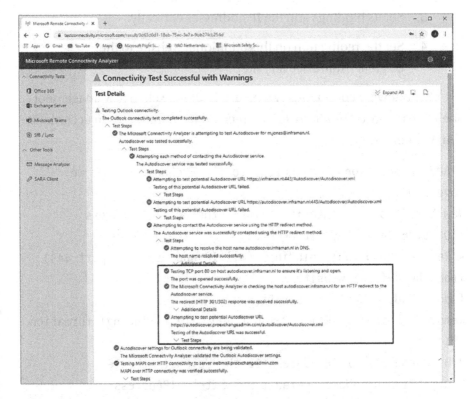

Figure 6-9. *Autodiscover Redirect*

Visible is that the tests for `https://inframan.nl/autodiscover/`
`autodiscover.xml` and `https://autodiscover.inframan.nl/`
`autodiscover/autodiscover.xml` fail, but succeed on the HTTP redirect
method. Just as in the earlier examples, there is no need to panic because
of the red circles with the white crosses; if there is one green circle, you
should be fine.

To implement the Autodiscover Redirect method on the Exchange
server, you must perform four steps:

1. Add an additional IP to the Exchange server.

2. Create an additional website on the
    Exchange server.

487

3. Set its bindings and the IP addresses correctly.

4. Set the redirection on this additional website to the original (Autodiscover) site.

The following commands can be used in the Exchange Management Shell to configure Autodiscover Redirect; adjust parameters in accordance with your environment:

```
# Add an additional IP address to the Exchange server we
logged on to
New-NetIPAddress -InterfaceAlias "Ethernet" -IPAddress
"10.38.96.241" -PrefixLength 24
# Remote the default bindings (all IP addresses on port 443)
from the default website
Import-Module WebAdministration
Remove-WebBinding -Name 'default web site' -BindingInformation
"*:443:"
# Bind the server IP address to the default website
New-WebBinding -Name "Default Web Site" -IPAddress
"10.38.96.241" -Port 443 -Protocol https
# Create new directories on disk for AutodiscoverRedirect
New-Item -ItemType Directory -Path $env:systemdrive\Inetpub\
AutodiscoverRedirect
New-Item -ItemType Directory -Path $env:systemdrive\Inetpub\
AutodiscoverRedirect\Autodiscover
# Create a new Website and Virtual Directory for
AutodiscoverRedirect
New-WebSite -Name AutodiscoverRedirect -Port 80 -PhysicalPath
"$env:systemdrive\inetpub\AutodiscoverRedirect" -IPAddress
"10.38.96.241"
```

```
New-WebVirtualDirectory -Name Autodiscover -Site
AutodiscoverRedirect -PhysicalPath "$env:systemdrive\inetpub\
AutodiscoverRedirect\Autodiscover"
# Point the virtual directory to the default website for
Autodiscover.
Set-WebConfiguration system.webServer/httpRedirect "IIS:\sites\
autodiscoverredirect\autodiscover" -Value @{enabled="true";
destination="https://autodiscover.proexchangeadmin.com/
autodiscover/autodiscover.xml"; exactDestination="false";
httpResponseStatus="Found"}
```

Multiple websites on one server need unique combinations of IP addresses and port number. Therefore, you see the default website listing on port 443 and the Exchange Back End website on port 444. This way, both can use the same IP address. Instead of using an additional IP address on the Exchange server, it is also possible to use a different port number, for example, create the AutodiscoverRedirect website on the same IP address, but bind it to port 81. Then create a virtual service on the load balancer for the AutodiscoverRedirect website, and connect to the Exchange server on port 82. This will save you any challenges of arranging and external publishing additional IP addresses.

You can also use IIS Manager, from another server when using Exchange on Windows Server Core, and connect to the IIS instance on your Exchange server. You can use the following steps to implement the Autodiscover Redirect method:

1. Configure an additional IP address on the Exchange server.

2. In IIS Manager, bind the default website to the original IP address of the Exchange server for port 443, as shown in Figure 6-10. Before you continue, make sure the Exchange server still

responds correctly with this new binding and no other application or service is interfering with your chosen IP address or port number.

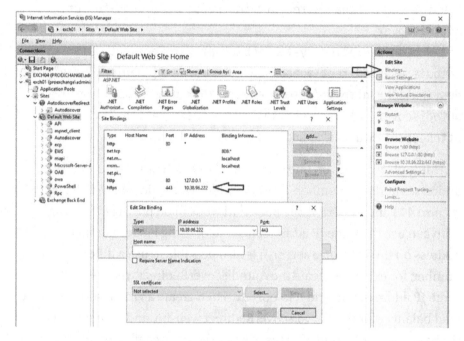

Figure 6-10. *Configuring Autodiscover Redirect using IIS Admin*

3. On the Exchange server, create two additional directories:

    C:\Inetpub\AutodiscoverRedirect

    C:\Inetpub\AutodiscoverRedirect\Autodiscover

4. In IIS Manager, create a new website, name it AutodiscoverRedirect, and use the C:\Inetpub\ Autodiscover as its physical path. Make sure the binding of this website is set to the additional IP address we configured earlier, as shown in Figure 6-11.

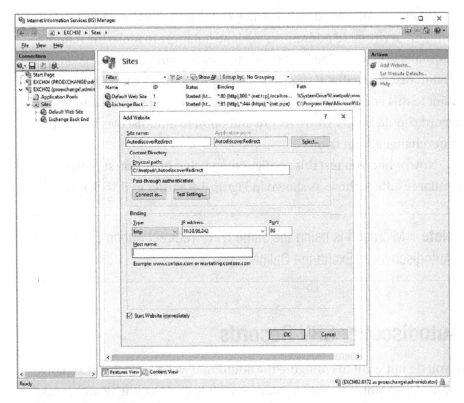

Figure 6-11. *Adding an Autodiscover Redirect website using IIS Admin*

5. In the AutodiscoverRedirect website in IIS Manager, you will see an Autodiscover Virtual Directory show up. Select this Autodiscover Virtual Directory, and in the Details pane, double-click **HTTP Redirect**.

6. In the HTTP Redirect window, check **Redirect request to this destination** and enter the normal Autodiscover URL, like `https://autodiscover.proexchangeadmin.com/Autodiscover`.

When the AutodiscoverRedirect website is up and running, configure a virtual IP address on the load balancer to make the redirect externally available. The final step is to create a public DNS A record for autodiscoverredirect.proexchangeadmin.com, which should point to this additional IP address. The autodiscover.inframan.nl DNS record should be a CNAME record and point to autodiscoverredirect. proexchangeadmin.com.

Now, when you test this configuration using RCA, you should see similar results to those as shown in Figure 6-9 earlier in this chapter.

Note   Microsoft is using the same HTTP redirect option for Autodiscover in Exchange Online.

Autodiscover SRV Records

If you do not want to configure the additional website on your Exchange server, for example, because you do not have spare public IP addresses, there is another option for Autodiscover to resolve to your Exchange server. This involves usage of service records (SRV) in public DNS. Be aware that not all clients have implemented support for SRV records as part of the Autodiscover process.

Suppose we have another SMTP domain in the proexchangeadmin. com environment named exchange16.com and that domain name is not present on the SSL certificate. For this domain, we can configure SRV records for Autodiscover. This service record is constructed as **_autodiscover._tcp.exchange16.com**, and it needs to point to **autodiscover.proexchangeadmin.com** on port **443** as shown in Figure 6-12.

Figure 6-12. *Autodiscover SRV records*

When checking with RCA, you will see that the Autodiscover Redirect option fails, but that the SRV option succeeds, as shown in Figure 6-13.

Note   When using SRV records for Autodiscover, you can use any FQDN you like. This way, you can configure your Exchange server with only webmail.proexchange.com and use an SRV record for Autodiscover and point it to webmail.proexchange.com. Again, be advised that not all clients implemented support for SRV records.

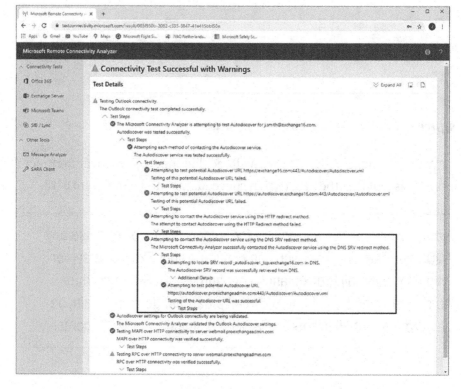

Figure 6-13. *RCA test for Autodiscover SRV records*

Autodiscover V2

Autodiscover (V1) and V2 are different versions of the Autodiscover service in Exchange, with the same purpose. The difference is how they achieve that goal.

Autodiscover V1 was introduced in Exchange Server 2007 and uses a combination of domain-joined client computers and Outlook client applications to locate the Autodiscover service endpoint via DNS or SCP records in Active Directory to retrieve configuration information. This method relies on a predefined method and fabricated endpoints, such as the root domain and autodiscover.cotoso.com. This hard-coded method may limit flexibility when steering the Outlook clients to update its settings. Autodiscover V1 also does not support Modern Authentication.

Autodiscover V2 was introduced in Exchange Server 2013 and uses a REST API–based architecture, which should provide more flexibility. With Autodiscover V2, clients can discover the Autodiscover service endpoint dynamically by querying Active Directory or Azure Active Directory, which can be especially useful in Exchange hybrid or Exchange Online deployments. Autodiscover V2 also supports Modern Authentication, making it more secure and reliable than V1.

Here is sample output of an Autodiscover V2 REST call to find the location of a mailbox for Exchange Web Services access:

```
[PS] ] C:\> Invoke-RestMethod -Method Get -Uri 'https://
autodiscover-s.outlook.com/autodiscover/autodiscover.
json?Email=michel@proexchangeadmin.com&Protocol=Ews'

Protocol Url
-------- ---
Ews      https://outlook.office365.com/EWS/Exchange.asmx
```

The endpoint hints at the mailbox residing in Exchange Online.

Here is another sample output, showing the endpoint to use for a mailbox still hosted on-premises:

```
[PS] ] C:\> Invoke-RestMethod -Method Get -Uri 'https://
autodiscover-s.outlook.com/autodiscover/autodiscover.
json?Email=jaap@proexchangeadmin.com&Protocol=Ews'

Protocol Url
-------- ---
Ews      https://webmail.proexchangeadmin.com/EWS/Exchange.asmx
```

Client Connectivity

Multiple clients and application programming interfaces (APIs) are available to use with Exchange Server, such as

- Outlook

- MAPI over HTTP

- Exchange Web Services

- REST API

- Web-based clients

- Mobile clients

These clients and client services will be discussed in more detail in the following paragraphs.

Outlook

For Outlook clients, Exchange servers are only accessible using Outlook Anywhere (RPC over HTTP) or MAPI (MAPI over HTTP) as the primary protocol. The latter is preferred due to its support for Modern Authentication, has faster reconnects (after hibernation or switching from a wired/wireless network), and uses a durable session on the back end, which can survive network changes on the client side. MAPI over HTTP is also the protocol of choice when connecting to Exchange Online, as RPC over HTTP for Exchange Online went out of support back in 2017.

Apart from MAPI over HTTP, Outlook clients use other web-based protocols, such as Autodiscover, Exchange Web Services (EWS), or HTTPS to download the Offline Address Book changes. Using EWS, Outlook clients can request availability information (Free/Busy) or set an out-of-office message. The Offline Address Book is downloaded by Outlook clients running in cached mode. Contrary to Outlook on Windows, Outlook for Mac fully utilizes Exchange Web Services for all communications.

Finally, Autodiscover is used by Outlook clients for initial profile configuration and reconfiguration if needed.

Outlook clients can run in cached mode or online mode, where cached mode is the default (and preferred) mode. When run in cached mode, Outlook works with a copy of a subset of mailbox data. All changes on the client side are made against this cache. Outlook periodically updates the cached information with changes on the back end and propagates changes in the cache to the back end (mailbox). Processing takes place on the client, thereby reducing processor cycles and (expensive) disk I/O on the Exchange server and allowing for network optimization due to operations being batched.

When Outlook runs in online mode, it directly runs against the Exchange server. It is obvious that this will increase the load on the Exchange server, plus the Outlook client will always need to be online and have a reliable connection with low latency for an acceptable end user experience. Another benefit of working online is that when multiple delegates manage a calendar, every delegate can see updates made by other delegates quickly; when cached mode is used, this can be a bit behind as Outlook only shows updates after the synchronization cycle.

Outlook in online mode is often used in terminal server environments, but when using a tool like FSLogix, it is possible to run Outlook in cached mode in terminal server environments as well. Cached mode is the recommended mode when working with Exchange Online, due its ability to work with higher latency and unreliable network connections. FSLogix is also often seen in terminal server environments in combination with Exchange Online.

MAPI over HTTP

MAPI over HTTP got introduced back in Exchange Server 2013 SP1 as the successor of RPC over HTTP, also known as Outlook Anywhere. RPC is considered a legacy protocol, developed in the 1960s for servers running on a local, stable network (like in the office) but not on less reliable networks such as Wi-Fi or the Internet. Even though Outlook Anywhere in itself is stable, when you have an intermittent network connection, your HTTPS connection can deal with that, but RPC over HTTP is less utilized for that.

Another issue with Outlook Anywhere is that it relies on the RPC Proxy service on Windows Server. As such, the RPC Proxy service is not a responsibility of the Exchange product group, but rather the Windows product group at Microsoft. To overcome this dependency, as well as address all the reliability and performance issues of RPC over HTTP, MAPI over HTTP was developed. With MAPI over HTTP, Outlook no longer uses RPC for its MAPI communication, but instead uses HTTPS directly. The difference is shown in Figure 6-14.

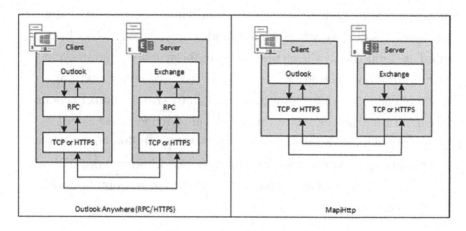

Figure 6-14. *RPC over HTTP versus MAPI over HTTP*

MAPI over HTTP is set on the Exchange organization level, but is also configurable on the mailbox level. To enable MAPI over HTTP for the whole organization, use EMS:

```
[PS] C:\> Set-OrganizationConfig -MapiHttpEnabled $TRUE
```

To enable it for a single mailbox, use Set-CASMailbox:

```
[PS] C:\> Set-CASMailbox -Identity <ID> -MapiHttpEnabled $TRUE
```

Please note that it can take some time for this change to take effect.

Note   For new Exchange deployments, this setting is already enabled. When you migrated from Exchange 2010 (or earlier) to Exchange 2013, and now migrating or having migrated to Exchange 2019, this setting might still be disabled, and you could still unknowingly be using RPC over HTTP. After publishing the MAPI Virtual Directories (see earlier in this chapter), you can enable this setting. Perhaps first only for some mailboxes to test publishing rules. Also, only clients supporting MAPI over HTTP will pick up this configuration aspect passed through Autodiscover and switch from RPC over HTTP to MAPI over HTTP.

Web-Based Clients

In theory, all Exchange clients are web-based nowadays, but in this section, we will focus on Outlook on the Web, formerly known and still commonly referred to as Outlook Web Access or just OWA. We will briefly talk about OWA and Office Online Server as an interesting add-on for OWA.

OWA is the primary and native web-based mail client of Exchange Server. It is an HTML5-based client, built by the Microsoft Exchange team and hosted on every Exchange server on top of IIS. OWA is supported on multiple browsers and devices, and it is a great tool to quickly check your email. Over time functionality within OWA has improved, and for most common daily tasks, OWA is a fine platform. We also use OWA when troubleshooting issues with Microsoft Outlook. Sometimes, you have support issues where a mail does not show up in Outlook, or you have issues because your client still has not updated the Offline Address Book, for example. Check the mailbox using OWA, and you can quickly rule out any of these client-side issues.

OWA also has an option for offline usage, something that was introduced years ago in Exchange Server 2013. OWA also supports server-based apps (Outlook apps) to enrich the user interface or offer additional functionality such as Bing Maps.

Offline Settings

Official Microsoft browser support is quite simple: latest versions of Microsoft Edge, Firefox, Safari, and Chrome are supported. Most modern browsers support the offline use of OWA, and it is easy to enable. From within the OWA site, click the settings icon and select **Offline settings**. Check the Turn on offline access checkbox and follow the wizard to enable offline usage.

Here are a couple of remarks on offline usage:

- Offline mail data is stored on the local computer. This can pose a security risk when other people are using the computer as well. Data is stored in a web database located in the user profile, located in C:\Users\<username>\AppData\Local\Microsoft\ Edge\User Data\Default\databases.

- OWA uses a predetermined amount of storage on the computer. If additional storage is needed, a pop-up box appears asking for permission to use more storage for offline mail data.

- When offline, a bookmark is the best way to access OWA offline.

- By default, only Inbox and Drafts folders are synchronized for offline use; other five most recently used folders are synced as well, and other folders can be selected.

It is possible to disable OWA offline use on an organizational level. To do so, modify OWA mailbox policies using the following command in EMS:

```
[PS] C:\> Set-OwaMailboxPolicy -Identity Default
-AllowOfflineOn NoComputers
[PS] C:\> Set-CASMailbox -Identity <username> -OWAMailboxPolicy
Default
```

In this example, the default OWA mailbox policy is modified and is then (re)assigned to an individual mailbox.

It is also possible to disable OWA offline use on the virtual directory. To do this, run the following command in EMS:

```
[PS] C:\> Set-OwaVirtualDirectory -Identity "EXCH01\Owa
(default web site)" -AllowOfflineOn NoComputers
```

Keep in mind when modifying the OWA Virtual Directory to keep settings aligned between all servers, to prevent erratic behavior. Alternatively, use OWA mailbox policies.

Outlook Apps

Outlook apps were introduced in Exchange Server 2013 and still exist in Exchange 2019. With Outlook apps, you can add functionality to OWA and Outlook. One nice example that is available by default is Bing Maps. When there is a street address in an email, Exchange will detect it, contact Bing Maps, and provide additional information when presenting the email.

By default, there are five apps available in Exchange:

- Action Items

- Bing Maps

- My Templates

- Suggested Meetings

- Unsubscribe

To add additional Outlook apps, open EAC and navigate to **Organization ➤ Add-ins**. Here, you will see the five default Outlook apps, but when you click the + icon and select **Add from the Office store**, you will be redirected to the Microsoft store. Filter on Exchange and you will see all available apps for Exchange, which can be used in OWA (shown as a web app) and Outlook.

Exchange Admin Center

The Exchange Admin Center is the HTML5-based management interface for Exchange Server. You can access EAC using your browser by navigating to a URL like `https://webmail.proexchangeadmin.com/ecp`. By default, EAC is accessible for everyone, both users and Exchange administrators. Depending on your permission, you can have a variety of functions available. Normal users have very limited permissions; they can only manage their own user and mailbox settings. Exchange administrators can use most functions available in EAC. We said most, because there are features not available by default in a typical Exchange deployment. For example, by default Exchange administrators cannot import or export mailboxes. For this, they need to be explicitly assigned permissions to do so.

Permissions are controlled via Role-Based Access Control (RBAC), which is discussed in Chapter 10.

It is possible to disable administrative access through EAC; to accomplish this, execute the following command in EMS:

```
[PS] C:\> Set-ECPVirtualDirectory -Identity "EXCH01\Ecp
(default web site)" -AdminEnabled $false
```

It will take approximately five minutes for this change to take effect. To expedite this change, you can reset the Internet Information Server using IISRESET.

Note   Only the administrative components of EAC will be disabled; the user components are still available. This is true for both external and internal access. So be careful with this setting, as after implementing this change, it will not be possible to make changes to the Exchange environment using EAC.

For a more granular approach, I recommend using Client Access Rules to restrict access. More on Client Access Rules in Chapter 9.

Exchange Web Services

Exchange Web Services is not a client, but rather an application programming interface (API). Through EWS, clients but also applications can programmatically access mailboxes hosted on Exchange Server. In the case of EWS, this access consists of clients sending SOAP requests to Exchange Web Services, after which EWS will return results in the form of XML responses.

Well-known EWS clients are Microsoft Outlook (for Free/Busy) and Outlook for Mac. There are also PowerShell scripts that perform certain tasks on Exchange mailboxes that use EWS Managed API to access mailboxes. There exist also third-party applications and devices that use EWS to interact with mailboxes, for example, room scheduling devices.

The Exchange Web Services architecture is shown in Figure 6-15.

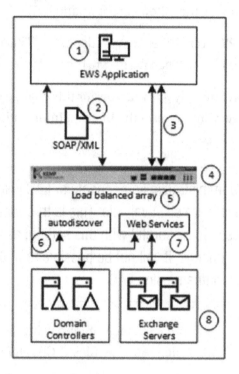

Figure 6-15. *Exchange Web Services architecture*

The following elements are shown in the Exchange Web Services architecture:

- An EWS application can be any client, application, or script. For custom applications or PowerShell scripts, you might have to install the Microsoft EWS Managed API, which can be downloaded from http://bit.ly/EWSAPIDownload.

- A SOAP/XML message is the request/response dialog when an application interfaces with the Exchange environment.

- The authentication method can be basic authentication, Windows Integrated Authentication (NTLM), or OAuth. The latter is used for authentication for Microsoft Teams or Exchange Online in Exchange hybrid deployments when accessing availability information on Exchange Server on-premises.

- The load balancer distributes client requests over multiple Exchange servers.

- An array of Exchange servers is a set of Exchange servers. Note that the Exchange server accepting requests may not be the Exchange server processing the requests.

- The Autodiscover service performs service discovery by using Active Directory to find the Exchange server hosting the user mailbox.

- Exchange Web Services is described by three files:

  - **Services.wsdl** describes the contract between the client and the server.

  - **Messages.xsd** defines the request and response SOAP messages.

  - **Types.xsd** defines the elements used in the SOAP messages.

- A Database Availability Group (DAG) increases availability of databases by storing multiple copies of mailbox data. DAGs are described in more detail in Chapter 3.

REST API

The REST API folder is a virtual directory that provides access to Exchange Web Services (EWS) via Representational State Transfer (REST) API. The REST API interface allows applications to access and interact with Exchange data, such as emails or calendar items.

The most common application that uses REST API with Exchange on-premises is Microsoft Teams. REST API is used by Teams to retrieve calendar information of on-premises mailboxes to display calendar information or show presence based on a user's status.

Using REST API to access mailboxes on-premises from Microsoft Teams requires Modern Authentication and federation with Azure Active Directory, which is set up during Exchange hybrid deployment.

Note that Teams also uses Autodiscover to discover the endpoint to use when trying to access mailboxes on-premises:

1. Teams sends an Autodiscover V2 request to Exchange Online.

2. Exchange Online checks the location of the mailbox; if this is a mailbox that is hosted in Exchange Online, the endpoint `https://outlook.office365.com/EWS/Exchange.asmx` is returned, and we are done.

3. If it is a mail user (related to a Synchronized Identity of an on-premises mailbox), the Autodiscover endpoint is determined using the domain-part, for example, autodiscover.proexchangeadmin.com.

4. Exchange Online returns a redirect (HTTP 302) including the endpoint to Teams.

5. Teams sends an Autodiscover request using the on-premises endpoint returned by the previous step.

6. Exchange on-premises returns an Autodiscover response containing the Exchange Web Services and REST API endpoints to use.

Teams' requests landing on your Exchange on-premises servers can be identified by looking at the IIS logs. They will contain log entries with specific user agents for Teams services. This information can also be used to troubleshoot integration issues, but for that I would primarily recommend using the Remote Connectivity Analyzer and one of its Teams test scenarios, for example, **Teams Calendar Events Based Presence** and **Teams Exchange Integration**.

The Teams user agent strings you might encounter in IIS logs and their originating service are

- *Calendar*: MicrosoftNinja/1.0 Teams/1.0 (ExchangeServicesClient/0.0.0.0) SkypeSpaces/1.0a$*+

- *Delegate*: SchedulingService

- *Presence*: Microsoft.Skype.Presence.App/1.0

Log entries are usually found for Autodiscover and Exchange Web Services requests, for example:

```
2023-04-29 20:22:52 fd86:b628:2775:1:9502:cdcc:d4b1:5950 GET /
autodiscover/autodiscover.json Email=michel%40proexchangeadmin.
com&Protocol=REST&RedirectCount=1 443 PROEXCHANGEADMIN\EX2$ fd8
6:b628:2775:1:9f8:2d9:c8a1:3c4a SkypeSpaces/1.0a$*+ 401 0 2 31
```

Note   Teams also caches calendar information in what is called the Presence service. This information allows Teams to update your presence based on your calendar (meetings and so on). How current this information is depends on the location of the mailbox. If the mailbox is hosted in Exchange Online, the presence information is subscription-based (push), meaning updates to your calendar should propagate quickly to the Presence service. If your mailbox is hosted on-premises, this information is updated every hour (pull).

At Microsoft Exchange Conference in 2022, it was announced that REST API will get deprecated over time and the Teams Presence service will switch to using Exchange Web Services instead for calendaring and presence. This should reduce discrepancies between someone's presence in Teams and in Outlook, as the latter uses Exchange Web Services, where Teams does its own thing using REST API.

Mobile Clients

Exchange ActiveSync (EAS) is the protocol used by most mobile clients connecting to the Exchange environment over the Internet. Mobile clients are mostly smartphones and tablets running iOS or Android. The Mail app on Windows 10 and Windows 11 also uses EAS to interact with mailboxes on Exchange Server.

Microsoft is licensing the EAS protocol and its interfaces to third parties and independent software vendors. It is up to the vendor to write applications and to follow the EAS protocol. One of the problems with this is that Microsoft does not enforce proper implementation or quality control. Therefore, each vendor has its own interpretation of the EAS protocol, resulting in some applications that run fine, but others that function less optimal.

Additionally, there are applications that have a major performance impact on the Exchange server. Mobile clients are typically very sensitive when it comes to SSL certificates, and not all SSL certificates are accepted by mobile clients. To get EAS working properly, there needs to be a supported third-party SSL certificate. Most mobile clients rely on the Autodiscover function of the Exchange server, as do Outlook clients, so having a fully working Autodiscover configuration is essential for running EAS successfully.

In addition to native mobile clients, Microsoft also makes Outlook for iOS and Outlook for Android available. Outlook Mobile is a cloud-backed application. It is a local app on the mobile device, combined with a scalable service in Exchange Online. As such, it uses a different approach when connecting to a mailbox in Exchange on-premises. Outlook Mobile is using an unmanaged mailbox in Exchange Online, and it communicates with this mailbox using native Microsoft Sync technology. The unmanaged mailbox in turn is using EAS to communicate with the on-premises Exchange server, as shown in Figure 6-16. The unmanaged mailbox in Exchange Online, which functions as a mailbox data hatch, contains four weeks of mail, all calendaring, and contact information, as well as a copy of the actual out-of-office status.

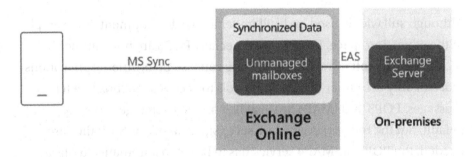

Figure 6-16. *Outlook Mobile communications for Exchange on-premises*

This behavior is clearly visible in the IIS logs. When connecting with Outlook Mobile on an iPhone, the following is logged in the IIS log file:

```
2023-04-04 09:45:54 10.38.96.222 POST /Microsoft-Server-
ActiveSync/default.eas Cmd=Ping&User=baron%40proexchange
admin.com&DeviceId=db4f7bbcccf845a185 da5b9f2d9783ec&De
viceType=Outlook&CorrelationID=<empty>;&cafeReqId=634618
5e-3f3d-4eac-8e66-98acac9920d7; 80 baron@proexchangeadmin.com
52.98.169.237 Outlook-iOS-Android/1.0 - 200 0 0 180023
```

The IP address 10.38.96.222 is the internal IP address of the Exchange server. The IP address 52.98.169.237 is an IP address belonging to Microsoft and is located in Dublin. The public IP address of the iPhone is 5.159.33.188; this IP address is not logged anywhere.

The connection and synchronization between the unmanaged mailbox and the on-premises mailbox is continuous and independent of user behavior. This ensures the best performance, as it takes away logic and dealing with differences between Exchange versions as the app only needs to know how to connect to instances of unmanaged mailboxes.

IMAP and POP

Although still widely used and still under active development, for example, in the education space, IMAP4 and especially POP3 are not commonly seen in a Microsoft infrastructure. There can also be business applications that can only use either of these protocols to access a mailbox to fetch messages. POP3 and IMAP4 are installed on the Exchange server by default, but the related services are set to start manually. So, if they are needed, the POP3 or IMAP4 service has to be set to automatically start.

Exchange Server allows the basic POP3 and IMAP4 protocols, but also allows the encrypted versions of the protocols, that is, POP3S (POP3 over SSL) and IMAPS (IMAP4 over SSL).

If you want to use a third-party certificate with POP3 or IMAP4, you must configure the respective service to use it, very similar to the process with IIS. For example, to enable an SSL certificate for POP3 and IMAP4, execute the following command in EMS:

```
[PS] C:\> Get-ExchangeCertificate -Server EXCH01 -Thumbprint
<thumbprint> |
Enable-ExchangeCertificate -Server EXCH01 -Services POP,IMAP
```

Restart the POP3 and IMAP4 services, and you are good to go.

The POP3 and IMAP4 protocols are only used for retrieving messages. The client should be configured for sending outbound mail via SMTP. This can be the same endpoint as used for IMAP4 or POP3.

High Availability

When running multiple Exchange servers, most likely you want to use a load balancer or application delivery controller for availability and scaling reasons. Using a load balancer, you can distribute the load from clients over multiple Exchange servers. This will distribute the load across the Exchange servers, and in the occasion that one server fails, client connections will be redistributed over the remaining Exchange servers.

Load balancing solutions can be hardware load balancers or software load balancers, which often are hardware load balancers but as a virtual machine package that can be run on commodity hardware instead of the appliance it comes with.

Note   There is still the option to use Microsoft's load balancing solution, Network Load Balancing (NLB). Although NLB is still supported, it has serious drawbacks. For example, it is not possible to install NLB on Mailbox servers that are part of a Database Availability Group. Also, NLB scales only to eight nodes, has little configuration options (layer 4 only), is unaware of service health (will keep sending traffic to unhealthy Exchange servers), and reconnects clients for changes in the load-balanced set of servers. For these reasons, NLB is not considered an alternative.

Load Balancing

In Exchange, there are two options when it comes to load balancing:

- Layer-4 (L4) load balancing, a relatively simple load balancing solution, where an inbound client connection is forwarded one on one to an Exchange server. The load balancing takes place on the network layer, and requests are distributed "as is"; no processing or intelligence takes place based on the request. The Exchange server, in turn, accepts the requests, and after authentication these are forwarded to the appropriate Mailbox server hosting the mailbox. L4 only allows clients to connect to the same server when needed (session affinity) based on their source IP address.

- Layer-7 (L7) load balancing, where the inbound SSL client connection is terminated at the load balancer and then forwarded to an Exchange server after optional re-encryption. The load balancing takes place on the application layer. The L7 load balancer can do intelligent things, since requests are decrypted, such as modifying HTTP headers or inserting session cookies to make sure clients always connect to the same Exchange server. Also, L7 load balancing allows for content switching, which is the process where different services are set up for the back end and distribution takes place based on the path (application or service) used by clients, for example, /EWS or /Mapi.

With connections to the Exchange server being stateless ("every server is an island," operating independently of each other), there is no need to worry about affinity. If an Exchange server fails the connection, requests are rerouted to another Exchange server. There will be a minimal performance penalty, due to the necessary reauthentication, but the connection on the Mailbox server is preserved.

The load balancer is usually configured with a virtual server with its own FQDN, such as webmail.proexchangeadmin.com, and an IP address. The IP address is referred to as the "virtual IP," or VIP. A client connects to this VIP, as the FQDN via DNS should resolve to the virtual IP of this virtual server, and thus connects to the load balancer. The load balancer keeps track of the source IP of the connection request and forwards the request to one of the Exchange servers, which are configured as "real servers" behind the virtual server.

Keep in mind that, in a layer-4 load balancer, the SSL connection is terminated at the Exchange server and not at the load balancer. Therefore, the load balancer cannot inspect any of the traffic between the client and the Exchange server. To overcome this problem, there are two possible options:

- Configure multiple VIPs, one for each service, so that the individual VIP can also be used to check for health (see Figure 6-17). This requires one IP address per service, as the combination of IP address and port needs to be unique per VIP, and every HTTPS-based service in Exchange Server uses port 443.

- Use a layer-7 load balancer so that the load balancer can inspect the traffic for the individual services. This can be combined with SSL offloading; a bit more on that later.

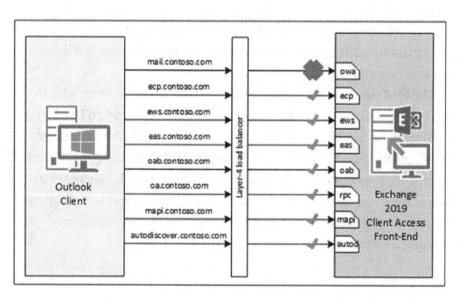

Figure 6-17. *Multiple VIPs with L4 load balancing configuration*

In Figure 6-17, there are eight VIPs configured, one VIP for each Exchange-related service. The VIPs are independent of each other; when OWA on an Exchange server fails, only OWA requests are redirected to another Exchange server, and requests for other services continue to be forwarded to this real (Exchange) server.

With a layer-7 load balancer, the load balancer can perform content inspection. This allows the load balancer to detect whether an incoming connection is, for example, for OWA or EWS based on the path used and redirect the requests to the respective virtual directory on the real (Exchange) server. So you can use a single VIP for both OWA and EWS (and all other HTTPS-based services), using the path of their virtual directory. When service failure is detected, the load balancer can initiate redirect requests for this service to other real servers or completely. Options like this depend on the features of the load balancer used.

In Figure 6-18 the failure of the OWA service is detected. In this case, the load balancer will redirect to another Exchange server, but all other virtual directories on this specific server will remain active and receive client requests.

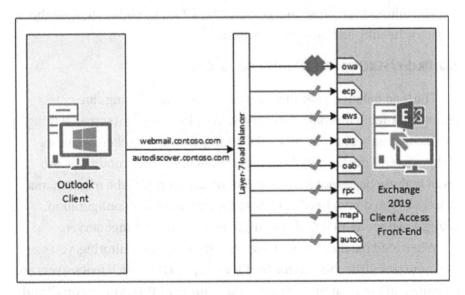

Figure 6-18. *Single VIP with L7 content-switching load balancing*

Note   To configure load balancers and application delivery controllers for Exchange, but also for other solutions, many vendors offer templates. These can be used to simplify the configuration process, in accordance with both Microsoft and vendor recommendations.

Health Check Monitors

We mentioned this a few times, but Exchange contains for every service a monitor. This monitor determines the health of every service, such as OWA or EWS, and presents this information on web pages. These web pages are accessible through a URL in the format **https://<FQDN or server IP>/<virtual directory>/healthcheck.htm**. For example, to check the status of EWS on the server EXCH01, you can check the page https://exch01/EWS/healthcheck.htm.

The information presented contains HTTP status code 200 when the service is healthy on that server, for example:

```
200 OK<br/>EXCH01.PROEXCHANGEADMIN.COM
```

The load balancer that supports this kind of monitoring can periodically fetch this page for every service, for every real server. If things are deemed unhealthy, it can decide to stop forwarding client requests to this server. Note that putting a server in maintenance mode will also result in these pages not returning 200, which simplifies the maintenance process as you do not need to change the load balancer configuration, taking a real server manually offline, to service an Exchange server.

When load balancers do not support this kind of monitoring, you can use more simplistic monitoring by, for example, checking if real servers are replying and then sending them a "ping." However, this is based on IP and therefore says nothing about the services, let alone which servers, as an answer on port 443 does not mean all HTTPS-based services are healthy; not replying at all does however can be an indication of server-level failure, in which case redirection of all traffic to that real server becomes a logical option.

SSL Offloading

When SSL offloading is enabled, the SSL connection is terminated at the load balancer; traffic between the load balancer and Exchange can remain unencrypted. With SSL offloading, it is possible to perform content inspection on the network level, which might be a requirement for some organizations.

SSL offloading is also needed for transparency purposes as described in the next section. SSL offloading for the individual web services is not enabled by default, so it must be enabled on each virtual directory on the Exchange server. To achieve this, execute the following commands in EMS:

```
Import-Module WebAdministration
Set-WebConfigurationProperty -Filter //security/access -name
sslflags -Value "None" -PSPath IIS: -Location "Default Web Site"
Set-WebConfigurationProperty -Filter //security/access -name
sslflags -Value "None" -PSPath IIS: -Location "Default Web
Site/OWA"
Set-WebConfigurationProperty -Filter //security/access -name
sslflags -Value "None" -PSPath IIS: -Location "Default Web
Site/ECP"
Set-WebConfigurationProperty -Filter //security/access -name
sslflags -Value "None" -PSPath IIS: -Location "Default Web
Site/OAB"
Set-WebConfigurationProperty -Filter //security/access -name
sslflags -Value "None" -PSPath IIS: -Location "Default Web
Site/EWS"
```

```
Set-WebConfigurationProperty -Filter //security/access -name
sslflags -Value "None" -PSPath IIS: -Location "Default Web
Site/Microsoft-Server-ActiveSync"
Set-WebConfigurationProperty -Filter //security/access -name
sslflags -Value "None" -PSPath IIS: -Location "Default Web
Site/Autodiscover"
Set-WebConfigurationProperty -Filter //security/access -name
sslflags -Value "None" -PSPath IIS: -Location "Default Web
Site/MAPI"
```

For Outlook Anywhere, SSL offloading is enabled by default. If for some reason the SSL offloading for Outlook Anywhere is not enabled, you can use the following commands in EMS to enable SSL offloading:

```
[PS] C:\> Get-OutlookAnywhere -Server EXCH01 | Set-
OutlookAnywhere –SSLOffloading:$true -ExternalClientsRequire
Ssl:$true –ExternalHostName webmail.proexchangeadmin.com
-ExternalClientAuthenticationMethod NTLM -InternalClientsRequir
eSSL:$true -InternalHostName webmail.proexchangeadmin.com
-InternalClientAuthenticationMethod NTLM
```

Most organizations do not allow unencrypted traffic between the load balancer and Exchange servers. In those cases, you need to enable the re-encrypt option on the load balancer. This way, the SSL connection is terminated on the load balancer, the load balancer can perform its tasks such as content switching, and after which it will talk through its own SSL connection to the Exchange server. The default self-signed certificate on the Exchange server can be used in this scenario. The self-signed certificate is only used for the encrypted connection, but not for server validation; a third-party certificate is therefore not required.

Note   If you consider enabling Extended Protection on your
Exchange servers, be advised that SSL offloading cannot be used
with Extended Protection. More on Extended Protection in Chapter 9.

Load Balancer Transparency

To work efficiently in a layer-7 configuration, two things need to happen:

1. Inbound traffic needs to flow through the load
    balancer.

2. Response traffic needs to flow through the load
    balancer on the way out.

To achieve this, the load balancer has an option to set L7 transparent
mode. When traffic reaches the load balancer, its source IP address is that
of the client sending requests, and the destination IP address is that of
the VIP. When configured in L7 transparent mode, the source IP address
of the client is preserved, but the destination IP is changed to the IP
address of the Exchange server. Return traffic is sent back to the original
address, flowing through the load balancer. The default gateway setting
of the Exchange server must be set to that of the balancer; otherwise,
Exchange will route return traffic via the default gateway of the regular
network. This might result in an asynchronous pattern, which might break
communications as return traffic could never reach the client, depending
on the network setup. This situation is shown in Figure 6-19.

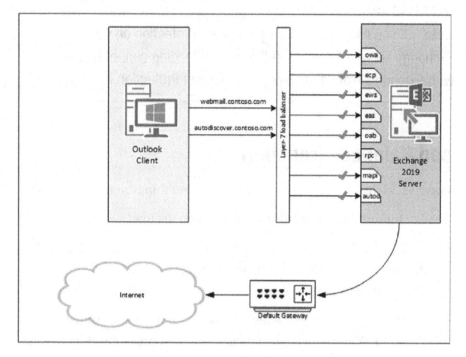

Figure 6-19. *Asynchronous load balancer communications*

When configured in L7 nontransparent mode, the load balancer
will change the source IP address of the client traffic to the internal IP of
the load balancer, and it will change the destination IP address to the IP
address of the Exchange server. The Exchange server will only see traffic
coming from the internal IP address of the load balancer, and return
traffic will always be routed via this internal IP address. In this scenario,
no changes need to be made to the network settings of the Exchange
server. An important downside of this setup is that logging on Exchange
will see the load balancer as the only client, which might complicate
troubleshooting.

Up-Level and Down-Level Proxying

One of the nice features of Exchange Server 2019, like its predecessors Exchange Server 2016 and Exchange Server 2013, is that from a Client Access Front End perspective, servers are compatible with each other and that they can do both up-level and down-level proxy. This means that client connections to a higher Exchange version, while their mailbox is hosted on Exchange Server with a lower version, will get proxied. Vice versa is also true; lower Exchange Server versions will proxy connections to higher Exchange Server versions.

A great benefit of this possibility is that when you have an array of Exchange 2016 servers sitting behind a load balancer, you can introduce Exchange 2019 servers to the VIP pool without issues.

Note   Up-level proxy only works for Exchange 2013 and up; Exchange 2013 and 2016 can down-level proxy to Exchange 2010 in coexistence scenarios. Also, you can only mix Exchange 2013, 2016, and 2019 for Client Access Front End services; you cannot mix these servers to make them part of the same Database Availability Group.

Azure AD Application Proxy

Azure AD Application Proxy is a feature of Microsoft Azure Active Directory (Azure AD) that allows you to securely publish internal web applications and access those applications from anywhere without the need for a virtual private network (VPN) or external publishing. Azure AD Application Proxy is only supported for Outlook Web Access; you cannot use it to publish any of the other services such as MAPI, which limits its usability.

To use Azure AD Application Proxy to publish your Exchange on-premises infrastructure, you need to synchronize identities from Active

Directory to Azure Active Directory, which can be accomplished using Azure AD Connect or Cloud Sync. This is required for authentication and authorization. More on Synchronized Identities in Chapter 4.

To configure Azure AD Application Proxy and publish your Exchange on-premises services, perform the following steps:

1. First, we need to configure Kerberos Constrained Delegation (KCD), which will allow the (computer running the) connector to delegate authentication requests on behalf of users. For this, we first need to create an Alternate Service Account for Exchange, which will represent the load-balanced namespace, for example, webmail.proexchangeadmin.com.

   Note: If you have already deployed previous versions of Exchange Server, you might have already performed this step. In the era of Exchange 2010, this was mandatory to use Kerberos authentication in combination with a CAS array (what you could now call a CAFE array).

   Here's how to create the computer account name that will function as the ASA:

   ```
   New-ADComputer -Name WEBMAILASA
   -AccountPassword (Read-Host 'Enter password'
   -AsSecureString) -Description 'Alternate
   Service Account for Exchange VIP'
   -Enabled:$True -SamAccountName WEBMAILASA
   ```

2. Enable AES-256 encryption for this account by running, which is required for Kerberos authentication

   ```
   Set-ADComputer WEBMAILASA -add @{"msDS-Suppo
   rtedEncryptionTypes"="28"}
   ```

3. Configure one Exchange server to use this ASA account, in EMS:

```
.\RollAlternateServiceAccountPassword.
ps1 -ToSpecificServers EXCH01
-GenerateNewPasswordFor PROEXCHANGEADMIN\
WEBMAILASA$
```

(make sure to specify GenerateNewPasswordFor as <DOMAIN>\<ASA>)

The output should look like something in Figure 6-20; you confirm the question about immediately changing the ASA password.

```
[PS] C:>.\RollAlternateServiceAccountPassword.ps1 -ToSpecificServers EXCH01 -GenerateNewPasswordFor
AD\WEBMAILASA$

========== Starting at 05/02/2023 10:43:34 ==========
Destination servers that will be updated:

Name PSComputerName
---- --------------
EXCH01  EXCH01.ad.proexchangeadmin.com

Credentials that will be pushed to every server in the specified scope (recent first):
UserName            Password
--------            --------
AD\WEBMAILASA$ System.Security.SecureString

Prior to pushing new credentials, all existing credentials that are invalid or no longer work will be removed from the
destination servers.

Pushing credentials to server EXCH01
Setting a new password on Alternate Serice Account in Active Directory

Password change
Do you want to change password for AD\WEBMAILASA$ in Active Directory at this time?
[Y] Yes  [N] No  [S] Suspend  [?] Help (default is "Y"): y
Preparing to update Active Directory with a new password for AD\WEBMAILASA$ ...
Resetting a password in the Active Directory for AD\WEBMAILASA$ ...
New password was successfully set to Active Directory.
Retrieving the current Alternate Service Account configuration from servers in scope
Alternate Service Account properties:

StructuralObjectClass QualifiedUserName Last Pwd Update     SPNs
--------------------- ----------------- ---------------     ----
computer          AD\WEBMAILASA$     5/2/2023 10:44:06 AM

Per-server Alternate Service Account configuration as of the time of script completion:
  Array: {webmail.proexchangeadmin.com}

Identity AlternateServiceAccountConfiguration
-------- ------------------------------------
EXCH01   Latest: 5/2/2023 10:43:45 AM, AD\WEBMAILASA$
      Previous: <Not set>
```

Figure 6-20.   *Creating ASA for Kerberos authentication*

4. For all other Exchange servers, you can copy the
    ASA configuration from the first Exchange server:

    ```
    cd $exscripts
    ```

    ```
    .\RollAlternateServiceAccountPassword.ps1
    -ToSpecificServer EXCH02 -CopyFrom EXCH01
    ```

5. To verify the ASA has been configured for every Exchange server, run the following command, and verify AlternateServiceAccountConfiguration has been configured for each server:

```
Get-ClientAccessService -IncludeAlternate
ServiceAccountCredentialStatus | fl Name,
AlternateServiceAccountConfiguration
```

6. Next, configure a Service Principal Name (SPN) for the service (http) and ASA account, associating the SPN with the ASA account. We need to do this for the OWA namespace, as well as Autodiscover. First, we can check if the namespace has not already been associated:

setspn -F -Q http/webmail.
procexchangeadmin.com

If the results show "No such SPN found," we are good to continue. Make sure you end the server name with a "$", as we are using the SAMAccountName, which ends in $ (to hide it), and use the format <DOMAIN>\<ASA$>, for example:

```
setspn -A http/webmail.proexchangeadmin.com
PROEXCHANGEADMIN\WEBMAILASA$
```

```
setspn -A http/autodiscover.
proexchangeadmin.com PROEXCHANGEADMIN\
WEBMAILASA$
```

To see which SPNs have been associated with the ASA, use

```
setspn -L PROEXCHANGEADMIN\WEBMAILASA$
```

7. Next, we need to configure KCD itself. In **Active Directory Users and Computers**, locate the object of the computer where you installed the connector, for example, OWACOMP. Open **Properties**, and select the **Delegation** tab. Select **Trust this computer for delegation to specified services only**, check **Use any authentication protocol**, and click **Add**. Click **Users and Computers**, and enter the name of ASA. Locate the http SPN entries you created in step 6, for example, **http/webmail. proexchangeadmin.com** and **http/autodiscover. proexchangeadmin.com**, and click **OK**. Click **OK** again to apply the change.

8. By default, the OWA Virtual Directory is configured for basic authentication and form-based authentication (FBA) for internal access and FBA for external access. The connector is located inside the network. To make single sign-on work, we need to use integrated authentication, disabling FBA. Use the following cmdlets to accomplish this for every Exchange server in your organization; ExternalAuthenticationMethods will be set to Negotiate, which is okay for Kerberos:

```
$Auth= @{ BasicAuthentication=$false;
DigestAuthentication=$false;
WindowsAuthentication=$true; ExternalAuthent
icationMethods='Negotiate'}
```

```
Set-OwaVirtualDirectory -Identity <Server> @Auth
```

```
Set-EcpVirtualDirectory -Identity
<Server> @Auth
```

Tip   This technique is called splatting. It allows you to specify parameters in a hash table, after which you pass the hash table to the command. This often can improve readability and like in this case can save you specifying things more than once.

9.   Restart IIS on those servers to make the change effective, for example:

```
IISRESET <Server> /RESTART /NOFORCE
```

10.   Open the Azure portal using an account with sufficient permissions, and navigate to **Azure Active Directory ➤ Enterprise Applications ➤ All Applications**.

11.   Click + to create a new application, enter a meaningful name such as OWA App, and select **Configure Application Proxy for secure remote access to an on-premises application**.

12.   Click **Create**.

13.   The next step is to download and install the Application Proxy Connector. The download link will be presented shortly after you clicked Create in the previous step. Copy the file **AADApplicationProxyConnectorInstaller. exe** to the system where you want to install the connector component. The connector is a lightweight agent, which will function as a bridge between the Azure Application Proxy service and Exchange on-premises. The connector requires outbound connectivity on ports 80 and 443 to

locations specified on this page, **https://bit.ly/ AzureAppProxyReqURLs**. The connector should be able to access the Exchange infrastructure.

Tip   Deploy multiple Application Proxy Connectors for redundancy.

---

14.   When installing the connector, you will be asked to authenticate against Azure AD. This account should have the application administrator role minimally, as setup will configure Azure Application Proxy in Azure AD.

Note   When installing the Application Proxy Connector on Windows Server 2019, you need to disable HTTP2 protocol support in the WinHttp component for Kerberos Constrained Delegation to work. Run `Set-ItemProperty 'HKLM:\SOFTWARE\Microsoft\Windows\ CurrentVersion\Internet Settings\WinHttp' -Name EnableDefaultHTTP2 -Value 0` to disable HTTP2, and restart the server for the change to become effective.

---

15.   Once the connector is configured, you can find Azure Application Proxy in **Azure Active Directory ➤ Application Proxy**. There, click **Configure an App**, and provide the following information:

- **Name** of the application, for example, My OWA App.

- **Internal Url** with the URL used internally— and thus by the connector—to access Exchange, for example, **https://webmail. proexchangeadmin.com/**.

- **External Url** with the URL you want to use to access the application (through Azure Application Proxy) externally, for example, `https://webmail-proexchangeadmin.msappproxy.net/`.

  Note that "proexchangeadmin" in this URL is generated, based on the name of your tenant.

  You can also use your own custom domain, such as webmail.proexchangeadmin.com. In that case, you need to configure a CNAME record in public DNS and set the target to the suggested msappproxy.net external URL, for example, webmail-proexchangeadmin. msappproxy.net.

- **Pre Authentication** to select if you want to use Azure Active Directory for pre-authentication. Using Azure AD for pre-authentication enables Azure AD–based security features, such as multifactor authentication and Conditional Access. The other option is Passthrough, in which case authentication is performed directly against the on-premises application, Exchange Server.

16. Next, assign users and groups to the application. To accomplish this, navigate to **Azure Active Directory ➤ Enterprise Applications** and open the application you created. Click **Assign Users and Groups** and enter the accounts that will be allowed access to the application.

17. The last step you might want to perform is
    configuring single sign-on when you have enabled
    pre-authentication. When omitting this step, after
    authentication to Azure AD, users will need to
    authenticate using the form-based authentication
    from Exchange on-premises. Open **Azure
    Active Directory ➤ Enterprise Applications
    ➤ <Application Name>** and click **Set up Single
    Sign On.** Assuming the connector is running on a
    domain-joined system, select Windows Integrated
    Authentication. Use the SPN http/<FQDN of
    the internal URL>, for example, **http/webmail.
    proexchangeadmin.com**, matching the SPN set in
    step 8. For delegated logon identity, choose **User
    Principal Name**, and click **Save.**

You can now test this publication through Azure Application Proxy.
Open a browser, and navigate to the external URL you specified in step 15,
for example, webmail-proexchangeadmin.msapproxy.net.

If you selected pre-authentication, you will be asked by Azure AD to
authenticate. This also might trigger additional security requirements,
such as the need to set up or approve MFA. Eventually, you should be
presented with the OWA application. Be advised that configuring Azure
Application Proxy can become complex quite quickly, and during testing
you will also encounter issues caused by cached Kerberos tokens or delays
in propagation of configuration changes to the connector. We can only
recommend to plan some time to set this up properly, and be patient.
Luckily, the Azure Application Proxy portal itself can be quite helpful with
troubleshooting, offering a testing tool and links to documentation on how
to solve common issues.

Azure Front Door

Another alternative to publishing Exchange on-premises through Azure services is Azure Front Door. Where Azure Application Proxy creates a proxy for on-premises applications, Azure Front Door is like a global load balancing solution. Similar to load balancers and application delivery controllers, Azure Front Door can route traffic and offer load balancing capabilities for on-premises web applications, such as Exchange on-premises.

Compared with Azure Application Proxy, Azure Front Door offers additional features, such as caching, compression, filtering options via Web Application Firewall (WAF), and DDOS protection. Together, this should optimize traffic to your Exchange on-premises environment and surrounding local network as it can route clients to the most optimal Internet egress when you have multiple public endpoints.

Also, certificates are provided at no additional costs, which should help when the need arises to add domains after mergers, to be added as email domain or public endpoints.

Be advised that Azure Front Door does come at a cost and requires an Azure subscription. The Azure Pricing Calculator might provide some guidance in estimating operational costs, using expected metrics such as bandwidth and number of policies.

Going into detail for every application delivery solution would be too much for the context of this book. If you want to learn more about Azure Front Door, visit **https://bit.ly/AzureFrontDoor**.

CHAPTER 7

Email Authentication

This chapter is about email authentication as part of email security and message hygiene. Email authentication is the process of making sure that the sender is allowed to send email on behalf of the domain of the sender. In other words, is my sending server edge01.proexchangeadmin.com allowed to send email on behalf of the proexchangeadmin.com domain?

The authentication process consists of the following techniques:

- *SPF*: Sender Policy Framework

- *DKIM*: DomainKeys Identified Mail

- *DMARC*: Domain-based Message Authentication, Reporting & Conformance

Additional techniques that are used for email authentication are

- *MTA-STS*: Mail Transfer Agent Strict Transport Security

- *ARC*: Authenticated Received Chain

These techniques are not Exchange Server–specific but email-generic techniques. As such, they are used by other platforms like Exchange Online, Gmail, and various Linux mail platforms as well.

When it comes to email authentication, there is configuration on the receiving side and on the sender side. The common denominator here is public DNS, which is used by the sender to publish configuration information and used by the receiver to check validity of the received message. This is the most difficult part of email authentication. As a

© Jaap Wesselius and Michel de Rooij 2023
J. Wesselius and M. de Rooij, *Pro Exchange Administration*,
https://doi.org/10.1007/978-1-4842-9591-5_7

sender, you must make sure that your public information is fully up to date so that the recipient mail server can validate it to make sure that your server truly is the server it says it is. Of course, the same is true for an organization that sends email to you so your server can authenticate the sending server.

Unfortunately, most techniques covered in this chapter are not implemented in Exchange 2019. There are a few open source solutions available for Exchange 2019, but to take full advantage of these features, you need a third-party solution or cloud solution like Exchange Online Protection in front of your Exchange 2019 environment.

In the following sections, the various techniques are explained, including the option to implement them.

Sender Policy Framework

SPF, or Sender Policy Framework, a well-known industry-wide standard, was first implemented in Exchange 2007. It was used in the Exchange 2007 Edge Transport server, a server role that was targeted as an SMTP relay server in front of an Exchange 2007 Hub Transport server. There was even a Microsoft official training, especially for Exchange security, targeting only the Edge Transport server.

A lot has changed in the past 15 years. The Edge Transport server is no longer used as an SMTP relay server directly connected to the Internet (it is still possible though, but I would not recommend it), and customers are now using a dedicated message hygiene solution. Message solutions are mostly in the cloud, like Exchange Online Protection, Mimecast, or TrendMicro, but there are still good on-premises message hygiene solutions available, like Cisco, Proofpoint, or Barracuda.

All vendors and solutions are using SPF as a second line of defense. The first line of defense is of course connection filtering, blacklists, whitelists, and real-time blacklists (RBL).

As a second line of defense, SPF is the process of validating if the SMTP server that is sending email is allowed to send email on behalf of this domain. In other words, when my Exchange server edge01. proexchangeadmin.com is sending out email, your mail server will check if my Exchange server is allowed to send out email on behalf of the proexchangeadmin.com domain.

Your mail server does this using a special SPF record in my public DNS domain. This SPF record contains information about all environments that can send out email of the proexchangeadmin.com domain. I deliberately say "environments" because it is typically not only the Exchange server, but it can also be Exchange Online Protection, but also other solutions like MailChimp or your online ERP system that sends out email on your behalf.

So how does this work? When I am sending an email to John at Contoso, my Exchange server with IP address 185.116.41.45 finds the Contoso mail server in public DNS and sets up a connection on port 25. When the connection is successfully established, my Exchange servers send the MailFrom: jaap@proexchangeadmin.com command to the Contoso mail server. The Contoso mail server already knows the IP address of the sending server, and then it checks the public SPF record if this IP address is listed.

The proexchangeadmin.com SPF record found in public DNS is

```
v=spf1 ip4:185.116.41.45 include:spf.protection.outlook.com -all
```

The Contoso mail server compares the IP address used in the connection with the IP address listed in the SPF record, and when there's a match, the email is successfully authenticated and processing of the email succeeds. This is schematically shown in Figure 7-1.

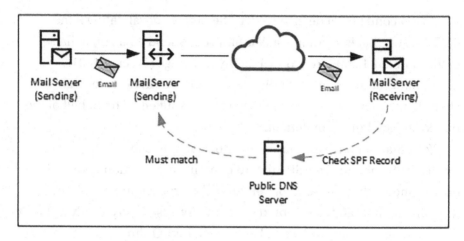

Figure 7-1. *SPF processing when accepting an email*

When an IP address is not found in the SPF record, authentication of the email fails. What happens next is defined by the qualifier and directive, at the end of the SPF record. In our example, the qualifier is "-" and the directive is "All". The different qualifiers and result codes are listed in Table 7-1.

Table 7-1. *SPF Mechanisms*

Qualifier	Result Code	Description
+	Pass	When "+All" is used, authentication is always successful, and "Pass" is added to the header of the email.
-	Fail	When "-All" is used, authentication is not successful when an IP address is not found in the SPF record. "Fail" is listed in the header of the email.
~	SoftFail	When "~All" is used and authentication is not successful, "SoftFail" is added to the header of the email. This can also happen when an error occurs during processing of the SPF record.
?	Neutral	When "?All" is used, nothing explicit can be said about the validity of the sending mail server.

As mentioned before, the SPF authentication results are shown in the header of the message. When sending a message to Google, for example, you can find something like this in the message header:

```
Received-SPF: pass (google.com: domain of s.summertown
@proexchangeadmin.com designates 185.116.41.45 as permitted
sender) client-ip=185.116.41.45;
```

Constructing the SPF Record

So what kind of information is recorded in the SPF record and how is this record constructed?

All SPF records start with the following:

```
v=spf1
```

This is followed by information about mail environments that are allowed to send mail on behalf of this domain. This can be identified by the following:

- *IPv4*: This is an IPv4 address that identifies the sending mail server. This has been used since the beginning of SPF records.

- *IPv6*: This is an IPv6 address that identifies the sending mail server. It took a long time, but finally IPv6 addresses are used more and more, and this is reflected in SPF records as well.

- *A record*: This is an A record that identifies the sending mail server.

- *MX record*: This is the public MX record for the domain.

- *Include*: This identifies other SPF records, typically for third-party environments like Exchange Online, Mimecast, Mailchimp, etc.

537

In the ProExchangeAdmin environment, there's only one Exchange 2019 Edge Transport server, and its public IP address is 185.116.41.45. When this is the only outbound connection, then the SPF record would be

```
v=spf1 ip4:185.116.41.45 -All
```

When Edge Transport is configured with the 2a02:20b0:112:1::2 IPv6 address, the SPF record would be

```
v=spf1 ip4:185.116.41.45 ip6:2a02:20b0:112:1::2 -All
```

In case of an Exchange hybrid scenario, where mail can be sent by the Edge Transport server or by Exchange Online, the Exchange Online SPF information would be added using the following include option:

```
v=spf1 ip4:185.116.41.45 ip6:2a02:20b0:112:1::2 include:spf.
protection.outlook.com -All
```

The "A" mechanism can be used as well, for example:

```
V=spf1 A -All
```

In this case, all A records for the current domain are tested. If there's a match in one of the A records, authentication succeeds. It is also possible to use A records from another domain to be tested. When ProExchangeAdmin is using the Exchangelabs mail servers, the SPF record can be

```
V=spf1 A:Exchangelabs.nl -All
```

The same is true for using the MX mechanism:

```
V=spf1 mx -all
```

All IP addresses of MX records of the current domain are tested, and if there's a match, authentication succeeds. Again, other MX records can be used as well. Just like the previous example where ProExchangeAdmin is using the Exchangelabs mail servers, the SPF record would be

```
V=spf1 mx:exchangelabs.nl -all
```

Important to note is that SPF record processing is sequential. It starts with the first entry, and if it fails, it succeeds with the next one and the next one. The last entry is the -All (in this example), which means that authentication for all other mail servers fails. When most mail is sent out using Exchange Online, it makes sense to put the Exchange Online include statement in the beginning of the SPF record.

Another important thing to note is that SPF processing can only do ten DNS lookups. When more lookups are derived from the SPF record, authentication will fail resulting in a "SoftFail" authentication, which can result in mail not being delivered or ending up in quarantine or in the user's Junk Mail folder.

For more information regarding the SPF records and how to construct an SPF record, visit the Open SPF website on `www.open-spf.org/`.

Checking the SPF Record

When you have constructed your SPF record, you want to check its validity. The easiest test is to send an email to your Gmail mailbox. When Google accept the message, then it's good!

Another option is to use the MxToolbox website `https://mxtoolbox.com`. MxToolbox offers a wide variety of interesting and useful tools for any messaging administrator. As shown in Figure 7-2, enter the domain name and click SPF Record Lookup.

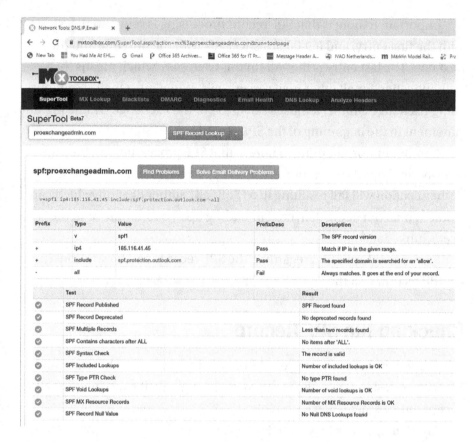

Figure 7-2. *Use MxToolbox to check the SPF record*

Another interesting tool is the Port25.com site. Port25.com offers a verifier, which is free to use.

To use this, you can send an email to check-auth@verifier.port25.com and wait for the results. In the body of the returned email, you should find something like

```
==============================================================
Summary of Results
==============================================================
SPF check:          pass
"iprev" check:      fail
DKIM check:         none

==============================================================
Details:
==============================================================

HELO hostname:   EDGE01.ProExchangeAdmin.com
Source IP:       185.116.41.45
mail-from:       S.Summertown@proexchangeadmin.com

--------------------------------------------------------------
SPF check details:
--------------------------------------------------------------
Result:          pass
ID(s) verified:  smtp.mailfrom=S.Summertown@proexchangeadmin.com

DNS record(s):
    proexchangeadmin.com. 300 IN TXT "v=spf1 ip4:185.116.41.45
include:spf.protection.outlook.com -all"
```

Note   The "iprev" check failure is a reverse DNS lookup. I haven't registered this in DNS.

Every Exchange 2019 server, or actually every Exchange server since version 2007, is using SPF to authenticate inbound messages. For outbound messages, there is nothing you must do on your Exchange server, except for constructing the SPF record in public DNS.

If the SPF record is not valid, there is the risk that recipients will not receive email messages that are sent out by your messaging environment. And that's the problem, especially with large organizations. There are so many partners, services, solutions, applications, and devices that send out email on behalf of your domain name that it's easy to forget one or two. And you cannot add an unlimited number of entries in your SPF record, which is automatically an issue.

Note   If you have domains that are not used for sending out email, you can also create an SPF record that consists only of the following: V=spf1 -all. Email that is sent out by any mail server is never authenticated using this record and thus is never valid.

DKIM

In the previous section, I have discussed how SPF works and how it uses public DNS to validate the authenticity of the sending SMTP servers. When SPF is implemented correctly, a receiving mail server can validate that the sending mail server is allowed to send email on behalf of the sender or their organization.

In this section I will discuss DKIM signing as an additional (and more complicated and more difficult to spoof) step in email validation.

DKIM, which stands for DomainKeys Identified Mail, is another message hygiene solution. It is not a true anti-spam solution, but a legitimate authentication solution. And when an email message is authenticated, it is most likely not spam, that is, as long as the sender's environment is not compromised of course.

DKIM is all about signing and verifying email messages. As such you can compare it to the signing capabilities of S/MIME, where S/MIME is client based and DKIM is server based.

DKIM consists of two operations:

- *Signing the message*: This can be achieved by the sending host itself or can be done by a third-party application or service. When signing a message, the signing module inserts a DKIM-Signature header to the message with the appropriate information. This signing module uses a private key to create a signature, therefore ensuring that only this server (or organization) can sign messages.

- *Verifying the message*: Just like signing this can be performed by the receiving host or by a third-party application or service. The verification module reads the information in the DKM-Signature field and verifies the signature using the sending organization's public key.

The private and the public key form a key pair. The private key is only known at the sending mail server; the public key is published in the sender's public DNS server and as such available to everyone that needs to validate the signed message.

Important to note is that not the entire message is signed but only an encrypted signature is added as an additional header of the email message. As such, mail servers that are capable of decrypting the signature can authenticate the email message. Email servers that are not capable of decrypting the signature just receive the email message as any other email message.

So how does this work? A user sends an email to an external recipient. The outbound mail server uses a private key to add an encrypted header, the DKIM signature, to the email message and sends out the message to the recipient mail server. This recipient mail server receives the message, detects the DKIM signature, and retrieves the public key from public DNS of the sending domain. Please note that the administrators of the sending mail server need to add this public key to DNS!

The public key is used to decrypt the DKIM signature, and when successful, the email message is authenticated and the email message is processed. This is shown schematically in Figure 7-3.

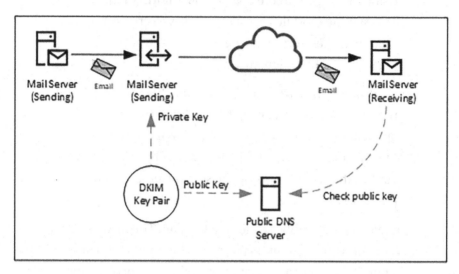

Figure 7-3. *DKIM and public/private keys*

So the DKIM-Signature header plays an important role in DKIM, and a typical DKM-Signature header can look like this:

```
DKIM-Signature: v=1; a=rsa-sha256; d=example.net; s=securemail;
c=relaxed/simple; q=dns/txt; l=1234; t=1117574938;
x=1118006938;
h=from:to:subject:date:keywords:keywords;
bh=MTIzNDU2Nzg5MDEyMzQ1Njc4OTAxMjMONTY3ODkwMTI=;
b=dzdVyOfAKCdLXdJOc9G2q8LoXSlEniSbav+yuU4zGeeruDOOlszZ
VoG4ZHRNiYzR
```

544

The following tags can be identified in a DKIM-Signature header:

- v: Version

- d: Domain

- s: Selector

- c: Canonicalization algorithm for body and header

- q: Query method

- l: Length of canonicalization part of the body

- t: Timestamp signature

- x: Expiration time

- h: List of signed header fields

- b: Hash of the selected message headers

- bh: Hash of the message body

To sign a message, the signing module first creates a hash of the message body, stored with the bh tag. Next is that selected headers in the message are hashed; these are stored in the b tag. So two hashes are being created. Both hashes are stored in the DKIM header of the message. Both are clearly visible in the preceding DKIM-Signature header example.

To sign a message, you need a key pair, but how do you get a key pair? Typically you get a key pair from the solution that is used.

The private key should be entered in the signing module on the sending mail server; this looks something like this:

```
--BEGIN RSA PRIVATE KEY--
MIICXAIBAAKBgQCy9cx399ZJ3xhCDcVmHOFkFWw5XAuWlsOnpBNO1hiMeUrOqI/c
+Abmjma2O/VB5oCPGHzRT3f78BlGryJKjEAyZKBE7U+GkaCGEVEjQqGEWnsF7tql
OkWW99Lx1VOEJItO9yMrRpmA6Ml01jH6rkBeADhUpgKAUDOfN+ZCnlVv1QIDAQAB
AoGAa4BluyUdjHJ/V+59zcE7g6t6v1oTe/pKcq2VC56AUKHr7NvOz4AOZSDVglKy
```

Guwlnc/P6swZ/zVTeapqpu1pAdtPig1f70GMDPA1YuqxaKXnH/jZz8g7o5L2F1pw
6CzoPDzXnCxoBAFuAyByonOIolFf9iPnMkm8o9d9La/YowECQQDZxkgPeRbHmySW
Usfq19vqH5Kz3YyjW+E/rMXMBE9qtfYaiQJBAJ+sVmGh8yXfhu/iAcYZi/R9Y/ug
Tu6mky+8HzIhc8kG1G8c4Xo4Y30j/RyG/OoiB5JgIkZgaMjaPN9pCwBkdfECQBjd
UwgNymikJWe9PmZviQ6VtH3Eyw3dk2+fo5odTZ/wAOtdetXBf2poL2eoBHoK2tt5
+T/o1Z/UGRMBV/l9xxECQEyUnkqkX+2YekxotCyVKt+whxdshZFAoPqGzIyN4Spq
w4j2w3xiPYSzpyXDx+6Dgpyb/Ru8MhNhakNRYIMjK64=
--END RSA PRIVATE KEY--

The public key (in BIND 9 DNS format) looks something like this:

```
securemail._domainkey.proexchangeadmin.com. IN TXT (
"v=DKIM1;t=s;p=MIGfMA0GCSqGSIb3DQEBAQUAA4GNADCBiQKBgQCmutszXoY
6C8/xlzy/Hrz954Gy"
"5zfOO8q/+brIO9o+WyYeoMkNjs2Ney9z20Ur7t1lP64KH7dx/
BKK6hlwRKxTw7OD"
"MU5HC5ZjtvLYuiiUz3KGuEMDSwsBpY4aAtD
hVG7CjYheSoIQ5kD2EcvnZJaQTPTa"
"tKLxEwImU2tYwPmqyQIDAQAB")
```

The selector in this example is "securemail", and the selector is the DNS record where the public key is stored. Once added to DNS, you can use the MxToolbox site to test the DKIM record as shown in Figure 7-4.

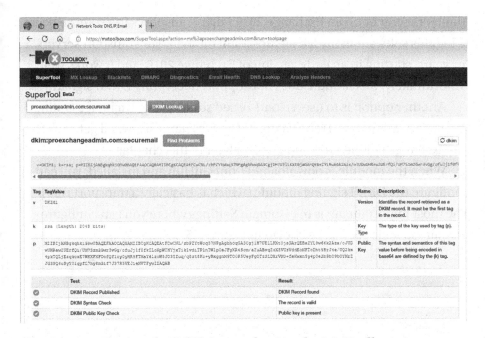

Figure 7-4. *Testing the DKIM record using the MxToolbox site*

So at this point everything is in place. There's a private key for signing messages, there's a public key stored in DNS, and you're ready to go. Messages are sent by the (sending) server, the receiving server will read the header of the message, and based on the selector key, the server can retrieve the public key to validate the signature.

Exchange and DKIM

You might have noticed that I used words like "mail administrator" or "mail server" in the previous section, and that was a deliberate choice. The reason for this is that Exchange Server does not support DKIM out of the box. To use DKIM in your Exchange environment, you need to use a third-party solution.

On GitHub (`https://github.com/Pro/dkim-exchange`), you can find a third-party DKIM solution that can create a DKIM signature for outbound messages. This module can be installed on an Exchange 2019

Mailbox server or on an Exchange 2019 Edge Transport server. I have been using this software in my lab environment on the Edge Transport servers for years, starting in an early version of Exchange 2016, and it works well. Unfortunately, this module does not support decrypting DKIM signatures.

Another option is to use a cloud-based solution like Exchange Online Protection, Mimecast, TrendMicro, or Cisco to name a few. I'll get back to the Exchange Online Protection option later in this chapter.

When the module is downloaded from GitHub and installed, you can configure the DKIM signing module (which is basically a transport rule). The most important tab is the Domain Settings where you can configure domain-specific settings as shown in Figure 7-5.

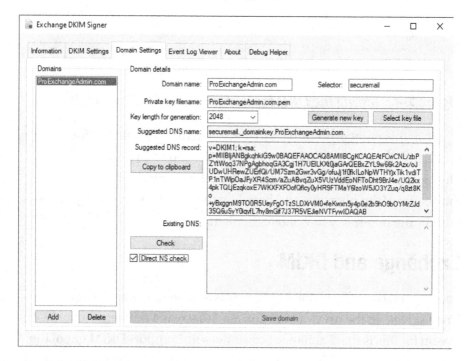

Figure 7-5. *Configuring the DKIM signing module downloaded from GitHub*

When a message is sent, the DKIM module will process the message, create an encrypted header (and thus sign the message), and add it to the email message header. When sending an email to a Gmail mailbox, you'll see the following information in the message header:

```
DKIM-Signature: v=1; a=rsa-sha256; d=ProExchangeAdmin.com;
s=securemail; c=simple/simple; t=1682592341; h=from:
subject:to:date:message-id; bh=CqCgDG9aWdQ2kpvO1KnhkOzYXVS
satabi8/jjaOl/RA=; b=Bq/3Igrz+eLPVGiFWIiXO+NozoeacPW1K8CIZFtBG
aqQ/P8j7cUOm6EUfZq7b2cE7HspHOpuplH4NIaSh3lZsHoQNH1yhXe9LHP+
Ongs9OQzO5uO8uMmiPJtN2SO6PFwM1OWtziZjquUR16206Ik
```

The DKIM-Signature looks legitimate, and there's more information in the message header, information regarding the authentication itself:

```
Authentication-Results: mx.google.com;
dkim=pass header.i=@ProExchangeAdmin.com header.s=securemail
header.b="Bq/3Igrz";
spf=pass (google.com: domain of s.summertown@proexchangeadmin.
com designates 185.116.41.45 as permitted sender)
```

At this point both SPF and DKIM are working correctly for the Exchange 2019 environment, and the Edge Transport server is properly signing email messages using DKIM.

DKIM and Exchange Online Protection

As explained in the previous section, Exchange 2019 does not support DKIM out of the box, and you need to use a third-party solution to enable DKIM. Exchange Online Protection is a great solution in front of your Exchange server environment for message hygiene purposes. Besides the anti-spam and anti-phishing capabilities, Exchange Online Protection also fully support SPF, DKIM, and DMARC.

The theory of DKIM in Exchange Online Protection is identical as explained in the previous section. Exchange Online Protection adds an encrypted header to outbound messages, but compared with the GitHub module in the previous section, Exchange Online Protection also authenticates inbound messages.

Instead of adding a public key in DNS, you create two CNAME records that point to public keys in Exchange Online Protection:

```
Selector1._domainkey.proexchangeadmin.com CNAME selector1-
proexchangeadmin-com._domainkey.tenant.onmicrosoft.com
Selector2._domainkey.proexchangeadmin.com CNAME selector2-
proexchangeadmin-com._domainkey.tenant.onmicrosoft.com
```

Use MxToolbox to check if the CNAME records were successfully created as shown in Figure 7-6.

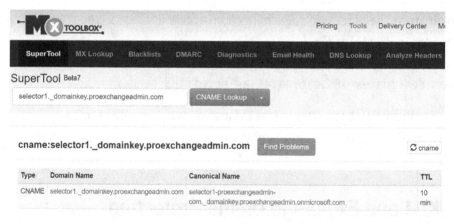

Figure 7-6. *Use MxToolbox to check the new CNAME records*

After creating the CNAME records, open the Microsoft Defender Portal on `https://security.microsoft.com` and navigate to Email & collaboration ➤ Policies & rules | Threat policies | Email authentication settings. On the DKIM tab, select the domain you want to enable DKIM and enable DKIM as shown in Figure 7-7.

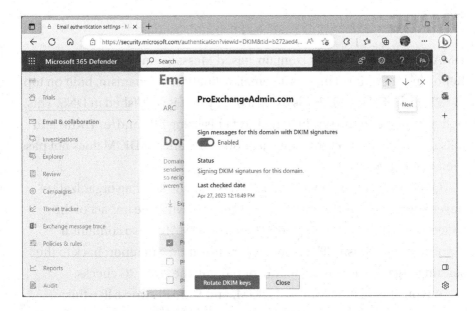

Figure 7-7. *Enable DKIM in Exchange Online Protection*

Note   It can take a couple of minutes before DKIM becomes active in your organization.

As explained earlier, Exchange Online Protection also authenticates DKIM signed messages. When sending an email from Gmail to the ProExchangeAdmin environment via Exchange Online Protection, you can see something like the following in the message header:

```
Authentication-Results: spf=pass (sender IP is 209.85.219.173)
smtp.mailfrom=gmail.com; dkim=pass (signature was verified)
header.d=gmail.com;dmarc=pass action=none header.from=gmail.com;
compauth=pass reason=100
```

At this point, both SPF and DKIM are configured. The next step is DMARC, which "runs" on top of SPF and DKIM.

DMARC

DMARC, which stands for Domain-based Message Authentication, Reporting & Conformance, is an email validation mechanism, built on top of SPF and DKIM. DMARC is using a policy that is published in DNS. This policy indicates if the sending mail server is using SPF and/or DKIM and tells the receiving mail server what to do if SPF and/or DKIM does not pass their respective checks.

One "problem" with SPF and DKIM is that the sending organization never knows how SPF and DKIM are used and what the impact of the usage is, whether it works or not. Therefore, DMARC also contains a reporting mechanism. The receiving organization can report back to the sending organization about failure or passing the DMARC checks.

A typical mail flow with SPF, DKIM, and DMARC works like this:

1. A user sends a new message to an external recipient. The mail server signs the message and inserts the DKIM header.

2. The mail server sends the message to the recipient's mail server.

3. The recipient's mail server checks DNS for the SPF record, the DKIM records, and the DMARC record containing the DMARC policy.

4. After checking the SPF and DKIM, the policy is applied, which determines what needs to happen.

5. If the DMARC check passes, the message is delivered to the recipient's mailbox.

6. If the DMARC check fails (block or quarantine), a report is sent back to the sender's organization.

This is shown in Figure 7-8.

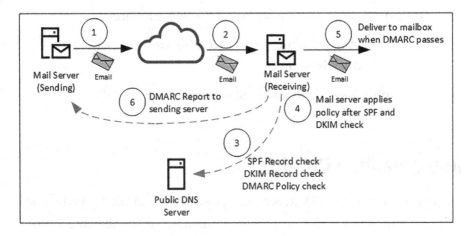

Figure 7-8. *DMARC processing with SPF and DKIM*

The DMARC policy that is published in DNS looks like this:

```
v=DMARC1;p=quarantine;sp=quarantine;pct=100;rua=mailto:
dmarcreports@proexchangeadmin.com
```

The following tags can be identified in this DNS record:

- v: Version

- p: Policy for organizational domain (none, quarantine, or reject)

- sp: Policy for subdomains of the organizational domain (none, quarantine, or reject)

- pct: Percentage of messages that are filtered

- rua: Reporting URI or address for aggregate reports

The following optional tags can be used as well:

- ruf: Reporting URI or address for forensic reports

- adkim: Alignment mode for DKIM (relaxed or strict, "s" or "r", which is default)

- aspf: Alignment mode for SPF (relaxed or strict, "s" or "r", which is default)

Implementing DMARC

As mentioned before DMARC is built on top of SPF and DKIM, so the first step is to implement both in your environment and make absolutely sure both work correctly.

Assuming you already have created a mailbox for receiving the reports, you can create a DMARC record with an organizational domain policy set to "none". This way DMARC will start working, but won't take any action while you can analyze the messages that are received in your reporting mailbox.

So, for the ProExchangeAdmin domain, the following DNS TXT record _dmarc.proexchangeadmin.com will be created:

```
v=DMARC1;p=none;sp=none;pct=100;rua=mailto:dmarceports@
proexchangeadmin.com
```

When entered you can use the http://mxtoolbox.com/dmarc.aspx site to check the DMARC record as shown in Figure 7-9.

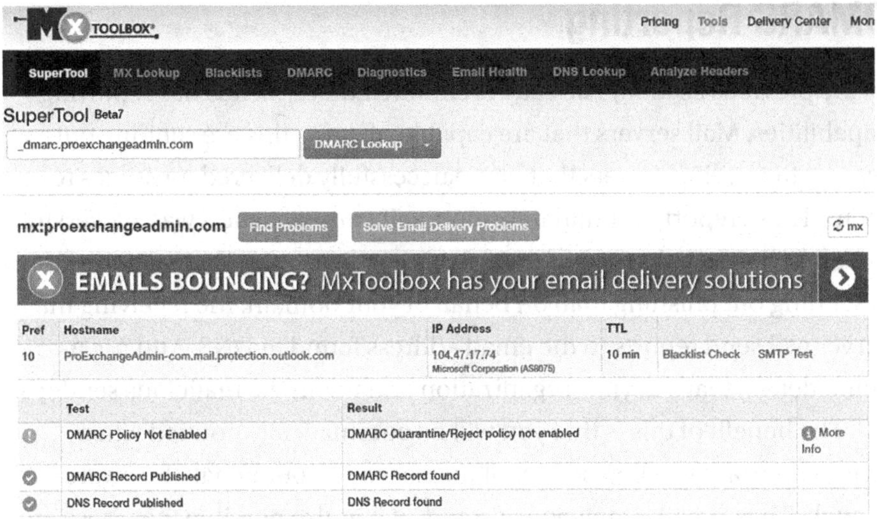

Figure 7-9. *Use MxToolbox to check the DMARC record*

When a user sends an email message to my Gmail mailbox, the following information can be retrieved from the email header:

```
Authentication-Results: mx.google.com;
dkim=pass header.i=@ProExchangeAdmin.com header.s=securemail
header.b=Qf06aPOd;
spf=pass (google.com: domain of munchausen@proexchangeadmin.com
designates 185.116.41.45 as permitted sender) smtp.mailfrom=S.
Summertown@proexchangeadmin.com;
dmarc=pass (p=NONE sp=REJECT dis=NONE) header.
from=proexchangeadmin.com
```

At this point, SPF, DKIM, and DMARC are successful, and email messages are successfully authenticated. A step closer to a better email world.

DMARC Reporting

In the previous section, I already mentioned that DMARC has reporting capabilities. Mail servers that are capable of doing this are sending out reports to sending servers that have successfully delivered messages to them. These reports contain information if authentication was successful, but also if it was not successful. And this can be useful. If a malicious user is sending out phishing mail on behalf of your domain, the receiving mail server will send reports to the email address found in DNS. And not a coincidence, that's in your organization and not in the malicious sender's.

The benefit of this is that you will be automatically notified when mail servers are sending out email messages on your behalf. Be aware though. These can be malicious users, but it is also possible that these are legitimate email messages from a (marketing) organization you are not aware of.

These reports are sent out on a regular basis and are nothing more than a plain XML file like the following example:

```
<?xml version="1.0" encoding="UTF-8" ?>
<feedback>
  <version>1.0</version>
  <report_metadata>
    <org_name>esa2.hc141-83.eu.iphmx.com</org_name>
    <email>MAILER-DAEMON@esa2.hc141-83.eu.iphmx.com</email>
    <extra_contact_info></extra_contact_info>
    <report_id>7f3291$c27796e=4be18cfbbbeb8603@esa2.hc141-83.
    eu.iphmx.com</report_id>
    <date_range>
      <begin>1682546403</begin>
      <end>1682632804</end>
    </date_range>
  </report_metadata>
```

```
<policy_published>
  <domain>proexchangeadmin.com</domain>
  <adkim>r</adkim>
  <aspf>r</aspf>
  <p>none</p>
  <sp>reject</sp>
  <pct>100</pct>
</policy_published>
<record>
  <row>
    <source_ip>185.116.41.45</source_ip>
    <count>1</count>
    <policy_evaluated>
      <disposition>none</disposition>
      <dkim>pass</dkim>
      <spf>pass</spf>
    </policy_evaluated>
  </row>
  <identifiers>
    <header_from>proexchangeadmin.com</header_from>
    <envelope_from>proexchangeadmin.com</envelope_from>
  </identifiers>
  <auth_results>
    <dkim>
      <domain>ProExchangeAdmin.com</domain>
      <selector>securemail</selector>
      <result>pass</result>
    </dkim>
```

```
    <spf>
      <domain>proexchangeadmin.com</domain>
      <scope>mfrom</scope>
      <result>pass</result>
    </spf>
   </auth_results>
  </record>
</feedback>
```

These reports are not something you want to read on a regular basis, but they contain a lot of information. As you can see in this example, email was sent out on behalf of the ProExchangeAdmin domain, it was sent by a mail server with IP address 185.116.41.45, and SPF and DKIM check were successful.

To take full advantage of the DMARC options, you need a DMARC analyzer. There are lots of commercial analyzers available that can help you with this, both commercial and open source.

DNSSEC and DANE

DNSSEC and DANE are strongly related to each other, and you cannot use DANE without DNSSEC, but still, they are two separate solutions.

DNSSEC

DNSSEC stands for Domain Name System Security Extensions and provides cryptographic authentication of data. In short, when doing a DNS lookup of a particular DNS record, the results that are returned to the DNS client (i.e., your mail server) are digitally signed by the DNS server.

By digitally signing the DNS responses, a malicious process called "DNS poisoning" is prevented, and you can be sure that the IP address that is returned truly is the correct response and not a response point to a malicious mail server.

This is not something in Exchange, but a service that is offered by your provider or by your own DNS server if you are running that by yourself.

DANE

DANE is built on top of DNSSEC and stands for DNS-based Authentication of Named Entities. DANE only works when DNSSEC is activated for the domain, and DANE checks the public fingerprint of a certificate that is used by the mail server. The fingerprint is stored in a so-called TLSA record.

The workings of DANE can be compared to the regular TLS mechanism, where SMTP traffic between mail servers is encrypted and validated using certificates. A self-signed certificate can be used for encryption purposes, but it cannot be used for validating the sending server or domain. This makes sense because the origin of the certificate cannot be trusted. Anyone can create a self-signed certificate for an Exchange server called EDGE01 or for an FQDN EDGE01. proexchangeadmin.com.

Only third-party certificates, where a valid path to the certificate root exists, can be used for validation purposes. A third-party certificate authority (CA) can issue valid certificates that can be trusted for validation, since I am the only one that can request an official certificate for the EDGE01.proexchangeadmin.com certificate.

The cool thing about DANE is that I can use a self-signed certificate and store the thumbprint of the certificate in public DNS. This way, a receiving mail server that supports DANE can use this self-signed certificate and validate it based on the information found in DNS. Since I am the only one that can add the thumbprint to public DNS and since DANE is using DNSSEC, this information cannot be tampered with.

Note   Of course, a third-party certificate can also be used for DANE. In this example I will be using a third-party certificate issued by DigiCert.

The first step is to create the thumbprint that will be published in DNS. This thumbprint can be retrieved using the following PowerShell commands:

```
[PS] C:\> $Path = C:\install\mycert.cer
[PS] C:\> Set-Content -Path $path -Value
[convert]::tobase64string((get-item cert:\currentuser\
my\$ DCBE9FAAD9AB5B9A96A226EA32C197B8073D55A1).RawData)
-Encoding Ascii
```

The contents of the mycert.cer file can be used in an online tool like huque.com to create a TLSA record as shown in Figure 7-10.

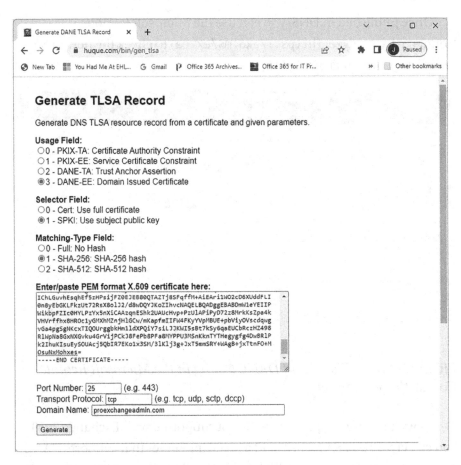

Figure 7-10. *Generate a TLSA record online*

This will generate a TLSA record similar to the following:

```
_25._tcp.edge01.proexchangeadmin.com. IN TLSA 3 1 1 (
      9ddeae70b1ebd6a198e6f79a54b9e0564a014d1869f1d06eb
      efc4719f924
      09c1
)
```

Once published in DNS, you can use the Microsoft Remote
Connectivity Analyzer (`https://aka.ms/exrca`) to check the new TLSA
record as shown in Figure 7-11.

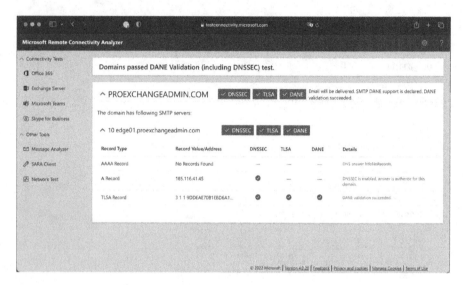

Figure 7-11. *DNSSEC and DANE testing in the Microsoft Remote
Connectivity Analyzer*

As with previous topics, DANE is not supported with Exchange 2019.
You can create a TLSA record, and a receiving server that supports DANE
can use this information, but for inbound mail Exchange 2019 will not do
anything with this.

Note   As of April 2023, Exchange Online supports TLSA for outbound
messages. Microsoft is still working on supporting TLSA on inbound
messages, but for the number of tenants in Exchange Online, this
is a huge task. Unfortunately, there are no plans to support TLSA for

Exchange 2019 inbound messages. For outbound messages from Exchange 2019, you can create the TLSA record in DNS. When a receiving server supports TLSA, this server can use the TLSA record for additional security.

MTA-STS

According to RFC8461, which defines MTA-STS, SMTP MTA Strict Transport Security (MTA-STS) is "a mechanism enabling mail service providers (SPs) to declare their ability to receive Transport Layer Security (TLS) secure SMTP connections and to specify whether sending SMTP servers should refuse to deliver to MX hosts that do not offer TLS with a trusted server certificate." In short, MTA-STS is a mechanism to enforce the use of TLS and enforce the use of a valid third-party server certificate.

To achieve this, a policy is published on a website, for example, https://mta-sts.proexchangeadmin.com/.well-known/mta-sts.txt, which contains something like

```
version: STSv1
mode: enforce
mx: edge01.proexchangeadmin.com
max_age: 604800
```

For the mode option, there are three different modes:

- *Enforce*: Sending MTAs MUST NOT deliver the message to hosts that fail MX matching or certificate validation or that do not support STARTTLS.

- *Testing*: Sending MTAs that also implement the TLSRPT (TLS Reporting) specification [RFC8460] send a report indicating policy application failures (as long as TLSRPT is also implemented by the recipient domain); in any case, messages maybe delivered as though there were no MTA-STS validation failure.

- *None*: In this mode, sending MTAs should treat the policy domain as though it does not have any active policy.

Max_age defines the time (in seconds) that the MTA-STS policy can be cached by a mail server. In this example, the policy is cached for 604800 seconds, which equals to 1 week.

Note   The subdomain mta-sts, the filename mta-sts.txt, and the directory .well-known (including the dot) are mandatory for the MTA-STS policy. It must also be secured using a valid third-party server certificate.

An MTA-STS support declaration TXT record in DNS must also exist. This record looks like

```
_mta-sts.proexchangeadmin.com. IN TXT "v=STSv1;
id=202305021641;"
```

The id is an identifier and defines the version of the MTA-STS record when changes are made to the MTA-STS record. A good practice is to create an identifier based on the date and time of the last change. In this example, it is May 2, 2023, at 4:51 PM.

There are several online tools available for checking the MTS-STS record. As mentioned several times in this book, MxToolbox is a great tool for checking the MTA-STS record as can be seen in Figure 7-12.

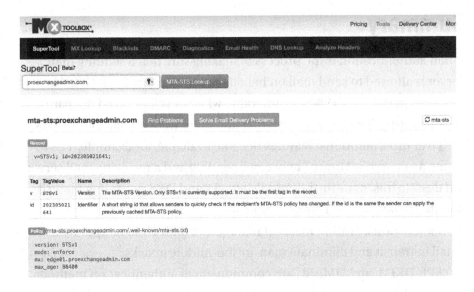

Figure 7-12. *Check the MTA-STS record in DNS using MxToolbox*

Another interesting option in MTA-STS is reporting. DMARC has a reporting function as well, but reports are only sent by receiving domains. Reporting in MTA-STS is performed daily by sending mail servers that support MTA-STS and TLSRPT.

To configure the reporting functionality, create a mailbox in Exchange 2019 or Exchange Online and assign it an email address like TLSReports@ ProExchangeAdmin.com. The next step is to configure the following DNS TXT record:

```
_smtp._tls.proexchangeadmin.com. 3600 IN  TXT v=TLSRPTv1;rua=ma
ilto:TLSReports@proexchangeadmin.com
```

Exchange Online supports MTA-STS, but Exchange 2019 does not support it. There are no plans to bring this functionality to Exchange 2019.

Summary

Email authentication is the process of making sure that a sending mail server is allowed to send mail on behalf of your domain. SMTP itself is designed in the early 1980s, a timeframe when developers did not care about security. There was no Internet and there were no malicious users.

Over time, additional features became available, for example, TLS to create an encrypted tunnel between a sending and a receiving mail server, but despite this, man-in-the-middle attacks and DNS poisoning made it possible to tamper with email in transit.

Email authentication makes it much more difficult to tamper with email in transit and eliminate man-in-the-middle attacks.

SPF, DKIM, and DMARC are common email authentication methods in use and supported by most cloud-based message hygiene solutions. Unfortunately, Exchange 2019 only supports SPF out of the box, and there's no support for DKIM and DMARC in Exchange 2019.

DNSSEC is growing, and more organizations and DNS providers are starting to support this, and by supporting DNSSEC, the use of DANE becomes possible as well. Using DANE an organization can create a certificate thumbprint in DNS that can be used by other mail servers to make sure there's a valid and trusted connection between the servers.

MTA-STS is more a "lightweight" version of DANE and the idea is the same. Create a policy in DNS where valid third-party server certificates are declared and that must be used for SMTP communication.

Microsoft is working hard to support MTA-STS, DNSSEC, and DANE in Exchange Online. Again, they are not supported in Exchange 2019, and there are no plans for supporting these in the future.

CHAPTER 8

Message Hygiene and Security

Ten or fifteen years ago, the Exchange Edge Transport server was used for message hygiene services. It was in the organization's perimeter network, and software like Forefront Protection for Exchange was installed on it. And in those days, it did a decent job.

In 2023 everything is different. Communications are different, threats are different, and lots of on-premises solutions have moved to cloud-based solutions, including message hygiene solutions.

The Edge Transport server role is still used in the perimeter network, but only as a gateway to prevent publishing an Exchange 2019 server directly to the Internet when security guidelines demand this. Forefront Protection for Exchange was discontinued years ago, and message hygiene is now performed by Exchange Online Protection.

© Jaap Wesselius and Michel de Rooij 2023
J. Wesselius and M. de Rooij, *Pro Exchange Administration*,
https://doi.org/10.1007/978-1-4842-9591-5_8

Exchange Online Protection is targeted specifically to message hygiene for Exchange, both Exchange 2019 and Exchange Online. As an add-on, there's also Microsoft Defender for Office 365 that takes email security to the next level. Of course, it all depends on the license you want to buy.

- Exchange Online Protection is available as a separate product that can be used in front of Exchange 2019. In this scenario, you need Azure AD Connect to synchronize your accounts to Azure Active Directory and create connectors in Exchange Online and in Exchange 2019 to facilitate mail flow.

- All Office 365 subscriptions that contain a license for Exchange Online automatically contain Exchange Online Protection. In an Exchange hybrid scenario, Exchange Online Protection for Exchange is enabled for all mailboxes, both in Exchange 2019 and in Exchange Online. The hybrid configuration will make sure the messages are correctly routed within the organization.

In this chapter, after an introduction we will focus on the features available in Exchange Online Protection.

Exchange Online Protection Introduction

Exchange Online Protection is Microsoft's cloud-based message hygiene solution. As such, it does not require any software installed in your organization. Subscribe to the service, create the necessary connectors between Exchange 2019 and Exchange Online Protection, and point your MX records to Exchange Online Protection and that's it. It just works. And if you only have mailboxes in Exchange Online, it's even simpler. Subscribe to Exchange Online, point your MX records to Exchange Online Protection, and you're good to go.

Exchange Online Protection has a long history. Originally it was called Forefront Online Protection for Exchange, a product developed by Frontbridge Technologies. Frontbridge Technologies was acquired by Microsoft in 2005, and the product was rebranded to Microsoft Exchange Hosted Services in 2006. Early 2009 the product was rebranded to Forefront Online Security for Exchange (FOSE), and late 2009 the product was again rebranded, but now to Forefront Online Protection for Exchange (FOPE). In 2013, Exchange Online Protection was introduced, and FOPE was transitioned to Exchange Online Protection, the product as we know it today.

As mentioned before, Exchange Online Protection can be used in combination with Exchange Online, with Exchange 2019, or in a hybrid scenario. From a message hygiene and security point of view, it makes no difference where the actual mailbox is located. This is schematically shown in Figure 8-1.

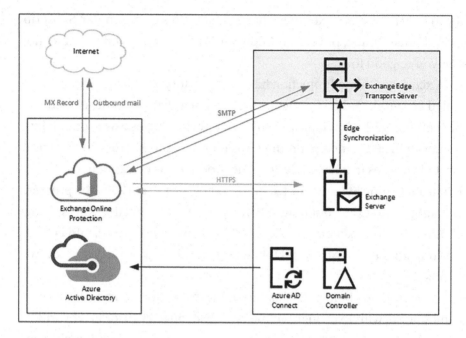

Figure 8-1. *Exchange Online Protection in front of Exchange 2019 or in a hybrid scenario*

The organization's MX record points to Exchange Online Protection for message hygiene. Legitimate messages are then sent to Exchange Online or to Exchange 2019, depending on the location of the recipient. The SMTP route via the Exchange 2019 Edge Transport server is optional. It is also possible to have a mail flow between Exchange Online and the Exchange 2019 Mailbox server, but some organizations depict an additional SMTP host in the demilitarized zone of the network.

Note   The Edge Transport server in Figure 8-1 is optional. It is also possible to deliver messages from Exchange Online Protection directly to the Exchange 2019 Mailbox server. However, some organizations do not allow their Mailbox servers connected directly to the Internet, hence the Edge Transport server.

Looking at Exchange Online Protection, message hygiene consists of several steps:

- *Connection filtering*: The first line of defense in Exchange Online Protection. Just like any other message hygiene solution, this is where the majority of all malware is blocked because of malicious sending servers.

- *Antimalware*: When a message passes the connection filtering, it is checked for malware. This is done both in the message and any attachments. Based on the configuration, if malware is found, the message can blocked, attachments can be removed, or the message can be delivered to a quarantine mailbox or the user's Junk Mail folder.

- *Mail flow rules*: Mail flow rules are also known as transport rules, which are discussed in Chapter 12. This chapter discusses transport rules in Exchange 2019, but the principles are the same as in Exchange Online. Based on predefined criteria, certain actions can be applied, for example, adding a recipient as a BCC, moderate a message, or send it to quarantine or the Junk Mail folder.

- *Content filtering*: The last step is content filtering where the message is inspected for spam, phishing, bulk, or spoofing. Based on the outcome of these checks, again actions can be applied just like the previous steps.

Exchange Online internals are shown in Figure 8-2.

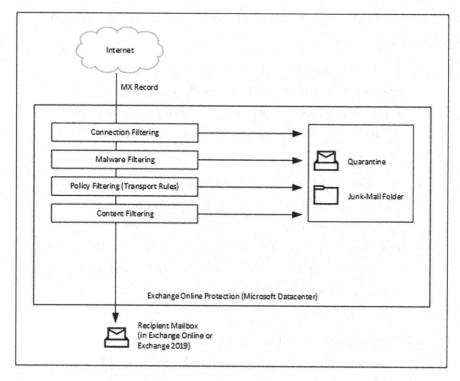

Figure 8-2. *Message hygiene steps in Exchange Online Protection*

Exchange Online Protection comes with preconfigured policies, and for a typical organization these work well. In the following sections, we'll go over the various components of Exchange Online Protection, how they work, and how to configure them for your own specifications.

Connection Filtering

As said in the beginning, the first line of defense is connection filtering. Exchange Online Protection, and many others, checks where a connection is coming from.

Many (commercial) organizations maintain lists of IP addresses that are known for sending malicious email, the so-called block lists.

Note   When hosting your own Exchange 2019 Edge Transport server that receives email from the Internet, you can use these real-time block lists as well. One of the well-known real-time block list providers is Spamhaus (`www.spamhaus.org`). There are more, and you can configure more than one real-time block list provider in your Exchange 2019 server.

Microsoft is not different; it hosts its own real-time block list, but can use other providers as well.

When a connection is set up by a sending SMTP server, Exchange Online Protection knows of course its IP address. It immediately checks the databases if this IP address is listed, and if it is listed, the connection is automatically dropped. It is dropped even before the sending host can send the HELO or EHLO command, therefore saving precious resources on the servers. This is a very effective way of fighting malicious email.

Besides the real-time block lists, more connection filtering options are available:

- *IP allow list*: Exchange Online Protection has a list of IP addresses that are allowed to connect, regardless of any real-time blacklist. When a sending SMTP server is on the IP allow list, all spam filtering is skipped. This is a per-tenant list and can be controlled using an IP allow list policy.

- *IP block list*: Exchange Online Protection also has a list of IP addresses that are blocked. When a sending SMTP server is listed on the IP block list, the connection attempt is automatically blocked. Just like the IP allow list, this is controlled using a IP block list policy, and it is a per-tenant setting.

- *Safe list*: The safe list is a list of SMTP servers, and this list comes from subscription at various providers. When a sending SMTP server is on the safe list, incoming messages are skipped from spam filtering and passed on immediately. No configuration is possible. You can only turn it on or off.

We'll discuss these three filtering options in the next sections.

IP Allow and IP Block Lists

As mentioned in the introduction, when a server is listed on the IP allow list, its messages bypass the spam filtering options. You can do this when you fully trust a sending SMTP host, it is safe to bypass the spam filtering options, and you don't want to miss any email from this particular sender.

The IP allow list is a tenant-wide configuration and is managed using a connection filter policy. You can find this connection filter policy in the Microsoft Defender Portal under **Email & collaboration ➤ Policies & rules ➤ Threat policies ➤ Anti-spam policies** (under **Policies**).

When you open this, you will find three default policies:

- Anti-spam inbound policy (default)

- Connection filter policy (default)

- Anti-spam outbound policy (default)

To add an IP address to the IP allow list, click **Edit connection filter policy** and add an IP address in the **Always allow messages from the following IP addresses or address range**. You can add a single IP address, multiple IP addresses, or IP ranges. This is shown in Figure 8-3.

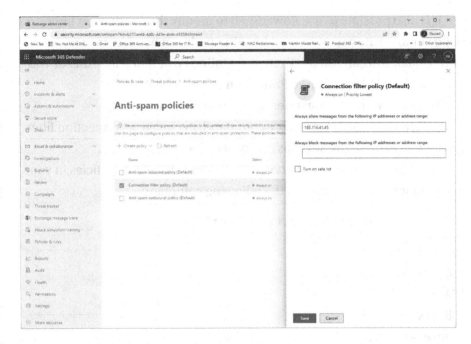

Figure 8-3. *Add an IP address to the IP allow list in the connection filter policy*

Note   Be as strict as possible to avoid any abuse of these whitelisted entries. Unfortunately, IPv6 addresses are still not supported here.

To add an IP address to the IP block list in the connection filter policy, add the IP address, IP addresses, or IP ranges in the other text box under **Always block messages from the following IP addresses or address range**.

Note   The IP allow list entries and IP block list entries are on the same window. Make sure you add the IP addresses to the appropriate text box.

It is also possible to use PowerShell to modify the connection filter policy or to create a new connection filter policy. When it comes to PowerShell, you can use the Exchange Online PowerShell module, or you can use the Exchange Online Protection PowerShell module.

To view the connection filter policy, you can use the Get-HostedConnectionFilterPolicy command; to change a connection filter policy, you can use the Set-HostedConnectionFilterPolicy.

For example, to get an overview of all connection filter policies in your organization, you can execute the following command:

```
[PS] C:\> Get-HostedConnectionFilterPolicy

AdminDisplayName            :
IsDefault                   : True
IPAllowList                 : {}
IPBlockList                 : {}
EnableSafeList              : False
DirectoryBasedEdgeBlockMode : Default
Identity                    : Default
Id                          : Default
IsValid                     : True
ExchangeVersion             : 0.20 (15.0.0.0)
Name                        : Default
DistinguishedName           : CN=Default,CN=Hosted Connection
                              Filter,CN=Transport Settings,
                              CN=Configuration,CN=proexcha
                              ngeadmin.onmicrosoft.com,
                              CN=ConfigurationUnits,DC=EURP19
                              4A002,DC=PROD,DC=OUTLOOK,DC=COM
ObjectCategory              : EURP194A002.PROD.OUTLOOK.COM/
                              Configuration/Schema/ms-Exch-
                              Hosted-Connection-Filter-Policy
```

```
ObjectClass                : {top, msExchHostedConnection
                             FilterPolicy}
WhenChanged                : 6/8/2023 2:49:54 PM
WhenCreated                : 8/13/2021 12:27:07 PM
WhenChangedUTC             : 6/8/2023 12:49:54 PM
WhenCreatedUTC             : 8/13/2021 10:27:07 AM
ExchangeObjectId           : faceea67-ec9d-403a-9e1e-
                             03a74c2f0fa6
OrganizationalUnitRoot     : proexchangeadmin.onmicrosoft.com
OrganizationId             : EURP194A002.PROD.OUTLOOK.COM/
                             Microsoft Exchange Hosted
                             Organizations/proexchangeadmin.
                             onmicrosoft.com - EURP194A002.
                             PROD.OUTLOOK.COM/Configuration
                             Units/proexchangeadmin.
                             onmicrosoft.com/Configuration
Guid                       : faceea67-ec9d-403a-9e1e-
                             03a74c2f0fa6
OriginatingServer          : AM5P194A002DC11.EURP194A002.PROD.
                             OUTLOOK.COM
ObjectState                : Unchanged
```

Or when you want to only view the default connection filter policy, you can execute the following command:

```
[PS] C:\> Get-HostedConnectionFilterPolicy -Identity Default
```

But since there is only one policy in a standard configuration, this makes no difference with the previous example of course.

To list only the IP block list, the IP allow list, and the safe list data, you can use the Format-List option with the appropriate parameters, like this:

```
[PS] C:\> Get-HostedConnectionFilterPolicy | Format-List Name,
IPBlockList,IPAllowList,EnableSafeList
```

```
Name            : Default
IPBlockList     : {}
IPAllowList     : {}
EnableSafeList  : False
```

To add an entry in the IP allow list and IP block list, the following command can be used:

```
[PS] C:\> Set-HostedConnectionFilterPolicy -Identity "Default"
-IPAllowList 185.116.41.45 -IPBlockList 172.17.17.0/24
```

This example modifies the default connection filter policy with the following settings.

Messages from 185.116.41.45 are never identified as spam, and messages from the IP range 172.17.17.0/24 are always identified as spam. Be aware that the IP allow list and IP block list are multi-valued attributes and as such you need the @{Add=" "} construct to add IP addresses to an existing IP allow list or IP block list, like this:

```
[PS] C:\> Set-HostedConnectionFilterPolicy "Default" -IPAllowList
@{Add="145.12.2.10","42.20.3.0/24"; Remove="188.96.113.45"}
```

In this example, the IP address 145.12.2.10 and the IP range 42.20.3.0/24 are added to the IP allow list, and the IP address 188.96.113.45 is removed from the IP allow list.

Tenant Allow/Block Lists (TABL)

Another option to create block lists and allow lists is to use the Tenant Allow/Block Lists (TABL) feature in Exchange Online Protection. Using TABL is the Microsoft-recommended way of creating lists of allowed or blocked senders. Using TABL, it is also possible to create a list of possible spoofed senders; these are outside senders that use a recipient in your organization as their "From address."

Allow or Block Addresses and Domains

When using TABL to block messages, the message is still accepted and processed, but the spam confidence level (SCL) is set to 9. In other words, these messages are tagged as *high-confidence spam* and are delivered to the user's Junk Mail folder in their inbox or to a quarantine mailbox if you have one configured.

When using TABL to block senders, not only inbound messages are blocked, but outbound messages to these senders are also blocked. When a user sends an email to a blocked sender, the following non-delivery report (NDR) is generated:

5.7.703 Your message can't be delivered because one or more recipients are blocked by your organization's tenant allow/ block list policy

To add an entry to the TABL feature, open the Microsoft Defender Portal on https://security.microsoft.com, navigate to **Policies & rules** ➤ **Threat policies** ➤ **Rules**, and select Tenant Allow/Block Lists. Click on + Block and add a sender or domain to the Domains & addresses text box. This is shown in Figure 8-4.

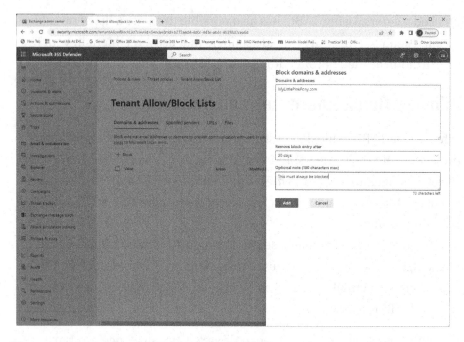

Figure 8-4. *Add a domain to the block list in the TABL feature*

When it comes to adding senders to the allow list, it is not possible to add them directly to the Microsoft Defender Portal as we just demonstrated using the block list. Instead, you must submit any false-positive messages to the IP allow list. Exchange Online Protection Machine Learning will "learn" from the entries. After 30 days, Exchange Online Protection will automatically remove the messages and entries, and messages coming from this IP address will continue to be delivered. If something malicious happens, the IP address will be removed again of course.

To use this, you must release a message from the Exchange Online quarantine mailbox and, once delivered, store the email message on your local hard disk. If you want to upload the file to Microsoft, leave it there. If you only want to use the message ID, open the email with Notepad and look for the X-MS-Exchange-Organization-Network-Message-Id header and copy the string that follows this header.

The next step is to open the **Microsoft 365 Defender portal** (security. microsoft.com), go to **Actions & Submissions**, click **Submissions**, and click **+ Submit to Microsoft for Analysis**.

There are two ways to send this information to Microsoft:

1. *Add the email network message ID*: You can find this information in the header of an email under the X-MS-Exchange-Organization-Network-Message- Id header. Copy and paste this information into the appropriate text box.

2. *Upload the email file in .msg or .eml format*: Instead of using the header information, you can also upload the complete email message into the Microsoft 365 Defender portal.

Select a recipient that was facing the issue and select a reason you want this to be changed. When done, click Submit to submit the information to Microsoft. This is shown in Figure 8-5.

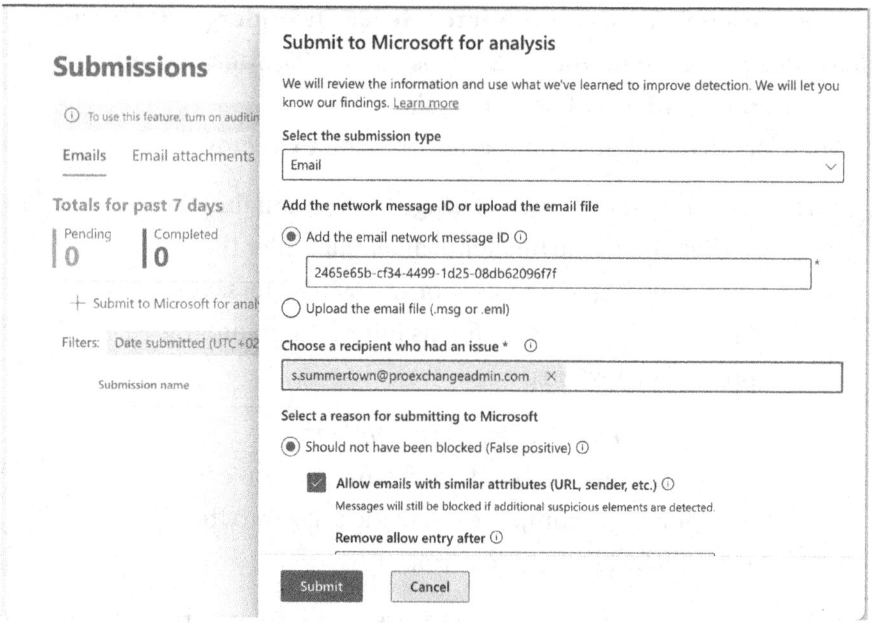

Figure 8-5. *Uploading email information to the Microsoft 365 Defender portal*

It takes some time to be processed, but the new entry should be visible in the Tenant Allow/Block Lists (TABL) in the Microsoft 365 Defender portal. You can find the Tenant Allow/Block Lists under **Email & collaboration ➤ Policies & rules ➤ Threat policies**.

Note   If the email address of the sender is not found to be malicious, a TABL entry is not created.

The third option is to use transport rules for a safe sender list based on IP addresses. To do this, you must follow these steps:

- Open the **Exchange Online Admin Center** and navigate to **Mail Flow ➤ Rules** and click **+ Add a Rule**.

- Select **Create a new rule**, and give the rule an identifiable name like "Allow mail from Exchangelabs IP Address."

- Apply this rule if **The sender** and **domain is...** and use the **add button** to add a domain name; in our example this is Exchangelabs.nl.

- Use the + icon again to add an additional condition and select **The sender** and **IP address is in any of these ranges...** and add the IP address of the sending server you are allowing.

- In the **Do the following** dropdown box, select **Modify the message properties** and **set the spam confidence level (SCL)** to –1. This is shown in Figure 8-6.

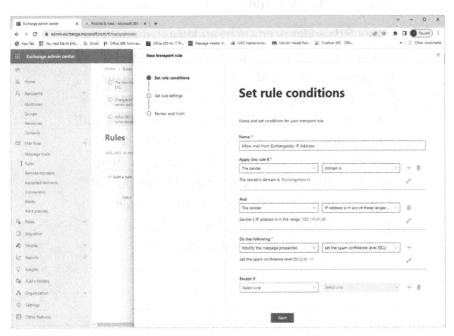

Figure 8-6. *Create a transport rule to allow messages from a certain IP address*

Note   A new transport rule is disabled by default immediately after creation. Open the new transport rule and enable it when done.

Spoofed Senders

Using TABL it is possible to create a list of spoofed senders. Spoofed senders are internal email addresses that can be used externally to send email on behalf of these email addresses. Newsletters and addresses like No-Reply are examples of spoofed senders.

To add these addresses to the list of spoofed senders, follow this procedure:

- On the **Tenant Allow/Block Lists** page, click **Spoofed senders** and click + **Add**.

- A spoofed sender needs to be added as a **domain pair**. Not only the spoofed sender like newsletter@contoso. com needs to be added, but also the infrastructure where it is coming from. A domain pair can be a username and sending IP address or a username and sending domain. So, for newsletters that are sent out by Mailchimp, it can be something like newsletter@ contoso.com, mailchimp.com. Select if the spoofed sender is internal or external and if the spoofed messages are allowed or blocked and click **Add** to continue. This is shown in Figure 8-7.

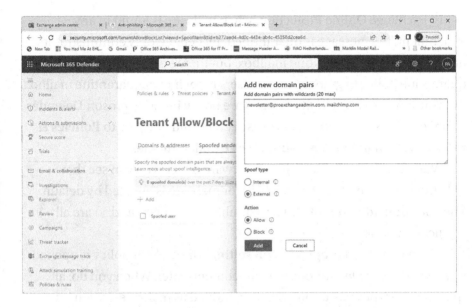

Figure 8-7. *Allowing a spoofed sender origination from Mailchimp*

Newsletters with a sender address newsletters@proexchangeadmin. com are now allowed to be received from Mailchimp, although they are officially spoofed messages.

Antimalware

When a message has passed the connection filtering features, it is scanned for malware. If malware is found in the message or the attachment(s), the message is delivered to quarantine. By default, only admins can view and interact with malware-quarantined messages. But admins can create and use quarantine policies to specify what users are allowed to do to quarantined messages.

Exchange Online Protection offers a multi-layered approach when it comes to antimalware filtering. It is designed to filter out malware for Windows, Mac, and Linux that travels through your organization.

In Exchange Online Protection, when malware is found in any attachment, the message is quarantined. By default, only administrators have access to the quarantine mailbox, but there's an option to create a quarantine policy to grant access to users to their own quarantine mailbox.

You can find the default antimalware policy in the Microsoft Defender Portal on `https://security.microsoft.com` and navigate to **Policies & rules ➤ Threat policies ➤ Antimalware** under **Policies**.

When you open the default antimalware policy, you can see that only the Zero-Hour Auto Purge (ZAP) for malware is enabled by default. The **common attachments filter** is disabled by default, and so are all notification options.

When you click **Edit protection settings**, the default policy is opened. Here you can enable the common attachments filter. When you do, all specified file types are automatically identified as malware, so you must be cautious when enabling this feature. On the other hand, the most dangerous file types are listed here, file types you don't want to have in your email environment at all.

The following file types are listed in the common attachments filter:

```
ace, apk, app, appx, ani, arj, bat, cab, cmd,com, deb, dex,
dll, docm, elf, exe, hta, img, iso, jar, jnlp, kext, lha, lib,
library, lnk, lzh, macho, msc, msi, msix, msp, mst, pif, ppa,
ppam, reg, rev, scf, scr, sct, sys, uif, vb, vbe, vbs, vxd,
wsc, wsf, wsh, xll, xz, z
```

The quarantine policy has the following options:

- DefaultFullAccessPolicy
- AdminOnlyAccessPolicy (default setting)
- DefaultFullAccessWithNotificationPolicy

And you can change the various notification options. This is shown in Figure 8-8.

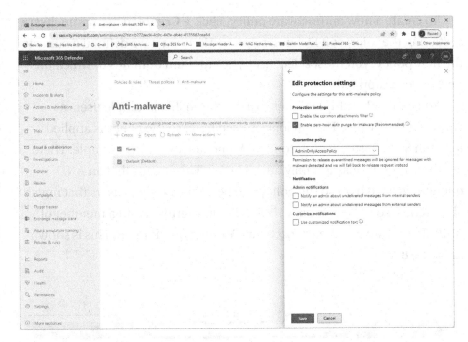

Figure 8-8. *The default antimalware policy in Exchange Online Protection*

Zero-Hour Auto Purge (ZAP) is an interesting feature of Exchange Online Protection. ZAP quarantines messages *after* they have been delivered to mailboxes in Exchange Online. ZAP is always turned on, and it is recommended to leave it on.

Note   The default policy is applied to all users in the organization, and it does not matter if the user's mailbox is in Exchange Online or in Exchange 2019. The default policy is always available and cannot be deleted. The default policy also has the lowest priority; custom policies always have a higher priority and are always processed first.

To create a new antimalware policy, click **+ Create** in the Antimalware section in the Microsoft Defender Portal. After you have defined a name for the new policy, you must select users, groups, and domains to which this new policy is applied.

You can add multiple values to a condition, like multiple users as shown in Figure 8-9. The OR logic is used here, so the policy is applied to Sarah Summertown or Baron von Munchausen in this example. There are three conditions, and they are *inclusive*. This means that an AND operator is used here so the policy will be applied only to users that match all criteria—so if the username is Sarah Summertown **and** a member of AllProUsers **and** has the ProExchangeAdmin.com domain. This is shown in Figure 8-9.

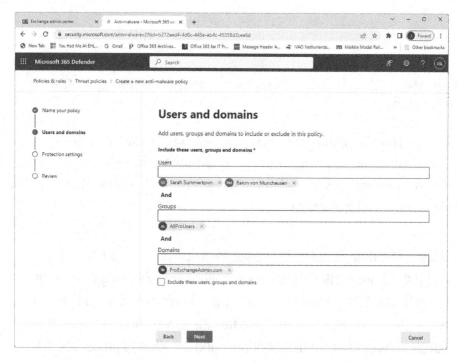

Figure 8-9. *Criteria when defining a new antimalware policy*

For a new policy, the common attachments filter is enabled by default, with the option to reject the message and send an NDR to the sender. As an option, you can enable Zero-Hour Auto Purge (ZAP), change the quarantine policy, and enable the notification setting that best matches your organization.

When you click **Next**, you can select the options available in an antimalware policy that are needed for your organization, like Zero-Hour Auto Purge, the right quarantine policy, or the notification settings. When you have made your selection, click **Next** again, review the settings, and click **Submit** to finalize the creation of the new antimalware policy.

After a few moments, the new policy should be available for users that match the criteria. For example, when you have selected the DefaultFullAccessWithNotificationPolicy quarantine policy, a user can access the quarantine mailbox and see what has been put in quarantine for them. After checking, the quarantined messages can be deleted or released.

Besides the default available quarantine policies as described, you can also create custom quarantine policies to get a more granular approach to quarantine.

To create a new quarantine policy, open the Microsoft 365 Defender portal and navigate to **Email & collaboration ➤ Policies & rules ➤ Threat policies** and click **Quarantine Policies** under **Rules**. Here you can find the three default quarantine policies, but there's no option to edit these default quarantine policies.

To create a new quarantine policy, click **+ Add a custom policy** and give the new policy an identifiable name. In the **Recipient Message Access** window, there are two options:

- *Limited access*: With this option, the users can view the quarantine messages, but they cannot release messages from quarantine.

- *Set specific access (advance)*: With this option, you can select the release action preference:

  - Allow users to request a message to be released from quarantine.

  - Users can release a message from quarantine.

- There are three more actions that can be taken on quarantined messages that can be selected here:

  - *Delete*: Delete the message from quarantine.

  - *Preview*: Preview the quarantined message in an additional HTML window before releasing or deleting the quarantined message.

  - *Block Sender*: Block the sender of the quarantined message.

When the new quarantine policy is created, you can use a custom antimalware policy to assign the quarantine policy to recipients.

It is also possible to create a new quarantine policy using Exchange Online PowerShell or Exchange Online Protection PowerShell. To create a new policy, execute the following command:

```
[PS] C:\> New-QuarantinePolicy -Name "Policy Name" -EndUser
QuarantinePermissionsValue <0 to 236> -EsnEnabled $true
```

The EndUserQuarantinePermissionsValue parameter uses a decimal value that's converted from a binary value. The binary value corresponds to the available end user quarantine permissions in a specific order. For each permission, the value 1 equals True and the value 0 equals False.

Table 8-1 lists the order and value for each individual permission.

Table 8-1. *Permissions That Can Be Used When Creating a New Quarantine Policy*

Permission	Binary value	Decimal value
Permission to delete	0000 0001	1
Permission to preview	0000 0010	2
Permission to release	0000 0100	4
Permission to request release	0000 1000	8
Permission to block sender	0001 0000	16
Permission to allow sender	0010 0000	32
Permission to download	0100 0000	64
Permission to view header	1000 0000	128

When creating a quarantine policy with permission to block the sender (fifth bit), permission to request release (fourth bit), permission to preview (second bit), and permission to delete (first bit), the binary value would be 0001 1011, which equals to a decimal value of 27. The EndUserQuarantinePermissionsValue in this case would be 27 in the PowerShell command earlier in this section.

The EsnEnabled option in the previous command enables quarantine messages when set to $True. Likewise, the quarantine messages are disabled when set to $False.

Content Filtering

The last step in Exchange Online Protection is content filtering, more specifically anti-spam and anti-spoofing. Harmful messages are identified as

- Spam
- High-confidence spam

- Phishing

- High-confidence phishing

- Bulk messages

- Spoofed messages

You can configure the action to take on the message based on the filtering verdict, like quarantine or move to the Junk Email folder. When a message successfully passes the content filtering in Exchange Online Protection, it is delivered to the user's mailbox.

Anti-spam

When using Exchange Online Protection, whether it be in combination with mailboxes in Exchange Online or in Exchange 2019, email messages are always protected against spam. The goal for Exchange Online Protection is to protect users from junk email, fraudulent email threats (phishing), and malware.

Anti-spam in Exchange Online Protection consists of the following four technologies:

- *Connection filtering*: This was discussed in a previous section.

- *Spam filtering or content filtering*: This is where messages are scanned and tagged as (high-confidence) spam, (high-confidence) phishing, or bulk email. Or messages are not tagged at all when they are legitimate messages of course.

- *Outbound spam filtering*: Exchange Online Protection also checks outbound messages to prevent users from accidentally sending out spam messages or checks if they don't send out too much messages in a certain timeframe (exceeding outbound limits).

- *Spoof intelligence*: Exchange Online Protection will take care of spoofing. Spoofing is a common technique that's used by attackers, and spoofed messages appear to originate from someone or somewhere other than the actual source. This technique is often used in phishing campaigns that are designed to obtain user credentials.

You can use the Microsoft Defender Portal on https://security. microsoft.com to view and configure the anti-spam policies. To do so, log in to the Microsoft Defender Portal and navigate to **Policies & rules ➤ Threat Policies ➤ Anti-spam** (under **Policies**). Here you will find the three default anti-spam policies:

- Anti-spam inbound policy (default)
- Connection filter policy (default)
- Anti-spam outbound policy (default)

When opening the default anti-spam inbound policy, you can see the following settings being enabled:

- *Bulk email action*: On.
- *Bulk email threshold*: Seven days.
- Spam, high-confidence spam, and phishing emails are sent to the user's Junk Mail folder.
- High-confidence phishing is sent to quarantine.
- Bulk messages are sent to the user's Junk Mail folder.
- Spam safety tips are enabled.

Note   Allowed senders, allowed domains, blocked senders, and blocked domains are not configured in the default policy.

It is possible to edit the existing default policy, but I always recommend creating a new policy that better fits your needs. To do so, follow these steps:

- Navigate to the anti-spam pages as mentioned earlier in this section and click **+ Create Policy**.

- Give the new policy an identifiable name and click **Next** to continue.

- Enter the users, groups, and domains you want this new policy to be applied to. If you don't want to have this policy applied to members of a group and don't want to apply this on an individual basis, you can leave the Users text box empty.

- In the **Bulk email threshold & spam properties** window, you can set specific filtering actions and threshold settings that will influence the anti-spam score, for example:

  - *Image links to a remote website*: When an image is not directly in the message, but only a link to a message on another site, the SCL is raised.

  - *Numeric IP address in URL*: When a link to another site does not contain an FQDN but only an IP address, the SCL is raised.

  - *Empty messages*: When an inbound message is empty, it is marked as spam.

  - *SPF record hard fail*: When the inbound message fails the SPF check, it is marked as spam.

  - *Contains specific languages*: If you never receive messages in Chinese, for example, messages in Chinese are automatically marked as spam.

- When you have configured all required options, click **Next** to continue.

- In the **Actions** window, you can set the actions that need to be taken when messages are tagged as spam, phishing, or bulk. This is shown in Figure 8-10.

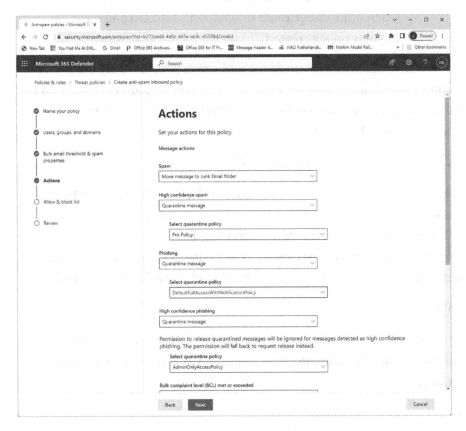

Figure 8-10. *Actions that need to be taken in the new anti-spam policy*

- Click **Next** to continue.

- In the **Allow & block list** window, you can configure the allow and block list options as appropriate. When done, click **Next** to continue.

- Review your settings, adjust them when needed, and when done click **Create** to finalize the wizard and have the new policy created.

It is also possible to manage the anti-spam policies using the Exchange Online or Exchange Online Protection PowerShell module. To get a list of all anti-spam policies, execute the Get-HostedContentFilterPolicy as shown in the following example:

```
PS C:\> Get-HostedContentFilterPolicy

Name                             SpamAction HighConfidence IsDefault
----                             ---------- -------------- ---------
Standard Preset Security Policy MoveToJmf  Quarantine     False
Pro anti-spam inbound policy     Quarantine Quarantine     False
Default                          MoveToJmf  MoveToJmf      True

PS C:\>
```

The next step is to get into to policy rules, which you can retrieve using the Get-HostedContentFilterRule command as shown in the following example:

```
PS C:\> get-HostedContentFilterRule

Name                          State   Priority HostedContentFilterPolicy
----                          -----   -------- -------------------------
Pro anti-spam inbound policy Enabled 0         Pro anti-spam inbound policy

PS C:\>
```

As with the previous example, you can use the Exchange Online PowerShell or the Exchange Online Protection PowerShell module to create new policies and rules. To create a new content filter policy, you can use the following command:

```
[PS] C:\> New-HostedContentFilterPolicy -Name "Pro Top 5"
-HighConfidenceSpamAction Quarantine -SpamAction Quarantine
-BulkThreshold 6

Name       SpamAction HighConfidenceSpamAction IsDefault
----       ---------- ------------------------ ---------
Pro Top 5 Quarantine Quarantine                     False

PS C:\>
```

This will create a new policy that puts messages in quarantine when the spam filtering verdict is spam or high-confidence spam and use the default quarantine policy for the quarantined messages. Bulk confidence level (BCL) 7 or higher triggers the verdict.

Here's how to create a new content filter rule:

```
[PS] C:\> New-HostedContentFilterRule -Name "Pro Top 5 Rule"
-HostedContentFilterPolicy "Pro Top 5" -SentToMemberOf
"ProExchange Management Group"
```

This will create a new rule that is associated with the policy we have created in the previous example and that will be applied to all members of the Distribution Group "ProExchange Management Group."

Anti-phishing

In Microsoft 365 organizations with mailboxes in Exchange Online or standalone Exchange Online Protection (EOP) organizations without Exchange Online mailboxes, anti-phishing policies provide anti-spoofing protection.

All recipients automatically have the default anti-phishing policy applied, but it is possible to create custom anti-phishing policies that better fit the needs of your organization. It is also possible to target specific anti-phishing policies to specific users or groups. A good example of this is a strict anti-phishing policy specifically for the top-level management of your organization, a group of users that is traditionally susceptible to phishing emails.

You view anti-phishing policies in the Microsoft 365 Defender portal or in PowerShell (Exchange Online PowerShell or the EOP).

Open the Microsoft Defender Portal on `https://security.microsoft.com` and navigate to **Policies & rules** ➤ **Threat policies** ➤ **Anti-phishing** (under **Policies**). Here you will find only one anti-phishing policy:

- Office 365 Antiphish Default (default)

In the default policy, spoof intelligence is enabled, and when a spoofed message is detected, it is moved to the user's Junk Mail folder. Furthermore, the **unauthenticated senders symbol** is enabled, and the **via** tag is enabled.

While this is sufficient for normal usage, there are situations where you want a more stringent anti-phishing policy. To create a new anti-phishing policy, follow these steps:

- On the **Anti-phishing** page in the Microsoft Defender Portal, click on **+ Create** and give the new anti-phishing policy an identifiable name. Click **Next** to continue.

- Select the **users**, **groups**, and **domains** you want this new policy to be applied to and click **Next** to continue.

- **Spoof intelligence** is enabled by default. It is possible to spoof certain recipients in your organization. For example, if a newsletter for your company is sent out by, for example, Mailchimp with a sender like **newsletter@contoso.com** or **noreply@contoso.com**, it is allowed to be spoofed. After all, you want your users to be able to receive these newsletters. Creating allowed spoofed senders is discussed earlier in this chapter. Click **Next** to continue.

- On the **Actions** page you can select what actions to take when a spoofed message is detected. For stringent policies, you can select **Quarantine the message**. You can also select the quarantine policy and select additional options like **first contact safety tip**, the **unauthenticated senders**, or the **via tag**. This is shown in Figure 8-11.

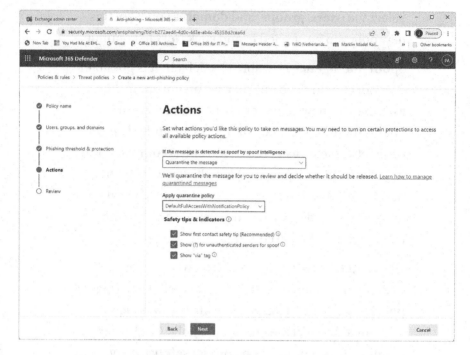

Figure 8-11. *Create a new and more stringent anti-phishing policy*

- Click **Next** to continue.

- Review your settings, and when all is okay, click **Create** to create the policy and finish the wizard.

When you have created your new anti-spam and anti-phishing policies, it is time to test them. Create a new external email and send it to the users you selected when creating the new policies. For example, when sending an email with a hyperlink based on an IP address instead of an FQDN, it should end in quarantine according to the newly created policies.

When all is well, the user should receive a message that messages are quarantined and that they can review the message, release the message, or block the sender. This is shown in Figure 8-12.

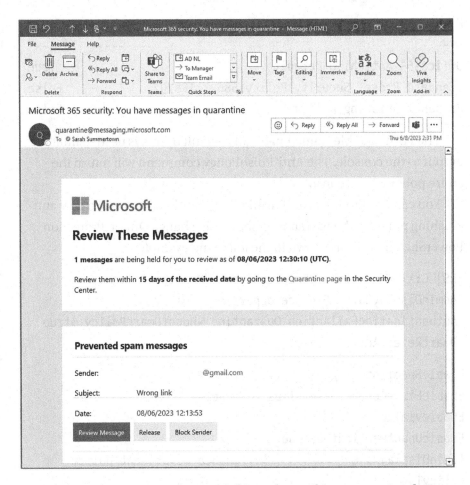

Figure 8-12. *A message that an inbound email is quarantined. For privacy reasons the sender is erased*

It is also possible to manage anti-phishing policies using Exchange Online and Exchange Online Protection PowerShell modules. To retrieve the existing anti-phishing policy, you can use the Get-AntiPhishingPolicy command as shown in the following example:

```
[PS] C:\> Get-AntiPhishPolicy | Format-Table Name,Enabled,
IsDefault
```

Name	Enabled IsDefault
Office365 AntiPhish Default	True
Standard Preset Security Policy1686231188792	False
Pro anti-phishing policy	False

The Format-Table Name,Enabled,IsDefault option is used to limit the output to the console. The Anti-PhishPolicy command will return the entire policy on the console.

You can use the New-AntiPhishPolicy command to create a new anti-phishing policy in the Exchange Online or Exchange Online Protection PowerShell module as shown in the following example:

```
[PS] C:\> New-AntiPhishPolicy -Name "Monitor Policy"
-AdminDisplayName "Finance department policy"
-AuthenticationFailAction Quarantine -HonorDmarcPolicy $true
-DmarcRejectAction Reject
```

```
EnableSpoofIntelligence    : True
EnableFirstContactSafetyTips : False
EnableViaTag               : True
EnableUnauthenticatedSender : True
AdminDisplayName           : Finance department policy
PolicyTag                  :
RecommendedPolicyType      : Custom
AuthenticationFailAction   : Quarantine
HonorDmarcPolicy           : True
DmarcRejectAction          : Reject
DmarcQuarantineAction      : Quarantine
SpoofQuarantineTag         : DefaultFullAccessPolicy
IsDefault                  : False
Identity                   : Monitor Policy
```

```
Id                         : Monitor Policy
IsValid                    : True
ExchangeVersion            : 0.20 (15.0.0.0)
Name                       : Monitor Policy
DistinguishedName          : CN=Monitor Policy,CN=AntiPhish,C
                             N=Transport
ObjectCategory             : EURP194A002.PROD.OUTLOOK.COM/
                             Configuration/
ObjectClass                : {top, msExchHostedContent
                             FilterConfig}
WhenChanged                : 6/19/2023 4:07:04 PM
WhenCreated                : 6/19/2023 4:07:04 PM
WhenChangedUTC             : 6/19/2023 2:07:04 PM
WhenCreatedUTC             : 6/19/2023 2:07:04 PM
ExchangeObjectId           : 874d19e5-a969-4645-bb86-
                             8ca76bca9527
OrganizationalUnitRoot     : proexchangeadmin.onmicrosoft.com
OrganizationId             : EURP194A002.PROD.OUTLOOK.COM/
                             Microsoft
Guid                       : 874d19e5-a969-4645-bb86-
                             8ca76bca9527
OriginatingServer          : AM5P194A002DC11.EURP194A002.
                             PROD.OUTLOOK.COM
ObjectState                : Unchanged
```

Likewise, you can use the New-AntiPhishPolicy command to create a new anti-phishing policy as shown in the following example:

```
[PS] C:\> New-AntiPhishRule -Name "Finance Department"
-AntiPhishPolicy "Finance Department policy" -SentToMemberOf
"Finance Department"
```

```
AntiPhishPolicy              : Monitor Policy
State                        : Enabled
Priority                     : 1
Comments                     :
Description                  : If the message:
                               Is sent to a member of group
                               'FinanceDepartment@proexchange
                               admin.com'
                               Take the following actions:
                               Apply AntiPhish policy "Monitor
                               Policy".

RuleVersion                  : 14.0.0.0
SentTo                       :
SentToMemberOf               : {FinanceDepartment@
proexchangeadmin.com}
RecipientDomainIs            :
ExceptIfSentTo               :
ExceptIfSentToMemberOf       :
ExceptIfRecipientDomainIs    :
Conditions                   :
Identity                     : Finance Department
DistinguishedName            : CN=Finance Department,CN=AntiPhish
                               Versioned,
Guid                         : 8be72911-6fd0-495f-af43-
                               7ef0840cfcd8
ImmutableId                  : 8be72911-6fd0-495f-af43-
                               7ef0840cfcd8
OrganizationId               : EURP194A002.PROD.OUTLOOK.COM/
                               Microsoft Exchange
Name                         : Finance Department
IsValid                      : True
```

```
WhenChanged          : 6/19/2023 4:10:15 PM
ExchangeVersion      : 0.1 (8.0.535.0)
ObjectState          : Unchanged
```

This rule will be associated with the "Finance department policy" that was created earlier in this section, and it will be applied to the members of the "Finance Department" Distribution Group.

Preset Security Policies

Preset security policies allow you to apply protection features to users based on Microsoft-recommended settings. Unlike custom policies that are infinitely configurable, virtually all the settings in preset security policies are not configurable and are based on Microsoft observations in the Exchange Online Protection data centers. The settings in preset security policies provide a balance between keeping harmful content away from users and avoiding unnecessary disruptions.

In Exchange Online Protection, there are two preset security policies:

- *Standard Protection*: A baseline protection profile that protects against spam, phishing, and malware threats

- *Strict Protection*: A more aggressive protection profile for selected users, such as high-value targets or priority users

Preset security policies use special versions of the individual protection policies that are available in Exchange Online Protection and Microsoft Defender for Office 365 when you have the proper license. These policies are created after you assign the Standard protection or Strict protection preset security policies to users.

The Exchange Online Protection policies are in all Microsoft 365 organizations with Exchange Online mailboxes and standalone EOP organizations without Exchange Online mailboxes:

- Anti-spam policies named Standard Preset Security Policy and Strict Preset Security Policy

- Antimalware policies named Standard Preset Security Policy and Strict Preset Security Policy

- Anti-phishing policies (spoofing protection) named Standard Preset Security Policy and Strict Preset Security Policy (spoof settings)

Note   Outbound spam policies aren't part of preset security policies. The default outbound spam policy automatically protects members of preset security policies. You can also create custom outbound spam policies to customize the protection for members of preset security policies.

It is not possible to modify the individual policy settings in the protection profiles. The Standard and Strict protection policy setting values, including the associated quarantine policies, are listed in Table 8-2.

Table 8-2. *Differences Between Standard and Strict Preset Security Policy*

	Standard	Strict
Antimalware policy	No difference	No difference
Anti-spam policy		
Bulk detection action	Move message to Junk Email folder (MoveToJmf)	Quarantine message (Quarantine)
Bulk email threshold	7	6
Spam detection action	Move message to Junk Email folder (MoveToJmf)	Quarantine message (Quarantine)
Anti-phishing policy		
Identified by spoof intelligence	Move message to Junk Email folder (MoveToJmf)	Quarantine message (Quarantine)
Impersonated user detected	Move message to Junk Email folder (MoveToJmf)	Quarantine message (Quarantine)
Phishing email threshold	3—More aggressive (3)	4—Most aggressive (4)
Safe attachments policy	No difference	No difference
Safe links policy	No difference	No difference

The differences and the stricter approach are clearly visible.

When a recipient is defined in multiple policies, the policies are applied in the following order:

- The Strict Preset Security Policy
- The Standard Preset Security Policy

- Defender for Office 365 evaluation policies (when applicable)

- Custom policies based on the priority of the policy (a lower number indicates a higher priority)

In other words, the settings of the Strict Preset Security Policy override the settings of the Standard Preset Security Policy, which overrides the settings from any anti-phishing, safe links, or safe attachments evaluation policies.

Directory-Based Edge Blocking (DBEB)

Directory-Based Edge Blocking is a service in Exchange Online Protection that automatically blocks recipients that are unknown to Exchange Online or Exchange Online Protection. It works both for mailboxes in Exchange Online and for mailboxes in Exchange 2019 that are protected by Exchange Online Protection.

When a message is blocked by DBEB, which happens before any filtering takes place, a non-delivery report is generated with the following error:

```
550 5.4.1 Recipient address rejected: Access denied.
```

Note   If you are in an Exchange-Only environment with all mailboxes in Exchange Online and no migration or hybrid scenario, DBEB is already in place.

If you are in hybrid scenario, things are a bit different. First, make sure the MX record for your domain points to Exchange Online Protection. Incoming mail must be routed here first. For DBEB to be effective, the accepted domain must be set to Authoritative. If it is set to InternalRelay, unknown recipients are forwarded using a Send Connector to Exchange 2019. And when in a hybrid configuration, this is the Send Connector created by the Hybrid Configuration Wizard.

All recipients must be known to Exchange Online Protection, so you must make sure that all recipients from Exchange 2019 are synchronized to Azure AD. From there, recipients are synchronized with Exchange Online.

Note   Azure AD Connect does not synchronize dynamic Distribution Groups to Azure Active Directory. As such, these are unknown to Exchange Online Protection and are blocked by DBEB. A similar situation is true when running public folders in Exchange 2019. There is a script called **Sync-MailPublicFolders.ps1** that synchronizes mail-enabled public folders in Exchange 2019 with Exchange Online. The problem is that these are not synced from Exchange Online to Azure AD. DBEB gets its information from Azure AD, and synchronized mail-enabled public folders are therefore blocked by DBEB. So, when running public folders in Exchange 2019, leave the accepted domain in Exchange Online to InternalRelay.

Summary

Message hygiene is performed by Exchange Online Protection and, when you have sufficient licenses, Microsoft Defender for Office 365. Exchange Online Protection is automatically included with every Exchange Online license, but Exchange Online Protection can also be purchased as a standalone message hygiene solution for on-premises Exchange 2019.

Exchange Online Protection protects inbound messages in a series of steps:

- Connection filtering with an IP allow list, an IP block list, and the Tenant Allow/Block Lists (TABL)

- Antimalware, where attachments are scanned for malicious documents

- Content filtering, which consists of anti-spam and anti-phishing measures

Besides these, Exchange Online Protection can also configure **preset security policies**, a set of predefined policies that can protect your environment without any additional configuration.

Directory-Based Edge Blocking is the Exchange Online Protection implementation of recipient filtering. All recipients in Exchange Online are automatically defined as valid recipients. When a recipient is not found, the inbound messages are blocked at the edge of Exchange Online Protection.

CHAPTER 9

Authentication

Organizations running Exchange on-premises usually have it running
as part of their business-critical infrastructure, whether it is Exchange
as part of their 24/7 infrastructure hosting mailboxes or public folders
or Exchange hybrid for managing mail recipients and handling mail
flow from or to Office 365. In both cases, there are uptime requirements,
and these requirements cannot be met without having the environment
properly secured.

Since Exchange 2007, Microsoft has positioned Exchange Server as
"secure by default." With the Trustworthy Computing initiative that started
in 2002, Microsoft began integrating Security Development Lifecycle (SDL)
principles into their development process. These efforts have involved
a security review for each feature and component, during which even
elementary aspects like default settings have been discussed.

Fast forward to 2023, where the preferred architecture principle is
Zero Trust. In the days of Exchange 2007, infrastructure was architected
following a perimeter-based security model using zones such as the
demilitarized zone (DMZ). Nowadays, the best practice is to adopt a Zero
Trust principle, a security framework and approach that assumes that no
user or device should be automatically trusted, whether they are inside or
outside the network perimeter. Instead, Zero Trust emphasizes the need
to verify and authenticate every access request, regardless of the user's
location or the network they are connecting from.

© Jaap Wesselius and Michel de Rooij 2023
J. Wesselius and M. de Rooij, *Pro Exchange Administration*,
https://doi.org/10.1007/978-1-4842-9591-5_9

With a complex product such as Exchange Server, and so intertwined with security matters on other levels, there is always the question of how to cover security. In the previous two chapters, we discussed security-related topics related to transport. In this chapter, we will discuss the following authentication-related security features:

- Hybrid Modern Authentication

- Multifactor authentication

- Conditional Access

- Client Access Rules

- SMTP AUTH

- Certificate Authentication

- Windows Extended Protection

- PowerShell Serialization Payload Signing

Features such as Hybrid Modern Authentication and multifactor authentication are originally designed with connectivity to Azure Active Directory in mind. This means Exchange on-premises can leverage Azure AD for authentication, where Azure AD can perform additional verification steps such as the originating location of the authentication request or enforce certain forms of authentication, such as blockage of basic authentication.

Note   Per Exchange Server 2019 Cumulative Update H1 2023 (CU13), it is also possible to run Exchange on-premises, leveraging AD FS 2019 as a Modern Authentication provider. This enables Modern Authentication support for pure on-premises deployments. There are several restrictions at the time of writing, such as limited client support (Outlook for Windows 16327.20200 or later only). We see it as an early step in offering an alternative to organizations remaining on-premises. More info at **https://bit.ly/ ModernAuthExchangeOnPremOnly**.

Hybrid Modern Authentication

In Chapter 5 we showed how to set up Exchange hybrid, and briefly in Chapter 6, we touched on what is Modern Authentication and what are the benefits of having Modern Authentication (OAuth) configured between on-premises and Office 365, with Azure Active Directory being trusted for authentication and authorization. With the option to hand off authentication and authorization to Azure Active Directory also come Azure Active Directory security features that build on Modern Authentication, such as multifactor authentication (MFA) or Conditional Access policies to provide access based on sign-in conditions or control over data. Perhaps more importantly, you can also start using identity-related (Entra) analytics in Office 365, such as risky sign-ins. However, for that to work, your Exchange on-premises infrastructure needs to use Modern Authentication exclusively. This is where Hybrid Modern Authentication comes into play.

Hybrid Modern Authentication (HMA) was introduced in previous editions of Exchange 2016 (CU8) and Exchange 2013 (CU19) in 2017. In short, HMA allows you to appoint Azure Active Directory as the primary authentication and authorization infrastructure for Exchange on-premises. Instead of supporting Modern Authentication and additionally legacy authentication such as NTLM or basic authentication, Exchange ultimately gets configured to exclusively support Modern Authentication. From a technical perspective, it means Exchange will be configured to consume authentication tokens from Azure Active Directory only.

Caution   Outlook Web Access and Exchange Control Panel cannot be used with HMA only, except when you have AD FS or use Azure App Proxy to publish OWA/ECP. More about publishing Exchange via Azure App Proxy in Chapter 6, or visit **https://bit.ly/ PubAppProxy** for generic instructions.

In order to deploy HMA with Exchange 2019, the following prerequisites should be met:

- Exchange hybrid should be deployed using Full Classic topology; Hybrid Modern or Classic Minimum topologies are not supported. This is described in Chapter 5.

- OAuth should be set up between Exchange on-premises and Exchange Online. This is the default for Exchange 2019, and the Hybrid Configuration Wizard (HCW) should have taken care of this step.

- Accounts should be synchronized to Azure Active Directory, either managed using same sign-on with Password Hash Synchronization (PHS), Pass-Through Authentication (PTA), or federation using AD FS or an alternative Security Token Service (STS) that is supported by Office 365.

- HMA cannot be used together with SSL offloading, as Exchange will be required to perform the encryption. SSL bridging is supported.

- MAPI/HTTP has to be enabled, which it is by default; RPC/HTTP will not work with HMA.

- Clients and services will need to support Modern Authentication (OAuth). This means Outlook 2016 or later, Outlook 2016 for Mac, or Outlook Mobile. Third-party apps such as the native Mail app on iOS (11.3.1 or later), Gmail app on Android, or third-party applications such as Thunderbird that support OAuth could be made to work as well.

- With HMA enabled, legacy authentication will keep functioning provided those authentication mechanisms are still enabled. However, with legacy authentication enabled, organizations will not benefit from the security boundary that is Modern Authentication and HMA in particular.

- Outlook for Mobile clients will leverage the caching mechanism in Exchange Online when HMA is enabled. This means that you need to allow this for HMA to work. More on this later in this section.

- If Exchange servers are sitting behind a proxy, make sure they are able to access Exchange Online, that is, you have InternetWebProxy configured or you allow them passage through your network security device.

Note   While out of support, a quick note for organizations running Outlook 2013 on Windows that it requires the following registry keys to enable OAuth support:

```
HKCU:\SOFTWARE\Microsoft\Office\15.0\Common\
Identity\EnableADAL=1
HKCU:\SOFTWARE\Microsoft\Office\15.0\Common\
Identity\Version=1
```

It is recommended to also enable OAuth for Autodiscover: `HKCU:\`
`Software\Microsoft\Exchange\AlwaysUseMSOAuthForAuto`
`Discover=1`

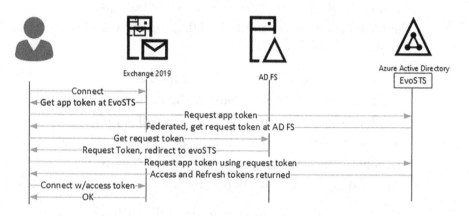

Figure 9-1. *Hybrid Modern Authentication with AD FS*

Before we dive into configuring Hybrid Modern Authentication, it
helps to get an understanding of how an authentication workflow with
HMA is set up. Figure 9-1 displays this process when using AD FS. We will
briefly walk you through its steps, also noting what happens for managed
domains, that is, when AD FS is not used. Note that there are no cached
tokens, and integrated authentication has been disabled in this example:

1) The user uses a client that supports Modern
   Authentication and attempts to connect to
   Exchange on-premises. During connection, the
   client reports it supports Modern Authentication, by
   means of an "**Authorization: Bearer**" header. The
   UPN is supplied as an **X-User-Identity** header.

2) Exchange receives the request, sees the header,
   and returns the URL of the endpoint that the client
   needs to use to retrieve an application token.

3) The client follows the URL and uses it to request an application token, providing the user UPN. Now, when that domain is not federated, the user gets to authenticate with Azure Active Directory and proceeds with step 8.

4) When EvoSTS determines that the domain is federated, it sends the client a redirect to the AD FS infrastructure.

5) The client navigates to the provided AD FS endpoint asking for a request token and needs to authenticate.

6) When the user authenticates successfully with AD FS (password, certificate), a request token is returned, and the client is directed to the EvoSTS.

7) The client uses the request token to request an app token.

8) The client receives an access from the EvoSTS, as well as a refresh token to request subsequent access tokens. Note that at this point any additional prerequisites also need to be satisfied, such as multifactor authentication or Conditional Access rules.

9) The client authenticates to Exchange using the access token.

We will now proceed to have a look at configuring Hybrid Modern Authentication. Configuration consists basically of the following three steps:

First, we need to add the Service Principal Names (SPNs) used by Exchange on-premises to Azure Active Directory. SPNs are used during the authentication and authorization process and require all URLs used within the Exchange on-premises environment to be known to Azure AD, which will become the default authentication method for authentication requests. To collect all URLs involved, use the following commands:

```
$U=  (Get-MapiVirtualDirectory).internalURL
$U+= (Get-MapiVirtualDirectory).externalURL
$U+= (Get-WebServicesVirtualDirectory).internalURL
$U+= (Get-WebServicesVirtualDirectory).externalURL
$U+= (Get-OABVirtualDirectory).internalURL
$U+= Get-OABVirtualDirectory).externalURL
$U+= (Get-AutodiscoverVirtualDirectory).internalURL
$U+= (Get-AutodiscoverVirtualDirectory).externalURL
$U+= (Get-ClientAccessService).AutodiscoverServiceInternalUri
$U | Where-Object {$_.Scheme -eq 'https'} |Select-Object
    -Unique Authority
```

This will collect all configured external and internal URLs on relevant endpoints, pick only those using HTTPS, and then return the unique set of entries. When you have only mail.contoso.com and autodiscover.contoso.com in use at your organization, this will return only mail.contoso.com and autodiscover.com. Another trick is to have a look at the certificate and collect all SANs, as that might return the requested information as well.

Note   If your Exchange deployment is connected to multiple tenants, you need to add these SPNs to every tenant that Exchange on-premises is configured in hybrid with.

We then need to verify these SPNs are configured in Azure AD. For this, we need to use the PowerShell Graph SDK module and first need to connect to it, providing the scope required to make changes later:

```
Import-Module Microsoft.Graph.Applications
Connect-MgGraph -Scopes Application.Read.All,Application.
ReadWrite.All,Directory.Read.All,Directory.ReadWrite.All
```

The AppId related to Exchange Online is 00000002-0000-0ff1-ce00-000000000000, so we can check the currently configured Service Principal Names using

```
Get-MgServicePrincipal -Search AppId:00000002-0000-0ff1-
ce00-000000000000 -ConsistencyLevel Eventual |
select -ExpandProperty ServicePrincipalNames
```

If the names collected from ExternalURL and InternalURL are not present yet, you need to add them to this list. Unfortunately, Update-MgServicePrincipal does not offer add/remove using hash tables, so we need to resort to a less gracious method:

```
$SP= Get-MgServicePrincipal -Search AppId:00000002-0000-0ff1-
ce00-000000000000 -ConsistencyLevel Eventual
Update-MgServicePrincipal -ServicePrincipalId $SP.Id -AppId
$SP.AppId -ServicePrincipalNames ($SP.ServicePrincipalNames +
'https://mail.contoso.com/')
```

Replace "mail.contoso.com" with every name collected from the ExternalURL and InternalURL values earlier.

Note   Like with any cloud-related operation, it might take a few moments for your change to become visible.

Next, verify OAuth is configured on relevant virtual directories in your Exchange on-premises environment. For Exchange 2019 this should already be the case or already been taken care of by the HCW, but it can never hurt to check:

```
Get-MapiVirtualDirectory | FL server,*url*,*auth*
Get-WebServicesVirtualDirectory | FL server,*url*,*oauth*
Get-OABVirtualDirectory | FL server,*url*,*oauth*
Get-AutoDiscoverVirtualDirectory | FL server,*oauth*
```

If any of the reported authentication methods does not indicate it is configured for OAuth, configure it using Set-MapiVirtualDirectory or other related cmdlets, depending on the type of virtual directory.

When everything is found to be configured correctly, we can activate HMA. Enabling HMA consists of two steps:

1) Configure the default authorization endpoint for Exchange on-premises. This can be accomplished by

    ```
    Set-AuthServer -Identity 'EvoSTS -
    <Guid>' -IsDefaultAuthorizationEndpoint $true
    ```

    where <Guid> is the Guid of your tenant organization. You can also derive this from the Get-IntraOrganizationConnector identity or have a look at the AuthServer's DomainName attribute to pick the right one.

Note   The default AuthServer 'EvoSTS - <Guid>' is created by the HCW. If you upgraded your hybrid deployment running older Exchange versions, your AuthServer configuration might still be called "EvoSTS" only.

---

2) Configure Exchange to start supporting clients using OAuth. This can be accomplished by

```
Set-OrganizationConfig -OAuth2Client
ProfileEnabled $true
```

After turning HMA on, it might take a short while for Exchange and clients to pick up new settings, and clients such as Outlook need a restart for the new authentication flow to become effective.

To validate HMA deployment from the back end, you can use a script called Test-EASHMA.ps1. It is available from the GitHub repository from Exchange Support and can be downloaded directly from **https://bit.ly/ TestEASHMA**. After downloading the script, run

```
.\Test-EASHMA.ps1 <User ID>
```

where User ID is the primary email address of an on-premises mailbox. Without additional parameters, the script will follow basic Autodiscover and bearer tests. The output should look something like Figure 9-2.

```
[PS] > C:\Tools>.\Test-HMAEAS.ps1 jaap@contoso.com

We sent an AutoDiscover Request to On-Premises for the Exchange ActiveSync Virtual Directory and below is the
response
The response should contain the Protocol ActiveSync with a valid URL
-----------------------------------------------------------------------------------------------------------------
https://mail.contoso.com/Microsoft-Server-ActiveSync

We sent an Empty Bearer Token Request to the On-Premises Exchange ActiveSync Virtual Directory and below is the
response
The response should contain a valid WWW-Authenticate=Bearer. Make sure the authorization_uri is populated
-----------------------------------------------------------------------------------------------------------------
request-id=bbfb885c-ec8b-47a4-814f-7c649799ab53
X-OWA-Version=15.2.1118.26
X-FEServer=EXCH01
Server=Microsoft-IIS/10.0
WWW-Authenticate=Bearer client_id="00000002-0000-0ff1-ce00-000000000000", trusted_issuers="00000001-0000-
0000-c000-000000000000@23091a2c-c494-48d9-a2b5-32c9d88d38b3", token_types="app_asserted_user_v1
service_asserted_app_v1", authorization_uri="https://login.windows.net/common/oauth2/authorize",Basic
realm="mail.contoso.com"
X-Powered-By=ASP.NET
Date=Sat, 18 May 2023 13:28:34 GMT
Content-Length=0


Autodetect has the following services listed for the user
This should have AAD pointing to Microsoft Online and On-Premises to the correct EAS URL
-----------------------------------------------------------------------------------------------------------------
Service:    office365
Protocol:   rest
Hostname:   outlook.office.com
Azure AD:   https://login.microsoftonline.com/common/oauth2/authorize
On-Premises: https://mail.contoso.com/Microsoft-Server-ActiveSync
```

Figure 9-2. *Test-EASHMA.ps1 testing output*

In the output, it is shown that Azure AD points to login.
microsoftonline.com and on-premises points to the Exchange on-premises
endpoint, so we're good to go.

You can perform a more thorough Exchange ActiveSync test by
specifying the additional -TestEAS switch, for example:

```
.\Test-EASHMA.ps1 <User ID> -TestEAS
```

Caution   If you have been experimenting with Azure AD authentication, make sure you have not disabled ActiveSync for this test. If you have been restricting applications that can access Office 365 data on behalf of a user, applications or scripts such as Test-EASHMA.ps1 may fail authentication because of these restrictions. Also, keep in mind admin and user consent configuration. More on this at **https://bit.ly/ConsentConfig**.

When using Outlook for Desktop, you can easily check if you are using Modern Authentication by pressing CTRL and right-clicking the Outlook icon in the system tray. This will display a small menu, in which you need to select **Connection Status**. After this, something similar to Figure 9-3 should show up.

CID	SMTP Ad...	D	P	Server name	Status	Protocol	Authn	Encrypt	RPCPort	Type	Req/Fail	Avg Resp	Avg Proc	Sess Type	Inte
23	Jaap@m...			https://mail.myexchangela...	Established	HTTP	Bearer*	SSL		Exchange Directory	15/0	88	57	Foreground	Eth
25	Jaap@m...		J	https://mail.myexchangela...	Established	HTTP	Bearer*	SSL		Exchange Mail	184/0	135	24	Foreground	Eth
37	Jaap@m...		J	https://mail.myexchangela...	Established	HTTP	Bearer*	SSL		Exchange Mail	127/1			Cache	Eth
30	Jaap@m...			https://mail.myexchangela...	Established	HTTP	Bearer*	SSL		Exchange Directory	1/0	62		Background	Eth

Figure 9-3. *Outlook Connection Status when using Modern Authentication*

The column "Authn" showing Bearer* is evidence that Modern Authentication is used. Note that in the example, cached mode is enabled, which creates multiple sessions (column Sess Type) per configured mailbox. The actual set may vary, depending on if you have also enabled caching of shared mailboxes, for example.

The behavior of clients that need to switch to Modern Authentication depends on the client. Outlook for Desktop will in principle switch gracefully after a restart and reauthentication because it will need to start working with tokens instead of the current set of credentials, that is, integrated or (saved) basic authentication. The same applies to Outlook for Mobile and iOS Mail per iOS version 15.6. Other mail clients or usage of profile management software, which manages profiles on managed devices or manually configured profiles not using Autodiscover during setup, might result in the need to recreate the profile or modify the profiles via device management, such as Intune.

When using Modern Authentication/OAuth with third-party clients, you need to register those as Enterprise Applications in Azure AD. The next section will shortly describe this process.

Caution   Before enabling HMA, be aware that if you have configured any Conditional Access policies, those immediately start to apply to users with mailboxes hosted in Exchange on-premises using clients supporting Modern Authentication. Anticipate the move for those users before making the switch.

Should circumstances arise that you need to disable HMA, you can do so by undoing the AuthServer configuration step, for example:

```
Set-AuthServer -Identity 'EvoSTS - <Guid>' -IsDefault
AuthorizationEndpoint $false
```

Optionally, you can also disable OAuth for clients that support it, but that is usually not required as Modern Authentication needs AuthServer as default for this to become decisive:

```
Set-OrganizationConfig -OAuth2ClientProfileEnabled $false
```

The other changes were usually already in place or complementary to existing configuration. You only need to undo them if you consider dismantling Modern Authentication functionality completely, but since this authentication method is the way forward, that is an unlikely scenario.

Tip   When you encounter issues with HMA, perhaps when running the Test-EASHMA.ps1 script, the Exchange Remote Connectivity Analyzer contains an **Outlook Mobile Hybrid Modern Authentication** module for configuration and connectivity tests. RCA can be accessed at **https://exrca.com**.

Now with OAuth being enabled and Azure Active Directory being the default authentication, be advised that legacy authentication is still configured for the virtual directories. You might leave those enabled, but you also might wish to start disabling basic authentication, especially for mobile clients.

For Outlook Mobile, you can leverage Device Access Rules. With basic authentication enabled, Outlook Mobile devices will report as device model **Outlook for iOS and Android**. When HMA is enabled and the Outlook for Mobile profile has been recreated, all inbound traffic for Outlook Mobile will use the caching engine in Office 365 and therefore will report as device type **OutlookService** in Exchange on-premises device logging.

To set up a Device Access Rule to block direct access by "Outlook for iOS and Android" devices:

```
New-ActiveSyncDeviceAccessRule -Characteristic DeviceModel
-QueryString 'Outlook for iOS and Android' -AccessLevel Block
```

To set up a Device Access Rule to allow "OutlookService" devices:

```
New-ActiveSyncDeviceAccessRule -Characteristic DeviceType
-QueryString 'OutlookService' -AccessLevel Allow
```

Note   Due to the architecture of Outlook for Mobile, if those clients use HMA, their traffic will be channeled through the caching service in Office 365. Evidence of this is traffic coming in from **52.125.128.0/20** and **52.127.96.0/23**, and the user agent for this traffic will report as **OutlookService**.

Eventually, you may wish to lock out basic authentication altogether on-premises in Exchange 2019 by means of an Authentication Policy. The default policy will allow basic authentication, but we can create a new one that will block basic authentication for all protocols.

Then, when the switchover to Modern Authentication–only is to be made, configure this new policy as default. This will also allow you to easily switch back, in case you missed a legacy application that still requires basic authentication, for example, and you need to re-enable it for the whole population.

To create a new Authentication Policy that blocks basic authentication for all protocols, use

```
$Param= @{
    BlockLegacyAuthActiveSync= $True
    BlockLegacyAuthAutodiscover= $True
    BlockLegacyAuthImap= $True
    BlockLegacyAuthMapi= $True
    BlockLegacyAuthOfflineAddressBook= $True
    BlockLegacyAuthPop= $True
    BlockLegacyAuthRpc= $True
    BlockLegacyAuthWebServices= $True
}
New-AuthenticationPolicy -Name 'Block Basic Auth' @Param
```

Tip   When using a long list of parameters, you can use a PowerShell technique called splatting as demonstrated earlier. This provides improved readability over long lines of parameters or (worse) using back ticks (`) as line breaks.

After creating an Authentication Policy, you then assign it to users, which is ideal for testing purposes:

```
Set-User -Identity <ID> -AuthenticationPolicy 'Block Basic Auth'
```

When you are done testing or are confident you can enable it for the whole organization, you can set the policy as the organization-wide default policy:

```
Set-OrganizationConfig -DefaultAuthenticationPolicy 'Block Basic Auth'
```

Should you wish to revert to the previous Authentication Policy, by default named OrgWideDefault, use

```
Set-OrganizationConfig -DefaultAuthenticationPolicy 'OrgWideDefault'
```

Note   Early 2023, the process started to disable basic authentication in Exchange Online for all tenants as a security measure. A sole exception to this program is SMTP AUTH, which still can use basic authentication; more on that later in this chapter. While deprecated, you might still encounter artefacts in Exchange Online; however, the wording is reversed, for example, AllowBasicAuthPop instead of BlockLegacyAuthPop.

Caution   Blocking legacy authentication in Exchange on-premises blocks **all** legacy authentication methods, including NTLM, for example. Be aware of this when you still need to migrate mailboxes, as MRS does not support OAuth.

Configuring an Enterprise Application

When using Modern Authentication/OAuth with third-party clients, you need to register those as Enterprise Applications in Azure AD. This is also where permissions for the application are granted. You can require additional restrictions and provide consent for users to allow them to use this application with Office 365 services.

Table 9-1. *Some Common Enterprise Applications*

Application	Application ID
Thunderbird	08162f7c-0fd2-4200-a84a-f25a4db0b584
Gmail app	2cee05de-2b8f-45a2-8289-2a06ca32c4c8
Apple Mail app(shows as iOS Accounts or Apple Internet Accounts)	f8d98a96-0999-43f5-8af3-69971c7bb423

The instructions for registering an Enterprise Application are as follows:

1. As an admin, open the Azure portal on **portal. azure.com**, navigate to Azure Active Directory, and select **Enterprise Applications**.

2. If somebody tried using the application before, it might already be present in the list of applications. Consult Table 9-1 and see if the application is already there. If not, you need to register it yourself. The easiest way to register the application is to construct a URL in the following format: **https:// login.microsoftonline.com/<TenantID>/oauth2/ authorize?client_id=<AppID>&response_ type=code&prompt=admin_consent**, where TenantID is your tenant ID and AppID is the ID of

the application (again, see Table 9-1 for examples). If all goes well, you will be presented with a dialog similar to the ones shown in Figure 9-4, asking you to provide consent for this application for the whole organization. Click **Accept** to agree.

3. Go to the Enterprise Application overview and open the application configuration, and click **Permissions**.

4. Depending on the application, you will find permissions have already been preconfigured when using the admin_content URL from step 2. For Thunderbird, for example, you will find Graph-delegated permissions have been configured for **IMAP.AccessAsUser.All**, **POP.AccessAsUser.All**, **SMTP.Send**, and **User.Read**. If your organization does not allow POP usage, you could remove the permission here to prevent Thunderbird users from using POP. Other applications using other protocols, such as Apple's Mail app that uses ActiveSync and Exchange Web Services, might show different preconfigured permissions such as **EAS.AccessAsUser.All**, **EWS.AccessAsUser.All**, and **User.Read**.

5. If the application is not listed or the application ID is unknown, try to configure it, and consult the Azure AD sign-in logs for log-in attempts helping you discover the ID you need to use for known applications.

The application is now made known in Azure AD and given consent and permission, and you are done.

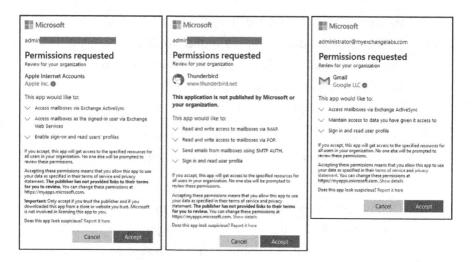

Figure 9-4. *Enterprise Application consent screens*

Multifactor Authentication

In general, authentication is based on something you know (e.g., your password), something you have (e.g., security token or smart card), or who you are (biometrics). By having two factors instead of one, the identities are more secure than they would be otherwise, as it creates an additional layer of protection on top of passwords, for example. *Multifactor authentication* (MFA) is the term used for this form of authentication, where users identify themselves by using more than one factor. Also, factors can be tied to managed devices with fingerprint matching or facial recognition, which are biometrics Windows Hello for Business can use to authenticate users and guard against potential spoofing.

Multifactor authentication should be considered for anyone accessing data and services, not only for administrator-type accounts. Studies have indicated that accounts are 99.9% more likely to be compromised when not using MFA. Also consider the targeted phishing and social hacking attempts to compromise C-level accounts alone. It is one of the reasons behind Microsoft's program to only allow Modern Authentication for Exchange Online, which is a requirement for MFA.

Note   Microsoft also had their own MFA server solution for running an MFA server on-premises. MFA Server will be deprecated at the end of September 30, 2024, when MFA Server will no longer service MFA requests. Organizations are requested to migrate to other MFA solutions, such as the Azure AD MFA service. For information on how to migrate from MFA Server, see **https://bit.ly/ MFAServerMigration**.

In Azure AD, with MFA enabled, users need to authorize their sign-in by confirming their identity through what is called an authentication method. The methods shown in Table 9-2 are available, together with how Microsoft grades them regarding strength, usability, and availability.

Table 9-2. *Azure AD Authentication Methods*

Authentication Method	Security	Usability	Availability
Password	Low	High	High
Voice	Medium	Medium	Medium
SMS	Medium	High	Medium
OATH software	Medium	Medium	High
OATH hardware (preview)	Medium	Medium	High
Certificate-based authentication (preview)	High	High	High
FIDO2 security key	High	High	High
Microsoft Authenticator app	High	High	High
Windows Hello for Business	High	High	High

While helpful, the fact is most organizations are still not using MFA to protect their accounts. Despite all the initiatives by Microsoft and the security world, Microsoft saw MFA protection of their Azure AD accounts jump from 1.8% in 2018 to 26.64% in 2022. It is progress, but still a minority, which should be worrying in today's world of leaks followed by password sprays and phishing campaigns. Therefore, SMS as MFA is still better than no MFA.

Another way to look at this is looking at the combination of methods, as most people still use passwords in combination with SMS or the Authenticator app. In order of increased security strength, this leads to the following categorization:

- *MFA*: Password plus mobile phone or office phone number for receiving authorization codes through voice call or SMS message

- *Password-less MFA*: Authenticator app password-less (phone sign-in) or password plus OATH One-Time Password (software or hardware) or password plus Authenticator with number matching

- *Phishing-resistant MFA*: Windows Hello for Business, FIDO2 security key, or certificate-based authentication

The Authenticator app Microsoft provides is available for iOS and Android. An Authenticator app should be considered an adequate security option, in balance with being manageable and convenient for end users as well. Number matching, where Authenticator app authentication approvals need users to match presented numbers, is now enabled for all Azure AD tenants. This is done to an increasing phenomenon known as MFA fatigue, where bad actors knowing user passwords spam users with authentication challenges hoping they get tired of approval requests they need to approve and at some point "just press Approve," after which the bad actor gets signed in.

Phone numbers for voice or text validation are considered insecure nowadays, as phone numbers can be spoofed. However, passwords with text messages are still a better option than passwords only.

Tip   The recommendation is to have a break-glass global admin account that is exempt from MFA rules or may sign in without MFA, for example, when that sign-in is performed from a trusted location using Conditional Access. That way, when needed, an admin can still perform administrative tasks when MFA is not possible due to a lost phone, or in case there are issues with Azure AD authentication.

The MFA feature is part of the Office 365 offering. Licensing requirements and features depend on your current subscription plan and what features your organization requires. While all Azure AD plans offer some form of MFA-related options, specific MFA-related features require an Azure AD Premium 1 or Premium 2 license:

Azure AD Free

- Protect all tenant users using Security Defaults.

- Users:

  - Use a mobile app as an additional authentication method.

- Global administrators:

  - Use Authenticator app, voice call, or SMS as an authentication method.

  - Remember MFA for trusted devices.

- Admin controls over global administrators' authentication methods.

Azure AD P1 or P2

Same MFA-related features as Azure AD Free, plus

- Admin controls over authentication methods.

- Users' extra options:

  - Voice call or SMS as an authentication method.

  - Remember MFA on trusted devices.

- Fraud alerting option.

- MFA reports, for example, usage, authentication methods.

- Additional configuration for a voice call method:

  - Custom call greeting

  - Custom Caller ID (US numbers only)

- Support MFA for on-premises applications.

While the feature set for Azure AD Free is rudimentary, it does provide organizations a basic level of protection for everyone, with few additional options for those with the global administrator role.

Do note that in addition to this all-or-nothing (Azure AD Free) or "per-user" configuration, organizations using Azure P1/P2 licenses will have additional options to require MFA, through Conditional Access policies, for example. This brings the full features of CA policies to MFA management, such as triggering MFA based on sign-in location, applying to groups, exclusions, etc.

Caution   Security Defaults is an all-or-nothing option. Its underlying policy is fixed and cannot be customized to suit your needs, serving as a starting point for organizations. When desired, Azure AD P1 or P2 licensing can be assigned to tailor MFA and related features such as Conditional Access and privileged access management.

To enable Security Defaults or inspect its status, navigate to the Azure portal, then open the blade at **Active Directory ➤ Azure Active Directory ➤ Properties**, and click the **Manage security defaults** link at the bottom. Be advised that enabling Security Defaults not only configures MFA for users and administrators but will also block legacy authentication methods, such as basic authentication.

Note   When enabling Security Defaults, the account used by AD Connect will be excluded from MFA.

To enable MFA for a user, there is an option in the Azure AD portal that can be found when you navigate to **portal.azure.com** and open **Azure Active Directory ➤ Users**. There, after selecting one or more users, you will find the option **Per-User MFA**. However, using this option is no longer the preferred option for using MFA, and this is why it sometimes is now referred to as the legacy MFA option. Most organizations have Azure AD P1 or P2, which makes using Conditional Access the preferred alternative. More on Conditional Access later in this chapter.

Should organizations have reasons to not use Security Defaults and they do not own Azure AD P1 or P2 licenses, they can still use the Per-User MFA option (legacy MFA). The downside to this is that it is only manageable through this web panel or PowerShell, and users are prompted for MFA every login. What comes to mind might be high-privileged accounts that need explicit MFA configuration.

Enable users for legacy MFA, which will trigger the enrollment process for them, if they have not enrolled already. You can also manage their user-related settings, which can trigger predefined actions:

- Require selected users to provide authentication methods again. When users are MFA enrolled, this forces them to update current authentication methods.

- Delete all existing app passwords generated by the selected users. This forces users to recreate app passwords for applications that do not support Modern Authentication. Since app passwords are strongly discouraged, you should never have to use this option.

- Restore multifactor authentication on all remembered devices, forcing users to use MFA again on devices on which they selected the "Remember Me" option. This option is controlled by the MFA Service Settings, configurable via **Azure Active Directory** ➤ **Users** ➤ **Per-User MFA** and selecting the **Service settings** view.

Note that when users are MFA enabled, apart from disabling them for MFA, you can also enforce them to use MFA. This can be achieved by selecting MFA-enabled users and selecting **Enforce**. Note that users can then only use applications that support Modern Authentication.

When you have enabled a user for multifactor authentication, that user needs to complete the enrollment process. The process is initiated when the user tries to access Office 365 resources. Alternatively, you can direct the user to **http://aka.ms/MFASetup**, where the user can complete the initial setup process. Administrators can configure custom MFA settings, such as fraud alert or custom greetings, from the Azure AD portal, via the blade at **Azure Active Directory** ➤ **Security** ➤ **MFA**.

Tip   When you want to manage the sign-in frequency of users using Conditional Access, make sure you disable the **Remember multifactor authentication on trusted device** in the legacy MFA configuration panel. Not doing so might create unexpected reauthentication prompts, as legacy MFA uses a persistent cookie to keep track of the session lifetime, while Conditional Access performs its own checks. Also, it overrides the behavior of applications such as Outlook that will only prompt every 90 days by default.

When required, administrators can manage legacy MFA user settings using PowerShell. Managing MFA this way not only allows organizations to easily configure MFA for existing users or in bulk but also to enhance the current provisioning process with MFA options. For example, by pre-populating contact methods and phone numbers, administrators can prevent users from having to enter their mobile phone or office number for verification.

Many blogs and information online still refer to using the PowerShell Microsoft Online module (MSOnline) for this. However, this module became unsupported in July 2023. This does not mean things stopped working; it just means things might break over time, also when used with more recent versions of PowerShell, for example. The recommended way to proceed is to use the PowerShell Graph SDK, already mentioned earlier in this chapter.

To manage the MFA methods, we only need the Identity SignIns module:

```
Install-module Microsoft.Graph.Identity.Signins
Connect-MgGraph -Scopes UserAuthenticationMethod.ReadWrite.All
Select-MgProfile -Name beta
```

To view users' currently configured authentication methods, use

```
[PS] > Get-MgUserAuthenticationMethod -UserId juliana@contoso.com
| select -ExpandProperty AdditionalProperties

Key              Value
---              -----
@odata.type      #microsoft.graph.phoneAuthenticationMethod
phoneNumber      +31 12345678
phoneType        mobile
smsSignInState   notAllowedByPolicy
@odata.type      #microsoft.graph.emailAuthenticationMethod
emailAddress     juliana@contoso.com
@odata.type      #microsoft.graph.passwordAuthenticationMethod
@odata.type      #microsoft.graph.windowsHelloForBusiness
                 AuthenticationMethod
displayName      LAPTOPJ
createdDateTime  2022-02-21T08:13:32Z
keyStrength      unknown
@odata.type      #microsoft.graph.microsoftAuthenticator
                 AuthenticationMethod
displayName      Ju's iPhone
deviceTag        tag
phoneAppVersion  3.4.2
clientAppName    microsoftAuthenticator
@odata.type      #microsoft.graph.softwareOathAuthenticationMethod
```

The "@odata.type" values show there are currently methods defined for phone authentication, email, password, Hello, Authenticator app, and software OATH OTP.

Note   Email authentication can be used for self-service password resets; it is not meant for MFA authentication.

Some details are also included, but you can also use one of the method-specific retrieval cmdlets, which are shown when you use Get-Command Get-MgUserAuthentication* | Select Name. It will show there is a cmdlet to retrieve the phone authentication method properties, for example:

```
[PS] > Get-MgUserAuthenticationPhoneMethod -UserId juliana@contoso.com

Id                                    PhoneNumber   PhoneType SmsSignInState
--                                    -----------   --------- --------------
3179e48a-750b-4051-897c-87b9720928f7 +31 12345678  mobile    notAllowedByPolicy
```

To add a method, use the related New-MgUserAuthentication* cmdlet, or use Update-MgUserAuthentication* to update a specific one, for example:

```
[PS] > New-MgUserAuthenticationPhoneMethod -UserId juliana
@contoso.com -phoneType mobile -phoneNumber '+31234567890'

[PS] > $PhoneMethod= Get-MgUserAuthenticationPhoneMethod -UserId
juliana@contoso.com
[PS] > Update-MgUserAuthenticationPhoneMethod -UserId juliana
@contoso.com -PhoneAuthenticationMethodId $PhoneMethod.Id
-phoneNumber '+31345678901'
```

Unfortunately, there is no way to enforce/enable/disable legacy MFA for users using PowerShell Graph SDK. We do not know if that is on the roadmap and have our doubt if it will ever arrive. The MSOnline PowerShell module, which supports this task (search for the term Set-MsolUser together with StrongAuthenticationRequirements), is going away soon. Also, Conditional Access, the recommended way to enforce MFA, is supported in the PowerShell Graph SDK through the *-MgIdentityConditionalAccessPolicy cmdlets.

After a while, administrators might want to create a report on which MFA methods are in use by which users. A simple script to accomplish this is found in Figure 9-5.

```
Get-MgUser | ForEach-Object {
  $Methods= Get-MgUserAuthenticationMethod -UserId $_.UserPrincipalName
  $Item= [PSCustomObject]@{
    Id= $_.UserPrincipalName
    Status= $False
    authApp= $null; authDevice= $null
    phoneAuth= $null; authPhoneNum= $null
    fido= $null; fidoDetails= $null
    helloForBusiness= $null; helloForBusinessDetails= $null
    emailAuth= $null; SSPREmail= $null
    tempPass= $null; tempPassDetails= $null
    passwordLess= $null; passwordLessDetails= $null
    softwareAuth= $null
  }
  ForEach( $Method in $Methods) {
    Switch ( $Method.AdditionalProperties["@odata.type"]) {
      "#microsoft.graph.microsoftAuthenticatorAuthenticationMethod" {
        $Item.authApp = $true
        $Item.authDevice = $method.AdditionalProperties["displayName"]
        $Item.Status= $True
      }
      "#microsoft.graph.phoneAuthenticationMethod" {
        $Item.phoneAuth = $true
        $Item.authPhoneNum= $method.AdditionalProperties["phoneType", "phoneNumber"] -join ' '
        $Item.Status= $True
      }
      "#microsoft.graph.fido2AuthenticationMethod" {
        $Item.fido = $true
        $Item.fidoDetails = $method.AdditionalProperties["model"]
        $Item.Status= $True
      }
      "#microsoft.graph.passwordAuthenticationMethod" {
        # Nothing to do here
      }
      "#microsoft.graph.windowsHelloForBusinessAuthenticationMethod" {
        $Item.helloForBusiness = $true
        $Item.helloForBusinessDetails = $method.AdditionalProperties["displayName"]
        $Item.Status= $True
      }
      "#microsoft.graph.emailAuthenticationMethod" {
        $Item.emailAuth = $true
        $Item.SSPREmail = $method.AdditionalProperties["emailAddress"]
        $Item.Status= $True
      }
      "microsoft.graph.temporaryAccessPassAuthenticationMethod" {
        $Item.tempPass = $true
        $Item.tempPassDetails = $method.AdditionalProperties["lifetimeInMinutes"]
        $Item.Status= $True
      }
      "#microsoft.graph.passwordlessMicrosoftAuthenticatorAuthenticationMethod" {
        $Item.passwordLess = $true
        $Item.passwordLessDetails = $method.AdditionalProperties["displayName"]
        $Item.Status= $True
      }
      "#microsoft.graph.softwareOathAuthenticationMethod" {
        $Item.softwareAuth = $true
        $Item.Status= $True
      }
    }
  }
  $Item
}
```

Figure 9-5. *Multifactor authentication method report script*

Sample output is shown in the following:

```
[PS] >.\MFAReport.ps1 | select Id,Status,authApp,PhoneAuth

Id                              Status authApp phoneAuth
--                              ------ ------- ---------
administrator@contoso.com       True   True
francis@contoso.com             False
jaap@contoso.com                True
juliana@contoso.com             True             True
```

Conditional Access

In Azure Active Directory (Azure AD), Conditional Access is a feature
that allows you to enforce specific access controls and security policies
based on certain conditions. It helps you protect data by allowing or
denying access based on factors such as users being authenticated using
multifactor authentication, but also conditions such as user location,
group membership, or device compliancy.

Note   Microsoft is moving things around for the new label of
everything identity-related, Entra. At time of proofing this book,
Microsoft rebranded all Azure AD related products and features as
well as licensing to Entra, for example Azure AD became Entra ID.
This means you will find configuration elements such as Conditional
Access in the Entra portal as well. The Entra portal is accessed via
https://entra.microsoft.com.

The subject of Azure AD's Conditional Access can be a book in
itself and more of an Azure AD topic rather than something for an
Exchange on-premises book. However, we would still like to touch on
some of its aspects, as earlier in this chapter we talked about multifactor

authentication, where we mentioned that Conditional Access is the preferred method to enforce MFA compared with MFA legacy (Per-User MFA). It also comes with additional benefits in the form of other Conditional Access features, that is, provided you have the proper license in place, which is Azure AD P1 at minimum. If you have Azure AD P2, you have additional features available to you, such as risk-based Conditional Access and Identity Protection.

Tip   An actual overview of Azure Active Directory plans and pricing can be found at **https://bit.ly/AADPlans**.

In this example, we will create a Conditional Access policy requiring users of a specific group (MFAGroup1 in this example) to use multifactor authentication when authenticating.

1) To create a Conditional Access policy to require MFA, open up the Azure AD portal.

2) Navigate to **Azure Active Directory ➤ Security ➤ Conditional Access**. Here you can create your own policy or use one of the templates as a starting point. For this example, we will create one manually by selecting **Create new policy**.

3) Give the policy a proper name, like **Require MFA for MFAGroup1 users**.

4) Assign the policy to specific **Users**, selecting **Include ➤ Select users and groups ➤ Users and Groups**, after which you need to pick the group **MFAGroup1** (the dialog only shows the first 50 entries, so you may need to type its first few characters).

5) Have the policy apply to all **Cloud apps or actions**
    (this will also apply to your Exchange on-premises
    when configured in Hybrid Modern Authentication),
    selecting **Include ➤ All cloud apps**.

Caution   Take note of the warning about locking yourself out, as
that might easily happen when experimenting too much with all the
Conditional Access options. In that case, know that it is possible to
have Conditional Access rules run in report-only mode instead of
active enforcement.

---

6) At this point we are not configuring conditions
    yet. We are going to require MFA, which is done at
    Grant. Select **Grant Access**, and check the **Require
    authentication strength** option, selecting the
    Multifactor authentication in the dropdown list.
    Click **Select** to confirm.

7) If you want to enforce this policy, set **Enable policy**
    on. Alternatively, you can leave it on **Report-only**
    to have it report when it would trigger in the Azure
    Sign-In view, which can be found at **Azure Active
    Directory ➤ Sign-In Logs**.

8) Finally, click **Create** to save this policy.

And that is all there is to it. You have now effectively required
members of the MFAGroup1 to authenticate using MFA, which is more
convenient than the legacy MFA where you have to configure MFA at the
individual level.

Note   The multifactor authentication strength is preconfigured and cannot be customized. You can create your own strength, removing unwanted methods, going to **Conditional Access ➤ Authentication Strength**. For example, if you want users to only have the option to use passwords plus software OATH OTP, select **New authentication strength**, give it a name, and check the **Password + Software OATH token** in the list of available methods. Add additional combinations as desired, click **Next** to verify your choices, and click **Create**. This option will now be available with Require authentication strength. Be advised that at the time of writing, the PowerShell Graph SDK does not support this new method, and you need to use the former multifactor authentication requirement.

A popular feature in Conditional Access is that organizations can selectively require MFA or block access to services when users are authenticating from devices located outside the corporate network. This is where named locations come in. By trusting a location to a Conditional Access rule, being an IPv4 or IPv6 range or country, organizations can lower or increase security requirements. It can also be used to allow accounts used by services running on-premises, for example, backup or archiving, to bypass MFA.

First, we need to define a named location:

1) In **Conditional Access**, select **Named Locations**.

2) Here you can add locations based on geography or IP ranges. In this example we will configure the organization's external IP range of 83.87.184.133/30. Be advised that the address is the external address range of the authentication request, not necessarily your internal IP address range. They might be the same though, depending on your network.

3) Click + **IP Ranges Location**.

4) Enter a name for the network definition such as CorpNet, and add **83.87.184.133/30** as the network using +.

5) Check **Mark as trusted location**, and click **Create** to save this definition.

To use this definition in an existing Conditional Access rule

1) Open up the rule in **Conditional Access ➤ Policies**.

2) Under **Conditions**, click **Locations**, and set **Configure** to **Yes**. Then, either **Exclude ➤ Selected locations** and pick the named location you defined earlier, or use the blanket **All trusted locations option** here.

3) Click **Save** to store your updated Conditional Access rule.

Tip   A time-saving feature that can assist in troubleshooting policies without waiting for the event to occur is What If, found on the Conditional Access Policies view. Click it, select the user to test with, and provide conditions you want to check against. Then click **What If** to see what policies would be hit (or missed).

We suggest you have a look at the templates provided for inspiration and you get an idea of the possibilities. Templates also allow for exporting/importing through JSON files, which makes it easier to transfer policy definitions between different tenants or for archival purposes.

Of course, this can also be configured using PowerShell Graph SDK. For this example, we will create a Conditional Access rule that will require MFA for members of our MFAGroup1, making an exception for the previously defined trusted named location CorpNet.

First, connect to Graph using the scopes required for Conditional Access:

```
Install-Module Microsoft.Graph.Identity.Signins
Connect-MgGraph -Scopes UserAuthenticationMethod.ReadWrite.All,
  Policy.ReadWrite.ConditionalAccess,Policy.Read.All,
  Application.Read.All
Select-MgProfile -Name beta
```

Tip   To determine which scope(s) you need in order to execute a Graph call successfully, you can use Find-MgGraphCommand and check the permissions property, for example,(Find-MgGraphCommand -Command New-MgIdentityCondition alAccessPolicy -ApiVersion beta).permissions. For ApiVersion, you can choose the common v1.0 endpoint or the beta one.

Defining parameters in body format can be challenging. You can use the following command to export a current definition using ConvertTo-Json, for example, after configuring it through the portal. You can use this to look up how to define certain properties:
(Get-MgIdentityConditionalAccessNamedLocation). Where({$_.DisplayName -eq 'CorpNet'}) | ConvertTo-Json -Depth 10 Depth is specified, as the default Depth of 2 is insufficient for displaying subelements.

How to create our Conditional Access rule is shown in Figure 9-6. Note that we need to look up the identifier of the group and the named location we want to use in the definition of the rule. Also, some Graph calls do not support searching, so for Get-MgIdentityConditionalAccessNamedLocati on, for example, we need to use a different method to locate the item.

```
[PS] > Get-MgGroup -Search DisplayName:MFAGroup1 -ConsistencyLevel Eventual

Id                    DisplayName Description GroupTypes AccessType
--                    ----------- ----------- ---------- ----------
b54c293d-7855-4157-a9c8-f666e03f7a86 MFAGroup1             {}

> Get-MgIdentityConditionalAccessNamedLocation | Where {$_.DisplayName -eq 'CorpNet'}

Id                    CreatedDateTime   DisplayName ModifiedDateTime
--                    ---------------   ----------- ----------------
073aca1d-e5e3-4cbb-8381-77438745bf8a 21-5-2023 13:49:41 CorpNet   21-5-2023 13:49:41

[PS] > $CARule= @{
 DisplayName = "Require MFA for MFAGroup1 users"
 State = "enabledForReportingButNotEnforced"
 Conditions = @{
  ClientAppTypes = @(
   "all"
  )
  Applications = @{
   IncludeApplications = @(
    "All"
   )
  }
  Users = @{
   IncludeGroups = @(
    "b54c293d-7855-4157-a9c8-f666e03f7a86"
   )
  }
  Locations = @{
   ExcludeLocations = @(
    "073aca1d-e5e3-4cbb-8381-77438745bf8a"
   )
   IncludeLocations = @(
    "All"
   )
  }
 }
 GrantControls = @{
  Operator = "OR"
  BuiltInControls = @(
   "mfa"
  )
 }
}
[PS] > > New-MgIdentityConditionalAccessPolicy -BodyParameter $params

Id                    CreatedDateTime   Description DisplayName           ModifiedDateTime
--                    ---------------   ----------- -----------           ----------------
f89c8912-8663-45c4-99f2-ffa76e94fb60 21-5-2023 16:17:36           Require MFA for MFAGroup1 users
```

Figure 9-6. *Using PowerShell Graph SDK to create a Conditional Access rule*

Tip While your CISO may look at this differently, feedback learns that creating a Conditional Access rule where you set the sign-in frequency too high (or even at "Every time") is horrible from a user experience perspective. An exception can be made for users flagged as risky users, should you have Azure AD P2.

Client Access Rules

One of the features introduced in Exchange 2019 is Client Access Rules, which inconveniently would share the same acronym as Conditional Access rules, so we will keep referring to these in full.

Client Access Rules allow admins to block or limit access to the Exchange Admin Center (EAC) or the Exchange Management Shell (EMS). It is a big plus for smaller companies that do not operate intelligent firewalls operating at the application layer to restrict access from outside the corporate network. Client Access Rules allow organizations to block or allow IP ranges, individual IP addresses, or subnets.

Managing Client Access Rules is only possible through the Exchange Management Shell. A Client Access Rule consists of the following elements:

- **Condition** or what client connections does this rule apply to. This condition can consist of one or more of the following predicates shown in Table 9-3.

- **Exception** or when should the rule not apply. Exceptions can be made for predicates in a similar way as Condition; see Table 9-3.

- **Action** defines what action needs to be taken.

- **Priority** defines the order in which rules are evaluated, where lower numbers have a higher priority.

Note   Client Access Rules are also available in Exchange Online, but those are being deprecated. Organizations are encouraged to migrate to Entra features such as Conditional Access or Continuous Access Evaluation. The official retirement of Client Access Rules in Exchange Online is September 2023, but that deadline might be extended to September 2024 for organizations that run complex rules that cannot be migrated. More on this at **https://bit.ly/DeprecationCAR**.

Table 9-3. *Client Access Rules Predicates*

Condition	Exception	Description
AnyOf Authentication Types	ExceptAnyOf AuthenticationTypes	For EAC: AdfsAuthentication or BasicAuthentication. For remote PowerShell: BasicAuthentication or NonBasicAuthentication. Can be multiple comma-separated values.
AnyOfClient IPAddresses OrRanges	ExceptAnyOfClient IPAddressesOrRanges	A single IP address, an IP address range, or CIDR specification. Can be multiple comma-separated values.
AnyOfProtocols	*ExceptAnyOfProtocols*	ExchangeAdminCenter or RemotePowerShell. Omitted means apply to both.

(*continued*)

Table 9-3. (*continued*)

Condition	Exception	Description
Scope	*N/A*	Users for end users or All for any type of connection including apps.
Username Matches AnyOfPatterns	*ExceptUsername Matches AnyOfPatterns*	Text pattern to identify an account in <Domain>\<User> format; can include wildcards. Escape non-alphanumeric characters. Can be multiple comma-separated values.
UserRecipient Filter	*N/A*	Use OPATH filter to identity users, for example, "Company -eq 'Contoso'". Can be multiple comma-separated filter criteria.

To get a list of currently configured Client Access Rules, use Get-ClientAccessRule. In a new deployment, the list will be empty.

A practical example would be to block access to EAC for all users from a non-management network. In this example, 172.16.10.0/24 is the management network:

```
[PS] > New-ClientAccessRule -Name "EAC Allow only MGMT"
-Action DenyAccess -AnyOfProtocols ExchangeAdminCenter
-ExceptAnyOfClientIPAddressesOrRanges 172.16.10.0/24
-Priority 1
```

You can also use Client Access Rules to block Exchange Management Shell access, for example:

```
[PS] > New-ClientAccessRule -Name "EMS Allow only MGMT"
-Action DenyAccess -AnyOfProtocols RemotePowerShell
-ExceptAnyOfClientIPAddressesOrRanges 172.16.10.0/24 -Priority 2
```

Rudimentary testing of Client Access Rules is possible using the Test-ClientAccessRule cmdlet, for example:

```
[PS] > Test-ClientAccessRule -RemoteAddress 10.10.1.1
-RemotePort 443 -Protocol ExchangeAdminCenter -User
Administrator -AuthenticationType BasicAuthentication

Identity           Name                  Action
--------           -------               ------
EAC Allow only MGMT EAC Allow only MGMT DenyAccess
```

When users are blocked from accessing EAC, they will be presented a message stating that *Access to the Exchange Admin Center has been blocked by your organization for security reasons.*

Tip   To disable remote PowerShell for users that do not need it, which are generally the non-admin population plus possibly service-type accounts, organizations are recommended to disable remote PowerShell. This can be accomplished by running the following for every non-admin/service account: `Set-User -RemotePowerShell Enabled $false`

SMTP AUTH

With all the incentives to phase out basic authentication, authentication for one protocol still stands out, which is SMTP AUTH. SMTP AUTH, which stands for Simple Mail Transfer Protocol Authentication, is the way SMTP allows a client or device to authenticate to an SMTP service in order for it to accept and deliver its message. It ensures only authorized accounts can send email messages through the server, preventing unauthorized usage.

Exchange on-premises supports the authentication methods as shown in Table 9-4 for send and Receive Connectors. We will refer to this table later on in this section.

Table 9-4. *Exchange On-Premises SMTP Authentication Mechanisms*

Authentication Mechanism	Description	Receive Connector	Send Connector
None	**None** means no authentication.	Yes	Yes
Basic authentication	Authenticates using credentials in plain text (**BasicAuth**), so should be used in combination with requiring encrypted transport (**BasicAuthRequireTLS**). The credential should be provided as well (**AuthenticationCredential**).	Yes	Yes
Exchange Server Authentication	**ExchangeServer** uses the credentials of the sender for authentication using Generic Security Services API and Mutual GSSAPI.	Yes	Yes
Externally secured	**ExternalAuthoritative** assumes the server is in a controlled environment and the connection is secured external to the server by a trusted source or target.	Yes	Yes
Integrated Windows Authentication (IWA)	**Integrated** uses NTLM and Kerberos authentication.	Yes	No

(continued)

Table 9-4. (*continued*)

Authentication Mechanism	Description	Receive Connector	Send Connector
TLS	**TLS** advertises StartTLS, depending on a certificate presence controlled by the FQDN or server name. The latter usually implies self-signed certificates, but external servers or clients might require a valid third-party certificate.	Yes	No

Note   When authenticating to Exchange Online or Exchange on-premises using Hybrid Modern Authentication, SMTP AUTH also supports Modern Authentication. Applications or devices need an Enterprise Application registration for this having the SMTP.Send permission. Earlier in this chapter, we talked about this in the section "Configuring an Enterprise Application."

When Exchange accepts messages from an authenticated source, it is treated differently. This is more prominent in Exchange Online, which will only accept and relay messages from an unknown sender if the messages are received through the Office 365 inbound connector, which has—normally—TLS enabled and certificate validation checks in place to increase trustworthiness of the source, even if the sender is unknown to it.

So, to improve credibility of the source, it is recommended to use SMTP AUTH for messages flowing into Exchange and limit usage of blanket approval to relay messages for whole sets of IP address ranges.

Problems arise for many organizations still operating older devices or applications that do not support SMTP AUTH, requiring them to keep an anonymous mail relay through Exchange on-premises. To create such a relay connector on Exchange 2019, use the following commands:

```
[PS] > New-ReceiveConnector -Name 'SMTP Relay EXCH01'
-Server EXCH01
-TransportRole FrontendTransport -Custom -Bindings 0.0.0.0:25
-RemoteIpRanges 172.16.10.0/24

Identity                    Bindings      Enabled
--------                    --------      -------
EXCH01\SMTP Relay EXCH01 {0.0.0.0:25} True

[PS] > Set-ReceiveConnector 'EXCH01\SMTP Relay EXCH01'
-AuthMechanism ExternalAuthoritative
-PermissionGroups ExchangeServers
```

This will create a dedicated Receive Connector on EXCH01 for devices and clients operating in the 172.16.10.0/24 range, so you need to repeat this step for additional Exchange servers you want to relay through, customizing RemoteIPRanges for IP ranges in the environment. Also, by specifying ExternalAuthoritive senders are deemed trustworthy, and messages will bypass antimalware and message size limitations.

Caution   If you have Security Defaults enabled, you might encounter that SMTP AUTH is blocked as part of the legacy authentication blockage. While SMTP AUTH using OAuth is available in those situations, not every device or application is able to support this. You can see the organization-wide setting using Get-TransportConfig | select SmtpClientAuthenticationDisabled. Use Set-TransportConfig -SmtpClientAuthenticationDisabled

$false to enable it globally. With globally disabling SMTP AUTH being recommended, you can then make exceptions for those accounts that require it using Set-CASMailbox, for example, Set-CASMailbox -Identity mfc01@contoso.com -SmtpClientAuthenticationDisabled $False. Be advised that you can also set this to $null, in which case the global setting will become effective for this account.

For Exchange Online, when you want devices or applications to deliver messages to Exchange Online, you have three options to choose from. A comparison of these options is shown in Table 9-5, as every choice has its own technical or license requirements or limitations.

Table 9-5. *Device/Application SMTP Delivery to Exchange Online*

Feature	Option 1: SMTP AUTH Submit	Option 2: Direct Send	Option 3: SMTP Relay
Send to recipients using your own domains	Yes	Yes	Yes
Send to other domains	Yes	No	Yes
Bypass anti-spam	Yes, if recipient is one of your mailboxes	No, add mail host to SPF record	No, add mail host to SPF record
Support mail sent by third party	Yes	Yes, add third-party host to your SPF record	No

(*continued*)

Table 9-5. (*continued*)

Feature	Option 1: SMTP AUTH Submit	Option 2: Direct Send	Option 3: SMTP Relay
Mail saved to Sent Items	Yes	No	No
Requires licensed mailbox	Yes	No	No
Requirement			
Requires open network port	Port 25 or 587	Port 25	Port 25
Device/application supports TLS	Required	Optional	Optional
Requires authentication	Credential	No	Static IP address/range
Limitations			
Throttling	10.000 recipients/day, 30 messages/min	Standard	"Reasonable limits"
Sender	Sent from single email address		
Resilience	Depends on device/application	Depends on device/application	Relaying server takes care of this

Note that the "reasonable limits" in Table 9-5 is to indicate that Exchange Online is not meant for sending out mass bulk mail, even if those messages are stemming from your own organization in an Exchange hybrid deployment.

Note   Alternative to sending messages through Exchange Online using SMTP is, apart from third-party services such as SendGrid or Mailchimp, is using Graph API. If your application supports calling external PowerShell scripts, you could use the PowerShell Graph SDK; see Figure 9-7 for an example.

```
#requires -modules Microsoft.Graph.Authentication, Microsoft.Graph.Users.Actions, Microsoft.Graph.Mail
Connect-MgGraph -Scope Mail.Send, Mail.ReadWrite
Select-MgProfile v1.0
$UserId= (Get-MgContext).Account
$Params = @{
   Message= @{
     Subject = "This is the message you are looking for."
     Body = @{
       Content= "Well, hello there."
       ContentType= "text"
     }
     ToRecipients = @(
       @{
         EmailAddress = @{
           Address = "michel@contoso.com"
         }
       }
     )
   }
   SaveToSentItems= "false"
}
Send-MgUserMail -UserId $UserId -BodyParameter $Params
```

Figure 9-7. *Sending mail using PowerShell Graph SDK*

Another option is to have applications or devices use a certificate, provided the application or device supports this. If you look at Exchange on-premises as an application, this is how connectors are configured between Exchange on-premises and Exchange Online in an Exchange hybrid deployment. However, it is more of an organizational validation, as both ends are configured to require TLS usage (implying certificates are used). When communicating, they present their certificate and verify the subject of the certificate presented by their counterpart, which can be any device or application. The subject (CN) or one of the Subject Alternative Names (SANs) on the certificate should match the domain the counterpart is expecting based on its configuration.

How to configure an application or device using SMTP AUTH client submission or Direct Send depends on the application or device. Overall, you will need to use the same parameters:

- *Endpoint or **smarthost***: For Exchange on-premises, this would be the FQDN of your SMTP load balancing VIP or DNS entry pointing to each individual Exchange server when using DNS Round Robin. For Exchange Online, this would be **smtp.office365.com**.

- **Port** for SMTP AUTH Client Submit is **587**; for Direct Send it is **25**.

- **Require TLS /StartTLS** should be **Enabled**/Required.

- **Email Address** or Sender should be an address with an accepted domain.

- Authentication for SMTP AUTH should be the credential of a mailbox on the receiving host, for example, the account related to an application mailbox in Exchange Online.

Considering all of the aforementioned factors in this section, keeping an Exchange on-premises server for mail flow is still the most convenient option when dealing with applications and devices, including Exchange hybrid scenarios. It is easier to set up and does not impose additional requirements and reconfiguration. Not unimportant, when applications or devices talk to Exchange Online directly, that application or device needs to be resilient. This means it should be able to deal with disruptions and resubmit when connectivity is re-established, for example. When using your Exchange on-premises server for relaying those messages, your

Exchange server will take care of this. You do not want to discover that your invoicing application was unable to send out monthly invoices per email due to problems with your Internet Service Provider and that the application has no easy way resend those.

Note   When using SMTP AUTH, Direct Send, or SMTP relay, make sure to add the sending host on the SPF record. See Chapter 7 for more information on SPF records.

Certificate Authentication

Certificate-based authentication (CBA) provides a secure method for authenticating Outlook on the Web (OWA) and Exchange ActiveSync clients, without the need for username and password entry. To implement CBA in Exchange, a client certificate must be issued to each user. To manage a large number of certificates, an automated internal public key infrastructure (PKI) is recommended, such as Active Directory Certificate Services (AD CS).

A few points of attention:

- The client certificate must be specifically issued for client authentication, which typically involves utilizing the User Certificate template in AD CS.

- The client certificate should include the User Principal Name (UPN) of the respective user in either the Subject or Subject Alternative Name field.

- The client certificate should be associated with the corresponding user account in Active Directory.

- Any service or device involved in accessing Outlook on
  the Web or ActiveSync, including proxy servers, must
  trust the entire chain of trust for client certificates. This
  includes the root certificate of the certification authority (CA) and any intermediate CAs utilized during the
  certificate issuance process. This is usually already
  present in the client or device for third-party certificates, but usually not for internally issued certificates.

For CBA in Outlook on the Web, the client certificate needs to be
installed on the local computer or device or on a smart card. For CBA in
ActiveSync, the client certificate needs to be installed on the local device.
You can automate the installation of certificates on devices by using a
mobile device management (MDM) solution like Intune.

To enable CBA with OWA, the client certificate needs to be installed on
the local computer, device, or a smart card. For CBA with ActiveSync, the
client certificate should be installed directly on the device.

Note   To automate certificate distribution across devices, a capable
mobile device management (MDM) solution such as Intune might help.
For an overview of how to accomplish this in Microsoft Intune using
certificate profiles, see `https://bit.ly/IntuneAuthCerts`.

To configure Exchange on-premises to support CBA, proceed as
follows:

1) Using PowerShell on each Exchange server, first
   install the Client Certificate Mapping Authentication
   feature:

   ```
   Install-WindowsFeature Web-Client-Auth
   ```

2) Configure the OWA, ECP, and ActiveSync Virtual
   Directories of Exchange using **IIS Manager** to verify
   Require SSL is checked and **Client certificates**
   is set to **Require**. Do this for **OWA**, **ECP**, and
   Microsoft-ActiveSync folders under **Default
   Website**.

   You can also perform this step using PowerShell, for
   example:

```
Set-WebConfigurationProperty -PSPath IIS:
-Location 'Default Web Site/OWA' -Filter
//security/access -name sslflags -Value
'Ssl, SslRequireCert'
```

```
Set-WebConfigurationProperty -PSPath IIS:
-Location 'Default Web Site/ECP' -Filter
//security/access -name sslflags -Value
'Ssl, SslRequireCert'
```

```
Set-WebConfigurationProperty -PSPath IIS:
-Location 'Default Web Site/Microsoft-
Server-ActiveSync' -Filter //security/access
-name sslflags -Value 'Ssl, SslRequireCert'
```

3) We can now disable all other authentication
   methods on those virtual directories, using the
   Exchange Management Shell:

```
$EASDisable= @{
    BasicAuthentication= $false
    WindowsAuthentication= $false
}
$ECPDisable= $EASDisable + @{
    DigestAuthentication= $false
    FormsAuthentication= $false
```

```
        AdfsAuthentication= $false
}
$OWADisable= $ECPDisable + @{
        OAuthAuthentication= $false
}

Get-EcpVirtualDirectory -Server EXCH01 |
Set-EcpVirtualDirectory @ECPDisable
Get-OwaVirtualDirectory -Server EXCH01 |
Set-OwaVirtualDirectory @OWADisable
Get-ActiveSyncVirtualDirectory -Server EXCH01 |
Set-ActiveSyncVirtualDirectory @EASDisable
```

4) The next step is to enable client certificate mapping for those virtual directories. In **IIS Manager**, open the **Configuration Editor** for **Default Website ➤ OWA**, navigate to **system. webServer ➤ security ➤ authentication ➤ clientCertificateMappingAuthentication**, and set **Enabled** to **True**. Perform this step for **ECP** and **Microsoft-ActiveSync** as well.

Alternatively, run the following through PowerShell:

```
Set-WebConfigurationProperty -PSPath
IIS: -Location 'Default Web Site/
OWA' -Filter //security/authentication/
iisClientCertificateMappingAuthentication
-name Enabled -Value true
Set-WebConfigurationProperty -PSPath
IIS: -Location 'Default Web Site/
ECP' -Filter //security/authentication/
iisClientCertificateMappingAuthentication
-name Enabled -Value true
```

```
Set-WebConfigurationProperty -PSPath IIS:
-Location 'Default Web Site/Microsoft-Server-
ActiveSync' -Filter //security/authentication/
iisClientCertificateMappingAuthentication
-name Enabled -Value true
```

5) If you are not using AD CS, you need to add the root certificate of that third-party certificate authority to the Enterprise NTAuth store. This store is located in Active Directory and signals Exchange that the issuer is trusted to issue user certificates.

To accomplish this, export the CA's root certificate to a Base64-encoded or DER (Distinguished Encoding Rules) binary-encoded X.509 .cer file. In this example, we will have exported it to C:\Cert\ CARoot.cer.

Next, on any Domain Controller, open an elevated prompt and run the following command as a member of the Enterprise Admins group:

```
certutil.exe -enterprise -addstore NTAuth
"C:\Cert\CARoot.cer"
```

6) Restart IIS on the Exchange server to make the settings effective:

IISRESET <SERVER> /NOFORCE /RESTART / TIMEOUT:900

Caution Using Set-ActiveSyncVirtualDirectory after this might disable client certificate mapping for ActiveSync, and you might need to repeat that part of step 4 in the preceding procedure.

When everything is set up correctly, you have obtained a user certificate, and your account in Active Directory is associated with that certificate. Now, when you open up OWA, you might still get asked to confirm the certificate presented by your browser to Exchange. Click OK, and you should be logged into OWA, no username or password needed.

Windows Extended Protection

Another feature we want to mention in this security-related chapter is Windows Extended Protection. Extended Protection is a security feature designed to protect against a specific type of attack called a man-in-the-middle attack. In this type of attack, an attacker intercepts the communication between two parties and secretly alters or steals the information being exchanged.

To prevent this, Extended Protection uses a security measure called channel binding information. This information is established through a Channel Binding Token (CBT). Think of it as a special code that is used to ensure the integrity of the communication channel.

The primary use of this Channel Binding Token is for SSL connections. By implementing the Channel Binding Token, Extended Protection adds an extra layer of security to these SSL connections.

Overall, Extended Protection with its Channel Binding Token helps make sure that the communication between the client and server is secure and has not been tampered with by any unauthorized third party.

Note   Exchange received support for Extended Protection with the August 2022 Security Updates for Exchange 2019 CU12 and CU11. Exchange 2019 CU13 and later contain this security feature. For those running Exchange 2019 alongside older Exchange versions, Exchange Server 2016 CU22 and CU23 and Exchange Server 2013 CU23 also received a Security Update including this feature. The related KB articles are KB5015322 for Exchange 2016/2019 and KB5015321 for Exchange 2013. Be advised that Microsoft announced Extended Protection will be enabled by default for new Cumulative Updates of Exchange 2019.

The ability to configure Extended Protection depends on the following prerequisites:

- Verify you run proper versions of Exchange (see Note earlier).

- If you are running in coexistence with Exchange 2013, Exchange 2013 servers cannot be hosting public folders. The solution is to move those public folders to Exchange 2016 or 2019 prior to enabling Extended Protection.

- If you have public folders, the public folder hierarchy mailboxes need to be hosted on Exchange 2019 CU11, Exchange 2016 CU22, or earlier versions of those products.

- If you are running Exchange hybrid, you need to be running it in Classic mode. Modern Hybrid mode uses Hybrid Agents and will lead to service disruption when Extended Protection gets enabled. Also, using Azure App Proxy for OWA will not work, as that terminates the SSL connection with a different certificate. To let the script bypass any Exchange server running a Hybrid Agent, use it with the SkipExchangeServerNames. Alternatively, you can use EWSBackend to have it bypass enabling Extended Protection for the EWSBackend Virtual Directory, used by Azure App Proxy.

- NTLMv1 is not supported. Check the registry key HKLM:\System\CurrentControlSet\Control\Lsa\ LmCompatibilityLevel, which should be set at 3 (NTLMv2) or higher.

- SSL offloading is not supported.

- SSL bridging is supported, provided Exchange and the load balancer use the same certificate.

- TLS configuration must be consistent between Exchange servers, that is, no mix of Exchange Servers with TLS 1.0/1.1/1.2 enabled or disabled.

- And last but not least is to test on compatibility when using third-party products, such as antivirus software. In those cases, it might be better to test things in a test environment, prior to testing in production.

When all the preceding prerequisites have been met, you can consider enabling Extended Protection. To support this configuration change, Microsoft made a script available that will perform all the underlying tasks for you. This script, **ExchangeExtendedProtectionManagement.ps1**, is available on GitHub via **https://bit.ly/ExchangeExtendedProtectionManagement**.

Pay attention, as by default the script will enable Extended Protection on any Exchange server it can access when calling it without parameters. You will get a configuration prompt, though. To show the current Extended Protection configuration for all Exchange servers it can access, run the following from the Exchange Management Shell (note: column IPFilterEnabled removed for readability):

```
[PS] >.\ExchangeExtendedProtectionManagement.ps1 -ShowExtended
Protection
Version 23.05.12.1808
Creating a new session for implicit remoting of
"Get-EventLogLevel" command...
Results for Server: EXCH01
```

```
Default Web Site              Value SupportedValue
  ConfigSupported RequireSSL     ClientCertificate
----------------              ----- --------------
---------------- ----------     --------
API                            None  Require
          False True (128-bit) Ignore
Autodiscover                   None  None
           True True (128-bit) Ignore
ECP                            None  Require
          False True (128-bit) Ignore
EWS                            None  Allow
           True True (128-bit) Ignore
Microsoft-Server-ActiveSync None  Allow
           True True (128-bit) Ignore
OAB                            None  Require
          False True (128-bit) Ignore
Powershell                     None  Require
          False False          Accept
OWA                            None  Require
          False True (128-bit) Ignore
RPC                            None  Require
          False False          Ignore
MAPI                           None  Require
          False True (128-bit) Ignore

Exchange Back End             Value SupportedValue
  ConfigSupported RequireSSL     ClientCertificate
------------------            ----- --------------
---------------- ----------     --------
API                            None  Require
          False True (128-bit) Ignore
```

```
Autodiscover                     None  None
            True True (128-bit) Ignore
ECP                              None  Require
         False True (128-bit) Ignore
EWS                              None  Require
         False True (128-bit) Ignore
Microsoft-Server-ActiveSync None  Require
         False True (128-bit) Ignore
OAB                              None  Require
         False True (128-bit) Ignore
Powershell                       None  Require
         False True (128-bit) Accept
OWA                              None  Require
         False True (128-bit) Ignore
RPC                              None  Require
         False True          Ignore
PushNotifications                None  Require
         False True (128-bit) Ignore
RPCWithCert                      None  Require
         False False         Ignore
MAPI/emsmdb                      None  Require
         False True          Ignore
MAPI/nspi                        None  Require
         False True          Ignore
```

If the column **Value** shows None, Extended Protection is not enabled for that virtual directory. **SupportedValue** indicates what the value would be if Extended Protection was enabled. The column **ConfigSupported** shows True when Extended Protection is supported for that virtual directory. This also applies to virtual folders, which do not support Extended Protection, such as Autodiscover.

To configure Extended Protection, run ExchangeExtendedProtection Management.ps1 without any parameters. A sample run in an environment with two Exchange servers, which is why you will see "duplicate" changes, is shown in Figure 9-8.

```
[PS] C:\Tools>.\ExchangeExtendedProtectionManagement.ps1
Version 23.05.12.1808

Enabling Extended Protection
Extended Protection is recommended to be enabled for security reasons. Known Issues: Following scenarios will not
work when Extended Protection is enabled.
   - SSL offloading or SSL termination via Layer 7 load balancing.
   - Exchange Hybrid Features if using Modern Hybrid.
   - Access to Public folders on Exchange 2013 Servers.
You can find more information on: https://aka.ms/ExchangeEPDoc. Do you want to proceed?
[Y] Yes [A] Yes to All [N] No [L] No to All [S] Suspend [?] Help (default is "Y"): y

The following servers have the TLS Configuration below
EXCH01, EXCH02

RegistryName     Location                                                   Value
------------     --------                                                   -----
SchUseStrongCrypto  SOFTWARE\Microsoft\.NETFramework\v2.0.50727              1
SystemTlsVersions   SOFTWARE\Microsoft\.NETFramework\v2.0.50727              1
SchUseStrongCrypto  SOFTWARE\Microsoft\.NETFramework\v4.0.30319              1
SystemTlsVersions   SOFTWARE\Microsoft\.NETFramework\v4.0.30319              1
SchUseStrongCrypto  SOFTWARE\Wow6432Node\Microsoft\.NETFramework\v2.0.50727       1
SystemTlsVersions   SOFTWARE\Wow6432Node\Microsoft\.NETFramework\v2.0.50727       1
SchUseStrongCrypto  SOFTWARE\Wow6432Node\Microsoft\.NETFramework\v4.0.30319       1
SystemTlsVersions   SOFTWARE\Wow6432Node\Microsoft\.NETFramework\v4.0.30319       1
DisabledByDefault  SYSTEM\CurrentControlSet\Control\SecurityProviders\SCHANNEL\Protocols\TLS 1.0\Client 1
Enabled            SYSTEM\CurrentControlSet\Control\SecurityProviders\SCHANNEL\Protocols\TLS 1.0\Client 0
DisabledByDefault  SYSTEM\CurrentControlSet\Control\SecurityProviders\SCHANNEL\Protocols\TLS 1.0\Server 1
Enabled            SYSTEM\CurrentControlSet\Control\SecurityProviders\SCHANNEL\Protocols\TLS 1.0\Server 0
DisabledByDefault  SYSTEM\CurrentControlSet\Control\SecurityProviders\SCHANNEL\Protocols\TLS 1.1\Client 1
Enabled            SYSTEM\CurrentControlSet\Control\SecurityProviders\SCHANNEL\Protocols\TLS 1.1\Client 0
DisabledByDefault  SYSTEM\CurrentControlSet\Control\SecurityProviders\SCHANNEL\Protocols\TLS 1.1\Server 1
Enabled            SYSTEM\CurrentControlSet\Control\SecurityProviders\SCHANNEL\Protocols\TLS 1.1\Server 0
DisabledByDefault  SYSTEM\CurrentControlSet\Control\SecurityProviders\SCHANNEL\Protocols\TLS 1.2\Client 0
Enabled            SYSTEM\CurrentControlSet\Control\SecurityProviders\SCHANNEL\Protocols\TLS 1.2\Client 1
DisabledByDefault  SYSTEM\CurrentControlSet\Control\SecurityProviders\SCHANNEL\Protocols\TLS 1.2\Server 0
Enabled            SYSTEM\CurrentControlSet\Control\SecurityProviders\SCHANNEL\Protocols\TLS 1.2\Server 1

TLS prerequisites check successfully passed!

All servers that we are trying to currently configure for Extended Protection have RPC (Default Web Site) set to false for SSLOffloading.
EXCH01: Backing up applicationHost.config.
EXCH01: Successful backup to C:\Windows\System32\inetSrv\config\applicationHost.cep.20230522230550.bak
EXCH01: Successfully updated applicationHost.config.
EXCH02: Backing up applicationHost.config.
EXCH02: Successful backup to C:\Windows\System32\inetSrv\config\applicationHost.cep.20230522230526.bak
EXCH02: Successfully updated applicationHost.config.

Successfully enabled Extended Protection: EXCH01, EXCH02
Do you have feedback regarding the script? Please email ExToolsFeedback@microsoft.com.
```

Figure 9-8. *Enabling Extended Protection*

You can see that you will be prompted to confirm your action, and you will be notified of some prerequisites the script cannot verify. After confirmation, the changes will be made on every Exchange server.

After enabling, ShowExtendedProtection will look something like this; the changed items are marked in inverse:

```
[PS] >.\ExchangeExtendedProtectionManagement.ps1
-ShowExtendedProtection
Version 23.05.12.1808
Results for Server: EXCH01

Default Web Site              Value    SupportedValue
  ConfigSupported RequireSSL    ClientCertificate
----------------              -----    --------------
--------------- ----------    --------
API                         Require Require
          True True (128-bit) Ignore
Autodiscover                  None    None
          True True (128-bit) Ignore
ECP                         Require Require
          True True (128-bit) Ignore
EWS                          Allow   Allow
          True True (128-bit) Ignore
Microsoft-Server-ActiveSync Allow    Allow
          True True (128-bit) Ignore
OAB                         Require Require
          True True (128-bit) Ignore
Powershell                  Require Require
          True False          Accept
OWA                         Require Require
          True True (128-bit) Ignore
```

```
RPC                          Require Require
          True True (128-bit) Ignore
MAPI                         Require Require
          True True (128-bit) Ignore

Exchange Back End             Value   SupportedValue
   ConfigSupported RequireSSL    ClientCertificate
----------------                 -----   --------------
----------------- ----------      --------
API                          Require Require
          True True (128-bit) Ignore
Autodiscover                 None    None
          True True (128-bit) Ignore
ECP                          Require Require
          True True (128-bit) Ignore
EWS                          Require Require
          True True (128-bit) Ignore
Microsoft-Server-ActiveSync Require Require
          True True (128-bit) Ignore
OAB                          Require Require
          True True (128-bit) Ignore
Powershell                   Require Require
          True True (128-bit) Accept
OWA                          Require Require
          True True (128-bit) Ignore
RPC                          Require Require
          True True (128-bit) Ignore
PushNotifications            Require Require
          True True (128-bit) Ignore
RPCWithCert                  Require Require
          True True (128-bit) Ignore
```

```
MAPI/emsmdb                     Require Require
              True True (128-bit) Ignore
MAPI/nspi                       Require Require
              True True (128-bit) Ignore
```

Note that during configuration, the script will make a copy of current configuration files. Should you discover that despite adequate analysis things do not work after enabling Extended Protection, you can use the script's Rollback mode, for example, .\ExchangeExtendedProtectionManagement. ps1 -RollbackType RestoreIISAppConfig, which will restore the .config files to their original version.

PowerShell Serialization Payload Signing

Certificate-based signing of PowerShell Serialization Payload is a security feature implemented to add an extra layer of protection against malicious tampering of serialized data in Exchange Management Shell (EMS) sessions.

This security feature, also known as Serialized Data Signing, was introduced with the January 2023 Exchange Server Security Update KB5022193, which is available for Exchange 2019 CU12 and CU11, Exchange Server 2016 CU23 (KB5022143), and even Exchange Server 2013 CU23 (KB5022188). Exchange 2019 CU13 already contains this feature.

In short, the conversation Exchange has server-to-server using PowerShell gets signed with the certificate with the subject **Microsoft Exchange Server Auth Certificate**. This certificate might sound familiar, as the Exchange Sever Auth Certificate is always present. It will get automatically replicated to all Exchange servers, including new servers. It is normally used for secure tasks, such as secure server-to-server communication.

Caution   With Serialized Data Signing, a new dependency is created on the Exchange Server Auth Certificate. It is therefore important to properly maintain and timely renew it before it expires.

The feature needs to be manually enabled, and it is an all-or-nothing setting; you cannot skip configuring a single server, as it would affect the ability to communicate with other Exchange servers.

Before enabling, make sure the current Exchange Server Auth Certificate is present, valid, and not about to expire. The procedure for rotating the certificate can be found at https://bit.ly/RenewExchangeServerAuthCert. A script to support this process is available at **https://bit.ly/MonitorExchangeAuthCertificate**. Download **MonitorExchangeAuthCertificate.ps1**, and run it without parameters to have it check your environment:

```
[PS] > .\MonitorExchangeAuthCertificate.ps1
Monitor Exchange Auth Certificate script version 23.05.09.1433
The script was run without parameter therefore, only a check of
the Auth Certificate configuration is performed and no change
will be made

Current Auth Certificate thumbprint:
8D7687A8F0FBFED87256B9874ADB27E59F13E73B
Current Auth Certificate is valid for 1065 day(s)
Exchange Hybrid was detected in this environment

Test result: No renewal action is required

Log file written to: C:\Program Files\Microsoft\Exchange
Server\V15\Logging\AuthCertificateMonitoring\AuthCertificate
MonitoringLog_20230523000553.txt
```

The script can also verify and renew the certificate when you specify the **ValidateAndRenewAuthCertificate** switch, create a scheduled task to periodically verify the certificate, etc.

After establishing that the Exchange Server Auth Certificate is in order, you can then enable Exchange servers for Serialized Data Signing. For Exchange 2019 and 2016, the feature can be enabled on an organizational level, which is the recommendation, or per server.

To enable Serialized Data Signing for all Exchange 2019 or 2016 servers, run the following using the Exchange Management Shell:

```
New-SettingOverride -Name "EnableSigningVerification"
-Component Data -Section EnableSerializationDataSigning
-Parameters @("Enabled=true") -Reason "Enabling Serialized Data
Signing"
```

To enable Serialized Data Signing on a single Exchange 2019/2016 server:

```
New-SettingOverride -Name "EnableSigningVerification"
-Component Data -Section EnableSerializationDataSigning
-Parameters @("Enabled=true") -Reason "Enabling Serialized Data
Signing" -Server <ExchangeServerName>
```

After either step, you need to trigger refreshing the VariantConfiguration argument, which will retrieve the updated EnableSigningVerification setting:

```
Get-ExchangeDiagnosticInfo -Process Microsoft.Exchange.
Directory.TopologyService -Component VariantConfiguration
-Argument Refresh
```

For Exchange 2013 you need to adjust the setting by setting a registry key on every Exchange 2013 server:

```
New-ItemProperty -Path HKLM:\SOFTWARE\Microsoft\ExchangeServer\
v15\Diagnostics -Name "EnableSerializationDataSigning" -Value 1
-Type String
```

When done enabling the feature on all Exchange servers, you need to restart the World Wide Web Publishing service and the Windows Process Activation Service (WAS) to apply the new settings:

```
Restart-Service -Name W3SVC, WAS -Force
```

Or when restarting remotely:

```
Invoke-Command -ComputerName <Server Name> -Command
{ Restart-Service W3SVC,WAS -Force }
```

Summary

In this chapter we talked about—mostly identity-related—authentication security features. We showed how Hybrid Modern Authentication can be used to hand off authentication to Azure Active Directory and benefit from the features offered by using Azure AD as an identity provider such as multifactor authentication and Conditional Access. We then continued with the Exchange 2019 built-in feature Client Access Rules, which enable limiting or granting access to interfaces such as the Exchange Admin Center to specific networks. Then we talked about authenticated SMTP delivery (SMTP AUTH) and its significance for how messages are treated in the Exchange ecosystem. Also, Exchange Online was discussed, where basic authentication has been disabled, with many organizations still having a significant heritage of legacy devices and applications that cannot perform Modern Authentication and what options organizations have regarding SMTP Transport. We also showed how the PowerShell Graph

SDK can be used for sending messages. We continued with showing how Certificate Authentication can be configured for Exchange on-premises, to allow users to authenticate using certificates instead of credentials. Finally, we talked about two not necessarily identity-related but still important topics when you want to secure your Exchange environment: Windows Extended Protection, which can be used to ensure integrity of secure communications between Exchange and clients to prevent man-in-the-middle-attacks, and PowerShell Serialization Payload Signing, which can be used to protect PowerShell-related payloads between Exchange servers using the Auth Certificate for encryption.

CHAPTER 10

Permissions and Access Control

To ensure the security and privacy of sensitive data stored in Exchange Server, it is essential to implement robust permissions and access control mechanisms. Permissions in Exchange Server allow administrators to define and manage user access rights to various resources, such as the Exchange configuration, mailboxes, or other administrative elements. By assigning appropriate permissions, organizations can maintain control over their Exchange environment and implement delegations when possible and where needed, while ensuring users have access to the resources they need while preventing unauthorized access.

In the previous two chapters, we discussed security-related topics related to transport and authentication. In this chapter, we will focus on the last, but certainly not least, security configuration elements in an Exchange ecosystem.

Permissions and access control in Exchange Server encompass the following concepts:

- **Role-Based Access Control (RBAC)** is a permissions model that allows administrators to assign specific roles to users or groups. Each role defines a set of tasks and operations that users can perform. RBAC simplifies administration by granting permissions based on

© Jaap Wesselius and Michel de Rooij 2023
J. Wesselius and M. de Rooij, *Pro Exchange Administration*,
https://doi.org/10.1007/978-1-4842-9591-5_10

predefined roles, such as the Organization Management role, Recipient Management role, or custom roles tailored to the needs of the organization.

Delegation allows administrators to assign specific management tasks to other users or groups without granting full administrative rights. For example, an administrator can delegate mailbox management tasks to the support team, without providing them with access to other administrative functions. RBAC allows for delegating management of objects, such as servers or recipients, based on certain aspects, such as the Organizational Unit those objects reside in. Also, built-in roles define for end users what they are able to manage themselves, such as the display name or perhaps Distribution Groups they are managers of.

– **Split permissions** is an operating mode of Exchange where management of Exchange and Active Directory objects is no longer integrated (shared).

Note that Exchange Server provides auditing for recording user actions, administrative changes, and access attempts. For information on compliance, see Chapter 12.

Client Access Rules and Conditional Access are also related to access control. However, these are located in Chapter 9 on authentication.

Role-Based Access Control

Exchange Server 2010 introduced Role-Based Access Control for Exchange. Before RBAC, Exchange used a limited permissions and delegation model, based on security groups, and its usage was basic and task orientated. Finer-grained control could be configured, but that required modifying

Access Control Lists (ACL) in Active Directory to enforce restrictions. This usually led to complications later, when upgrading to a more recent version of Exchange, or other side effects with third-party products. A small fact for the pub quiz is that the original Role-Based Access Control saw daylight as Authorization Manager, which was introduced for Windows Server 2003 and was a security framework for .NET applications.

Role-Based Access Control, as the name implies, is a Role-Based Access Control permissions model that still exists today in Exchange Server 2019 and has not changed a lot over the years. It allows for fine-grained control over the Exchange environment and even the underlying Active Directory objects when not using the split permissions model, which by default is not the case. This control goes as far as having the ability to control and limit access not only on the cmdlet level but also on what parameters can be used.

Note   While RBAC is also available in Exchange Online, some common roles are better managed through built-in Azure Active Directory roles. For example, the **Exchange Administrator** Azure AD role synchronizes to **ExchangeServiceAdmins_<Guid>** in Exchange Online (member of Organization Management), just as **Global Administrator** synchronizes to **TenantAdmins_<Guid>** and **Exchange Recipient Administrator** to **HelpDeskAdmins_<Guid>**.

The benefit of using Azure AD roles is that these roles can grant workload transcending permissions, as well as enable Privileged Identity Management (PIM). PIM can grant administrative access to eligible roles per request and for a limited time. More on **PIM at https://bit.ly/PIMAzure**.

The implementation of RBAC revolved around the Universal Security Group (USG) Exchange Trusted Subsystem. That group is effectively the Exchange ecosystem and by default not only has full access rights on every Exchange object in the organization but also can manage objects on the Active Directory level by being a member of the Administrators local security group and the Windows Permissions security group. All installed Exchange servers are members of the Exchange Trusted Subsystem.

Note   Exchange servers with the Edge Transport server role are not part of RBAC security, since it typically is not a member server in the Exchange domain.

Be advised that because of this architecture, you cannot use AdminSDHolder protected accounts, such as administrator accounts, for daily operations. The SDProp (Security Descriptor Propagator) process ensures that the same security configured on the AdminSDHolder object, located at **DC=<domain context> ➤ CN=System ➤ CN=AdminSDHolder**, is applied to protected accounts every hour. This prevents the Exchange Trusted Subsystem from managing user accounts, such as registering an ActiveSync device for an admin. Often, a quick fix is to enable the "Include inheritable permissions from this object's parent" setting on the object, but this is not recommended, and the setting will be reset by the AdminSDHolder process. Protected accounts can be located through the AdminCount property being set to 1. For more information on protected accounts and groups, see **https://bit.ly/ ADProtectedAccounts**.

Through the RBAC system, you are effectively proxying your actions through Exchange Server, which, based on the RBAC configuration, determines what you are allowed to do and what not. This not only goes for administrators but also for end users. An example of the latter is having the ability to manage Distribution Groups or modify properties such as your display name.

The RBAC model is based on the concept of assigning who can do what and where, as follows:

- Who is determined by role groups you are a member of. These role groups contain roles. Users can be assigned to multiple role groups.

- What is determined by roles, which define permitted actions. When assigned to multiple roles, the cumulative set of permissions are granted.

- Where is determined by the scope of the role.

While Exchange contains several predefined roles and role groups that suffice for most organizations, it allows the creation of custom roles and custom role groups. These custom roles can be assigned through EAC or EMS. The RBAC configuration of defined administrator or user roles with the option of changing memberships can be found in EAC ➤ Permissions ➤ Admin Roles, as shown in Figure 10-1. Creating custom elements for RBAC can only be done through EMS. User roles function to manage assignment policies, which are discussed later in this chapter.

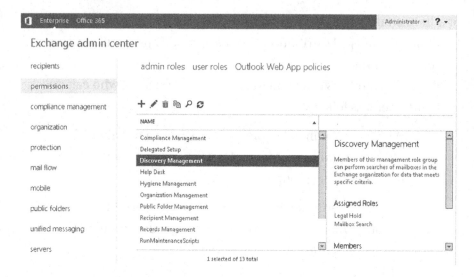

Figure 10-1. *Locating predefined roles in the Exchange Admin Center*

Caution   The reason directly loading the Exchange module is not supported is that this not only bypasses RBAC but also may result in non-working Exchange cmdlets. For example, your account may lack the Active Directory permission to create a user object, but running New-MailUser via the Exchange Management Shell might create the underlying user object, because of permissions granted to the Exchange Trusted Subsystem through RBAC.

There are three exceptions to this rule and when you might need to run **Add-PSSnapIn Microsoft.Exchange.***:

1) Required by some cmdlets when managing Exchange hybrid without Exchange Server, for example, Set-RemoteDomain

2) When managing Edge Transport servers

3) When RBAC is misconfigured or messed up

In those scenarios there is no Exchange server to handle your actions, and you need to load the PowerShell Snap-In module to talk directly to Active Directory.

Apart from opening the Exchange Management Shell shortcut, to load the Exchange Management Shell in a supported way, honoring RBAC configuration, you have two options:

1) Load the functions from the **RemoteExchange.ps1** script, which by default is located in the $exbin subfolder by dot-sourcing it; then call the function to connect to an automatically selected Exchange server:

```
. 'C:\Program Files\Microsoft\Exchange
Server\v15\bin\RemoteExchange.ps1'
Connect-ExchangeServer -auto
```

You can also connect to a specific Exchange server, specifying the FQDN:

```
Connect-ExchangeServer -ServerFqdn ex1.
contoso.com
```

2) Connect to Exchange remotely by setting up a remoting session, as follows:

```
$Session= New-PSSession -ConfigurationName
Microsoft.Exchange -ConnectionUri <FQDN>/
PowerShell/
Import-PSSession $Session
```

Caution   When managing Exchange Online, you are probably familiar with the Exchange Online Management module version 3 (or later). This module is not used to manage Exchange on-premises. Exchange on-premises supports remote PowerShell only and does not support the REST calls that the EXOMv3 module uses for management.

The RBAC configuration is stored in Active Directory. Take AD replication latency into account when making changes to RBAC configuration when operating multiple AD sites.

RBAC Components

The components used in the RBAC model, as well as their relationships, are shown in Figure 10-2. The following sections will talk about these components, their relationships, and how to put them into action.

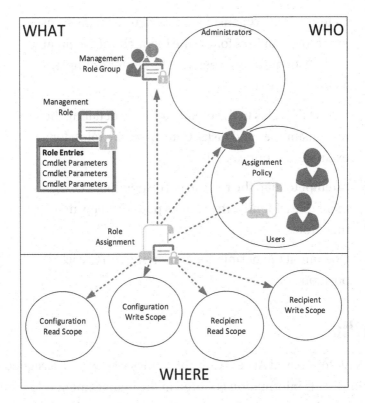

Figure 10-2. Role-Based Access Control components

Caution   Role-Based Access Control is managed by the Organization Management role group. You could potentially create a situation where you lock yourself out.

To understand the RBAC model, you must know the concepts, components, and possibilities. This will also help you understand how to customize RBAC to perhaps address specific requirements of your organization. When planning for RBAC customization, keep the following in mind:

- Determine the organizational structure. In most cases, job responsibilities follow the hierarchy of the organization. Distinguish between role levels, for example, senior vs. junior.

- Define the roles in the organization by detailing their responsibilities and tasks. Categorize the roles, for example, support vs. sales.

- Attempt to map the roles to corresponding management roles. Identify the gaps as potential new management roles.

- Document the permission requirements for each position.

The Who

The Who in Role-Based Access Control defines who will be assigned permissions. This information is stored in the management role groups, or role groups. Role groups are Universal Security Groups (USGs) with special flags to indicate they are role groups. By assigning role groups to one or more management roles, you are effectively granting those role groups the permissions that are part of the management role's list of management role entries.

Table 10-1 lists all built-in role group definitions, as well as short descriptions of their pre-defined capabilities.

Note   A management role group is a Universal Security Group with msExchRecipientTypeDetails set to 1073741824.

Table 10-1. *Built-In Role Groups*

Role Group	Description
Organization Management	Members of this management role group have permissions to manage Exchange objects and their properties in the Exchange organization. Members can also delegate role groups and management roles in the organization. This role group shouldn't be deleted.
Recipient Management	Members of this management role group have rights to create, manage, and remove Exchange recipient objects in the Exchange organization.
View-Only Organization Management	Members of this management role group can view recipient and configuration objects and their properties in the Exchange organization.
Public Folder Management	Members of this management role group can manage public folders. Members can create and delete public folders and manage public folder settings such as replicas, quotas, age limits, and permissions as well as mail-enabled and mail-disabled public folders.
Help Desk	Members of this management role group can view and manage the configuration for individual recipients and view recipients in an Exchange organization. Members of this role group can only manage the configuration each user can manage on their own mailbox. Additional permissions can be added by assigning additional management roles to this role group.

(continued)

Table 10-1. (*continued*)

Role Group	Description
Records Management	Members of this management role group can configure compliance features such as retention policy tags, message classifications, transport rules, and more.
Discovery Management	Members of this management role group can perform searches of mailboxes in the Exchange organization for data that meets specific criteria.
Server Management	Members of this management role group have permissions to manage all Exchange servers within the Exchange organization, but members don't have permissions to perform operations that have global impact in the Exchange organization.
Delegated Setup	Members of this management role group have permissions to install and uninstall Exchange on provisioned servers. This role group shouldn't be deleted.
Hygiene Management	Members of this management role group can manage Exchange anti-spam features and grant permissions for antivirus products to integrate with Exchange.
Compliance Management	This role group will allow a specified user, responsible for compliance, to properly configure and manage compliance settings within Exchange in accordance with their policy.

(*continued*)

Table 10-1. (*continued*)

Role Group	Description
Security Reader	Members of this role group may include cross-service administrators, as well as external partner groups and Microsoft Support. While present and pre-canned with role group entries, there is no relationship with Azure Active Directory unlike the group of the same name in Exchange Online, and may be regarded as a placeholder for now.
Security Administrator	Members of this role group may include cross-service administrators, as well as external partner groups and Microsoft Support. While present and pre-canned with role group entries, there is no relationship with Azure Active Directory unlike the group of the same name in Exchange Online, and may be regarded as a placeholder for now.
UM Management	This role group is only present when migrated from an earlier release of Exchange, as UM is not available on Exchange 2019.

You can view current role groups and the assigned roles running **Get-RoleGroup** from the Exchange Management Shell, as shown in Figure 10-3.

```
[PS] >Get-RoleGroup

Name              AssignedRoles
----              -------------
Organization Management      {Active Directory Permissions, Address Lists,
                  ApplicationImpersonation, ArchiveApplication, Audit
                  Logs, Cmdlet Extension Agents, Compliance Admin,
                  Data Loss Prevention, Database Availability Groups,
                  Database Copies, Databases, Disaster Recovery,
                  Distribution Groups, Edge Subscriptions, E-Mail
                  Address Policies, Exchange Connectors...}
Recipient Management         {Distribution Groups, Mail Recipient Creation, Mail
                  Recipients, Message Tracking, Migration, Move
                  Mailboxes, Recipient Policies, Team Mailboxes}
View-Only Organization Management {Monitoring, View-Only Configuration, View-Only
                  Recipients}
Public Folder Management     {Mail Enabled Public Folders, Public Folders}
UM Management                {UM Mailboxes, UM Prompts, Unified Messaging}
Help Desk                    {User Options, View-Only Recipients}
Records Management           {Audit Logs, Journaling, Message Tracking, Retention
                  Management, Transport Rules}
Discovery Management         {Legal Hold, Mailbox Search}
Server Management            {Database Copies, Databases, Exchange Connectors,
                  Exchange Server Certificates, Exchange Servers,
                  Exchange Virtual Directories, Monitoring, POP3 And
                  IMAP4 Protocols, Receive Connectors, Transport
                  Queues}
Delegated Setup              {View-Only Configuration}
Hygiene Management           {ApplicationImpersonation, Receive Connectors,
                  Transport Agents, Transport Hygiene, View-Only
                  Configuration, View-Only Recipients}
Compliance Management        {Audit Logs, Compliance Admin, Data Loss Prevention,
                  Information Rights Management, Journaling, Message
                  Tracking, Retention Management, Transport Rules,
                  View-Only Audit Logs, View-Only Configuration,
                  View-Only Recipients}
Security Reader              {Security Reader}
Security Administrator       {Security Admin}
```

Figure 10-3.   View built-in role groups using EMS

Custom Role Group

In addition to using the built-in role groups, you can create your own role group. In fact, you need to, as you cannot alter the built-in (precanned) role groups.

To create a role group, you must be a member of the **Organization Management** role group. To manage a role group, you must be the manager of the role group, which is determined by the **ManagedBy** property, or use the **BypassSecurityGroupManagerCheck** to bypass management checks, similar to managing Distribution Groups as an administrator when you are not the manager.

To create a role group, you use the **New-RoleGroup** cmdlet. Give the role group a name and assign to it one or more existing management roles using the Roles parameter, as follows:

```
New-RoleGroup -Name 'Staff Mailbox Manager' -Roles 'Staff
Mailboxes'
```

Users or groups can be directly added to the role group using the Members parameter, or manage the members using **Add RoleGroupMember** or **Remove-RoleGroupMember**. For example, here's how to add a user Frank to Staff Mailbox Manager:

```
Add-RoleGroupMember -Identity 'Staff Mailbox Manager' -Member
'Frank'
```

The **New-RoleGroup** cmdlet allows you to specify management roles using the Roles parameter, scopes using the various Scope parameters, and desired role group members using the Members parameter. This way, you can accomplish role assignments using one cmdlet, assuming the required building blocks are built-in or created.

This will also allow you to change the manager of the role group. For example, you could use the following cmdlet:

```
New-RoleGroup -Name 'Exec Recipient Management' -Roles 'Mail
Recipients','Staff Mailboxes'
 -CustomRecipientWriteSope 'Exec Recipients' -ManagedBy
 'Frank' -Members 'Peter','Judith'
```

This will accomplish the following:

1. A new role group named Exec Recipient Management is created.

2. Users Peter and Judith are added as members of this role group.

3. User Frank is configured as manager of the role group.

4. The following management role assignments are created, where each assignment will be configured with Exec Recipients as CustomRecipientWriteScope:

    *   Mail recipients-Exec Recipient management

    *   Staff mailboxes-Exec Recipient management

More on scopes later. Alternatively, you can use Set-RoleGroup to modify an existing role group.

Linked Role Groups

Some organizations have multiple Active Directory forests, which are trusting each other. A common example of this is a resource forest containing all Exchange-related resources, trusting an account forest where all the users and group accounts reside in. In those scenarios, you can use linked role groups. This will create role groups in the trusting Exchange (resource) forest that will be linked to Universal Security Groups (USGs) in the trusted account forest. Two-way trusts are not required.

Assuming the trust has been set up correctly, you can create a linked role group with the following command:

```
New-RoleGroup -Name '<Role Group Name>-Linked' -LinkedForeign
Group <Name of foreign USG> -LinkedDomainController <foreign
DC fqdn> -LinkedCredential (Get-Credential) -Roles <Roles>
```

You can then use the Roles property of the role groups to get a list of roles to assign to the linked role group. For example, to create a linked role group for the Server Management role group, you use the following:

```
New-RoleGroup -Name 'Server Management-Linked' -LinkedForeign
Group 'Server Management Admins' -LinkedDomainController
dc1.contoso.com -LinkedCredential (Get-Credential) -Roles
(Get-RoleGroup -Identity 'Server Management').Roles
```

Tip   To assist in converting existing built-in role groups to linked role groups, use the procedure described at **http://bit.ly/ ConvertToLinkedRoleGroups**.

The What

The What is defined by the management roles and management role entries. A management role defines permitted actions, with its set of cmdlets and parameters that can be used. Exchange 2019 has around 90 predefined management roles. You can obtain a list of these by using Get-ManagementRole.

Management role entries consist of cmdlets and their parameters. When the management role entry is part of a management role, that management role can use those cmdlets in combination with the specified parameters. Exchange 2019 has over 2,800 management role entries. Note that parameters can be a subset of the parameters that would normally be available.

You can obtain a list of current management role entries for a particular management role using Get-ManagementRoleEntry -Identity '<Management Role>*'. Alternatively, you can query the RoleEntries attribute of the management role. To view all the management role entries, use '*' as the management role—for example, Get-ManagementRoleEntry -Identity '**'.

Management Roles and Management Role Entries

To get an idea of how this works, let us inspect the "Reset Password" management role. You can retrieve the management role object and view its attributes by using the Get-ManagementRole cmdlets, with results shown in Figure 10-4.

```
[PS] >Get-ManagementRole -Identity 'Reset Password'

Name        RoleType
----        --------
Reset Password ResetPassword

[PS] >Get-ManagementRoleEntry -Identity 'Reset Password\*'

Name            Role            Parameters
----            ----            ----------
Set-Mailbox     Reset Password  {Password, ResetPasswordOnNextLogon, RoomMailboxPassword}


[PS] >Get-ManagementRole -Identity 'Reset Password' | Select -ExpandProperty RoleEntries | fl

PSSnapinName : Microsoft.Exchange.Management.PowerShell.E2010
Name        : Set-Mailbox
Parameters  : {Password, ResetPasswordOnNextLogon, RoomMailboxPassword}
```

Figure 10-4. *Reset Password management role entries*

As shown in in Figure 10-4, the latter two cmdlets show that the Reset Password management role permits use of the cmdlet **Set-Mailbox**, in conjunction with the parameters **Password**, **ResetPasswordOnNextLogon**, or **RoomMailboxPassword**. Simply said, users with the Reset Password role can use Set-Mailbox to configure the password for user mailboxes or rooms and configure the requirement for users to reset their password after they log on.

Custom Management Roles

You can create custom management roles by using the New-ManagementRole cmdlet. In Exchange, there are two types of management roles: normal and unscoped (more on the unscoped roles later). The normal management role requires you to specify an existing role, which will become known as the parent. This can be a predefined management role or another custom management role. The parent is used as a template but also functions as a limiter; you can remove any superfluous cmdlets or parameters at any level, but you cannot add cmdlets or parameters that are not part of the parent management role.

Note   When you assign a Set-* cmdlet to a management role, you also need to assign the corresponding Get-* cmdlet. Simply said, in order to be able to set things, you also need to be able to get them.

In this example, you will create a simple custom role for mail recipients. This predefined role is used for managing mail-enabled objects in the organization. You use this command:

```
New-ManagementRole -Name 'Custom Mail Recipients' -Parent 'Mail Recipients'
```

You can verify the capabilities of this new custom role, which will be identical to the capabilities of the Mail Recipients role, by using

```
Get-ManagementRoleEntry -Identity 'Custom Mail Recipients\*'
```

Now, suppose you want to remove the capability of using one of the role entries, such as a cmdlet. To accomplish this, use the Remove-ManagementRoleEntry cmdlet, specifying <Management Role>\<Management Role Entry>, like this:

```
Remove-ManagementRoleEntry -Identity 'Custom Mail Recipients\
Set-UserPhoto'
```

To (re-)add an entry to a management role, for example, after accidently removing it, use

```
Add-ManagementRoleEntry 'Custom Mail Recipients\Set-UserPhoto'
```

Note that you can only add entries that are also present in the parent role. Optionally, when adding, you can use **Parameters** with **Add-ManagementRoleEntry** to explicitly specify parameters that you want to allow.

Caution   When stripping role entries from a custom management role that will be using EAC, be careful not to remove the Set-ADServerSettings cmdlet. This cmdlet is used during initialization of the session to enable the View Entire Forest option needed to discover the permissions of the currently logged-on user.

Managing Parameters

To modify the parameters that you can use, use the **Set ManagementRoleEntry** cmdlet together with **AddParameter** or **RemoveParameter** depending on the required operation, as well as **Parameter** specifying the parameters.

For example, if you want to remove the ability to use the Preview parameter with Set-UserPhoto, you can use

```
Set-ManagementRoleEntry -Identity 'Custom Mail Recipients\
Set-UserPhoto' -Parameter Preview -RemoveParameter
```

To reinstate this Preview parameter, use

```
Set-ManagementRoleEntry -Identity 'Custom Mail Recipients\
Set-UserPhoto' -Parameter Preview -AddParameter
```

As mentioned earlier, re-adding Preview works here because it is also available in the parent Mail Recipients role.

To quickly retrieve roles that use certain cmdlets, parameters, scripts, or script parameters, you can use the **Get-ManagementRole** cmdlet with the parameters **Cmdlet**, **CmdletParameters**, **Script**, or **ScriptParameters**.

You can also use **GetChildren** to retrieve roles that are "children" of the parent role or use **Recurse** to return a role and all of its offspring. For example, this returns all roles that allow **Set-Mailbox**:

```
Get-ManagementRole -Cmdlet Set-Mailbox
```

This cmdlet will return all roles allowing use of a parameter called **EmailAddresses** with any cmdlets:

```
Get-ManagementRole -CmdletParameters EmailAddresses
```

Unscoped Top-Level Management Roles

A special management role is the unscoped top-level management role. This is a management role whose purpose is to provide administrators or specific user accounts permissions to execute scripts or non-Exchange cmdlets. As the name implies, unscoped roles have no scope, as they have no related parent role, contrary to normal management roles.

To create an unscoped management role, you need to be assigned to the **Unscoped Role Management Group**. To quickly assign the administrator account to this group, use

```
New-ManagementRoleAssignment -Name 'Unscoped Role Management-
Administrator' -User 'Administrator' -Role 'Unscoped Role
Management'
```

If you want to grant permission to a group, use the **SecurityGroup** parameter instead of **User**:

```
New-ManagementRoleAssignment -Name 'Unscoped Role Management-
Organization Management' -SecurityGroup 'Organization
Management' -Role 'Unscoped Role Management'
```

Note   You may need to restart EAC or the EMS session to see the results of RBAC changes to your currently logged-on account.

It is best practice to name the management role assignment by combining the name of the management role group and the user or group you have assigned the role group to. When not specified, this combination will be used as the management role assignment.

Now, when granted the Unscoped Role Management assignment, you can specify the switch **UnScopedTopLevel** when using the **New-ManagementRole** cmdlet:

```
New-ManagementRole -Name 'Maintenance Scripts' -UnscopedTop
Level
```

Since we do not use templates like with normal management roles, the newly created unscoped management role will initially be empty regarding permissions. The account that created the unscoped management role will initially get assigned to it, which is necessary to perform delegation of the role to other accounts. It is also something you may notice when, for example, you want to remove the group or assignment. More on that later.

Unscoped management roles are special in that they allow you to assign scripts or non-Exchange cmdlets permissions to run. The scripts you want to use must reside in the **$exinstall\RemoteScripts** folder, though. When the default Exchange installation folder is used, this location will resolve to **C:\Program Files\Microsoft\Exchange Server\ v15\RemoteScripts**.

Note   The scripts you want to use with unscoped management roles need to reside in the **$exinstall\RemoteScripts** folder on every Exchange server or only on those within a specific region or site depending on your scope.

To allow the execution of scripts via management role entries for an unscoped management role, specify its name as well as any parameters you would allow:

```
Add-ManagementRoleEntry -Identity '<role name>\<script name>'
-Parameters <param1, param2,..> -Type Script -UnscopedTopLevel
```

Note   You need to specify every individual parameter required; there is no wildcard option to add all possible parameters at once.

For example, to allow a custom unscoped management role **Maintenance Scripts** to execute the script **ClearLogs.ps1** using the parameter **Days**, after distributing this script to every RemoteScripts folder, use the following to allow it through a role entry:

```
Add-ManagementRoleEntry -Identity 'Maintenance Scripts\
ClearLogs.ps1'
-Parameters 'Days' -Type Script -UnscopedTopLevel
```

Caution   When adding scripts to role entries, know that the cmdlet only performs basic validation for the parameters specified. It is not dynamic, so any changes to the script or removal of the script will not be detected, and you need to adjust the related role entries manually.

Earlier, we created an unscoped management role group Maintenance Scripts, which we have given permission to run the script ClearLogs.ps1. All we need to do now is create a role group for the role we created and add accounts that need to run this script to this group:

```
New-RoleGroup -Name 'RunMaintenanceScripts' -Roles 'Maintenance
Scripts'
Add-RoleGroupMember -Identity 'RunMaintenanceScripts'
-Member svcExchange
```

The output of these cmdlets as well as the result is shown in Figure 10-5.

```
[PS] >New-ManagementRole -Name 'Maintenance Scripts' -UnscopedTopLevel

Name        RoleType
----        --------
Maintenance Scripts UnScoped

[PS] >Add-ManagementRoleEntry -Identity 'Maintenance Scripts\ClearLogs.ps1' -Parameters 'Days' -Type Script -
UnscopedTopLevel
[PS] >New-RoleGroup -Name 'RunMaintenanceScripts' -Roles 'Maintenance Scripts'

Name          AssignedRoles    RoleAssignments        ManagedBy
----          -------------    ---------------        ---------
RunMaintenanceScripts {Maintenance Scripts} {Maintenance Scripts-RunMaintenanceScripts}
{ad.myexchangelabs.com/Microsoft Exchange Security
                                Groups/Organization Management,
                                ad.myexchangelabs.com/Users/Administrator}

[PS] >Add-RoleGroupMember -Identity 'RunMaintenanceScripts' -Member svcExchange
```

Figure 10-5. *Create a custom role group to run a specific script*

Notice that there are two assignments created, each with a different role assignment delegation type (property not shown):

- The account creating the role gets a DelegationOrgWide-type assignment. This assignment is automatic after role creation, allowing the creator to delegate permissions for the role.

- The assignment created using New-RoleGroup is a normal-type assignment. This allows the role assignee to execute the role entries associated with that role group.

Note   If the user executing the **Add-RoleGroupMember** cmdlet is not part of the **ManagedBy** property of the role group (i.e., accounts that can manage their membership), specify the **BypassSecurityGroupManagerCheck** switch to bypass built-in group management checks.

Now, when the account svcExchange opens a remote EMS session, it will have only the ClearLogs.ps1 script at its disposal. You can quickly test this using the Connect-ExchangeServer cmdlet, with the User and Prompt parameters to provide the account name, and let it prompt for the password. The -Auto switch is added to make it connect to any available server:

```
[PS] >Connect-ExchangeServer -Auto -User svcExchange -Prompt
VERBOSE: Connecting to exch01.contoso.com.
VERBOSE: Connected to exch01.contoso.com.
```

To see which commands are available from the Exchange session, return only commands that have the same module name as the PowerShell session that is connected using the *\svcExchange account (our test connection):

```
[PS] >Get-Command -Module (Get-PSSession | Where {$_.runSpace.
ConnectionInfo.Credential.UserName -like '*\svcExchange'}).
computerName
```

CommandType	Name	Version	Source
Function	ClearLogs.ps1	1.0	ex2.ad.myexchangelabs.com

Note also that you allowed only the role to execute the script. There is no single Exchange cmdlet available. If you want to be able to execute Exchange cmdlets through this script or directly, you need to allow them as well, by adding them as role entries using **New-ManagementRoleEntry**.

This may take a while to set up, as you need to go through scripts to collect information on cmdlet and parameter usage, but it grants you very fine-grained control over permissions, which should make your security officer happy and may prevent disasters from occurring.

Caution   When allowing execution of scripts through roles, you need to allow cmdlets and parameters referenced in the script as well. When you overlook this requirement, these will not be available in the security context of the role, and your script will not function.

You can also use unscoped management roles to grant permissions to execute cmdlets provided through other PSSnapIn modules as well. In those cases, use the following syntax:

```
Add-ManagementRoleEntry -Identity <role name>\<cmdlet name>
-PSSnapinName <snap-in name> -Parameters <param1, param2, ..>
-Type Cmdlet -UnscopedTopLevel
```

For example:

```
Add-ManagementRoleEntry -Identity 'Maintenance Scripts\
Get-QADUser' -Parameters 'Identity' -PSSnapinName Quest.
ActiveRoles.ADManagement -UnscopedTopLevel
```

Note that this module needs to be installed and registered on all relevant Exchange servers that could potentially be running the cmdlet.

Clean Up Unscoped Top-Level Management Roles

The cmdlet to remove script or non-Exchange cmdlet assignments for unscoped management roles is similar to removing normal management role entries:

```
Remove-RoleGroup RunMaintenanceScripts
```

Only user-defined management roles can be removed. Before you can remove a management role, you first need to remove any dependencies on that management role or use the Recurse parameter to perform a cascaded delete:

```
Remove-ManagementRole -Identity 'Maintenance Scripts' -Recurse
```

Finally, to remove the management role, specify the parameter UnScopedToplevel as well:

```
Remove-ManagementRole -Identity 'Maintenance Scripts'
-UnScopedTopLevel -Recurse
```

The Where

The Where component determines where the cmdlets are allowed to operate. From an Active Directory perspective, this can be the entire Exchange organization or scoped down to an Organizational Unit or Active Directory site, for example. The entire Exchange organization is the default scope. The scope can also be targeting subsets of recipients, Exchange servers, or databases, filtering on objects with specific properties.

RBAC defines two types of management scopes:

- **Regular** or non-exclusive scopes define which objects in Active Directory can be accessed—for example, on Organizational Unit (OU) or the server level.

- **Exclusive scopes** are like regular scopes, except that they include access to Active Directory objects. Only members of groups with exclusive access can access those Active Directory objects; others will be denied access.

When defining scopes, be aware of the following rules and terminology:

- When you create a custom management role, it will inherit the non-exclusive scope configuration of the parent management role. These inheritable scopes are called implicit, as they are set by the parent.

- Custom scopes are called explicit scopes, as they are not inherited and explicitly defined.

More on implicit and explicit scopes later in the section.

Note   Unscoped top-level management roles have no scope definition. The scope properties of these roles will state "Not Applicable."

Regular Scopes

There are two types of regular scopes: recipient and configuration scopes. A recipient scope refers to recipient objects, such as mailboxes, Distribution Groups, or mail-enabled users. A configuration scope refers to Exchange configuration objects, such as an Exchange server or mailbox databases.

For each of these types, you can configure a read or write scope. Together, this results in being able to assign the following types of scopes to every management role:

- **Recipient Read Scope** determines which recipient objects the assignee is allowed to read from Active Directory.

- **Recipient Write Scope** determines which recipient objects the assignee is allowed to create or modify from Active Directory.

- **Configuration Read Scope** determines which configuration objects the assignee is allowed to read from Active Directory.

- **Configuration Write Scope** determines which configuration objects, such as Exchange servers or databases, the assignee is allowed to create or modify from Active Directory.

Note   An assigned write scope cannot exceed the boundaries of the related read scope. In other words, you cannot configure what you cannot view.

Implicit Scopes

Implicit scopes are predefined for management roles and are configured through the **ImplicitRecipientReadScope**, **ImplicitRecipientWriteScope**, **ImplicitConfigReadScope**, and **ImplicitConfigWriteScope** properties of the management role. Child management roles inherit the scopes of their parent roles.

When a management role is assigned, the implicit scopes associated with that role are automatically applied to the assignment, unless explicit scopes are specified (which will be explained later). If an explicit scope is configured, it will override the implicit scopes, creating a non-inheritable explicit scope. However, implicit read scopes are an exception to this rule, as they always take precedence over explicit scopes.

Please refer to Table 10-2 for a list of all available implicit scope definitions.

Table 10-2. *Implicit Scope Definitions*

Name	Recipient Configuration	Description
Organization	Read/Write	Recipient objects in the Exchange organization
MyGAL	Read	Read the properties of any recipient within the current user's GAL
Self	Read/Write	The current user's properties

(continued)

Table 10-2. (*continued*)

Name	Recipient Configuration	Description
MyDistributionGroups	Read/Write	Distribution Groups managed by the current user
OrganizationConfig	Read/Write	Exchange server or database objects in the Exchange organization
None		Blocks a scope

Explicit Scopes

Explicit scopes are customizable scopes that override implicit write scopes. These scopes are defined through management role assignments, providing a way to use implicit roles consistently while allowing for exceptions through explicitly configured scopes.

Management role assignments have specific properties for defining predefined relative scopes. These scopes are a subset of the implicit scopes and are based on the relationship between the role assignee and recipients. The options for predefined relative scopes are as follows:

- **Organization** scope allows assignees to modify recipients across the entire Exchange organization. For example, if a role allows configuration of the display name and user photo, assigning this scope will enable the assignee to configure those properties for all recipients in the Exchange organization.

- **Self** scope allows assignees to modify their own properties. For example, if a role allows configuration of the display name and user photo, assigning this scope will only allow the assignee to perform those actions on their own properties.

- MyDistributionGroups allows assignees to create and manage Distribution Groups where they are listed as the owner through the ManagedBy property.

Predefined relative scopes are assigned to management role assignments using the **RecipientRelativeWriteScope** property.

Custom Scopes

When implicit scopes, possibly in combination with predefined relative scopes, meet your requirements, you can use a custom scope. This allows you to define specific targets, such as particular Organizational Units, recipients, or databases. As with predefined relative scopes, custom scopes override the implicit scopes, except for the read scope.

To create custom scopes that can be reused for more than one management role, you can define and assign management scope objects. This also makes them more manageable. More on management scopes later in this section.

When you want to define custom scopes, you can choose from the following type of custom scopes:

- **OU** scope targets recipients within the configured OU. It is configured through the **RecipientOrganizationalUnitScope** property of management role assignments.

- **Recipient filter** scope uses a management scope object to filter recipients based on properties such as recipient type, department, manager, or location by using an OPATH filter. The filter is configured through the **RecipientRestrictionFilter** property of the management scope. In addition, you can combine the recipient filter with **RecipientRoot** to define the filter starting point. The management scope is configured through the **CustomRecipientWriteScope** property.

– **Configuration scope** uses a management scope object to target specific servers based on server lists or filterable properties, such as the Active Directory site of server role, or to target specific databases based on database lists or filterable database properties.

– **Server** scope is configured using the **ServerRestrictionFilter** parameter using an OPATH filter or the **ServerList** parameter. Note that configuration objects related to the server, like Receive Connectors or virtual directories, can also be managed for servers that are in scope.

– **Database scope** is configured using the **DatabaseRestrictionFilter** parameter using an OPATH filter or the **DatabaseList** parameter. Database configuration settings like quota settings, maintenance schedule, or database mounting can be managed for databases that are in scope. In addition, the assignee can also create mailboxes in databases that are in scope.

Note   When you specify an alternative root location for the recipient filter scope using RecipientRoot, you need to specify RecipientRoot in canonical form (contoso.com/nl/users), not the distinguished name.

Caution   Defined scopes related to Active Directory locations are not dynamic. For example, when you move or rename Organizational Units, you need to adjust related scopes as well.

Management Scopes

Now that we touched on all the possible elements that may come into play when constructing and configuring management scopes, we can talk about the management scopes themselves. We will also provide a few examples to improve understanding of the subject, as it can be overwhelming at first.

Management scopes are created using the **New-ManagementScope** cmdlet. Depending on whether you want to provide a recipient scope or server scope, you provide the corresponding parameters and the filter value itself.

For example, to create a scope for the following objects

- All recipients who are members of a certain group named Staff. This can be achieved by specifying the distinguishedName of the group, for example, cn=Staff, ou=Users,dc=contoso,dc=com.

- They must reside below a top-level OU named NL in contoso.com, whose canonical definition would be contoso.com/NL.

you would use

```
New-ManagementScope -Name 'Scope-NL-Staff' -RecipientRoot
'contoso.com/NL' -RecipientRestrictionFilter {membergroup
-eq 'cn=Staff,ou=Users,dc=contoso,dc=com'}
```

Along the same lines, to create a scope for the Active Directory site London, you could use

```
New-ManagementScope -Name 'Scope-Site London' -Server
RestrictionFilter {ServerSite -eq 'CN=London,CN=Sites,
CN=Configuration,DC=contoso,DC=com'}
```

To create a scope for a fixed set of servers, you can use the ServerList parameter:

```
New-ManagementScope -Name 'Servers Amsterdam' -ServerList
AMS-EXCH01,AMS-EXCH02
```

To create a scope for a databases starting with "NL-", you use

```
New-ManagementScope -Name 'Databases NL' -Database
RestrictionFilter {Name -like 'NL-*'}
```

Note that Recipient or Server filters use OPATH definitions for recipient or configuration restrictions. More information on scope filtering can be found at **http://bit.ly/RBACScopeFilters**.

Exclusive Scopes

The last type of scope to discuss is the exclusive scope. An exclusive scope targets a specific set of recipients or configuration objects in Active Directory. These objects then become inaccessible for other management role assignments when accessing the same type of object—hence the word exclusive. Even if other assignments have those objects in scope, if they are targeted with an exclusive scope, they can only be managed through the management roles with the exclusive scope assignment.

For example, if you define an exclusive recipient assignment for a top-level OU named NL, other assignments will be blocked from accessing the NL container structure, including assignments with an organization-wide scope. Common usage for roles with these scopes is high-profile recipients, for which manage-recipient role with an exclusive scope is assigned, thus blocking management of these recipients by other management roles.

To create an exclusive scope, use the **Exclusive** switch when creating or reconfiguring a management role assignment. For example, here's how to create an exclusive scope using a recipient filter for all recipients located in the VIP OU tree:

```
New-ManagementScope -Name 'Scope-Exec Recipients' -RecipientRoot
'contoso.com/VIP' RecipientRestrictionFilter {Name -like '*'}
-Exclusive
```

Now suppose you want to assign a group called Exec Admins the role of Mail Recipients, using the scope we have just created. You would use the **ExclusiveRecipientWriteScope** instead of the **CustomRecipientWriteScope** for the exclusive scope:

```
New-ManagementRoleAssignment -SecurityGroup 'Exec Admins'
-Role 'Mail Recipients' -ExclusiveRecipientWriteScope
'Exec Recipients'
```

The reason for using ExclusiveRecipientWriteScope is to confirm that you are specifying an exclusive scope. If you use CustomRecipientWriteScope, Exchange will notify you that the scope you have specified is exclusive. This way, Exchange not only takes care of configuring the CustomRecipientWriteScope with the scope you provided, but it also sets the RecipientWriteScope to the ExclusiveRecipientScope type to indicate that the scope is exclusive.

You can check the previously set assignment using Get-ManagementRoleAssignment, knowing that Exchange will use the <Role>-<Role Assignee Name> convention when naming assignments. If that name already exists, it will append sequence numbers. To check this, use the following command; Figure 10-6 shows a similar example of the output:

```
Get-ManagementRoleAssignment -Identity 'Mail Recipients-Exec
Admins'| fl *role*,*scope*,*assign*
```

```
[PS] >Get-ManagementRoleAssignment -Identity 'Mail Recipients-Exec Admins'| fl *role*,*scope*,*assign*

RoleAssigneeType          : SecurityGroup
RoleAssignee              : ad.myexchangelabs.com/NL/Exec Admins
Role              : Mail Recipients
RoleAssignmentDelegationType : Regular
RoleAssigneeName          : Exec Admins
CustomRecipientWriteScope   : Scope-Exec Recipients
CustomConfigWriteScope      :
RecipientReadScope        : Organization
ConfigReadScope           : OrganizationConfig
RecipientWriteScope        : ExclusiveRecipientScope
ConfigWriteScope          : OrganizationConfig
AssignmentMethod          : Direct
AssignmentChain           :
RoleAssigneeType          : SecurityGroup
RoleAssignee              : contoso.com/NL/Exec Admins
RoleAssignmentDelegationType : Regular
RoleAssigneeName          : Exec Admins
```

Figure 10-6. *View management role assignments*

As shown, the members of the Exec Recipients group are now the only users allowed to manage recipients in the VIP OU (and below). Organization-level managers of mail recipients, including administrators with organization management permissions, cannot.

Note   Exclusive scopes can overlap. Objects that are part of multiple exclusive scopes are accessible for assignees of any of these scopes.

The interaction of regular scopes and exclusive scopes and possibility their overlap are shown in Figure 10-7. As shown, Recipient Admin can manage recipients in the recipient scope (could be a complete organization), except for recipients that are part of the Exec Recipients or Another VIP exclusive scopes. Exec Admins can manage recipients in Exec Recipients, including the recipient that is part of the Exec Recipients as well as the Another VIP exclusive scope.

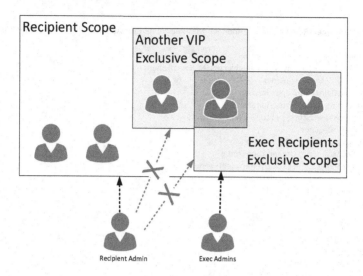

Figure 10-7. *Regular and exclusive scope interaction*

1+1+1=3: Management Role Assignments

After defining the management roles (what), the management scopes (where), and the role groups (who), it is now time to connect these pieces of the RBAC puzzle. This is accomplished by so-called management role assignments.

In an earlier example in this chapter, we showed how to use New-ManagementRoleAssignment to assign a user or Universal Security Group to an unscoped management role. Besides these direct role assignments, end users can be granted permission through role assignment policies. But before moving on to management role assignments, let us briefly look at the possible parameters when creating these assignments:

- The Name parameter can be used to specify the name of the management role assignment. If a name is not provided, <Role>-<Role Assignee Name> will be used by default. If the name already exists, sequence numbers will be appended to create unique names.

- The Computer parameter specifies the computer account to assign the management role to.

- The SecurityGroup parameter specifies the management role group or Universal Security Group to assign the management role to.

- The User parameter specifies the name or alias of the user to assign the management role to.

- The Policy parameter specifies the name of the management role assignment policy to assign the management role to. The IsEndUserRole property of the specified role needs to be $true, indicating it is a user role.

- The Role parameter specifies the management role to assign.

- The CustomConfigWriteScope parameter specifies the regular management scope for configuration objects. If CustomConfigWriteScope is specified, you cannot use ExclusiveConfigWriteScope.

- The CustomRecipientWriteScope parameter specifies the regular management scope for recipient objects. If CustomRecipientWriteScope is specified, you cannot use ExclusiveRecipientWriteScope or RecipientOrganizationalUnitScope.

- The Delegating switch specifies if the user or USG is allowed to grant the assigned management role to other accounts.

- The `ExclusiveConfigWriteScope` parameter specifies the exclusive management scope for configuration objects. If `ExclusiveConfigWriteScope` is specified, you cannot use `CustomConfigWriteScope`.

- The `ExclusiveRecipientWriteScope` parameter specifies the exclusive management scope for the recipient objects. If `ExclusiveRecipientWriteScope` is specified, you cannot use `CustomRecipientWriteScope` or `RecipientOrganizationalUnitScope`.

- The `RecipientOrganizationalUnitScope` parameter specifies the OU to scope the role assignment. Use the canonical form when specifying the OU, for example, contoso.com/OU.

- The `RecipientRelativeWriteScope` parameter specifies the type of restriction to apply to the recipient scope. Valid options are `Organization`, `MyGAL`, `Self`, `MyDistributionGroups`, and `None`.

- The `UnScopedTopLevel` switch needs to be specified if the role provided is an unscoped top-level management role.

Tip   When assigning management roles, the parameters Computer, SecurityGroup, User, or Policy are mutually exclusive; you can only use one of these parameters per assignment.

Now let us look at a few examples to see how this works by creating assignments using management roles, management scopes, and role groups. The examples assume you have country-specific administrators who have the task of managing recipients in a top-level OU called

NL. These administrators are members of a Universal Security Group (USG) named NL Admins. Since you only want to filter on an OU, specifying the RecipientOrganizationUnitScope parameter suffices for accomplishing this:

```
New-ManagementRoleAssignment -SecurityGroup 'NL Admins'
-Role 'Mail Recipients' -RecipientOrganizationalUnitScope
'contoso.com/NL'
```

Here's what have we accomplished:

- Created a management role assignment. Since we omitted the name, it received the default name Mail Recipients-NL Admins.

- The assignment is effective on the Organizational Unit named NL in ad.myexchangelabs.com and below.

- The role assigned is Mail Recipients.

- The role is assigned to members of the security group NL Admins.

Now, assume you want those NL administrators to only manage recipients below the Organizational Unit NL and only if they are in the Amsterdam office indicated by their Active Directory property City being set to "Amsterdam."

Before you can assign a scope to a role assignment, we first need to create a scope definition for it:

```
New-ManagementScope -Name 'Scope-NL-Amsterdam' -RecipientRoot
'contoso.com/NL'
-RecipientRestrictionFilter { City -eq 'Amsterdam' }
```

You can now adjust the previously created assignment and have it use the configured management scope as CustomRecipientWriteScope:

```
Set-ManagementRoleAssignment -Identity 'Mail Recipients-
NL Admins'
-CustomRecipientWriteScope 'Scope-NL-Amsterdam'
```

To retrieve information regarding effective permissions, you can use the Get-ManagementRoleAssignment cmdlet with the EffectiveUsers switch. This will return what users are granted the permissions given by a management role through the role groups, assignment policies, and USGs that are assigned to them. For example, to return all assignments where the account AdminNL has effective permissions, you would use

```
[PS] >Get-ManagementRoleAssignment -GetEffectiveUsers |
Where { $_.EffectiveUserName -eq 'AdminNL' } | Select
EffectiveUserName, Role, RoleAssignee, Identity


EffectiveUserName Role
   RoleAssignee              Identity
----------------- ----

   ------------              --------
AdminNL            Mail Recipients
   contoso.com/NL/NL Admins Mail Recipients-NL Admins\AdminNL
```

You can see that there is an assignment for the Mail Recipients role, for which the AdminNL user has permissions through the role assignee, which in this case is a USG.

Tip   Use Get-ManagementRoleAssignment with the EffectiveUsers switch to return effective user permissions for the role assignments.

Role Assignment Policy

End users can also be assigned permissions by way of role assignment policies. One policy is the default policy, the **Default Role Assignment Policy**. This policy contains relative scopes that, when enabled, allow users to manage certain attributes of their own user object or other items, such as Distribution Groups managed by the end user. The default policy gets assigned when new mailboxes are created. When required, you can modify this default policy or create your own explicit role assignment policy and assign this to specific users.

When using the Exchange Admin Center, these role assignment policies can be found via **Permissions ➤ User Roles** and opening up the **Default Role Assignment Policy**. Part of the default settings are shown in Figure 10-8. Note that not all end user roles are shown (scroll down), which all together control what tasks a user is or is not allowed to perform.

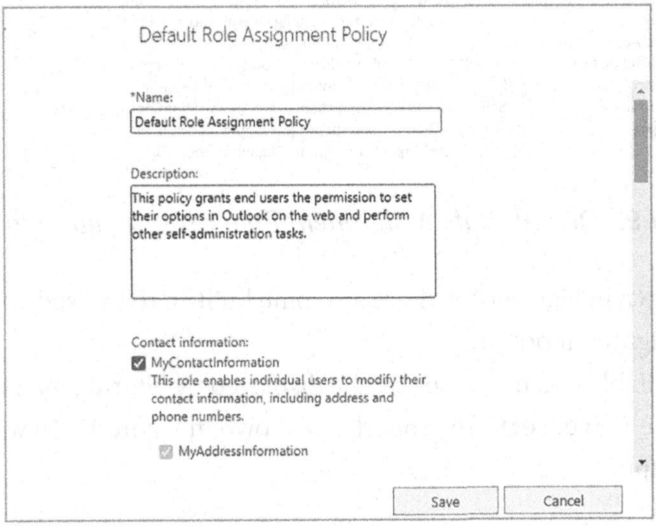

Figure 10-8. *Default Role Assignment Policy*

To retrieve the same information using EMS, use
Get-RoleAssignmentPolicy:

```
Get-RoleAssignmentPolicy | Where { $_.IsDefault }
```

The property **Roles** contains the roles assigned, and **RoleAssignments** contains the role assignments that have been created by the policy. To inspect which assignments are made, as well as the scopes that were used in making the assignments, retrieve the Default Role Assignment Policy, and send each element of the RoleAssignments property to perform a Get-ManagementRoleAssignment; the latter will provide the desired scope information.

```
[PS] >(Get-RoleAssignmentPolicy | Where { $_.IsDefault }).RoleAssignments | Get-ManagementRoleAssignment | ft
Role,Recipient*Scope,Config*Scope

Role                         RecipientReadScope RecipientWriteScope  ConfigReadScope  ConfigWriteScope
----                         ------------------ -------------------  ---------------  ----------------
MyTeamMailboxes                  Organization      Organization OrganizationConfig OrganizationConfig
MyDistributionGroupMembership         MyGAL           MyGAL           None            None
My Custom Apps                     Self           Self OrganizationConfig OrganizationConfig
My Marketplace Apps                Self           Self OrganizationConfig OrganizationConfig
My ReadWriteMailbox Apps            Self             Self OrganizationConfig OrganizationConfig
MyBaseOptions                      Self           Self OrganizationConfig OrganizationConfig
MyContactInformation                Self           Self OrganizationConfig OrganizationConfig
MyTextMessaging                    Self           Self OrganizationConfig OrganizationConfig
MyVoiceMail                        Self           Self OrganizationConfig OrganizationConfig
```

Figure 10-9. *Default Role Assignment Policy role assignments*

As shown in Figure 10-9, there are some built-in roles used specifically for the assignment policy.

All available end user roles can be displayed by filtering management roles on the IsEndUserRole property, as shown in Figure 10-10 with default output.

```
[PS] >Get-ManagementRole | Where { $_.IsEndUserRole } | ft Name,*Scope

Name          Impl.RecipientReadScope Impl.RecipientWriteScope Impl.ConfigReadScope Impl.ConfigWriteScope
----          ----------------------- ------------------------ -------------------- --------------------
My Custom Apps                Self              Self OrganizationConfig   OrganizationConfig
My Marketplace Apps           Self              Self OrganizationConfig   OrganizationConfig
My ReadWriteMailbox Apps      Self              Self OrganizationConfig   OrganizationConfig
MyBaseOptions                 Self              Self OrganizationConfig   OrganizationConfig
MyContactInformation          Self              Self OrganizationConfig   OrganizationConfig
MyProfileInformation          Self              Self OrganizationConfig   OrganizationConfig
MyRetentionPolicies           Self              Self OrganizationConfig   OrganizationConfig
MyTextMessaging               Self              Self OrganizationConfig   OrganizationConfig
MyVoiceMail                   Self              Self OrganizationConfig   OrganizationConfig
MyDiagnostics                 Self              Self OrganizationConfig   OrganizationConfig
MyDistributionGroupMembership    MyGAL         MyGAL              None                None
MyDistributionGroups            MyGAL MyDistributionGroups OrganizationConfig         None
MyMailboxDelegation             MyGAL MailboxICanDelegate OrganizationConfig          None
MyTeamMailboxes           Organization      Organization OrganizationConfig   OrganizationConfig
MyAddressInformation          Self              Self OrganizationConfig   OrganizationConfig
MyDisplayName                 Self              Self OrganizationConfig   OrganizationConfig
MyMobileInformation           Self              Self OrganizationConfig   OrganizationConfig
MyName                        Self              Self OrganizationConfig   OrganizationConfig
MyPersonalInformation         Self              Self OrganizationConfig   OrganizationConfig
```

Figure 10-10. *Default end user role assignments*

These built-in roles contain the role entry information that determines which cmdlets the assignee is allowed to run. Table 10-3 contains an overview of each built-in role and a description of its purpose.

Table 10-3. *Built-Un User Roles*

Name	Description
My Custom Apps	This role will allow users to view and modify their custom apps.
My Marketplace Apps	This role will allow users to view and modify their marketplace apps.
My ReadWriteMailbox Apps	This role will allow users to install apps with ReadWriteMailbox permissions.
MyBaseOptions	This role enables individual users to view and modify the basic configuration of their own mailbox and associated settings.

(*continued*)

Table 10-3. (*continued*)

Name	Description
MyContactInformation	This role enables individual users to modify their contact information, including address and phone numbers.
MyProfileInformation	This role enables individual users to modify their name.
MyRetentionPolicies	This role enables individual users to view their retention tags and view and modify their retention tag settings and defaults.
MyTextMessaging	This role enables individual users to create, view, and modify their text messaging settings.
MyVoiceMail	This role enables individual users to view and modify their voice mail settings when running an earlier version of Exchange.
MyDiagnostics	This role enables end users to perform basic diagnostics on their mailbox such as retrieving calendar diagnostic information.
MyDistributionGroupMembership	This role enables individual users to view and modify their membership in Distribution Groups in an organization, provided that those Distribution Groups allow manipulation of group membership.
MyDistributionGroups	This role enables individual users to create, modify, and view Distribution Groups and modify, view, remove, and add members to Distribution Groups they own.
MyMailboxDelegation	This role enables administrators to delegate mailbox permissions.

(*continued*)

Table 10-3. (*continued*)

Name	Description
MyTeamMailboxes	This role enables individual users to create site mailboxes and connect them to SharePoint sites.
MyAddressInformation	This role enables individual users to view and modify their street address and work telephone and fax numbers. This is a custom role with MyContactInformation as the parent role.
MyDisplayName	This role enables individual users to view and modify their display name. This is a custom role with MyProfileInformation as the parent role.
MyMobileInformation	This role enables individual users to view and modify their mobile phone and pager numbers. This is a custom role with MyContactInformation as the parent role.
MyName	This role enables individual users to view and modify their full name and notes. This is a custom role with MyProfileInformation as the parent role.
MyPersonalInformation	This role enables individual users to view and modify their mobile website, address, and home telephone number. This is a custom role with MyContactInformation as the parent role.

To create a new assignment policy, use **New-RoleAssignmentPolicy**:

```
New-RoleAssignmentPolicy -Name 'Limited Configuration' -Roles
MyBaseOptions,MyAddressInformation,MyDisplayName
```

This cmdlet created the policy. Suppose we want this policy to be the new default policy. We need to reconfigure it using **Set-RoleAssignmentPolicy**, specifying its name as well as the IsDefault switch:

```
Set-RoleAssignmentPolicy -Identity 'Limited Configuration'
-IsDefault
```

To add and remove roles to and from an assignment policy, use **New-ManagementRoleAssignment** and **Remove-ManagementRoleAssignment**, respectively.

To assign a policy to a mailbox, use **Set-Mailbox** with the **RoleAssignmentPolicy**:

```
Set-Mailbox -Identity 'Philip' -RoleAssignmentPolicy 'Limited
Configuration'
```

To retrieve all mailboxes that have a specific assignment policy configured, filter on the RoleAssignmentPolicy property. There are more ways to accomplish this task. The command would be something like

```
Get-Mailbox -ResultSize Unlimited | Where {
$_.RoleAssignmentPolicy -eq 'Limited Configuration'}
```

However, while simple this is not very efficient. It will retrieve all mailboxes, before applying the filter. Better is to use Get-Mailbox' Filter parameter, which allows server-side filtering on **RoleAssignmentPolicy**:

```
Get-Mailbox -ResultSize Unlimited -Filter "RoleAssignmentPolicy
-eq 'Limited Configuration'"
```

Tip   When available, using server-side filtering is not only more efficient; it also should return results faster. To see which attributes can be used using server-side OPATH filtering, see **https://docs. microsoft.com/en-us/powershell/exchange/filter- properties**.

Finally, to remove an assignment policy, use **Remove-AssignmentPolicy**:

```
Remove-RoleAssignmentPolicy -Identity 'Limited Configuration'
```

Split Permissions

In most common deployments, Exchange Server is installed using the shared permissions model, which is the default installation mode. Often organizations are not even aware they are using the shared permissions model. In shared permissions, you can create and manage security principals in Active Directory through Exchange cmdlets. This is possible as the Exchange Trusted Subsystem is a member of the Exchange Windows Permissions security group, which has permissions in Active Directory for performing tasks such as creating user objects or modifying group objects.

More specifically, in shared mode, the following management roles are used to create security principals in Active Directory:

- **Mail Recipient Creation** role, assigned by default to the Organization Management and Recipient Management role groups

- **Security Group Creation and Membership** role, assigned by default to the Organization Management role group

However, depending on the security needs of your organization or the way your environment is managed, you may need tighter management of security principals in Active Directory. It can also be Exchange is managed by a different team than Active Directory and the team responsible for Active Directory strictly governs management of security principals.

In a shared model, creating a new mailbox automatically also creates a new user object in Active Directory. While this might be convenient, it perhaps is also something your organization does not allow. In those cases, have a look at implementing the split permissions model.

When considering implementing a split permissions model, there are two options:

- *RBAC split permissions*: This model is recommended over Active Directory split permissions. The model is flexible, and security principal management remains under RBAC control. The Exchange Trusted Subsystem is still a member of the Exchange Windows Permissions USG. Exchange servers, services, and specific groups can manage security principals such as Distribution Groups or role groups.

  Configuring RBAC split permissions is a manual process.

- *Active Directory split permissions*: This model totally isolates management of Exchange configuration and Active Directory security principals. The Exchange Trusted Subsystem will not be a member of the Exchange Windows Permissions USG. This may result in your having to use separate tools for managing Exchange and Active Directory, including managing Distribution Groups. This model might also cause community scripts or third-party products to not work, as they do not have (implicit) permissions on Active Directory.

Configuring AD split permissions is an automated process.

Tip When using split permissions, the task of installing Exchange Server can be delegated using the **Delegated Setup** role group. Administrators can provision placeholder information in Active Directory by using `setup.exe / NewProvisionedServer:<server name>`. After that, members of the Delegated Setup role group can deploy that server. If those delegates need to perform configuration as well, they need to be added to the **Server Management** role group. When needed, create an assignment using a scope to limit its management boundary.

RBAC Split Permissions

Implementing split permissions on the RBAC level is relatively simple and makes use of RBAC features. In RBAC split permissions mode, the **Mail Recipient Creation** role and the **Security Group Creation and Membership** role are used to create security principals in Active Directory.

Enabling RBAC split permissions is a manual process and will effectively transfer the permission for creating security principals to a user-defined role group, rather than using the built-in **Organization Management** and **Recipient Management** role groups.

To configure RBAC split permissions

1. Create a role group that will contain AD administrators that have permission to create security principals.

2. Make regular and delegating role assignments between the **Mail Recipient Creation** role and the new role group. Do the same for the **Security Group Creation and Membership** role.

3. Remove the regular and delegating role assignments between the **Mail Recipient Creation** role and the **Organization Management** and **Recipient Management** role groups. Do the same for the **Security Group Creation and Membership** role group.

4. Add AD administrators to the created role.

5. Optionally, reconfigure the **ManagedBy** property of the role group, as this by default will be the creator of the role group.

For example, assume we are creating a role group ADAdmins, which will become the designated role group for AD administrators as mentioned in step 1. To grant them sole permissions to create and manage security principals in Active Directory, perform the steps in the example shown in Figure 10-11, which will enable RBAC split permissions using this role group, assuming you are currently using shared permissions.

```
[PS] >New-RoleGroup -Name 'ADAdmins' -Roles 'Mail Recipient Creation', 'Security Group Creation and Membership'

[PS] >New-ManagementRoleAssignment -Role 'Mail Recipient Creation' -SecurityGroup 'ADAdmins' -Delegating
[PS] >New-ManagementRoleAssignment -Role 'Security Group Creation and Membership' -SecurityGroup 'ADAdmins' -
Delegating

[PS] >Add-RoleGroupMember 'ADAdmins' -Member <User ID>

[PS] >Get-ManagementRoleAssignment -RoleAssignee 'Organization Management' -Role 'Mail Recipient Creation' |
Remove-ManagementRoleAssignment
[PS] >Get-ManagementRoleAssignment -RoleAssignee 'Recipient Management' -Role 'Mail Recipient Creation' |
Remove-ManagementRoleAssignment
[PS] >Get-ManagementRoleAssignment -RoleAssignee 'Organization Management' -Role ' Security Group Creation and
Membership' | Remove-ManagementRoleAssignment

[PS] >Set-RoleGroup -Identity 'ADAdmins' -ManagedBy 'ADAdmins'
```

Figure 10-11. *Configuring RBAC split permissions*

Note the following:

1. Only members of the ADAdmins role group will now be able to manage security principals, such as users and groups.

2. The following cmdlets become unavailable for Exchange administrators: New-Mailbox, New-MailContact, New-MailUser, New-RemoteMailbox, Remove-Mailbox, Remove-MailContact, Remove-MailUser, and Remove-RemoteMailbox.

3. Certain features in EAC or OWA/ECP might become unavailable for Exchange administrators, because the cmdlets mentioned previously became unavailable.

Tip   If you want the ADAdmins role group to also manage Exchange attributes on new objects, assign the Mail Recipients role.

Active Directory Split Permissions

Anyone who has installed Exchange in a new environment using setup is probably familiar with the dialog that is asking if you want to apply the Active Directory split permissions security model. With Active Directory split permissions, the **Recipient Management** and **Organization Management** roles will not be able to create security principals in Active Directory. Active Directory administrators will be responsible for creating security principals in Active Directory. Exchange administrators, being Recipient or Organization Management group members, will be responsible for configuring and managing the Exchange-related attributes on those security principals.

Thus, after configuring AD split permissions, Exchange admins can only mailbox-enable an existing user, not create a new mailbox-enabled user, or mail-enable a (distribution) group, not create a new Distribution Group. They can also not manage Distribution Group memberships, which in the shared permissions model, they are always able to using the **BypassSecurityGroupManagerCheck** override switch.

The AD split permissions model is configured through the setup wizard by checking the Apply Active Directory Split Permissions mode or by running setup.exe /PrepareAD /ActiveDirectorySplitPermissions :true from the command line. This will not reconfigure Exchange, but will take care of setting up Active Directory to support AD split permissions. When your organization has multiple domains, you need to run setup. exe /**PrepareDomain** per domain or /**PrepareAllDomains** to propagate required changes.

Depending on whether you are enabling Active Directory split permissions during the initial setup of Exchange or are switching from shared permissions or RBAC split permissions mode, enabling Active Directory split permissions results in the following changes:

1. An OU named **Microsoft Exchange Protected Groups** is created.

2. The **Exchange Windows Permissions** USG is created in the **Microsoft Exchange Protected Groups** OU. When the **Exchange Windows Permissions** USG already exists, it is moved to **Microsoft Exchange Protected Groups**.

3. When the **Exchange Trusted Subsystem** USG is a member of the **Exchange Windows Permissions Group**, it is removed from that group.

4. When they exist, any non-delegating role assignment to role group **Mail Recipient Creation** or **Security Group Creation and Membership** is removed.

5. Any existing access control entry (ACE) assigned to the **Exchange Windows Permissions** USG is removed from the domain object, for example, CN=contoso,CN=com. This will be repeated for all domains in the forest, depending on usage of the / PrepareAllDomains switch during setup.

After enabling the Active Directory split permissions model, the following cmdlets will become unavailable: New-Mailbox, New-MailContact, New-MailUser, New-RemoteMailbox, Remove-Mailbox, Remove-MailContact, Remove-MailUser, and Remove-RemoteMailbox. The following cmdlets are accessible, but cannot be used to manage Distribution Groups: Add-DistributionGroupMember, New-DistributionGroup, Remove-DistributionGroup, Remove-DistributionGroupMember, and Update-DistributionGroupMember.

Certain features in EAC or OWA/ECP might become unavailable as related cmdlets or permissions become unavailable.

Tip   You can switch back from Active Directory split permissions to shared permissions using `setup.exe /PrepareAD /Active DirectorySplitPermissions:false`. Changes mentioned will be made in the opposite direction, such as the addition of required ACEs to domain objects for **Exchange Windows Permissions** and adding the **Exchange Trusted Subsystem** to **Exchange Windows Permissions**. When switching, role assignments for **Mail Recipient Creation** and **Security Group Creation and Membership** are not automatically recreated, and you need to do this manually:

```
New-ManagementRoleAssignment 'Mail Recipient
Creation-Organization Management' -Role 'Mail
Recipient Creation' -SecurityGroup 'Organization
Management'
```

```
New-ManagementRoleAssignment 'Security Group
Creation and Membership-Org Management' -Role
'Security Group Creation and Membership'
-SecurityGroup 'Organization Management'
New-ManagementRoleAssignment 'Mail Recipient
Creation-Recipient Management' -Role 'Mail Recipient
Creation' -SecurityGroup 'Recipient Management'
```

Restart Exchange servers in order for them to pick up these changes.

Summary

In this chapter on managing permissions and access control, we explored the Exchange Role-Based Access Control (RBAC) model. This model is built on the principles of "who," "what," and "where," which together determine access rights. We explained the components of RBAC and how they work together to provide granular control over permissions.

To meet the specific needs of your organization, we demonstrated how to customize the built-in roles. By using task-oriented commands and leveraging RBAC for controlled script execution, you can fine-tune the roles to align with your requirements. We also covered delegated deployments, showcasing how RBAC enables you to delegate specific tasks to designated divisions based on Active Directory or recipients matching attribute filters, for example.

Furthermore, we explained Exchange permission models, shared permissions and the two split permissions options. We highlighted the differences between these models and discussed what the key differences are. Shared permissions allow multiple administrators to have broad access and suit SMB organizations better, whereas split permissions emphasize separation of duties, which can mitigate potential risks.

By understanding and implementing RBAC, organizations gain enhanced security and streamlined management of permissions in their Exchange environment. Customizable roles, controlled script execution, and delegated deployments provide flexibility while maintaining control. Choosing between shared permissions and split permissions model depends on the organization and its security framework, trading simplicity for separated recipient management and security principal management.

PART IV

Compliance

CHAPTER 11

Backup and Restore

Restoring data is one of the most important aspects of any IT organization, and that includes restoring data on your Exchange server. Restoring can be individual items, something that's often requested by users, or restoring a mailbox database or even an entire server.

In this chapter we will have a look at backing up your Exchange server, since a good backup is the number one prerequisite for any restore action. We will be exploring backup technologies in Exchange Server and will cover

- VSS, or Volume Shadow Copy Service, backups, sometimes also referred to as "snapshot backups." We'll explore the default Windows Server Backup (WSB) and a low-level tool called Diskshadow, which shows you what's happening when you're creating a VSS backup.

- Restoring techniques, to both a standard location and an alternative location.

- Recovery techniques, using ESEUTIL.

- Disaster recovery techniques, to rebuild an entire server.

All solutions documented in this chapter are for Exchange 2019, but they are equal for Exchange 2016 and even Exchange 2013. Let's get started.

© Jaap Wesselius and Michel de Rooij 2023
J. Wesselius and M. de Rooij, *Pro Exchange Administration*,
https://doi.org/10.1007/978-1-4842-9591-5_11

Back Up an Exchange Server

Backing up an Exchange 2019 server is a process of storing your Exchange server configuration and data, like the Exchange binaries, registry information, and mailbox databases, on another medium. This medium, in turn, can be stored on another location as a safeguard if you face the loss of an entire location.

But not only mailbox databases need to be backed up; you can also back up information like your transport log files or protocol log files, SSL certificates, or maybe even the entire Exchange 2019 server.

Explained earlier in this book, a mailbox database consists of the following components:

- The mailbox database, where the actual data is stored

- The transaction log files, where the transactions are stored as soon as processing of a transaction is finished in memory

- The checkpoint file, which keeps track of which transactions are stored in the transaction log files but have not yet been flushed to the mailbox database

- The reserved transaction log files, which are stored in case a disk where the transaction log files are stored becomes full

It is important to remember that all transactions are always stored in the transaction log files before they are flushed into the mailbox database. You need to understand the workings of the mailbox database and its database technologies to understand the backup and restore technologies used in Exchange Server, but it also is useful to know for recovery purposes.

Backup Technologies

The Exchange mailbox databases are backed up using snapshots. Microsoft utilizes a framework for this called the Volume Shadow Copy service (VSS). Let's look at what VSS is and how it works with Exchange Server.

VSS Backup

Windows Server 2003 was the first Microsoft operating system capable of creating snapshot backups using the Volume Shadow Copy service (VSS) framework. Unfortunately, in those days it was not possible to create VSS backups of Exchange Server itself. Exchange Server 2007 running on Windows Server 2008 was the first version of Exchange Server capable of using the VSS technology, and VSS backups have been in use in Exchange Server ever since.

There are two kinds of snapshot backups:

- *Clone*: This is a full copy or split mirror. In this scenario, a complete copy, or mirror image, is maintained until an application or administrator effectively "breaks" the mirror. From this point on, the original and the clone are fully independent of each other. The mirror copy is effectively frozen in time.

- *Copy on write*: This is a differential copy. A shadow copy is created that is different from a full copy of the original data, made before the original data has been overwritten. Effectively, the backup copy consists of the data in the shadow copy combined with the data in the original location. Both copies need to be available to reconstruct the original data.

The VSS consists of the VSS service itself, as well as requestors, writers, and providers. The central part is the VSS running on the computer. It is responsible for coordinating all activities concerning backups and restores.

The requestor typically is the backup application. This can be the default out-of-the-box Windows Server Backup, or it can be any third-party backup solution.

The writer is the application-specific part of VSS. Writers exist for Microsoft Exchange, Active Directory, IIS, NTFS, SQL Server, and so on. The Exchange writer is responsible for coordinating all Exchange-related activities, such as flushing data to the mailbox database, freezing the mailbox database during the VSS snapshot, and so on.

The provider works with storage. It can be the Windows provider, which can create copy-on-write snapshots of a disk, or it can be a vendor-specific hardware provider.

Thus, the VSS is at the core, as can be seen in Figure 11-1. The arrows show the communication paths within the VSS function.

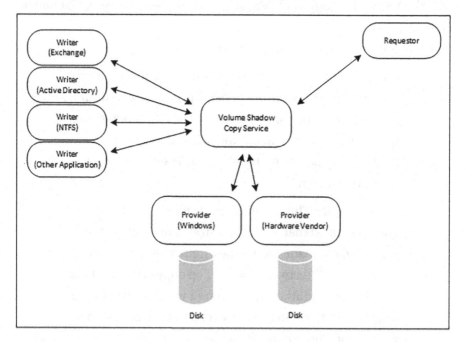

Figure 11-1. *VSS with its requestor, writers, and providers*

For a VSS backup to be created, the following steps occur sequentially:

1. The backup application or requestor sends a command to the VSS to make a shadow copy of the mailbox database.

2. The VSS sends a command to the Exchange writer to prepare for a snapshot backup.

3. The VSS sends a command to the appropriate provider to create a shadow copy of the mailbox database. (The storage provider can be a hardware storage provider provided by the hardware vendor or the default Windows storage provider.)

4. The Exchange writer temporarily stops or pauses the mailbox database and puts it into read-only mode; all data in the server memory is then flushed to the mailbox database. Also, a log file rollover is performed to make sure that all data will be in the backup set. This holds for a couple of seconds while the snapshot is taken. All write I/Os are queued at this point. Please note that the Exchange writer does not perform any consistency checks on the mailbox database.

5. The shadow copy is created.

6. The VSS releases the Exchange server to resume ordinary operations, and all queued write I/Os are completed.

7. The VSS queries the Exchange writer to confirm that the write I/Os were successfully held while the snapshot was taken. If the write operations were not successfully held, there could potentially be an

inconsistent shadow copy. If this is the case, the shadow copy is deleted, and the requestor is notified of the failed snapshot.

8. If the snapshot was successful, the requestor verifies the integrity of the backup set (the clone). If the clone integrity is good, the requestor informs Exchange Server that the snapshot was successful.

9. The snapshot can now be transferred to a backup device.

10. When all data is successfully moved to the backup device, the requestor informs the VSS that the backup was successful and that the log files can be purged.

Steps 1 through 6 usually take between 10 and 15 seconds. Note that this is the time it takes to take the actual snapshot; it does not include the time needed to write all the data to the backup device, which is step 9 in the preceding list. Depending on the size of the mailbox database, this step can take up to several hours to complete.

You might be familiar with a VSS administrative tool called VSSADMIN. You can use VSSADMIN to quickly check the various components in the VSS infrastructure. For example, to list all the VSS writers on a server, simply use the VSSADMIN List Writers command in a command prompt window:

```
PS C:\> vssadmin list writers
vssadmin 1.1 - Volume Shadow Copy Service administrative
command-line tool
(C) Copyright 2001-2013 Microsoft Corp.

Writer name: 'Task Scheduler Writer'
    Writer Id: {d61d61c8-d73a-4eee-8cdd-f6f9786b7124}
```

```
    Writer Instance Id: {1bddd48e-5052-49db-9b07-b96f96727e6b}
    State: [1] Stable
    Last error: No error

Writer name: 'VSS Metadata Store Writer'
    Writer Id: {75dfb225-e2e4-4d39-9ac9-ffaff65ddf06}
    Writer Instance Id: {088e7a7d-09a8-4cc6-a609-ad90e75ddc93}
    State: [1] Stable
    Last error: No error

Writer name: 'System Writer'
    Writer Id: {e8132975-6f93-4464-a53e-1050253ae220}
    Writer Instance Id: {afb086bc-3d0b-4b61-9f19-624b46ba503b}
    State: [1] Stable
    Last error: No error

Writer name: 'IIS Config Writer'
    Writer Id: {2a40fd15-dfca-4aa8-a654-1f8c654603f6}
    Writer Instance Id: {c57e39a3-400b-4747-a463-b10ea27430b1}
    State: [1] Stable
    Last error: No error

Writer name: 'Microsoft Exchange Writer'
    Writer Id: {76fe1ac4-15f7-4bcd-987e-8e1acb462fb7}
    Writer Instance Id: {c2413ca8-3e1a-49d9-94c5-c12ab6f972f2}
    State: [1] Stable
    Last error: No error

Writer name: 'IIS Metabase Writer'
    Writer Id: {59b1f0cf-90ef-465f-9609-6ca8b2938366}
    Writer Instance Id: {77d9a79d-a5db-419d-9b9e-133e404637a9}
    State: [1] Stable
    Last error: No error
```

```
Writer name: 'Registry Writer'
   Writer Id: {afbab4a2-367d-4d15-a586-71dbb18f8485}
   Writer Instance Id: {5d656df2-d27e-46f5-bfd5-19fe0d172abf}
   State: [1] Stable
   Last error: No error
```

Similarly, you can list the VSS providers, existing shadow copies, or volumes eligible for creating shadow copies.

VSSADMIN is an old (but still useful) tool and is replaced by a tool called Diskshadow. Diskshadow is more powerful and reveals more information about the VSS infrastructure, and it can even create backups. Both tools are available on Windows Server 2019.

Back Up a Mailbox Database

For backing up your mailbox databases, there are various applications available. Which one you use is a matter of personal experience or company license, but the most important factor in making your choice is that the application be "Exchange aware." Windows Server comes with Windows Server Backup (WSB), which is also capable of backing up Exchange 2019 mailbox databases.

It is a simple but limited backup application, but I encounter it frequently when visiting customers.

Using Windows Server Backup in PowerShell

Exchange Server 2019 contains a VSS plug-in that can be used with WSB. Although WSB has limited functionality, it can create backups and restore them if needed. Another advantage of WSB is that it is free and comes with Windows Server.

To install Windows Server Backup, execute the following command in PowerShell:

```
PS C:\> Add-WindowsFeature Windows-Server-Backup

Success Restart Needed Exit Code        Feature Result
------- -------------- ---------        --------------
True    No             Success          {Windows Server Backup}
```

> **Note**   To get an overview of all available WSB cmdlets, you can use the following URL: http://bit.ly/WSBCommands. You can also run Get-Command *wb* in PowerShell; this will show all Windows Server Backup–related commands directly on the console.

Windows Server Backup is policy based. To create a new policy, we first create a variable $WBPolicy and populate it with all the options that are needed, such as

- *Schedule*: When the backup will be running

- *VSS options*: Whether a full backup or a copy backup will be created

- *Volumes to back up*: The volumes containing the mailbox databases

- *Target disk*: A disk where the backup will be stored

The first step is to create a variable with the new Windows Server Backup policy. To do this, execute the following command in PowerShell:

```
PS C:\> $WBPolicy = New-WBPolicy
```

To

- Add the schedule

- Create a VSS full backup

- Select the volumes to back up

- Select the disk to write the backup to

execute the following commands in PowerShell:

```
PS C:\> $Schedule = Set-Date "01/06/2022 11:30:00"
PS C:\> Set-WBSchedule -Policy $WBPolicy -Schedule $Schedule
PS C:\> Set-WBVssBackupOptions -Policy $WBPolicy –VssFullBackup
PS C:\> $Volumes = Get-WBVolume -AllVolumes | Where-Object
{$_.MountPath -like "C:\ExchDbs\*"}
PS C:\> Add-WBVolume -Policy $WBPolicy -Volume $Volumes
PS C:\> $Disks = Get-WBDisk
PS C:\> $Target = New-WBBackupTarget -Disk $Disks[4] -Label
"Backup"
PS C:\> Add-WBBackupTarget -Policy $WBPolicy -Target $Target
```

To store the policy on the Exchange server, execute the following command in PowerShell:

```
PS C:\> Set-WBPolicy -Policy $WBPolicy -Force
```

This Windows Server Backup policy will create a VSS full backup of both mountpoints (where the Exchange databases and log files are located) daily; it will run every day at 1:30 AM. The data will be stored on an additional disk, dedicated for backup purposes.

The backup will start automatically during the next cycle that has been configured with the schedule option, but to start the backup immediately, execute the following command in PowerShell:

```
PS C:\> Get-WBPolicy | Start-WBBackup
```

When this command is executed, a full VSS backup of the volumes containing the mailbox databases will be created. It will start with a VSS snapshot of these volumes, followed by a consistency check of the mailbox databases to ensure the mailbox databases' integrity.

When the consistency check is finished successfully, the data is backed up to the backup location; the backup can take a couple of hours if you have a large mailbox database.

If you check the application log in the event viewer, you'll see the following entries:

- Event ID 2021 (MSExchangeRepl): Successfully collected the metadata document in preparation for backup.

- Event ID 2110 (MSExchangeRepl): Successfully prepared for a full or a copy backup of database MDB01.

- Event ID 2023 (MSExchangeRepl): VSS writer successfully prepared for backup.

- Event ID 2005 (ESE): Shadow copy instance started. This will be a full shadow copy.

- Event ID 2025 (MSExchangeRepl): VSS successfully prepared for a snapshot.

- Event ID 2001 (ESE): MDB01 shadow copy freeze started.

- Event ID 2027 (MSExchangeRepl): VSS writer instance has successfully frozen the databases.

- Event ID 2003 (ESE): MDB01 shadow copy freeze ended.

- Event ID 2029 (MSExchangeRepl): VSS writer instance has successfully thawed the databases.

- Event ID 2035 (MSExchangeRepl): VSS writer has successfully processed the post-snapshot event.

- Event ID 2021 (MSExchangeRepl): VSS writer has successfully collected the metadata document in preparation for backup.

- Event ID 224 (ESE): MDB01 deleting log files C:\ExchDbs\Disk1\LogFiles\E0000000001.log to C:\ExchDbs\Disk1\LogFiles\E000000075E.log.

- Event ID 2046 (MSExchangeRepl): VSS writer has successfully completed the backup of database MDB01.

- Event ID 2006 (ESE): MDB01 shadow copy completed successfully.

- Event ID 2033 (MSExchangeRepl): VSS writer has successfully processed the backup completion event.

- Event ID 2037 (MSExchangeRepl): VSS writer backup has been successfully shut down.

When you check the location of the log files using Windows Explorer, you'll notice that most of the log files have indeed been purged. The information in the mailbox database itself has also been updated with backup information.

You can use the Get-MailboxDatabase command with the -Status option to retrieve information regarding the backup status of a mailbox database:

```
[PS] C:\> Get-MailboxDatabase -identity MDB01 -Status |
Select Name,*backup*

Name                          : MDB01
BackupInProgress              : False
```

```
SnapshotLastFullBackup          : True
SnapshotLastIncrementalBackup   :
SnapshotLastDifferentialBackup  :
SnapshotLastCopyBackup          :
LastFullBackup                  : 1/9/2023 5:01:44 PM
LastIncrementalBackup           :
LastDifferentialBackup          :
LastCopyBackup                  :
RetainDeletedItemsUntilBackup   : False
```

You can also use the ESEUTIL /MH MDB01.edb command to check
the header for backup information. Be aware that the mailbox database
needs to be dismounted for this. If you use ESEUTIL, you will see
something like this:

```
Previous Full Backup:
        Log Gen: 1887-1888 (0x75f-0x760) - OSSnapshot
          Mark: (0x761,1,0)
          Mark: 01/09/2023 16:01:44.582 UTC

Current Full Backup:
        Log Gen: 0-0 (0x0-0x0)
          Mark: (0x0,0,0)
          Mark: 00/00/1900 00:00:00.000 LOC
```

You might ask yourself why this information is written under Previous
Full Backup, while the entry under Current Full Backup is empty. This
is because when you create a backup, the entry Current Full Backup is
written with information regarding the backup as it runs. When the backup
is finished, the entries are moved from the Current Full Backup section to
the Previous Full Backup section, and the Current Full Backup is emptied.

When a backup is restored to disk and you check the header information after a restore, you can always identify the database as a backup that has been restored instead of a "normal" mailbox database because it will show as Previous Full Backup.

Using Windows Server Backup GUI

I can imagine that, for backup purposes, you do not want to use PowerShell. Still a lot of Exchange administrators think that PowerShell is complex and difficult. Let us look at the graphical user interface (GUI) as well, assuming you have Exchange Server 2019 running on Windows 2022 or Windows 2019 Desktop Experience.

To create a backup of your Exchange databases, you use the following steps:

1. In the Administrative Tools section, select Windows Server Backup. This is an MMC snap-in. In the Actions pane, select Backup Once.

2. In the Backup Options page, select Different Options and click Next to continue.

3. In this example we want only to back up the mailbox database, so select the Custom option and click Next to continue.

4. The mailbox database is located on mountpoint C:\ExchDbs\Disk1. Use the Add Items button to select this disk.

5. To change the type of backup that is being created, click the Advanced Settings button, select the VSS Settings tab, and select the VSS Full Backup radio button. Click OK to return to the previous page and click Next to continue.

6. WSB has the option of backing up to a remote share or to a local disk, whichever you prefer. On our server there is an additional backup disk (disk X), so select Local Drives and click Next to continue.

7. In the Backup Destination dropdown box, select the disk where the backup needs to be stored; on our server this would be disk X. Click Next to continue.

8. The selection is now complete. Click Backup to start the actual backup process.

Note By default, WSB will create a copy backup instead of a full backup. This is understandable, as it will not interfere with a normal backup cycle when you are using another backup solution and you want to test using WSB. If you want to make a regular backup using WSB, make sure you change this setting. This is a common pitfall with WSB.

The backup will now start with the creation of the VSS snapshot, and it will perform a consistency check of the mailbox data, as shown in Figure 11-2. Be aware that this information can be visible for a small amount of time, especially when the mailbox database is not that large and the consistency check takes only a few seconds. This backup status check is the only visual indication you have that an Exchange-aware backup is running.

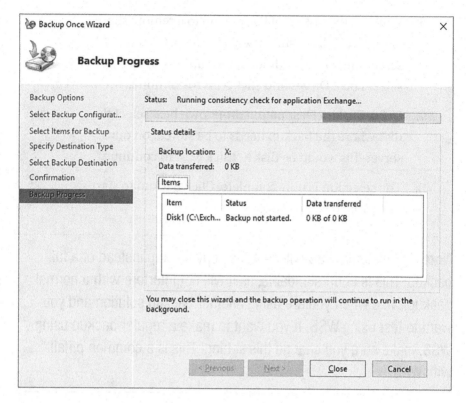

Figure 11-2. *Windows Server Backup automatically checks for database consistency*

When the consistency check is finished successfully, the data is backed up to the backup location, and after a while (which can take a couple of hours if you have a large mailbox database), the backup is completed.

Note Another common pitfall I see regularly is that admins think they are creating an Exchange-aware backup, but instead create a file-level backup of an Exchange database. While this creates a backup of the mailbox database, it does not perform a consistency check, and it does not purge the transaction log files. As such it is extremely difficult, if not even impossible, to gracefully restore such a backup.

Back Up Other Configuration Information

The previous section discussed how to back up mailbox databases in Exchange, since this is the most important aspect of an Exchange server's role. There are more things that need to be backed up, however, either in a regular backup sequence or maybe after there have been configuration changes, for example:

- Log files (not transaction log files), as Exchange logs quite a lot of information in log files—for instance, IIS log files located in C:\inetpub\logs\logfiles, which contains logging from all HTTPS-based clients like Outlook Web App, Exchange Web Services, Autodiscover, Outlook Anywhere, and ActiveSync.

- SMTP logs, located in C:\Program Files\Microsoft\ Exchange Server\V15\TransportRoles\Logs\ Hub\ ProtocolLog. These are disabled by default, but when enabled these might be included in a daily backup routine.

- Message tracking information, located in C:\Program Files\Microsoft\Exchange Server\V15\TransportRoles\ Logs\MessageTracking.

- An entire directory, depending on the (legal) backup requirements of your company. It might be necessary to back up the entire logging directory in C:\Program Files\Microsoft\Exchange Server\V15\Logging.

- Config files, such as transport configuration files located in C:\Program Files\Microsoft\ Exchange Server\V15\Bin. This file is used to relocate the SMTP message database and log files to another location. No need to include this in a daily backup sequence, but it is necessary to back up after configuration changes.

- SSL certificate. No need to back up this daily, but you should back up after the initial installation of the certificate. It is needed when rebuilding an Exchange server or maybe when adding additional Exchange servers. Make sure that when you create a backup of your SSL certificate, you also include the private key in the certificate backup. If not, it is useless when rebuilding your Exchange server.

- System state or entire server, depending on your disaster recovery plan. You might want to back up the server's system state, or maybe the entire server, for rebuilding purposes.

When using server virtualization, it is an option to back up the entire virtual machine using a backup solution. Veeam, for example, is a third-party vendor that offers backup solutions in a virtual environment. Veeam can back up the VMs, and using the Hyper-V Integration Components or VMware tools, the VSS backup information is sent to the operating system inside the VM. This way the virtual machine is also aware that a snapshot is being made.

Restoring Exchange Server

Backing up your Exchange environment does make sense, but restoring the backup is even more important. In all my years as an Exchange consultant, I have regularly met customers who thought that their backup solutions were fine, but they did not have any idea how to restore them if needed. The worst way to find out is during a disaster, when you must restore information rapidly, as there likely are hundreds of users and managers complaining. Most often, the restoration will fail at this moment because of the lack of experience.

In this section I will focus on restoring mailbox databases, since these are where all the data is. Later in this chapter, I will explain how to restore the Exchange servers as part of a disaster recovery operation.

There are two options for restoring mailbox databases:

1. Restore the mailbox database to its original location. In this scenario, the original mailbox database is taken offline and is overwritten by the mailbox database in the backup set. Since all the information is also stored in the log files, the information processed by the Mailbox server since the last backup was created will automatically be replayed by the Mailbox server. If all goes well, no information, or almost no information, will be lost, and the mailbox database will be in the same state as before.

2. Restore the mailbox database to another location. In this scenario, the mailbox database from the backup set is restored to another location, most likely a dedicated restore disk on your Mailbox server. When the mailbox database is restored to another location, the original mailbox database can continue running and thus continue servicing client requests.

A recovery mailbox database can be used as well. This is a special mailbox database, not visible for regular clients (only for the Exchange administrator), that can be used to restore a particular mailbox; you can move this mailbox into the production mailbox database or export it to a PST file.

Restoring to Its Original Location

A lot of interesting technologies are used to make the mailbox database backup process as smooth as possible without interrupting any users. Restoring a mailbox database to its original location is straightforward work.

The mailbox database must be taken offline, and thus, users will face some downtime because Exchange Server is not available anymore. The mailbox database is then restored from the backup set, additional log files are replayed automatically, and the mailbox database can then be mounted again. There is nothing fancy to do when restoring a mailbox database.

In the previous section, WSB was used to back up the mailbox database, so you must use WSB again to restore the mailbox database. For testing purposes, you can log onto the mailbox before the restore action and send some messages around to see if these are replayed after the backup is restored. To restore a previous backup using WSB, you can use these steps:

1. Log onto EAC as an administrator and navigate to Servers ➤ Databases. Select the appropriate mailbox database and dismount it.

2. When the mailbox database is still selected, open its properties and select Maintenance. Check the "This database can be overwritten by a restore" checkbox as shown in Figure 11-3.

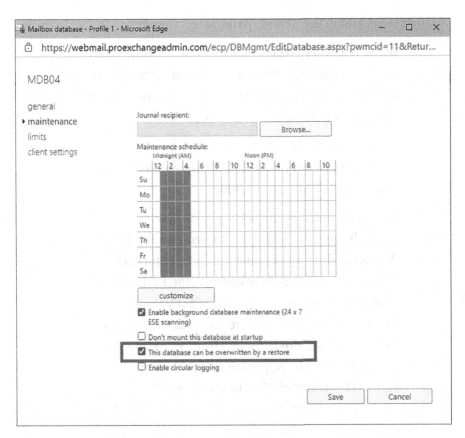

Figure 11-3. *Setting the option "This database can be overwritten by a restore"*

Note   This option can be set in PowerShell by using the command `Set-MailboxDatabase -Identity MDB01 -AllowFileRestore $true`.

Open WSB, and in the Actions pane, select Recover.

3. In the Recovery Wizard that starts, select where the backup is located. This can be on a disk attached to the server itself, or it can be a remote location. Select "This server" and click Next to continue.

4. In the Select Backup Date window, select the backup set you want to restore to this server. Once selected, click Next to continue.

5. Next is the Select Recovery Type window, which is very important. WSB is Exchange-aware, and thus an Exchange backup is an application backup. This way, the backup is restored as the Exchange writer would like it to be. If you select Volumes, for example, the backup is restored as an ordinary file backup, and this is useless from an Exchange perspective. Select Applications as shown in Figure 11-4 and click Next to continue.

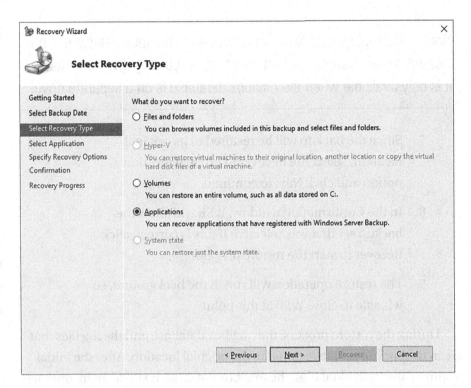

Figure 11-4. *Select the Applications radio button when restoring a mailbox database*

6. In the Select Application window, make sure Exchange is selected. The remaining log files since the last backup was taken can be automatically replayed into the mailbox database; this is the default behavior. If you do not want this to happen, check the "Do not perform a roll-forward recovery" checkbox. Click Next to continue.

Note   This option is only available when the mailbox database is not
located on the system drive and boot drive, typically drive C:\. That is,
it is only available when the mailbox database is on a separate drive.

---

7. Since the backup will be restored to its original
    location, select the Recover to original location
    option and click Next to continue.

8. In the Confirmation window, WSB will show the
    backup set that was selected. If this is correct, click
    Recover to start the restore process.

9. The restore operation will run in the background, so
    it is safe to close WSB at this point.

During the restore process, the mailbox database and the log files that
are in the backup set are restored to the original location. After the initial
restore of the individual files, the mailbox database is still in an inconsistent
(i.e., dirty shutdown) state. Exchange will try to start a soft recovery process
with the log files that are also restored from the backup set.

When finished, any additional log files that are written to disk after
the previous backup was taken are replayed into the mailbox database as
well, so no mail data will be lost when restoring a mailbox database from a
backup, up to the point in time the backup was created.

Note   Exchange Server has always been very sensitive when it
comes to transaction log files and with replaying these into the
mailbox database. If only one log file is missing, the replay of the log
files during recovery will fail. Therefore, you should never delete any
of the log files manually; or do so only if you are 150% sure of what
you are doing or if Microsoft Support instructs you to do so!

During the restore process, several events are written to the event log, indicating the progress of the restore operation or if any problems have arisen during the process. For example:

- Event ID 4347 (MSExchangeRepl): Exchange Replication service VSS writer will restore a backup set to database MDB04\EXCH04, which is the same database from which the backup was originally taken.

- Event ID 4367 (MSExchangeRepl): Exchange Replication service VSS writer successfully restored the backup set. To bring the restored database to a clean shutdown state, database recovery will be performed using the information in the restore environment document MDB04\EXCH04.

- Event ID 4370 (MSExchangeRepl): Exchange Replication service VSS writer will perform database recovery on database MDB04.edb as part of the restore process for MDB04\EXCH04, followed by several events from ESE, indicating the recovery steps for the restored mailbox database.

- Event ID 40008 (MSExchangeIS): Mount completed successfully for database <<GUID>>.

- Event ID 3156 (MSExchangeRepl): Active Manager successfully mounted database MDB04 on server EXCH04.proexchangeadmin.com.

- Event ID 737 (Backup): The operation to recover component(s) "e3c4d2b5-678e-443e-9f55-777c447 eb220" has completed successfully at "2023-05-10T09: 04:34.488000000Z."

If you log onto your mailbox and check any messages that were sent after the last backup was taken, you will see that these are still available in the mailbox and thus successfully recovered.

Restoring to Another Location

Restoring a mailbox database to its original location is only useful when the original mailbox database is lost, for whatever reason. Restoring to its original location means you must dismount the mailbox database, resulting in an outage for users. So, in a normal production situation, you do not want to dismount your mailbox database for restoring purposes unless there's no other option.

Restoring a backup to another location has the advantage of leaving the original mailbox mounted, allowing users to continue working. Also, when using this method, there is no risk in accidentally overwriting the mailbox database with a database that is restored, since the original database is still mounted and thus reports as "file in use."

The procedure for restoring the mailbox database to another location does not differ that much from restoring the mailbox to its original location.

The Restore Process

If you want to restore to another location, you follow these steps:

1. Log onto the Exchange server, open WSB, and in the Actions pane, select Recover.

2. In the Recovery Wizard that starts, select where the backup is located. This can be on a disk attached to the server itself, or it can be a remote location. Select the appropriate option here and click Next to continue.

3.   In the Select Backup Date window, select the
     backup set you want to restore to this server. Once
     selected, click Next to continue.

4.   Next, the Select Recovery Type window is very
     important. WSB is Exchange-aware, and thus
     an Exchange backup is an application backup.
     This way, the backup is restored as the Exchange
     writer would like it to be. If you select Volumes, for
     example, the backup will be restored as an ordinary
     file backup, and this is useless from an Exchange
     perspective. Select Applications and click Next to
     continue.

5.   In the Select Application window, make sure
     Exchange is selected and click Next to continue.

6.   Since the backup will be restored to another
     location, select the Recover to another location
     option, and use the Browse button to select a disk
     and directory where you want to restore the mailbox
     database. Typically, a dedicated restore LUN is
     used for this purpose. In our example, we use G:\
     RestoreDB to restore the mailbox database from
     backup. This is shown in Figure 11-5.

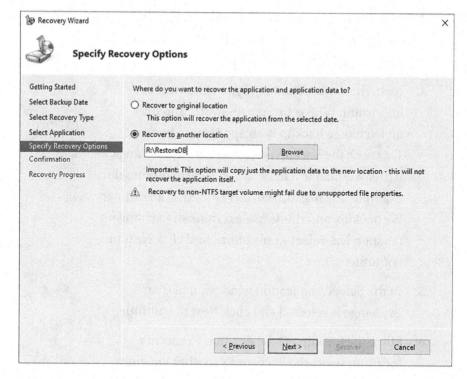

Figure 11-5. *Restoring a mailbox database to an alternative location*

7. The selection is shown in the Confirmation window.
   If all is okay, then click the Restore button to start
   the recover process.

8. Since only the mailbox database and its log files are
   restored from backup, the process finishes much
   faster than when restoring to its original location.
   In this process, no additional recovery steps are
   performed, so you must do this manually.

The mailbox database and the accompanying log files are now
restored from the backup set. The file location is also restored, so now
there is a mailbox database MDB04 located in R:\RestoreDB\<GUID>\C_\

and the log files are stored in R:\RestoreDB\<GUID>\C_\LogFiles. This
file is taken from a running copy of the mailbox database, and thus the
mailbox database is in a dirty shutdown state. You can check this using the
ESEUTIL /MH command, which would produce something like this:

```
State: Dirty Shutdown
Log Required: 4195-4197 (0x1063-0x1065)
Log Committed: 0-4197 (0x0-0x1065)
Log Recovering: 0 (0x0)
Log Consistent: 4197 (0x1065)
```

To bring this database back into a consistent state, the mailbox
database must be recovered—something that can be achieved using the
ESEUTIL tool with the following options:

- /r for recovery

- /l for the location of the transaction log files

- /s for the location of the checkpoint file

- /d for the location of the mailbox database file

This will result in the following command and output:

```
R:\>ESEUTIL /R E00 /lR:\RestoreDB\f2b5ce50-9a1d-48dd-9538-
bb9d87adfda0\F_\MDB04\Logfiles /sR:\RestoreDB\
f2b5ce50-9a1d-48dd-9538-bb9d87adfda0\F_\LogFiles /dR:\
RestoreDB\f2b5ce50-9a1d-48dd-9538-bb9d87adfda0\F_\MDB04
Extensible Storage Engine Utilities for Microsoft(R)
Exchange Server
Version 15.01
Copyright (C) Microsoft Corporation. All Rights Reserved.

Initiating RECOVERY mode...
    Logfile base name: E00
```

```
        Log files: R:\RestoreDB\f2b5ce50-9a1d-48dd-9538-
        bb9d87adfda0\F_\MDB04\Logfiles
     System files: R:\RestoreDB\f2b5ce50-9a1d-48dd-9538-
        bb9d87adfda0\F_\LogFiles
  Database Directory: R:\RestoreDB\f2b5ce50-9a1d-48dd-9538-
  bb9d87adfda0\F_\MDB04

Performing soft recovery...
                 Restore Status (% complete)

      0    10   20   30   40   50   60   70   80   90   100
      |----|----|----|----|----|----|----|----|----|----|
      ..................................................

Operation completed successfully in 25.390 seconds.
```

Please note the absence of a space between the option and the value.

Now when you check the database again using the ESEUTIL /MH command, the database will be in a clean shutdown state and ready to use. A use case for this kind of restore is the recovery database as discussed in the next section.

Recovery Database

A recovery database in Exchange is a special mailbox database, invisible to normal users, where you can mount a normal database restored from backup. This means that you will have one normal mailbox database MDB04 running in its original location and one recovery mailbox MDB04 running in recovery mode.

Creating a recovery mailbox database is not very different from creating a regular mailbox database, but it can be managed only by using EMS. When creating the recovery mailbox database, you must use the -Recovery switch to tell Exchange that a recovery mailbox database is created.

To create a recovery mailbox database using the database we have restored in the previous section, you would use an EMS command like this:

```
[PS] C:\> New-MailboxDatabase -Name "MDB04 Recovery" -Recovery
-Server EXCH04 -EdbFilePath R:\RestoreDB\<GUID>\C_\MDB04.edb
-LogFolderPath R:\RestoreDB\<GUID>\C_\LogFiles
```

When the recovery mailbox database is created, it can be mounted, again only using EMS since the recovery mailbox database is not visible in EAC. To mount the recovery mailbox database, execute the following command in EMS:

```
[PS] C:\> Mount-Database -Identity "MDB04 Recovery"
```

Now that the recovery mailbox database is up and running, you can view what's inside this database. An ordinary Get-Mailbox command is not going to work, since this is targeted to the normal mailbox database, but the Get-MailboxStatistics command does work to get a recovery mailbox database data. Just use the following command to retrieve the mailbox data from the recovery mailbox database:

```
[PS] C:\> Get-MailboxStatistics -Database "MDB04 Recovery" |
Select-Object DisplayName,ItemCount | Format-Table -Autosize

DisplayName                                          ItemCount
-----------                                          ---------
SystemMailbox{e3c4d2b5-678e-443e-9f55-777c447eb220}     46
HealthMailbox-EXCH04-MDB04                              186
In-Place Archive -HealthMailbox-EXCH04-002             183
In-Place Archive -HealthMailbox-EXCH04-MDB04            28
HealthMailbox-EXCH04-002                               177
Boardroom                                               21
HealthMailbox-EXCH02-003                               183
HealthMailbox-EXCH02-007                                20
```

In-Place Archive -HealthMailbox-EXCH02-003	197
HealthMailbox-EXCH01-003	173
HealthMailbox-EXCH02-007	20
In-Place Archive -HealthMailbox-EXCH01-003	179
In-Place Archive -HealthMailbox-EXCH02-007	28
In-Place Archive -HealthMailbox-EXCH01-007	44
HealthMailbox-EXCH005-001	169
HealthMailbox-EXCH005-006	20
Jaap Wesselius	371
DMARC Reports	21
Marina Baggus	251

This information can be used to restore mailbox content from the recovery mailbox database into the normal production mailbox database by using the New-MailboxRestoreRequest command in the EMS.

To retrieve mailbox content from the administrator mailbox inside the recovery mailbox database into the normal administrator mailbox, you can use the following command:

```
[PS] C:\> New-MailboxRestoreRequest -SourceDatabase "MDB04
Recovery" -SourceStoreMailbox Jaap -TargetMailbox Jaap
```

The content will be imported into the normal mailbox, but content will not be overwritten. If items already exist in the target mailbox, an additional copy of the item is created so that no information gets lost.

Note   If you are uncertain what will happen during a command like the New-MailboxRestoreRequest, you can always use the -WhatIf switch. The command will be the same, but it will not be executed. The results, however, will be shown on the console. If you are satisfied with the results, you can then rerun the command but without the -WhatIf parameter.

The preceding example will restore the entire mailbox from the recovery mailbox database, but it is possible to use a more granular approach. For instance, you can use the -IncludeFolders parameter to specify the folder in the mailbox that needs to be restored. To include the contents from the Inbox, the option -IncludeFolders "Inbox/*" can be used; or in case of restoring only the Deleted Items folder, the option -IncludeFolders "DeletedItems/*" can be used, for example:

```
[PS] C:\> New-MailboxRestoreRequest -SourceDatabase "MDB04
Recovery" -SourceStoreMailbox Jaap -TargetMailbox Jaap
-IncludeFolders "DeletedItems/*"
```

Note   There is a dependency here on the regional settings of the mailbox. In English, you have an "Inbox," while in Dutch the same folder is called "Postvak In"; in Spanish, it is "bandeja de entrada." You must be aware of the regional setting of the mailbox when performing this command.

For certain purposes, it is possible to restore mailbox content from the mailbox in the recovery mailbox database to another mailbox that's not the original mailbox—for example, a legal mailbox. Suppose there's a mailbox called "Legal" and this mailbox is used to gather information from a mailbox from a backup. A command similar to this can be used:

```
[PS] C:\> New-MailboxRestoreRequest -SourceDatabase "MDB04
Recovery" -SourceStoreMailbox Jaap -TargetMailbox legal
-TargetRootFolder "Recovery Items"
```

Dial-Tone Recovery

A recovery database is also used in a process called dial-tone recovery. In this recovery scenario, you get the users back online as quickly as possible after a mailbox database crash, and you work on mailbox database recovery in the background.

Suppose a mailbox database has crashed beyond repair, but you need to get users back online immediately. In this case you can remove all corrupted files from the disk and mount the mailbox database again. Since Exchange does not find any mailbox database files, it creates a new mailbox database and new log files (after showing a warning message).

Users who had their mailboxes in the crashed mailbox database can now start their mail client, and new mailboxes will automatically be created in the new mailbox database. Of course, that database is empty, but users are online again. They can send mail, but more important, they can receive mail again. The last thing you want to have happen is for external customers to send email to your organization and they receive error messages like "Mailbox info@contoso.com is not available."

Since users are online, they can continue to work, and you can work in the background on restoring the last mailbox database backup to a recovery mailbox database. When the mailbox database is restored and all remaining log files are replayed into the recovered mailbox database, you can swap the two mailbox databases. The recovered mailbox database is then moved to the production location, while the newly created mailbox database, which now also has items in it, is moved to the recovery mailbox database location.

The trick you perform at this point is to mount the newly created mailbox database as a recovery mailbox database and move the new content, using the New-MailboxRestoreRequest command as explained in the previous section, into the restored mailbox database. Once finished, you will have the mailbox database up and running again, without having lost any data.

The good part here is that you can restore the mailbox database from a backup, but your users are able to log on again and continue sending and receiving email. Yes, at that moment they will not have their "old" mailbox content available (not only email items, but also the temporary mailbox does not contain any information or additional permissions), but at least they are online during the restore procedures.

Note   Some third-party backup applications use a granular restore technology, whereby it is possible to restore individual items directly from the VSS backup. What happens is that the VSS backup is completely indexed after the backup, indexing all individual email messages. These messages can then be restored directly from the backup, where the Mapi/Http is used for storing directly into the mailbox.

Recovering an Exchange Server

The previous section discussed mailbox database technologies: how they work, how to back them up, and how to restore them. It showed how it is possible to restore a mailbox database to its original location or to an alternative location. In the last scenario, you created a recovery mailbox database, restored data from this recovery mailbox database, or used it in a dial-tone scenario.

But what happens if an entire server is lost and beyond repair? Then you need to rely on your disaster recovery skills.

Rebuilding an Exchange Server

When the Exchange server is lost, it needs to be rebuilt, and the services, configuration, and data need to be restored. Although this is a rare situation, I saw a lot of rebuilding requests during the HAFNIUM issues in early 2021.

Earlier in this chapter, I described where all the information is stored that is needed to rebuild an Exchange server, for example:

- Mailbox data is stored in the mailbox database, which should be on additional disks. If you are in luck, these are still safe after losing your Exchange server.

- Configuration data is sometimes stored in config files, located somewhere in the C:\Program Files\Microsoft\ Exchange Server\v15 directory.

- All kinds of log files are also stored in the C:\Program Files\Microsoft\Exchange Server directory.

- SSL certificates are stored somewhere safe.

- Server configuration is stored in Active Directory.

Now, if you have taken care of the first four items listed previously, the last one about Active Directory is interesting. All configuration data that is not in the config files is stored in Active Directory, and that can be used when rebuilding the Exchange server. But instead of entering all the details manually during setup, this information is retrieved from Active Directory during installation.

Rule number 1 in a crisis situation is: Don't panic and don't destroy any data—not from disks and not from Active Directory. Otherwise, this action will backfire on you at some point!

To successfully rebuild an Exchange server, you can use the following steps:

1. Reset the computer account in Active Directory. When the server has crashed beyond repair and you must rebuild your server, do not remove the computer object from Active Directory. Instead, reset the computer object in Active Directory, as follows:

   a. Log onto a Domain Controller or any other member server that has the Active Directory tools installed, and open the Active Directory Users and Computers MMC snap-in.

   b. Locate the computer object, right-click it, and select Reset Account (see Figure 11-6). This will reset the computer object so you can join a new Windows server (using the same name) to Active Directory.

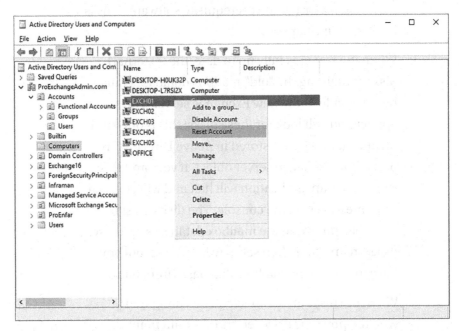

Figure 11-6. Resetting the computer object in a disaster recovery scenario

2. Install a new Windows server with the same specifications as the "old" Mailbox server. Use the same operating system and bring it up to date with the same hot fixes and service packs as were applied to the old Exchange server. Very important: Use the same server name as was for the old Exchange server. That is, when the old server name was EXCH01, the new server name needs to be EXCH01 as well.

3. Join the new server, using the original name, to the Active Directory domain. When joined, reboot the server and log onto the new server as a domain administrator.

4. When logged on as an administrator with sufficient permissions, install the prerequisite software. This is explained in Chapter 2.

5. When the server is fully up to date, the (external) disks containing the "old" mailbox databases must be accessible to the new Exchange server. The setup application will look for these disks; this is one kind of information that is stored in Active Directory as part of the Exchange server object. If you omit this step, the setup application will halt and will generate error messages on the console. The disks must be available, but when the mailbox databases on these disks are missing, then setup will succeed, but you have to restore the mailbox databases from backup.

6. When the disks are connected and configured with the previous drive letters or mount points,
   . the Exchange server can be recovered. If you

don't have the installation media available of the Exchange server you want to recover, you can always download the latest CU and recover directly to that version. This CU "upgrade" is fully supported by Microsoft.

To recover an Exchange server, open a command prompt, navigate to the installation media, and enter the following command:

```
Z:\> Setup.exe /Mode:RecoverServer /
IAcceptExchangeServerLicenseTerms_DiagnosticDataOn

Microsoft Exchange Server 2019 Cumulative Update 13
Unattended Setup

Copying Files...
File copy complete. Setup will now collect additional
information needed for
installation.
Languages
Mailbox role: Transport service
Mailbox role: Client Access service
Mailbox role: Mailbox service
Management tools
Mailbox role: Client Access Front End service
Mailbox role: Front End Transport service
Performing Microsoft Exchange Server Prerequisite Check
```

```
    Configuring Prerequisites                              Completed
    Prerequisite Analysis                                  Completed

Configuring Microsoft Exchange Server

    Preparing Setup                                        Completed
    Stopping Services                                      Completed
    Copying Exchange Files                                 Completed
    Language Files                                         Completed
    Restoring Services                                     Completed
    Language Configuration                                 Completed
    Mailbox role: Transport service                        Completed
    Mailbox role: Client Access service                    Completed
    Mailbox role: Mailbox service                          Completed
    Exchange Management Tools                               Completed
    Mailbox role: Client Access Front End service          Completed
    Mailbox role: Front End Transport service              Completed
    Finalizing Setup                                       Completed
```

The Exchange Server setup operation completed successfully. Setup has made changes to operating system settings that require a reboot to take effect. Please reboot this server prior to placing it into production.

7. This will install Exchange server, and all the configuration information that is normally entered in the setup application is now retrieved from Active Directory. When the setup application is finished and the server is reinstalled, reboot the server.

After rebooting, you can check the mailbox databases that were on the (external) disk drives; they should be good, although dismounted. When you mount the mailbox databases on the recovered server, you are good to log into your mailbox using OWA. The last steps are to restore or reconfigure additional items like the SSL certificate, virtual directories, additional config files, or other log files, as explained earlier in this chapter.

When done, though your server has been unavailable for some time, it is now restored to its original location. If you (and your users) are unhappy with the downtime, you should refer to the "Database Availability Group" in Chapter 2. When using a DAG, downtime can be minimized, even when recovering an Exchange server.

ESEUTIL and Corrupt Databases

Although rare these days, it can happen that you end up with a corrupted mailbox database and no backup of your mailbox database. Most of the times this is caused by malfunctioning hardware like a dead battery on a disk controller or a faulty backup device. In this case, you must rely on tools that can repair your mailbox database. ESEUTIL is such a tool, and it comes with Exchange Server; you can use ESEUTIL to repair a corrupted mailbox database.

When a mailbox database is corrupted, that means it has corrupted pages in it, and most likely it will not mount. When you perform an integrity check on the mailbox database using ESEUTIL /G, it will report that the mailbox database is corrupted, as shown in the following:

```
R:\MDB04>Eseutil /G mdb04.edb

Extensible Storage Engine Utilities for Microsoft(R)
Exchange Server
Version 15.01
Copyright (C) Microsoft Corporation. All Rights Reserved.
```

```
Initiating INTEGRITY mode...
        Database: mdb04.edb
  Temp. Database: .\TEMPINTEG4784.EDB

Checking database integrity.

              Scanning Status (% complete)

      0    10   20   30   40   50   60   70   80   90   100
      |----|----|----|----|----|----|----|----|----|----|
      ...............................................................

Integrity check completed.  Database is CORRUPTED!

Operation terminated with error -1206 (JET_
errDatabaseCorrupted, Non database file or corrupted db) after
14.469 seconds.
```

ESEUTIL also has an option to repair a mailbox database, but it is
a very destructive way of repairing. What it does is open the mailbox
database and check all the pages in the database. When a page is found to
contain corrupted pointers (i.e., pointers to other pages containing data),
it will remove these pointers from the page. The result is that no pages
contain invalid pointers anymore, but the data that was referenced using
those pages is automatically lost.

It is not possible to predict which pages and pointers are corrupted,
and thus it is not possible to anticipate what data you will be missing.
Unfortunately, your users will find this out in the end.

You can start a repair with ESEUTIL /P MDB04.edb. A warning
message is shown saying that you should only run Repair on damaged or
corrupted databases. The caution is that Repair will not apply information
in the transaction log files to the database and may cause information to be
lost. And it will ask you if you want to continue.

If you do, click the OK button to continue. ESEUTIL will perform a consistency check first, then scan the database, and repair any damaged information that it found. This is shown in the following example:

```
R:\MDB04>Eseutil /p mdb04.edb

Extensible Storage Engine Utilities for Microsoft(R)
Exchange Server
Version 15.01
Copyright (C) Microsoft Corporation. All Rights Reserved.

Initiating REPAIR mode...
        Database: mdb04.edb
  Temp. Database: TEMPREPAIR13252.EDB

Checking database integrity.

              Scanning Status (% complete)

     0    10   20   30   40   50   60   70   80   90   100
     |----|----|----|----|----|----|----|----|----|----|
     ....................................................

Scanning the database.

              Scanning Status (% complete)

     0    10   20   30   40   50   60   70   80   90   100
     |----|----|----|----|----|----|----|----|----|----|
     ....................................................

Repairing damaged tables.

              Scanning Status (% complete)

     0    10   20   30   40   50   60   70   80   90   100
     |----|----|----|----|----|----|----|----|----|----|
     ....................................................
```

Repair completed. Database corruption has been repaired!

Note:

It is recommended that you immediately perform a full backup
of this database. If you restore a backup made before the
repair, the database will be rolled back to the state
it was in at the time of that backup.

Operation completed successfully with 595 (JET_
wrnDatabaseRepaired, Database corruption has been repaired)
after 13.125 seconds.

One question that always pops up is how long it takes for a mailbox
database repair to be completed. As a rule of thumb, I use 10 GB per hour
for processing. So, if you have a 250 GB mailbox database you must repair,
it will take approximately 25 hours to complete. There is no need to panic
when you do not see any dots moving on the console; ESEUTIL just needs
time to do its work.

This is the reason Microsoft recommends not using large mailbox
databases (i.e., larger than 200 GB) when a DAG is not used. If you are
using a 500 GB mailbox database in a single Mailbox server environment
and you run into a situation like this, you will have a hard time ensuring
service delivery (which should be documented in the SLA).

It is recommended that you create a new mailbox database after a
corrupted mailbox database has been repaired and move all data from the
old mailbox database to the new mailbox database.

This can be done in two ways:

- Create a new mailbox database on the Exchange server
  and move all the mailboxes from the old and repaired
  mailbox database to the new mailbox database. Once
  they are moved, the old mailbox database can be
  removed. Do not forget to create a new backup of the

new mailbox database when done. The advantage is that users can continue to work during the move of the mailboxes.

- Use ESEUTIL /D to perform an offline defragmentation. The net effect of this is that a new mailbox database is created with the old name. When you use ESEUTIL /D to perform an offline defragmentation, it will create a new mailbox database file next to the old mailbox database file. Then it will read all information from the old file and merge it into the new file. However, to do this you first have to dismount the mailbox database, and it can only be mounted after ESEUTIL has finished. Again, this can take a considerable amount of time, and the users cannot continue to work, which is a huge disadvantage.

This way not only is a new file created but also new indices, new tables, new pointers, and so on—so basically you end up with a new mailbox database. When the copy process is complete, the old (and previously corrupted) mailbox database will be deleted.

Summary

In this chapter we have discussed backup and restore technologies and procedures in Exchange 2019.

Using this information, you must have some knowledge of backup technologies and how to restore mailbox databases and replay transaction log files that are automatically stored in the backup. You can do this in an original location, thus overwriting an existing mailbox database, or use an alternative location for restoring a mailbox database.

Using the ESEUTIL tool, you can work with mailbox databases offline, check header information, check the mailbox database integrity, or replay additional transaction log files.

While this is all possible, it is better to stay away from these technologies and use a Database Availability Group to create highly available mailbox databases. When one server fails or when a mailbox database fails, you have additional servers and mailbox database copies online available that will automatically take over the services. When this happens, you can repair the faulty server or create a new copy of the mailbox database.

This is not only much easier than work with a backup and restore; your services will remain online and your users can continue to work.

CHAPTER 12

Policy and Compliance

Many organizations utilize email for communicating both internally and with other organizations. Because everybody has become used to sending and receiving email on all sorts of devices and because some of the underlying complexities and potential adverse consequences are unknown to end users, many companies want their communications to conform to certain rules—whether those rules are company policies for sending email containing sensitive information to external organizations or are operations to comply with external laws and regulations, such as the Sarbanes-Oxley Act in the United States or the European Union's Data Protection Directive.

Exchange 2019 has features that address some of those concerns. Some features were introduced back in Exchange 2010 and some features were introduced in Exchange 2013, and Microsoft continues to improve these features.

In this chapter we discuss the following compliance-related features:

- In-place archiving

- Messaging Records Management (MRM)

- In-place hold and litigation hold

- In-place eDiscovery

© Jaap Wesselius and Michel de Rooij 2023
J. Wesselius and M. de Rooij, *Pro Exchange Administration*,
https://doi.org/10.1007/978-1-4842-9591-5_12

- Mail flow rules

- Journaling

- Data loss prevention (DLP)

- Administrator audit logging

- Mailbox audit logging

In-Place Archiving

The in-place archive mailbox is an extension of a regular mailbox, and it is hosted on an Exchange server or in Exchange Online. This feature was introduced with Exchange Server 2010 as a personal archive or archive mailbox; as of Exchange Server 2013, this feature is known as in-place archiving, and the archive is known as the in-place archive mailbox.

In-Place Archive Mailbox

An in-place archive mailbox can be used to offload contents from the primary mailbox, therefore controlling the size of the mailbox. Exchange 2019 supports mailbox databases up to 2 TB in size, and mailbox sizes are not limited from an Exchange perspective.

Things are different in Exchange Online, where depending on the license the mailbox is limited to 50 GB or 100 GB. In Exchange Online, you must offload items to an in-place archive where the total size is over 100 GB. This is something to keep in mind when you are planning a migration from Exchange 2019 to Exchange Online.

For large mailboxes, there's also a client implication. When running Outlook in cached mode, it builds a .OST file holding the mailbox cache, and this cache is a representation of the mailbox contents. When the mailbox is 2 GB in size, the .OST file is also 2 GB in size. For a fat client this is not a problem, but when using a 125 GB mailbox, Outlook wants to build a 125 GB .OST file, which becomes unmanageable quickly. Image what happens when a user logs on to a different computer, and Outlook starts building a new .OST file.

Performance of the workstation becomes less of an issue. In the old days when using a 5400 rpm disk, a large .OST file became quickly unworkable, but with the current SSD disks in workstations, this is no longer an issue.

To manage the size of the OST file, Outlook contains an option in the form of a slider, hidden in the Outlook profile settings. This slider limits the information that can be stored in the offline cache to a certain age, and then Outlook can retrieve the non-cached mailbox information from the online mailbox as required. The default setting for the slider is to cache one year of mail data. The maximum time span is "unlimited"; the minimum time span is three days.

It is also possible to control the slider via a Group Policy Object (GPO). For this to work, you need to download the Office 2016 Administrative Template files (ADMX/ADML) and Office Customization Tool from the Microsoft download center. More information about managing Outlook and the slider can be found at `https://bit.ly/OutlookSlider`.

Note   Archive mailboxes are always accessed in online mode. Keep this in mind when considering use of in-place archive mailboxes. This is even more important when using in-place archive mailboxes in Exchange Online!

Second, and perhaps more important, is that the archive mailbox serves as a much better alternative for the infamous personal folders, or .PST files. This is because archive mailboxes are stored in Exchange (or the cloud when using Exchange Online in-place archive mailboxes), and this has several advantages over .PST files:

- The information is stored in Exchange and does not require inventory and collection of .PST files for discovery, which might be inaccessible and can be tampered with.

- Information stored in Exchange is not prone to theft or loss as are .PST files, which are often hosted on laptops or are transported using USB sticks.

- Archive mailboxes are treated just like mailboxes and thus can be incorporated into your Exchange backup solution, or you can replicate the information using a Database Availability Group.

- Information stored in archive mailboxes can be discovered from a compliance perspective, just like regular mailboxes.

Offloading your mailbox contents to an in-place archive mailbox can be done manually, or retention policies can be used to move the items from the primary mailbox to the in-place archive mailbox, depending on criteria such as the age of the item. Retention policies are discussed in the next section of this chapter.

In-place archive mailboxes also come with certain limitations you should be aware of:

- They are not supported by all clients. For example, mobile devices will not allow you to access your archive mailboxes, not even with Outlook Mobile.

- In-place archive mailboxes and their related primary mailboxes are tightly coupled; you can't simply detach an in-place archive mailbox and attach it to a different primary mailbox. This is because both the primary mailbox and the in-place archive mailbox have the same legacyExchangeDN property. A possible workaround for this limitation would be to export the contents of the archive mailbox and import it elsewhere. Be advised, though, that if the primary mailbox is deleted, the archive mailbox will be deleted as well.

Note   In-place archiving is a premium feature and requires an Enterprise CAL when used on-premises. More information about licenses can be found at `https://bit.ly/OLLicense`. As such, it has specific Outlook licensing requirements. To quickly check how many mailboxes are configured with archive mailboxes, use `(Get-Mailbox -Archive).Count` command.

In contrast to Exchange Online where mailboxes sizes are limited to 100 GB, mailboxes in Exchange 2019 are not limited in size, and they can grow far beyond 100 GB. However, if you ever have plans to move to Exchange Online, this is something to be aware of. You can use the in-place archive mailbox to keep your mailbox below the 100 GB size limit, which makes moving to Exchange Online easier. But the 100 GB size limit in Exchange Online also counts for the in-place archive in Exchange Online. In Exchange Online there's the concept of auto-expanding in-place archive mailboxes, where in-place archive mailboxes can virtually grow to 1.5 TB in size, but moving in-place archives of over 100 GB in size from Exchange 2019 to Exchange Online is complex and time consuming.

Enabling Archive Mailboxes

When you consider using in-place archive mailboxes, check if the clients used in your organization support archive mailboxes.

To create an in-place archive mailbox for Sarah's mailbox, execute the following command in the Exchange Management Shell:

```
[PS] C:\> Enable-Mailbox -Identity S.Summertown -Archive

Name                Alias          ServerName   ProhibitSendQuota
----                -----          ----------   -----------------
Sarah Summertown    S.Summertown   Exch01       Unlimited
```

The target database for the archive mailbox will automatically be picked by the mailbox resources management agent. You can also create an archive mailbox on a specific mailbox database by specifying the archive database in the Enable-Mailbox command:

```
[PS] C:\> Enable-Mailbox –Identity David –Archive –
ArchiveDatabase MDB02

Name                 Alias           ServerName   ProhibitSendQuota
----                 -----           ----------   -----------------
David Honeychurch    D.Honeychurch   Exch02       Unlimited
```

When using an Exchange hybrid configuration, it is also possible have the primary mailbox in Exchange 2019 and have the in-place archive in Exchange Online, assuming you have the correct license in Exchange Online of course. To add an in-place archive to an existing mailbox in Exchange 2019, execute the following command in the Exchange Management Shell:

```
[PS] C:\>Enable-Mailbox -Identity P.Mortimer -RemoteArchive
-ArchiveDomain proexchangeadmin.mail.onmicrosoft.com
```

Name	Alias	ServerName	ProhibitSendQuota
Philip Mortimer	P.Mortimer	EXCH01	Unlimited

The next time Azure AD Connect runs, it will synchronize the correct properties with Exchange Online, and the in-place archive will be provisioned.

After an in-place archive mailbox is enabled, additional mailbox properties will get populated. For example, when you are retrieving the mailbox properties using the Get-Mailbox command, you will see additional archive-related attributes:

```
[PS] C:\> Get-Mailbox -Identity P.Mortimer | Select *Archive*
```

```
ArchiveDatabase              : MDB01
ArchiveGuid                  : 9755aeb3-aca3-4d45-
                               b110-90b90981dff7
ArchiveName                  : {In-Place Archive -Philip
                               Mortimer}
JournalArchiveAddress        :
ArchiveQuota                 : 100 GB (107,374,182,400 bytes)
ArchiveWarningQuota          : 90 GB (96,636,764,160 bytes)
ArchiveDomain                :
ArchiveStatus                : None
ArchiveState                 : Local
AutoExpandingArchiveEnabled  : False
DisabledArchiveDatabase      :
DisabledArchiveGuid          : 00000000-0000-0000-0000-
                               000000000000
ArchiveRelease               :
```

The property ArchiveDatabase contains the name of the database where the archive is stored. When the in-place archive is stored in Exchange 2019, it shows the actual mailbox database. When the in-place archive is stored in Exchange Online it shows nothing.

The property ArchiveStatus indicates the status of the archive and can be set to None or Active; the latter is used to indicate when the Exchange Archive mailbox is ready.

The property ArchiveState indicates the state of the archive and can be Local or None in case of Exchange 2019, or it can be HostedPending or HostedProvisioned in case of Exchange Online.

The property ArchiveDomain contains the SMTP domain of the tenant hosting the in-place archive mailbox. When the in-place archive is in Exchange 2019, the ArchiveDomain property remains blank; when the in-place archive is in Exchange Online, it contains the SMTP of the tenant, for example, contoso.mail.onmicrosoft.com.

Caution   If you enable a primary mailbox for an in-place archive mailbox on-premises, it will create a new archive. If you want to reuse a formerly disabled archive, see the section on reconnecting archive mailboxes.

When you have added an archive mailbox to a mailbox, the Autodiscover response will contain an additional alternative mailbox section that provides information to the client, such as that there is an in-place archive mailbox configured for this mailbox. The client can leverage Autodiscover to connect to the in-place archive mailbox. Because the information is contained in the initial Autodiscover response, no additional configuration is required on the client, and the in-place archive mailbox will automatically be configured and added onto the supported clients.

In the excerpt of the Autodiscover response shown in Figure 12-1, you can see that there is an additional mailbox of type Archive configured, which has the identity shown at the LegacyDN attribute and is accessible through the provided Server attribute.

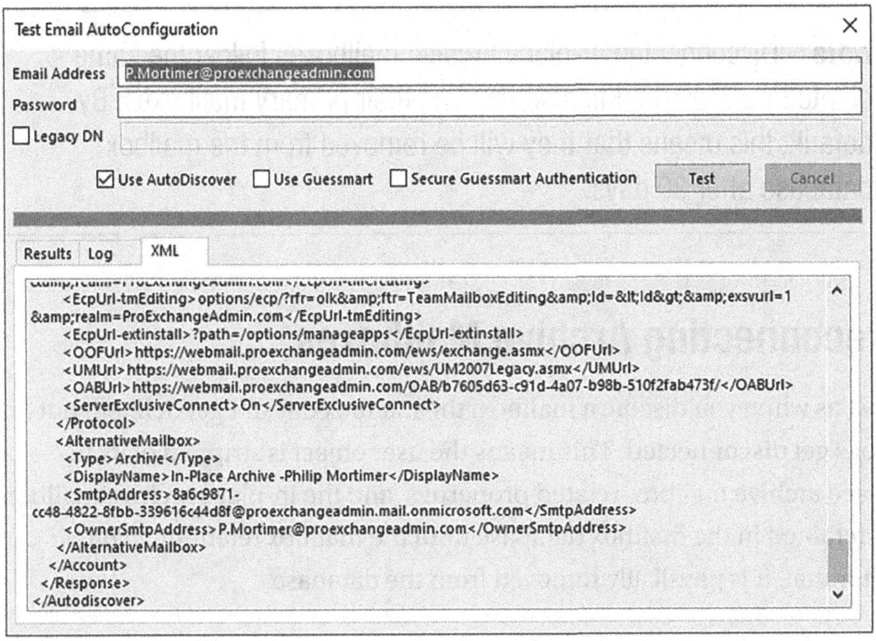

Figure 12-1. *Autodiscover archive mailbox alternative mailbox section*

Disabling In-Place Archive Mailboxes

To disconnect an in-place archive mailbox from the primary mailbox, use the Disable-Mailbox cmdlet in conjunction with the -Archive parameter. For example, to disable the in-place archive mailbox for the mailbox of Sarah, use the following command:

```
[PS] C:\> Disable-Mailbox –Identity S.Summertown –Archive
```

When the in-place archive is in Exchange Online, the disconnect command is similar:

```
[PS] C:\> Disable-Mailbox -Identity S.Summertown -RemoteArchive
```

Note   Disconnected in-place archive mailboxes follow the same deleted mailbox retention settings as their primary mailboxes. By default, this means that they will be removed from the mailbox database after 30 days.

Reconnecting Archive Mailboxes

Just as when you disable a mailbox, the mailbox doesn't get deleted, but it does get disconnected. This means the user object is stripped of its in-place archive mailbox–related properties, and the in-place archive mailbox is retained in the mailbox database until the mailbox retention expires; after that, it is physically removed from the database.

Note   If you want to reconnect a disabled in-place archive mailbox to its original mailbox, just enable the in-place archive mailbox for the primary mailbox.

As with mailboxes, you can reconnect a disabled on-premises in-place archive mailbox to a mailbox-enabled user, and this will be the original primary mailbox. To get a list of all disconnected in-place archive mailboxes, use the following command:

```
[PS] C:\> Get-MailboxDatabase | Get-Mailboxstatistics |
Where {$_.DisconnectDate -and $_.IsArchiveMailbox} | ft -a
```

```
DisplayName                        ItemCount LastLogonTime
-----------                        --------- -------------
In-Place Archive -Sarah Summertown 182       12/16/2022 3:58:43 PM
In-Place Archive -Michel De Rooij  40
In-Place Archive -Karen Young      33
```

To connect an on-premises archive to its original primary mailbox, use the Connect-Mailbox cmdlet in conjunction with the Archive parameter. For example, to reconnect the in-place archive mailbox for Sarah Summertown that was disabled in the previous step you can use the following command:

```
[PS] C:\> Connect-Mailbox -Identity "In-Place Archive -Sarah
Summertown" -Archive -User S.Summertown -Database MDB2
```

Note   If you get an error message saying "Object reference not set to an instance of an object" try adding the -AllowLegacyDNMismatch switch.

Checking and Modifying Archive Mailbox Quotas

Primary mailboxes and their related in-place archive mailboxes can have different quota settings. You can query the archive mailbox quota settings for all mailboxes by using the following command:

```
[PS] C:\>Get-Mailbox -Archive | Select Name,
Archive*Quota | FT -A
```

```
Name             ArchiveQuota                        ArchiveWarningQuota
----             ------------                        -------------------
John Smith       100 GB (107,374,182,400 bytes)      90 GB (96,636,764,160 bytes)
Michel De Rooij  100 GB (107,374,182,400 bytes)      90 GB (96,636,764,160 bytes)
David Honeychurch 100 GB (107,374,182,400 bytes)     90 GB (96,636,764,160 bytes)
```

```
Karen Young        100 GB (107,374,182,400 bytes) 90 GB (96,636,764,160 bytes)
Philip Mortimer    100 GB (107,374,182,400 bytes) 90 GB (96,636,764,160 bytes)
Glenn Kendall      100 GB (107,374,182,400 bytes) 90 GB (96,636,764,160 bytes)
```

You can modify the archive mailbox quota settings using the Set-Mailbox command, for example,

```
[PS] C:\> Set-Mailbox -Identity P.Mortimer -ArchiveQuota
200GB -ArchiveWarningQuota 190GB
```

Note   Unlike regular mailboxes, you don't have to use the -UseDatabaseQuotaDefaults parameter when changing quota settings on an in-place archive mailbox.

Relocating the Archive Mailboxes

The primary mailbox and the archive do not need to be hosted in the same mailbox database. This means you can have dedicated Mailbox servers for hosting primary mailboxes and for hosting archives.

When you want to relocate only the in-place archive mailboxes to a different database, you can utilize the New-MoveRequest cmdlet in conjunction with the -ArchiveOnly parameter. In addition, you can use the -ArchiveTargetDatabase parameter to specify the target database for the archive mailboxes. For example, to relocate all the archive mailboxes to a database called MDB2, you use the following command:

```
[PS] C:\> Get-Mailbox -Archive | New-MoveRequest -ArchiveOnly -
ArchiveTargetDatabase MDB2
```

Do not forget to clean up your move requests when the archives have been moved successfully; you do this by using this command:

```
[PS] C:\> Get-MoveRequest | Where {$_.Status -eq 'Completed'} |
Remove-MoveRequest -Confirm:$False
```

Note   You can use the New-MoveRequest command with the -ArchiveOnly parameter also when you want to move the in-place archive mailbox to Exchange Online. The -ArchiveTargetDatabase parameter is omitted when moving the in-place archive mailbox to Exchange Online.

Exporting and Importing Archive Mailboxes

Should you need to physically move the contents of an in-place archive mailbox to a different mailbox, you can opt to export and import the information. To export or import mailbox contents, you first need to have the mailbox import/export management role. You can use the Exchange Admin Center to assign this role, or you can use the following PowerShell command:

```
[PS] C:\> New-ManagementRoleAssignment -Role 'Mailbox Import
Export' -User Administrator
```

Next, you create a network share for hosting the .PST files. Exporting and importing require a network share because it is undetermined which Exchange server will ultimately handle the import or export request in a multi-Exchange server environment. Make sure the Exchange Trusted Subsystem has read/write permissions on this share.

To export the contents out of an in-place archive mailbox, you use New-MailboxExportRequest command in conjunction with the –IsArchive parameter, and use –FilePath to specify the full UNC filename of the .PST file, for example:

```
[PS] C:\> New-MailboxExportRequest –Mailbox P.Mortimer –
FilePath '\\FS01\PST\Philip_Archive.pst' -IsArchive
```

To import the contents in a subfolder, you use TargetRootFolder, for example:

```
[PS] C:\> New-MailboxImportRequest –Mailbox P.Mortimer –
FilePath '\\FS01\PST\Philip_Archive.pst' –IsArchive –
TargetRootFolder 'Imported Archive'
```

When you're finished, you can remove the import and export requests using Remove-MailboxExportRequest and Remove-MailboxImportRequest commands.

Directly after you enabled the in-place archive mailbox, Exchange starts moving items from the primary mailbox to the in-place archive mailbox, independent of whether the mailbox is in Exchange 2019 or in Exchange Online. The process that is responsible for this is the Messaging Records Management, which is discussed in the next section.

Messaging Records Management

In the world of ever-growing mailbox sizes, organizations require controls to manage the volume of email stored within their corporate environments. When these mailboxes are left unmanaged and unrestricted, there could be disruption of email services and higher storage costs. Additionally, organizations may have a legal obligation to store certain electronic communications for a given period. This makes email management crucial in many organizations.

Messaging Records Management (MRM) is the feature of Exchange that deals with the organization and management of email by using an established set of rules. In MRM, mailboxes are managed by definition of the retention policies that have been assigned to those mailboxes. Those retention policies consist of retention policy tags that identify the rules that could be applied to the mailbox or elements of the mailbox. A retention policy tag can be part of one or more retention policies. The retention policies are enforced by the managed folder assistant (MFA). Let's discuss these elements next.

Note   Exchange 2019 comes with a default set of retention policies and retention policy tags that are set on a primary mailbox as soon as you enable an in-place archive mailbox on this primary mailbox.

Retention Policy Tags

A retention policy tag defines what retention setting is to be used for a message or folder to which that tag is assigned. There are three types of retention tags:

- *Default policy tag (DPT)*: This is assigned to items that do not otherwise have a tag assigned. A retention policy can have only one DPT.

- *Retention policy tag (RPT)*: This tag is assigned to default well-known folders, such as Inbox, Deleted Items, Calendar, and so on.

- *Personal tag*: This tag can be assigned by users using Outlook or Outlook Web Access to apply retention settings to specific items or folders.

Note   Personal tags are a premium feature and require an Enterprise CAL or Exchange Online Archiving License.

In this section we will create new policy tags first with EAC to make it more visible. Later in this section we will continue with PowerShell.

To create a retention policy tag using EAC, you do the following:

1. Open the Exchange Admin Center and navigate to Compliance Management ➤ Retention Tags.

2. Click the + sign and select one of the following options:

   - Applied automatically to entire mailbox (default) to create a default policy tag

   - Applied automatically to a default folder to create a retention policy tag

   - Applied by users to items and folders (personal) to create a personal tag

3. Depending on the type of tag you choose, you are now asked to complete the creation of the retention policy tag by providing details such as name, retention period, and action to take.

This is shown in Figure 12-2.

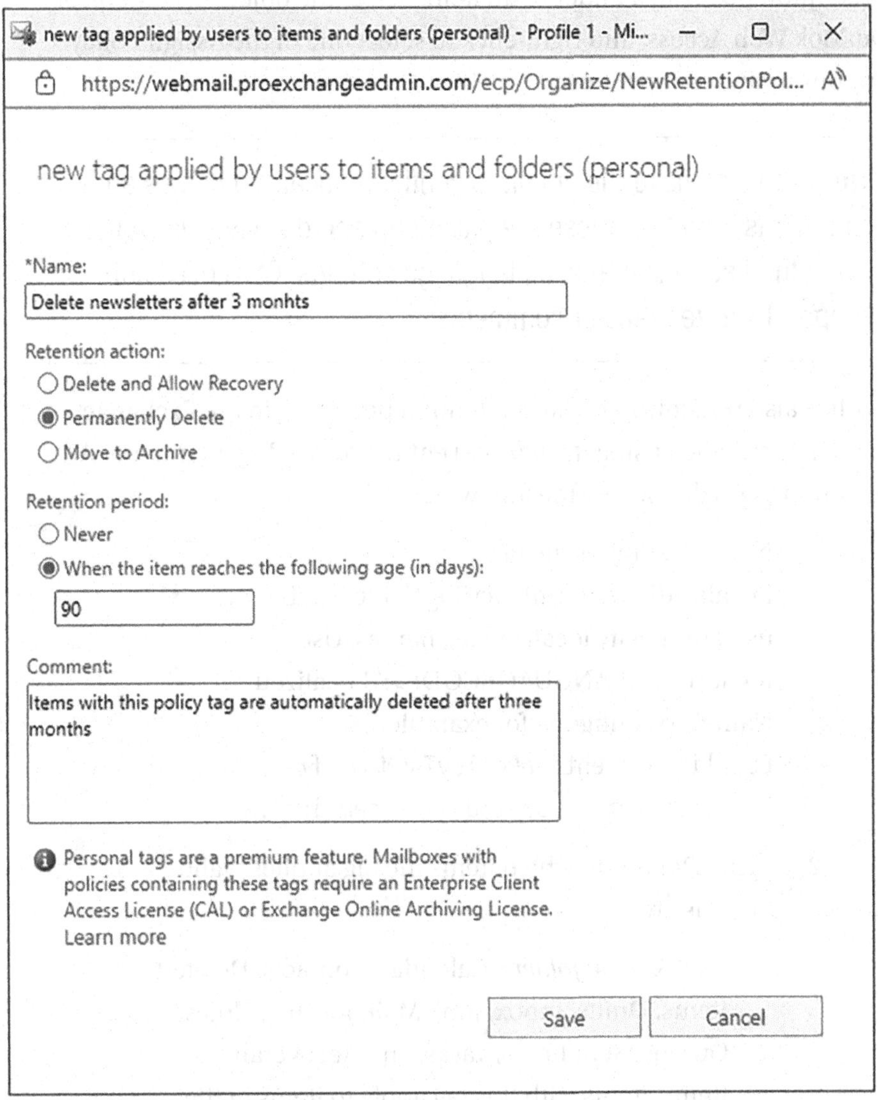

Figure 12-2. Creating a new retention policy tag in EAC

After adding the new retention policy tag to a policy, you can apply a retention policy to a folder or an item. Select the object in Outlook or Outlook Web Access, and right-click to select one of the Assign Policy options in the popup menu.

Tip   You also have the option to configure localized names and comments on a tag. These are picked up and displayed in Outlook when the user has matching language settings. OWA does not support localized tags or comments.

It is also possible to create a retention policy tag in the Exchange Management Shell using the `New-RetentionPolicyTag` command. A retention tag is defined by the following:

1. Name: Identifies the tag; LocalizedRetentionPolicyTagName can be used to specify localized tag names. Use the format <LANGUAGECODE>:"Localized Name" to configure, for example, `LocalizedRetentionPolicyTagName fr-FR:''retirer au bout d''une semaine'`.

2. Type: Defines to which items the tag applies. Valid options are

   - *Well-known folders*: Calendar, Contacts, Deleted Items, Drafts, Inbox, Junk Mail, Journal, Notes, Outbox, Sent Items, Tasks, and Recoverable Items. Items with this tag apply to items in the corresponding mailbox folder.

   - All: This tag is considered a default policy tag and items with this tag apply to all items.

- RssSubscriptions: Items with this tag apply to the mailbox folder for RSS feeds.

- SyncIssues: Items with this tag apply to the mailbox folder where synchronization issues are stored.

- ConversationHistory: Items with this tag apply to the mailbox folder where Lync IM conversations are stored.

- Personal: Items with this tag are personal tags.

3. AgeLimitForRetention: Specifies the age limit after which the action defined by retention action should be performed.

4. RetentionEnabled: Set to $true if the tag is enabled.

5. RetentionAction: Defines the action to take when the retention limit has been reached. Possible actions are

   - MarkAsPastRetentionLimit: Items with this tag are marked as past the retention limit. This will only result in a visual clue in Outlook—that is, a notice that the item has expired will be shown, and it will appear in strikethrough font.

   - DeleteAndAllowRecovery: Items with this tag will be soft-deleted and moved to the Deleted Items folder.

   - PermanentlyDelete: Items with this tag will be hard-deleted and cannot be recovered. When the mailbox is on hold, those items can be found using in-place discovery.

- MoveToArchive: Items with this tag will be move to the archive (when configured). You can use this tag only for All, Personal, and Recoverable Item types.

6. Comment: Used to specify a comment for the tag; LocalizedComment can be used to specify localized comments. Use the same format as with LocalizedRetentionPolicyTagName to create localized information.

7. MessageClass: Used to limit the tag to certain items. Currently only one message class is supported: UM voice mail messages. To select these, specify MessageClass IPM.Note.Microsoft.Voicemail* as the message class. The default message class value is *, which means the tag applies to all items.

A default policy tag is created by establishing a policy tag with the All type. For example, to create a default policy tag that moves items to the archive after a year, you use the following command:

```
[PS] C:\> New-RetentionPolicyTag -Name 'Default 1 year move to
archive' -Type All -AgeLimitForRetention 365 -RetentionAction
MoveToArchive
```

To create a retention policy tag for a well-known folder, you specify the type of the folder. For example, to create a policy to soft-delete calendar items after two years, you use the following command:

```
[PS] C:\> New-RetentionPolicyTag –Name 'Delete Calendar
Items after 2 year' -Type Calendar –AgeLimitForRetention
730 –RetentionAction DeleteAndAllowRecovery
```

To create a personal tag, you use the Personal type. For example, to create a personal tag that can be used to tag items that should never be processed for retention, you use the following command:

```
[PS] C:\> New-RetentionPolicyTag –Name 'Never Move to Archive'
-Type Personal -RetentionEnabled $false -RetentionAction
MoveToArchive
```

To configure a localized string for an existing policy tag in French for example, you can use the following command:

```
[PS] C:\> Set-RetentionPolicyTag -Name '1 Week Delete'
-LocalizedRetentionPolicyTagName fr-FR:'retirer au bout d''une
semaine'
```

Note   The two quotes in the string are not a typo, but it's a PowerShell notation of a quote inside a string.

Assigning Personal Tags

Personal tags can be assigned by end users using Microsoft Outlook, Outlook Web Access, or programmatically (Exchange Web Services). To assign a personal tag, you follow these steps:

1. Open Outlook or Outlook Web Access.

2. Right-click the folder or item you want to assign a personal tag to and select Assign Policy.

3. Pick a personal tag from the list. You may also see the following options:

   • Use Folder Policy, which is to revert to the folder retention policy.

- Set Folder Policy, to set the parent folder retention policy.

- View Items Expiring Soon, to show items that will expire within the next 30 days.

You can automatically apply personal tags to items using inbox rules. For example, you can create a rule to automatically apply the "1 Year Delete" tag to electronic newsletters to have them automatically removed from your mailbox by the managed folder assistant after a year.

In Exchange 2019, the following retention tags are available by default:

- *Default*: Two-year move to archive

- *Personal*: One-year move to archive, five-year move to archive, or never move to archive

- 1 Week Delete

- 1 Month Delete

- 6 Month Delete

- 1 Year Delete

- 5 Year Delete

- Never Delete

- *Recoverable Items*: 14-day move to archive

Understanding System Tags

The tags mentioned earlier are in fact non-system tags, which implies that there also is something called "system tags." System tags are used by Exchange internally for automatic management of, for example, arbitration mailboxes.

You can retrieve a list of retention tags, including system tags, by using the Get-RetentionPolicyTag including the -IncludeSystemTags parameter:

```
[PS] C:\> Get-RetentionPolicyTag  -IncludeSystemTags | Select
Name,Type,SystemTag
```

Name	Type	SystemTag
AutoGroup	Personal	True
ModeratedRecipients	Personal	True
AsyncOperationNotification	Personal	True
Personal 1 year move to archive	Personal	False
Default 2 year move to archive	All	False
Personal 5 year move to archive	Personal	False
Personal never move to archive	Personal	False
1 Week Delete	Personal	False
1 Month Delete	Personal	False
6 Month Delete	Personal	False
1 Year Delete	Personal	False
5 Year Delete	Personal	False
Never Delete	Personal	False
Recoverable Items 14 days move to archive	RecoverableItems	False
Move to in-place archive after 2 years	Personal	False
Delete newsletters after 3 months	Personal	False

System tags can be queried just like regular retention tags, as shown in the following example:

```
[PS] C:\>Get-RetentionPolicyTag -Identity AutoGroup | Select
Name,Age*,*Action

Name       AgeLimitForRetention            RetentionAction
----       --------------------            ---------------
AutoGroup 30.00:00:00                      DeleteAndAllowRecovery
```

> **Note**   It is generally recommended you leave the default retention tags as is.

Retention Policies

A retention policy is a collection of retention tags assigned to a mailbox. A default policy tag is applied to the assigned mailbox overall, and a retention policy can only contain one default policy tag. Retention policies can also contain retention policy tags that are applied to the related folder in the assigned mailbox. Finally, the user of the mailbox can select those personal tags made available by assigning a retention policy containing those personal tags to that mailbox, thus explicitly overriding any existing retention settings.

In an Exchange Server deployment, by default there are two retention policies available:

- Default MRM Policy: This is the default retention policy assigned to mailboxes. Note that it contains the default two-year move to archive retention policy tag, which configures the mailbox to automatically move its contents to the in-place archive when such an archive is configured for the mailbox.

- ArbitrationMailbox: This policy is by default assigned to system mailboxes and contains, for example, the retention policy tag AutoGroup, which deletes items after 30 days.

To see which retention policy tags are part of a retention policy, inspect the RetentionPolicyTagLinks attribute:

```
[PS] C:\>Get-RetentionPolicy -Identity 'Default MRM Policy' |
Select -ExpandProperty RetentionPolicyTagLinks | select na
me

Name
----
Delete newsletters after 3 months
Recoverable Items 14 days move to archive
Never Delete
5 Year Delete
1 Year Delete
6 Month Delete
1 Month Delete
1 Week Delete
Personal never move to archive
Personal 5 year move to archive
Default 2 year move to archive
Personal 1 year move to archive
```

To create a retention policy using EAC, you do the following steps:

1. Open the Exchange Admin Center and navigate to Compliance Management ➤ Retention Policies.

2. Select the + sign.

3. In the new retention policy dialog, enter the name of the policy to create. In the retention tags section, use the + and – signs to add or remove retention tags.

This is shown in Figure 12-3.

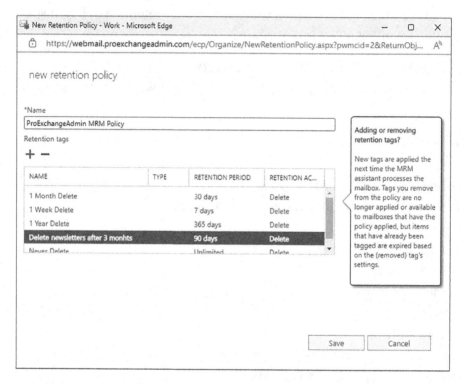

Figure 12-3. *Creating a new Exchange MRM policy*

To create a new retention policy using the Exchange Management Shell, use the New-RetentionPolicy command and provide retention policy tags as a parameter, separating tags using a comma (thus providing the tags as an array), as follows:

```
[PS] C:\> New-RetentionPolicy –Name 'ProExchangeAdmin MRM Policy'
-RetentionPolicyTagLinks 'Default 1 year move to archive','1 Month
Delete', '1 Week Delete','1 Year Delete','Never Delete'
```

To add a retention policy tag to a retention policy, you need to add it as an element:

```
[PS] C:\> Set-RetentionPolicy -Name 'ProExchangeAdmin MRM
Policy' -RetentionPolicyTagLinks @{Add='Delete newsletters
after 3 months'}
```

Should you need to remove a retention policy tag from a retention policy, you can remove the element:

```
[PS] C:\> Set-RetentionPolicy -Name 'ProExchangeAdmin MRM
Policy' -RetentionPolicyTagLinks @{Remove='1 Week Delete'}
```

Warning   Do not use `Set-RetentionPolicy` `'ProExchangeAdmin MRM Policy' -RetentionPolicyTag Links '1 Week Delete'` as this would overwrite any current retention policy tag entries with the value specified. Always use the @{Add= 'value'} or @{Remove='value'} construction.

Assigning a Retention Policy

For a retention policy and its tags to become effective or available in case of personal tags, it needs to be assigned to a mailbox. To assign a retention policy to a mailbox using EAC, you do the following steps:

1. Open the Exchange Admin Center and navigate to Recipients ➤ Mailboxes.

2. Select the mailbox you want to assign a retention policy to and click the Edit icon.

3. Select the Mailbox Features section.

4.   Select the desired retention policy in the Retention
     Policy dropdown box.

5.   Click Save to save the new setting.

Tip   If you select multiple mailboxes, you can use the Bulk Edit
option. Select More Options… and click Update below the Retention
Policy heading. You will then see a dialog where you can pick a
retention policy that you want to apply to the mailboxes you have
selected.

When using the Exchange Management Shell, the Set-Mailbox
cmdlet is used to configure a retention policy. For example, to apply the
ProExchangeAdmin MRM policy retention policy to Philip's mailbox,
you enter

```
[PS] C:\> Set-Mailbox -Identity P.Mortimer -RetentionPolicy
'ProExchangeAdmin MRM Policy'
```

If you want to assign the retention policy to a certain group of people,
you can utilize PowerShell's ability to pipe objects to Set-Mailbox. For
example, if you want to clear retention policy on mailboxes starting with P,
you assign each one the retention policy value $null, as follows:

```
[PS] C:\> Get-Mailbox -Identity P* | Set-Mailbox -
RetentionPolicy $null
```

Managed Folder Assistant

The managed folder assistant (MFA) is responsible for enforcing retention
policies on items in mailboxes. It is a background process that checks
items in each mailbox against the policy that has been configured on
the mailbox (DPT), folder (RPT), and personal tags level. The process is
throttled to limit the number of resources and cycles consumed.

It is possible to configure the MFA to process all mailboxes on an Exchange server with a certain time period known as a "work cycle." The default setting for a work cycle is one day, so all mailboxes on that Exchange server are processed by the MFA per day.

You can monitor MFA activity by looking in the Application event log for Event ID 9018, generated by the MSExchange mailbox assistants. It will mention what database was processed by the MFA, how many mailboxes were processed, and how long it took. If the MFA could not complete a work cycle, it will also mention how many mailboxes could not be processed.

It is possible that the events do not show up in the Application event log. The EventLevel for the MFA is set to "Lowest," so not all events are logged. It is possible to increase this setting using the Set-EventLogLevel command in EMS.

Possible values are

- Lowest

- Low

- Medium

- High

- Expert

To raise the level to "Expert" for troubleshooting purposes, execute the following command:

```
[PS] C:\> Set-EventLogLevel -Identity
"MSExchangeMailboxAssistants\Service" -Level Expert
```

To change the settings in Exchange 2019, a SettingOverride must be used. To configure the work cycle for MFA and process mailboxes every two days, use the following command:

```
[PS] C:\> New-SettingOverride -Name "MFA WorkCycle Override"
-Component TimeBasedAssistants -Section ELCAssistant
-Parameters @("WorkCycle=2.00:00:00") -Reason "Process
mailboxes every 2 days"
```

```
RunspaceId          : 0ee5f64d-ed65-4308-9591-849dd0ce27b4
ComponentName       : TimeBasedAssistants
SectionName         : ELCAssistant
AppId               : EXO
FlightName          :
ModifiedBy          : ProExchangeAdmin.com/Users/Administrator
Reason              : Process mailboxes every 2 days
MinVersion          :
MaxVersion          :
FixVersion          :
Server              :
IsFlight            : False
Parameters          : {WorkCycle=2.00:00:00}
Status              : Accepted
XmlRaw              : <S CN="TimeBasedAssistants" SN="ELCAssistant"
                      MB="ProExchangeAdmin.com/Users/
                      Administrator"
                      R="Process mailboxes every 2 days"><Ps><P>
                      WorkCycle=2.00:00:00</P></Ps></S>
AdminDisplayName    :
ExchangeVersion     : 0.1 (8.0.535.0)
Name                : MFA WorkCycle Override
DistinguishedName   : CN=MFA WorkCycle Override,CN=Setting Overrides,
                      CN=Global Settings,CN=PROEXCHANGE,CN=Microsoft
```

```
Exchange,CN=Services,CN=Configuration,DC=ProExchange
Admin,DC=com
Identity          : MFA WorkCycle Override
Guid              : c39c402d-2489-4d64-8c39-aaadf3247fbc
ObjectCategory    : ProExchangeAdmin.com/Configuration/Schema/
                    ms-Exch-Config-Settings
ObjectClass       : {top, msExchConfigSettings}
WhenChanged       : 1/2/2023 1:05:02 PM
WhenCreated       : 1/2/2023 1:05:02 PM
WhenChangedUTC    : 1/2/2023 12:05:02 PM
WhenCreatedUTC    : 1/2/2023 12:05:02 PM
OrganizationId    :
Id                : MFA WorkCycle Override
OriginatingServer : DC01.ProExchangeAdmin.com
IsValid           : True
ObjectState       : Unchanged
```

The WorkCycle format is d.hh.mm.ss: the default setting is one day. It can be changed but be careful with system resource planning.

To apply the new work cycle, execute the following command:

```
[PS] C:\> Get-ExchangeDiagnosticInfo -Process Microsoft.
Exchange.Directory.TopologyService -Component
VariantConfiguration -Argument Refresh

RunspaceId : 0ee5f64d-ed65-4308-9591-849dd0ce27b4
Result     : <Diagnostics>
               <ProcessInfo>
                 <id>5164</id>
                 <serverName>EXCH01</serverName>
                 <startTime>2023-01-02T09:14:00.9443462Z
                 </startTime>
                 <currentTime>2023-01-02T12:05:54.7167519Z
                 </currentTime>
                 <lifetime>02:51:53.7724057</lifetime>
```

```
                    <threadCount>24</threadCount>
                    <handleCount>2319</handleCount>
                    <workingSet>213.2 MB (223,567,872 bytes)</workingSet>
    <fastTrainExchangeVersion>15.2.1258.7</fastTrain
    ExchangeVersion>
  </ProcessInfo>
  <Components>
    <VariantConfiguration>
      <Overrides Updated="2023-01-02T12:05:54.8287489Z">
        <SettingOverride>
          <Name>MFA WorkCycle Override</Name>
          <Reason>Process mailboxes every 2 days</Reason>
          <ModifiedBy>ProExchangeAdmin.com/Users/Administrator
          </ModifiedBy>
          <ComponentName>TimeBasedAssistants</ComponentName>
          <SectionName>ELCAssistant</SectionName>
          <Status>Accepted</Status>
          <Message>This override synced to the server but
          whether it applies to the services running on
                this server depends on the override parameters,
                current configuration and the context.</Message>
          <Parameters>
            <Parameter>WorkCycle=2.00:00:00</Parameter>
          </Parameters>
        </SettingOverride>
      </Overrides>
    </VariantConfiguration>
  </Components>
</Diagnostics>
Identity    :
IsValid     : True
ObjectState : New
```

To check the new settings, execute the following commands:

```
[PS] C:\> [xml]$diag=Get-ExchangeDiagnosticInfo -Process
MSExchangeMailboxAssistants -Component VariantConfiguration
-Argument "Config,Component=TimeBasedAssistants"
[PS] C:\> $diag.Diagnostics.Components.VariantConfiguration.
Configuration. TimeBasedAssistants.ElcAssistant

[PS] C:\>$diag.Diagnostics.Components.VariantConfiguration.
Configuration. TimeBasedAssistants.ElcAssistant
```

```
Classification                                  : InternalMaintenance
MaxConcurrency                                  : 1024
Enabled                                         : True
EnabledDuringBlackout                           : False
MailboxNotInterestingLogInterval               : 1.00:00:00
SpreadLoad                                      : True
SlaMonitoringEnabled                            : True
CompletionMonitoringEnabled                     : True
ActiveDatabaseProcessingMonitoringEnabled       : True
SlaUrgentThreshold                              : 0.1
SlaNonUrgentThreshold                           : 0.5
WorkCycle                                       : 2.00:00:00
GroupMailboxADGroupProcessingEnabled            : True
SpreadLoadPaddingPercent                        : 10
```

Adjusting the work cycle will impact the frequency of which retention policies are checked and enforced on mailboxes hosted on the Mailbox server with the adjusted ManagedFolderWorkCycle setting.

You can also manually start the MFA to perform a work cycle. To manually trigger the MFA, use the Start-ManagedFolderAssistant and specify the mailbox you want the MFA to run against. For example, to run the MFA for Philip's mailbox, you would use the following command:

```
[PS] C:\> Start-ManagedFolderAssistant –Identity P.Mortimer
```

Note   The managed folder assistant will resume processing where it left off, so there is no problem if the MFA cannot complete a work cycle at a particular time. However, retention policy application and executing retention policy actions might be delayed for unprocessed mailboxes.

The in-place archive mailbox is a good solution for keeping the primary mailbox size manageable, but it is not an archiving solution where mail is automatically kept unaltered for a certain amount of time. To achieve this, the in-place hold, litigation hold or journaling feature is available. These are discussed in the next sections.

In-Place Hold and Litigation Hold

There could be circumstances when an organization needs to preserve its email records, such as for a legal investigation. It may also be necessary to freeze the contents of a mailbox, preventing it from being processed by the managed folder assistant (MFA) as part of the Messaging Records Management (MRM) process. A possible task of the managed folder assistant is, for example, the automatic removal of items after a certain period.

To support requests to preserve mailbox information, Exchange contains a feature called in-place hold. This feature was introduced with Exchange Server 2010 as litigation hold, but litigation hold is still available in Exchange 2019. In-place hold allows organizations to freeze mailbox contents, prevent manual or automatic updating, and/or not remove expired items that have passed the retention period.

In-place hold integrates with in-place eDiscovery, allowing you to limit the hold items by using criteria such as keywords or senders. It is also possible to specify a time span or to search for specific item types, such as email or calendar items.

Note   When the managed folder assistant processes a mailbox, and it finds five or more query-based holds applying to the same mailbox, it will put the whole mailbox on in-place hold. If the number of matching queries drops below five, the MFA will revert to query-based in-place hold again.

Normally, when a mailbox is not on in-place hold, deleted messages are moved to the Deleted Items folder. When items get deleted from the Deleted Items folder or when the user shift-deletes the messages, those messages get moved to the Recoverable Items\Deletions folder. This is the folder in which contents are displayed when, for example, you use the Recover Deleted Items option in Outlook. When the managed folder assistant processes the mailbox, the deleted items that had passed the retention period are purged.

When a mailbox is put on in-place hold, though, items that would normally be purged from the Recoverable Items\Deletions folder are instead moved to the Recoverable Items\Discovery Holds folder. These items remain there until the in-place hold is lifted.

Note   To use query-based in-place hold, such as queries based on sender or start time, the user requires both the mailbox search and litigation hold management roles. Without the mailbox search management role, the user cannot specify the criteria and can only put whole mailboxes on in-place hold. The Discovery Management role group is assigned both these management roles.

When a mailbox is put on in-place hold, copy-on-write is used when updating or removing messages from the mailbox. This is to preserve original copies of modified messages and to prevent tampering. Copies of original messages are stored in the Recoverable Items\Versions folder. This is shown in Figure 12-4.

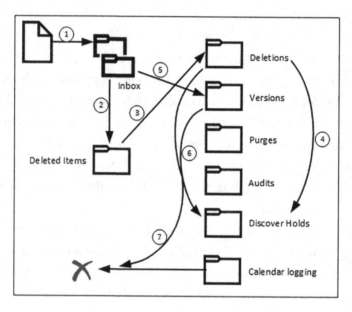

Figure 12-4. *How in-place hold and copy-on-write work*

Here is how in-place hold and copy-on-write work in detail:

1. A message is delivered to the mailbox. The message can be stored in Inbox or any of the other folders.

2. When the user deletes a message, it is moved to the Deleted Items folder.

3. When the Deleted Items folder is emptied, the messages are removed from the Deleted Items folder, or when the user hard-deletes a message (shift-deletes), those messages are moved to the

Recoverable Items\Deletions folder. The contents
of this folder are displayed when the user selects
Recover Deleted Items from Outlook or the
Outlook WebApp.

4. Messages from the Recoverable Items\Deletions
folder are purged when the user removes those
messages from the Recoverable Items folder in
Outlook or Outlook Web Access. When the mailbox
is on in-place hold, messages are moved to the
Recoverable Items\Discovery Holds folder instead
of getting purged.

5. When the user edits a message, a copy of the
original message is stored in the Versions folder
using copy-on-write.

6. When the mailbox is on in-place hold, expired
messages from the Recoverable Items\Deletions
folder and Recoverable Items\Versions folder
are moved to the Recoverable Items\Discovery
Holds folder if they are touched by any current in-
place hold query. The managed folder assistant is
responsible for keeping track of messages in relation
to any in-place hold queries.

7. Expired messages will be purged from the
Recoverable Items\Deletions and Recoverable
Items\Versions folders when the mailbox is no
longer on in-place hold. Messages not touched by
any current in-place hold query are also purged
from the Recoverable Items\Discovery Holds folder
when they expire.

Not listed previously is that when a user shift-deletes an item, it will go straight to the Recoverable Items\Deletions folder.

To get a sense of how this looks under the hood, you can use tools like MFCMAPI, available from `https://github.com/stephenegriffin/mfcmapi`. Note that to be able to view the recoverable items in MFCMAPI, you need to go to Tools ➤ Options and check the following options:

- Use the MDB_ONLINE flag when calling OpenMsgStore.

- Use the MAPI_NO_CACHE flag when calling OpenEntry.

Warning   Low-level utilities like MFCMAPI can be powerful tools providing lots of insight, but they can also operate on the low-level structures and contents of your Exchange data and create inconsistencies or corruption. Tools like these offer great power to administrator, and consequently using them comes with great responsibility.

From MFCMAPI, you can open the mailbox via Session Logon (selecting an Outlook profile), double-click the Mailbox store entry, and expand the root container. This is shown in Figure 12-5.

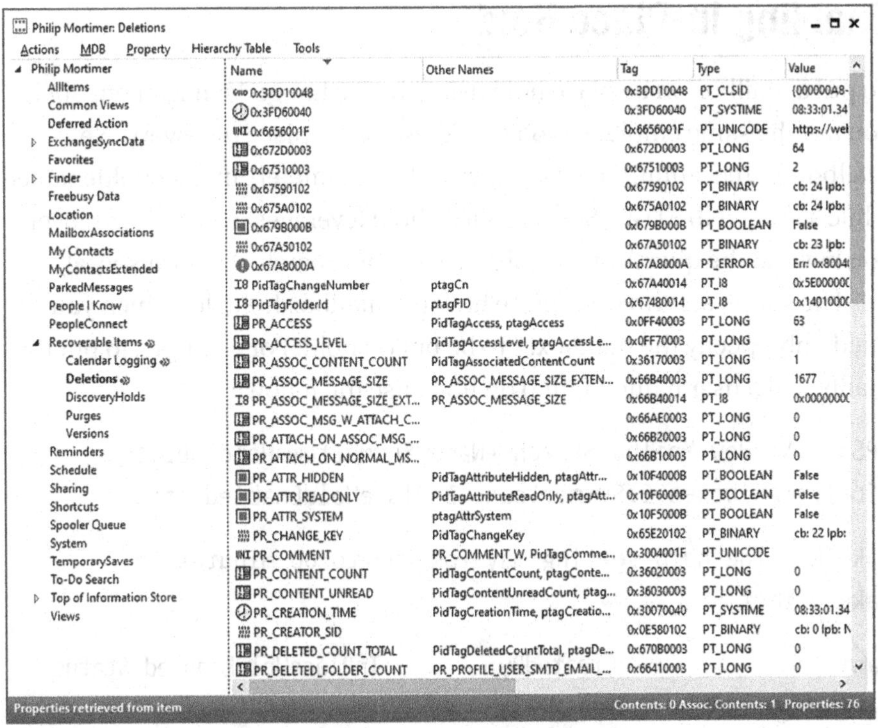

Figure 12-5. *Recoverable Items folder in a mailbox on in-place hold*

Within the Recoverable Items folder, you will find the Deletions, Versions, and Discovery Holds folders, among others, and you can inspect their contents.

Note   You cannot change messages in the Versions folder; when you try to save an edited item, the save attempt will fail. You can remove messages from the Versions or Discovery Holds folder, but these will end up in the Purges folder. Messages cannot be removed from the Purges folder, thereby preventing (malicious) removal or alteration of original messages.

Enabling In-Place Hold

To put a mailbox on in-place hold using the Exchange Management Shell, you use the same cmdlet as you would use for in-place discovery, New-MailboxSearch, additionally specifying the parameter -Inplaceholdenabled while setting it to $True. Since in-place hold leverages in-place eDiscovery, you have all the query options of New-MailboxSearch at your disposal.

The simplest form of in-place hold is a mailbox hold, for which you need only specify the mailboxes to be put on hold. For example, to put the mailbox of a user named Philip on hold, use the following:

```
[PS] C:\> New-MailboxSearch -Name SummertownHoldQuery1
-SourceMailboxes S.Summertown -InPlaceHoldEnabled $true

WARNING: The hold setting may take up to 60 minutes to
take effect.

Name                   CreatedBy          InPlaceHoldEnabled Status
----                   ---------          ------------------ ------
SummertownHoldQuery1 PRO\Administrator True                  NotStarted
```

Note   Use of switches and Boolean parameters is not always consequent, despite serving the same purpose. For example, when you want to enable creation of an in-place archive, you specify New-Mailbox -Archive; but when you want to put a mailbox on hold, you need to set -InPlaceHoldEnabled to $true.

The fact that a mailbox is put on hold does not manifest itself in any way for the end user. If it is required and deemed acceptable, you could send the user a notification or utilize the RetentionComment and RetentionURL mailbox settings to put a notice on the account settings section in Outlook, for example:

```
[PS] C:\> Set-Mailbox -Identity S.Summertown -RetentionComment
'Your mailbox is put on In-Place Hold' -RetentionUrl 'http://
intranet.proexchangeadmin.com/faq/mailboxhold'
```

This message and its clickable URL will be displayed on the Outlook account page, as shown in Figure 12-6.

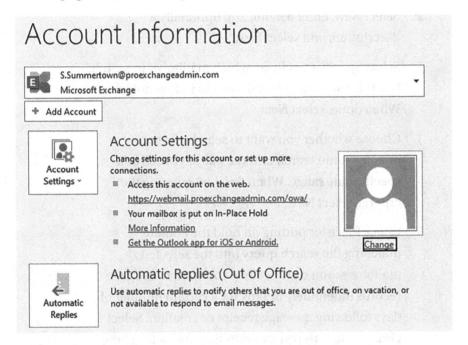

Figure 12-6. *Outlook notification of in-place hold*

You can clear the message by setting these properties to $null:

```
[PS] C:\> Set-Mailbox -Identity S.Summertown -RetentionComment
$null -RetentionUrl $null
```

To define an in-place hold from the Exchange Admin Center, you perform the following steps:

1. Open the Exchange Admin Center and navigate to Compliance Management ➤ In-Place eDiscovery & Hold.

2. Select New, enter a name and optionally a description, and select Next.

3. Select Specify to indicate which mailboxes to search. Use the + sign to add mailboxes to put on hold. When done, select Next.

4. Choose whether you want to search all content or enter some search criteria, like keywords or a specific date range. When finished entering the criteria, select Next.

5. Check Place for putting on hold the content matching the search query into the selected mailboxes. You can specify if you want to keep the records indefinitely or only for a certain number of days following message receipt or creation. Select Finish to save the query definition and activate the in-place hold.

Note   If an in-place archive is configured for the primary mailbox and the mailbox is put on in-place hold, the in-place hold will be applied to the in-place archive as well.

Disabling In-Place Hold

To disable in-place hold, you set the InPlaceHoldEnabled attribute of the related in-place discovery search to $true, as follows:

```
[PS] C:\> Set-MailboxSearch -Name SarahHoldQuery1 -
InPlaceHoldEnabled $false
```

When an in-place hold is lifted, the mailbox and its messages will again fall under the applicable retention policy regime. Any messages stored in the Recoverable Items\Versions folder as part of the in-place hold will get removed by the managed folder assistant.

Caution   When an in-place hold is removed, it may release messages from being placed on hold, thus possibly expiring and removing those messages if they no longer match any other current in-place hold query. After an in-place hold is lifted, the managed folder assistant purges all messages from the Discovery Holds, Versions, and Purges folders.

Note that this does not remove the underlying search; to remove the discovery search definition, use Remove-MailboxSearch, for example:

```
[PS] C:\> Remove-MailboxSearch -Name SarahHoldQuery1
```

Litigation Hold

Litigation hold uses the LitigationHoldEnabled property of a mailbox to place mailbox content on hold. Whereas in-place hold provides granular hold capability based on query parameters and the ability to place multiple holds, litigation hold only allows you to place all items on hold. You can also specify a duration period to hold items when a mailbox is placed on litigation hold. The duration is calculated from the date a mailbox item is received or created. If a duration isn't set, items are held indefinitely or until the hold is removed.

Note   When a mailbox is placed on one or more in-place holds and on litigation hold (without a duration period) at the same time, all items are held indefinitely or until the holds are removed. If you remove litigation hold and the user is still placed on one or more in-place holds, items matching the in-place hold criteria are held for the period specified in the hold settings.

Enabling Litigation Hold

To enable litigation hold on a mailbox, the LitigationHoldEnabled property needs to be set to $True. Optional properties are

- LitigationHoldDate: This property specifies the date the mailbox is placed on litigation hold. This property is populated automatically when the mailbox is placed on hold.

- LitigationHoldDuration: This property specifies how long items in the mailbox will be held if the mailbox is placed on litigation hold. The duration is calculated from the date an item is received or created. The value of this property is an integer and represents the number of days. The default value is "unlimited," which means items are held indefinitely (or until the hold is removed).

- LitigationHoldOwner: This property specifies the user who placed the mailbox on litigation hold. It this property is omitted during enabling the litigation hold, it is populated automatically.

To enable litigation hold for a user and set the duration to five years (equals 1800 days), you can use the following command in the Exchange Management Shell:

```
[PS] Set-Mailbox -Identity P.Mortimer -LitigationHoldEnabled
$True -LitigationHoldDuration 1800
```

Note   It may take up to 60 minutes before the litigation hold becomes active.

You can use the Get-Mailbox command to check the litigation hold settings, for example:

```
[PS] C:\>Get-Mailbox -Identity P.Mortimer | Select
litigation* | fl

LitigationHoldEnabled   : True
LitigationHoldDate      : 12/28/2022 2:30:49 PM
LitigationHoldOwner     : Administrator@ProExchangeAdmin.com
LitigationHoldDuration  : 1800.00:00:00
```

Note   When you place a mailbox on in-place hold or litigation hold, the hold is placed on both the primary and the archive mailbox. If you place an on-premises primary mailbox on hold in an Exchange hybrid deployment, the cloud-based archive mailbox (if enabled) is also placed on hold.

It is also possible to enable the litigation hold using the Exchange Admin Center for a mailbox. To do this, open the Exchange Admin Center and navigate to Recipients ➤ Mailboxes and select the mailbox. Open its properties and select the mailbox features. In the features popup window, scroll down to litigation hold.

When enabling the litigation hold using EAC, you can

- Set the litigation hold duration, just like the PowerShell command, in days.

- Add a note. This note is shown to the user in Outlook after enabling the litigation hold.

- Add a URL. This can direct the user to a website for more information regarding the litigation hold. Just like the note, this will appear in Outlook after the litigation hold is set.

This is shown in Figure 12-7.

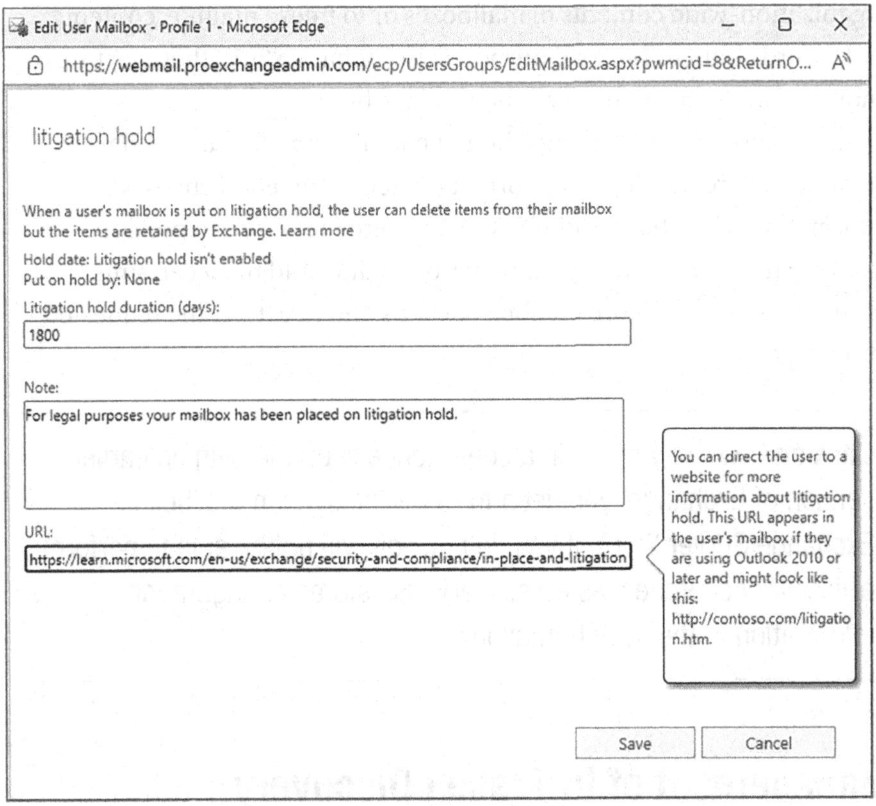

Figure 12-7. Enable the litigation hold using the Exchange Admin Center

Again, this can take up to 60 minutes before the litigation hold becomes active.

In-Place eDiscovery

Electronic discovery, or eDiscovery, refers to the discovery of or the ability to discover exchange of information. Exchange Server 2010 introduced multi-mailbox search and legal hold, which were features to discover organization-wide contents of mailboxes or to freeze mailbox contents and record changes for legal purposes. In Exchange 2019 these features are known as in-place eDiscovery and in-place hold.

Early versions of Exchange did not contain such features and had no options to retain deleted information, let alone retain changed information. If Exchange administrators were requested to provide mailbox information for a certain period, that would most certainly result in having to restore mailbox backups and to extract the requested information.

Caution   When you are in a coexistence scenario with an earlier version of Exchange, you need to move the system mailbox to Exchange Server 2019. If you do not, you will not be able to perform eDiscovery searches, as eDiscovery also stores configuration information in the system mailbox.

Management of In-Place eDiscovery

In-place eDiscovery of information stored in Exchange and management of in-place hold on mailboxes are secure processes dealing with potentially confidential information, and thus they are subject to privacy legislation. To be able to create eDiscovery searches, the user needs to be a member of the RBAC role group Discovery Management. This group is empty by default.

To add users to the Discover Management group and to perform eDiscovery searches or put mailboxes on in-place hold, you use the following command (where Philip is the identity of the user you want to be able to create eDiscovery searches):

```
[PS] C:\> Add-RoleGroupMember -Identity 'Discovery Management'
-Member P.Labrousse
```

To list the current members of the Discovery Management role group, you use

```
[PS] C:\> Get-RoleGroupMember -Identity 'Discovery Management'

Name                RecipientType
----                -------------
Professor Labrousse UserMailbox
```

When the investigation is over, do not forget to remove the user from the role group using the following command:

```
[PS] C:\> Remove-RoleGroupMember -Identity 'Discovery
Management' -Member P.Labrousse
```

Note   When enabling Discovery Management for a user, be sure you are in line with the legal guidelines of your company. You are searching through other users' mailboxes, so this can be a privacy breach. Therefore, Discovery Management is not enabled for any user by default.

Although this book is primarily targeted toward PowerShell, sometimes a GUI can be very useful, especially for nonrepetitive tasks. To use EAC to perform these tasks, open EAC and navigate to Permissions ➤ Admin Roles and open the Discover Management group. In the Members section, add Professor Labrousse to this group.

Discovery Mailbox

A discovery mailbox is a mailbox that can be used for storing contents retrieved as part of an in-place eDiscovery search. During setup, Exchange 2019 creates a default discovery mailbox (when no discovery mailbox is available) whose name starts with DiscoverySearchMailbox followed by a GUID. You can create additional discovery mailboxes when you need them, for example to support multiple searches. Because they are like ordinary mailboxes, you can remove a discovery mailbox when it is no longer needed.

To create an additional discovery mailbox, you use the New-Mailbox in conjunction with the –Discovery switch, for example:

```
[PS] C:\> New-Mailbox DiscoverySearch2 -Discovery -UserPrincipalName
DiscoverySearch2@proexchangeadmin.com
Name               Alias            ServerName   ProhibitSendQuota
---------          ------           ----------   ------------------
DiscoverySearch2   DiscoverySearch2 exch02       50 GB (53,687,091,200 bytes)
```

Note   You can use the -Database switch on the New-Mailbox command to use a dedicated mailbox database.

To list the currently known discovery mailboxes, you use Get-Mailbox and filter on RecipientTypeDetails, for example:

```
[PS] C:\> Get-Mailbox | Where {$_.RecipientTypeDetails
 -eq 'DiscoveryMailbox'}
Name                     Alias             ServerName
  ProhibitSendQuota
----                     -----             ----------
  ------------------
DiscoverySearchMailbox... DiscoverySearchMa... exch01
  50 GB (53,687,091,200 bytes)
DiscoverySearch2          DiscoverySearch2     exch02
  50 GB (53,687,091,200 bytes)
```

Note   Discovery mailboxes by default have a fixed mailbox quota of 50 GB, and so they might fill up easily, depending on the underlying query. Be sure to properly manage the storage used by these large discovery mailboxes.

Searching Mailboxes

The easiest way to perform a discovery search is using EAC. Remember that as an admin we are used to PowerShell, but users that perform these searches are most likely not. To perform a discover search, follow these steps:

1. Open the Exchange Admin Center and navigate to Compliance Management ➤ In-Place eDiscovery & Hold. Click the + icon to start a new search.

2. Enter a name for the search and optionally add a description. Click Next to continue.

3. Specify a specific mailbox to search or select the "Search all mailboxes" radio button to perform a search on all mailboxes. Be aware, this can take a serious amount of time. Click Next to continue.

4. Choose whether you want to search all content or enter search criteria, such as keywords or a specific date range. When you are finished entering the criteria, click Next to continue. This is shown in Figure 12-8.

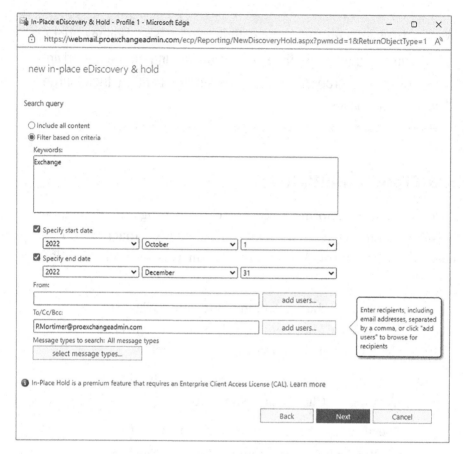

Figure 12-8. *Search query for a new in-place eDiscovery and in-place hold*

5. When needed, you can place the search results on in-place hold by selecting the checkbox. You can also specify to hold the items indefinitely or for a certain amount of time.

6. Select Finish to store the eDiscovery search.

Tip   When specifying search query keywords, you can use the
"and" or "or" Boolean operator to construct queries using multiple
keywords. For example, to search for "Fabrikam" and "Options,"
enter FABRIKAM AND OPTIONS. To influence the evaluation order,
you can use parentheses, that is, X AND Y OR Z is not the same as
X AND (Y OR Z). To include spaces in a search string, put the string
in quotes—for example, "WINGTIP TOYS". To look for words in each
other's vicinity, you can use the NEAR(N), where N is the number of
words before or after to take into account—for example, FABRIKAM
NEAR(5) OPTIONS. Finally, you can use the asterisk (*) for wildcard
matching—for example, CON* matches words starting with CON
(e.g., consultant, connection, construction).

After defining the discovery search criteria, the results will be shown
in the in-place discovery and hold section. Exchange will then start to
estimate the amount of data and number of unsearchable items. Note
that the query will only be activated when you view or export the results,
meaning the query will also return items added after the discovery search
was created.

Note   Unsearchable items are items that cannot be or are
not indexed because of unrecognized, nonindexed file types or
encryption. IRM protected messages can be indexed.

After defining the discovery search, you have the following options:

- Update the search results figures, such as the amount of
  data and the number of items.

- Preview the search results on-screen.

- Copy the search results to a discovery mailbox. Besides the option to exclude unsearchable items, you can cancel duplicate items so as to have items only returned once, even if they match multiple criteria. Also, you can have Exchange send you an email with a summary of the results.

- Export the discovered items to a .PST file. This option can be useful if you need to ship the information to third parties.

You can also utilize the Exchange Management Shell to perform discovery searches using the New-MailboxSearch cmdlet. When using New-MailboxSearch to perform discovery searches, you have the following parameter options:

- **Name** to set the name of the search.

- **EndDate** to set the end of the search time span.

- **StartDate** to set the start of the search time span.

- **EstimateOnly** to indicate you only want an estimate of the number of items.

- **ExcludeDuplicateMessages** to remove duplicates items from the results.

- **IncludeUnsearchableItems** to include items not indexed by Exchange Search.

- **LogLevel** to set the level of logging. Options are Suppress, Basic, or Full.

- **MessageTypes** to limit the search to a specific message type. Valid options are Email, Meetings, Tasks, Notes, Docs, Journals, Contacts, and IM. When omitted, all items are searched.

- **Recipients** to limit the search to certain recipients (examines TO, CC, and BCC fields).

- **SearchQuery** to specify terms to search for.

- **Senders** to limit the search to certain senders (FROM).

- **SourceMailboxes** to specify the mailboxes to be searched.

- **StatusMailRecipients** to specify users who should receive status reports.

- **TargetMailbox** to set the mailbox that should receive a copy of the search results.

Note   When a start date or end date is specified, it is matched against the receive date or creation date (depending on the item type) of discovered items.

To create a discovery search titled SarahSearch2 for Sarah's mailbox on items received or created between March 1, 2021, and June 30, 2021, of type Email, with the keywords "IT Knowledgebase" and the destination set to DiscoverySearch2, you use the following command:

```
[PS] C:\> New-MailboxSearch SarahSearch2 -SourceMailboxes
S.Summertown -StartDate 1/1/2022 -EndDate 12/31/2022 -
TargetMailbox 'DiscoverySearch2' -SearchQuery 'cloud' -
MessageTypes Email

Name          CreatedBy          InPlaceHoldEnabled Status
----          ---------          ------------------ ------
SarahSearch2 PRO\Administrator False                 NotStarted
```

To get a list of your current discovery search entries, you use the Get-MailboxSearch cmdlet. To run a discovery search, use Start-MailboxSearch. When you have selected to copy the discovered data to a discovery mailbox, you start the mailbox search, which clears any existing results for that specific mailbox search from that discovery mailbox, as follows:

```
[PS] C:\> Start-MailboxSearch -Identity SarahSearch2
```

Note   You cannot change the properties of a running discovery search. To do that, you need to restart the search by using Stop/Resume in EAC or by using the cmdlets Stop-MailboxSearch and Start-MailboxSearch.

To modify a discovery search, you use Set-MailboxSearch, for example:

```
[PS] C:\> Set-MailboxSearch -Identity SarahSearch2 -
StatusMailRecipients p.labrousse@proexchangeadmin.com
```

When the search is finished, the configured StatusMailRecipients will receive a status report, which will look like what is shown in Figure 12-9.

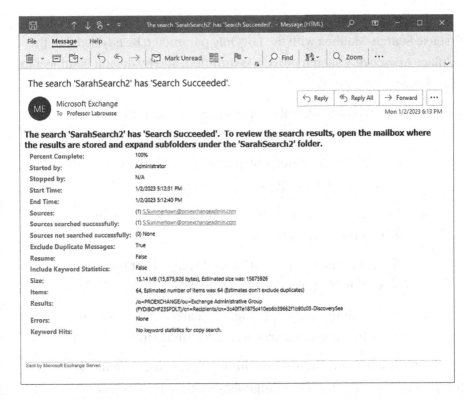

Figure 12-9. *In-place eDiscovery search report*

While the search is running, you will notice a folder named <SEARCH NAME>. This folder is used to temporarily store the search results and will be renamed after the search is finished.

Finally, you have the option to delete the contents from mailboxes using discovery search. For this purpose, you can use Search-Mailbox with the -DeleteContent parameter in combination with a search query, for example:

```
[PS] C:\> Search-Mailbox –Identity S.Summertown -DeleteContent
-SearchQuery "Viagra"
```

To preview the information that would potentially be deleted, you can first use Search-Mailbox with the LogOnly parameter. Be advised that the in-place eDiscovery search process is throttled, and by default is subject to the following limitations:

- The maximum number of concurrent searches per user is two (DiscoveryMaxConcurrency).

- The maximum number of mailboxes searches per discovery is 5,000 (DiscoveryMaxMailboxes).

- The maximum number of keywords per search is 500 (DiscoveryMaxKeywords).

- The maximum number of items displayed per page in preview is 200 (DiscoveryMaxSearchResultsPageSize).

- The maximum running time of a search before it times out is 10 minutes (DiscoverySearchTimeoutPeriod).

Should you need to adjust these limitations, you can create a new throttling policy with the ThrottlingPolicyScope set to Organization, so it applies to all users in the organization. For example, to create a custom throttling policy named OrgInPlaceDiscoveryPolicy using different limits, use the following:

```
[PS] C:\> New-ThrottlingPolicy –Name OrgInPlaceDiscoveryPolicy
-DiscoveryMaxConcurrency 10 -DiscoveryMaxMailboxes 1000 –
ThrottlingPolicyScope organization

Name                          ThrottlingPolicyScope IsServiceAccount
----                          --------------------- ----------------
OrgInPlaceDiscoveryPolicy Organization                  False
```

To verify the current settings, use Get-ThrottlingPolicy, for example:

```
[PS] C:\> Get-ThrottlingPolicy OrgInPlaceDiscoveryPolicy |
fl Discovery*
```

```
DiscoveryMaxConcurrency                  : 10
DiscoveryMaxMailboxes                     : 1000
DiscoveryMaxKeywords                      : 500
DiscoveryMaxPreviewSearchMailboxes        : 5000
DiscoveryMaxStatsSearchMailboxes          : 100
DiscoveryPreviewSearchResultsPageSize     : 200
DiscoveryMaxKeywordsPerPage               : 25
DiscoveryMaxRefinerResults                : 10
DiscoveryMaxSearchQueueDepth              : 32
DiscoverySearchTimeoutPeriod              : 10
```

Mail Flow Rules

One of the critical components in an Exchange infrastructure is the Transport service, which is responsible for processing messages traveling within or entering or leaving an Exchange organization.

Part of an organization's compliance and security requirements could be that messages transported within the organization or messages entering or leaving the Exchange infrastructure must comply with certain rules. Here is where the Exchange mail flow rules or sometimes called transport rules can come into play. An example of such a restriction is an ethical wall, also known as a Chinese wall, whose purpose is to prevent conflict of interest and disclosure of valuable information.

Note   Transport rules can be used to accomplish lots of other goals as well, such as adding disclaimers. They are building blocks for features like data loss prevention and information rights management. If you are interested in these areas, consider employing the transport rules to achieve your ends.

Basically, transport rules are rules that define operations for messages that satisfy certain conditions. Examples of such rules are dropping or redirecting messages or applying information rights management templates. To manage transport rules, you need to be assigned an Organization Management or Records Management role. Transport rules are organization-wide unless their specific conditions narrow the scope, and they are processed by the transport rule agent.

Create a Transport Rule

Let us assume you're working for a law firm where lawyers are working on a case, both representing client A (distribution list LawyersClientA) and client B. Both clients have their own group of lawyers, and these lawyers are not allowed to send mail to each other. So you want to create an ethical wall (EW) between the users in those groups via a transport rule.

To create a transport rule using EAC, you do the following:

1.   Open the Exchange Admin Center and navigate to Mail Flow ➤ Rules.

2.   Select the + sign and select "Restrict messages by sender or recipient..." (This is the ninth option).

3.   Enter a name—for example, EthicalWall—and in the "Apply this rule if..." dropdown box, select the "The message is between members of these groups" option and select RepCaseAClientA and RepCaseAClientB.

4.   Configure "Do the following" as "Reject the message and include an explanation" and add an explanation like "You are not allowed to send a message to this recipient for legal purposes."

5.   Note that the message will be returned in a delivery service notification (DSN) message using a default return code of 5.7.1, a common code for access-denied types of DSN messages.

6.   Optionally, configure "Audit this rule with severity level" if you want to generate audit log entries when the rule is triggered.

7.   Click Save to save and activate the rule.

Creation of the ethical wall transport rule is shown in Figure 12-10.

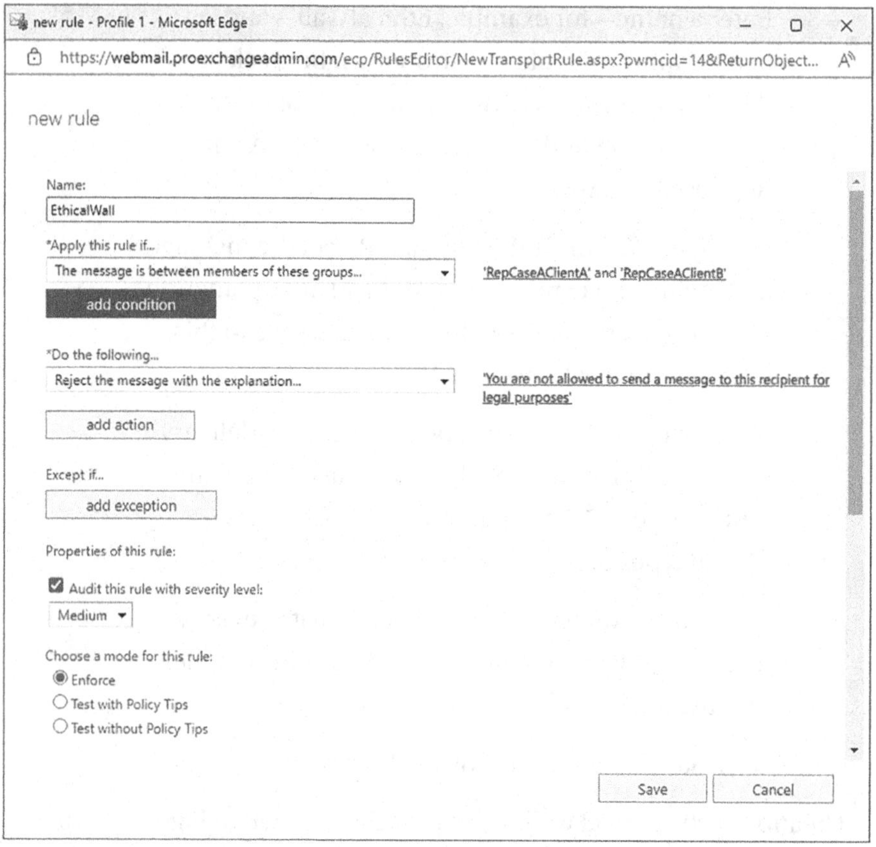

Figure 12-10.   *Create an ethical wall transport rule in EAC*

Personally, I think that creating a transport rule like the one shown is much easier in Exchange PowerShell. To create a transport rule using the Exchange PowerShell, use the New-TransportRule cmdlet. For example, to institute the same transport rule, use the following command:

```
[PS] C:\> New-TransportRule -Name 'ChineseWall'
-BetweenMemberOf1 RepCaseAClientA -BetweenMemberOf2
RepCaseAClientB -RejectMessageReasonText You are not allowed
to send a message to this recipient for legal purposed '
-Mode Enforce
```

Optionally you can use the RejectMessageEnhancedStatusCode parameter to override the default DSN status code of 5.7.1 for rejected messages.

Caution   Transport rules are stored in Active Directory. Therefore, you may experience delays when implementing changes, and you should consider replication latency before those changes will be propagated to Mailbox servers throughout the organization.

Another example of using transport rules for compliance is about a corporate disclaimer. For such disclaimers, you can select to have the disclaimer applied only to messages sent outside of the organization. To accomplish this, you use the scope NotInOrganization (displayed in EAC as Outside the organization). Possible scope options for sender (FromUserScope) or receiver (SentToScope) are

- InTheOrganization: The sender or receiver is located in Active Directory, or the domain name is an accepted, non-external relay domain name using an authenticated connection.

- NotInTheOrganization: The domain name of the sender or receiver isn't an accepted domain or is an external relay accepted domain.

- ExternalPartner (ToUserScope only): The domain name of the receiver is configured to use a domain secure security setting.

- ExternalNonPartner (ToUserScope only): The domain name of the receiver is not using a domain secure security setting.

A complication with disclaimers is that inserting text in the body of a message may invalidate any signed or encrypted messages. Because only a signed or encrypted message can be excluded (not both), you can leverage the Exchange message classification to tag the message, using transport rules to tag that encrypted or signed message. In the disclaimer transport rule, you can then select to not apply the rule to tagged messages.

Note   If your company policy is to disallow sending signed or encrypted messages externally, you can replace the action of adding the disclaimer by an action that will drop the message, quarantine it, or forward it for moderation.

Message classifications can only be created from the Exchange Management Shell, using the New-MessageClassification. In this example, you would use the label SignedOrEncrypted, as follows:

```
[PS] C:\> New-MessageClassification 'SignedOrEncrypted' -
DisplayName 'Signed or Encrypted Message' -SenderDescription
'Signed or Encrypted Message' -PermissionMenuVisible:$false

Identity                        Locale DisplayName
--------                        ------ -----------
Default\SignedOrEncrypted              Signed or Encrypted Message
```

Note   PermissionMenuVisible determines if the message classification can be assigned to messages in Outlook or Outlook Web App. Setting this parameter to $false disables this option.

You create the transport rules that will tag messages using this message classification. First, you create a transport rule that applies the message classification 'SignedOrEncrypted' to encrypted messages as follows:

```
[PS] C:\> New-TransportRule -Name 'Tag Encrypted
Messages' -Enabled $true -MessageTypeMatches 'Encrypted' -
ApplyClassification 'SignedOrEncrypted'
```

```
Name                        State   Mode    Priority Comments
----                        -----   ----    -------- --------
Tag Encrypted Messages Enabled Enforce 2
```

Next, you create a transport rule that applies the message classification SignedOrEncrypted to signed messages, as follows:

```
[PS] C:\> New-TransportRule -Name 'Tag Signed Messages' -
Enabled $true -MessageTypeMatches 'Signed' -ApplyClassification
'SignedOrEncrypted'
```

```
Name                        State   Mode    Priority Comments
----                        -----   ----    -------- --------
Tag Signed Messages Enabled Enforce 3
```

Finally, you create the transport rule that applies the disclaimer to outgoing messages:

```
[PS] C:\> New-TransportRule -Name 'Disclaimer' -Enabled $true
-SentToScope 'NotInOrganization' -ExceptIfHasClassification
'SignedOrEncrypted' -ApplyHtmlDisclaimerLocation 'Append'
-ApplyHtmlDisclaimerFallbackAction 'Wrap' -ApplyHtmlDisclaimer
Text '<P>This email and any files transmitted with it are
confidential and intended solely for the use of the individual
or entity to whom they are addressed.</P>'
```

```
Name       State   Mode    Priority Comments
----       -----   ----    -------- --------
Disclaimer Enabled Enforce 4
```

The ApplyHtmlDisclaimerFallbackAction parameter specifies where to put the disclaimer text. In the example, it is appended to the message. By setting ApplyHtmlDisclaimerFallbackAction to Wrap, the message will be wrapped in a new message containing the disclaimer. The parameter ApplyHtmlDisclaimerText specifies the text to use for the disclaimer. Note that the disclaimer text can be HTML, allowing you to use HTML IMG tags, which reference externally hosted images for embedding, or to use a link to point to an online disclaimer.

If you want to use disclaimers for internal communications as well, you will face an additional challenge. As the message passes each Transport service, a disclaimer is added, thereby potentially resulting in multiple disclaimers. Of course, you can add an additional exception that will check the body of the message for disclaimer text fragments. A different and perhaps more elegant approach, though, is to insert a sentinel in the message header after a disclaimer has been appended and add the condition to exclude messages containing the sentinel.

To implement such a condition and transform the disclaimer created earlier in a global disclaimer, you use the following command, where you set the SentToScope to $null to make it apply to all messages:

```
[PS] C:\> Set-TransportRule -Identity 'Disclaimer' –
SetHeaderName 'X-Disclaimer' –SetHeaderValue '1' –
ExceptIfHeaderContainsMessageHeader 'X-Disclaimer' –
ExceptIfHeaderContainsWords '1'
```

Now, when you receive a message, a disclaimer is added to the message as shown in Figure 12-11.

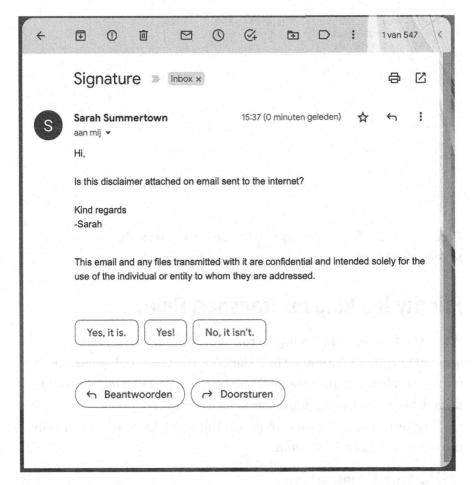

Figure 12-11. *Disclaimer added to a message using transport rules*

Now, when you receive a message with a disclaimer, you can see "proof" in the header, which will contain an entry X-Disclaimer: 1, as shown in Figure 12-12. That is, the header will contain an additional header entry, X-Disclaimer, which will be set to 1 for messages subject to the rule you just created.

```
From: Sarah Summertown <S.Summertown@proexchangeadmin.com>
To: "jaapwess@gmail.com" <jaapwess@gmail.com>
Subject: Signature
Thread-Topic: Signature
Thread-Index: AdkfgNroDAt649e4R+igrore0AuOnw==
Date: Tue, 3 Jan 2023 14:37:25 +0000
Message-ID: <d01531451cde46fa93a5d7d4ca763dc1@proexchangeadmin.com>
Accept-Language: en-US
Content-Language: en-US
X-MS-Has-Attach:
X-MS-TNEF-Correlator:
x-originating-ip: [10.83.4.116]
x-disclaimer: 1
Content-Type: multipart/alternative;
boundary="_000_d01531451cde46fa93a5d7d4ca763dc1proexchangeadmincom_"
MIME-Version: 1.0
Return-Path: S.Summertown@proexchangeadmin.com
```

Figure 12-12. *The additional X-Disclaimer header in the previous message*

Priority Ranking for Transport Rules

When you have multiple transport rules configured, the way they are ordered becomes important. For instance, if you have configured one transport rule to tag messages and another transport rule to process the tagged messages, the tagging needs to take place first.

To query the current list of transport rules and their assigned priority, use the Get-TransportRule cmdlet:

```
[PS] C:\>Get-TransportRule

Name                     State    Mode    Priority Comments
----                     -----    ----    -------- --------
EthicalWall              Enabled  Enforce 0            ...
ChineseWall              Enabled  Enforce 1
Tag Encrypted Messages   Enabled  Enforce 2
Tag Signed Messages      Enabled  Enforce 3
Disclaimer               Enabled  Enforce 4
```

The priority property determines the order in which the rules are applied, starting with 0. As you can see in the previous output, the rules to tag messages are third and fourth, and the rule taking actions based on those tags comes next.

Tip   When you have lots of rules, you can speed up the overall processing by the transport rule agent of the message by setting the StopRuleProcessing property of a transport rule to $true. When conditions are met and with this property set to $true, additional transport rules with lower priority will not be evaluated.

When you want to reassign the priority for a transport rule, you can use the Set-TransportRule cmdlet with the –Priority parameter. For example, if you created the disclaimer rule from the example first, it would have a higher execution priority than the tagging rules, as rules are assigned priorities based on their order of creation. To reset the priority of a transport rule with the identity of disclaimer to 2, you use the following command:

```
[PS] C:\> Set-TransportRule -Identity Disclaimer -Priority 2
```

If you assign a priority that is already in use, it will insert the rule on that position and the priorities of the other rules will shift one position down.

Journaling

Some organizations may be required to record **all** inbound and outbound email messages from a compliance perspective. Exchange can help fill that requirement by leveraging the transport rules discussed previously. When considering the transport rule options, you may have spotted that one possible action a transport rule can perform is copying to a certain recipient. That, in combination with rules that define the conditions under which to journal messages, makes up the journaling option in Exchange.

In Exchange Server, all email is handled by the Transport service. The journaling agent is a transport agent that processes messages on Mailbox servers, either when they are submitted or when they are routed. Exchange provides the following journaling options:

- *Standard journaling*: Configured on the mailbox database and can be used to journal all messages that are either received by or sent through mailboxes hosted on that mailbox database.

- *Premium journaling*: Can utilize rules, allowing you to journal based on criteria such as the recipient, Distribution Group, or internal vs. external messages.

Note   Premium journaling requires an Enterprise CAL.

So far, a journal rule, or even journaling in general, may sound like just an implementation of a transport rule, but there is a difference. While transport rules can be used to forward messages, journaling generates integral copies of the original messages in the form of journal reports, including the original messages as an attachment with the original header information. This makes journal reports suitable as evidence, as contrasted with forwarded messages retrieved by means of a transport rule.

A journal report for an externally sent message may differ from that for an internal message. This is because internal messages contain more information in the header regarding source and destination. The information provided in journal reports contains

- *Sender*: This is the SMTP address of the sender of the message.

- *Subject*: This is the subject of the journaled message.

- *Message-ID*: This is the internal message ID generated by Exchange when the message is submitted in the organization by the Transport service.

- *To*: These are the SMTP addresses of the message recipients. This list includes recipients indicated as TO, CC, or BCC addresses. If groups are expanded, it will also be mentioned at this line.

Options for Journaling Rules

When you are defining a journal rule, there are three parameters you need to consider:

1. *The scope of the messages to be journaled*: Possible scope options are internal messages only, external messages only, or all messages.

2. *The recipients you want to journal*: These can be an Exchange mailbox, Distribution Group, mail user, or contact. By being specific in whose messages to journal, you can minimize the required storage but still comply with legal and regulatory requirements for evidence collection.

3. The mailbox where the journal reports should be sent

Tip   To reduce the amount of storage needed to maintain journal reports, you can omit voice mail and missed-call notifications from UM-enabled users. This is an organization-wide setting and can be enabled using `Set-TransportConfig -VoicemailJournalingEnabled $false`. Or, you can enable journaling of voice mail and missed-call notification messages using `Set-TransportConfig -VoicemailJournalingEnabled $true`. To retrieve the current setting, use `Get-TransportConfig | Select VoiceMailJournalingEnabled`.

The journaling mailbox is a configured mailbox where the journal reports are collected. The configuration of this journaling mailbox itself depends on the policies that have been set by the organization or by regulatory or legal requirements. For example, you can define a retention policy on the mailbox so there will be some form of automatic housekeeping on the mailbox itself. Also, you can make sure the quota setting doesn't prevent the journal mailbox from receiving journal reports, as the size of that journal mailbox can grow quite big depending on the number of journal reports generated. So make sure your journal mailboxes are properly managed.

Note   You can utilize multiple journal mailboxes for different journal rules. On a side note, you cannot utilize a mailbox hosted in Office 365 for journaling.

In addition, the journal mailbox needs to be treated as a special, secured mailbox, as it may contain sensitive information. It is recommended that you configure your journal mailboxes as follows, where 'Journal' is the name of the journal mailbox in this example:

```
[PS] C:\> $ExRcpt= (Get-OrganizationConfig).
MicrosoftExchangeRecipientEmailAddresses | select
-ExpandProperty SmtpAddress
[PS] C:\> Set-Mailbox -Identity 'Journal' -
RequireSenderAuthenticationEnabled $true
-HiddenFromAddressListsEnabled $true
-AcceptMessagesOnlyFromSendersOrMembers $ExRcpt
```

Doing this will

- Lock the mailbox and not allow external senders to send messages to it.

- Hide it from the address books so users will not see it.

- Only allow the Exchange server to send messages to that mailbox.

Note (Get-OrganizationConfig).
MicrosoftExchangeRecipientEmailAddresses
will return the SMTP addresses of the named Microsoft
Exchange recipients. It will contain an entry in the format
MicrosoftExchange329e71ec88ae4615bbc36ab6ce41109e@domain
for each configured accepted domain. Note that the primary address
is used as sender for internal DSN messages.

Warning If you ever decide to change the primary SMTP address
of a Microsoft Exchange recipient by configuring it directly or
indirectly through email address policies, make sure you adjust the
AcceptMessagesOnlyFromSendersOrMembers setting accordingly.

Besides establishing the journaling mailbox, you can also define an alternative journal recipient, often used in cases when Exchange encounters problems delivering the journal report to the configured journal recipient. The alternative journal recipient will receive NDRs with the journal report attached, allowing you to resend the original message if the journaling mailbox becomes available again. If there is no alternative journal recipient configured, Exchange will just re-queue the journal report.

Journal reports do not generate NDR reports unless an alternate recipient is configured. If an alternate journal recipient is configured, it will receive an NDR with the original journal report. If no alternative journal recipient is configured, Exchange will re-queue the journal report indefinitely and those messages will never expire.

The alternative journal recipient is an organization-wide setting, collecting journal reports for all unavailable journal recipients. Because it collects journal reports for all failing journal recipients, it might grow very fast when an outage hits multiple original journal recipients. Also, because it possibly collects NDRs of journal reports for all journal recipients, be sure to check with your legal department to see if sending all those journal reports to an alternative journal recipient is allowed under existing regulations and applicable laws.

Note   Multiple journaling reports could be generated if the number of recipients exceeds the ExpansionSizeLimit setting in %ExchangeInstallPath%\EdgeTransport.exe.config, which could happen after group expansion. The default value is set to 1,000 recipients. Multiple journal reports are also generated when a message is bifurcated—that is, the message is split as it gets routed to different destinations.

Create a Standard Journal Rule

To create a standard journal rule using EAC, you do the following:

1. Open the Exchange Admin Center and navigate to Servers ➤ Databases.

2. Select the database you want to enable journaling on and click the Edit icon.

3. Select Maintenance.

4. For selecting the journal recipient, click Browse and select the journal mailbox you want to use for collecting journal reports generated for mailboxes hosted on this database.

5. Click Save to confirm.

To accomplish this using the Exchange Management Shell, use the Set-MailboxDatabase cmdlet. For example, to enable standard journaling to database MDB1 using journaling mailbox Journal Box 1, use the following command:

```
[PS] C:\> Set-MailboxDatabase -Identity MDB01 -
JournalRecipient Journal
```

To check which mailbox database has been configured for standard journaling, use the following command:

```
[PS] C:\> Get-MailboxDatabase | Where {$_.JournalRecipient} |
Select Identity,JournalRecipient

Identity JournalRecipient
-------- ----------------
MDB01    ProExchangeAdmin.com/Accounts/Functional
         Accounts/Journal
```

To disable standard journaling, set the JournalRecipient to $NULL, as follows:

```
[PS] C:\> Set-MailboxDatabase -Identity MDB01 -
JournalRecipient $null
```

Create a Premium Journal Rule

To create a premium journal rule using EAC, you do the following:

1. Open the Exchange Admin Center and navigate to Compliance Management ➤ Journal Rules.

2. Select the + sign to add a journal rule.

3. Configure "Send journal reports to..." with the SMTP address of the journal report recipient.

4. Enter a name for the journal rule at Name.

5. At "If the message is sent to or received from.," configure the recipient, which can be a user or Distribution Group for which you want to generate journal reports. You can also generate journal messages for all recipients by selecting "Apply to all messages."

6. Finally, at "Journal the following messages...," you can specify the scope of the journal rule. This can be global (all messages), messages generated within the Exchange organization (internal messages only), or messages with an external recipient or sender SMTP address (external messages only).

7. Click Save to save the rule.

This is shown in Figure 12-13.

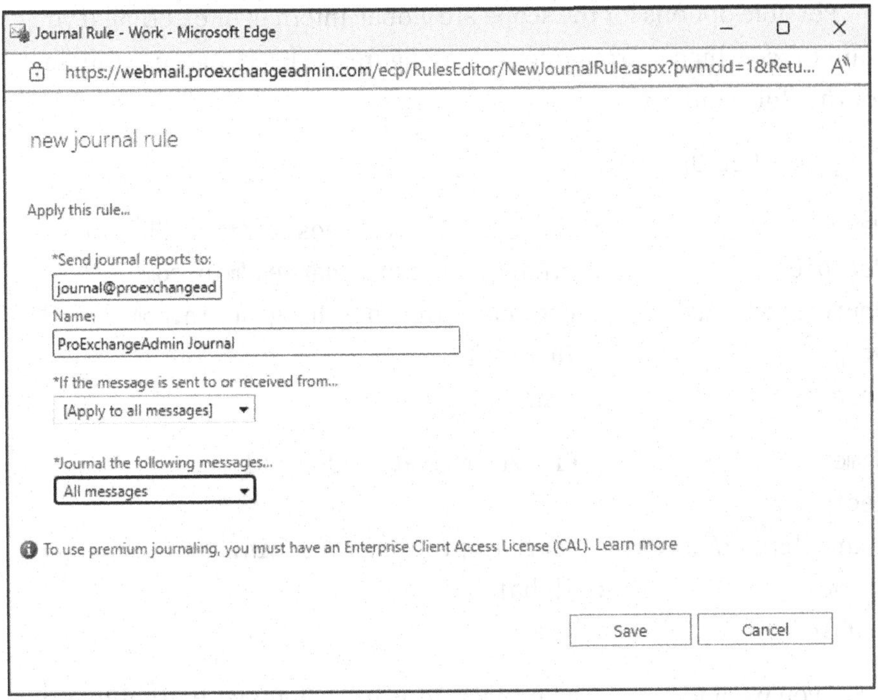

Figure 12-13. *Journal rule creation*

The cmdlet to create a journal rule is New-JournalRule. To create
the journal rule in the preceding example, you would use the following
command:

```
[PS] C:\> New-JournalRule –Name 'Journal all messages to/from
Philip' –JournalEmailAddress PremJournal@proexchangeadmin.com
-Recipient P.Mortimer@proexchangeadmin.com –Scope Internal –
Enabled $true

Name               : Journal all messages to/from Philip
Recipient          : P.Mortimer@proexchangeadmin.com
JournalEmailAddress : PremJournal@proexchangeadmin.com
Scope              : Internal
Enabled            : True
```

Possible options for the scope are global, internal, or external. If you want to see which journal rules are configured in Exchange, use the Get-JournalRule cmdlet:

```
[PS] C:\>Get-JournalRule
```

```
Name               : Journal all messages to/from Philip
Recipient          : P.Mortimer@proexchangeadmin.com
JournalEmailAddress : PremJournal@proexchangeadmin.com
Scope              : Internal
Enabled            : True

Name               : ProExchangeAdmin Journal
Recipient          :
JournalEmailAddress : journal@proexchangeadmin.com
Scope              : Global
Enabled            : True
```

If you want to remove a journal rule, use the Remove-JournalRule cmdlet, as in this command:

```
[PS] C:\> Remove-JournalRule –Name 'Journal all messages
by Philip'
```

Configure an Alternative Journal Recipient

The alternative journal recipient is an organization-wide setting and is configured using the Set-TransportConfig cmdlet using the JournalingReportNdrTo parameter. You can also configure it from EAC:

1. Open EAC and navigate to Compliance Management ➤ Journal Rules.

2. In the top section, just above the + icon, you can see the "Send undeliverable journal reports to" section.

3. Click Select Address, select an alternative journal
    mailbox, and click Save to continue.

To configure the alternative journal recipient to AlternativeJournal@
proexchangeadmin.com, execute the following command:

```
[PS] C:\> Set-TransportConfig -JournalingReportNdrTo
AlternativeJournal@proexchangeadmin.com
```

To remove the alternative journal recipient, set it to $null.

Warning   When an alternative journal recipient is configured, you
must make sure either the original journal recipient or the alternative
journal recipient is available. If the alternative journal recipient is
configured, messages that cannot be delivered to the original journal
recipient are not re-queued and the related NDR, which Exchange will
try to deliver to the alternative journal recipient, will be lost.

Data Loss Prevention

Part of compliance is not only having the instruments to verify that an
organization or its employees are operating within applicable regulations
and laws, but also providing the controls to manage sensitive data and
prevent data leakage, such as credit card information. With email being
used to send business reports as well as those invitations for dinner to
family, users could be unaware of the sensitivity of the information they
are sending or ignorant of the potential business impact of sending certain
information over the public network which is the Internet.

An Exchange feature that focuses on managing or preventing the
exposure of sensitive information is data loss prevention (DLP). For
this purpose, DLP policies can be seen as a package of transport rules

that prevent users from sending sensitive information by filtering those messages. Alternatively, you can use policy tips to notify users that they might be sending sensitive information. Policy tips are like mail tips, and they are shown as a notification in Outlook.

Note   It can happen that after configuring policy tips, they do not show up in the Outlook client, but do show up in Outlook on the Web. That's most likely not caused by the version of Outlook, but the version of the mso20win32client.dll software installed on the client. More information can be found in the Microsoft article "DLP Policy Tip notifications are not displayed in Outlook for Windows" on `https://bit.ly/NoPolicyTips`.

Exchange has a feature named document fingerprinting, which can be used to identify sensitive material in your organization. By uploading sensitive text-based forms used by your organization, you can create DLP policies to match those forms. For example, you can add HR documents and create a DLP policy to prevent messages containing those HR documents from leaving the Exchange organization.

Note   Data loss prevention is a premium feature that requires an Enterprise CAL when used with Exchange 2019.

Creating DLP Policies

There are two ways to create a DLP policy in Exchange Server. The first method is to use a template. This template can be an Exchange-supplied one or one provided by a third-party or yourself. After creating a DLP policy using a template, you can then customize the transport rules.

Note   To be able to create DLP policies, the user needs to be a member of the Compliance Management group.

You can see which templates are available by using the Get-DlpPolicyTemplate cmdlet in Exchange PowerShell:

```
[PS] C:\>Get-DlpPolicyTemplate
```

Name	Publisher	Version
Australia Financial Data	Microsoft	15.0.3.0
Australia Health Records Act (HRIP Act)	Microsoft	15.0.3.0
Australia Personally Identifiable Information (PII) Data	Microsoft	15.0.3.0
Australia Privacy Act	Microsoft	15.0.3.0
Canada Financial Data	Microsoft	15.0.3.0
Canada Health Information Act (HIA)	Microsoft	15.0.3.0
Canada Personal Health Act (PHIPA) - Ontario	Microsoft	15.0.3.0
Canada Personal Health Information Act (PHIA) - Manitoba	Microsoft	15.0.3.0
Canada Personal Information Protection Act (PIPA)	Microsoft	15.0.3.0
Canada Personal Information Protection Act (PIPEDA)	Microsoft	15.0.3.0
Canada Personally Identifiable Information (PII) Data	Microsoft	15.0.3.0
France Data Protection Act	Microsoft	15.0.3.0
France Financial Data	Microsoft	15.0.3.0
France Personally Identifiable Information (PII) Data	Microsoft	15.0.3.0
Germany Financial Data	Microsoft	15.0.3.0
Germany Personally Identifiable Information (PII) Data	Microsoft	15.0.3.0
Israel Financial Data	Microsoft	15.0.3.0
Israel Personally Identifiable Information (PII) Data	Microsoft	15.0.3.0
Israel Protection of Privacy	Microsoft	15.0.3.0
Japan Financial Data	Microsoft	15.0.3.0
Japan Personally Identifiable Information (PII) Data	Microsoft	15.0.3.0
Japan Protection of Personal Information	Microsoft	15.0.3.0
PCI Data Security Standard (PCI DSS)	Microsoft	15.0.3.0
Saudi Arabia - Anti-Cyber Crime Law	Microsoft	15.0.3.0
Saudi Arabia Financial Data	Microsoft	15.0.3.0
Saudi Arabia Personally Identifiable Information (PII...	Microsoft	15.0.3.0
U.K. Access to Medical Reports Act	Microsoft	15.0.3.0
U.K. Data Protection Act	Microsoft	15.0.3.0
U.K. Financial Data	Microsoft	15.0.3.0
U.K. Personal Information Online Code of Practice (PI...	Microsoft	15.0.3.0
U.K. Personally Identifiable Information (PII) Data	Microsoft	15.0.3.0
U.K. Privacy and Electronic Communications Regulations	Microsoft	15.0.3.0
U.S. Federal Trade Commission (FTC) Consumer Rules	Microsoft	15.0.3.0

```
U.S. Financial Data                                    Microsoft 15.0.3.0
U.S. Gramm-Leach-Bliley Act (GLBA)                     Microsoft 15.0.3.0
U.S. Health Insurance Act (HIPAA)                      Microsoft 15.0.3.0
U.S. Patriot Act                                       Microsoft 15.0.3.0
U.S. Personally Identifiable Information (PII) Data     Microsoft 15.0.3.0
U.S. State Breach Notification Laws                    Microsoft 15.0.3.0
U.S. State Social Security Number Confidentiality Laws Microsoft 15.0.3.0
```

To create a template-based DLP policy using EAC, you do the following:

1. Open the Exchange Admin Center and navigate to Compliance Management ➤ Data Loss Prevention.

2. Select the + sign and select New DLP policy from template.

3. Enter a name for the DLP policy, optionally a description. Then, in "Choose a template," you pick the template to use as a basis for your DLP policy.

4. When expanding "More options," you can choose to test the DLP policy first by selecting "Test DLP policy with Policy Tips" or "Test DLP policy without Policy Tips." This is especially helpful when customizing DLP policies, as an improperly configured DLP policy could result in unwanted behavior, like blocking the mail flow of valid messages. You can also initially disable the DLP policy, which is recommended if you need to customize it, as the DLP policy becomes effective after saving it, potentially affecting mail flow.

5. Click Save to create the policy.

This is shown in Figure 12-14.

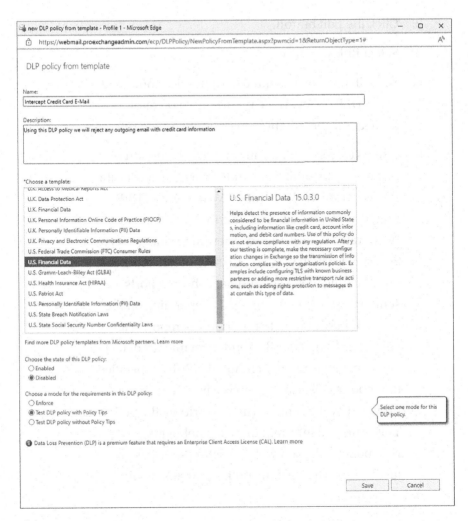

Figure 12-14. *Creating a DLP policy using a template*

If you are happy with the template, you can leave the DLP policy as is. When you want to inspect or customize the DLP policy, in EAC you do the following:

1. In Compliance Management ➤ Data Loss Prevention, select the DLP policy.

2. Click the Edit button.

3. Select Rules.

4. You will now be presented a list of rules contained in the DLP policy. You can turn them on or off individually or edit them to customize each rule.

5. When you select Edit, you will have the option to inspect or customize the underlying transport rule that is part of the DLP policy. When testing DLP policy rules, you can temporarily add an action "Generate incident report" (new in Exchange Server 2013 SP1), which you can use to generate reports for matching messages and have those reports sent to the recipients specified. Depending on the selected information to report, these reports can contain information like sender, recipients, detected classifications, and matching rules. When specified, the reports will also contain the justification provided by the sender when overriding the policy. This is helpful information when debugging your DLP policy rules or when collecting statistics on justifications to see if the policy perhaps requires adjustment.

6. When you have finished, click Save to store your customized transport rule.

This is shown in Figure 12-15.

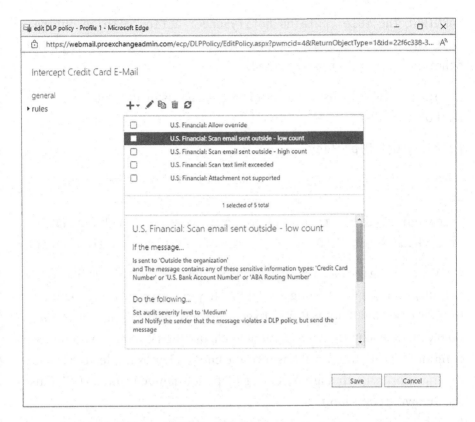

Figure 12-15. Editing a DLP policy rule

If you want to create a DLP policy using the Exchange Management Shell, use the New-DlpPolicy cmdlet, specifying a name and the template to use as a basis for your DLP policy. You can also specify mode (audit, audit and notify, or enforce—the latter will block sending messages with detected possible sensitive information without notification) and the initial state (enabled or disabled) of the transport rule. For example, to create a new DLP policy named Contoso USPA based on the US Patriot Act template, you use the following command:

```
C:\> New-DlpPolicy –Name 'ProExchangeAdmin USPA' –Template
'U.S. Patriot Act' –Mode AuditAndNotify –State Enabled
```

WARNING: The rule contains NotifySender action with an option
that may reject the message. In case the message gets rejected,
other actions won't be applied.

You can view the list of current DLP policies using the Get-
DlpPolicy cmdlet:

```
[PS] C:\>Get-DlpPolicy
```

```
Name                            Publisher State    Mode
----                            --------- -----    ----
Intercept Credit Card E-Mail Microsoft Disabled AuditAndNotify
ProExchangeAdmin USPA        Microsoft Enabled  AuditAndNotify
```

You can use the Get-TransportRule cmdlet to retrieve the collection
of transport rules that belong to a DLP policy, or you can access them
from EAC ➤ Mail Flow ➤ Rules. To get the transport rules part of a DLP
policy in the Exchange Management Shell, use the DlpPolicy parameter in
conjunction with the Get-TransportRule cmdlet. For example, to retrieve
the transport rules that are part of a DLP policy named Contoso USPA, use
the following command:

```
[PS] C:\> Get-TransportRule -DlpPolicy 'ProExchangeAdmin USPA'
```

```
Name                                                          State
  Mode            Priority Comments
----                                                          -----
  ----            -------- --------
U.S. Patriot Act: Allow override                            Enabled
  AuditAndNotify 10
U.S. Patriot Act: Scan email sent outside - low count  Enabled
  AuditAndNotify 11
U.S. Patriot Act: Scan email sent outside - high count Enabled
  AuditAndNotify 12
```

```
U.S. Patriot Act: Scan text limit exceeded          Enabled
  AuditAndNotify 13
U.S. Patriot Act: Attachment not supported          Enabled
  AuditAndNotify 14
```

Note   Regular transport rules can be distinguished from transport rules that are part of a DLP policy in that their DLP policy attribute is not set and their DLP ID is configured as 00000000-0000-0000-0000-000000000000. For DLP policy rules, the DLP ID matches the Immutable ID attribute of the DLP policy.

You can customize policy tips with localized messages or a URL, which you can use to direct users to a page explaining the communications compliance standards. To add these custom elements, go to Compliance Management ➤ Data Loss Prevention, and select "Customize policy tips" (the cogwheel).

To create custom policy tips using the Exchange Management Shell, use the New-PolicyTip cmdlet. The Name parameter defines what policy tip you want to override, where locale is a supported language locale, as follows:

1. <Locale>\NotifyOnly: To customize the message used for notifications in <Locale>.

2. <Locale>\RejectOverride: To customize the message used for notifications in <Locale> when the user is still allowed to send the message.

3. <Locale>\Reject: To customize the message used when used for notifications in <Locale> and when the sending of the message is prevented.

4. Url: To add a link to a URL for policy tips. There can be only one URL policy tip. The URL will be accessed when the sender clicks the link in "Learn more about your organization's rule," which will be shown in the policy tip.

For example, to customize the Dutch locale notification when users are notified of possibly sending a message with sensitive information, you could use

```
[PS] C:\> New-PolicyTipConfig -Name 'nl\RejectOverride' -Value
'Uw bericht bevat mogelijk gevoelige informatie.'

Identity           Value
--------           -----
nl\RejectOverride  Uw bericht bevat mogelijk gevoelige
                   informatie.
```

Note   If the transport rule is configured to only notify users and you configure a custom policy tip for "en\RejectOverride," your custom notification message will not be displayed. You will need to configure a notification message for all three possible modes.

To configure a compliance URL to show with the policy tip, you could use

```
[PS] C:\> New-PolicyTipConfig -Name 'Url' -Value 'http://
compliance.proexchangeadmin.com'

Identity Value
-------- -----
Url      http://compliance.proexchangeadmin.com
```

To retrieve the current set of customized policy tips, use Get-PolicyTipConfig.

Optionally, you can use the locale parameter to only return the custom policy tips for a given locale, for example, Get-PolicyTipConfig -Locale NL as shown in the following:

```
[PS] C:\>Get-PolicyTipConfig -Locale NL

Identity          Value
--------          -----
nl\RejectOverride  Uw bericht bevat mogelijk gevoelige informatie.
```

The way DLP policy tips manifest themselves to users is like how mail tips operate. A small notification bar is shown when sensitive information is detected and the DLP policy and related DLP policy rules are configured to generate a notification, as shown in Figure 12-16.

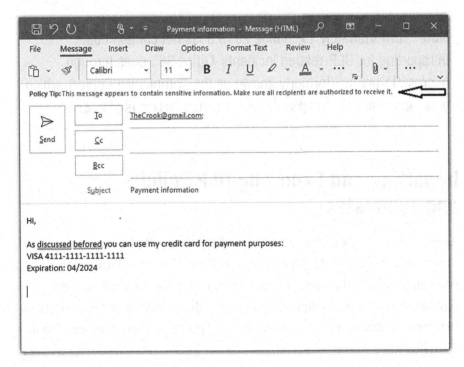

Figure 12-16. *DLP policy tip shown in Outlook*

When such a message is sent (when allowed by the DLP policy) and you have configured to generate incident reports for DLP policy rules, the configured recipients will receive a report as well as a copy of the message attached. The information in the report depends on the selected fields and may include such items as matching rules and data classifications that were detected, including the number of occurrences.

If you want to adjust a DLP policy, use the Set-DlpPolicy cmdlet, for example:

```
[PS] C:\> Set-DlpPolicy –Identity 'ProExchangeAdmin USPA' -Mode
Enforce -State Enabled
```

When you want to remove a DLP policy, you use Remove-DlpPolicy, for example:

```
[PS] C:\> Remove-DlpPolicy –Identity 'ProExchangeAdmin USPA'
```

Note   Unfortunately, Exchange 2019 does not contain built-in reporting for DLP-related incidents. Office 365 does through Microsoft Purview (formerly known as the Compliance Center), which you can access on `https://compliance.microsoft.com`.

Importing and Exporting DLP Policies and Templates

As mentioned earlier, you can import DLP policy templates, or you can import or export a DLP policy collection from XML files. Either way, you can quickly implement a customized DLP policy in an Exchange environment. You can duplicate the DLP policies from a test environment to your production environment. The DLP policy settings are stored in an XML file.

Warning   When you import a DLP policy collection, that collection of policies will overwrite any existing DLP policies defined in your Exchange organization.

To import a DLP policy template file, you use the Import-DlpPolicyTemplate cmdlet. For example, to import a DLP policy from a file named C:\ProExchangeTemplate.xml, you would use the following command:

```
[PS]C:\> Import-DlpPolicyTemplate -FileData ([Byte[]]$(Get-
Content -Path 'C:\ProExchangeTemplate.xml' -Encoding Byte
-ReadCount 0))
```

To import a DLP policy template in EAC, follow these steps:

1. Open EAC and navigate to Compliance Management ➤ Data Loss Prevention.

2. Click the + icon and select the Import Policy option.

Alternatively, you can create a new DLP policy directly from a file-based template using New-DlpPolicy with the TemplateData parameter, for example:

```
[PS]C:\> New-DlpPolicy –Name 'DLPPolicy' –TemplateData
([Byte[]]$(Get-Content -Path 'C:\ProExchangeTemplate.xml'
-Encoding Byte -ReadCount 0))
```

Tip   Besides importing DLP policy template files from third parties, you can develop your own template file. For more information on developing your own DLP policy template files, see http://bit. ly/ExchangeDevDLPTemplate.

You can also import or export the complete collection of DLP policies. To export the current DLP policy collection, use Export-DlpCollection. For example, to export the DLP policy collection to a file named C:\Temp\ProExchangeDLP.xml, you would use the following command:

```
[PS] C:\> Set-Content -Path 'C:\Temp\ProExchangeDLP.xml' -Value
(Export-DlpPolicyCollection).FileData -Encoding Byte
```

The XML file will contain all DLP policies, all DLP policy settings, and the related transport rules as shown in the following. This XML file is shown in Figure 12-17.

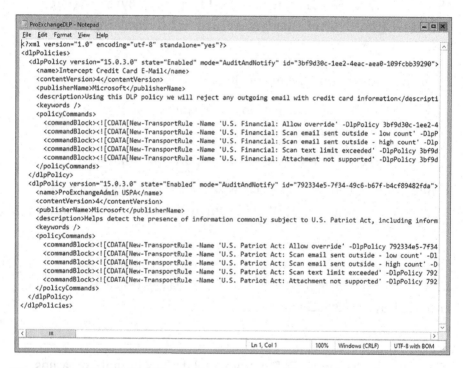

Figure 12-17. *DLP policy collection XML file*

To import a file containing a DLP policy, you use the Import-DlpPolicyCollection cmdlet. For example, to import the DLP policy collection settings stored in C:\ContosoDLP.xml, you would use the following command:

```
[PS] C:\> Import-DlpPolicyCollection -FileData ([Byte[]]$(Get-
Content -Path 'C:\ContosoDLP.xml' -Encoding Byte -ReadCount 0))
```

Caution   Export-DlpPolicyCollection seems to contain a bug, as it exports the New-TransportRule cmdlets to create the related DLP policy rules, but it forgets to state some mandatory values. For example, it does not save the AttachmentProcessingLimitExceeded value in the XML file, after which Import-DlpPolicyCollection will complain because no value is specified for the AttachmentProcessingLimitExceeded parameter. Try correcting the cmdlets in the XML file and then retry the importing when you encounter this obstacle.

Customizing Your DLP Policy

An alternative to using a template to create a DLP policy is to create a custom DLP policy when you have specific requirements. That DLP policy will be empty after creation, so you need to add your own transport rules to it.

To create a custom DLP policy using EAC, you do the following:

- Open the Exchange Admin Center and navigate to Compliance Management ➤ Data Loss Prevention.

- Click the arrow next to the + sign and select New for setting a custom policy.

- Enter a name, optional description, and initial state for the policy.

- Click Save to save the empty DLP policy definition.

You can now start adding rules to it by clicking the Edit icon and selecting the rules section, where you can add your custom rules.

If you want to add a custom rule using the Exchange Management Shell, you use New-DlpPolicy, for example:

```
[PS] C:\> New-DlpPolicy -Name 'CustomDLP' -State Enabled -Mode
AuditAndNotify
```

After you have established that, you can start adding custom transport rules to the DLP policy using the New-TransportRule cmdlet with the DlpPolicy parameter to attach the transport rules to the DLP policy.

In addition, you can use the mode to determine how the rule operates. Choices for mode are Audit (rule is evaluated but actions are skipped), AuditAndNotify (audit with policy tips), or Enforce (audit and notify plus actions are performed). For example, to create a transport rule to generate policy tips for all messages in which a credit card number is detected and further attach it to a DLP policy named "CustomDLP," you would use the following command:

```
[PS] C:\> New-TransportRule -Name 'Custom DLP: All messages
with Credit Card Number' -DlpPolicy 'CustomDlp' -Mode
AuditAndNotify -MessageContainsDataClassifications @{Name =
'Credit Card Number'} -SetAuditSeverity Medium -NotifySender
NotifyOnly

Name                                                       State
  Mode            Priority Comments
----                                                       -----
  ----            -------- --------
Custom DLP: All messages with Credit Card Number Enabled
  AuditAndNotify 15
```

Here is a short explanation of the DLP-specific parameters used in this example:

- **DlpPolicy** is used to specify the DLP policy to attach the rule to.

- **NotifySender** is a DLP-specific parameter that determines how a user is notified when entering DLP policy–violating information. It needs to be specified together with the MessageContainsDataClassifications parameter. The options for NotifySender are

- **NotifyOnly** notifies the sender that the message is sent.

- **MessageContainsDataClassifications** is a predicate and is used to specify rules for searching for sensitive information.

- **RejectMessage** notifies the sender that the message is rejected.

- **RejectUnlessFalsePositiveOverride** notifies the sender; the sender can send the message, marking it as a false positive.

- **RejectUnlessSilentOverride** is when the message is rejected unless the sender overrides policy restriction.

- **RejectUnlessExplicitOverride** is when the message is rejected unless the sender overrides, allowing the sender to specify justification.

If any of the reject options are selected for NotifySender, you can specify a rejection status code and reason using the RejectMessageEnhancedStatusCode and RejectMessageReasonText parameters.

You can also define thresholds for the minimum and maximum numbers of occurrences, as well as for the confidence level, which is a percentage indicating how sure the DLP engine is that the information is a match. For example, something that looks like a credit card number near something else that looks like an expiration date is more likely to be credit card information than something that looks like a series of numbers. Note that when the parameter is omitted, as in the example, a default minimum of one occurrence and 100% maximum confidence level is set.

Not shown in the example but other DLP-specific predicates are ExceptIfHasClassification (to exclude one specific data classification) and ExceptIfHasNoClassification (to apply the rule to messages without a classification). Predicates HasSenderOverride and ExceptIfHasSenderOverride can be used to control rule evaluation whether or not the sender has selected to override DLP policy for the message.

You can verify the creation of the DLP policy rule using Get-TransportRule with the DlpPolicy parameter.

Note   For more information on creating your own sensitive information, or even your own template containing these definitions, see `http://bit.ly/ExchangeSensitiveInformation`. To get a list of currently defined types of sensitive information, use Get-DataClassification|Sort Name.

DLP Document Fingerprinting

Another interesting feature in Exchange Server is DLP document fingerprinting. This fingerprinting allows you to enhance DLP by customizing your sensitive information types by uploading documents. These documents should represent the information you are trying to protect, for example HR documents or tax forms. You can then create DLP policy rules to detect these types of documents and take appropriate action.

Note   Documents uploaded for document fingerprinting are not stored in Exchange Information Store. Instead, a hash is generated using the contents of the document used by the DLP engine for detecting matching information. The hashes are stored with the data classification object in Active Directory. There could be one or more document fingerprints per data classification.

To create document fingerprints using EAC, you do the following:

1. Open the Exchange Admin Center and navigate to Compliance Management ➤ Data Loss Prevention.

2. Select Manage Document Fingerprints.

3. In the document fingerprints window, select the + sign to create a new document fingerprint.

4. In the new document fingerprint window, enter a name for the kind of document fingerprint you are creating and a mandatory description.

5. In the document list section, select the + sign to add a new document for which you want to create a fingerprint. The document fingerprinting supports the same file types as transport rules. For a list of supported file types, see `http://bit.ly/ExchangeTransportRulesFileTypes`.

6. When you are done uploading the documents to fingerprint, click Save and click close.

Tip   You can add multiple documents to a single document fingerprint. This allows you to create a single fingerprint for the same type of information in various formats—for example, .docx and .pdf—or different versions of the document. You can also configure a localized name to display in supported clients for the fingerprint via Edit document fingerprints ➤ Language settings—for example, "EN/ HR Documents" and "DE/HR Documents."

If you want to create a new document fingerprint using the Exchange Management Shell, use New-FingerPrint to create the document fingerprint after which you can provide that information to New-DataClassification to create the data classification holding one or more document fingerprints.

For example, to create a new data classification "HR Form" using the document fingerprints of the files c:\HR-Template-EN.doc and c:\HR-Template-NL.doc, you use the following commands:

```
[PS] C:\>$Fingerprint1= New-Fingerprint -FileData (Get-Content
'C:\Temp\HR Finance document.docx' -Encoding Byte) -Description
'HR document v1'
[PS] C:\>$Fingerprint2= New-Fingerprint -FileData (Get-
Content 'C:\Temp\HR Employment document.docx' -Encoding Byte)
-Description 'HR document v2'
[PS] C:\>New-DataClassification -Name 'ProExchangeAdmin
HR documents' -Fingerprints $Fingerprint1, $Fingerprint2
-Description 'Message contains HR documents'
```

```
Invariant Name                Localized Name
  Publisher         Classification Type
--------------                --------------
---------                --------------------
ProExchangeAdmin HR documents ProExchangeAdmin HR documents
  ProExchangeAdmin Fingerprint
```

You can validate the classification using Get-Classification, for example:

```
[PS] C:\> Get-DataClassification -Identity 'ProExchangeAdmin HR
documents'
```

```
Invariant Name                Localized Name
  Publisher         Classification Type
--------------                --------------
---------                --------------------
ProExchangeAdmin HR documents ProExchangeAdmin HR documents
  ProExchangeAdmin Fingerprint
```

If you want to add a fingerprint to an existing data classification, you use Set-DataClassification, as follows:

```
[PS] C:\> $FingerprintPDF= New-Fingerprint -FileData (Get-
Content 'C:\Temp\HR-Template.pdf' -Encoding Byte) -Description
'HR document PDF'
[PS] C:\> $Fingerprints= (Get-DataClassification -Identity
'ProExchangeAdmin HR documents').Fingerprints + $FingerprintPDF
[PS] C:\> Set-DataClassification -Identity 'ProExchangeAdmin HR
documents' -Fingerprints $Fingerprints
```

Changes made to a DLP policy may not take effect immediately. Microsoft Outlook caches DLP policies in two local XML files that are refreshed every 24 hours. The files are in the folder %UserProfile%\ AppData\Local\Microsoft\Outlook, and their file names start with

- PolicyNudgeClassificationDefinitions (cached data classifications)

- PolicyNudgeRules (cached rule information)

Keep this in mind when implementing policy changes in production or when you are testing DLP policies. Luckily, there is a workaround.

Note   Outlook will use the locally cached DLP policy information to evaluate the message and attachments against document fingerprints or other DLP policy rules, using the same DLP engine as Exchange. This means attachments are not send over the network for evaluation.

To force Microsoft Outlook to download the latest DLP policies, close Outlook and remove the following entry from the registry:

```
HKEY_CURRENT_USER\SOFTWARE\Microsoft\Office\16.0\Outlook\
PolicyNudges\LastDownloadTimesPerAccount
```

After removal, start Outlook again. When you create a message, the updated DLP policies will be downloaded.

Caution   Document fingerprinting does not work for password-protected files or files containing solely images. Also, documents will not be detected if they do not contain all the text used in the document employed to create the document fingerprint. Use documents or forms with blank fields, for example, to create the fingerprints.

Now, you need to create a DLP policy rule in which you specify this data classification data to match your sensitive information contents. To do this, follow these steps:

1. Open EAC and navigate to Compliance Management ➤ Data Loss Prevention.

2. Open the DLP policy and select Rules.

3. Click the + icon to select a new rule. In the "Apply this rule if" dropdown box, select the "The message contains any of these sensitive information types," and select the document fingerprint that was created in the previous step.

4. In the "Do the following" dropdown box, select "Reject the message with an explanation" and enter the text "This message contains sensitive HR information."

5. Click Save and Close to continue.

To create such a DLP policy in the Exchange Management Shell, use the New-TransportRule you would also use to create a custom DLP policy rule, for example:

```
[PS] C:\> New-TransportRule –Name 'CustomDLP: HR docs'
-MessageContainsDataClassifications @{'Name'='ProExchangeAdmin
HR documents'} -NotifySender 'RejectUnlessExplicitOverride'
-RejectMessageReasonText 'Delivery not authorized, message
refused' -SetAuditSeverity 'Medium' -Mode 'AuditAndNotify'
-DlpPolicy 'CustomDLP'

WARNING: The rule contains NotifySender action with an option
that may reject the message. In case the message gets
rejected, other actions won't be applied.
```

883

Name	State	Mode	Priority	Comments
CustomDLP: HR docs	Enabled	AuditAndNotify	16	

Now, when a user tries to send a message using a document with an attachment that matches the document fingerprint, the sender will get a non-delivery report.

Auditing

Administrators in an Exchange organization have power, and with power comes responsibility. From a compliance perspective, organizations may require tracking of administrative changes, such as monitoring who made changes to a certain Receive Connector or auditing the access to high-profile mailboxes.

The following auditing options are available in Exchange 2019:

- *Administrator audit logging*: This allows organizations to audit administrative changes in their Exchange organization.

- *Mailbox audit logging*: This allows organizations to audit mailbox access and changes.

Both will be discussed in the following sections.

Administrator Audit Logging

The administrator audit logging feature allows auditing of who did what and where in the Exchange organization. Exchange Server can audit all changes performed by administrators in the Exchange Management Shell. Actions performed in the Exchange Admin Center are also logged because EAC constructs and runs cmdlets in the background.

Tip   In Exchange 2019, you can view the last 500 commands that were executed on your behalf from EAC by opening the Show Command Logging window.

"Changes" here means that view-only cmdlets like Get-* and Search-* won't be logged. Use of the following cmdlets is always logged:

- Set-AdminAuditLogConfig

- Enable-CmdletExtensionAgent

- Disable-CmdletExtensionAgent

The cmdlets Disable-CmdletExtensionAgent and Enable-CmdletExtensionAgent are logged because they can be used to turn the administrator audit log agent on or off. The administrator audit log agent is responsible for evaluating cmdlets against the auditing configuration and logging entries.

Administrator audit logging entries are stored in the Microsoft Exchange system mailbox, SystemMailbox{e0dc1c29-89c3-4034-b678-e6c29d823ed9}. You can access this mailbox—for example, if you want to move it to a different database—by using Get-Mailbox with the Arbitration parameter, for example:

```
[PS] C:\> Get-Mailbox -Arbitration –Identity
'systemMailbox{e0dc1c29-89c3-4034-b678-e6c29d823ed9}'
```

Name	Alias	ServerName	ProhibitSendQuota
SystemMailbox{e0dc1c29...	SystemMailbox{e0d...	exch01	Unlimited

If you want to move the system mailbox to a database named "MDB02," for instance, you will use the following command:

```
[PS] C:\> Get-Mailbox -Arbitration –Identity
'systemMailbox{e0dc1c29-89c3-4034-b678-e6c29d823ed9}' |
New-Moverequest –TargetDatabase 'MDB02'
```

If you are concerned about the amount of logged data in the system mailbox after enabling administrator audit logging, you can check the size of the system mailbox, as follows:

```
[PS] C:\> Get-Mailbox -Arbitration -Identity
'systemMailbox{e0dc1c29-89c3-4034-b678-e6c29d823ed9}' |
Get-MailboxStatistics | Format-Table TotalItemSize
```

Caution   When you are in a coexistence scenario with a previous version of Exchange server, you need to move the system mailbox to Exchange 2019. If you do not, Exchange 2019 tasks will not be logged in the audit log and audit log searching will not work.

Administrative auditing logging is a global setting enabled by default in Exchange Server. It can be disabled using the following:

```
[PS] C:\> Set-AdminAuditLogConfig -AdminAuditLogEnable $False
```

To enable administrative audit logging, you use:

```
[PS] C:\> Set-AdminAuditLogConfig -AdminAuditLogEnable $True
```

If you want to view the current administrative audit logging settings, you use the Get-AdminAuditLogConfig command:

```
[PS] C:\> Get-AdminAuditLogConfig

RunspaceId                     : 09a0503e-7e07-47e6-92eb-
                                 f495865eb3e6
AdminAuditLogEnabled           : True
LogLevel                       : None
TestCmdletLoggingEnabled       : False
AdminAuditLogCmdlets           : {*}
AdminAuditLogParameters        : {*}
AdminAuditLogExcludedCmdlets   : {}
```

```
AdminAuditLogAgeLimit              : 90.00:00:00
LoadBalancerCount                  : 3
RefreshInterval                    : 10
PartitionInfo                      : {}
UnifiedAuditLogIngestionEnabled    : False
UnifiedAuditLogFirstOptInDate      :
AdminDisplayName                   :
ExchangeVersion                    : 0.10 (14.0.100.0)
Name                               : Admin Audit Log Settings
Identity                           : Admin Audit Log Settings
Guid                               : 0b43c4d7-da63-4bb1-
                                     afcc-8227ab9f116b
ObjectClass                        : {top,
                                     msExchAdminAuditLogConfig}
WhenChanged                        : 11/26/2022 10:31:10 PM
WhenCreated                        : 11/26/2022 10:04:28 PM
WhenChangedUTC                     : 11/26/2022 9:31:10 PM
WhenCreatedUTC                     : 11/26/2022 9:04:28 PM
OrganizationId                     :
Id                                 : Admin Audit Log Settings
OriginatingServer                  : DC01.ProExchangeAdmin.com
IsValid                            : True
ObjectState                        : Unchanged
```

As you can see in this example, there are options for administrator audit logging. There are options to restrict logging to certain cmdlets or parameters. These administrator audit logging options are explained next.

Caution   The administrator audit logging setting is stored in Active Directory, and depending on replication, it may not immediately be applied. Also, for any current Exchange Management Shell session, it may take up to one hour for the new setting to become effective.

Administrator Audit Logging Options

To restrict logging to only specific cmdlets or only if specific parameters are used, you use `Set-AdminAuditLogConfig` in combination with the AdminAuditLogConfig commands and AdminAuditLogConfigParameters parameters. For example, to log only the cmdlets `New-Mailbox` and `Remove-Mailbox`, you would use

```
[PS] C:\> Set-AdminAuditLogConfig -AdminAuditLogCmdlets 'New-Mailbox','Remove-Mailbox'
```

You can also choose to exclude certain cmdlets from being logged using the AdminAuditLogExcludeCmdlets parameters, for example:

```
[PS] C:\> Set-AdminAuditLogConfig -AdminAuditLogExcludeCmdlets 'set-Mailbox'
```

You can restrict logging when certain parameters are used. For example, to log only the name, identity, Windows email address, and email address parameters, you would use

```
[PS] C:\> Set-AdminAuditLogConfig -AdminAuditLogParameters 'Name', 'Identity', 'WindowsEmailAddress', 'EmailAddresses'
```

To cover a set of related cmdlets or parameters, you can use wildcards. For example, to log only cmdlets related to the mailbox and only those parameters containing "address," you would use

```
[PS] C:\> Set-AdminAuditLogConfig -AdminAuditLogCmdlets '*-Mailbox' -AdminAuditLogParameters '*Address*'
```

The default values for AdminAuditLogCmdlets and AdminAuditLogParameters are *, which causes any cmdlet in combination with any parameter to be logged. If you want to reset these values to their default, you use

```
[PS] C:\> Set-AdminAuditLogConfig –AdminAuditLogCmdlets '*' –
AdminAuditLogParameters '*' –AdminAuditLogExcludeCmdlets $null
```

By default, administrative audit logging is restricted to a 90-day period. After 90 days, the log entries are deleted. You can increase or decrease this limit by using the AdminAuditLogAgeLimit parameter, specifying the number of days, hours, minutes, and seconds that entries should be kept. The format to specify this parameter is dd.hh:mm:ss. For example, to set the limit to 180 days, you use

```
[PS] C:\> Set-AdminAuditLogConfig –AdminAuditLogAgeLimit
180.00:00:00
```

Administrative audit logging only logs information like the cmdlet ran, when it ran, the context, and any specified parameters and values. By configuring the log level to Verbose, it will also log the previous values of any changes attributes: Set-AdminAuditLogConfig –LogLevel Verbose. To return to the default logging, you set the log level to None.

By default, test cmdlets are not logged. To log the test cmdlets, set TestCmdletLoggingEnabled to $true, for example:

```
[PS] C:\> Set-AdminAuditLogConfig –
TestCmdletLoggingEnabled $true
```

To disable it again, set TestCmdletLoggingEnabled to $false.

Custom Logging Entries

In addition to the administrator audit logging cmdlets, you can create custom entries in the administrator audit log. This can be useful when you want to create markers for when to run scripts or for maintenance stop and starting events, for example.

To create a custom administrative audit log entry, use the Write-AdminAuditLog cmdlet, with the Comment parameter to pass the message to log. For example, to log the start of a scheduled maintenance cycle, you could use

```
[PS] C:\> Write-AdminAuditLog —Comment 'start of scheduled maintenance'
```

Caution   The maximum size of the comment text is 500 characters.

Auditing Log Searches

Logging information for auditing purposes would be useless if there were no ways to search through or retrieve the logged information. To search the administrator audit log using EAC, navigate to Compliance Management ➤ Auditing, and select "Run the admin audit log report..." to perform a search, to view the administrator audit log, or to export the administrator audit log when you want to perform a search in the administrator audit log and view it on the screen as shown in Figure 12-18.

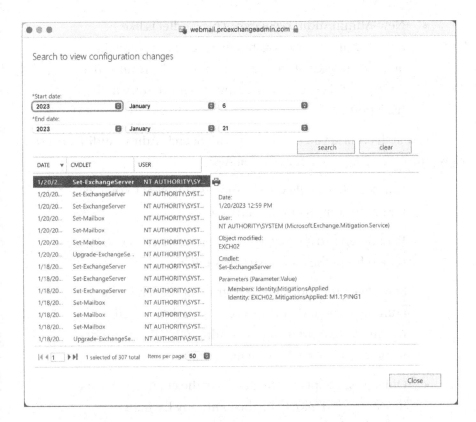

Figure 12-18. Inspecting the administrator audit log

EAC is a bit limited when it comes to searching the audit log, as you can only further specify the start and end dates for reports on the administrator audit log. When you want to check the administrative audit log using EMS using additional search criteria, Exchange provides two cmdlets:

- Search-AdminAuditLog: Use this cmdlet to search through the administrator audit log entries based on search criteria. These searches are synchronous.

- New-AdminAuditLogSearch: This cmdlet is like Search-AdminAuditLog, but instead of returning the audit log entries, it can be used to send the results to a recipient. These searches run asynchronously in the background.

The search criteria you can specify with Search-AdminAuditLog and New-AdminAuditLogSearch are as follows:

- Cmdlets: To specify which cmdlets you want to search for in the administrator audit log.

- Parameters: To specify which parameters you want to search for in the administrator audit log.

- StartDate and EndDate: To restrict the search in the administrator audit log to a certain period. When running an export using New-AdminAuditLogSearch, a start date and end date are mandatory.

- ObjectIds: To specify the names of the changed objects to search for. This can be the name any Exchange-related configuration item, such as mailboxes, aliases, database, Send Connector, and the like.

- UserIds: To search for cmdlets in the administrator audit log run by specific users.

- IsSuccess: To restrict the search to successful or failed events.

- ExternalAccess: When used in Exchange Online or Office 365, using $true will return audit log entries generated by Microsoft service administrators; using $false will return audit log entries generated by the tenant administrators.

- StatusMailRecipients: Specifies the SMTP addresses of the recipients who should receive the audit log report. This parameter is only valid when using New-AdminAuditLogSearch.

- Name: Specifies the subject of the email. This parameter is only valid when using New-AdminAuditLogSearch.

Note   It can take up to 15 minutes for Exchange to generate and deliver the report. The raw information in XML format attached to the report generated by New-AdminAuditLogSearch can have a maximum size of 10 MB.

For example, to search the audit log for entries where the Add-TransportRule cmdlet was used on an object (in this case, transport rule) named "HR Documents" since June 21, 2021, 3:15, you would use the following:

```
[PS] C:\>Search-AdminAuditLog -Cmdlets Set-SendConnector
-StartDate '12/01/2022 12:00'

RunspaceId          : 09a0503e-7e07-47e6-92eb-f495865eb3e6
ObjectModified      : EdgeSync - Default-First-Site-Name to
                      Internet
CmdletName          : Set-SendConnector
CmdletParameters    : {SmartHostAuthMechanism,
                      DNSRoutingEnabled, SourceTransportServers,
                      Identity, AddressSpaces,
                      SmartHosts, DomainSecureEnabled}
ModifiedProperties  : {}
Caller              : ProExchangeAdmin.com/Users/Administrator
ExternalAccess      : False
```

```
Succeeded          : True
Error              :
RunDate            : 12/6/2022 2:43:31 PM
OriginatingServer  : PROX2013 (15.00.1497.043)
IsValid            : True
ObjectState        : New
```

Tip   As with many cmdlets, only the first 1,000 entries are returned. When necessary, use -ResultSize Unlimited to return all matching audit log entries.

To return all cmdlets run by administrators against objects named Philip Mortimer, you would use

```
[PS] C:\> Search-AdminAuditLog -UserIds Administrator -
ObjectIds P.Mortimer
```

To return all audit log entries where the New-ManagementRoleAssignment or Remove-ManagementRoleAssignment cmdlets were run, you would use

```
[PS] C:\> Search-AdminAuditLog -Cmdlets New-
ManagementRoleAssignment, Remove-ManagementRoleAssignment
```

To run the same query against the past 24 hours and send the results to a recipient named philip@proexchangeadmin.com, you would use

```
[PS] C:\> New-AdminAuditLogSearch -Name
'ManagementRoleAssignment Changes'
 -Cmdlets New-ManagementRoleAssignment, Remove-
ManagementRoleAssignment
 -StatusMailRecipients p.mortimer@proexchangeadmin.com
-StartDate (Get-Date).AddDays(-1) -EndDate (Get-Date)
```

You can also search for specific parameter usage and or use ExpandProperty to get an overview of all changed values using parameters. For example, if you want to show changes in the circular logging settings of mailbox databases in the last seven days, you will use

```
[PS] C:\> Search-AdminAuditLog -Cmdlet Set-MailboxDatabase
-StartDate (Get-Date).AddDays(-7) -EndDate (Get-Date) | Select
RunDate,CmdletName -ExpandProperty CmdletParameters
```

You can retrieve a list of current searches using Get-AuditLogSearch. This will return both administrator audit log searches and mailbox audit logging searches. You can optionally specify "created after" and "created before" to limit the time span of the items returned. The returned information contains the name, the name of the job or email subject, and the recipients of the report. The time span used for the report is returned as an UTC time stamp in StartDateUtc and EndDateUtc. The attribute "Type" can be used to differentiate between administrator audit log searches ("Admin") and mailbox audit log searches ("Mailbox"):

```
[PS] C:\> Get-AuditLogSearch | Format-Table Name, Type,
CreationTime, StartDateUtc, EndDateUtc, StatusMailRecipients -
AutoSize
```

This cmdlet will return a list of current audit log searches and the audit log entries are returned as a set of objects. The structure of the returned administrator audit log entries is as follows:

- ObjectModified: Contains the object modified.

- CmdletName: Contains the cmdlet run.

- CmdletParameters: Contains the parameters specified with the cmdlet.

- ModifiedProperties: Is only populated when the log level is set to Verbose. When set, this field will contain the modified properties of "ObjectModified."

- Caller: Contains the user account that ran the cmdlet.

- Succeeded: Reports if the cmdlet ran successfully.

- Error: Contains the error message if the cmdlet did not run successfully.

- RunDate: Contains the time stamp when the cmdlet ran.

- OriginatingServer: Indicates which server ran the cmdlet.

As you can see, the CmdletParameters, as well as the ModifiedProperties when applicable, will by default only display the parameter name or the name of the attribute changed. To see the related value, expand the CmdletParameters or ObjectModified attribute.

For example, to find the last logged New-TransportRule cmdlet and view what parameters and configuration values were used, you can use the following commands:

```
[PS] C:\> $LogEntry= Search-AdminAuditLog -Cmdlets New-
TransportRule | Sort StartDate -Desc | Select -First 1
[PS] C:\> $LogEntry
[PS] C:\> $LogEntry.CmdletParameters
```

Mailbox Audit Logging

Along with the auditing administrative changes, an organization might require tracking the access or changes made to individual mailboxes, especially mailboxes potentially containing sensitive information from a business or privacy perspective. This also applies to non-personal mailboxes, which are mailboxes attached to a disabled user account and which are used by multiple mailbox users commonly referred to as "delegates."

Mailbox audit logging can audit access and changes performed by the mailbox owners, delegates, and administrators. After enabling the mailbox audit logging, you can additionally limit the audit log to record only log certain operations—for example, creation, movement, or deletion of messages. You can also specify the logon type to audit—for instance, owner, delegate, or administrator.

You cannot enable mailbox audit logging using EAC. To enable mailbox audit logging from EMS, use the Set-Mailbox cmdlet, setting AuditEnabled to $true, for example:

```
[PS] C:\> Set-Mailbox -Identity 'P.Mortimer' -
AuditEnabled $true
```

To verify that the auditing is enabled and see what cmdlets will be logged, check the audit attributes of the mailbox, as follows:

```
[PS] C:\> Get-Mailbox -Identity 'P.Mortimer' | Select
Name, Audit*

Name             : Philip Mortimer
AuditEnabled     : True
AuditLogAgeLimit : 90.00:00:00
```

```
AuditAdmin          : {Update, Move, MoveToDeletedItems,
                       SoftDelete, HardDelete, FolderBind, SendAs,
                       SendOnBehalf,
                       Create, UpdateFolderPermissions,
                       UpdateInboxRules, UpdateCalendarDelegation}
AuditDelegate       : {Update, SoftDelete, HardDelete, SendAs,
                       Create, UpdateFolderPermissions,
                       UpdateInboxRules}
AuditOwner          : {UpdateFolderPermissions, UpdateInboxRules,
                       UpdateCalendarDelegation}
```

To disable mailbox audit logging, you use

```
[PS] C:\> Set-Mailbox –Identity 'Info' –AuditEnabled $false
```

Mailbox Audit Logging Options

As seen earlier when verifying the mailbox audit logging settings, there are several options that can be used to determine what is logged per type of logon—that is, owner, delegate, or administrator. Not all actions can be logged for all logon types. Table 11-1 lists the mailbox audit logging options.

Table 11-1. *Mailbox Audit Logging Options*

Action	Description	Owner	Delegate	Administrators
Copy	Item is copied to another folder	No	No	Yes*
Create	Creation of an item (e.g., item received). Folder creation is not audited	Yes	Yes*	Yes
FolderBind	Folder access	No	Yes	Yes*
HardDelete	Permanent deletion of an item	Yes	Yes*	Yes
MessageBind	Item access	No	No	Yes
Move	Item is moved to another folder	Yes	Yes	Yes*
MoveToDeletedItems	An item is deleted (moved to Deleted Items)	Yes	Yes	Yes*
SendAs	A message is sent using SendAs permissions	-	Yes*	Yes*
SendOnBehalf	A message is sent using SendOnBehalf permissions	-	Yes	Yes
SoftDelete	An item is moved from Deleted Items to Recoverable Items	Yes	Yes*	Yes
Update	Updating of item properties	Yes	Yes*	Yes*

*Default option

To log a specific action for a certain logon type, use the parameter AuditOwner for logging owner actions (this includes delegates with full access mailbox permissions), AuditDelegate for logging actions performed by delegate, and AuditAdmin for logging actions performed by administrators.

Note   FolderBind operations are consolidated. Only the first occurrence of FolderBind per folder in a three-hour time span generates a mailbox audit log entry.

For example, to enable mailbox audit logging on a shared mailbox called "Info" and only log Send As actions for delegates, you would use

```
[PS] C:\> Set-Mailbox –Identity 'S.Summertown' -AuditEnabled
$true -AuditDelegate SendAs -AuditAdmin None -AuditOwner None
[PS] C:\> Get-Mailbox -Identity 'S.Summertown' | Select
Name,Audit*

Name            : Sarah Summertown
AuditEnabled    : True
AuditLogAgeLimit : 90.00:00:00
AuditAdmin      : {}
AuditDelegate   : {SendAs}
AuditOwner      : {}
```

When mailbox audit logging is enabled, the audit log entries are stored in the mailbox itself, in the Audits folder located in the Recoverable Items folder. When a mailbox is moved, the recoverable items are also moved, including any existing audit log entries.

The default retention period of mailbox audit log entries is 90 days. You can adjust that retention period by using Set-Mailbox with the AuditLogAgeLimit parameter. For example, to set the retention period of the mailbox audit log for Sarah's mailbox to 180 days, you would use

```
[PS] C:\> Set-Mailbox -Identity S.Summertown -
AuditLogAgeLimit 180
```

Note   If the mailbox is on in-place hold, the mailbox audit logs entries will not be removed after the retention period.

If you are concerned about the amount of logged audit data in the mailbox after you have enabled the mailbox audit logging, you can use the following commands to check the size of the folder mailbox:

```
[PS] C:\> Get-Mailbox -Identity S.Summertown | Get-
MailboxFolderStatistics -FolderScope RecoverableItems | Where
{$_.Name -eq 'Audits'} | Select FolderSize
```

In this command, Get-MailboxFolderStatistics retrieves statistical information on the folders. By using FolderScope, you can configure it to look into a specific well-known folder. As mentioned earlier, the mailbox audit log entries are stored in the Recoverable Items folder in a subfolder named "Audits." So you set the scope to Recoverable Items to only return that folder. Next, you use Where to filter the folder name "Audits," of which you display its FolderSize property.

Searches of the Mailbox Audit Logging

To search a mailbox audit log using EAC, you navigate to Compliance Management ➤ Auditing. Exchange EAC provides seven options for generating mailbox audit log reports:

- *Run a non-owner mailbox access report*: This option
  allows you to generate a report on non-owner access
  to mailboxes. You can select the search period, the
  auditing-enabled mailboxes to investigate, and the type
  of access.

- *Run an administrator role group report*: This option
  allows you to search for changes made to role groups.
  This can identify security breaches.

- *Run an in-place eDiscovery and hold report*: This
  option lets you search for changes made to in-place
  eDiscovery and in-place holds.

- *Run a per-mailbox litigation hold report*: This options
  lets you search for mailboxes that have litigation hold
  enabled or disabled.

- *Export mailbox audit logs*: This option allows you
  to export the mailbox audit logs and send them
  as an attachment to selected recipients. As with
  administrator audit logging, the searching and
  reporting options are limited when managed through
  EAC. In EMS, mailbox audit logging provides the
  following cmdlets for searching and reporting:

- *Search-MailboxAuditLog*: Use this cmdlet to search
  the mailbox audit logs based on search criteria. These
  searches are synchronous.

- *New-MailboxAuditLogSearch*: This cmdlet is similar to
  Search-MailboxAuditLog but instead of returning the
  audit log entries, it can be used to send the results to
  a recipient. These searches run asynchronously in the
  background.

- *Run the admin audit log report*: This option will show you the admin audit log, similar to the Search-AdminAuditLog in EMS.

- *Export the admin audit log*: This option is an additional to the previous option and lets you export the results to an XML file and have it sent to specified recipients.

The search criteria you can specify with SearchMailboxAuditLog and New-MailboxAuditLogSearch are the following:

1. Identity: To specify the mailboxes to search for audit log entries. This parameter is only available when using Search-MailboxAuditLog.

2. Mailboxes: To specify the mailboxes to search for audit log entries. When neither Identity nor Mailboxes is specified, all mailbox auditing–enabled mailboxes will be searched.

3. LogonTypes: To specify the logon types to search. Valid logon types are

    - Admin for administrator logon types

    - Delegate for delegate logon types, including users with Full Access

    - External for Microsoft service administrators in Exchange Online or Office 365

    - Owner for primary owner

4. ShowDetails: To retrieve details of each audit log entry. This parameter is mandatory when LogonTypes is set to Owner and can't be used together with the Mailboxes parameter. This parameter is only available when using Search-MailboxAuditLog.

5.   StartDate and EndDate: To restrict the search in the mailbox audit log to a certain period. When running an export using New-AdminAuditLogSearch, the start date and end date are mandatory.

6.   ExternalAccess: To search for audit log entries generated by users outside of your organization such as Microsoft service administrators in Exchange Online or Office 365.

7.   StatusMailRecipients: Specifies the SMTP addresses of the recipients that should receive the audit log report. This parameter is only available when using New-MailboxAuditLogSearch.

8.   Name: Specifies the subject of the email. This parameter is only available when using New-MailboxAuditLogSearch.

When used without specifying parameters, Search-MailboxAuditLog will return all auditing-enabled mailboxes, as follows:

```
[PS] C:\> Search-MailboxAuditLog
```

To see what auditing information is returned by mailbox audit logging, let us pick a single audit log entry while specifying ShowDetails to include detailed information, as follows:

```
[PS] C:\> Search-MailboxAuditLog -ShowDetails -ResultSize 1
```

A lot of information is available per audit log entry. You may notice a few unpopulated fields, which are due to the operation. Folder names are not logged for SendAs operations. Here is a short list of some of the important fields:

- LastAccessed: Contains the time stamp when the operation was performed.

- Operation: Is one of the actions Copy, Create, FolderBind, HardDelete, MessageBind, Move, MoveToDeletedItems, SendAs, SendOnBehalf, SoftDelete, and Update.

- OperationResult: Shows if the operation succeeded, failed, or partially succeeded.

- LogonType: Shows who performed the operation, whether the owner, a delegate, or administrator.

- FolderPathName: Contains the folder name that contains the item.

- ClientInfoString: Contains information about the client or Exchange component that performed the operation.

- ClientIPAddress: Contains the IPv4 address of the client computer used.

- InternalLogonType: Contains the type of logon performed by the non-owner.

- MailboxOwnerUPN: Contains the UPN of the mailbox owner.

- DestMailboxOwnerUPN: Contains the UPN of the destination mailbox owner for cross-mailbox operations; CrossMailboxOperation contains information about whether the operation is across mailboxes.

- LogonUserDisplayName: Contains the display name of the logged-on user who performed the operation.

- ItemSubject: Contains the subject line of the item affected.

- MailboxResolvedOwnerName: Contains the display name of the mailbox.

For example, to search all auditing-enabled mailboxes for log entries generated for non-owner access by delegate or administrator logon types, you could use

```
[PS] C:\> Search-MailboxAuditLog -LogonTypes
Delegate,Admin -ShowDetails | Format-Table LastAccessed,
MailboxResolvedOwnerName, Operation, LogonType,
LogonUserDisplayName, ClientIPAddress, ItemSubject -AutoSize
```

Note   Use ResultSize to limit the number of entries when using Search-MailboxAuditLog.

In this example, you query the mailbox "Info," which is mailbox auditing enabled, for non-owners' access to a specific folder. Because you cannot specify the operations to search for directly as a Search-MailboxAuditLog parameter, you can pipe the output through Where-Object, where you filter entries so that only objects where the operation is FolderBind (i.e., folder access) and the folder path name is "\Inbox" are returned. Of the objects returned, you then select certain fields for displaying:

```
[PS] C:\> Search-MailboxAuditLog -Identity 'Info' -LogonTypes
Delegate, Admin -ShowDetails | Where { $_.Operation -
eq 'FolderBind' -and $_.FolderPathName -eq '\Inbox' } |
Format-Table LastAccessed, InternalLogonType, LogonType,
LogonUserDisplayName, FolderPathname
```

When required, you can narrow your search to a certain period by specifying the start date and end date as well.

In addition to Search-MailboxAuditLog you can use New-MailboxAuditLogSearch to gather mailbox audit log information in the background and have it sent as an email attachment to specific recipients. The parameters you can use are similar to those you can use with Search-MailboxAuditLog, only you can't use identity for reporting on a specific mailbox; you need to specify the message subject (name) and recipients (status mail recipients).

That said, to create a background mailbox audit log query on delegate access to a mailbox called "Info" from December 1, 2022, to February 1, 2023, you could use

```
[PS] C:\> New-MailboxAuditLogSearch -StartDate '12/1/2022' -
EndDate '2/1/2023' -Mailboxes 'Info' -ShowDetails -LogonTypes
Delegate -Name 'Mailbox Info - delegate access audit report'
-StatusMailRecipients p.mortimer@proexchangeadmin.com
```

You can use Get-AuditLogSearch to list current audit log searches. The generated export of audit information is in XML format is sent as an attachment to Philip.

The XML contains the same elements as the Search-MailboxAuditLog output, allowing organizations to perform additional processing or reporting using the information contained in the XML file. For example, when you store the attached XML file locally, you can import it using PowerShell by using

```
[PS] C:\> [xml](Get-Contents .\SearchResults.xml)
```

Note   Do not try to import an XML file using Import-CliXml. The purpose of Import-CliXml is to import serialized powerShell objects, usually generated using the Export-CliXml cmdlet.

A simple query to retrieve the information contained in SearchResults. xml and select certain information from audit log events is as follows:

```
[PS] C:\> [xml](Get-Contents .\SearchResults.xml) | Select
-ExpandProperty SearchResults | Select -ExpandProperty
Event | Format-Table LastAccessed, LogonType, Operation,
LogonUserDisplayName, FolderPathName -AutoSize
```

Bypass of Mailbox Audit Logging

Applications may implicitly use administrator permissions when processing mailboxes, generating excessive amounts of audit log information for mailboxes that have mailbox auditing enabled for MessageBind or FolderBind operations. Examples of such applications are backup or archiving solutions. Audit log information generated by these applications are likely not of interest to the organization with regard to compliance, and are viewed only as creating "noise" in the mailbox audit logs while also claiming valuable system resources in the process.

To create exceptions for these types of applications, Exchange Server 2013 can be configured to bypass mailbox auditing using mailbox auditing bypass associations. These bypass associations can be assigned to user or computer accounts. The cmdlet to configure bypass associations is Set-MailboxAuditBypassAssociation. To configure bypass for an account named 'BesAdmin', for example, you would use

```
[PS] C:\> Set-MailboxAuditBypassAssociation -Identity
'BesAdmin' -AuditBypassEnabled $true
```

To remove the bypass association for 'BesAdmin', you set AuditBypassEnabeld to $false:

```
[PS] C:\> Set-MailboxAuditBypassAssociation -Identity
'BesAdmin' -AuditBypassEnabled $false
```

To retrieve the accounts currently associated with mailbox auditing bypass, you use

```
[PS] C:\> Get-MailboxAuditBypassAssociation | Where {
$_.AuditBypassEnabled } | Select Name
```

Caution   When configuring mailbox auditing bypass associations, bear in mind that some organizations need to closely monitor these bypass associations, as these accounts will not generate mailbox audit log information. Alternatively, organizations can leverage Role-Based Access Control to restrict those configuring bypass associations using the Exchange Management Shell. You can also monitor the msExchBypassAudit attribute of user objects in Active Directory.

Summary

In this chapter we discussed the compliance features in Exchange 2019, features that can help you meet your business requirements stipulated by law or regulations.

In-place archiving, in combination with Messaging Records Management, can be helpful in monitoring the contents of the primary mailbox by using retention policies to automatically offload contents into the in-place archives or to remove them after a certain period.

Litigation hold and in-place hold will make a mailbox immutable and can help you keep content in mailboxes, regardless of users deleting items from their mailbox or editing items in their mailbox. Litigation hold keeps all items in a mailbox, while in-place hold is query based and thus more granular.

In-place discovery can be used to search for information, allowing organizations to create exportable sets of content using discover mailboxes for external investigations.

To investigate activities related to mailboxes, organizations can leverage their mailbox auditing to log mailbox access or specific operations on mailboxes or even on specific folders.

Transport rules automatically process messages or control mail flow. Data loss prevention including document fingerprinting helps organizations control leakage of sensitive information.

Finally, regarding the Exchange environment itself, organizations can use administrator auditing to log or report changes in the Exchange environment.

Please be aware that for years these compliance features were similar in Exchange Online, but in Exchange Online, these features are no longer Exchange specific but include other services as well. As such they are now combined in Microsoft Purview (the old Compliance Center).

Index

© Jaap Wesselius and Michel de Rooij 2023

J. Wesselius and M. de Rooij, *Pro Exchange Administration*,

https://doi.org/10.1007/978-1-4842-9591-5

D

R

Printed in the United States
by Baker & Taylor Publisher Services